CONTEMPORARY Black Biography

ISSN-1058-1316

CONTEMPORARY Black Biography

Profiles from the International Black Community

Volume 26

Dave Oblender, Editor

GALE GROUP

Detroit
New York
San Francisco
London
Boston
Woodbridge, CT

STAFF

David G. Oblender, *Editor*
Ashyia N. Henderson, *Contributing Editor*
Shelly Dickey, *Managing Editor, Multicultural Department*

Maria Franklin, *Permissions Manager*
Margaret Chamberlain, *Permissions Specialist*

Dorothy Maki, *Manufacturing Manager*
Stacy Melson, *Buyer*

Kenn Zorn, *Product Design Manager*
Michael Logusz, *Graphic Artist*

Barbara Yarrow, *Imaging and Multimedia Content Manager*
Randy Bassett, *Image Database Supervisor*
Pamela A. Reed, *Imaging Coordinator*
Robyn V. Young, *Senior Editor, Imaging and Multimedia Content*
Robert Duncan, *Sr. Imaging Specialist*
Leitha Etheridge-Sims, Mary Grimes, *Image Cataloguers*

Victoria B. Cariappa, *Research Manager*
Barbara McNeil, *Research Specialist*
Barbara Leevy, *Research Associate*
Sarah Genik, *Research Assistant*

ISBN 0-7876-4617-2
ISSN 1058-1316

10 9 8 7 6 5 4 3 2 1

Contemporary Black Biography Advisory Board

Contents

Introduction ix

Photo Credits xi

Cumulative Nationality Index 189

Cumulative Occupation Index 199

Cumulative Subject Index 215

Cumulative Name Index 253

Alexander, Clifford ... 1
Staunch equal rights supporter

Baker, LaVern ... 4
Talented rhythm and blues vocalist

Barney, Lem ... 7
Hall of Fame cornerback

Beach, Michael ... 9
Multi-talented actor

Blake, Asha ... 12
Likeable television personality

Bruce, Isaac ... 15
Emerging NFL star

Bryant, John ... 18
Savvy investment banker

Butler, Jerry ... 22
"Icy" smooth vocalist

Carmichael, Stokely ... 25
Defiant advocate for revolution

Carter, Rubin ... 29
Resilient prisoners' rights activist

Carter, Vince ... 33
Phenomenal NBA superstar

Cayton, Horace ... 36
Troubled sociologist

Chapman, Tracy ... 40
Popular folk-rock vocalist

Chinn, May Edward ... 43
Dedicated medical doctor

Clendenon, Donn ... 46
Gifted baseball player and attorney

Cosby, Bill ... 49
Beloved comedian, actor, and author

Curtis, Christopher Paul ... 55
Award-winning children's author

Doley, Harold, Jr. ... 58
Pioneering securities broker

Duncan, Michael Clarke ... 60
Rising film star

Elliott, Sean ... 63
Courageous basketball player

Evans, Mari ... 66
Proud poet and educator

Foster, Henry W., Jr. ... 68
Compassionate physician

Harmon, Clarence ... 71
Energetic mayor of St. Louis

Henderson, Cornelius Langston ... 74
Civil engineering pioneer

Howard, M. William, Jr. ... 76
Staunch advocate for racial justice

Jackson, Milt ... 79
Versatile jazz vibraphonist

Jordan, Ronny ... 82
Creative acid jazz musician

Joyner, Marjorie Stewart ... 84
Trailblazing inventor and philanthropist

Lloyd, Earl ... 87
First African American to play in the NBA

Mabrey, Vicki ... 90
Seasoned journalist

Manley, Edna....................92
Mother of Jamaican art

Mathis, Greg....................95
Inspirational judge

Metcalfe, Ralph....................98
Respected Olympic track star

Moore, Chante....................101
Diverse singer and songwriter

Morial, Ernest "Dutch"....................104
Accomplished man of "firsts"

Motley, Marion....................107
Intimidating Hall of Fame football player

Newsome, Ozzie....................111
Classy Hall of Fame tight end

Newton, Thandie....................113
Elegant actress

Osborne, Jeffrey....................116
Silky-smooth balladeer

Pride, Charley....................119
Respected country music pioneer

Redding, J. Saunders....................122
Productive author and literary critic

Redding, Louis L....................126
Tireless foe of segregation

Robertson, Oscar....................129
Basketball legend

Rush, Bobby....................132
Evolutionary congressman from Illinois

Shabazz, Betty....................135
Dignified activist and health administrator

Silver, Horace....................138
Soul jazz architect

Sizemore, Barbara....................143
Dynamic educator

Smith, Mary Carter....................148
Notable storyteller

Taylor, Mildred D....................151
Award-winning novelist

Thomas, Debi....................154
First black Winter Olympic medalist

Thomas, Isiah....................157
Fiercely competitive entrepreneur

Thompson, Bennie G....................163
Congressional champion of liberal causes

Thompson, John W....................167
Talented computer executive

Tsvangirai, Morgan....................170
Zimbabwe's hope for peaceful change

Verdelle, A.J....................173
Promising novelist

Waters, Benny....................176
Legendary jazz musician

Watt, Melvin....................180
Capable congressman

Williams, Clarence, III....................183
Hardworking stage and screen actor

Witt, Edwin....................185
Inspirational physician

Introduction

Contemporary Black Biography provides informative biographical profiles of the important and influential persons of African heritage who form the international black community: men and women who have changed today*s world and are shaping tomorrow*s. *Contemporary Black Biography* covers persons of various nationalities in a wide variety of fields, including architecture, art, business, dance, education, fashion, film, industry, journalism, law, literature, medicine, music, politics and government, publishing, religion, science and technology, social issues, sports, television, theater, and others. In addition to in-depth coverage of names found in today*s headlines, *Contemporary Black Biography* provides coverage of selected individuals from earlier in this century whose influence continues to impact on contemporary life. *Contemporary Black Biography* also provides coverage of important and influential persons who are not yet household names and are therefore likely to be ignored by other biographical reference series. Each volume also includes listee updates on names previously appearing in CBB.

Designed for Quick Research and Interesting Reading

- ***Attractive page design*** incorporates textual subheads, making it easy to find the information you*re looking for.
- ***Easy-to-locate data sections*** provide quick access to vital personal statistics, career informa- tion, major awards, and mailing addresses, when available.
- ***Informative biographical essays*** trace the subject*s personal and professional life with the kind of in-depth analysis you need.
- ***To further enhance your appreciation*** of the subject, most entries include photographic portraits.
- ***Sources for additional information*** direct the user to selected books, magazines, and newspapers where more information on the individuals can be obtained.

Helpful Indexes Make It Easy to Find the Information You Need

Contemporary Black Biography includes cumulative Nationality, Occupation, Subject, and Name indexes that make it easy to locate entries in a variety of useful ways.

Available in Electronic Formats

Diskette/Magnetic Tape.*Contemporary Black Biography* is available for licensing on magnetic tape or diskette in a fielded format. Either the complete database or a custom selection of entries may be ordered. The database is available for internal data processing and nonpublishing purposes only. For more information, call (800) 877-GALE. ***Online.****Contemporary Black Biography* is available online through Mead Data Central*s NEXIS Service in the NEXIS, PEOPLE and SPORTS Libraries in the GALBIO file.

We Welcome Your Suggestions

The editors welcome your comments and suggestions for enhancing and improving ***Contemporary Black Biography.*** **If you would like to suggest persons for inclusion in the series, please submit these names to the editors. Mail comments or suggestions to:**

The Editor
Contemporary Black Biography
Gale Group
27500 Drake Rd.
Farmington Hills, MI 48331-3535
Phone: (800) 347-4253

Photo Credits

PHOTOGRAPHS AND ILLUSTRATIONS APPEARING IN *CONTEMPORARY BLACK BIOGRAPHY,* VOLUME 26, WERE RECEIVED FROM THE FOLLOWING SOURCES:

All Reproduced by Permission:***Alexander, Clifford,***photograph. AP/Wide World Photos. ***Baker, LaVern,*** photograph. Courtesy of Jack Vartoogian. ***Beach, Michael,*** photograph. ***Blake, Asha,*** photograph. Courtesy of Liaison Agency. ***Bruce, Isaac,*** photograph. Courtesy of Liaison Agency. ***Bryant, John,*** photograph. ***Butler, Jerry,*** photograph. AP/Wide World Photos. ***Carmichael, Stokely,*** photograph. AP/Wide World Photos. ***Carter, Rubin "Hurricane",*** photograph AP/Wide World Photos. ***Carter, Vince,*** photograph. AP/Wide World Photos. ***Chapman, Tracy,*** photograph. AP/Wide World Photos. ***Chinn, May Edward,*** photograph. AP/Wide World Photos. ***Clendenon, Donn,*** photograph. AP/Wide World Photos. ***Cosby, Bill,*** photograph. AP/World Wide Photos. ***Curtis, Christopher Paul,*** photograph. AP/Wide World Photos. ***Duncan, Michael Clarke,*** photograph. Courtesy of Liaison Agency. ***Elliott, Sean,*** photograph. AP/Wide World Photos. ***Foster, Henry W.,*** photograph. Courtesy of Henry W. Foster, Jr. ***Jackson, Milt,*** photograph. AP/Wide World Photos. ***Lloyd, Earl*** photograph. AP/Wide World Photos. ***Mabrey, Vicki,*** photograph. Courtesy of Liaison Agency. ***Metcalfe, Ralph,*** photograph. AP/Wide World Photos. ***Moore, Chante,*** photograph by Ken Settle. ***Morial, Ernest "Dutch" Nathan,*** photograph. Amistad Research Center. ***Motley, Marion,*** photograph. AP/Wide World Photos. ***Newsome, Ozzie,*** photograph. AP/Wide World Photos. ***Newton, Thandie,*** photograph. Courtesy of Liaison Agency. ***Osborne, Jeffrey,*** photograph. Courtesy of Liaison Agency. ***Pride, Charley,*** photograph by Ira Schwartz. AP/Wide World Photos. ***Redding, Jay Saunders,*** photograph. Fisk University Library. ***Robertson, Oscar,*** photograph. Courtesy of the University of Cincinnati. ***Shabazz, Betty,*** photograph. AP/Wide World Photos. ***Silver, Horace,*** photograph. Verve Records. ***Sizemore, Barbara,*** photograph. ***Smith, Mary Carter,*** photograph. ***Thomas, Debi,*** photograph by Richard Drew. AP/Wide World Photos. ***Thomas, Isiah,*** photograph. AP/Wide World Photos ***Thompson, Bennie,*** photograph. AP/Wide World Photos. ***Thompson, John W.,*** photograph. ***Tsvangirai, Morgan,*** photograph. AP/Wide World Photos. ***Waters, Benny,*** photograph by Jack Vartoogian. ***Watt, Mel,*** photograph. Courtesy of Liaison Agency. ***Williams, Clarence III,*** photograph. Courtesy of Liaison Agency. ***Witt, Edwin,*** photograph.

Clifford Alexander

1933—

Government official, attorney

One of the first African Americans to rise to the highest levels of the United States government, Clifford L. Alexander served in a succession of presidential administrations during the turbulent 1960s and 1970s. A top advisor to President Lyndon Johnson, he became the head of the Equal Employment Opportunities Commission, supervising governmental anti-discrimination efforts just as the civil rights movement was moving into high gear. The culmination of his career was his service as Secretary of the Army during the administration of President Jimmy Carter. Since leaving government service, he has remained active as a supporter of equal opportunity for African Americans.

Clifford Leopold Alexander was born on September 3, 1933, in New York City; his father was Jamaican by birth, and his mother came from the industrial New York suburb of Yonkers. Alexander's administrative savvy might have been inherited from his father, who served as manager at a YMCA branch in the family's Harlem neighborhood, and also worked as a bank manager. From his mother, he gained instincts for survival in political bureaucracies: she worked for New York City's welfare department for a time, served on a mayoral commission that worked to improve race relations in New York following World War II-era unrest, and finally became the first African American woman to serve as a Democratic representative in the electoral college, the group of state delegations whose voting formalizes the results of the U.S. presidential election every four years.

Educational ambition ran strong in the family, and Alexander attended some of New York's top private schools: the Ethical Cultural School and the Fieldston School. He graduated from the latter and won admission to Harvard University. As a student at Harvard, Alexander was elected student body president. He was the first African American to hold the post. A talented basketball player, Alexander considered a professional career in the sport. However, the academic contacts he made at Harvard exerted a stronger hold on him. Alexander particularly impressed McGeorge Bundy, at the time a Harvard dean, and later a Washington insider who became one of the architects of the U.S. involvement in the Vietnam conflict.

Graduating with honors from Harvard in 1955, Alexander enrolled at the equally strenuous Yale Law School. Although he held a job with the Mutual Life

At a Glance . . .

Born September 21, 1933, in New York, NY; married to Adele; children: Elizabeth, Mark Clifford. *Education:* Harvard University, B.A., 1955; Yale University Law School, law degree, 1958. *Military service:* U.S. National Guard, 1958-59.

Career: Management consultant and former government official; became assistant district attorney, New York, 1959; executive director, Manhattanville-Hamilton-Grangeneighborhood agency, 1961-63; executive director, HARYOU youth agency, 1962-63; NationalSecurity Agency staff member, 1963-64; special assistant and deputy counsel to PresidentLyndon Johnson, 1964-67; chairman, Equal Employment Opportunity Commission, 1967-69; practiced with prominent Washington law firms, 1969-76; Secretary of the Army during the Carter administration, 1977-81; president, Alexander & Associates, 1981-.

Awards: Frederick Douglass Award, 1970; Outstanding Civilian Service Award,Department of the Army, 1980; Distinguished Public Service Award, Department of Defense,1981.

Addresses: *Office*—Alexander & Associates, 400 C. St. NE,Washington, DC 20002.

Insurance firm on the side, he was able to graduate from Yale Law School in only three years. Alexander enlisted in the National Guard in 1958, completed a six-month tour of active duty the following year, and returned to New York to resume his legal career. His first job after leaving the military was as an assistant district attorney for New York County (Manhattan), a position that is often used as a stepping stone to higher political ambitions.

Not yet out of his twenties and newly married to fellow Fieldston student Adele Logan, Alexander quickly moved into high-level positions in the public sector. In 1961 he became executive director of a city housing agency, the Manhattanville-Hamilton-Grange Neighborhood Conservation District. Responsible for enforcing city codes relating to apartment dwellings, Alexander oversaw the correction of more than 3,000 violations during his nine months in office. In 1962, he took a job as executive director of Harlem Youth Opportunities Unlimited.

Alexander's work in these agencies attracted the attention of top officials in the administration of President John F. Kennedy, who was seeking to increase the very small number of African Americans serving in national government posts. After obtaining a job at the National Security Agency in 1963, Alexander reported to Bundy. Among his duties, he was required to monitor the increasingly worrisome reports coming in from diplomats and intelligence officials about the escalation of the fighting in Vietnam. Following President Kennedy's assassination, Alexander was appointed as deputy special assistant to President Lyndon Johnson.

In the wake of the Rev. Martin Luther King Jr.'s march on Washington and the widespread attempts to dismantle the system of institutionalized segregation in the southern states, civil rights became an important national issue. Alexander became one of Johnson's closest advisors on civil rights issues. He helped shepherd the Voting Rights Act of 1965 through Congress, and often bore the brunt of President Johnson's temperamental nature. "Johnson certainly knew how to make you feel fully responsible for what he perceived to be your negligence," Alexander recalled in a 1995 *American Visions* memoir. As associate (later deputy) special counsel to the President, Alexander proved to be an effective advocate for other African American who were seeking governmental jobs.

Alexander's work for Johnson was rewarded in 1967 when he was named chairman of the Equal Employment Opportunities Commission (EEOC). As one of the agencies that took the lead in enforcing new federal anti-discrimination statutes, the EEOC grew dramatically during Alexander's tenure, and launched investigations of hiring practices within major industries. By Alexander's own estimation, the EEOC assisted 70,000 individuals, in comparison to 5,000 individuals assisted under the previous regime. Among the large corporations questioned about their hiring practices were the three major television networks of the day, NBC, CBS, and ABC. Network officials assured Alexander that their programming would strive to portray minority characters in a more favorable, less stereotypical manner.

Shortly after Republicans took control of the White House following the election of Richard Nixon in 1968, Alexander resigned as chairman of the EEOC. He accused the Nixon administration of failing to support the commission's goals, left the EEOC permanently, and returned to his private law practice in Washington. Alexander remained interested in Democratic politics and, in 1974, ran an unsuccessful campaign for mayor of Washington D.C. against veteran politician Walter Washington. He also worked as a Washington-area television talk show host during this period.

When the Democrats regained the White House in 1977, President Jimmy Carter named Alexander as

Secretary of the Army. In this role, Alexander guided the largest branch of the nation's armed forces as it made a critical transition to an all-volunteer force. He was also responsible for managing a budget of 34 billion. Alexander served as Secretary of the Army until President Ronald Reagan took office in 1981.

Like other government officials who had held high office, Alexander could have rested on his laurels and made a comfortable living as a Washington attorney or lobbyist. Instead, he began a new career as a consultant, and used his influence to continue furthering the goal of equality in employment which he had championed for much of his adult life. In 1981 he founded Alexander and Associates, which devoted its efforts to advising companies on how to increase minority hiring. Alexander's most famous client was major league baseball, where African Americans have be traditionally underrepresented in management and administration roles.

In latter stages of his career, Alexander has emerged as an important spokesman for progressive ideals in matters of race. "You [whites] see us as less than you are," he declared bluntly in testimony before the Senate Banking, Housing, and Urban Affairs Committee concerning the status of African American men in American society. Quoted in the *New York Times,* Alexander went on to say that "[y]ou think that we are not as smart, not as energetic, not as well suited to supervise you as you are to supervise us." In a 1999 essay in the *New York Times,* Alexander wrote about the hearings being held concerning the underrepresentation of minorities in television. Looking back on the hearings he himself had conducted in the late 1960s, he noted that the situation of minorities in television was "depressingly familiar," and sadly concluded that "history teaches us that skepticism rather than optimism is the order of the day."

Sources

Books

Hawkins, Walter L., *African American Biographies: Profiles of 558 Current Men and Women,* McFarland and Company, 1992.

Smith, Jessie Carney, ed., *Notable Black American Men,* Gale, 1999.

Periodicals

American Visions, February 1995, p. 42.

New York Times, May 22, 1991, p. D23; August 18, 1999, p. A25.

Washington Post, May 22, 1997, p. A25.

—James M. Manheim

LaVern Baker

1929–1997

Rhythm and blues vocalist

Her voice carried a fascinating mixture of sophistication and down-to-earth power that evoked Bessie Smith and the other vocalists of the classic era, and she did much to set in place the outlines of early rock and roll. LaVern Baker was one of the most original and significant African American vocalists of the 1950s and early 1960s. Yet she might have risen to an even greater level of renown had her career not peaked during an era in which the recordings of African American artists were routinely "covered" or copied by white vocalists, robbing African American creators of their full rewards in monetary compensation and social recognition.

Baker was born Delores Williams on November 11, 1929, in Chicago. Her aunt was the classic blues vocalist Memphis Minnie, and she began to sing with friends at an early age. The raw power in her voice, as it did for so many other African American singers, came from gospel; Baker joined the choir at her Baptist church at the age of 12. By her late teens, she was singing blues and pop in Chicago nightclubs. She had a separate alias for each of the two images she wanted to project; for the down-home crowds recently arrived in Chicago, she took the name of Little Miss Sharecropper, while for other club dates she used the name Bea Baker. The name might have been derived from Memphis Minnie's real name, Merline Baker.

Recorded as "Little Miss Sharecropper"

One of the musicians who recognized Baker's talent early on was swing bandleader Fletcher Henderson, who heard her in a nightclub in 1947. Baker made some blues recordings under the Little Miss Sharecropper name in 1949, and while these vanished without a trace, her reputation in Midwestern clubs continued to rise. She toured extensively, both as a solo artist and with the Todd Rhodes Orchestra. Appearing at Detroit's legendary Flame Show Bar, she made another influential ally in future soul superstar Al Green, who managed Baker for a time and landed her a recording slot with the Columbia label. She also took vocals, not always credited, on recordings by Rhodes and bandleader Maurice King.

Baker rose to stardom when she was signed to the Atlantic label in 1953; it was there that she finally adopted the stage name of LaVern Baker. Atlantic, under the direction of producers and founders Ahmet Ertegun and Jerry Wexler, had pioneered a distinct

At a Glance . . .

Born Delores Williams on November 11, 1929, in Chicago, IL; early in career used stage names Little Miss Sharecropper and Bea Baker; died March 10, 1997, in New York, NY.

Career: Rhythm-and-blues recording artist. Recorded debut single as Little Miss Sharecropper, 1949; signed to Atlantic label and began to record as LaVern Baker, 1953; reachedpop top 20 with "Tweedlee Dee"; success diluted by white cover versions of"Tweedlee Dee" and other songs; reached pop top ten with "I Cried aTear," 1959; left Atlantic for Brunswick Records, 1963; suffered attack of pneumonia in Vietnam, 1969, with extensive convalescence in Philippines; became entertainment director at U.S. military base at Subic Bay, Philippines, 1969; performed at Atlantic Records 40th anniversary party, New York, 1988; replaced Ruth Brown in Broadway musical *Black and Blue,* 1990; recorded and performed extensively, 1990s.

Awards: Rhythm & Blues Foundation Career Achievement Award, 1990; inducted into Rock and Roll Hall of Fame, 1991.

rhythm-and-blues sound favoring sharp, precise arrangements that nevertheless kept in touch with the emerging rhythms of the streets. The material and sound that the label sent Baker's way showcased her skills perfectly. Baker's second recording session for Atlantic yielded the hit "Tweedlee Dee" in 1954. The recording rose to Number Fourteen on the pop charts and reached the one-million sales mark. As was common practice at the time, however, white recording executives moved to minimize Baker's success by releasing a cover version of "Tweedlee Dee" by a white artist. Georgia Gibbs's version of "Tweedlee Dee" on the Mercury label reached the Number Two chart position, and copies of Baker's songs by Gibbs and other vocalists continued to appear during many of Baker's prime recording years in the late 1950s. Unlike many other African American artists, Baker protested this unfair practice. She filed suit, claiming that her own interpretation of "Tweedlee Dee" constituted a copyrightable arrangement, but her suit was unsuccessful. Baker also wrote a letter to a U.S. congressman describing the injustices that were being visited upon African American recording artists—but in return received only a publicity packet.

Baker pressed on, and recorded a tribute album to Bessie Smith in 1958. The following year, she reached the pop Top Ten charts with the sultry "I Cried a Tear." The song featured saxophone work by King Curtis, who offered a close instrumental counterpart for Baker's own style. At one point, embarking on an Australian tour with a group of early rock and roll acts, Baker mailed Gibbs a flight-insurance document she had purchased at the airport. She enclosed a letter saying Gibbs might need insurance against the possibility that, with Baker absent, she wouldn't have any more material to copy. Baker had another minor hit with "Saved," a quasi-gospel number penned by the masters of white rhythm-and-blues composition, Jerry Leiber and Mike Stoller.

With her highly rhythmic vocals backed by Atlantic's zippy accompaniment tracks, Baker must be counted not only as a major rhythm-and-blues artist, but as one of the pioneers of rock and roll as well. However, as both African American and white music moved in new stylistic directions in the 1960s, Baker's popularity declined somewhat. She moved to the Brunswick label in 1963, but derived much of her income from live concert appearances during the 1960s. During the Vietnam War, she gave concerts to entertain U.S. troops.

Baker's later years would seem an ideal subject for cinematic treatment. In 1969, while on tour in Vietnam, she fell seriously ill with pneumonia. She survived, but faced a lengthy period of recuperation in the Philippines. After her recovery she decided to stay there, and landed a job as entertainment director at the U.S. military base at Subic Bay. She raised a family in the Philippines, and did not return to the U.S. mainland for nearly 20 years. The stay might have been permanent had not the American popular music industry finally begun to honor its legends—in particular its underappreciated African American legends.

In 1989, Baker came back to the United States to attend the 40th-anniversary celebration at Atlantic Records. Baker performed at the star-studded event, which was held at New York's Madison Square Garden. After that, new opportunities began to flow Baker's way. She made extended appearances on Broadway as a replacement for vocalist Ruth Brown in the rhythm-and-blues-themed musical *Black and Blue,* recorded two new albums and a song for the soundtrack of the film *Dick Tracy,* and performed club dates in New York. Baker was honored in 1990 with induction into the Rock and Roll Hall of Fame and with a Career Achievement Award from the Rhythm & Blues Foundation.

Tragically, illness cast a dark shadow upon Baker's life. Afflicted with diabetes for many years, she was finally forced to undergo a double amputation of her legs. As was typical of the determination she had shown throughout her career, Baker returned to performing.

Down Beat magazine lauded the "heart-wrenching set" she performed in Newport, Rhode Island at the Rockport Rhythm & Blues Festival during the last year of her life. Baker died in New York City on March 10, 1997.

Selected discography

LaVern Baker, Atlantic, 1953.
LaVern, Atlantic, 1956.
Sings Bessie Smith, Atlantic, 1958.
Blues Ballads, Atlantic, 1959.
Saved, Atlantic, 1959.
See See Rider, Atlantic, 1959.
Soul on Fire: The Best of LaVern Baker, Rhino, 1991.
Woke Up This Morni', DRG, 1992.
Blues Side of Rock 'n' Roll, Star Club, 1993.

Sources

Books

Contemporary Musicians, volume 25, Gale, 1999.
Larkin, Colin, ed., *The Encyclopedia of Popular Music,* Muze UK, 1998.
Romanowski, Patricia, and Holly George-Warren, *The New Rolling Stone Encyclopedia of Rock and Roll,* Fireside, 1995.

Periodicals

Down Beat, July 1997, p. 12.
New York Times, March 12, 1997.

Other

Additional information for this profile was obtained from http://www.allmusic.com

—James M. Manheim

Lem Barney

1945—

Former football player, broadcaster, finance director

One of the most versatile defensive backs to ever play in the NFL, Lem Barney of the Detroit Lions was a threat to the opposing team whenever he touched the ball. The Hall of Fame cornerback had sprinter speed and gained 1,057 yards on 56 interceptions during his ten-year career. When he retired from football in 1977, Barney retained his celebrity status as an advocate for youth and civic affairs and as a church leader. Additionally, Barney worked as a sports broadcaster and public relations executive for the Michigan Consolidated Gas Company. A 1993 arrest for drug possession tarnished his image somewhat, but Barney wove through the charges and negative publicity as if they were opposing tacklers and was eventually acquitted. He went on to become a finance director for former teammate Mel Farr at his auto dealership in Detroit, and continued to work on behalf of his community.

Born Lemuel Jackson Barney in Gulfport, Mississippi in 1945, Barney had an early affinity for football. A player since grade school, he went on to excel at the high school level as a defensive back and was also utilized as a punter, quarterback, kick returner, and holder. At Jackson State University in Mississippi, Barney had 26 interceptions in three seasons and was the team's punter. After earning a bachelor's degree in health and science in 1967, Barney was a second round draft pick of the Detroit Lions, a team he would play for throughout his career.

In his first professional game with the Lions, Barney returned an interception for a touchdown against the legendary Green Bay Packers. "I remember every detail," Barney told James Buckley, Jr of NFL Publishing. "They got the ball first. First play is a run for 3 yards. Second play, [quarterback] Bart Starr tries a short out to Boyd Dowler. I read it, dive for the ball and grab it, do a forward somersault, get up and run 24 yards for the score. First pass ever thrown my way in the NFL and I took it in. I thought to myself, "'Lord, this is going to be easy.'" Barney went on to become the team's co-leader in interceptions and was named the NFL's Defensive Rookie of the Year in 1967.

"Interceptions were my forté," Barney admitted to Buckley. "I liked to think of myself as a defensive weapon turned offensive weapon. The keys were, and are, knowledge of your opponents and the guts to say that once the ball is in the air, it's as much mine as his." Although Barney made the Pro Bowl seven times, the Detroit Lions failed to achieve anything of note while he was on the roster. "We had some great players when I arrived in 1967," Barney told George Puscas of the *Detroit Free Press,* "then when [head coach Joe] Schmidt resigned after 1971 and [defensive coach Jim] David left, it was a struggle. We had four different coaches and didn't top .500 my last five years."

Befriended Marvin Gaye

During the late 1960s, Barney and Lions teammate Mel Farr became close friends with Motown singer Marvin Gaye. The trio would play golf and hang out together and, at one point, Gaye considered trying out for the Detroit Lions. The tryout never occurred.

At a Glance . . .

Born Lemuel Jackson Barney on September 8, 1945 in Gulfport, MS; married to Martha, 1967. children: Lem III, LaTrece. *Education:* Bachelor's degree in health and science, Jackson State University, 1967.

Career: Professional football player for the Detroit Lions, 1967-77; sang backgroundvocals on the song "What's Going On" by Marvin Gaye, 1971; manager ofcivic affairs, Michigan Consolidated Gas Company, 1979-93; college football broadcaster, BlackEntertainment Television, 1980-; finance director, Mel Farr Automotive Group, 1993-.

Awards: Defensive Rookie of the Year, NFL,1967; elected to seven Pro Bowls;inducted into the Pro Football Hall of Fame, 1992; inducted into the Afro-American Sports Hallof Fame, 1992.

Addresses: *Office*—Mel Farr Automotive Group, 24750 Greenfield Road,Oak Park, MI 48237.

Barney and Farr did, however, crossover to Gaye's profession and the two can be heard at the beginning of Gaye's 1971 classic song, "What's Going On." For their efforts, Barney and Farr received a gold record.

Following his retirement from professional football in 1977, Barney remained active within the community. He became involved with a number of organizations such as the United Way, Metro Detroit Youth Foundation, Detroit Adult Service Center, Children's Hospital and many others. In 1979, he was hired as manager of civic affairs for the Michigan Consolidated Gas Company. One year later, Barney began a career as a color commentator of college football games for Black Entertainment Television.

Enshrined in the Hall of Fame

In 1992 Barney was elected to the Pro Football Hall of Fame, becoming only the fifth cornerback to be inducted. "I never was on a championship team," Barney reflected to Puscas of the *Detroit Free Press,* "not in grade school, high school, college or pro. Now I can feel like I really belong." For the ceremony, Barney chose his former defensive coach Jim David to induct him. "If there was ever anybody better than Lem, I never saw or heard of him," David declared to Puscas. "Nobody before or since measured up to him... He had speed and quickness and great acceleration. He had good hands, too, and a willingness to hit. And he was smart, really a smart player; he never beat us with a dumb play."

Less than a year after his induction into the Hall of Fame, Barney was arrested after a traffic accident in Detroit on charges of drunken driving and possession of cocaine and marijuana. Many were shocked that the man who would often speak at school assemblies and instruct students to avoid drugs, would have been involved in such activity. Barney was fired from his job at Michigan Consolidated Gas Company and, after a year of negative publicity, was cleared of the charges. He then went to work as a financial director for former teammate Mel Farr, who owned a chain of automobile dealerships.

Barney continues to work with Farr and is still active with a number of organizations in the Detroit area. He is also a lay minister at the Springhill Missionary Baptist Church. Barney told Puscas that he lives his life with "the teachings and virtues that my mom and dad gave us, and the golden rule that you do unto others as you would have them do unto you—that's all I try to do every day."

Sources

Periodicals

Detroit Free Press, June 7, 1987, p. 3K; January 27, 1992, p. 3C; July 31, 1992, p. 1D; November 20, 1992, p.1B; March 20, 1993, p. 3A; March 23, 1993, p. 3A; March 24, 1993, p. 1C; March 29, 1993, p. 1B; April 10, 1993, p.10A; April 16, 1993, p. 6B; April 22, 1993, p. 1B; May 5, 1994, p. 1B; May 6, 1994, p. 1B.

Detroit News, December 16, 1999.

Jet, April 12, 1993, p. 50.

New York Times, January 26, 1992, p. S-7; August 2, 1992, p. S-8.

Other

Additional information for this profile was obtained from www.NFL.com/Lions/news/981126barney.html; and www.profootballhof.com/famers/barney.html

—Brian Escamilla

Michael Beach

1963—

Actor

In an environment that has neglected to include African American actors or pigeonholed them as villains or troubled characters, Michael Beach has managed to become one of the most versatile actors around, playing those roles and others, on television, film, and in the theater since the 1980s. Although known for his various roles as a cheating husband, he has moved away from this image to take on a variety of interesting personas ranging from cop to minister to doctor. He also has played other complex and demanding parts, including a man who is HIV positive in the award-winning TV show, *ER*; a spouse attempting to hang onto his failing marriage in the box office smash, *Soul Food*; and a sociopathic drug runner in the well-received independent film, *One False Move*.

Beach has starred on the popular NBC drama, *Third Watch,* in a part created for him by the producers of the show who worked with him on *ER*. On *Third Watch* he skillfully plays "Doc" Parker, a caring paramedic. Beach clearly enjoys the human side of the drama. "What I love about this character is, he's not a Joe medical guy," he told the *New York Daily News*. "He's more of a people person." To understand the role, Beach hung around with actual paramedics, firefighters and police. He acknowledged in the *New York Daily News* that this was difficult for him because "the technical stuff doesn't come easily to me." Beach's face became familiar to television audiences after he appeared on *ER*. He hoped that his role on *Third World* would give him more exposure to the viewing audience. "What I'm trying to do is get my face out there and get some face and name recognition," he commented to the *New York Daily News*.

Beach was cast for the part in *Third Watch*, which has a multi-ethnic cast, before the NAACP publicized the lack of racial diversity on the top television networks. He was disturbed by the absence of African American actors as leading or supporting characters on other new TV shows, and has agreed with the NAACP's position. "Now I'm finding a lot of my friends are being placed in series who were not in the pilot," Beach told the *New York Daily News*. "It's unfortunate that it has to come to that, but what is it going to take for a catalyst to make the networks open their eyes? Not just for blacks, but for Asians? And the world is full of a lot of people."

At a Glance . . .

Born October 30, 1963, and raised in the Roxbury section of Boston, MA; married to Tracey; children: four. *Education:* graduated from The Julliard School in New York.

Career: Actor; began acting in high school and while attending The Julliard School;performed in off-Broadway, regional, and Los Angeles plays; wrote and directed others; stagecredits include *Much Ado About Nothing* and *Ascension Day*; film credits include *Streets Of Gold*, 1986; *Suspect*, 1987; *Lean On Me*, 1989; *TheAbyss*, 1989; *Internal Affairs*, 1990; *Cadence*, 1991; *Guilty As Charged*, 1991; *Late For Dinner*, 1991; *One False Move*, 1992; *True Romance*, 1993; *Short Cuts*, 1993; *Bad Company*, 1995; *Waiting ToExhale*, 1995; *White Man's Burden*, 1995; *A Family Thing*, 1996; and *Soul Food*, 1997; television performances include *Vengeance: The Story of TonyCimo*, 1986; *Open Admissions*, 1988; *ER*, 1994-; *Rebound*, 1996;*Ms. Scrooge*, 1997; *Fortunate Son*, 1998; *The Ruby Bridges Story*, 1998;*Third Watch*, 1999; and *Made Men*, 1999; has also has performed in television-shows such as *Law and Order*, *Touched By An Angel*, *NYPD Blue*, and*The Street*.

Awards: First Place, NAACP National Drama Competition, 1982; Drama Award for Outstanding Achievement, 1984; and the New York Shakespeare Festival Award, 1986.

Addresses: *Home*—Los Angeles, CA; *Office*—c/o Eddie Michaels & Associates, Inc., 9025 Wilshire Blvd., Ste. 450, Beverly Hills, CA 90211.

Beach already has played a lot of lead roles. He played the leading man in an HBO action film entitled *Made Men* with Timothy Dalton in 1999. He also starred opposite Lela Rochon in the 1998 ABC television movie *The Ruby Bridges Story*, which was based on a true story of desegregation in a public school in New Orleans. While *People Weekly* gave the movie a so-so rating, the magazine observed, "Michael Beach gives grown-up depth to the character of Ruby's father, Abon." Beach's other television credits include starring with Don Cheadle in the 1996 HBO film, *Rebound*, which was directed by fellow *ER* cast member Eric LaSalle. He also co-starred with Cicely Tyson as a preacher in a 1997 USA Network film, *Ms. Scrooge*, a revised version of the Charles Dickens' classic, *A Christmas Carol*. For *People Weekly*, *Ms. Scrooge* didn't pass muster. "But," stated the magazine, "there is one shining moment: The miser's clergyman nephew (Michael Beach) delivers a folksy but profound homily that captures the meaning of Christmas better than any dozen carols." Beach also had the starring role in a short film, *Fortunate Son*, which he first learned about when a man stopped him on the street in Los Angeles and asked him if he would read his script. The film was produced and shown during Black History Month on the Showtime channel in 1998.

Beach has worked with highly visible actors and directors. In what many critics consider to be his first major film role, Beach starred opposite Angela Bassett and Whitney Houston in *Waiting to Exhale* in 1995. He also starred with Vanessa Williams and Vivica Fox in the 1997 hit movie *Soul Food;* Billy Bob Thornton in *One False Move;* Robert Duvall and James Earl Jones in the comedy drama, *A Family Thing;* and *White Man's Burden* with Harry Belafonte. Beach's other film credits include *Bad Company*, *Guilty as Charged*, *Late for Dinner*, *Lean on Me*, *Suspect*, *Streets of Gold*, and *Cadence*. He has also worked with some of Hollywood's most respected directors, among them Robert Altman in *Short Cuts*, Tony Scott, in *True Romance*, Jim Cameron in *The Abyss*, and Mike Figgis in *Internal Affairs*. The 1992 film, *One False Move*, received a fair amount of press coverage. *The New Yorker* called it "skillfully acted and welcomely unpredictable" and added that Beach played his sociopathic character with "inhuman brilliance."

Beach's acting abilities were recognized almost from the start of his career in the 1980s. In addition to his television work on *Third Watch* and *ER*, he has appeared in films such as *Evening Class*, *Hit List*, and *Another Round*. He also has played roles in the CBS television films *Open Admissions* and *Vengeance: The Story of Tony Cimo*. *Open Admissions* was actually a play filmed for television. It concerns a college where open admissions for minorities is mandatory, but the system is not benefitting pupils. Its strong casting was praised by *The New York Times*. The *New York Times* reviewer also enjoyed Beach's performance, "Mr. Beach is admirable as the student who changes from a cheery, upbeat fellow to one who finally understands that he is not yet equipped and is not learning anything, thanks to the system and his teacher, although he is being shoved ahead automatically. From the moment he appears with a smile, through the scenes where he realizes his helplessness, to the final scenes where the situation is, if not resolved, at least moving in the right direction, Mr. Beach makes an onlooker feel deeply about his fate." Beach has also landed regular spots on the series *Under Suspicion* and *The Street*, and has guest-starred on shows such as *Law and Order*, *Street Justice*, *Touched by an Angel*, and *NYPD Blue*. Beach has portrayed several villainous characters. In *Waiting to Exhale*, his character abandons his African American spouse for his white secretary while in *ER,* his unfaithful character infects another character with HIV. Beach's character in *Soul Food,* a depressed attorney whose wife Teri (played by Vanessa Williams) doesn't support his artistic inclinations, has an affair with Teri's cousin. His role in *Soul Food* upset many African American women. "I'll be walking through the mall," Beach told *People Weekly,* "and they'll be yelling at me, 'Why are you always mistreating women? Can't you be nice?'" After *Soul Food* was released, Beach seemed to be steering clear of characters who were unsavory. "A lot of people tell me they want to see me play a good husband," he told *TV Guide.* He was relieved to play the parts of men with good hearts: a minister in *Ms. Scrooge,* and a strong-willed father in the racially charged *Ruby Bridges Story.* Beach prefers to play fully developed characters. As he told *Essence,* "In *Exhale,* the Black male characters were just there for the women to react or respond to...The Black men in *Soul Food* are much more rounded. You see how we feel and think, what we experience and how we love."

Born on October 30, 1963, Beach was raised in the tough Roxbury section of Boston, Massachussetts. Before he became interested in acting, he was a star athlete. Fate and luck played a role in his career aspirations. Beach was headed to an elite prep school on a football scholarship when an ankle injury thwarted his athletic ambitions. He started acting in high school after a friend convinced him to audition for a school play, *The Diary of Anne Frank.* Beach loved acting from the start, although he recalled in *Entertainment Weekly* that one instructor "was extremely upset that they cast me as a Dutch Jew." Later, he won first prize at the 1982 NAACP National Drama Competition. Beach received training as an actor at The Julliard School in New York, where he met other talented African American actors including Eriq LaSalle, Ving Rhames, and Andre Braugher.

While studying at Julliard, Beach received the Drama Award for Outstanding Achievement in 1984. Two years later, he captured the New York Shakespeare Festival Award. Beach has acted in more than 18 plays, and has written and directed many others. He has appeared in off-Broadway productions, in regional theater, and in plays in Los Angeles, including *Much Ado About Nothing* and *Ascension Day.* His first film break came in 1986, when he appeared with Wesley Snipes in *Streets of Gold.*

When he is not on the set of *Third Watch* in New York City, Beach and his wife, Tracey, a homemaker, live in Los Angeles with their four children. Apart from acting, he loves spending time with his family. Beach's decision to star in *Ms. Scrooge* was made with his family in mind. "I did that to be able to sit down and watch something with my kids," he stated in *TV Guide.* "Normally they can't see the stuff that I do." Beach continues to hope that African American films will gain wider respect and acceptance in the industry. "Now my only wish is for Black films to be on par with the rest of Hollywood," he explained in *Essence.* "*Exhale* was one step in that direction, and *Soul Food* is a step beyond."

Sources

Books

Who's Who among African Americans, Gale, 1998, p.76.
Who's Who in Hollywood, Facts on File, 1992, vol. A-L, p. 106.

Periodicals

Entertainment Weekly, January 12, 1996, p. 40; October 17, 1997; January 14, 2000, p. 83.
Essence, November 1997, p. 66.
New Republic, February 20, 1995, p. 30.
New York, July 27, 1992, p. 47.
New York Daily News, September 17, 1999.
New York Times, September 8, 1988, p. C22; April 10, 1988, pp. 39, 45.
New Yorker, July 27, 1992, p. 54.
People Weekly, December 8, 1997, p. 17; December 29, 1997-January 5, 1998, p. 138; January 19, 1998, p. 13.
Time, August 3, 1992, p. 75.
TV Guide, November 8, 1997, p.5.

Other

Additional information for this profile was obtained from Eddie Michaels & Associates, Inc., Public Relations and Marketing, and from the Internet.

—Alison Carb Sussman

Asha Blake

1961(?)—

Journalist

Television journalist Asha Blake was offered a career-making assignment in the summer of 1999 when NBC executives tapped her to be one of three co-hosts for an extended hour of the *Today* show, called *Later Today*. Blake's jump to such national prominence came after years of professional transience and job uncertainty. Blake had been a popular local anchor in Minneapolis, Detroit, and Los Angeles for more than a decade, and always won praise for her combination of cool professionalism and personal warmth. "Blake had that hard-to-define quality that spells network material," declared Julie Hinds in the *Detroit Free Press*. "She had an on-air ease that made her seem down-to-earth, as well as the looks that are a prerequisite for the national spotlight."

Of Indo-Caribbean heritage, Blake was born in early 1960s in Guyana, a country on South America's northeast coast. The daughter of two educational professionals, she grew up in Toronto, Canada and then Minnesota, a part of the Midwest not necessarily noted for its large ethnic population. The family settled in Circle Pines, a northern suburb of Minneapolis-St. Paul, and Blake was the homecoming queen at Centennial High School. She earned a journalism degree from the University of Minnesota, and first appeared on television as the host of a local music show in the Minneapolis-St. Paul area.

One of Blake's first post-college jobs compelled her to move to New Mexico, where she worked as a radio announcer with her own music program. A television station in Grand Junction, Colorado, hired Blake as a reporter in the mid-1980s, and from there she went on to a stint at a Little Rock, Arkansas outlet. She returned to the Minneapolis-St. Paul area in 1987 when KARE-TV offered her a slot as a general assignment reporter.

In 1990, Blake fell while jogging and suffered two herniated discs in her spine. She spent a few weeks in the hospital, and was forced to recuperate at home in a back brace for several more weeks. As she told *Minneapolis-St. Paul Star-Tribune* reporters Neal Justin and Susie Hopper, "There were some days I just wanted to drink red wine because it would take the pain away...I had never understood chronic pain. It was a life-changing experience for me." Blake soon began covering consumer health issues at the station, and became KARE-TV's medical reporter. As the station's medical reporter, she wrote, produced, and delivered

At a Glance . . .

Born c. 1961, in Guyana; daughter of an education specialist and a teacher; married Mark Dusbabek (affiliated with a gold-equipment firm) 1994; children: Sasha Rose. *Education:* Received degree from University of Minnesota Journalism School.

Career: Began television career as a reporter at KJCT-TV, in Grand Junction, CO;worked as a reporter for KTHV-TV, Little Rock, AR; KARE-TV in Minneapolis, MN, began asgeneral assignment reporter, became medical reporter, 1987-93; WDIV-TV, Detroit, weekendanchor and medical reporter, 1993-96; ABC News, New York City, New York bureau correspondent and co-anchor of *World News This Morning, World News Now,*and *Good Morning America Sunday,* 1996-98; KNBC-TV, Los Angeles, CA, late afternoon newscast anchor, 1998-99; *Later Today,* NBC News, New York City, co-host,1999-00.

Awards: Two Emmy award nominations for reporting while at WDIV-TV, Detroit.

Member: South Asian Journalists' Association.

Addresses: *Office—Later Today,* NBC News, 30 Rockefeller Plaza, NewYork, NY 10012. *Agent*—Ken Lindner & Associates, 2049 Century ParkEast, Suite 3050, Los Angeles, CA 90067.

stories on breast cancer, vaccinations, and medical fraud, among other topics. "That really changed my life in many ways," Blake recalled about her back injury in a speech before an audience of television critics in the summer of 1999, according to Tim Kiska of the *Detroit News.* "I was in so much pain. I devoted my life, at that point, to health and wellness information."

Passed Over for Anchor Spot

Blake earned solid ratings and an appreciative audience while at KARE, and also became a national correspondent for the *USA Today* newspaper. After six years at the station, she was one of the few qualified staffers eligible for a permanent anchor spot when one became available. This opportunity arose in the spring of 1993, when Blake subbed on the morning news desk at KARE. Although her appearance led to a jump in the station's ratings, the vacant anchor job was given to a blond-haired, blue-eyed newscaster with far less experience. "Blake's numbers, her seven-plus years working in this market and her smooth anchoring style should have made her a shoo-in to keep the anchor spot," opined *Minneapolis-St. Paul Star-Tribune* editorial columnist Clinton Collins Jr. in a column about the scarcity of minorities in local Minneapolis-St. Paul television news organizations.

Later that year, Blake was offered a job with NBC affiliate WDIV-TV in Detroit—a city that was the first in the nation to feature an African American woman as co-anchor on all three of its evening news broadcasts. She took the offer, and spent three successful years there as a medical reporter, weekend anchor, and late-evening news anchor. Blake earned two Emmy award nominations, which helped to elevate her status within the television news industry. In broadcasting journalism, Detroit is considered the last step before a job with a national news organization; the market is known for the quick-breaking nature of its news stories, which challenge reporters' skills both at the desk and in the field.

Impervious Professional Demeanor

Blake excelled at WDIV, and remained cool one evening in early 1995 when weathercaster Michelle Leigh made a on-air remark which equated African American men with gorillas. Blake and her African American co-anchor Emory King, "looked at Leigh in silence for a few seconds, then signed off," reported *Jet* magazine. Leigh was fired from the station. Executives from the major networks began courting Blake and, after her three years in Detroit, she knew that her career might not advance any further at WDIV. "There wasn't a lot of upward mobility at the station because the people above—whom I like very much—weren't going anywhere," she told Kiska in the *Detroit News.* WDIV's popular African American evening co-anchor, Carmen Harlan, was a local fixture and unlikely to move out of the city or retire in the near future.

Blake's career considerations also had to take into account more personal concerns. During her time in Detroit, Blake married former Minnesota Viking football player Mark Dusbabek, whom she had met at a charity event in Minneapolis. For a time, Dusbabek worked in the financial markets in Chicago and commuted from Detroit. However, when the couple had a daughter, life became a bit more hectic. A move to another city seemed like an added complication, but as Blake told Hinds in the *Detroit Free Press* interview, "you weigh the quality of life versus your job. It wasn't easy. I hadn't always thought, 'Hey, I've got to get to a network.'"

In October of 1996, Blake joined the team at ABC News in New York. She was disappointed to be leaving Detroit, where she had become a popular local media presence. "I don't know if I'll find as good a place ever in life," she told Cheryl Johnson of the *Minneapolis-St. Paul Star-Tribune.* "They tried to keep me here. They were going to offer me more money, but it couldn't compare" to the ABC News contract. Blake began as a medical correspondent at the network's New York bureau, and was tapped to anchor *World News Now,* the network's well-received overnight news show. She occasionally appeared as a co-anchor for *Good Morning America Sunday.* Dusbabek took a year off from his job to stay home with their daughter, Sasha Rose. In October of 1998, Blake returned to the affiliate level with NBC, but in a city that is arguably the most intense local news market in the United States: Los Angeles. She spent the next several months anchoring the late-afternoon newscast for KNBC-TV.

In the summer of 1999, Blake was selected as one of the co-hosts of *Later Today,* a one-hour extension of NBC's extremely successful morning news show, *Today. Today,* a staple of the network's news division since the early days of television, was a perennial ratings-winner. However, the rest of NBC's daytime line-up was usually bested by the offerings of other networks. A particular favorite among women viewers was an innovative ABC program called *The View,* which featured four female journalists who chatted amongst themselves about current events, and then interviewed guests in the second half of the show. It was hoped that a combination of Blake and Florence Henderson, who played Carol Brady on the popular 1970s show *The Brady Bunch,* and Jodi Applegate, a reporter on the regular *Today* show, would achieve similar ratings success. "NBC has talked for years about expanding *Today,*" stated Associated Press reporter David Bauder in a report that appeared in the *Detroit News.* "Even with the program's rating success, NBC's desultory daytime lineup could never take advantage of its head start."

Blake was tapped for the *Later Today* job by *Today* show executive producer Jeff Zucker, who was a new father when Blake was delivering the overnight news on *World News Now* for ABC. Zucker often tuned in during middle-of-the-night feedings. Henderson had been a member of the *Today* show cast in the late 1950s, and Applegate had strong words of praise for her co-host Blake. "She's every bit as down to earth, cute and fun as you think she is," Applegate told *Minneapolis-St. Paul Star-Tribune* reporters Justin and Hopper. "You really can't fool the camera when you're doing something like *Later Today,* which is why a lot of people don't succeed at it. It really has to be you."

Reviews for *Later Today* were initially lukewarm, but Blake was impervious to the thought of having to relocate again. "I've moved so much that I don't put things on the wall until we've been somewhere for a year," the veteran journalist told Justin and Hopper in the *Minneapolis-St. Paul Star-Tribune* article when she started the *Later Today* job. "If you walk into my office in the next year, you won't see anything up on the wall. You get used to it in the business." Unfortunately, *Later Today* was canceled in August of 2000. But with her warm personality and strong penchant for good journalism, viewers won't have to wait long for Asha Blake to return to the spotlight.

Sources

Detroit Free Press, September 1, 1999.
Detroit News, July 31, 1999.
Jet, February 20, 1995, p. 46.
Minneapolis-St. Paul Star-Tribune, August 18, 1993, p. 19A; July 2, 1996, p. 4B; October 5, 1999, p. 1E.
New York Post, September 1, 1999.
St. Paul Pioneer Press, June 23, 1996, p. 1A.

—Carol Brennan

Isaac Bruce

1972—

Professional football player

"Guys look at me and think I'm too skinny," Isaac Bruce told *Sports Illustrated for Kids* in the early years of his career. "They probably ask what I'm doing playing in the NFL. So I always try to make a big play. And when I block, I try to knock the defender on his butt." That determination allowed the six-foot-tall Bruce, who at 185 pounds may not fit the image many people have of a professional football player, to emerge as one of the brightest new stars in the game of football during the late 1990s.

Nicknamed "Reverend Ike" because of his plans to enter the ministry after the end of his playing career, Isaac Isidore Bruce was born on November 10, 1972, in Fort Lauderdale, Florida. The 13th of 15 children, he attended Dillard High School in Fort Lauderdale. He is a cousin of Derrick Moore, a running back who played for the Detroit Lions and the Carolina Panthers during the mid-1990s. During his senior year in high school in 1989, Bruce gave an indication of his emerging talent on the gridiron. He was named to Fort Lauderdale's All-City squad, and led Dillard to a Florida state championship in the school's division.

Starred at Memphis State

Following his graduation from high school, Bruce moved to California and attended West Los Angeles and Santa Monica Junior College. In 1992, he transferred to Memphis State University in Tennessee. Bruce majored in physical education at Memphis State, and enjoyed a fine collegiate football career. He graduated from Memphis State with a total of 113 pass receptions, 15 touchdowns, and 1,586 total yards.

Bruce's abilities on the football field caught the attention of pro scouts, and he was highly regarded as the 1994 NFL draft approached. Selected in the second round by the Los Angeles Rams, he quickly fulfilled the team's high expectations. Bruce's first pass reception in the NFL came on September 11, 1994, during a game against the Atlanta Falcons, and it marked the beginning of a rapid rise to fame. Despite missing the last four games of his rookie season due to a sprained right knee, Bruce ranked seventh on the team in yardage gained, and was named Rams Rookie of the Year by several Southern California sports journalists' groups.

At a Glance . . .

Born Isaac Isidore Bruce November 10, 1972, in Fort Lauderdale, FL. *Education:* attended West Los Angeles and Santa Monica Junior College; graduated from Memphis State University, Memphis, TN, with a degree in physical education. *Religion:* Church of God in Christ.

Career: Professional football player; star player in collegiate career at Memphis State;drafted in second round by Los Angeles Rams, 1994; followed team to St. Louis; set record asall-time leading gainer among wide receivers (record eclipsed at season's end by another-player) in second year, 1995; led the NFL in yardage gained, 1996; plagued by injuries, 1997 and1998; recovered from injuries and led the Rams to the NFL championship, 1999.

Addresses: *Office*—c/o St. Louis Rams, One Rams Way, St. Louis, MO63045.

As his second professional season approached, Bruce became one of the NFL's most closely watched young players. He began to flash his characteristic wit when he recalled a pregame kiss from Rams owner Georgia Frontiere in an interview with the *Sporting News,* saying it was the "[f]irst time I ever smelled money on someone's breath." Following the team's relocation to St. Louis, Bruce became the starting wide receiver. He compiled 119 receptions for 1,781 yards and 13 touchdowns. The 1,781-yard total briefly made Bruce the NFL's all-time leading gainer among wide receivers. However, he was edged out at the season's end by Jerry Rice of the San Francisco 49ers.

During the 1996 season, Bruce again served notice that his name would be showing up frequently in the record books. With 84 receptions for an NFL-league-leading 1,338 yards, he set a record for most pass receptions (224) in a player's first three NFL seasons. Rounding out the 1996 campaign with seven receptions for 104 yards in the postseason Pro Bowl all-star game, Bruce seemed firmly ensconced as a celebrity star and as one of the greatest wide receivers ever to play the game. However, the next two seasons would threaten to ground Bruce's high-flying career.

St. Louis Rams coach Dick Vermeil told *Sports Illustrated* that Bruce was the best player he had ever coached, "a complex, gifted athlete, probably the best vertical, one-on-one, bursting-type receiver in the league." For his own part, Bruce told the magazine, "I don't think I'm the best, I know I am." During the 1997 and 1998 seasons, however, Bruce appeared to be another example of a young athlete who had pushed too hard and burned out too fast. In the first game of the 1997 season against the Denver Broncos, Bruce had to leave the field without catching a pass due to a hamstring injury. He missed the rest of the game and the next four games as well.

Bruce returned to the lineup later in the season, and at times his raw ability showed through. In a game against the Atlanta Falcons, he recorded ten receptions for a career-high 233 yards, the best performance by an NFL receiver that season. In 1998, Bruce suffered a recurrence of the hamstring injury that had plagued him during the previous season. He missed eight games and was finally placed on the injured reserve list early in December. The Rams management grumbled about his Bruce's proneness to injury, and it became clear just how much the team's fortunes depended on those of its star wide receiver. During the 1997 and 1998 seasons, the Rams compiled a dismal 9-23 record.

Bruce bounced back strongly in 1999, played in all 16 games, and caught 77 passes. His offensive reliability led the Rams to the NFL playoffs and to a divisional championship win over the Minnesota Vikings. Against the Vikings, Bruce had four receptions for a total of 133 yards. Another pivotal event of the 1999 season occurred off the field. Bruce's car flipped over on a Missouri interstate highway when a tire blew out as he returned from a basketball game with his girlfriend. Bruce and his girlfriend were unhurt, and he credited divine intervention for their good fortune.

"Y'all are afraid to write the word Jesus," Bruce told *Sports Illustrated* after the accident. Notable among athletes for his strong and publicly expressed religious faith, he also attributed his successful 1999 season to his religious activities. Bruce had fallen behind on tithe contributions to his church, Memphis's Bountiful Blessings Cathedral of Deliverance Church of God in Christ. However, after he wrote a check in a six-figure amount to cover the balance, he returned to peak form. Whatever the source of his inspiration on the playing field, Bruce entered the 21st century as one of professional football's rising stars.

Sources

Books

Bonavita, Mark, and Brendan Roberts, eds., *The Sporting News Pro Football Register,* 1998 edition-,Times Mirror,1998.

Periodicals

New York Times, December 12, 1999, p. 41.
Sporting News, August 28, 1995, p. 34.
Sports Illustrated, November 6, 1995, p. 114; October 12, 1998, p. 68; January 24, 2000, p. 38; February 9, 2000, p. 50.
Sports Illustrated for Kids, September 1996, p. 74.

Other

Additional information for this profile was obtained from http://www.stlouisrams.com

—James M. Manheim

John Bryant

1966—

Businessman, investment broker

John Bryant is a young African American businessman whose track record exemplifies achievement. Having accomplished more by the end of his twenties than most do in a lifetime, he is a shining example of what can be realized through intelligence, personality, determination, and extremely hard work. Bryant is the founder and CEO of Bryant Group Companies, Inc. in Los Angeles, an investment holding company that serves as an umbrella for three of his businesses. These include Bryant Group Consulting, a leadership development and marketing development company, Bryant Group Africa, a firm which imports carved Shona stone and other fine art from Zimbabwe and South Africa, and Bryant Group Capital, an investment and merchant banking firm. Bryant is also the founder and Chairman of Operation HOPE, Inc., a non-profit investment banking organization in Los Angeles, the first of its kind in the United States.

Created as a response to the civil unrest following the Rodney King verdicts in Los Angeles in 1992, Operation HOPE had, by the year 2000, funded over 60 million in inner city loans in conjunction with its partner banks. It has also provided personal finance education to over 50,000 people through its Banking on the Future programs in Los Angeles and New York. Niki Butler Mitchell, author of *The New Color of Success,* wrote in 1999 that Bryant "arguably is the one person most responsible for rebuilding the war-torn communities of South Central Los Angeles."

Bryant has been cited by Presidents Bush and Clinton for his contributions to business and community. He has been lauded by the media: *Time* magazine named him "One of America's 50 Most Promising Leaders of the Future" in 1994. In 1995, *Black Enterprise* magazine listed him as "One of 25 Future Leaders to Watch." The following year, *Swing* magazine included Bryant on its list of 30 "Most Powerful Twentysomethings in America." According to the *Los Angeles Times,* Bryant likes to look back on his accomplishments and remark, "Not bad for a little black boy from Compton."

John Bryant Smith was born on February 6, 1966, in Compton, California. He was the youngest of three children born to Johnie Smith, a flat-finish cement contractor, and his wife, Juanita, a sewing machine operator at McDonnell-Douglas. His parents divorced when he was small. Bryant's mother used her sewing skills to create formal, crushed-velvet suits with bow ties

At a Glance . . .

Born John Bryant Smith February 6, 1966, to Johnie Smith (a cement finishing contractor) and Juanita Smith (a sewing machine operator); married Arlene Bryant, divorced. *Education:* attended Los Angeles City College. *Religion:* African Methodist Episcopal.

Career: Actor, c.1980-83, roles on *Twilight Zone* and *Diff'rent Strokes*; entrepreneur, c.1983-86; investment banker with Wade, Cotter and Company,1986-91; founder of Specialty Lending Group, Wade, Cotter, 1986; founder, CEO, Bryant GroupCompanies, Inc., 1991-; founder, chairman, Operation HOPE, Inc., 1992-; The New Leaders Organization, 1995; United Nations Conference on Trade and Development (UNCTAD), Goodwill Ambassador to United States, 1998-99; special advisor to UNCTAD, 1999; Corporate Council of CEOs, 1999; Adjunct Instructor in Business Management, UCLA Extension.

Selected memberships: Board of directors, California African American MuseumFoundation; national board of directors, Teach for America; board of directors, Operation HOPE,Inc.; board of governors, Kravis Leadership Institute, Claremont McKenna College.

Selected awards: "One of 25 Future Leaders to Watch," *Black Enterprise* magazine, 1995; One of "Top 103 Most Influential People," *Los Angeles Times*, 1999; Knight Commander, Society of Signum Fidei, House ofLippe, 1998; panel participant with Vice President Al Gore, Family Reunion 8, Family andCommunity Policy Conference, Nashville, Tennessee, 1999.

Addresses: *Office*—Operation HOPE, Inc., 707 Wilshire Blvd, Suite 3030, Los Angeles, CA 90017.

for her son. "She sent me to school in Compton dressed like that," Bryant told the *Los Angeles Times* in 1998. "I used to have my rear end kicked every day. I was the outcast, like the overweight kid or the kid with the thick glasses." Nevertheless, Bryant took his mother's efforts to make him into an individual to heart. "First and foremost, my mother was my role model," he wrote in Julian C.R. Okwu's 1997 book, *Face Forward: Young African American Men in a Critical Age.* "To a limited degree, my father, who owned his own business without much of a traditional education, was also an example. My mother once told me that the man can set my salary but I decide my income." Bryant put these lessons to work very early. He started his first business when he was only ten-years-old by selling candy to other children. He had observed that his classmates were chronically late to school because they detoured to a local market to buy candy. Conversations with the store's proprietor revealed the secrets of buying wholesale. With $40 in seed money provided by his mother, Bryant bought, wholesale, the kind of candy his friends liked. He then set up shop on the way to school each morning. Bryant had figured out niche marketing at the age of ten. His candy business was extremely successful. At its peak, he was making $300 a week.

When he was 12-years-old, Bryant dropped his last name–Smith–and began to use his middle name as his last. The following year, he moved in with his father and worked for a time with him in his cement contracting business. The experience convinced Bryant that he did not want to work in the construction industry. He enrolled in the Hollywood Professional School, and was soon rubbing elbows with famous teenage actors. Eventually, he landed bit parts on *The Twilight Zone* and *Diff'rent Strokes.*

In retrospect, Bryant admitted that he was not a very good actor. "There was too much hype and I always found myself playing one role: myself," he told the *Los Angeles Times.* The acting jobs paid well, and Bryant quickly spent what he had earned. By the time he reached the age of 17, the roles had evaporated and his acting career was over almost as soon as it had begun.

Bryant eventually earned a GED, and talked his way into a job at an upscale Malibu restaurant. While working at the restaurant, he met financier Harvey Baskin. Baskin was impressed with the young man, and taught him the art of deal-making and investment banking. Armed with this new knowledge, Bryant looked for ways to make money. A series of disastrous business ventures followed, and he ended up losing everything.

Bryant has frequently remarked that the condition of being broke is an economic state, whereas being poor is a debilitating, defeating frame of mind. At this point in his life, Bryant was broke, but he was not poor. "I couldn't fall from the floor, which is where I was," he stated in *Face Forward,* "so the only place I had to go was up." He was still receiving a small residual check every month and, reasoning that an office had more money-making potential than an apartment, Bryant chose to rent office space and live in his Jeep. For six months he lived in his vehicle, getting up each day and going to work until he was able to rent a room in a house.

In 1986 Bryant was hired by Wade, Cotter, and Company, a specialty investment firm. "This was definitely an affirmative action gig," he told Mitchell. Although a self-described "charity case" at Wade, Cotter, Bryant made the most of this opportunity. In the business of equity lending, he soon realized that there was a certain amount of racism inherent in the system. Poor people, mostly African Americans, were being taken advantage of. They were being targeted for equity loans that they could not afford to repay. Knowing that it was possible to get the same return on loans made to people who were actually capable of repaying the notes, Bryant persuaded Wade, Cotter to let him try. He made them an offer they could not refuse: he would work without salary in return for the company name, its contact list, and 50 percent of any profit. There were no profits the first year for WCC Funding Corporation. However, Bryant brought in $9 million in sales the following year. He produced $15 million in sales during the third year, and $24 million the next. In 1991, Bryant bought out the division and established his own company, Bryant Group Capital.

A mostly white jury acquitted white Los Angeles police officers of charges arising from the beating of Rodney King in 1992. This acquittal provided the flashpoint for riots in South Central Los Angeles. As area businesses were looted and burned, outraged residents and community leaders gathered at local churches to cope with the present and plan for the future. Bryant was one of those residents. He found direction from the Reverend Cecil L. Murray, his pastor at the West Adams First AME Church. Murray urged Bryant to utilize his banking background to help the city.

In the days immediately following the riots, Bryant took $5000 of his own money and founded Operation HOPE, a non-profit organization dedicated to brokering home and small business loans. He also organized and led the first Bankers' Bus Tour through South Central Los Angeles. It would become an annual undertaking. The Tour chartered a bus, and drove bankers through areas they had never seen before: well-kept homes and quiet neighborhoods as well as the barren commercial areas in desperate need of revitalization. For the bankers on the bus, the tour was an eye-opener, marking the beginning of a gradual shift in thinking about the impoverished areas of Los Angeles.

The Community Reinvestment Act of 1977 is a federal law which requires FDIC-insured lenders to lend and invest more in impoverished areas or suffer penalties. By emphasizing this law and helping investors to understand that their impressions of the assets in those areas were not well-founded, Bryant's Bus Tour and Operation HOPE began to draw attention and capital to the inner city. By stepping into the breach, Bryant and OHI were able to show lenders that there was a vast, untapped economic market in Los Angeles.

Operation HOPE, Inc., working under the slogan that it is possible to "do well by doing good," has grown steadily since its creation in 1992. In concert with lending institutions such as First Federal Bank of California, Hanmi Bank, Washington Mutual, and Bank of America, OHI had by April of 2000 brokered "more than $60 million in lending commitments for inner-city home ownership and small business ownership," according to an OHI publication. Additionally, through its Banking on the Future program, OHI has educated over 50,000 adults and students about credit and basic personal finances.

OHI has opened several inner city banking centers as well. Calling the banking center effort "a private bank for LA's working poor," Bryant told the *Los Angeles Business Journal* in 1998 that he envisions banking centers "in every urban community" in the United States. Explaining that investments and donations by commercial banks provide the funding for the centers, Jason Booth of the *Los Angeles Business Journal* also described their range of services. "Members...can open checking and savings accounts with participating banks, make financial investments, apply for mortgage loans and credit cards, and use computers to write resumes or do their banking over the Internet," he wrote.

Bryant and OHI organized the First Annual Inner City Economic Summit in Los Angeles in the spring of 2000. Sponsors included Wells Fargo Bank, *Fortune, Time,* Union Bank of California, the Milken Institute, and UPS. Vice President Al Gore was the featured speaker. The summit attracted CEOs, federal agency heads, and other leaders. Its mandate, according to the *Los Angeles Times,* was "to develop strategies to foster economic renewal in neglected communities." Seminars examined topics such as small business ownership, home ownership, and bridging the digital divide.

Bryant's efforts to pump life into the many facets of inner city economics have won him praise from Presidents Bush and Clinton, as well as recognition from several media sources. He has been included on several high-profile lists of future leaders to watch. Bryant has received many awards, among them the Reginald F. Lewis Entrepreneurship Award from the Howard University School of Business, and the Bridge Builder Award from the Korean American Coalition. He was asked to be a panel participant at the White House Pacific Rim Economic Conference in 1995 as well as the IV African-African American Summit in 1997. Bryant was also chosen by the United Nations Conference on Trade and Development (UNCTAD) as their first Goodwill Ambassador to the United States. In 1999, he was asked to serve as special advisor to UNCTAD in 1999. In 1998, Bryant was the first African American to be knighted by the German noble House of Lippe. His title is Knight Commander, Signum Fidei.

Although his achievements might imply otherwise, Bryant became a leader almost by accident. He told the *Los Angeles Times Magazine* in 1995, "I started out...trying to help the community. This was going to be my contribution–being in the right place at the right time, with the right thing to say. I got sucked into leadership." Nevertheless, he has risen to the challenge. In his Chairman's Letter in the 1998 OHI Annual Report, he wrote, "...at the end of the day, I do what I do because I am selfish. I work hard on behalf of others...because I believe that you don't get credit in life, or from God, for doing what you are supposed to do anyway.... I believe that you only get credit in life, and from God, for helping other people. And let's just say that I want a gold or platinum card with no limit on it."

Sources

Books

Mitchell, Niki Butler. *The New Color of Success.* Rocklin, CA: Prima Publishing, 1999.

Okwu, Julian C.R. *Face Forward: Young African American Men in a Critical Age.* San Francisco: Chronicle Books, 1997.

Periodicals

American Banker, June 6, 1995, p.23.

Black Enterprise, September, 1997, p.22.

Empowering Communities, Operation HOPE, Inc. Newsletter, Vol. 8, Issue 1, Spring, 2000.

Los Angeles Business Journal, June 22, 1998, p.18.

Los Angeles Times, April 12, 1992, p.E1; August 23, 1993, p.B5; June 9, 1994, p.B1; April 27, 1995, p.B2; October 25, 1995, p.D1; May 28, 1997, p.D2; December 22, 1998, p.A1; December 22, 1999, p.C1; April 12, 2000, p.C6; April 18, 2000, p.C2.

Los Angeles Times Magazine, May 1995, p.56.

U.S. Banker, October 1999.

U.S. News and World Report, June 15, 1998, p.15.

Other

Additional information for this profile was obtained from Operation Hope, Inc., Annual Report, 1998; Xpress Press News Service, 1999, at www.x-presspress.com; and a corporate biography of John Bryant, provided by Operation HOPE, Inc., 2000.

—Ellen Dennis French

Jerry Butler

1939—

Vocalist

Known as "The Iceman," Jerry Butler perfected a smooth, delicate baritone that has captivated music fans of many different backgrounds over his five decades of performing and recording. He was credited as "one of the architects of R&B" by *Ebony* magazine. As both a solo artist and during his long partnership with Curtis Mayfield, Butler forged new styles that grew from his own musical background of gospel and doo-wop and helped propel African American popular music to a new level of general appeal. Unlike those of many other virtuoso vocal stylists, his career has encompassed both singing and songwriting.

Butler was born in the small community of Sunflower, Mississippi, on December 8, 1939. Before he had reached the age of three, his family joined the African American migration north to Chicago. Jerry was the oldest of four children. His younger brother, Billy, also embarked upon a musical career. At the age of 14, Butler took over as the family's main breadwinner, but still found time to attend Chicago's Washburn High School. He also became interested in gospel music, joining the choir of the Traveling Souls Spiritual Church when he was only 12-years-old.

The choir put Butler in contact with other musically talented young men, just as the streetcorner-harmony style known as doo-wop, after the exquisitely harmonized nonsense syllables that permeated the music, was peaking in popularity. It was natural that these gospel singers would gather into secular groups after hours. One of Butler's choirmates was a singer and guitarist named Curtis Mayfield. The two had already worked together in a gospel ensemble called the Modern Jubilaires. In 1957, along with three other compatriots, Butler and Mayfield formed the Impressions. Clearly a standout even in Chicago's crowded harmony-group scene, the Impressions were signed to their hometown Vee Jay label in 1958.

Stardom was just around the corner for the Impressions. The group rocketed to the R&B top three with "For Your Precious Love," and the song also reached number eleven on the pop charts. Sudden success caused bickering among the youthful Impressions, especially after "For Your Precious Love" appeared with a label crediting "Jerry Butler and the Impressions" for the performance. Butler embarked on a solo career, but remained creatively close to Mayfield. The pair

At a Glance . . .

Born on December 8, 1939, in Sunflower, MS; oldest of four children; married, wife's name Annette; children: Randall and Anthony.

Career: Joined choir, Traveling Souls Spiritual Church at age 12; with Curtis Mayfield, formed the Impressions, 1957; signed to Vee Jay label with the Impressions, 1958; left Impressions for solo career but continued to work with Mayfield; signed with Mercury label,1967; worked with Gamble and Huff production team on classic soul LP albums *The Ice Man Cometh* and *Ice on Ice,* 1969; formed beer distributorship that became Iceman Beverage Company, 1973; signed with Motown label, 1976; signed with Philadelphia International label, 1978; elected to Cook County, Illinois, Board of Commissioners, 1985.

Awards: Three Grammy nominations, for Album of the Year, Male Vocalist of theYear, and Song of the Year, 1969.

Addresses: *Office*—Cook County Board of Commissioners, 118 N. ClarkSt., Suite 567, Chicago, IL 60602.

teamed up on Butler's 1960 hit "He Will Break Your Heart," which also reached the pop Top Ten. Butler stayed with the Vee Jay label until it became defunct in the mid-1960s. He scored several more hits, such as the durable "I Stand Accused" from 1964.

The Impressions, under Mayfield's leadership, developed into one of the most successful soul vocal groups of the 1960s. Later in that decade, Butler left the Impressions and embarked on a solo career. Recording for the Mercury label, he found the perfect sonic complement for his voice in the work of the Philadelphia production team of Kenneth Gamble and Leon Huff. Gamble and Huff pioneered the so-called "Philly soul" sound, which cultivated a smoother, more intricately arranged style than those favored by their competitors in Detroit and Memphis. The addition of Butler's vocals to the sound resulted in some of the biggest hits of his career.

"Hey Western Union Man" reached the number sixteen slot on the pop charts in 1968, and "Only the Strong Survive" climbed even further, to number four, the following year. Butler's two albums from the late 1960s, *Ice on Ice* and *The Ice Man Cometh*, were indispensable components of any soul music record collection at the time. They earned Butler three Grammy award nominations, for Album of the Year, Male Vocalist of the Year, and Song of the Year, in 1969. In addition to the contributions of Gamble and Huff, the success of Butler's albums at this point in his career may be attributed to his own meticulous approach to the styling of a song. "I'm from the old school," he was quoted as saying in *African American Biographies.* "I believe that anything that's worth doing is worth doing well."

By 1970, Butler was a soul-music institution. His split from Gamble and Huff that year initiated a moderate downturn in his popularity, but he remained a consistent hitmaker for many years. Butler was especially noted for his duets with Gene Chandler and Brenda Lee Eager in the early 1970s. He signed with the Motown label in 1976, but returned to Gamble and Huff's Philadelphia International label two years later. The shift resulted in an increase in Butler's popularity for a time. He kept up a steady stream of new releases that reached into the 1990s, recording for the Fountain and Ichiban labels. Butler also remained in the limelight as a live performer. In 1999, he hosted a half-century-of-doo-wop tribute program on the Public Broadcasting Service. He also remained a fixture on the Chicago club scene.

As his career in music reached a plateau, Butler branched out into other areas. He started a beer distributorship in 1973, which eventually grew into the Iceman Beverage Company, a subsidiary of the giant Chicago brewery G. Heileman (the maker of Old Style beer). Butler had always been known as an entertainer with a social conscience, a tendency that dated back to the early years of his career in the South when he and his entourage had faced difficulty in finding accommodations in segregated hotels. At the height of his career, Butler performed benefits for such groups as the Southern Christian Leadership Council (SCLC), the National Association for the Advancement of Colored People (NAACP), and the Congress of Racial Equality (CORE). He also became involved in several political campaigns.

In 1985, Butler became one of the few entertainers to make a successful transition into politics, winning election to the Cook County, Illinois, Board of Commissioners after an eleven-month campaign. This governmental body supervised state-owned facilities—hospitals, schools, prisons, parks, and more—in the second-most populous county in the nation, an area that included the city of Chicago. Butler won reelection consistently and remained on the county board at the turn of the century. Honored with induction into the Rock and Roll Hall of Fame in 1991, Butler is a much-loved elder statesman of African American music. Married to the former Annette Smith, he is the father of two sons, Randall and Anthony.

Selected discography

"For Your Precious Love" (single), Vee Jay, 1958 (with the Impressions).
He Will Break Your Heart, Vee Jay, 1960.
Love Me, Vee Jay, 1961.
Aware of Love, Vee Jay, 1961.
Moon River, Vee Jay, 1962.
Folk Songs, Vee Jay, 1963.
Soul Artistry, Mercury, 1967.
The Soul Goes On, Mercury, 1968.
The Ice Man Cometh, Mercury, 1968.
Ice on Ice, Mercury, 1969.
You & Me, Mercury, 1970.
Special Memory, Mercury, 1970.
Best of Jerry Butler, Mercury, 1970.
The Sagittarius Movement, Mercury, 1971.
The Spice of Life, Mercury, 1972.
The Love We Have, The Love We Had, Mercury, 1972 (with Brenda Lee Eager).
The Power of Love, Mercury, 1973.
Sweet Sixteen, Mercury, 1974.
Love's on the Menu, Motown, 1976.
Suite for the Single Girl, Motown, 1977.
Nothing Says I Love You Like I Love You, Philadelphia International, 1978.
Best Love I Ever Had, Philadelphia International, 1981.
Ice 'n' Hot, Fountain, 1982.
The Best of Jerry Butler, Rhino, 1987.
Iceman: The Mercury Years, Mercury, 1992.
Time & Faith, Ichiban, 1993.

Sources

Books

Erlewine, Michael, et al., eds., *The All Music Guide to Rock,* 2nd ed., Miller Freeman, 1997.
Hawkins, Walter L., *African American Biographies: Profiles of 558 Current Men and Women,* McFarland and Company, 1992.
Larkin, Colin, ed., *The Encyclopedia of Popular Music,* Muze UK, 1998.
Romanowski, Patricia, and Holly George-Warren, eds., *The New Rolling Stone Encyclopedia of Rock and Roll,* Fireside, 1995.
Stambler, Irwin, *The Encyclopedia of Pop, Rock & Soul,* St. Martin's Press, 1989.

Periodicals

Billboard, November 20, 1999, p. 27.
Ebony, April 1999, p. 104.

—James M. Manheim

Stokely Carmichael

1941–1998

Activist, lecturer, author

"Flailing at the white society he condemns, the young man galvanizes his audience with the strident call for 'Black Power.'" Such was the sensational portrait of Stokely Carmichael offered by *Life* magazine in the late 1960s. Considerable emphasis was placed on Carmichael's "stridency," and the fear of this incendiary speaker, organizer, and author was palpable in much mainstream rhetoric about him. Over many years of organizing and activism, Carmichael moved from the peaceful integrationist doctrine of the civil rights marchers to a more radical pro-revolutionary position, eventually inspiring so much hatred from U.S. institutions that he opted for self-imposed exile in Guinea, West Africa. And decades after his first inflammatory speeches, he demonstrated only a deepened commitment to revolutionary politics.

After the dovish sermons and speeches of the Reverend Martin Luther King, Jr., whites were unprepared for the uncompromising demands of African American militants such as the Black Panthers and the All Afrikan People's Revolutionary Party, and Carmichael was an important figure in both organizations. Carmichael himself has been credited for the "Black Power" slogan, which frightened whites and turned off even activists like King. Fellow militant Eldridge Cleaver quoted Carmichael's strategy: "The civil rights movement was good because it demanded that blacks be admitted into the system. Now we must move beyond the stage of demanding entry, to the new stage of changing the system itself." "Black Power," wrote James Haskins in 1972's *Profiles in Black Power,* "has become the philosophy of the black revolution, and because of that Stokely Carmichael is assured a place in history."

Carmichael was born in Port-of-Spain, Trinidad, in 1941. His carpenter father, Adolphus, moved with Stokely's mother, Mabel, to the United States when their son was two years old, leaving him in the care of two aunts and a grandmother. Adolphus—who had been swept up by the cause of Trinidadian independence but left his homeland to better his family's economic fortunes—moonlighted as a cab driver, while Mabel found work as a maid. Stokely attended Tranquility Boys School, learning, he would recall angrily years later, the mentality of the colonized. "I remember that when I was a boy," he wrote in "What We Want," which originally appeared in a 1967 issue of the *New York Review of Books* and was later reprinted in *Chronicles of Black Protest,* "I used to go to see Tarzan movies on Saturday. White Tarzan used to beat

At a Glance . . .

Born June 29, 1941, in Port-of-Spain, Trinidad; died November 15, 1998, in Conakry, Guinea; immigrated to the United States, 1952; son of Adolphus (a carpenter) and Mabel (also known as Mae Charles) Carmichael; married singer Miriam Makeba, 1968 (divorced). married physician Marlyatou Barry (divorced); children: Bokabiro. *Education:* Howard University, B.A., 1964.

Career: Civil rights activist and organizer; organizer with Student Nonviolent Coordinating Committee (SNCC, also known as Student National Coordinating Committee), Atlanta, GA, 1964-66, chairman, 1966-67; director of civil rights activities, Mississippi SummerProject, 1964; organizer for All Afrikan People's Revolutionary Party; honorary prime minister of Black Panther Party, 1967-69; self-imposed exile in Conakry, Guinea, 1969-98, changed name to Kwame Ture; lecturer and author.

Awards: Honorary LL.D. from Shaw University.

up the black natives. I would sit there yelling, 'Kill the beasts, kill the savages, kill 'em!' I was saying: Kill me. It was as if a Jewish boy watched Nazis taking Jews off to concentration camps and cheered them on." Carmichael joined his parents in New York City's Harlem when he was 11, later attending the prestigious Bronx High School of Science after his parents moved to the Bronx. He had been the only African American member of a street gang called the Morris Park Dukes, but settled down after discovering the lure of intellectual life. His status as a foreigner and self-described "hip" demeanor assured him of popularity among many of his liberal, affluent white schoolmates, he said in an interview with *Life;* he dated white girls and attended parties on swank Park Avenue.

Carmichael was interested in politics even then, especially the work of African American socialist Bayard Rustin, whom he heard speak many times. "Bayard played a crucial role in my life," Carmichael told *Fire in the Streets* author Milton Viorst. "He was one of the first people I had direct contact with that I could really say, 'That's what I want to be.' He was so at ease with all the problems. I mean, he was like Superman, hooking socialism up with the black movement, organizing blacks." On one occasion, Carmichael volunteered to help his mentor organize African American workers in a paint factory. But the friendliness—doctrinal and otherwise—of Rustin and other African American intellectual leftists with the white liberal establishment would eventually alienate Carmichael.

Before beginning college, Carmichael had become aware of the flowering of the civil rights movement in the South and the injustice experienced by African Americans and others who challenged segregation. "Suddenly I was burning," he told *Life*'s Gordon Parks. Carmichael soon joined antidiscrimination pickets in New York and sit-ins in Virginia and South Carolina. He began his studies at Howard University in Washington, D.C., in 1960. "Several white schools offered me scholarships," he informed Parks, but Howard seemed "a natural. It was black. I could keep in touch with the movement there."

While at Howard, Carmichael met members of the Student Nonviolent Coordinating Committee (SNCC), an Atlanta-based organization that received funds from the Southern Christian Leadership Conference (SCLC). During his freshman year he participated in the first of the famous "Freedom Rides" sponsored by the Congress of Racial Equality, traveling south and getting beaten and arrested in Jackson, Mississippi, for his activism. It was the first of many incarcerations in the career of a confrontational activist.

In 1964 Carmichael graduated from Howard with a bachelor's degree in philosophy, but he intended to stay very much involved in the civil rights movement. That summer saw six civil rights workers murdered in the South, in addition to many arrests, beatings, and other indignities and harassment. Carmichael soon became an organizer for SNCC and participated in the group's drive to register African American voters—the first of these well-publicized efforts—in Lowndes County, Alabama. SNCC helped start the Lowndes County Freedom Association, a political party that chose a black panther as its symbol to fulfill a state requirement that all parties have visual symbols to assist voters. The panther was indigenous to Alabama and seemed both a dignified symbol for empowered African Americans and an effective response to the white rooster that symbolized the Alabama Democratic party. In his book *Freedom Bound,* historian Robert Weisbrot related that Carmichael and other SNCC activists, despite their differences with the SCLC and Martin Luther King's resolute nonviolence, continued to associate themselves with King because older African American Alabamans regarded the Reverend, in Carmichael's own words, "like a God."

A turning point in Carmichael's experience came, however, as he watched from his locked hotel room while outside, African American demonstrators were beaten and shocked with cattle prods by police. The horrified Carmichael began to scream and could not stop. As Carmichael's activism deepened, however, and as he saw the violence doled out to violent and nonviolent resisters alike, he began to distance himself from King's tactics. In 1965 he replaced the moderate John Lewis as head of SNCC and began to trumpet the message of "Black Power." White members of the group were not encouraged to stay, and Carmichael and other SNCC leaders began to talk about "revolution."

Carmichael's articulation of "Black Power," evidenced by his 1967 book of that title (co-written with Charles V. Hamilton), and his article "What We Want" advanced the idea that mere integration was not the answer to American racism, and that America formed only a piece in the puzzle. Carmichael and Hamilton linked the struggle for African American empowerment definitively to economic self-determination domestically and the end of imperialism and colonialism worldwide. "What We Want" described the need for communal control of African American resources—"Ultimately, the economic foundations of this country must be shaken if black people are to control their lives"—but also delved into the crippling psychological effects of racism. "From birth," Carmichael wrote, "black people are told a set of lies about themselves," concluding, "We are oppressed not because we are lazy, not because we're stupid (and got good rhythm); but because we're black."

The term "Black Power," however disconcerting to moderate African American leaders, absolutely terrified mainstream whites; it was not interpreted to mean "empowerment" but rather African American domination and possibly even race war. Journalists demanded repeatedly that Carmichael define the phrase, and the activist soon came to believe that no matter what his explanation, they would continue to make it sound sinister. *Life*'s Parks, an African American journalist, pressed Carmichael and received a somewhat exasperated reply: "*For the last time,* Black Power means black people coming together to form a political force and either electing representatives or forcing their representatives to speak their needs," rather than relying on the established parties. "Black Power doesn't mean anti-white, violence, separatism or any other racist things the press says it means. It's saying, 'Look, buddy, we're not laying a vote on you unless you lay so many schools, hospitals, playgrounds and jobs on us." Nonetheless, as Haskins recorded in *Profiles in Black Power,* Carmichael gave the term a different spin when he spoke to African American audiences: "When you talk of 'black power,' you talk of building a movement that will smash everything Western civilization has created."

As the revolutionary fervor of the 1960s deepened, SNCC became a Black Power vehicle, more or less replacing the hymn-singing integrationism of earlier days. Yet Carmichael had gone as far as he could with the organization, deciding not to run for reelection as its leader in 1967, just before SNCC fell apart. Carmichael's political emphasis had shifted as well; he began speaking out not only against the war in Vietnam but against what he called U.S. imperialism worldwide. *Time* reported with supreme disdain that Carmichael had traveled the world denouncing the United States, speaking to cheering throngs in Cuba, and declaring, "We do not want peace in Vietnam. We want the Vietnamese people to defeat the United States." The magazine called him a purveyor of "negritude and nihilism" and noted that many U.S. politicians wanted to jail him for sedition on his return to the country he called "hell."

When he did return, in 1968, U.S. marshals confiscated Carmichael's passport. Meanwhile, the radical Oakland, California-based Black Panther party made him honorary prime minister; he would resign from the position the following year, rejecting Panther coalitions with white activists. He based himself in Washington, D.C., and continued to speak around the country. In March of 1968 he announced his engagement to South African singer-activist Miriam Makeba; they were wed two months later. The Tanzanian ambassador to the United States hosted their reception. Carmichael and Makeba were permitted to honeymoon abroad after they agreed not to visit any "forbidden" countries; even so, many nations refused them entrance. In 1969 Carmichael left the United States for Guinea, a country in west Africa. He moved there in part to assist in the restoration to power of the deposed Ghanaian ruler Kwame Nkrumah, who lived in Guinea and served as an exponent of the sort of anti-imperialist, pan-African empowerment Carmichael had espoused in the United States.

While in Guinea, Carmichael took the name Kwame Ture in honor of African socialist leaders Kwame Nkrumah and Ahmed Sekoe Toure. Over the ensuing decades, he solidified his commitment to revolution as the answer to racism and injustice. While speaking at Michigan State University in 1993, Carmichael made it clear that he still considered capitalism the source of most of the problems he had been studying during his career as an activist. "Those who labor do not enjoy the fruits of their labor," he said, as quoted in the *Michigan Chronicle.* "We know that to be slavery." However, Carmichael's 1992 afterword to a new edition of *Black Power* showed that he felt real progress had been made in certain respects in the U.S., "From 1965 to 1992, no one could deny that change has occurred," he acknowledged in the *Chronicle*—and that a "coalition of oppressed minorities plus poor whites represents the real force for change. The 1992 Los Angeles rebellion [civil unrest following the acquittal by a white jury of the four police officers who had been videotaped beating African American motorist Rodney King] reflects this reality; other oppressed nationalities joined the rebellion in mass character." Carmichael told the crowd at Michigan State that the riots "were good for us." He insisted in his conclusion to the *Black Power* afterword that "mass political organization on a Pan African scale is the only solution. Thus, Black Power can only be realized when there exists a unified socialist Africa."

In 1996, Carmichael was diagnosed with prostate cancer. He received treatment for the disease in Cuba and, with financial assistance from Nation of Islam leader Louis Farrakhan, was admitted to a hospital in New York. To raise money for Carmichael's medical expenses, benefits were held in New York, Denver, and Atlanta. The government of Trinidad and Tobago also awarded him a $1,000 a month grant.

Although Carmichael's battle with prostate cancer steadily weakened him, he continued to advocate revolution and an end to racism. When friends telephoned to wish him well, he would answer with his characteristic response, "Ready for the revolution!" In early 1998, Carmichael made his final appearance in the United States at a testimonial dinner held in his honor in Washington, D.C. Among those in attendance were Congressmen Bobby Rush and John Lewis, Louis Farrakhan, and former Washington, D.C. mayor Marion Barry.

Carmichael died on November 15, 1998. At a memorial service held at Gamal Nasser University in Conakry, Guinea's capital city, Carmichael was eulogized by his longtime friend Bob Brown. According to *Jet* magazine, Brown told those assembled that "Kwame is a struggler. He struggled all his life. He struggled until the last second of the last minute of the last hour of the last day." Memorial services for Carmichael were also held in Philadelphia, New York, Chicago, and other cities throughout the United States. Carmichael was laid to rest in a public cemetery in Conakry. As reported by *Jet,* Carmichael's son, Bokabiro, remarked during the burial that his father would be "very happy, happy because he will remain in Guinea."

Selected writings

"What We Want," *Chronicles of Black Protest,* edited by Bradford Chambers, New American Library, 1968.

(With Charles V. Hamilton) *Black Power: The Politics of Liberation in America,* Random House, 1967, revised edition, 1992.

Stokely Speaks: Black Power Back to Pan-Africanism, Random House, 1971.

Sources

Books

Eldridge Cleaver: Post-Prison Writings and Speeches, edited by Robert Scheer, Random House, 1969.

Haskins, James, *Profiles in Black Power,* Doubleday, 1972.

Johnson, Jacqueline, *Stokely Carmichael: The Story of Black Power,* Silver Burdett Press/Simon & Schuster, 1990.

Viorst, Milton, *Fire in the Streets: America in the 1960s,* Simon & Schuster, 1979.

Weisbrot, Robert, *Freedom Bound: A History of America's Civil Rights Movement,* Norton, 1990.

Periodicals

Jet, November 30, 1998, p. 5; December 14, 1998, p. 26.

Life, May 19, 1967, pp. 76-80.

Michigan Chronicle, February 24, 1993, p. 1.

New York Times, August 5, 1966.

Time, December 15, 1967, p. 28.

—Simon Glickman and David G. Oblender

Rubin Carter

1937—

Former boxer, activist

Rubin Carter was a fighter from his early days in a small New Jersey town. After several run-ins with the law, he joined the Army and developed into a champion boxer. A promising career as a professional boxer was shattered, however, when he and a friend were wrongly accused of murder and sent to prison. Over the course of two decades, Carter would fight to clear his name and regain the freedom that had been taken from him.

Carter was born on May 6, 1937 in Delawanna, New Jersey to a middle class family in a racially mixed neighborhood. His father, Lloyd, was an entrepreneur and owned several small businesses throughout Carter's childhood. He was a deacon in the local Baptist church and a strict disciplinarian. All of the beatings that Carter received from his father did little to curb his penchant for fighting. Carter stuttered as a youth and would not suffer being teased. He beat up bullies or anyone else who made fun of him. Carter was expelled from school for fighting with a teacher who he felt was mistreating his sister. He even punched the local preacher. At the age of nine, Carter stole some new clothes and gave them to his brothers and sisters. His father saw the new clothes and, after beating his son, turned him in to the police.

Carter continued to have brushes with the law and, after he and three other boys attacked a man and stole his watch, was convicted of robbery and assault. He was sent to the Jamesburg Home for Boys and stayed there for two years until he escaped. To avoid the authorities, Carter joined the Army. He endured the hideous physical punishment of paratrooper training and became a member of the elite Army unit. While stationed in Germany, he learned to box at the Army's fieldhouse. His first fight, which he was goaded into after he had been drinking, came against the Army's heavyweight champ. Using borrowed boots and gloves, Carter knocked out the heavyweight champ. He was immediately transferred to a special service for boxers.

In his first year, Carter compiled a 35-5 record and won the European Lightweight Championship. He began going to classes—including a Dale Carnegie class, which helped him to conquer his stuttering problem. He even adopted Islam and changed his name for a while. Carter was discharged from the Army on May 29, 1956, and was arrested less than a month later for his escape from Jamesburg Home for Boys. He went to Annandale prison for five months, was arrested again for robbery and assault, and spent time in the

At a Glance . . .

Born Rubin Carter, May 6, 1937 in Delawanna, NJ; son of Lloyd Carter (an entrepreneur); children: Theodora and Raheem.

Career: Joined the Army and became a boxer, 1954; arrested for assault and robbery and spent four years in prison until his release, 1961; lost middleweight championship bout, 1964; tried and convicted of a triple homicide, 1966; released from prison after the New Jersey Supreme Court overturned the conviction, 1976; retried and sent to prison, 1976; freed from prison, 1985; charges are officially dropped, 1988; the movie based on Carter's life, *The Hurricane,* is released, 1999.

Awards: European Lightweight Champion, 1956;

Addresses: *Residence*—Toronto, Canada; *Office*—c/o The Association of the Wrongly Convicted, 155 Delaware Avenue, Toronto, Ontario, Canada.

Rahway and Trenton state prisons until his release in September of 1961. During his four years in prison, he rededicated himself to boxing, training, and lifting weights. When he emerged from prison and became a professional boxer, Carter established himself as a brutal competitor. He fought for the middleweight title in 1963 after knocking out Emile Griffith in two minutes and 13 seconds of the first round. Carter lost his championship bid in December of 1964 in a close bout with champion Joey Giardello. After the Giardello bout, Carter finished out his career at 7-7-1 with an overall record of 28 wins, 11 losses, and one draw.

The Ominous Night

Carter was married in 1963 and soon after he and his wife, Mae Thelma, had a daughter named Theodora. On the night of June 16, 1966, after watching television with his daughter, Carter decided to go out for the night. He went out to a bar called the Nite Spot, and met an ex-sparring partner who Carter believed had stolen three guns from his last training camp. Carter took the man to look for the guns, but could not find them nor confirm that the man had stolen from him. He returned to the bar and stayed until last call at 2:00 A.M. Carter didn't want to go home, but had run out of money. He asked a 19-year-old at the bar to drive him home to get more money. The young man, John Artis, agreed to drive Carter home along with a local drifter named John Royster.

Earlier in the evening, two African American men had entered the Lafayette Grill through the side door. One of the men carried a shotgun, and immediately killed the bartender. The other man, who was carrying a pistol, killed a patron at the bar and wounded another man and a woman. The police believed that the killing was an act of racial retaliation for the murder of an African American bartender by a white man earlier in the evening.

During the search for the two gunmen, Carter, Artis, and Royster were stopped by the police. One of the policemen knew Carter, and the three men were released almost immediately. Carter stopped home, picked up more money, and the trio set out again. After driving around for awhile, the men decided to call it a night. Artis dropped off Royster first and then, on the way to Carter's house, the police stopped the car. This time, the police acted very differently. Carter and Artis were taken to the Lafayette Grill and put up against the wall while the car was searched. They were then taken to the hospital. The police showed Carter and Artis to one of the shooting victims, who told police that neither man had shot him. The two men were then taken to the police department and held for 16 hours. Both men were questioned, passed lie detector tests, and were released. The next day, the assistant county prosecutor denied that Carter had ever been a suspect. Believing that the matter was settled, Carter left for Argentina to fight in his next bout.

On October 14, 1966, Carter was picked up by the police and charged with the murders at the Lafayette Grill. Prosecutors now had two witnesses who claimed that they saw Carter and Artis fleeing the scene of the crime. One of the witnesses, Alfred Bello, was an ex-convict who had been questioned on the night of the murders. Originally, Bello had told the police that he did not see who committed the shootings. The shooting victim who had seen Carter and Artis in the hospital, William Marins, had also changed his story and identified Carter and Artis as the perpetrators. There was conflicting evidence about the getaway car, and the police department failed to collect fingerprints or conduct paraffin tests on Carter or Artis to see if they had fired any weapons. Bello took the stand, and said that he saw a white Dodge with three men in it. He then heard shots, and saw Carter and Artis leave the bar laughing—one with a shotgun and another with a pistol. Bello also admitted that moments after the murders, he entered the bar and took money out of the cash register. Despite the numerous contradictions, inconsistencies, and the unreliable nature of the prosecution's witnesses, the jury took less than two hours to convict Carter and Artis on three counts of murder.

Back to Prison

Carter was returned to Trenton State Prison, were he had previously served five years. He refused to wear prison clothes or shave, and swore that he would kill any prison official who touched him. Carter was immediately sent to solitary confinement, and remained there until doctors found a detached retina on his right eye. He had an operation in prison and, instead of fixing the old boxing injury, the operation left him blind in one eye. Although Carter was released from solitary confinement, he still refused to work or wear a striped prison uniform. Younger prisoners gave him food, which he ate in his cell. He also refused to attend his own parole hearings.

After losing his first appeal before the New Jersey Supreme Court in 1969, Carter was transferred to Rahway State Prison. He became a leader among the inmates and wrote his autobiography entitled *The Sixteenth Round: From Number One Contender to Number 45472.* Thanks to the efforts of an investigator from the public defenders office, Fred Hogan, Carter's case was receiving attention in the media. Hogan, who knew Carter as a boxer, told Dave Anderson of *The New York Times* about his involvement in the case: "I knew in my heart that there was no way that Rubin did that. And the more Rubin told me about the trial, the more I knew it stunk." Hogan gathered his own evidence, and even interviewed the state's key witnesses. He turned over all of his findings to Selwyn Raab, a reporter for the *New York Times.* In an article published on September 27, 1974, in the *New York Times,* both Bello and the government's other key witness admitted that they had lied under oath. Carter hired a public relations man to publicize his case to the media. He became a cause-celebre during the mid-1970s, and even appeared on television shows. Carter was also the subject of an eight-minute-and-33-second epic written and performed by Bob Dylan called "Hurricane." After the New Jersey Supreme Court overturned their conviction by a 7-0 vote, Carter and Artis were released from prison. Despite his newfound freedom, Carter was not happy: he had lost an eye, he had spent another vast period of his life in prison, and the Passaic County prosecutor vowed to send him back to jail.

By the fall of 1976, Carter's fortunes had suffered another drastic setback. He was in debt, his family was on welfare, and key supporters were being driven away by infighting and other issues. Carter was even accused of assaulting one of his most stalwart advocates, former parole officer Carolyn Kelly. Kelly claimed that Carter had beaten her and threatened to kill her. He denied the charge, and claimed that Kelly was taking her revenge for being rejected romantically. This was only the beginning of the bad news, however. Carter and Artis were retried for the murders at the Lafayette Grill. After another racially charged trial, the two men were again found guilty. Carter was sent back to prison and, in December of 1976, his son Raheem was born.

Carter spent four more years behind bars before appearing at a prosecutorial misconduct hearing in 1981. All of the witnesses repeated their testimonies from the earlier trials. Alfred Bello, the state's star witness in both trials, conceded that he had a serious alcohol problem and remembered very little about the night in question. Carter appeared disinterested with the hearing. Instead, he read philosophy and concentrated on finding inner peace.

Around this time, Carter struck up a friendship with Lesra Martin, a 15-year-old teenage boy from Brooklyn who lived with a commune in Toronto. Martin was encouraged to contact and visit Carter by members of the commune. He visited Carter in prison and, when he related the details of his visit to his fellow commune members, they took up Carter's cause with enthusiasm. The group and its leader, Lisa Peters, sent him gifts of food, clothing, and a television set. Peters and Carter grew close, sometimes conversing on the phone for up to eight hours at a time. Although the commune members had helped Carter legally, materially, and emotionally, he began to feel somewhat trapped by their worshipful attention. When members of the commune suggested that Carter move to Canada and join the commune after his release from prison, he broke off his relationship with Peters and her group. However, by the end of 1983, Carter and Peters had reestablished their relationship. She and two other commune members even moved to New Jersey to be closer to him.

Carter and his legal team, which included commune members Terry Swinton and Sam Chaiton, decided to go through federal court and ask for habeas corpus relief. His lawyers filed the writ on February 13, 1985, after three months of work. From the beginning, Judge H. Lee Sarokin rejected the racial revenge theory around which the prosecution had based their case against Carter. Despite this positive development, Carter remained in prison.

On November 7, 1985, Judge Sarokin ruled that the State of New Jersey had violated the constitutional rights of Carter and Artis on two occasions. First, the state failed to make public the results of the lie detector test which it had given to its star witness, Alfred Bello. Secondly, by using the racial revenge theory as the basis for its case, the state appealed to racial prejudice and violated Carter and Artis's equal protection and due process rights. Following the judge's ruling, Carter was released without bond to await his next legal hurdle.

Before Christmas of 1985, the prosecutor's office again tried to put Carter behind bars. The Third Circuit Court ruled against the prosecution, but Carter was sufficiently threatened. Motions and appeals were filed throughout 1986, and investigators from Passaic

County tried to visit Carter at his home. In August of 1987, the prosecution lost another appeal to a three-judge panel. Despite yet another loss, the prosecutor's office pushed to have the case heard before the Supreme Court. After the Supreme Court ruled that it wouldn't hear the case, the prosecution had no other recourse. On February 19, 1988, a State Superior Court judge dismissed all charges against Carter and Artis.

After his release from prison, Carter lived with the commune members in Canada who had helped free him from prison. He was briefly thrown out of the commune, but returned in 1989 when he developed tuberculosis. Carter and Peters were married, but only so that he could receive a more official status in Canada. Carter lived with the commune until early 1994, and left the group after he could no longer conform to the commune's strict rules. In late 1999 the movie *The Hurricane,* starring Denzel Washington, was released. The film whitewashed Carter's earlier troubles with the law, deleted key parts of his story, and invented characters to further dramatize Carter's life. One of the movie's producers, Rudy Langlais, defended the film and claimed to Matthew Purdy of the *New York Times* that "The Rubin Carter case is part of the myth, part of the sacred history of New Jersey." However Selwyn Raab, the reporter who originally brought Carter's case to the attention of the media in 1974, wrote in the *New York Times* that the truth was much more frightening that any Hollywood recreation: "The actual story...exposes an underlying frailty in the criminal-justice system that convicted Mr. Carter not once but twice. The convictions were obtained not by a lone, malevolent investigator but by a network of detectives, prosecutors and judges who countenanced the suppression of evidence and the injection of racial bias into the courtroom."

Carter still lives in Canada, and serves as the executive director of the Association in Defense of the Wrongly Convicted. He travels around North America working to eliminate the death penalty. Carter also devotes his energies to furthering the cause of prisoners' rights.

Sources

Books

Hirsch, James S., *The Miraculous Journey of Rubin Carter.* Houghton Miflin Company: New York, 2000.

Periodicals

The New York Times, December 28, 1999; February 6, 2000; February 13, 2000.

—Michael J. Waktins

Vince Carter

1977—

Professional basketball player

As one of the NBA's brightest young stars, Vince Carter has electrified the league. In only his second professional season, he led the Toronto Raptors to their first-ever playoff appearance. With his amazing dunks and stellar scoring touch, Carter is often mentioned as the heir apparent to Michael Jordan as the NBA's premier player.

Vincent Lamar Carter was born on January 26, 1977 in Daytona Beach, Florida. Although he excelled at basketball from an early age, his mother Michelle Robinson and his stepfather Harry made sure that he grew up as more than just an athlete. By the time he reached the seventh grade, Carter stood 5'8" and could already dunk a basketball, but he also played the baritone and the alto and tenor saxophone. He also wrote songs for the marching band and penned Mainland High School's homecoming song. Carter even attended band camp, a fact that he proudly passed along to *Sports Illustrated*'s Jon L. Wertheim: "Guys hear that and make fun of me, but trying different things and doing what I like is more important than being popular." He also ran track and played volleyball. After leading his school as a drum major, for which he was also offered a college scholarship to Bethune-Cookman College, Carter led Mainland to the 1994-95 Florida Class 6A championship. Carter left Mainland High School as one of the most highly recruited high school basketball players in the country. He accepted a scholarship to attend the University of North Carolina. Carter was not one of those rare talents who uses college as a stepping stone to the NBA, however. Because both of his parents were educators, he took his studies very seriously. Carter's mother forced him to sign a contract stating that if he were to leave college early in pursuit of NBA glory, he would go back to school and graduate.

At the University of North Carolina, Carter was part of a star-studded cast which included Antawn Jamison, the man who would later be drafted one spot before him in the NBA draft. As many high school basketball phenoms have discovered at North Carolina, freshmen players must earn their way onto the starting rotation. Carter finished his freshman season with only a 7.5 points per game average. During his sophomore year, he doubled both his production and his playing time. Carter averaged 13 points per game, and led North Carolina to the Final Four before losing to the eventual national champions—Arizona. In his third year at North Carolina, he again led his team to the Final Four

At a Glance . . .

Born Vincent Lamar Carter, January 26, 1977 in Daytona Beach, FL; son of Michelle Robinson (a teacher); *Education:* Attended the University of North Carolina.

Career: Starred in the band and on the basketball court at Mainland High School,1991-95; attended the University of North Carolina, 1995-98; picked fifth overall in the NBAdraft and traded to the Toronto Raptors, 1998-; member of USA Basketball's Sydney Olympics team, 2000.

Awards: Second Team AP All-American, First Team All-ACC, 1997-98; NBA Rookie of the Year, 1998-99.

Member: Established the Embassy of Hope Foundation, 1998; named a "Goodwill Ambassador" by Big Brothers/Big Sisters of America, 1998.

Addresses: *Home*—Daytona Beach, FL; *Office*— The Toronto Raptors, 150 York Street, Toronto, Ontario, Canada M5H 355.

and solidified his reputation as a complete player—an athlete who could also play defense, rebound, and hit key shots. After his third year at North Carolina, there was little doubt that Carter would leave school to pursue the riches of the NBA. He was named a second team All-American by the Associated Press, and was a first team All-ACC selection. Carter declared himself eligible for the NBA, but not before being reminded by his mother that he must complete his education. He returned to the university during the summer months, and continued his education.

In June of 1998, the Golden State Warriors selected Carter with the fifth pick of the NBA draft and then traded him to the Toronto Raptors for Antawn Jamison, his former North Carolina teammate. Carter immediately energized the woeful Raptors franchise, and led the team to challenge for its first playoff berth. By appearing nightly on ESPN and other sports programs, he began to attract an increasing number of Canadians to professional basketball. Sports stores sold out of Carter's number 15 jersey almost immediately, and his rookie card was pedaled for as much as ten dollars. Carter told Michael Farber of *Sports Illustrated* that he was surprised by his impact on the city and the league: "I didn't plan for it to be this way. My goal was to fit in, gradually work my way to being an impact player. My whole scheme fell through from Day One..." Carter ended the strike-shortened 1998-99 season by winning the NBA's Schick Rookie of the Year Award, and by becoming a unanimous selection to the league's All-Rookie team. During his rookie season in the NBA, Carter led the Raptors in blocked shots, field-goal percentage, and scoring.

Carter began his second year as the heir apparent to retired NBA great Michael Jordan. He did little to quiet the speculation that he was ready assume the mantle of NBA demi-god. Carter's mother told Mike Wise of *The New York Times* that her son was accustomed to the being mentioned in the same breath as Michael Jordan: "the Michael Jordan comparison is something he's been dealing with since high school. On one hand, it's very flattering. You can't overlook the similarities. By the same token, it gets a little old, too. Vince gets tired of hearing it." Carter won the slam dunk contest during the All-Star game weekend, and the NBA seemed to officially designate him as league savior. His good looks and squeaky-clean reputation, coupled with the amazing moves and eye-popping dunks, put the league's hype machine into high gear. The evidence of Carter's popularity and importance to the NBA came one day after he won the slam dunk contest. NBC shifted the Toronto Raptors game into the national spotlight, and moved the originally scheduled New York Knicks game out of the main programming slot. Carter was featured in a pre-game introductory piece, interviewed at halftime, and again after the game. During the broadcast, his name was mentioned 165 times and his face was the subject of 105 close-ups. Carter also scored a Jordanesque 51 points during the game.

Despite his stellar season, Carter received some bad news just before his heroic All-Star weekend. He was omitted from the U.S. Olympic team when Ray Allen was chosen for the final roster spot. After all the adulation, the Olympic rebuff changed Carter's attitude slightly. He told the Associated Press about being left off the team: "It has helped me step up. I said, 'OK, you just have to show the world what you can do night in and night out.'" Although Carter was eventually added to the team after one of the original players on the roster suffered a knee injury, the supposed slight caused him to focus his energies more on winning than flashy, entertaining play. Carter led his team to the playoffs in 2000—a first for the Toronto franchise. The young Raptors faced the New York Knicks in the first round. Toronto had beaten the Knicks three times during the regular season. However, the New Yorkers quickly disposed of the Raptors in a three-game sweep. Carter, who was shadowed throughout each game by defensive wizard Latrell Sprewell, was held to 15 of 50 field goal attempts through the three games of the series. Despite this disappointing end, Carter enjoyed a tremendous season. Teammate Antonio Davis summed up Carter's responsibilities for Wise of *The New York Times:* "Some of the time I hear him talking and some of the things he had to do after practice or something he had to before practice, it's like wow. And you still made it to practice on time, you got your work in after practice? That's tough, trying to lift your team and sell the league at the same time. He's going to help the league by being himself. He's doing a great job of it."

Sources

The New York Times, December 21, 1999; February 29, 2000.

Sports Illustrated, April 19, 1999; November 1, 1999.

Other

Additional material for this essay was found on the worldwide web at http://cnnsi.com/basketball/nba/news/2000/03/21/carter_feature_ap/; and http://www.nba.com/playerfile/bio/vince_carter.html

—Michael J. Watkins

Horace Cayton

1903–1970

Sociologist

Horace Cayton spent his lifetime attempting to reconcile his two halves. Inheritor both of wealth and of the slave legacy, Cayton found himself trapped between these two worlds, filled as they were with racial implications. By establishing himself as a preeminent sociologist dealing with the plight of urban African Americans, he concurrently attempted to resolve his own inner struggle for identity.

Cayton was born on April 12, 1903 in Seattle, Washington. His mother, Susie Revels Cayton, was the daughter of Hiram Revels of Mississippi. Revels was elected during the Reconstruction era of the 1870s as the first African American to serve in the United States Senate. Cayton's grandfather became a symbol of achievement for all African Americans by attaining the highest position an African American had ever held in this country. Following his term in Congress, Revels was appointed president of Alcorn State College in Alcorn, Mississippi. At the other extreme, Cayton's father, Horace Cayton, Sr., was the son of a slave and a white plantation owner's daughter.

Both of Cayton's parents were quite accomplished. His father, like his grandfather, was born a slave and migrated to Seattle after the Emancipation. After working as a political reporter for the *Seattle Post Intelligencer,* Cayton Sr. became the editor of the *Seattle Standard,* an African American-owned newspaper. In 1894 he published the first edition of the *Seattle Republican,* which for 21 years was a leading voice for civil rights, and, for a time, the city's second largest newspaper. When the *Seattle Republican* folded, Cayton inaugurated *Cayton's Weekly* in August of 1916, a journal for Seattle's African American community. Outspoken and politically-minded, he was the acknowledged African American leader in Seattle for many years. Cayton's mother was also college educated. A writer and editor for the *Seattle Republican,* she maintained an independent writing business as well, taught at Rusk College, and was also very active in Seattle's cultural affairs.

At the time of Horace's birth, the Cayton family was prosperous, middle-class, and living in Capitol Hill, the heart of wealthy, white Seattle. He was taught to be proud of the accomplishments of his middle and upper middle class heritage and status of his family, and his mother ensured that he was highly cultured. As a child, he even studied the violin. As Cayton explained in his autobiography, "With such sterling examples to guide us, surrender to prejudice seemed cowardly and unnecessary. Our goals were dictated by our past; we were obligated by our family history to achievement in our fight for individual and racial equality."

As Seattle's African American population increased, so did racial tensions in the city. Cayton experienced his share of discrimination. His father, moreover, was very vocal in his condemnations of the South. Not only was Cayton exposed to such viewpoints, but he also suffered the ramifications of them. At one point, for example, Cayton's father ran a story in his paper about a cruel lynching in Mississippi. When the article appeared, subscriptions to the newspaper dropped dramatically, thereby plunging the family into financial

At a Glance . . .

Born Horace Roscoe Cayton April 12, 1903 in Seattle, WA; died in 1970 in Paris, France; son of Horace Roscoe Cayton Sr. (newspaper owner, editor, publisher), and Susie Revels Cayton (journalist, teacher); married Bonnie Branch (divorced); twice married and divorced Irma Jackson; married Ruby Wright (divorced). *Education:* University of Washington, B.A. in sociology, 1931; University of Chicago, graduate work in sociology, 1931-35.

Career: Research assistant to Harold Gosnell in political science, University ofChicago, 1931-33; research assistant in sociology, University of Chicago, 1933-34; special assistant to Secretary of the Interior Harold Ickes, 1934; professor of economics and labor, Fisk University, Nashville, TN, 1935-36; research assistant in anthropology, University of Chicago,1936-37; leader, Works Projects Administration project, Chicago, IL, 1936-39; director, Chicago Parkway Community House, Chicago, IL, 1940-49; columnist, *Pittsburgh Courier,* 1934-61; researcher, American Jewish Committee, New York, NY, 1950-51; correspondent tothe United Nations for the *Pittsburgh Courier,* New York, NY, 1952-54; researcher, National Council of Churches, New York, NY, 1954-58; instructor, City College of New York,1957-58; professor, University of California at Berkeley, 1961-68.

Selected awards: Anisfield-Wolf Award for *Black Metropolis,* 1945; Grant, National Foundation for the Arts and Humanities, 1968.

turmoil. Perhaps as a direct result of being caught amidst the changing patterns of racial relations in Seattle, Cayton grew up confused and troubled about issues of race, identity, class, and place. From his early childhood years onward, he grappled with his place in society at large. Accepted by neither whites nor African Americans and without any idea of how to act in either world, Cayton embarked upon a life-long quest for self-discovery.

The fact that Cayton was troubled surfaced during his high school years. Despite the strong example set by his parents, he dropped out of high school during his sophomore year and worked as a mess man on the Alaska Company's SS "Ketchikan." On the ship, there was no pressure to find one's place in a confusing world and certainly no pressure to succeed. Finally, Cayton found himself in an environment where he understood the rules of the game.

Eventually, Cayton returned to Seattle and resumed his studies. However, he soon dropped out of school again. Suffering from extreme feelings of alienation, Cayton drifted into crime. Various illegal activities, which culminated in his arrest for driving a getaway car from a gas station robbery, landed Cayton in the State Training School in Chehalis, Washington. Within six months, he was released. Still searching for an identity, Cayton began to travel widely. Along the way, he supported himself with various manual labor jobs, working most extensively as a longshoreman. Once again, Cayton returned to Seattle and finished high school at a Young Men's Christian Association preparatory school. In 1925, he enrolled at the University of Washington and earned a bachelor of arts degree in sociology in 1931. Concurrently, Cayton worked as a sheriff's deputy in King County, becoming the first African American to be appointed to this position. This job helped to solidify his commitment to sociology, for he came to realize that he was more interested in learning about life than in punishing criminals. Ultimately, Cayton left the force because he did not want to utilize the incredible power that policemen held over the lives of others.

During college, Cayton met and fell in love with a fellow classmate, a white social worker named Bonnie Branch. The two were married in 1929. This relationship proved devastating for Cayton. In many ways, he and his wife removed themselves from society in anticipation of the isolation that they felt would be cast upon them for their interracial relationship. Forever anxious of society's judging voice, they denied themselves acceptance into either world. Unfortunately, during Cayton's graduate school years, the two drifted apart and eventually divorced.

Upon graduating from the University of Washington, Cayton won a fellowship to study sociology at the University of Chicago. He eagerly left Seattle and relocated to Chicago. Between 1931 and 1935, Cayton completed all of the coursework for his doctoral degree, although he never finished his dissertation. Through his study of sociology, he noted in his memoir, he "became aware that there was a greater Negro community throughout America in which I might play an important and vital role if I could gain acceptance there." Cayton also came to the realization that African Americans were not the only group to have experienced prejudice.

In 1934, in conjunction with his work at the University of Chicago, Cayton was offered a job as Special Assistant to the Secretary of the Interior Harold Ickes. The job gave him the opportunity to study the effects of the New Deal legislation on African American labor. Based in New York, Cayton spent one year interviewing and observing the formation of the Congress of Industrial Organizations (CIO) and the role of the African American worker in the steel, meat-packaging, and railroad car shop industries across the United States. He also traced the economic effects of racism on African American workers during their movement from agricultural-based occupations to industrial-based employment. As a result of his inquiries, Cayton wrote his first book, entitled *Black Workers and the New Unions,* in conjunction with George S. Mitchell.

Such professional success, however, did not help to ease Cayton's personal struggles. Following his divorce, he was wary of entering into another interracial relationship. However, he felt more comfortable among white people, especially the university crowd. As Cayton claimed in *Long Old Road,* he "didn't relish taking a Negro wife and settling down in some southern university to teach sociology for the rest of [his] life." In the throes of a deep depression, he accepted an invitation to travel in Europe. He soon discovered a world seemingly free of racial tension, a world in which race did not dictate everything. However, after a several-month stay in Europe, he ultimately decided to return to the United States.

Upon his return, Cayton accepted a teaching job in economics and labor at Fisk University in Nashville, Tennessee. He quickly discovered that he could not tolerate the blatant racism of the South, and returned to Chicago in 1936. Now married to Irma Jackson, an African American woman, Cayton settled into life in an African American section of Chicago. Perhaps for the first time in his life, he felt secure within the African American community.

Professionally, Cayton continued to blossom. In conjunction with W. Lloyd Warner, he outlined a large research project that focused on Chicago's African American community. With the help of government funding, the two men submitted a proposal to study the problem of juvenile delinquency. Their ultimate goal was to study the entire social structure of the African American community and its relationship to the rest of Chicago. When the funds were awarded, Cayton became the only African American to lead a large white-collar Works Progress Administration (WPA) project. This earned him stature within the African American community. He was later joined in the project by St. Clair Drake, an African American anthropologist from the University of Chicago. In 1941, an additional grant from the Julius Rosenwald Fund allowed Cayton and Drake to organize the materials gathered during the WPA project and supplement them with information from the 1940s. The project formed the basis of Cayton's major work, *Black Metropolis,* which was published in 1945.

Black Metropolis blended the two dominant social scientific methodologies used during the interwar years for the study of race relations: the Chicago school of sociology, which viewed race relations as a dynamic process of assimilation; and the anthropological study of case and class. The book focused on the effects of the rapid migration of African Americans into Chicago. As Richard Wright discussed in the introduction to the book, the facts of urban life were presented in their "scariest form, their crudest manifestation" with the expressed purpose of preserving the humanity of African Americans. Cayton and Drake argued that racism prevented African Americans from assimilating into the dominant culture and relegated them to a separate, subordinate status, which made them unique among ethnic groups in the United States. With the purpose of educating white America, the book further exposed and explained African American conduct, personality, and culture which emerged from the conditions imposed by the white world. Ultimately, Cayton and Drake concluded their book with a call for the government to work more aggressively to help African Americans achieve equality. Like his father, Cayton expressed an on-going concern for racial equality and civil rights, a theme to which he repeatedly returned in his regular column for the *Pittsburgh Courier.*

In 1940 Cayton assumed the position of director of the Chicago Parkway Community House, a large community center for African Americans. In this role, he was a regular speaker at community affairs and attended city-wide activities as the African American representative. Cayton soon transformed the House into a focal point for African American cultural life, and luminaries such as Langston Hughes, Arna Bontemps, Paul Robeson, and Richard Wright often visited.

Overcome with Depression

As a result of his own accomplishments, Cayton once again found himself a part of the well-to-do African American upper class. However, he remained possessed by profound feelings of loneliness and hostility. Through repeated psychoanalysis, Cayton came to understand that he despised white people. He also realized that he feared them. Such self-discovery was extremely painful, and seemed to increase his emotional and psychological burdens. A stint at Yaddo, the writer's colony in Saratoga, New York, brought Cayton some relief because he was able to write. However, he returned to Chicago deeply disturbed. On the verge of a mental collapse, Cayton abandoned Chicago in 1949, moved to New York City, and completely severed all ties with the world.

During the 1950s, Cayton was in and out of various New York treatment centers for alcoholism and drug addiction. At one point, he had plummeted so far that he found himself selling his own blood. Unable to hold steady employment, he floated between various research positions. As Cayton later admitted, racial hatred played a part in his breakdown.

Cayton moved to California in 1960 to join his brother, Revels, with whom he was never particularly close. In 1961, he ended his column with the *Pittsburgh Courier* and began teaching at the University of California at Berkeley. Cayton began work on his autobiography, which was published in 1965. According to John P. Jackson, Cayton viewed *Long Old Road,* as "a form of therapy, a way to grapple with the demons of racism and loneliness that had plagued him for most of his adult life." In 1968, he received a grant from the National Foundation for the Arts and Humanities to write a biography of Richard Wright. Cayton traveled to Paris to conduct his research and, in 1970, died there of natural causes.

Cayton's contributions to the world of sociology and, in particular, to an understanding of the African American community in Chicago, remain significant. However, while his studies enabled him to decipher social facts, they proved powerless in helping him to cope with the anger, rage, and ambivalence generated by racism. Tragically, Cayton's inner struggle to find his place in the jumbled world of race relations created a conflict within him that he was never able to resolve.

Selected writings

Black Metropolis, University of Chicago Press, Chicago, IL, 1945.
Black Workers and the New Unions, McGrath Publishing Co., College Park, MD, 1939.
Changing Scene: Current Trends and Issues, 1965.
Long Old Road, University of Washington Press, Seattle, WA, 1965.

Sources

Books

Black Metropolis, University of Chicago Press, Chicago, IL, 1945.
Cayton Legacy, University of Washington Press, Seattle, WA, 1989.
Long Old Road, University of Washington Press, Seattle, WA, 1965.

Periodicals

Atlantic Monthly, June 1986, pp. 31-55; July 1986, pp. 54-68.

Other

Additional information for this profile was obtained from the Seattle General Strike Project website, June 7, 1999.

—Lisa S. Weitzman

Tracy Chapman

1964—

Folk-rock vocalist

With a unique style that combined folk music with an African American sensibility, singer-songwriter Tracy Chapman took the pop-music world by storm in 1988. That year, her debut album was released. It sold upwards of ten million copies, and its lead single "Fast Car" became almost universally known among music fans. One of the few late twentieth-century musicians in any genre outside of hip-hop to succeed in delivering a political message to a wide audience, Chapman also helped pave the way for the resurgence of strong, independent female voices in the popular music of the late 1990s.

Chapman was born on March 30, 1964, in Cleveland, Ohio. Her parents divorced when she was four, and her mother found it extremely difficult to raise Chapman and her older sister Aneta. "Sometimes there was no electricity, or the gas would be shut off," Chapman told *Time.* "I remember standing with my mother in the line to get food stamps." Her mother was a music lover with a large record collection and a determination to nurture her daughter's musical talents. Chapman played the ukulele in elementary school, and later studied clarinet and organ.

Watched "Hee Haw"

It might seem easy to assume that Chapman's bent toward political folk music came about after she entered the elite educational institutions to which she later gained admission. In fact, both her interest in politics and her attraction to the guitar began while she was still in Cleveland. "As a child, I always had a sense of social conditions and political situations," she told *Rolling Stone.* "I think it had to do with the fact that my mother was always discussing things with my sister and me—also because I read a lot." Another influence, surprisingly enough, came from country music. "One of the things that made me want to learn how to play guitar was watching Buck Owens and Roy Clark and Minnie Pearl on *Hee Haw* when I was 8 years old," she told *Time.* "The guitars they played were beautiful."

Chapman won an ABC (A Better Chance) scholarship to the prestigious Wooster School, a prep school in Danbury, Connecticut. She honed her songwriting skills in the school's coffeehouse, starred on its basketball and soccer teams, and was heavily recruited by several top colleges as she approached her graduation in 1982. Enrolling at Tufts University outside Boston,

At a Glance . . .

Born in Cleveland, Ohio, on March 30, 1964; *Education:* Graduated from Tufts University.

Career: Singer-songwriter; released debut album, *Tracy Chapman,* 1988; participated in 1–Nation Amnesty International tour, 1988; released *Crossroads,* 1989; released *Matters of the Heart,* 1992; released *New Beginning,* 1995; performed on Lilith Fair tour, 1996; released *Telling Stories,* 2000.

Awards: Three Grammy awards, including Best New Artist, for *Tracy Chapman,* 1988.

Addresses: *Recording company*—Elektra Records, 75 Rockefeller Plaza,New York, NY 10019.

Chapman began studying veterinary medicine, but later switched to anthropology and ethnomusicology—the study of music from outside Western traditions. She continued singing and, on one occasion, played for loose change in the busy public spaces of Harvard Square. Chapman gained a strong following in the numerous folk coffeehouses and clubs of Boston and nearby Cambridge. She numbered among her admirers a fellow Tufts student, Brian Koppelman, whose father Charles Koppelman was an executive at the large SBK music publishing firm. Chapman's contact with the elder Koppelman, who was bowled over by her songs, led to others. She teamed with veteran manager Elliot Roberts, who had worked with folk-rock stars Joni Mitchell and Neil Young, and was signed to the Elektra record label.

Chapman began her career almost reluctantly, showing little interest in financial gain and, at one point, turning down an offer from an independent label so as not to interrupt her studies. Promising though her first steps might have seemed, neither Chapman nor anyone at Elektra could have been prepared for the success of her debut album *Tracy Chapman,* which was released in 1988. The album reached the Number One position on *Billboard* magazine's pop charts, a rare accomplishment for an unknown newcomer. "Fast Car," a vivid, densely packed narrative of a young woman who dreams of a better future but is dragged down by a series of troubles, became one of the most widely heard songs of the late 1980s.

The album owed its success to a variety of virtues. Often compared with folk/jazz vocalist Joan Armatrading, Chapman also resembled 1960s folk icon Richie Havens in her ability to bring a distinctively African American sensibility to the predominantly white-oriented genre of folk music. However musically distant her style might seem from those of the rap artists who were beginning to flourish in the late 1980s, Chapman shared with the rappers an ambitious way with words and a desire to tell the stories of the American underclass. Some of her songs had a vaguely Caribbean sound, and she drew on the heavily verbal qualities of genres from that part of the world. That aspect of Chapman's music was reinforced visually by her trademark short dreadlocks.

Such songs as "Talkin' Bout a Revolution" espoused an uncompromising political message that was light-years away from the shiny dance pop that was the norm during the late 1980s. Chapman became the subject of intense publicity for some months after the release of her debut album. She won Best New Artist and Best Female Pop Vocal Performance Grammy awards, and several other major awards. Expectations ran high for Chapman's sophomore release, *Crossroads,* which was released in 1989.

Crossroads sold four million copies, a smash hit by any standards except for those of an artist whose debut album had sold ten million. Sales slipped further with the release of Chapman's third album, *Matters of the Heart,* in 1992. Some critics speculated that the public had grown tired of Chapman's political themes. However, like many other folk-oriented artists, Chapman had been writing songs for many years before making her first recording. She had gradually exhausted her storehouse of material and, as she recorded subsequent albums, was unable to write new material under the glare of publicity and celebrity. Indeed, when Chapman's *New Beginning* album put her back near the top of the charts in 1995, it was due to the success of a song, "Give Me One Reason," that she had written a decade earlier while still in college. Fans still flocked to Chapman's concerts, and public admiration of her music's distinctiveness remained strong. She became a star attraction on the all-female Lilith Fair tour in 1996. After the release of the *New Beginning* album, Chapman took a leave of absence from the recording process. "I felt like my life was on this cycle that was beyond my control," she told *Time.* "Making records and touring, making records and touring, and in that process not being at home and not being settled. They weren't particularly happy times."

Chapman re-emerged in 2000 with her fifth album, *Telling Stories.* Reviews were mixed, with *Interview* praising the album's "intimate and personal" quality and noting approvingly that Chapman "doesn't make an album until she's got something to say." *Entertainment Weekly* was less enthusiastic, remarking that "Chapman remains an enigma: an intelligent, level-headed craftsperson unable to convey any emotion beyond resignation." Whatever the future direction of her career, Chapman had already fulfilled the ambition of the woman she depicted in the song "Fast Car": to "be someone, be someone."

Selected discography

Tracy Chapman, Elektra, 1988.
Crossroads, Elektra, 1989.
Matters of the Heart, Elektra, 1992.
New Beginning, Elektra, 1995.
Telling Stories, Elektra/Asylum, 2000.

Sources

Books

Contemporary Musicians, volume 4, Gale, 1991; volume 20, Gale, 1997.
Graff, Gary, ed., *MusicHound Rock: The Essential Guide,* Visible Ink, 1996.
Larkin, Colin, ed., *The Encyclopedia of Popular Music,* Muze UK, 1998.
Smith, Jessie Carney, ed., *Notable Black American Women, Book II,* Gale, 1996.

Periodicals

Billboard, February 12, 2000, p. 11.
Entertainment Weekly, February 18, 2000, p. 86.
Interview, March 2000, p. 88.
Life, August 1988, p. 60.
The Nation, July 6, 1992, p. 30.
Playboy, July 1988, p. 26.
Rolling Stone, September 22, 1998, p. 54.
Time, March 12, 1990, p. 70; February 28, 2000, p. 92.

Other

Additional information for this profile was obtained from http://www.allmusic.com

—James M. Manheim

May Edward Chinn

1896–1980

Physician

May Edward Chinn led an unusual life for a woman of her time and race. She was a pioneer in many respects. Chinn was the first African American woman to graduate from Bellevue Hospital Medical College, the first African American woman intern at Harlem Hospital, the first female physician to ride with ambulance crews of Harlem Hospital for emergency calls, the first African American woman, and for several years the only woman, to practice medicine in Harlem, and the first African American woman to receive admitting privileges at Harlem Hospital. Despite the many restrictions placed on African American doctors, Chinn creatively conquered these obstacles in order to provide the quality of care her patients deserved. She had an intense interest in the early detection, diagnosis, and treatment of cancer, which led her to a rewarding 29-year staff position with the renowned Strang Clinic. She continued her private practice in Harlem until she retired at the age of 81.

Chinn was born April 15, 1896 in Great Barrington, Massachusetts. Her father, William Lafayette Chinn, the son of a slave and a plantation owner, had escaped slavery when he was a child. Her mother had been born on a Virginia reservation, her parents a Chickahominy Indian and a slave. Believing New York City to be a place of opportunity, the Chinn family moved there when May was three years old. The Chinns experienced the severe poverty that marked the African American and immigrant experience in New York City at the turn of the century. Chinn's mother believed that education was the key to escaping poverty, and was determined that her daughter would receive quality schooling. Chinn's father found it difficult to find work, but her mother worked steadily at cleaning houses. Despite her meager salary, Chinn's mother managed to send her daughter to a boarding school for African American children in New Jersey. However, Chinn contracted osteomyelitis of her jaw while at the Bordentown Manual Training and Industrial School and had to return home in 1901. She underwent nine surgeries to combat the infection.

Chinn's mother had gotten a job cleaning and cooking at the Tiffany family mansion in upstate New York. The Tiffanys were well known for the stained-glass lamps that bore the family name. When Chinn came back from boarding school, she lived in the Tiffany mansion because her mother was live-in help. The Tiffany family treated Chinn as if she were their own child. She ate

At a Glance . . .

Born in 1896 in Great Barrington, MA; died on December 1, 1980, in New York, NY; daughter of William Lafayette Chinn and Lulu Ann Chinn. *Education:* Columbia University Teachers College, B.S. 1921; Belleview Hospital Medical School, MD, 1926; Columbia University, M.S., 1933.

Career: Intern, Harlem Hospital, 1926-28; general practice physician, 1926-78; attending physician, Strang Clinic, Memorial Hospital, New York, NY, 1944-73; consultant to the Phelps-Stokes Fund, Harlem, 1978-80.

Selected awards: Honorary doctorate, Columbia University; Distinguished Alumnus Award, Columbia Teachers College.

Member: National Urban League, American Cancer Society, New York County and New York State Medical Societies; American Medical Society.

with the Tiffany children, received lessons in French and German, and attended plays and concerts with them. It was during this time that Chinn developed her love of music.

When Chinn's mother finished working for the Tiffany mansion, the family was reunited in New York City. She encouraged her daughter to take piano lessons, and moved the family from place to place so that Chinn could attend the best schools. Chinn learned to play the piano, sang, and gave recitals.

On Chinn's 16th birthday, her parents gave her a piano. An older, widowed businessman also asked for her hand in marriage, but she refused. Although Chinn's mother supported her decision, her father began to resent her interest in music and her refusal to marry. Despite her father's disapproval, she sang and acted in musical productions and developed a lifelong interest in securing human rights for women and African Americans.

Chinn dropped out of high school in the eleventh grade, a decision which greatly upset her mother. To support herself, she worked in a factory and gave piano lessons to young children. Chinn's life changed dramatically when a friend convinced her to take the entrance exam for Columbia University's Teachers College. She scored so well on the exam that she was able to enroll in the college, even though she had not finished high school. Although Chinn's mother was very pleased, her father was unwilling to pay for her college education. He believed that a woman should not be educated, but find satisfaction only as a wife and mother. However, Chinn's mother had secretly saved money, and was able to pay for her daughter's first two years of tuition.

Chinn planned to study music at Columbia, believing that she would be able to teach piano and perform at concerts as a career. However, she was the only woman and African American in the class. A naturally shy person, Chinn could not bear her professor's ridicule and uncooperative attitude. The professor strongly believed that African Americans could not excel as classical musicians. Chinn realized that in order for her to gain experience as a performer she would have to go to Europe, where discrimination against African Americans was less prevalent. If she stayed in the United States, she would probably be only able to perform as a nightclub singer. In the midst of her dilemma another professor, Jean Broadhurst, encouraged Chinn to pursue a career in science after reading her research paper on sewage disposal. Chinn eventually decided to begin training to become a clinical pathologist.

The Chinn family lived in Harlem, which at the time was a neighborhood of white, upper-middle-class people and one filled with upscale shops, department stores, theaters, and an opera house. Chinn lived with her parents and walked to her classes at Columbia University. As Harlem's African American community grew, so did its culture. African American writers, musicians, and singers moved to Harlem. Chinn met several of these artists, including Paul Robeson, who would become a highly successful actor and singer. She began accompanying Robeson on piano and traveled with him to his performances. The two eventually separated as they became immersed in their own careers.

After graduating from college, Chinn decided to become a doctor. When she made her decision to become a doctor, only 65 of the 150,000 doctors in the United States were African American women. She applied to Bellevue Medical Hospital and was accepted. Chinn began her medical studies in 1922, and attended classes during the day while working in a pathology laboratory at night. In 1926, she became the first African American woman to graduate from Bellevue Medical College.

During her internship at Harlem Hospital, Chinn faced discrimination. As the hospital's first African American female doctor, she was resented by her male colleagues. Chinn began going on emergency calls with the ambulances in order to escape the unfriendly atmosphere. No woman had ever gone on emergency calls before.

Upon completing her internship, Chinn began a medical practice in Harlem. She continued to live with her parents in the same building as her practice, and hoped to eventually earn enough money to support her parents. Racial discrimination was rampant during the 1920s and 1930s, and Chinn was prohibited from practicing medicine in most New York City hospitals. African American doctors had to set up their own hospitals in order to perform surgery and other procedures. Chinn operated her private practice during the day. At night, she offered her services as the night-duty physician at the Edgecombe Sanitarium, a small hospital owned by seven African American doctors. She spent many hours helping poor women, African Americans, and other minorities would could not receive medical treatment elsewhere. Her medical practice and reputation as a compassionate doctor began to grow steadily. As Harlem changed from a prosperous cultural community into a crowded, crime- and poverty-infested community, Chinn's practice changed as well. Living conditions for many people in Harlem were poor. She often operated on patients in their own homes because African American doctors were still barred from practicing medicine in most hospitals. Beds or ironing boards were used as operating tables, and instruments were sterilized on coal stoves. After witnessing the horrible living conditions of her patients, Chinn became interested in public health issues. She went back to Columbia, and earned a master's degree in public health.

In 1928 Chinn studied with Dr. George Papanicolaou, the developer of the pap test for cervical cancer. She was especially interested in treating women and yearned to know more about their special problems, including cancer. Chinn wanted to find new ways to detect and treat various forms of cancer. Because she was unable to gain entry into most hospitals and clinics, she used a bit of trickery to gain entry so that she could observe cancer biopsies being performed. Eventually, she learned enough to begin performing her own biopsies.

In 1940 Chinn finally gained admitting privileges at Harlem Hospital, thanks to Mayor LaGuardia's committees established after the 1935 Harlem riots. The committee findings helped to bring about change. Chinn quickly gained a reputation as a skilled medical doctor. In 1944 the founder of the Strang Clinics, Dr. Elise Strang L'Esperance, invited Chinn to join her staff. The Strang Clinics were known for their study and prevention of cancer. Chinn worked for the Strang Clinics for 29 years while maintaining her private practice in Harlem.

Chinn continued to develop her interest in civil rights. She joined Dr. Martin Luther King. Jr.'s march on Washington in 1963, and listened as he delivered his famous "I Have A Dream" speech. Chinn worked on other important causes throughout her life. In 1975, she founded a society to help African American women who wanted to attend medical school. At the age of 81, Chinn retired from private practice. In 1978, she became a consultant to the Phelps-Stokes Fund and treated children in day care centers in Harlem. On December 1, 1980, Chinn passed away after collapsing at a reception held at Columbia University to honor one of her friends.

Sources

Books

Butts, Ellen R. and Schwartz, Joyce R., *May Chinn. The Best Medicine,* Scientific American, 1995.

Other

Additional information for this profile was obtained from www.sdsc.edu/ScienceWomen/chinn.html

—Sandy J. Stiefer

Donn Clendenon

1935—

Former baseball player, lawyer, drug abuse counselor

On March 1, 1969, Donn Clendenon retired from professional baseball. Seven months later, he was named Most Valuable Player of the 1969 World Series as a member of the world champion New York Mets. All of this occurred due to trades, contracts and other concerns that are part of the business of baseball. However, it also has to do with the personality of Clendenon and how he worked to bounce back from seemingly adverse situations. A gifted student and athlete, he consistently worked other jobs while playing professional baseball and received his law degree six years after retiring from the sport for good in 1972. A ten month addiction to cocaine and a 1988 arrest for possession nearly put an end to his law practice. After spending four years as a certified drug counselor, he returned to practicing law in 1996. Clendenon is also battling the effects of chronic lymphocytic leukemia, a disease which took the lives of his father and grandfather.

Born in Neosho, Missouri in 1935 to Claude and Helen Clendenon, Donn was only six months old when his father died from leukemia. At the time of his death, Claude Clendenon was a professor of psychology and mathematics and chairman of the mathematics department at Langston University, an all-black university in Langston, Oklahoma. Clendenon's mother demanded high academic achievement from her son in deference to his father's accomplishments. At the age of 15, Clendenon was second in his class at Booker T. Washington High School in Atlanta. Two years later, he graduated as a letterman in nine sports, and received a host of scholarship offers.

When he was only six years old, Clendenon's mother married a man named Nish Williams. In addition to academic excellence, Clendenon's new stepfather also made other demands. As a former standout baseball player in the Negro Leagues during the 1930s, Williams decided he was going to make his stepson into a professional baseball player. "I knew that if I didn't play baseball," Clendenon recalled in his book, *Miracle in New York,* "that I just might not get my allowance—and no allowance meant no money for gas and no spending money." Williams served as a coach on virtually every baseball team that Clendenon played on, including his college team at Atlanta's Morehouse College.

Clendenon also received pointers from some of the players Williams knew from the Negro Leagues, includ-

At a Glance . . .

Born Donn Alvin Clendenon July 15, 1935 in Neosho, MO; son of Claude and Helen Morre Clendenon; married Deanna, 1965; divorced; married Anne, 1993. children: Eric Val, Donn Alvin, Jr., Donna. *Education:* Morehouse College, BA, 1956; Duquesne University School of Law, 1978.

Career: Professional baseball player for the Pittsburgh Pirates, 1961-68, New YorkMets, 1969-71, and St. Louis Cardinals, 1972; management trainee, Mellon Bank and Trust,1961-62; Allegheny County detective, 1962-64; management trainee, U.S. Steel, 1964; labor relations/personnel, Scripto Pen Company, 1967-71; owner, Donn Clendenon's night club and restaurant, 1968-71; personnel consultant, General Electric, 1971-72; Mead Corporation,1972-78; law partner, Bostick, Gerren & Clendenon, 1978-80; director of personnel, DapInc., 1978-80; president and CEO, Western International Contractors Inc., 1980-85; presidentand CEO, Chicago Economic Development, 1985-86; attorney, Anderson, Carlson, Carter& Hay, 1986-88; counselor, Keystone-Carroll Treatment Center, 1988-92; law partner,Clendenon, Henney & Hoy, 1992-; author, *Miracle in New York,* 1999.

Awards: World Series Most Valuable Player, 1969.

Addresses: *Home*—2709 Sandstone Circle, Sioux Falls, SD 57103.

ing such legendary names as Satchel Paige, Jackie Robinson, Roy Campanella, and Don Newcombe. Following his excellent athletic performance in high school, Clendenon was prepared to attend UCLA on a scholarship. However, some coaches from nearby Morehouse College visited his mother, and convinced her that he should attend college closer to home. Clendenon attended Morehouse, and became a 12-sport letterman in football, basketball, and baseball.

From Morehouse to the Majors

Morehouse College was the premier academic institution for young African American men. Just before Clendenon arrived in 1952, the freshman class were assigned big brothers to help the students acclimate themselves to Morehouse and college life. Although the policy had ended, a Morehouse graduate volunteered to be Clendenon's big brother. His name was Martin Luther King, Jr.

During summers off from Morehouse, Clendenon played semi-pro baseball for Atlanta's Black Crackers, a team coached and managed by Nish Williams. Although his mother wanted him to be a doctor, Clendenon decided that he wanted to teach. After graduating from Morehouse, Clendenon taught fourth grade for a while, and then went to the Pittsburgh Pirates try-out camp in Florida. "Nish convinced me that I could , in effect, have my cake and eat it too if I went into professional sports," Clendenon wrote. "I could have a dozen good years as a professional athlete; make some money; develop a name for myself; and use the off-season to pursue my future plans."

Beginning in September of 1956, Clendenon began a five-year stint with a team in the Pittsburgh Pirates farm system. In September of 1961, the Pirates called him up to join the major league club. For the next seven seasons, Clendenon became known as a power hitter. Led by Hall of Famers Roberto Clemente and Willie Stargell, the Pirates became known as "the Lumber Company" because of their ability to score many runs. However, Clendenon also became known as a batter who'd swing at just about anything. In 1963 and 1968, he led the National League in strike-outs.

As a member of the Pirates, Clendenon averaged 17 home runs and 76 RBIs with an overall .278 batting average. Following the 1968 season, the Pirates did not put Clendenon on their protected player list, and he was drafted by the expansion Montreal Expos. A few months later, he was traded to the Houston Astros. The Astros had just hired Harry Walker as their manager. Walker had been the Pirates manager from 1965 to 1967, and Clendenon did not want to play for him again. "Our personalities definitely clashed," Clendenon recalled in *Miracle in New York,* "and it took me too long to learn to just ignore him."

Although he was a member of the Pittsburgh Pirates, Clendenon worked during the off-season. He worked initially as a management trainee at the Mellon Bank and Trust Company. Beginning in 1962, he held a job as an Allegheny County detective for the district attorney's office, where he worked with underprivileged juveniles. In 1964, Clendenon went to work at U.S. Steel as a management trainee. While working at U.S. Steel, he decided to attend law school, and enrolled at Duquesne University School of Law in 1965. Job pressures, the demands of baseball, and his stepfather's illness forced him to drop out of law school in 1967. He eventually returned to school, and graduated in 1978.

Because he was earning a steady income from his non-baseball jobs, Clendenon decided that he no longer needed to play professional sports. On March 1, 1969, he announced his retirement from baseball.

Houston was upset with Clendenon because they had lost a player that they had traded for. With the assistance of baseball commissioner Bowie Kuhn, the Astros and Expos hammered out a deal. Montreal sent two pitchers and $100,000 to Houston and the Expos eventually signed Clendenon to a three-year deal.

Clendenon played only one month for the Expos. On June 15, 1969, he was traded to the New York Mets, a move favored by both Clendenon and the Mets. The Mets felt that, with the addition of Clendenon, they finally had a championship caliber team. "He [Clendenon] was the catalyst on the team," outfielder Art Shamsky recalled to Stanley Cohen, author of *A Magic Summer.* "You can talk about our pitching, which was great, and whatever else, but until June we were just a potentially good team. When Clendenon joined us, he gave us the right-handed power we needed, some more experience, and we became a really good team from that point on." Third baseman Wayne Garrett agreed, telling Cohen, "Clendenon was probably the key to our whole season, because when he came over we really came alive."

The 1969 New York Mets are part of baseball lore. When Clendenon joined the team, they were 11 1/2 games behind the first-place Chicago Cubs. By the All-Star break, the Mets had closed the gap to 4 1/2 games. With a pitching staff that included Tom Seaver, Nolan Ryan, Tug McGraw, and Jerry Koosman, the Mets eventually won the National League pennant and met the Baltimore Orioles in the World Series. After losing the first game of the series, the Mets won the next four to capture the world championship. Clendenon hit three home runs and was named the World Series Most Valuable Player.

After playing a final season for the St. Louis Cardinals in 1972, Clendenon retired from baseball for good. At the time of his retirement, he worked for the Mead Corporation. During the mid-1980s, Clendenon became addicted to cocaine. "I was 49 turning 50; that was kind of like a birthday present for me," he reminisced to William C. Rhoden of the *New York Times.* "I was hooked immediately." After an arrest for cocaine possession in 1988, Clendenon was forced to resign from the law firm of Anderson, Carlson, Carter & Hay, where he had worked as an attorney.

Clendenon sought treatment for drug abuse at a facility in Utah. Following a few years of sobriety, he eventually became a certified drug counselor and worked at the Keystone-Carroll Treatment Center in South Dakota. In the early 1990s Clendenon was diagnosed with chronic lymphocytic leukemia, the deadly disease that killed both his father and grandfather. "Every day I wake up is a blessing," he told Rhoden in 1999. "I will die from it or a side effect of it. It's going to eventually take me, I know. But I keep fighting."

Sources

Books

Bock, Duncan and John Jordan, *The Complete Year-By-Year N.Y. Mets Fan's Almanac,* Crown Publishers, 1992.

Clendenon, Donn, *Miracle in New York,* Penmarch Publishing, 1999.

Cohen, Stanley, *A Magic Summer: The '69 Mets,* Harcourt Brace Jovanovich, 1988.

Periodicals

New York Times, February 26, 2000, p. B-15.

Newsday (New York), May 21, 1989, p. S-7.

Sport, November 1992, p.18.

USA Today, October 13, 1989.

—Brian Escamilla

Bill Cosby

1937—

Comedian, actor, author

Bill Cosby, one of television's funniest and most popular comedic actors, has spent his long career making people laugh. Cosby first gained prominence as a comedian in the early 1960s, when he vaulted from telling jokes in Philadelphia night-spots to the top of the nightclub circuit and then to television. Cosby became the first African American to star in a television drama when he appeared on *I Spy* in 1965. In the 1980s, in the role of Dr. Heathcliff Huxtable, he headed television's first educated, middle-class African American family in the wildly successful *The Cosby Show.* Though best known for his television appearances, Cosby has made more than 20 comedy albums, appeared in films, published a string of humorous books, and pitched products for Jell-O, Kodak, and a variety of other companies.

Cosby's humor springs from life's absurdities. As a young comic, he told long funny stories about his childhood in Philadelphia and his experiences at Temple University. In the 1970s and 1980s, he wove humorous yarns from family events, such as a child's trip to the dentist. In the 1990s, he addressed aging and the consequences of raising wealthy children.

William Henry Cosby, Jr., was born in 1937 in the Germantown district of North Philadelphia. He grew up in the all-African American Richard Allen housing project where his mother, Anna Cosby, struggled to raise him and his younger brothers, Russell and Robert. His father, William Cosby, Sr., served as a mess steward in the U.S. Navy and was away for months at a time. As a child, Cosby loved comedy radio shows. "I always listened for the comedy," he told the *Los Angeles Times:* "Jack Benny, Burns & Allen, Jimmy Durante, Fred Allen... .When comedy was on, I was just happy to be alive." By the fifth grade, Cosby was getting up in front of his class and making everybody laugh, including his teacher.

Cosby's high IQ led teachers to place him in a class for gifted students, but outside interests eventually derailed his school career. Between work and playing football, basketball, baseball, and running track, he found little time for schoolwork. When Cosby was told that he would have to repeat the tenth grade at Germantown High, he dropped out. "The truth is," he recalled in the *Los Angeles Times,* "I'd just grown very tired of myself and thought perhaps there was a career for me in the

At a Glance . . .

Born William Henry Cosby, Jr., July 12, 1937, in Germantown, PA; son of William Henry, Sr. (a U.S. Navy mess steward) and Anna (a domestic worker) Cosby; married Camille Hanks, January 25, 1964; children: Erika, Erinn, Ennis (deceased), Ensa, Evin. *Education:* Attended Temple University, 1961-62; University of Massachusetts, M.A., 1972, Ed.D., 1977. *Military service:* U.S. Navy, 1956-60.

Career: Actor, comedian, recording artist, author. Nightclub comedian, 1963-.Television actor, appearing in *I Spy,* 1965-68, *The Bill Cosby Show,* 1969-71,*The Cosby Show,* 1984-92, *The Cosby Mysteries,* 1994; and *Cosby,*1996-; creator of children's animated series *Fat Albert and the Cosby Kids,*1972-79, and *The New Fat Albert Show,* 1979-84; host of *You Bet Your Life,*1992-93. Film appearances include roles in *Uptown Saturday Night,* 1974; *Let's Do It Again,* 1975; *Mother, Juggs & Speed,* 1976; *California Suite,* 1978; *The Devil and Max Devlin,* 1981; *Leonard Part VI,* 1987; and *Ghost Dad,* 1990. Commercial spokesperson for Jell-O Pudding, Kodak Film, and other products; creator of the "Little Bill" children's book series, 1997-.

Member: United Negro College Fund; NAACP; Operation PUSH; Sickle CellFoundation.

Awards: Eight Grammy awards for best comedy album; four Emmy awards; NAACP Image Award; Golden Globe Award; four People's Choice awards; Academy of Television Arts and Sciences Hall of Fame inductee, 1994; Kennedy Center Awards Honoree,1998.

Addresses: *Office*—P.O. Box 4049, Santa Monica, CA 90404.*Agent*—The Brokaw Co., 9255 Sunset Blvd., Los Angeles, CA 90069.

service. If you stayed in for 20 years, you knew at least you'd get a certain amount of money for the rest of your life." Cosby enlisted in the Navy in 1956.

Away from school, Cosby realized the importance of an education and used his four years in the Navy to prepare for the day when he would continue his schooling. Cosby learned physical therapy, traveled around the western hemisphere, and earned a high school equivalency diploma through correspondence courses. In 1961, at the age of 23, Cosby won a track and field scholarship to Temple University.

For two years, Cosby studied physical education, ran track, and played right halfback on Temple's football team. During his sophomore year, however, Cosby got his first job telling jokes while tending bar at a Philadelphia coffeehouse called the Cellar. His salary was five dollars a night. According to Cosby, this was the real beginning of his comedy career. "I understood that if people enjoy conversation with the bartender, they leave tips," he told the *Los Angeles Times* "So I began collecting jokes, and learning how to work them up, stretch them out."

From the Cellar he moved to a Philadelphia nightclub called the Underground and finally, in the spring of 1962, to New York City's Greenwich Village, where for $60 a week and a room without plumbing he worked the Gaslight Cafe. At the Gaslight, he told long funny stories which brought everyday events to absurd but sweet conclusions. His comedy was one of understatement, wild sound effects, a rubbery face, and far-ranging characterizations. The Gaslight soon tripled Cosby's salary, and within months the William Morris Agency signed him to a management contract. He soon cut a comedy album and traveled the comedy club circuit, performing at the "hungry i" in San Francisco, Mr. Kelly's in Chicago, and the Flamingo in Las Vegas. Cosby's temporary leave from Temple soon became permanent. No longer a student, Bill Cosby was now a comedian. Cosby was "a new kind of black comedian," wrote Donald Bogle, author of *Blacks in American Film and Television:* "In suit and tie, he looked like a well-brought-up, serious college student, a smart fellow geared to make it. Unlike Redd Foxx or Slappy White, who... had performed material directly pitched towards black audiences, Cosby was [a] crossover." Asked to explain the absence of racial material in his humor, Cosby told a *Newsweek* interviewer in 1963, "I'm trying to reach all the people. I want to play John Q. Public."

In 1965, television producer Sheldon Leonard saw Cosby on the *Tonight Show Starring Johnny Carson.* Leonard was impressed and cast Cosby as Alex Scott, an undercover CIA agent in NBC's action adventure series, *I Spy.* The part of the witty, multilingual Scott was intended for a white actor—no African American had ever had a lead role in a dramatic series. Nevertheless, Cosby played it with ease. He won three Emmy Awards and began what would be his pattern of playing successful, educated African Americans in a medium dominated by negative images of African Americans.

I Spy left the air after three hit seasons, but Cosby returned to television in 1969 in the *Bill Cosby Show* as Chet Kincaid, a physical education teacher helping disadvantaged kids in a fictional Los Angeles neighborhood. The show remained on the air for two years, but was not a hit. In fact, Cosby's acting career foundered a bit in the early 1970s. The *Bill Cosby Show* was canceled in the spring of 1971; his first film feature, *Hickey and Boggs,* was poorly received, and his 1972 comedy/variety television show, the *New Bill Cosby Show,* failed to find an audience.

Cosby next found success with the unlikely program *Fat Albert and the Cosby Kids,* an animated kids show which debuted in 1972 and became a fixture on Saturday morning television. *Fat Albert*'s storylines came from Cosby's comedy albums and boyhood memories, and Cosby served as executive producer and host. After each humorous but instructive adventure of Fat Albert, Weird Harold, Mush Mouth, and the other characters, Cosby would appear on screen and draw a lesson from the show's events that aimed to help kids put their experiences in perspective. According to *Vibe* contributor Cathleen Campbell, "The message was the same every time: We have the power to turn alienation into a sense of community, the power to rediscover and reinvent." The critically acclaimed program remained in production until 1984.

In the mid-1970s, Cosby teamed with actor-director Sidney Poitier for two successful movie comedies, 1974's *Uptown Saturday Night,* and 1975's *Let's Do It Again.* In *Uptown Saturday Night* he portrayed Wardell Franklin, a taxi driver trying to recover a stolen lottery ticket from the mob, in a performance the *New Yorker* praised as "very funny." Though *Let's Do It Again* was less successful, critics hailed Cosby as a major comedic talent. Still, the comedian struggled to find consistent success. *Mother, Jugs & Speed,* a 1976 film co-starring Raquel Welch and Harvey Keitel, flopped, as did *Cos,* a variety show for kids, and the 1977 film *A Piece of the Action,* which reunited him with Poitier.

Though his successful career as an entertainer made a college degree unnecessary, Cosby spent much of the 1970s earning advanced degrees in education at the University of Massachusetts at Amherst. The university allowed him to substitute life experience for his uncompleted bachelor's degree and his work in prisons and on the children's television program *The Electric Company* for its teaching requirement. Cosby wrote a 242-page dissertation called "An Integration of the Visual Media via Fat Albert and the Cosby Kids into the Elementary School Curriculum as a Teaching Aid and Vehicle to Achieve Increased Learning," and in May of 1977, he was awarded a doctorate of education.

Cosby determined by the mid-1970s that he would take advantage of his wide public visibility, and his acumen as a businessman and corporate spokesman prompted *Forbes* magazine to call the comedian: "Bill Cosby, capitalist." With newly hired lawyer Herbert Chaice, Cosby began to seek ways to gain a portion of the profits he generated. Their strategies led to Cosby's attaining interests in the Coca-Cola Company, for which he had long been a spokesman, and in other business ventures. Cosby also became a ubiquitous pitchman whose commercials for Jell-O, Kodak, Del Monte, Ford Motor Company, and other businesses made him one of the most recognizable people in America.

While Cosby remained a strong nightclub act in this period, his film and television work continued to be less than impressive. He and Richard Pryor portrayed bumbling dentists in 1979's *California Suite,* roles which the *New Yorker* complained had "racist overtones." He appeared in Disney's *The Devil and Max Devlin* and was featured in the in-concert film *Bill Cosby—Himself.* He also worked as a guest host for the *Tonight Show* where, according to Donald Bogle, he "came across as rather arrogant and occasionally insensitive, looking a little like a Vegas burnout case."

In 1982, Cosby let it be known that he was interested in a weekly series. Production companies, recognizing his popularity, approached him with offers. Cosby chose a show pitched by former ABC executives Tom Werner and Marcy Carsey, and demanded a salary and an equal split of all of the show's profits. Werner and Carsey agreed to this rare arrangement, and on September 20, 1984, *The Cosby Show* debuted on NBC. As Dr. Heathcliff Huxtable, Cosby and his lawyer wife, played by Phylicia Rashad, dealt with the ups and downs of family life. The show's humor was warm and universal. The *New York Times* called it "the classiest and most entertaining new situation comedy of the season." It reached number three in its first year, was number one for the next four seasons, and remained in the top 20 until its final episode in 1992. *The Cosby Show* had 80 million regular viewers at the height of its popularity and its ratings pulled NBC from third to first place among the networks.

The show—which mirrored Cosby's own life with his wife, Camille, and their five children—generated a large sociological debate, since it portrayed African Americans and parents as they had never been seen on television before. The *New York Times*'s Bill Carter wrote that "it restored the television image of the parent as loving authority figure, and it gave viewers, black and white, an unwaveringly positive look at family life, as lived in a home headed by two professional parents who happened to be black." Some attacked *The Cosby Show* for presenting an unrealistically idealized portrait of the African American family. The Huxtables were too well off, too smart, too "perfect," said critics. Cosby responded that his television family offered a positive alternative to harsher images available on television and elsewhere.

Asked if he thought *The Cosby Show* would have been as popular if it had been more aggressive on racial issues, Cosby told the *Los Angeles Times:* "No. Because I don't know how to do that without getting angry at racial bigotry. That's not funny to me." Henry Louis

Gates, Jr., chairman of Harvard University's African American Studies Program, told the *New York Times* that Cosby "put race and economic issues on the back burner so we could see a black family dealing with all the things black people deal with the same as all other people. It was the first time most of us as black people have felt a sense of identity with and resemblance to the kind of values we have in common, our relationships with our parents and our siblings."

"No series in the history of television...has ever been more about education," wrote Dennis A. Williams in *Emerge.* The Huxtable parents consistently reminded their children of the importance of a college education, and the opening credit that listed "William H. Cosby, Jr., Ed.D." was a powerful reminder of where education could take a person. Both *The Cosby Show* and its spinoff, *A Different World* (set in a fictional black college), made higher education a viable option to thousands of young African Americans. During their run, applications to African American colleges went up dramatically. "You've got to figure we made a heck of an impression on people who wanted to go to college," Cosby told the *Los Angeles Times.*

When *The Cosby Show* went into syndication in 1987, Bill Cosby, as half owner of the show's profits, became a very rich man. According to *Forbes,* competing independent stations doubled previous records in their bidding for the program. By 1992 total syndication for the show reached $1 billion, of which Cosby received $333 million. With all of this money, Cosby and his wife, Camille, became active philanthropists. In 1988 they donated $20 million to Spelman College in Atlanta, the biggest single contribution ever made to a black college.

During *The Cosby Show*'s eight-year run, Cosby published four books: *Fatherhood* (1986), *Time Flies* (1987), *Love and Marriage* (1989), and *Childhood* (1991). Each of the fast-paced and hilarious books hit the best seller list, though critical reaction was mixed. The *New York Times*'s Karen Ray complained that *Fatherhood* contained "only one joke...stretched and stretched some more." But Laura Green wrote in the same paper that readers of *Love and Marriage* would "giggle with self-recognition." Less successful were the movies he made during this period. Critics and audiences agreed that *Leonard Part VI* (1987) and *Ghost Dad* (1990) were undisputed and undistinguished duds.

As the children in *The Cosby Show* grew older and went off to college or got married, some critics complained of a decline in quality. But the show remained popular as Cosby showcased African American entertainers, used the character of Theo to mirror his own son's struggle with a learning disability, and brought in women writers to focus on a female character's first period and the problems of a teen-age girl who is pressured to have sex. Williams applauded *The Cosby Show* for being the most ethnically diverse program on television, but "most significantly," he wrote, "Cosby combines unspoken racial pride and its color-blind premise in a conscious promotion of personal achievement that might please both Thurgood Marshall and Clarence Thomas." In the spring of 1992, *The Cosby Show* ended its fabulously successful run. "I don't have anything left to say," Cosby told the *New York Times.* "That may be why it's not a sad, sad moment. I'm satisfied."

Not one to rest on his laurels, Cosby returned to television the following fall with a syndicated version of the old Groucho Marx game show *You Bet Your Life. You Bet Your Life* was supposed to be a sure money maker, but was canceled midway through its first season due to low ratings. Cosby went back to NBC for a series of light television mystery movies in 1993, to be followed by *The Cosby Mysteries* series in 1994. *The Cosby Mysteries* failed to find a sustained audience, and was canceled. Although Cosby has always avoided racial humor in his comedy, the highly-respected star began to speak out about portrayals of African Americans in American entertainment in the 1990s. Upon his 1994 induction into the Academy of Television Arts and Sciences Hall of Fame, Cosby asked network television executives to "stop this horrible massacre of images [of African Americans] that are being put on the screen now. I'm begging you, because it isn't us." A few months earlier, Cosby told *Newsweek:* "Someone at the very top has to say, 'OK, enough of this... .' Today's writers look on TV as just a joke machine. And when it comes to African Americans, the joke's on us."

Undaunted by the failure of *The Cosby Mysteries,* Cosby returned to primetime television in 1996 with a new sitcom entitled *Cosby.* The show centers around the life of Hilton Lucas (Cosby), an airline employee who loses his job as a result of downsizing. Without a steady job, Lucas spends time around the house dispensing advice to those around him about how to cope with the challenges of daily life. Phylicia Rashad, who played Cosby's wife on *The Cosby Show,* co-stars as Lucas's wife Ruth. The show focuses around Ruth and Hilton's relationship, and episodes have also tackled complex social issues such as drug addiction and absentee parents. In 1996, *Cosby* won the People's Choice Award as America's Favorite New Television Comedy Series.

Confronted With Tragedy

In early 1997, Cosby was faced with one of the most difficult periods of his life. On January 16, 1997, Cosby's only son, Ennis, was robbed and murdered on a Los Angeles highway after he stopped to fix a flat tire. Shortly after the murder, a 19-year-old Ukrainian immigrant named Mikhail Markhasev was arrested and charged with the crime. In 1998, Markhasev was convicted of Ennis's murder and sentenced to life in prison without the possibility of parole.

On the same day that Ennis was murdered, a Southern California woman named Autumn Jackson came forward and alleged that she was Cosby's illegitimate daughter. Jackson and an accomplice had threatened to expose the story to the media unless they received $40 million dollars from Cosby. The pair were arrested in New York City by the FBI and were charged with extortion. Cosby acknowledged that he had an affair with Jackson's mother, Shawn Upshaw, and had paid her $100,000 so that she would not disclose their affair. He also paid some of Jackson's educational expenses. However, Cosby strongly denied that he was Jackson's father. Jackson was found guilty of extortion and ordered to publicly apologize to Cosby. She was also sentenced to a 26-month term in prison. After serving only 14 months, Jackson's conviction was overturned by an appeals court. The court then reversed itself and restored her conviction in 1999.

Despite the tremendous grief he felt over the loss of his son, Cosby did not retreat into isolation and self-pity. Rather, he remained in the public eye and conducted himself with grace and dignity. Cosby returned to the set of *Cosby* and immersed himself in his work. As he told *Cosby* executive producer Norman Steinberg, which was reported in *People,* "A lot of people depend on me. I have to open my store. This is what I do." While appearing at a benefit held in October of 1997 in New York, *People* reported that Cosby told those assembled, "Now I don't want you to think that because of what happened to me this year, I'm going to meet you at the bus station and ask you if you found Christ. No, no."

Cosby concentrated his efforts on finding ways to honor and preserve his son's memory, a son whom he referred to as "my hero." Shortly after Ennis's death, the Cosby family launched a charitable organization called the Hello Friend/Ennis William Cosby Foundation. The organization is focused on promoting the early detection and treatment of dyslexia, a condition that Ennis had worked to overcome in his own life. "Hello, Friend" was added to the organization's title because this was Ennis's trademark greeting. Cosby also created a series of books for children featuring a character called "Little Bill". The "Little Bill" books feature children with learning problems and are designed to help parents to teach values to their children. In an interview on CBS "This Morning", which was quoted on *black voices.com,* Cosby remarked that his son wanted to write stories "about children with learning differences. Of course with his murder, this cut everything short. So I dedicated all of this to him." In 1998, Cosby released an album featuring various jazz artists entitled *Hello Friend: To Ennis With Love.* In 1998, Cosby was among five performers who were saluted at the Kennedy Center Honors in Washington, D.C. A ceremony was held at the Kennedy Center and was attended by President and Mrs. Clinton. In her remarks, which were quoted in *Jet,* Phylicia Rashad praised her friend and television co-star, "It doesn't take a lot of intelligence to put people down, but it takes Bill's intelligence, his sensibility, and his grace to embrace the whole world with care and to uplift it with laughter."

Cosby published a book entitled *Congratulations! Now What?: A Book For Graduates* in 1999. Using his characteristic humor, Cosby offered words of wisdom and advice to new college graduates. In her review of *Congratulations! Now What?* on *amazon.com,* Brenda Pittsley noted that "graduates—and their now-broke parents—will find a reason to smile on every page." Ray Olson, in his review of the book for *Booklist,* remarked that "no comedian knows better how to speak the worst fatalisms and reduce an audience to tears of both laughter and sentiment. Fine, fine humor."

Cosby has continued to speak out against the generally poor quality of television programming. "The problem with television programming today is that we are now in the age of stooping as in to bend down to make yourself lower." he remarked to *Jet.* "The bar is not being raised at all. There is too much focus on orifices and the size of organs and body parts. Many of the writers write like they never had a course in Western Literature. They seem to be taking their language off the street corners." Cosby has consistently held himself to a higher standard. He has created a body of work that offers wholesome entertainment for people of all ages. As CBS Television President Leslie Moonves told *Jet,* "At its best, television is a medium that entertains as well as informs. Throughout his career, Bill Cosby has accomplished this with grace, humor, and unparalleled passion for his craft."

Selected writings

The Wit and Wisdom of Fat Albert, Windmill Books, 1973.

Bill Cosby's Personal Guide to Tennis Power; or Don't Lower the Lob, Raise the Net, Random House, 1975.

Fatherhood, Doubleday, 1986.

Time Flies, Doubleday, 1987.

Love and Marriage, Doubleday, 1989.

Childhood, Putnam, 1991.

The Best Way to Play, (Little Bill series), Cartwheel Books, 1997.

The Meanest Thing to Say, (Little Bill series), Cartwheel Books, 1997.

Shipwreck Saturday, (Little Bill series), Cartwheel Books, 1998.

Hooray for the Dandelion Warriors! (Little Bill series-),Cartwheel Books, 1999.

Congratulations! Now What?: A Book For Graduates, Hyperion, 1999.

The Day I Was Rich, (Little Bill series), Scholastic Trade, 1999.

The Day I Saw My Father Cry, (Little Bill series),Cartwheel Books, 2000.

Sources

Books

Bogle, Donald, *Blacks in American Film and Television,* Simon & Schuster, 1988.
Cohen, David, and Charles M. Collins, editors, *The African Americans,* Viking Studio Books, 1993.
Salley, Columbus, *The Black 100: A Ranking of the Most Influential African-Americans, Past and Present,* Citadel Press, 1992,

Periodicals

Booklist, May 1, 1999.
Broadcasting, February 22, 1993, p. 5.
Ebony, June 1977.
Emerge, May 1992, pp. 22-26.
Essence, March 1994, p. 84.
Forbes, September 28, 1992, p. 85.
Jet, December 28, 1998, p. 34; April 3, 2000, p. 60.
Los Angeles Times, December 10, 1989, p. Calendar-6; April 26, 1992, p. Calendar-7; August 28, 1992, p. F1.
Newsweek, June 17, 1963; December 6, 1993, pp. 59-61.
New Yorker, June 17, 1974, p. 89; January 8, 1979, p. 49.
New York Times, September 20, 1984, p. C30; December 18, 1987, p. C30; January 21, 1988, p. C26; November 8, 1988, p. A1; January 12, 1989, p. D21; May 14, 1989, sec. 7, p. 23; February 21, 1991, p. C13; October 27, 1991, sec. 7, p. 20; April 26, 1992, sec. 2, p. 1.
Playboy, December 1985.
People, December 29, 1997, p. 54-55.
Time, July 16, 1990, p. 86; February 28, 1994, pp. 60-62.
Vibe, November 1993, p. 120.

Other

Additional information for this profile was taken from *Bill Cosby: In Words and Pictures* (an *Ebony/Jet* special issue), by Robert E. Johnson, Johnson Publishing; www.blackvoices.com; and www.amazon.com

—Jordan Wankoff and David G. Oblender

Christopher Paul Curtis

1954(?)—

Author

The life story of Christopher Paul Curtis has a fairytale ending. After working more than a dozen years on an automobile assembly line, Curtis wrote two critically acclaimed children's books. His 1999 novel *Bud, Not Buddy* won the Newbery Medal, which is one of the most coveted prizes in children's literature. The success of these books enabled Curtis to fulfill his lifelong dream of becoming a writer.

Curtis grew up in Flint, Michigan. After graduating from high school, he enrolled at the University of Michigan, Flint to study political science. However, in 1972, Curtis succumbed to the temptation of the relatively good wages to be made at the nearby Fisher Body automobile plant where his father worked. When the boredom of working for ten hours a day on an automobile assembly line became unbearable, he began to write to challenge himself intellectually. For thirty minutes, he would hang thirty car doors on the passenger side of Buicks as they slowly moved past on the assembly line. While his partner hung the next thirty doors, Curtis put pen to paper. Some of the works he composed were letters to Kaysandra, a registered nurse whom he met in 1977 and married 11 years later. Curtis quit working at the plant in 1985, and worked at a variety of other jobs. In 1988, he managed democratic Senator Donald Reigle, Jr.'s election campaigns in Flint and Saginaw.

In 1993, Kaysandra Curtis encouraged her husband to take a year off to write and earn his bachelor of arts degree. While attending classes at the University of Michigan in Flint, Curtis won Hopwood Awards for his essays and for the manuscript of what would eventually become his first published children's book *The Watsons Go to Birmingham —1963.* Although Curtis did not intend to write a children's book, the story he wanted to tell came to him in the voice of a ten-year-old boy. He wrote his tale of the close-knit Watson family, known as the "Weird Watsons," while sitting in the children's department of the Windsor Public Library, in Windsor, Ontario. When he needed a break, he would help someone with homework or talk to the children. Curtis's son Steven, a much better typist than his father, typed the daily portion of manuscript into the computer each night. Steven also critiqued his father's work. "Lots of people can say they like it or they don't, but not many can say what exactly doesn't work. He can," Curtis related to Linnea Lannon of the *Knight-Ridder/Tribune News Service.* Curtis submitted his manuscript to Delacorte's annual writing contest for first young adult novel, one

At a Glance . . .

Born May 10, 1954 in Flint, MI; son of Herman (an auto worker) and Leslie Curtis; married Kaysandra (a registered nurse); children: Steven, Cydney. *Education:* University of Michigan-Flint, B.A., 1996.

Career: Writer. Fisher Body Plant, Flint, MI, assembly line worker, 1972-85; assistantto Senator Don Reigle, Lansing, MI; Automatic Data Processing, Allen Park, MI.

Awards: Hopwood Awards for essays, University of Michigan, Flint; Best Books,*Publishers Weekly* and *New York Times Book Review,* 1996; Coretta Scott KingText Honor, Best Books for Young Adults, and Newbery Honor Book, for *The Watsons Goto Birmingham—1963,* 1996; John Newbery Award and Coretta Scott King Awardfor *Bud, Not Buddy,* 2000.

Addresses: *Home*—Windsor, Ontario, Canada.

of four hundred manuscripts the publisher received that year. Although *The Watsons Go to Birmingham* did not fit the criteria for the contest, an editor pulled it out of the pile because of its eye-catching title and eventually decided to publish it. When the novel appeared in 1995, critics lavished praise upon it and actress Whoopi Goldberg bought film rights to the story.

Set in 1963 and told from the point of view of ten-year-old Kenny, readers meet the close-knit, Watson family, which includes the bossy older brother, Byron, and younger sister Joetta. When 13-year-old Byron starts getting into trouble in Flint, Michigan, his parents decide to take him to Alabama to live for a time with his Grandmother Sands. While traveling south in their car, the Watson children become aware of racial prejudice they had not experienced in the North. While they are in Alabama, a bomb explodes in a Sunday school classroom, one that Joetta had previously occupied. Although she is safe because she left school early, four other girls are killed. The entire community is shocked and the Watsons return to Michigan with new insights. While writing his debut novel, Curtis relied on the experiences of family members and personal memories. The bombing incident was based on the actual bombing of the Sixteenth Avenue Baptist Church in Birmingham, Alabama, which took place in September of 1963.

Critics applauded *The Watsons Go to Birmingham* for Curtis's characterizations, humor, and combination of factual and fictional events. According to Lannon, "It is a mark of Curtis' skill that he so easily makes the transition from humorous family vignettes to a life-threatening run-in with racism." Because readers have gotten to know and like the fictional Watson family, they react with distaste to the racism the Watsons encounter. "Curtis has created a wholly original novel in this warmly memorable evocation of an African American family and their experiences both terrible and transcendent," added Martha V. Parravano in her review for *Horn Book*. One day while Curtis was writing in the library, a librarian approached him with a big smile on her face. She gave the surprised Curtis a hug and said to call home because *The Watsons Go to Birmingham* had just won the two most important awards in children's literature. "I still have a moment of disbelief when I am introduced as a Newbery or Coretta Scott King Honor winner," Curtis later told Teri Lesesne in an interview for *Teacher Librarian*. "Not only do the awards make it possible for the book to get much wider recognition and placement, they also help immeasurably in boosting one's self confidence, something writers are always in need of."

After his usual early morning game of basketball at the YMCA, Curtis went to the library and began working on a new novel. The new novel, *Bud, Not Buddy*, was published in 1999. "I actively tried not to think about the reception of *The Watsons* while I was working on number two," Curtis told Lesesne. "I love the whole writing process and simply got back into the joy of writing." In *Bud, Not Buddy,* Curtis did not plan a specific plot in advance, but focused instead on the personality of the main character. The main character and narrator is ten-year-old Bud Caldwell, an orphan who wants to find his birth father. Caldwell escapes from an orphanage in Flint and journeys 120 miles to Grand Rapids, where he believes his father is working as a leader for the band Herman E. Calloway and the Dusky Devastators of the Depression!!!!!! Again, a likeable main character, humor, and a concrete sense of place made this novel a standout. Although the novel is set in the 1930s during the Great Depression, Curtis was not trying to teach readers about history. He was using his grandfathers (one a band leader, the other a Negro League baseball pitcher) as models for characters. As Curtis explained to Michael D. Schaffer of the *Knight-Ridder/Tribune News Service,* "I really believe the story comes first. You get kids' attention first... .Then they can gain an idea of what is going on." During his search for his father, Bud encounters a number of kind strangers, becomes involved in both humorous and frightening situations, and eventually finds a treasure, though one different than he expects.

Reviewers found much to like about *Bud, Not Buddy.* Writing in *Booklist,* Michael Cart summed up the novel's appeal, "Curtis turns his novel into a celebration of the human capacity for simple goodness. Bud is, throughout, an altogether engaging character, and his search for a father—and the extended family that he finds instead—will warm readers' hearts and refresh their spirits." In the *New York Times Book Review,* Lois Metzger described *Bud, Not Buddy* as a "powerfully felt novel," one that is "funny, eloquent, deeply sad and delightful (usually all at once)." "Surely Curtis' second novel will attract and delight countless readers with its genial good humor and its generosity of spirit," predicted Cart. When Curtis won the Newbery Medal and the Coretta Scott King Award in 2000 for *Bud, Not Buddy*, he had much to celebrate. He became the first African American to win the Newbery Medal since 1976, when Mildred Taylor won for *Roll of Thunder, Hear My Cry*. With these prestigious honors, Curtis's books were destined to become classics of children's literature, and allow him the financial security to write full time.

Curtis credits his wife for his tremendous success because she believed in his dream and gave him the freedom to pursue it. "I never thought it would be possible to make a living as a writer, but my wife Kay had more faith in me and gave me the courage and opportunity to take a chance," Curtis told Lesesne. "I do believe we all have stories brewing inside of us, that it takes just the right amount of maturity, skill, dedication and luck to get them down into a published book." Curtis has many more stories to tell, stories that are just waiting to be scrawled onto yellow legal pads at a table in the childrens' section of the Windsor Public Library.

Sources

Books

Contemporary Authors, Gale (Detroit), 2000.
Something about the Author, volume 93, Gale (Detroit), 1997.
St. James Guide to Young Adult Writers, St. James Press (Detroit), 1999.

Periodicals

Booklist, August, 1995, p. 1946; July, 1997, p. 1830; February 15, 2000, p. 1094.
Bulletin of the Center for Children's Books, January, 1996, pp. 157-58.
Horn Book, March-April, 1996, pp. 195-96.
Jet, February 21, 2000, p. 36.
Kirkus Reviews, October 1, 1995, p. 1426.
Knight-Ridder/Tribune News Service, December 27, 1995, p. 1227K1113; January 26, 2000, p. K6367.
Library Journal, February 1, 1997, p. 127.
New York Times Book Review, November 21, 1999, p. 32.
People, April 17, 2000, p. 113+.
Publishers Weekly, October 16, 1995, p. 62; December 18, 1995, pp. 28-30.
School Library Journal, October, 1995, p. 152.
Teacher Librarian, March, 1999, p. 54.
Time, January 31, 2000, p. 68.

—Jeanne M. Lesinski

Harold Doley Jr.

1947—

Securities broker

In the early 1970s, New Orleans securities broker Harold Doley Jr. became one of the first African Americans to own a seat on the New York Stock Exchange. A pioneer among minorities in the rarefied world of American corporate finance, Doley and his firm have done extraordinarily well in the decades since, and he even served in the Reagan administration partly as a result of his extensive ties to African governments for investment purposes. In the early 1990s, Doley and his wife purchased a lavish Hudson River-area estate built by Madam C. J. Walker, the first African American woman to become a millionaire.

Doley was the son of Harold Doley Sr., a New Orleans grocer. The Doley family was of mixed heritage, and Doley had red hair and a light complexion. The family's roots in New Orleans stretched back six generations. The Doley's were free blacks in the antebellum South, and like many others of their status, enjoyed the refuge provided by the relatively liberal atmosphere of New Orleans. As a child, Doley attended New Orleans's segregated schools. For college he chose Xavier University, a private institution that was considered a training ground for African Americans from established Louisiana families like his own.

Entered the World of Finance

At Xavier, Doley began a student investment club, whose stocks performed admirably, and he looked forward to a career in finance. "I graduated from college on a Friday night and started in the brokerage business on Monday morning," he recalled in a 1976 interview with Roy Reed of the *New York Times.* He went to work as an account executive with Bache Halsey Stuart, Inc., a brokerage house, in its New Orleans office. Doley recognized that solid financial success came from the creation of wealth through established channels. "Look at the blue bloods of this country," he told the *New York Times*'s Reed. "The Harrimans, the Morgans—all of them have their names on the doors of Wall Street investment houses. That's where they got their start. They make up a cohesive, powerful group. And so far that group has not been tapped. I aim to penetrate."

In 1973, Doley borrowed $90,000 and bought a seat on the New York Stock Exchange (NYSE). This feat landed him a guest appearance on NBC's *Today* show. At the time, there were just two other African American-owned firms with a presence on the nation's oldest and largest trading floor. Doley spent some time as an independent broker in New York before returning to New Orleans to found Doley Securities Inc. in 1975, and began trading on the NYSE on behalf of his clients. About two-thirds of his investors were African American-owned institutions, such as the National Insurance Association. One-third of his clients were white investors. In the *New York Times* article, Reed pointed out that there were 50,000 stockbrokers in the United States according to 1975 figures, and just 200 were African American. Doley's on-the-floor trading was handled by a white associate and longtime Wall Street mentor. "I don't look at my firm as a minority firm," he told Reed, "but as a member firm on the New

At a Glance . . .

Born March 8, 1947, in New Orleans, LA; son of Harold Sr. (a grocer) Doley Sr.; married Helena Cobette (a school guidance counselor); children: Harold III; Aaron. *Education:* Xavier University, B.S.; attended Harvard University Office of Public Management program. *Politics:* Republican.

Career: Bache Halsey Stuart, Inc., New Orleans, account executive, early 1970s; Howard Weil Labouisse & Friedrichs Inc., assistant vice president, 1973-76; DoleySecurities Inc., New Orleans, LA, founder, 1975, and chair, 1975-; Minerals Management Service, U.S. Department of the Interior, director, 1982-83; African Development Bank, Abidjan ,Ivory Coast, ambassador and executive director, 1983-85; instructor at Southern University.

Member: New York Stock Exchange, Interracial Council for Business and Opportunity; advisory board, Lloyds of London.

Awards: Awards from Harvard Management School of Business and the *Wall Street Journal;* honorary degrees from Clark-Atlanta University, Bishop College, and ShawUniversity.

Addresses: *Office*— Doley Securities Inc., 616 Baronne St., New Orleans, LA 70113; 237 Park Ave., New York NY 10017.

York Stock Exchange whose president and owner happen to be black. I'm sure my clients don't do business with me based on the color of my skin but because we provide proper services."

Because of the success of his firm, Doley became a well-known figure in New Orleans financial circles. He was tapped to help negotiate the merger of two large African American-owned insurance firms, and became involved in the creation of Republic National Bank, one of New Orleans's two African American-owned banks. His success and commitment to change also gave him entry into numerous charitable and professional organizations in New Orleans. Doley also became increasingly involved in Republican politics, which brought him to the attention of officials in the first Reagan administration during the early 1980s. He was offered a post as head of the Minerals Management Service, a new agency within the Department of the Interior that granted companies leases to explore federal lands for mineral wealth. Doley was charged with the task of collecting overdue payments from these companies, and put in place a better accounting system to collect revenues. Doley Securities had also been doing some business with governments in Africa by this time, primarily by raising private American funds for investment opportunities there. Doley's stint with the Minerals Management Service had forged an alliance with controversial Secretary of the Interior James Watt and, in 1983, Doley was appointed by President Reagan as the American ambassador to the Ivory Coast. He was also named executive director of the African Development Bank located in the capital city of Abidjan. This consortium bank of 53 African nations had assets of $40 billion and was created to finance infrastructure development, such as roads and hospitals, on the African continent. Doley, James Watt told Tony Chapelle in the *New York Times,* "was determined to take on an ambassador's job. I thought it was a dumb idea. I'm cause-oriented, and I didn't think the job of ambassador advanced the cause of anything. But we didn't want to lose him. So somehow I learned about the African Development Bank. I thought that there, Mr. Doley could increase people's standard of living."

Doley and his second wife, Helena, spent two years living in the Ivory Coast. Upon his return to the United States, he continued to be active in African investment opportunities, founding the U.S.-Africa Chamber of Commerce and selling bonds for the African Development Bank through his firm. In 1993, Doley purchased Villa Lewaro, the opulent mansion built by Madame C. J. Walker, who earned a fortune with her line of hair-care products in the early years of the twentieth century. Named by Italian opera singer Enrico Caruso in honor of Walker's daughter, A'Lelia Walker Robinson, Villa Lewaro had been bequeathed to the National Association for the Advancement of Colored People, then later sold. In the 1980s, a developer tried to purchase the home to demolish it and build condominiums on the site, but the presence of two trees—one of them 300 years old—helped save the estate and earn it a spot on the National Register of Historic Places. Doley had long been fascinated by Madam Walker's literal rags-to-riches story. "She was a genius," he told Lynette Holloway of the *New York Times,* "and to walk the halls that she once walked and to sleep in the room where she once slept is a feeling that is indescribable."

Sources

New York Times, December 26, 1976, p. 13; September 18, 1994, p. F3; April 11, 1996, p. C1; January 10, 1999.

—Carol Brennan

Michael Clarke Duncan

1957—

Actor

Noted most of all for his physical stature—he stands six feet, five inches tall and weighs 315 pounds—Michael Clarke Duncan burst into the American national consciousness with his portrayal of a death row inmate with miraculous powers in the 1999 film *The Green Mile.* He was nominated for an Academy Award for his performance in that film, and it seemed certain to jump-start his film career. As noteworthy as his impressive physical presence, though, was the personal odyssey that led him to the top of his profession.

Duncan was born in Chicago on December 10, 1957. He and his sister, Judith, were raised on the city's south side by their single mother Jean, who despite the family's modest circumstances had ambitions for her children. She steered her son away from the drugs and alcohol that were beginning to gain a foothold on Chicago's South Side, and encouraged him to concentrate on academics. Duncan's size made him a natural for his high school's football team. His mother, however, feared the injuries that come from playing football, and urged him to pursue other extracurricular activities. Dreams of fame on the silver screen led Duncan into acting.

Worked as Ditch Digger

Duncan attended historically black Alcorn State University in Mississippi for a time, but his mother's serious illness led him to return to Chicago to help support the family. He attended Kankakee Community College in Illinois and played basketball there. The family's financial difficulties forced Duncan to take a job that was inconsistent with both his educational and acting goals. For several years, he worked as a gas-company ditch digger.

Duncan's journey back into the world of acting was a roundabout one. Finding it easy to pick up side work as a bouncer thanks to his commanding physical appearance, Duncan began working in nightclubs. In one nightclub, he met a theatrical producer who happened to be looking for a security guard for his traveling company. Duncan quit his gas-company job, signed on, and found that being in the theater world reignited his passion for acting. In 1995, he relocated to Los Angeles.

Success did not happen instantly, as Duncan lived the life of a struggling actor and went to audition after

At a Glance . . .

Born December 10, 1957, in Chicago, IL; raised by single mother, Jean; one sister (Judith). *Education:* attended Alcorn (Mississippi) State University and Kankakee (Illinois) Community College.

Career: Actor; worked as ditch digger and nightclub bouncer after college years; landedjob as security guard for traveling theater troupe; moved to Los Angeles to pursue acting career,1995; worked as bodyguard for actors Will Smith and Martin Lawrence; began to land smallparts as guards and bouncers, 1997; broke through with starring role in *Armageddon,*1998; recommended by costar Bruce Willis for starring role opposite Tom Hanks in *TheGreen Mile,* 1999; costarred with Willis and Matthew Perry in *The Whole NineYards,* 2000.

Awards: Best Supporting Actor, Golden Globe Awards; Best Supporting Actor, ScreenActors Guild awards; Best Supporting Actor, Broadcast Film Critics Association; NAACP ImageAward; Male Star of Tomorrow award, ShoWest exhibitors' meeting (all for *TheGreen Mile,* 1999-2000).

Addresses: *Business*—Delores Robinson Entertainment, 112 S. AlmontDr., Los Angeles, CA 90048.

fruitless audition. Facing bankruptcy, he went back into security work, and served as a bodyguard for actors such as Will Smith and Martin Lawrence. One night, while sitting in his roach-infested motel room, Duncan began to reexamine his priorities. As he related to *People* magazine, he told himself, "You have no life, no money, and you're talking to bugs on a wall. Something is wrong here." Duncan considered giving up acting, and tried to parlay his security experience into a job with the Los Angeles Police Department.

Landed Roles as a Bouncer

Ironically, things began to improve for Duncan when he landed bit parts as a bouncer. In the films *Back in Business* (1997), *The Players Club* (1998), and *Bulworth* (1998), he appeared as a bouncer or guard. In addition, television and commercial work began to flow his way. However, Duncan's big break occurred in 1998 when he earned a role in the hit film *Armageddon.* In the film, he played an oilfield worker who was part of a crew sent to deflect an asteroid that threatened to wipe out the Earth. While working on *Armageddon,* Duncan developed a friendship with co-star Bruce Willis, one of Hollywood's top actors. "A lot of people told me that when Bruce Willis gets in character you can't look at him," Duncan told *People.* "But we became friends right off the bat."

Duncan tried to cheer up Willis after the latter's breakup with actress Demi Moore. Willis returned the favor by recommending Duncan to director Frank Darabont, who was in the midst of screening a cast for his new film, *The Green Mile.* "There are not a lot of roles for big, black, bald-headed men," Duncan was quoted as saying in *Entertainment Weekly.* However, the *Green Mile* role seemed custom made for him, and he landed the part. Duncan poured his heart and soul into the role. "I'm an emotional person," he told *Entertainment Weekly.* "All those tears you see in the movie were mine."

In the film, which was adapted from a story by Stephen King, Duncan played a 1930s Death Row inmate named John Coffey, who is imprisoned for the murder of two young girls. With his peaceful, spiritual demeanor, Coffey seems incapable of having committed the murders. Coffey also possesses miraculous healing powers that lead to a friendship with prison guard Paul Edgecomb (played by Tom Hanks), who begins to question Coffey's guilt. As Duncan explained to *Jet,* "John Coffey is one of the biggest men that anybody has ever seen. He's 7 feet tall and 330 pounds—an apparent cold-blooded murderer with two dead girls in his arms. But John Coffey is also a very special individual who understands Paul, sees the kindness that is in Paul and most of the other guards. And that's kind of the ironic twist to it."

Duncan earned extremely positive reviews for his performance in *The Green Mile,* for which he garnered a Best Supporting Actor Golden Globe award and an Oscar nomination in 2000. *Jet* praised his "powerful, heartfelt performance," and *Entertainment Weekly* opined that "Duncan imbues a potentially stereotypical character—the saintly African American—with a tangible human soul." Duncan also was named Male Star of Tomorrow at the ShoWest exhibitors' convention in Las Vegas, and earned a best supporting actor award from the Broadcast Film Critics Association, and an NAACP Image Award nomination. Although Duncan was eventually edged out for the Oscar, his career seemed ready to advance to a new level.

In the year 2000, Duncan reunited with Bruce Willis in the comedy *The Whole Nine Yards.* This film, in the words of allmovie.com writer Rebecca Flint, "cast him [Duncan] as a brutish thug who terrorizes mild-mannered dentist Matthew Perry". Duncan is single and lives alone in Los Angeles. "Right now," he told *People,* "it's just me and the business—and she's being pretty good to me."

Sources

Periodicals

Entertainment Weekly, March 1, 2000, p. 71; June 16, 2000, p. 67.
Jet, December 20, 1999, p. 58.
New York Times, March 19, 2000, p. AR13.
People, August 17, 1998, p. 110; January 1, 2000, p. 103.
Variety, February 7, 2000, p. 18.

Other

Additional information for this profile was obtained from http://www.allmovie.com; and http://www.imdb.com (The Internet Movie Database).

—James M. Manheim

Sean Elliott

1968—

Professional basketball player

Sean Elliott was born in Tucson, Arizona, on February 2, 1968 and grew up to be one of the most miraculous basketball players of his time. A prolific scorer in college, Elliott became a two-time National Basketball Association (NBA) All-Star. He was also a key member of the 1998-99 NBA champion San Antonio Spurs—a feat he contributed to while his kidneys were failing. Elliott played throughout the playoffs with a badly malfunctioning kidney due to the disease focal segmental glomerular sclerosis, but he kept most of his teammates in the dark regarding his condition. After the season, he was told that he would have to receive dialysis if he did not have a kidney transplant. On August 16, 1999, Elliott underwent kidney transplant surgery. His brother, Noel, gave one of his healthy kidneys to his younger brother. Most NBA observers believed that Elliott's basketball career was finished. However, on March 14, 2000, he played in an NBA game and remained in the Spurs lineup for the remainder of the season.

After graduating from Cholla High School in 1986, Elliott decided to attend the University of Arizona. He had a brilliant collegiate career, and surpassed Kareem Abdul-Jabbar as the Pac-10's all-time leading scorer. Elliott was named the College Player of the Year during his senior season, and was a two-time All-American. The San Antonio Spurs selected him third overall in the 1989 draft, and Elliott joined another rookie named David Robinson to make the Spurs the hottest young team in the league. During the 1988-89 season, the Spurs finished with a lowly 21-61 record. However, with the addition of the two new players, the Spurs finished 56-26 during the 1989-90 season, won the Midwest Division title, and advanced to the Western Conference Semifinals. Elliott finished his rookie season averaging ten points per game, and was named to the Second-Team All-Rookie squad. In his second season with the Spurs, he improved his scoring average to 15.9 points per game and was the only San Antonio player to appear in all 82 games that season. During his third season in the NBA, Elliott again played in all 82 games and compiled a franchise-record 3,120 minutes for the season. He increased his scoring average to 16.3 points per game, and scored in double figures in 71 of his 82 games. For the 1992-93 season, Elliott continued to improve despite missing 12 games of the season with a bad back. In 1993, he appeared in his first All-Star game as a member of the Western Conference squad. Elliott finished the year with a 17.2 point

At a Glance . . .

Born on February 2, 1968. *Education:* University of Arizona, attended.

Career: Starred at Cholla High School in Tucson, AZ, 1982-86; attended the University of Arizona, 1986-89; third overall pick of the NBA draft by the San Antonio Spurs, 1989; traded to the Detroit Pistons, 1993; traded back to the Spurs, 1994; underwent kidney transplant after Spurs championship season, 1999; made NBA comeback, 2000.

Awards: First Team All-American, 1987-88, 1988-89; won the John Wooden Award as the college Player of the Year, 1988-89; named to the Second Team NBA All-Rookie Team,1990; Western Conference All-Star, 1993, 1996.

Addresses: *Office*—c/o The San Antonio Spurs, The Alamo dome, 100 Montana, San Antonio, TX, 78203-1031

scoring average, and a feeling that he had finally found success in the NBA.

After a season in which he was named an All-Star and had seen his scoring average rise for the third consecutive year, Elliott should have felt secure in his position on a team that was a perennial playoff contender. However, he was traded to the Detroit Pistons, a team which was undergoing a painful rebuilding process. The Spurs traded Elliott for Dennis Rodman, hoping that Rodman's rebounding skills would help David Robinson to score more points. During a routine medical checkup, Elliott learned of his potentially serious kidney problem. Doctors prescribed steroids to treat his condition, which caused his face and body to bloat. Because of his malfunctioning kidneys, Elliott was retaining water, which caused further swelling. He told Jackie MacMullan of *Sports Illustrated* about some of the physical challenges of that season: "I'd get my ankles taped before the game, and afterward my ankles were really skinny where the tape had been, but the rest of my leg was fat and swollen from the water buildup. They started calling me Peg Leg." The Detroit fans and media criticized Elliott for being fat and out of shape, although this was not the case. The Pistons and their newest player both realized that the trade was a bad fit. On February 4, 1994, the Pistons tried to trade Elliott to the Houston Rockets for Robert Horry. However, the trade was rescinded because Elliott failed his physical. The Houston Rockets medical personnel discovered his kidney ailment, and the trade was voided. Elliott was forced to finish out the season in Detroit, where his scoring average dipped to 12.1 points per game.

Because of his potentially serious medical condition, Elliott seemed destined to remain in a Detroit Pistons uniform. General managers throughout the NBA knew of his medical problems and were unwilling to take a chance on him. However, before the start of the 1994-95 season, the Spurs traded a first and second round draft pick to Detroit and reacquired Elliott. With Robinson, Rodman, and Elliott in their lineup, the Spurs became a force to be reckoned with. Elliott enjoyed a tremendous season, averaging 18.1 points per game. The Spurs finished with the best regular season record in the NBA at 62-20, but lost in the conference finals to the Houston Rockets. The following season, Elliott reclaimed his position as one of the best small forwards in the game. He was named to the All-Star team and averaged a career-high 20 points per game.

After seven years in the NBA, Elliott was finally bitten by the injury bug. He played the first half of the 1996-97 season with tendinitis in his right leg before undergoing surgery. In the 39 games that he did appear in, Elliott averaged 14.9 points and 4.9 rebounds and scored in double figures in 33 of those games. After losing half of 1996-97 season to injury, he was again sidelined for the second half of the 1997-98 campaign and appeared in only 36 games. For the first time in his professional career, Elliott averaged less than ten points per game.

Prior to the start of the 1998-99 season, NBA owners decided to lockout their players. Once this labor dispute was resolved Elliott and the San Antonio Spurs, which now included Robinson and Rookie of the Year Tim Duncan, looked like the team to beat. Elliott started all 50 games of the season, averaged 11.2 points per game, and was an instrumental part of San Antonio's championship run. However, he faced a much more serious opponent—kidney failure. During March of the 1998-99 season, Elliott was told to prepare himself for a kidney transplant. He continued to play, and kept his condition a secret. Elliott told NBA.com about his decision to keep his kidney problems to himself: "I had a responsibility to those guys on the team, to the people who come to watch the games and to the coaching staff not to bring my problems to the court. If I was able to go out there and play and do my job, then that's what I had to do. I didn't want anybody treating me any differently." Elliott contributed to the team throughout the playoffs as the Spurs defeated the New York Knicks in five games to win the NBA championship. Almost immediately after the season, Elliott announced that he would need a kidney transplant. On August 16, 1999, Elliott underwent surgery and received a new kidney.

Shortly after the surgery, Elliott began to seriously think about returning to the NBA. He stayed with the Spurs during the 1999-2000 season, and worked as a television commentator. Teammates and coaches discouraged Elliott's comeback attempt. Despite being hospitalized with the flu in December of 1999, he continued to gain strength and doctors assured Spurs officials that there was no medical reason why he could not return to the court. By the middle of the 1999-2000 season, Elliott returned to the Spurs as an active player. He became the first professional athlete to return to his sport after receiving a kidney transplant. Gregg Popovich of the Spurs told Mike Wise of *The New York Times* why he thought that Elliott had endured so much to come back: "These challenges are something he's accepted. Because of who he is, he's decided he wants to overcome them. Frankly, I don't think he's concerned with whether he plays 10 minutes a game or 30 minutes a game. He want's to be able to say, 'I came back, I beat it and I contributed to my team.'"

On March 14, 2000, seven months after receiving a new kidney, Elliott returned to the Spurs lineup. The highlight of Elliott's return came in the third quarter in a game against the Atlanta Hawks when he drove around Hawks forward Roshown McLeod, and dunked the ball with authority. Hawks center Dikembe Mutumbo commented on the play to the Associated Press: "I was surprised the way he [Elliott] dunked the ball. He has a lot of courage. I was really touched. The whole thing is amazing that someone can recover that fast to come back and do something they love—play basketball." Elliott appeared in 18 more games, averaged over 20 minutes of playing time, and scored six points per game.

Sources

Sports Illustrated, January 31, 2000.
The New York Times, March 12, 2000.

Other

Additional material for this essay was obtained at http://www.nba.com/Spurs/elliott_miracle.html; http://www.nba.com/playerfile/bio/sean_elliott.html; and http://www.nba.com/games9900/20000314/atlsas/recap.html

—Michael J. Watkins

Mari Evans

1923—

Poet, writer, educator

Poet and writer Mari Evans initially gained fame in 1970 when her second collection of poetry, *I Am a Black Woman,* was published. "The volume heralded the arrival of a poet who took her subject matter from the black community," Wallace R. Peppers wrote in *Dictionary of Literary Biography,* "and who celebrated its triumphs, especially the focus on the beauty of blackness that characterized the black arts and civil rights movements, and who would mourn its losses, especially the deaths of Martin Luther King, Jr. and Malcolm X." Since then, Evans has published several volumes of poetry and children's books, and written for television, radio, and the theater. Her work has appeared in over 30 textbooks and has been translated into several languages, including German, Swedish, French, and Dutch.

Evans was born on July 16, 1923, in Toledo, Ohio. As she was growing up, her father was her greatest influence. Evans recalled in the essay "My Father's Passage," which was included in *Black Women Writers (1950-1980): A Critical Evaluation,* that her father saved her "first printed story, a fourth-grade effort accepted by the school paper, and carefully noted on it the date, our home address, and his own proud comment." After attending public school in Toledo, Evans enrolled at the University of Toledo, where she majored in fashion design. However, the subject did not hold her attention for long, and she left without taking a degree.

Beginning in the mid-1960s, Evans began to make her name in the public arena. From 1965 to 1966, she was a John Hay Whitney fellow. Three years later, she received a Woodrow Wilson Foundation grant. From 1968 to 1973, Evans was the producer, director, and writer for the highly acclaimed television program "The Black Experience" for WTTV in Indianapolis, Indiana.

In 1968, Evans published her first volume of poetry, *Where Is All the Music?* Like many African American poets of the time, she celebrated her heritage while rejecting the conciliatory attitude of African American poets from the 1920s and 1930s. "Though she was born during the Harlem Renaissance, Mari Evans' poetry reveals little of the inclination toward compromise with white values and forms that was cherished by most black intellectuals of that period," Alan R. Shucard wrote in *Contemporary Poets.* "Quite the contrary, her work is informed by the uncompromising black pride that burgeoned in the 1960s." In the poem "Who Can Be Born Black," Evans showed her awareness of the differences between Harlem Renaissance poets and poets of her own generation. Evans' poem is a response to Countee Cullen's mid-1920s sonnet, "Yet Do I Marvel," a long list of the horrors God has created, the worst of which is "To make a poet black, and bid him sing." In contrast, Evans wrote, "Who/can be born black/and not/sing/the wonder of it/the joy/the/challenge...Who/can be born black/and not exult!"

In 1970 Evans published her second poetry collection entitled *I Am a Black Woman,* which brought her wide critical attention, and an award for the most distinguished book of poetry by an Indiana writer. Each of

At a Glance . . .

Born Mari Evans, July 16, 1923, Toledo, OH; married and divorced; children: William, Derek. *Education:* studied fashion design at the University of Toledo.

Career: Instructor in African American literature and writer in residence, Indiana University-Purdue, 1969-70; assistant professor of African American literature and writer inresidence, Indiana University-Bloomington, 1970-78; visiting assistant professor, Northwestern University, 1972-73; visiting assistant professor, Purdue University, 1978-80; visiting assistant professor, Washington University, St. Louis, 1980; visiting assistant professor, Cornell University, 1981-83; assistant professor and distinguished writer, Cornell University, 1983-85; associate professor, State University of New York-Albany, 1985-86; visiting distinguished writer, Miami University, Coral Gables, 1989; writer in residence, Spelman College, 1989-90.

Selected awards: John Hay Whitney fellow, 1965-66; Woodrow Wilson Foundationgrant, 1968; Indiana University Writers Conference Award, 1970; First Annual Poetry Award, Black Academy of Arts and Letters, 1970; Copeland Fellow, Amherst College, 1980; National Endowment for the Arts grant, 1981-82.

Member: First World Foundation, African Heritage Studies Association, Authors Guild, Authors League of America.

the poems in the collection is written from the viewpoint of a different character, and marked her movement toward more politically-based poetry. This is most evident in her third volume of poetry, *Nightstar: 1973-1978,* which was published in 1981. "At the heart of Mari Evans' *Nightstar* is a questioning of the ways in which we know ourselves and are known, and a recognition of the subtleties of identity," Romey T. Keys wrote in the book's introduction. "Her language can compass a range of people and things, sounds and sights, places and times."

Evans launched her academic career in 1969, which has included positions at several prestigious universities. From 1969 to 1970, she was an instructor in African American literature and writer in residence at Indiana University-Purdue. The following year, Evans moved to Bloomington, Indiana, and accepted a job as assistant professor of African American literature and writer in residence at Indiana University. She taught at Indiana University until 1978. From 1972 to 1973, she combined her job at Indiana University with an appointment as a visiting assistant professor at Northwestern University in Evanston, Illinois. Her academic career continued with teaching appointments at Purdue University from 1978 to 1980, at Washington University in St. Louis in 1980, at Cornell University from 1981 to 1985, and at the State University of New York-Albany from 1985 to 1986. Evans has also taught at Miami University-Coral Gables, and Spelman College in Atlanta.

Apart from the world of academia, Evans has served as a consultant to several organizations. From 1969 to 1970 she worked with the Discovery Grant Program for the National Endowment for the Arts. She also served as a consultant in ethnic studies for the Bobbs-Merrill Publishing Company from 1970 to 1973.

In addition to poetry, Evans has written plays, essays, and short fiction. Choreographed versions of two of her plays, *A Hand Is on the Gate* and *Walk Together Children,* have had successful off-Broadway runs. She has written several books for children, including *J.D.* (1973), *I Look at Me!* (1974), *Singing Black* (1976), and *Jim Flying High* (1979). Evans also edited an anthology, *Black Women Writers (1950-1980): A Critical Evaluation,* which was published in 1984.

By the mid-1980s, Evans' place in the annals of African American literature was assured. As Peppers wrote in *Dictionary of Literary Biography:* "Her volumes of poetry, her books for adolescents, her work for television and other media, and her recently published volume on black women writers between 1950 and 1980 ensure her a lasting place among those who have made significant contributions to Afro-American life and culture."

Sources

Contemporary Authors, Gale Research, 1989.
Contemporary Poets, St. James Press, 1980.
Dictionary of Literary Biography, edited by Trudier Harris and Thadious M. Davis, Gale Research, 1985.
Nightstar, 1973-1978, by Mari Evans, Center for Afro-American Studies, University of California-Los Angeles, 1981.

—Carrie Golus

Henry W. Foster Jr.

1933—

Physician, educator, presidential advisor

When Dr. Henry Foster's 1995 nomination to the post of U.S. Surgeon General failed to gain Senate approval, it represented a rare setback in an otherwise successful career. Over the course of a 40-year career in medicine, Foster has continually championed the cause of quality health care for disadvantaged populations. From maternal care for the rural poor to pregnancy prevention for urban teens, Foster has been a leading advocate for the development of health service delivery systems that meet the needs of poverty-stricken communities. While a few members of the Senate objected loudly to some of his past practices, the positive impact of Foster's work on the lives of the individuals and families he has served is beyond dispute.

Henry Wendell Foster Jr. was born September 8, 1933 in the Pine Bluff, Arkansas, to Henry Wendell Foster Sr. and Ivie Foster. The Fosters were a family of educators. Henry Sr. held a masters degree from the University of Arkansas in Little Rock, and was a high school teacher and football coach. He was revered in Pine Bluff for leading the Merrill High School football team to two national championships. Ivie's resume included a stint as an art instructor at Arkansas Agricultural, Mechanical, and Normal College, and both of her parents were schoolteachers as well.

Henry Sr. was a strict disciplinarian. He also emphasized the importance of education as a way of escaping the poverty experienced by many African Americans in the South. Foster took his father's advice to heart, and excelled academically at Corbin High School, which was located on the Pine Bluff campus of the University of Arkansas.

Foster acquired an intense interest in aviation at an early age, stemming from an educational airplane ride arranged by his father as a science field trip. By the time he graduated from Corbin, he was serious enough about flying to consider a career as a pilot. Faced with the reality that opportunities in aviation were scarce for African American men, and inspired by his childhood doctor Cleon Flowers, Foster chose to become a medical professional.

Following graduation from high school, Foster enrolled at Morehouse College. In addition to excelling academically, he engaged in an active social life as a member of the Kappa Alpha Psi fraternity. Foster graduated from Morehouse in 1954, and went on to the University of Arkansas Medical School, where he was the only

At a Glance . . .

Born Henry Wendell Foster Jr. on September 8, 1933, in Pine Bluff, AR; son of Henry Wendell (a high school teacher) and Ivie (a college art instructor) Foster; married St. Clair Anderson, 1960; children: Myrna Faye, Wendell III; *Education:* Morehouse College, BS in biology, 1954; University of Arkansas School of Medicine, MD, 1958.

Career: Detroit Receiving Hospital, intern, 1958-59; Larson Air Force Base, chief, obstetrics and gynecology, 1959-61; Malden Hospital, Malden, MA, general surgery resident,1961-62; Meharry Medical College, Nashville, TN, obstetrics and gynecology resident, 1962-65; John A. Andrew Memorial Hospital, Tuskegee Institute, chief of obstetrics and gynecology,1965-73; Meharry Medical College, department chair, obstetrics and gynecology, 1973-90, dean,School of Medicine, 1990-93, acting president, 1993-94; Association of Academic Health Centers, senior scholar-in-residence, 1994-95; senior advisor to the President on Teen Pregnancy Reduction and Youth Issues, 1996- ; expert consultant to the Secretary of Department of Healthand Human Services and to the Director of Centers for Disease Control and Prevention, 1996-.

Selected awards: Thousand Points of Light Award (for "I Have a FutureProgram"), 1991; President's Award, Morehouse College National Alumni Association, 1995; Meritorious Service Award, National Medical Assocation, Obstetrics andGynecology Section, 1996; Outstanding Service Award, Meharry Medical College Departmentof Surgery, 1997; Certificate of Appreciation, Vanderbilt University, School of Nursing, 1999.

Addresses: *Office*—Department of Health and Human Services, 200 Independence Avenue, SW, Room 717-H, Washington DC, 20201-0004.

African American in a class of 96 students. In spite of the racial tension surrounding him—Arkansas was in the throes of forced school desegregation during this period—Foster thrived at the University of Arkansas. He became the university's first African American student to be elected into Alpha Omega Alpha, the school's honor society in medicine.

Foster graduated from medical school in 1958, and began an internship at Detroit Receiving Hospital, which was connected to Wayne State University. It was there that he met St. Clair "Sandy" Anderson, a nurse at the nearby Dearborn Veterans Administration Hospital. The pair married on February 6, 1960.

Meanwhile, Foster entered the U.S. Air Force in 1959. The Air Force was experiencing a shortage of obstetricians at the time, and Foster was given the option of enrolling in a three-month obstetrics and gynecology course, which would result in a permanent assignment as a civilian specialist. After completing the training program at Carswell Air Force Base in Texas, Foster was sent to Moses Lake, Washington, where he worked with local obstetrician Anson Hughes. During his stint in the military, Foster delivered nearly 500 babies.

After being discharged from the Air Force in 1961, Foster moved to Boston for a year of general surgical training at Malden Hospital. Upon completing his training at Malden, he accepted a residency at Meharry Medical College in Nashville, Tennessee. Foster completed his residency at Meharry in 1965. That year, he took a job at the John A. Andrew Memorial Hospital at the Tuskegee Institute in Alabama. Foster primarily served an African American, poor, and rural population that was spread over several counties. It was there that he became acutely aware of the shortcomings of the medical system in the rural South. Foster discovered that he was treating his patients for serious problems that could have been prevented had they received basic medical care.

Foster initiated a series of reforms at Tuskegee Institute that would serve as a model for delivering health care services in poor, rural areas. He made the hospital an education and research center, and convinced officials at Meharry Medical College to set up a rotation in obstetrics and gynecology at Tuskegee for third-year medical students. The impact of Foster's initiatives was dramatic. The region saw a substantial decrease in its infant mortality rate. Visiting health officials from developing countries were frequently brought in to observe how these kinds of gains had been achieved. In 1970, Foster realized a lifelong dream when he purchased his own airplane. He used the airplane both for recreational flying and medical emergencies.

Foster received many awards for his skill and dedication. He was elected to the Institute of Medicine of the National Academy of Sciences in 1972, becoming one of the youngest physicians ever to receive membership in that prestigious association. The following year, Foster left Alabama to return to Meharry as chair of the department of obstetrics and gynecology. He would remain in that position until 1990. In 1975, he also joined the faculty of Vanderbilt University as a clinical professor of obstetrics and gynecology. Although he was no longer based in a rural setting, Foster continued to focus his efforts on the needs of at-risk populations, specifically young mothers living in poverty. He received $12 million in funding from the Robert Wood Johnson Foundation in 1980 to launch the High-Risk Young People's Program. This program was designed to make health services more accessible to vulnerable populations, particularly infants and poor mothers. In 1987, Foster unveiled his widely acclaimed "I Have a Future" program. The goal of this initiative, funded primarily by the Carnegie Foundation, was to educate disadvantaged teens in Nashville about the importance of responsible sexual behavior. It also emphasized the importance of a positive self-image and encouraged participants to go to college. The project received national attention in 1991, when President George Bush designated it as one of his "Thousand Points of Light."

In 1990, Foster was named dean of the school of medicine at Meharry. Soon after, Meharry president David Satcher was named head of the Centers for Disease Control in Atlanta. For the 1993-94 academic year, Foster served as acting president of Meharry Medical College. When a new president was appointed in 1994, Foster took the opportunity to spend a sabbatical year conducting research at the Association of Academic Health Centers in Washington, DC.

The series of events for which Foster is most widely known took place in 1995, when President Bill Clinton nominated him for the post of U.S. Surgeon General. Foster's nomination to replace the fired Jocyelyn Elders—the first African American surgeon general and a close friend of Foster's—quickly became controversial. Conservatives in the Senate voiced strong opposition to Foster's nomination based on his advocacy of birth control, his association with Planned Parenthood, and, most importantly, the fact that he had performed 39 abortions. Although he received a favorable recommendation from the nominating committee, Foster fell victim to procedural maneuvering that prevented his nomination from going to a vote. Thwarted by a Republican filibuster, Foster was ultimately denied the chance to join the Clinton cabinet.

Disappointed but not discouraged, Foster continued to battle for better health care for the poor. In the wake of the failed nomination, President Clinton tapped Foster as his senior advisor on teen pregnancy reduction and youth issues. He also serves as an expert consultant to the Secretary of the Department of Health and Human Services and to the director of the Centers for Disease Control and Prevention. From these positions, Foster is able to provide an influential voice in the creation of national policy on many issues that impact the lives of disadvantaged families across the United States.

Sources

Periodicals

American Medical News, May 15, 1995, p. 4.
Jet, February 20, 1995, p. 13; February 26, 1996, p. 22.
Newsweek, February 20, 1995, p. 26.
People Weekly, March 13, 1995, p. 69.
Time, May 15, 1995, p. 34.
U.S. News & World Report, March 6, 1995, p. 36.

Other

Additional material for this profile was provided by Dr. Foster's office at the U.S. Department of Health and Human Services.

—Robert R. Jacobson

Clarence Harmon

1940(?)—

Mayor of St. Louis

In April of 1997, Clarence Harmon became the second African American mayor of St. Louis. Harmon, who had previously served as the city's chief of police, had never held elected office before. "As a boy growing up in St. Louis, the thought of one day standing before you as mayor-elect never occurred to me," he said in his inaugural address which was published on the city of St. Louis' web site. "...In those days, becoming mayor wasn't a realistic dream."

Harmon's victory came after a bitter primary election campaign against Freeman Bosley Jr., the city's first African American mayor. Bosley had the solid support of the African American community, including the city's African American weekly paper and the local branch of the National Association for the Advancement of Colored People (NAACP). Meanwhile, Harmon had gained the support of many white voters, and Bosley, among others, branded him a traitor to his race. The election, like the campaign, was split along racial lines: most white voters cast their ballots for Harmon, while most African Americans supported Bosley. After his election as mayor, Harmon promised to put the bitter campaign behind him and heal the city's wounds. "I want to begin by telling you that despite the challenges before us, I am hopeful about St. Louis," he said in his inaugural address. "And I'm hopeful because of what I see as I look out among you. I see a St. Louis of people. People of all colors, of all cultures, of various ideologies. A St. Louis that belongs to no one group but to all of us."

Harmon began his public service career in 1969 as an officer with the St. Louis Metropolitan Police Department. During his 26 years on the force, he rose steadily through the ranks, receiving four letters of commendation for outstanding performance of duty. At the same time, Harmon took the time to pursue his goal of higher education. "When I was young, my parents taught me education was a gift not to be squandered," he recalled later in a mayor's office press release. "They told me that education cannot be taken away, and with an education you can achieve your dreams."

Harmon began his studies at St. Louis Community College in Forest Park, where he did well enough to be inducted into the honor society Phi Theta Kappa in 1973. He completed his undergraduate education at Northeast Missouri State University, earning a bachelor of science degree. He continued his studies at Webster University, where he earned two master's degrees: one in public administration, and one in criminal justice administration. Later in his career, Harmon was a Danforth Foundation Fellow at the John F. Kennedy School of Government at Harvard University.

First African American Police Chief

From 1988 to 1990, Harmon served as an area commander for the police department. During this time, he developed a community-oriented policing service program which was designed to involve the

At a Glance . . .

Born Clarence Harmon in St. Louis, MO; married to Janet Kelley-Harmon; children: four. *Education:* studied at St. Louis Community College; B.S., Northeastern Missouri State University; master's degrees in criminal justice administration and criminal justice administration, Webster University; Danforth Foundation Fellow at the John F. Kennedy School of Government, Harvard University. *Politics:* Democrat.

Career: St. Louis Police Department, police officer, 1969-95; commander of area I,1988-90; secretary, Board of Police Commissioners, until 1991; chief of police, 1991-95;director of business development, United Van Lines, 1995-97; mayor of St. Louis, 1997-.

Awards: Four letters of commendation for performance of duty, St. Louis PoliceDepartment; Phi Theta Kappa Society, Most Distinguished Alumnus Award, 2000.

Member: International Association of Chiefs of Police; board of directors, American Association of Industrial Management, United Way, Missouri Botanical Garden, Fair St. Louis; board of trustees, Webster University and St. Louis Science Center.

Addresses: *Home*—St. Louis, MO. *Office*—Mayor, City ofSt. Louis, 1200 Market Street, City Hall, Room 200, St. Louis, MO 63103.

city's citizens in crime prevention. He also served as secretary to the St. Louis Board of Police Commissioners. In 1991, Harmon became the first African American chief of police in the 130-year history of the police department. According to an unnamed writer in the *New York Times*, Harmon "was a popular chief who was considered to be effective fighting crime and challenging a department promotion system that depended on political connections." In 1995, Harmon was named Police Chief of the Year by the Missouri Police Chiefs Association.

During his tenure as police chief, Harmon began to have disagreements with the city's mayor, Freeman Bosley Jr. After just four years on the job, Harmon resigned and retired from the force. According to the *New York Times,* "a battle with Mayor Bosley over control of the department" convinced Harmon to tender his resignation. "The two men feuded for years," John F. Harris wrote in the *Washington Post.*

From 1995 to 1997, Harmon was the director of business development for United Van Lines, a nationwide moving company. He also served as director of United Van Lines' market research and analysis department. However, Harmon had grander plans for the rest of his career. In 1996, he announced that he planned to run for mayor.

Elected Mayor of St. Louis

In the previous election, Bosley had become the city's first African American mayor. Harmon decided to challenge Bosley in the Democratic party's primary. In heavily Democratic St. Louis, where a Republican mayor has not been elected since 1945, the winner of the primary is almost certain to win the mayoral election. In his campaign, Harmon stressed four areas he believed were crucial to the city's future: education, neighborhood stabilization, job creation and crime. He faulted Bosley for the fact that large companies, such as Ralston Purina, were considering leaving the city. At the same time, St. Louis' only public hospital was on the verge of closing, because the city had failed to pay its share of the hospital's budget.

The campaign soon descended into ugly racial allegations, which spread far beyond St. Louis: both the *New York Times* and the British magazine the *Economist* ran articles about the dispute. "Only in a city as racially divided as St. Louis could a political contest between two blacks take on a racial tone," wrote an unnamed writer in the *Economist*. While Harmon had captured the respect and support of white voters in the city, many African Americans regarded him with suspicion. The local branch of the NAACP claimed that during Harmon's term as police chief, white officers were routinely treated better than African Americans. The *St. Louis American,* a weekly African American paper, called Harmon "a more subdued, palatable candidate, propped up by business and white voters." According to an article in the *Economist,* Harmon was "older, more articulate and with a professional demeanor...a Colin Powell figure—or an Uncle Tom, depending on your point of view."

The Democratic primary, which was held in March of 1997, drew 100,000 of the city's 204,000 voters. When the ballots were counted, Harmon won 56 percent of the vote, while Bosley captured 43 percent. Support for each candidate was clearly split along racial lines: 94 percent of white voters voted for Harmon, 83 percent of African Americans supported Bosley. While the population of St. Louis is roughly half African American and half white, higher voter turnouts in white districts had carried the day. According to an article in the *Economist,* "The upset victory of Clarence Harmon over Freeman Bosley, the incumbent, for the Democratic nomination for mayor marked one of the sharpest divisions in the city's troubled history."

In the mayoral election the following month, Harmon easily defeated two white candidates to become St. Louis' second African American mayor. Harmon captured 73 percent of the vote, while Marit Clark, a Democratic alderwoman running as an independent, won 22 percent, and Jay Dearing, a Republican, won 5 percent. Not everyone perceived the mayoral election to be a low point in the city's race relations. Ken Warren, a political scientist at St. Louis University, told the *New York Times* that the election proved white voters were beginning to transcend racial divisions. "They could have voted for Clark or Dearing, but they didn't," Warren was quoted as saying. "So clearly this demonstrates that St. Louisans did not vote on racial lines like they usually have in the past."

Since his election, Harmon has fought hard to keep businesses in St. Louis. He was able to convince Middendorf Meats, Union-Pacific, Bissinger Candies, and Ralston Purina—businesses that had considered leaving St. Louis—to remain in the city. Before Harmon took office, the number of jobs in the city was declining. However, during his first two years in office, he managed to reverse that trend.

Harmon has also spearheaded the revitalization of St. Louis' downtown, with plans for a new convention center hotel, transportation hub, and bridge. He has worked with developers to turn abandoned buildings into loft condominiums and rental units, while encouraging the construction of new housing.

Increased gun control is another of Harmon's long-term goals. In March of 2000, he announced that the city had reached a settlement with gun manufacturer Smith & Wesson, in which the company agreed to make a safer product and change its distribution practices. "After years fighting for safer gun laws, this is an historic moment that means a lot to me personally," Harmon was quoted as saying in a press release.

In his April 2000 "State of the City" address, Harmon listed many of his other accomplishments in the revitalization of St. Louis. These included building three new public schools, offering tax credits for preserving historic buildings, and replacing high-rise public housing with mixed-income neighborhoods. "Viewing it objectively, I believe it would be a fair characterization to say our city is recovering from a long illness, gaining strength each day," Harmon said in a speech published on the city's web site. "...We showed a disillusioned and disengaged citizenry that government is responsive and change is possible."

Sources

Chicago Tribune, Mar. 3, 1997; Mar. 5, 1997.
Economist, Mar. 8, 1997.
New York Times, Mar. 10, 1997; Apr. 3, 1997.
Washington Post, Apr. 6, 1997.

—Carrie Golus

Cornelius Langston Henderson

1888(?)–1976

Civil engineer

Cornelius Langston Henderson was a pioneering African American civil engineer who broke racial barriers in his field to work on two historic projects in the Great Lakes area during the 1920s. Henderson spent all of his career with the Canadian Bridge Company, an Ontario-based firm that created massive steel trusses, cables, and other segments of a suspension bridge that spanned the Detroit River between the United States and Canada. As a structural steel engineer, he helped to design and oversee the installation of these steel sections, and is credited with giving the Canadian approach a particular grace. Henderson was also involved in similar engineering work for an underground tunnel, opened in 1930, that allowed for automobile traffic between Detroit and Windsor, Ontario.

Henderson was born in 1887 or 1888 in Detroit, a city where his family had strong roots. A relative, the Reverend James Henderson, was pastor of Ebenezer African Methodist Episcopal Church in the city, and was considered a leading African American citizen of the day. As a child, however, Henderson moved with his family to Atlanta, Georgia, when his father was hired as president of Morris Brown College. As a young adult, he enrolled in Payne University in Alabama, from which he graduated in 1906.

Racial violence and the oppressive segregation laws in the South drove Henderson northward, like many other African Americans at the beginning of the 20th century. He entered the University of Michigan in Ann Arbor to study civil engineering. When he graduated in 1911, he became only the second African American to graduate with such a degree. Despite his impressive academic honors, Henderson had trouble finding work for a time because of racial barriers in the field. He contemplated taking a teaching job at the Tuskegee Institute in Alabama. "He didn't talk racial-wise," his son, Cornelius Henderson Jr., told the *Detroit Free Press*'s Jeanne May in 1987. "Nobody much talked racial-wise. They knew it was hard to get jobs, but—you just went out there and did what you had to do to get a job."

Fortunately, Henderson found work across the border from Detroit in Walkerville, Ontario, with the Canadian Bridge Company. He was hired at an entry-level position in the drafting department, where he spent the first four years of what would become a nearly 50-year career with the company. Henderson eventually advanced to other positions that better utilized his civil-engineering credentials, especially when the company won two lucrative contracts in the 1920s from ventures that planned to physically link the cities of Detroit and Windsor. The two were separated by the Detroit River, which is linked with Lake Erie, and the spot was a major transportation hub on the Great Lakes. The river was narrow, however, and shipping traffic came to a standstill when ice formed during the winter months. Commerce between the cities, conducted by ferries and freight carriers, also suffered.

A railroad tunnel had been completed underneath the Detroit River in 1910, and in the 1920s Henderson worked on an ambitious project for which Canadian Bridge had been hired: the creation of a tunnel allowing

> ### *At a Glance . . .*
>
> Born c. 1888 in Detroit, MI; died August 23, 1976, in Detroit, MI; children: Cornelius Jr. *Education:* Earned degree from Payne University, 1906; University of Michigan, B.A., 1911.
>
> **Career:** Canadian Bridge Company, Walkerville, Ontario, Canada, design engineer, 1911-58.
>
> **Member:** National Technical Association, president; Engineering Society of Detroit.

automobile traffic between the United States and Canada at a juncture close to the downtown areas of both cities. He supervised the construction of the steel tubes for the tunnel—cylindrical sections were installed aboveground at the shorelines, and then a trench was dug deep underneath the Detroit River. The steel tubes were welded together, waterproofed, and covered over. During the final leg of the project, the tunnel was connected to the entry and exit points on either side of the border. Completed in 1930, the Detroit-Windsor Tunnel was considered an engineering marvel of the day.

As a structural steel designer, Henderson was also involved with another important project for which his employer had been contracted to provide steel materials. Plans for a bridge to connect Detroit and Windsor were officially underway by 1921, but the project was both a costly and controversial one. A coalition of Great Lakes shippers objected to the planned bridge, since an easy overland span would shorten the transit route for goods between the eastern United States and the Midwest. Despite the controversy, construction on the bridge began in 1927. It was designed as a suspension bridge, and the Canadian Bridge Company was contracted for the Canadian side of the project, in part, because of their ability to keep up with advances in steel technology. New engineering methods ensured that long steel cables and trusses could be used as an integral part of the bridge design. Previous attempts to span the river had called for traditional stone or masonry arches, which meant that ship traffic would be slowed and even endangered.

The Ambassador Bridge, so named in 1928 because it spanned two countries, was heralded as a symbol of the friendly ties between the United States and Canada. The bridge opened for business in November of 1929 to great fanfare. It bridged a two-mile span a few miles south of downtown Detroit and Windsor, and stood 152 feet above the river at the center, a height that easily allowed the largest vessels to pass underneath. Canadians and Americans lined up all night in their cars to cross when the structure opened. Early in its history, pedestrian traffic was also allowed. For a few short years, the Ambassador Bridge was the longest suspension bridge in the world, and was also one of the first bridges designed exclusively for automobile traffic. It remains the longest suspension bridge at an international border. The opening of the Ambassador Bridge occurred just two weeks after the 1929 stock market crash, which ushered in the Great Depression. In 1930, 1.6 million vehicles crossed the Ambassador Bridge, a figure that would not be exceeded for 15 years. Henderson worked for the Canadian Bridge Company for 47 years, and retired in 1958. The company eventually became the Canadian arm of U.S. Steel. He worked on many other engineering projects around the world during his long career, and traveled to Australia, New Zealand, South America, and the Caribbean for his job. Before his retirement, Henderson served as president of the National Technical Association, and was a member of the Engineering Society of Detroit. As a hobby, he enjoyed playing the violin. Henderson was also involved in the design of Detroit Memorial Park, the first African American cemetery in an area of Detroit occupied exclusively by African Americans. After his death on August 23, 1976, he was buried at Detroit Memorial Park. His son Cornelius also became a civil engineer, and worked for the city of Detroit for many years.

Sources

Books

Mason, Philip P. *The Ambassador Bridge: A Monument to Progress,* Wayne State University Press, 1987.

Notable Twentieth-Century Scientists, first edition, Gale, 1995, pp. 895-896.

Periodicals

Detroit Free Press, February 16, 1984, p. 1B; July 15, 1987, p. 4A; November 29, 1993, p. 5B.

Detroit News, August 24, 1976.

—Carol Brennan

M. William Howard, Jr.

1946—

Clergyman

M. William Howard, Jr. has been involved in civil rights and racial justice issues for most of his adult life, and has served at local, national, and world levels in his ecumenical work. From his days at Morehouse College and the civil rights movements of the 1960s, his service in key positions with the National Council of Churches and World Council of Churches, and his position as head of the New York Theological Institute, he has constantly worked to better the lives of millions of people. Howard has met many influential people and world leaders, and has traveled throughout the world. He has had his addresses and writing published in magazines, journals, newsletters, and newspapers, has appeared on a number of television and radio shows, and has received several honorary degrees, keys to cities, and awards.

Moses William Howard, Jr. was born on March 3, 1946, in Americus, Georgia, to M. William Howard and Laura (Turner) Howard. He attended segregated Sumter High School in Americus and graduated in 1963. During the turbulent 1960s, Howard took part in African American demonstrations for civil rights, and was a follower of Dr. Martin Luther King, Jr. He attended Morehouse College in Atlanta, Georgia, and served as a researcher on the autobiography of Benjamin E. Mays. Mays was a nationally noted educator and the sixth president of Morehouse College. He was also a mentor to Martin Luther King, Jr., who was a 1948 Morehouse College graduate. Howard received his bachelor of arts degree from Morehouse in 1968. He married Barbara Jean Wright in 1970 and the couple would have three children. Howard received his master of divinity degree in 1972 from Princeton Theological Seminary in Princeton, New Jersey and was ordained in the American Baptist Church in 1974.

Howard's clerical career began in 1970 when he became associate pastor for the First Baptist Church in Princeton, New Jersey, where he served for two years. He also served as the chaplain for United Campus Ministry at Rutgers University in New Brunswick, New Jersey from 1971 to 1972. That year, he became the executive director of the African American Council for the Reformed Church in America, and would go on to serve for 20 years as a member of the national staff. Having grown up in the South, Howard was familiar with racism and segregation. As he told *Christianity Today,* "If I were to say that picking cotton in the hot sun in southwest Georgia, and hearing grandmothers being referred to as 'girl' by teen-age, white men has not informed my ministry, I would be telling you a lie."

In 1974 Howard began his association with the National Council of Churches (NCC), a community of Protestant and Eastern Orthodox member church bodies. The council maintains programs dealing with religious and social issues, including civil rights, domestic social justice, worldwide relief and development, Christian education, and many other areas. Howard would serve in several leadership capacities. He was moderator of the Third World Peoples Conference on Development, and served as Chair, Commission on Justice, Liberation and Human Fulfillment from 1974 to 1978. During this time he also served the World Council of Churches, become an advisor to the Fifth Assembly,

At a Glance . . .

Born March 3, 1946 in Americus, GA; son of Moses William Howard, Sr., and Laura (Turner) Howard; wife's name Barbara Jean (Wright) Howard; children: Mathew Weldon, Adam Turner, Maisha Wright. *Education:* Morehouse College, Atlanta, GA, B.A. 1968; Princeton Theological Seminary, Princeton, NJ, MDiv, 1972.

Career: Associate pastor, First Baptist Church, Princeton, NJ, 1970-72; chaplain,United Campus Ministry, Rutgers University, New Brunswick, NJ, 1971-72; executive director, African-American Council, Reformed Church in America, 1972-92; president, New York-Theological Seminary, New York, NY, 1992-99; pastor, Bethany Baptist Church, Newark, NJ,1999-.

Selected awards: Toussaint L'Ouverture Freedom Award, Haitian Community,1980; Distinguished Alumnus Award, Princeton Theological Seminary, 1982; New JerseyCitizen Action Award "International Human Rights Activist," 1985; Outstanding Achievement Award, New York City NAACP, 1993.

Selected memberships: Board of trustees, Trenton State College; The Children's Defense Fund; National Urban League; president, North American Regional Conference on Action Against Apartheid; president, American Committee on Africa; U.S. General Services Administration Steering Committee for the African Burial Ground.

Addresses: *Office*—Bethany Baptist Church, 275 W. Market St., Newark,NJ. 07103.

Nairobi, Kenya, and participated in a Pre-Assembly youth meeting in Tanzania. Howard also served for two years as the moderator for the Commission on the Program to Combat Racism. The World Council of Churches, which was founded in 1948, is an international fellowship of more than 330 churches, denominations, and fellowships in 100 countries and territories throughout the world with about 400 million Christians as members. It was formed to serve and advance the ecumenical movement.

During Pope John Paul II's visit to the United States in 1979, Howard read the Gospel during an ecumenical service. That same year, he became the youngest person and the second African American president of the NCC, the largest ecumenical body in the nation. By 2000 the membership rolls of the NCC had increased to 35 Protestant, Orthodox, and Anglican member churches with nearly 52 million congregants. When Howard became president of the NCC his goal, among others, was to strengthen the existing racial and social justice programs. In a *Christianity Today* article, he was referred to as "a specialist in racial justice" for his work in the movement against apartheid in South Africa. When Howard's term as president of the NCC ended, he served for two years as chair of the Information Committee. He also became a delegate of World Consultation on Racism in the Netherlands.

During the 1980s Howard served as a member on several committees or boards, including the American Cancer Society, People for the American Way, Trenton State College, the Children's Defense Fund, and the National Urban League. In the fight against apartheid, he served as Chairman on the United Nations Seminar Against Bank Loans to South Africa. When Reverend Jesse Jackson made his bid for the presidency of the United States in 1984, Howard served as floor leader at the Democratic National Convention in San Francisco. That same year, he served as president of the North American Regional Conference on Action Against Apartheid, the largest United Nations-sponsored conference of anti-apartheid activities ever held in the United States and Canada. Howard served as president of the board of directors for the American Committee on Africa, and presented testimonies on southern Africa and human rights issues before the U.S. Congress and the United Nations. In 1990, he was chairman of the Religious Sub-Committee of the New York Nelson Mandela Welcome Committee.

Howard has also served in several special assignments. In 1979, he conducted Christmas services for U.S. Embassy personnel held hostage in Teheran, Iran. In 1980, Howard chaired a fact-finding mission to the Middle East and held talks with King Hussein of Jordan, Menachem Begin, Shimon Peres, and Teddy Kolleck of Israel. He has traveled extensively to serve in various ecumenical capacities and has visited Armenia, Bermuda, Canada, Cuba, Egypt, Germany, Great Britain, Guatemala, Hong Kong, Iran, Israel, Jamaica, Jordan, Kenya, Lebanon, Mexico, The Netherlands, Peoples Republic of China, Puerto Rico, Russia, Somalia, South Africa, Switzerland, Syria, and Zimbabwe. He headed the National Council of Churches' first post-revolution delegation to Cuba in 1977. In 1984, Howard chaired a delegation led by Reverend Jesse Jackson that obtained the release of a U.S. Navy pilot who was shot down and taken prisoner during a bombing mission over Lebanon.

In 1992 Howard became president of New York Theological Seminary (NYTS), beginning an eight-year tenure with the graduate school of theology. Under his leadership NYTS, the largest Christian seminary in the state of New York with nearly 500 students, was accredited for a ten-year period by the Association of Theological Schools. In addition, the school's information systems and technology departments received two comprehensive upgrades, the board of trustees was reorganized and strengthened, the endowment was almost doubled, new teaching programs were inaugurated, and the seminary partnered with two universities in New York to offer joint programs for the master of divinity degree in urban studies and social work. Howard answered the call to pastor Bethany Baptist Church in Newark, New Jersey in 2000. He told the *New York Amsterdam News*, "God's sending me to Bethany feels like the next logical step in the progression of my ministry—closer to people and the challenges they face."

Sources

Periodicals

Christianity Today, December 1, 1978, p. 48.
Ebony, March 1994, p. 92.
New York Amsterdam News, September 23, 1999, p. 44.

Other

Additional information for this profile was obtained from the National Council of Churches web site at www.yearbooknews.com/html/nccusa.html; informational materials from the New York Theological Seminary; the Pullen Library of the Georgia State University web site at wwwlib.gsu.edu; and the World Council of Churches web site at www.wcc-coe.org

—Sandy J. Stiefer

Milt Jackson

1923–1999

Jazz vibraphonist

The unquestioned master of the vibraphone in modern jazz, Milt Jackson exemplified the true jazz musician's ability to understand the music's duality of group thinking and individualism. While most players would have been proud to be present at even one of jazz's great historical moments, Jackson played in groups that helped forge two innovative jazz styles: bebop and classical-influenced jazz. Versatile and skillful when playing as part of a group, Jackson also compiled an impressive record of accomplishments as a soloist over the course of his 60-year career, and his lyrical, soulful vibraphone style was unmistakable.

Jackson was born on January 1, 1923, in Detroit, a city with a vigorous jazz scene for much of the twentieth century. The second of five brothers, Jackson started out in gospel music under the influence of his very religious mother. By the age of seven, he was accompanying his brother A.J. on the guitar as the two sang gospel hymns. While still a youngster, Jackson had already become an experienced gospel performer, traveling across the Canadian border every Sunday with a Detroit gospel choir to broadcast on the Windsor, Ontario radio station CKLW. He began taking piano lessons at the age of eleven, but stopped two years later when his mother became unable to afford them.

Mastered Vibes in High School

In high school, Jackson quickly outstripped his fellow music students, mastering several instruments and finishing the material for one course before the semester was even half over. Jackson told *Down Beat* that his teacher, Luis Cabrera, came up with an unusual solution: "Why don't you take up the vibes?" Jackson recalled Cabrera as saying. "That'll give you something to do, plus keep you out of trouble." Never a commonly played instrument, the vibraphone and its larger cousin the vibraharp (which was actually the instrument Jackson played) had just begun to be heard in jazz. The instrument's leading performers were Lionel Hampton and Red Norvo, and Jackson heard Hampton play at Detroit's Graystone Ballroom and Michigan State Fairgrounds.

Jackson took to the vibes immediately. "I was fascinated by the instrument," he told *Down Beat*. Rather than following Hampton and Norvo, Jackson worked to develop his own style. He experimented with different settings on the instrument's electronic oscillator,

At a Glance . . .

Born Milton Jackson, January 1, 1923, in Detroit, MI; died of liver cancer in New York, NY, October 9, 1999. married to Sandy; *Education:* Attended public schools in Detroit. *Military service:* Served in U.S. Army, 1942-44.

Career: Jazz vibraphonist. Sang in church; took up guitar at age seven and piano at age eleven; played several instruments in high school music classes and took up the vibraphone; joined Dizzy Gillespie band, 1945; recorded with Thelonious Monk band, 1947-52; performed with Woody Herman big band, 1949-50; rejoined Gillespie, 1951-52; formed Milt JacksonQuartet, soon renamed Modern Jazz Quartet, 1952; performed with Modern Jazz Quartet,1952-74; extensive solo recording career.

eventually settling on a slow speed that produced a trademark vocal-sounding vibrato. Jackson's innovative bent stood him in good stead in the early 1940s, as the angular, revolutionary new jazz style known as bebop took shape. His jazz apprenticeship was interrupted by military service in 1942, but after he returned to Detroit he found work performing in the city's club circuit. His was a round-the-clock existence in those years. From his fellow musicians, Jackson acquired the nickname "Bags" because of the bags that often formed under his eyes.

Jackson's big break came when jazz trumpeter Dizzy Gillespie, then making giant strides forward in defining the musical language of bebop, heard him play in Detroit in 1945 and hired him for a series of West Coast dates. Jackson played vibes on some of Gillespie's legendary recordings of the mid-1940s, including "A Night in Tunisia" and "Two Bass Hit." He moved with Gillespie's band to New York, the epicenter of the bebop revolution. The decision was a difficult one for the deeply religious young man, but it put him at the creative vortex of the jazz world. Jackson's parents were leery of the move at first, but he won them over by bringing renowned vocalist Ella Fitzgerald home to dinner one evening. "And my mother went and called up everyone and said her son was playing with Ella Fitzgerald," Jackson recalled to *Down Beat.*

Jackson made other valuable contacts in New York, and when he was ready to leave Gillespie's group in 1947, he moved on to another ensemble that was both cutting-edge and top-flight: that of pianist Thelonious Monk. Jackson's precise style suited Monk's terse, minimalist musical landscapes well, and once again he was heard on recordings that became jazz classics: Monk's "Misterioso," "Epistrophy," and others. Recording with Monk for the Blue Note label, Jackson impressed more and more jazz enthusiasts with his instantly identifiable sound.

Though identified with bebop, Jackson could adapt his talents to more traditional styles. In 1949 he joined bandleader Woody Herman's big band, touring Cuba with an associated small ensemble, the Woodchoppers. Nourished by the Afro-Cuban rhythms within many of Gillespie's crucial innovations, Jackson reunited with Gillespie in 1951, recording on Gillespie's Dee Gee label with such future jazz superstars as John Coltrane and Kenny Burrell. With Gillespie's rhythm section, he also cut a few sides under the name of the Milt Jackson Quartet.

Three members of this rhythm section—Jackson, pianist John Lewis, and drummer Kenny Clarke—went on, with new bassist Percy Heath, to form the Modern Jazz Quartet in 1952. This group, with its unique mixture of styles, brought a new level of sophistication to jazz in the 1950s. Lewis's cool playing, influenced by European classical technique and sometimes even drawing on classical compositions, provided the perfect foil for Jackson's essentially bluesy style. Jackson remained with the Modern Jazz Quartet until the breakup of the group in 1974.

Jackson's versatility kept leading him into other collaborations as well, with musicians of the most diverse styles and aspirations. Jackson played on Miles Davis's *Miles Davis and the Modern Jazz Giants* album of 1954, rejoined Coltrane for the album *Bags and Trane,* and, on an entirely different note, recorded two albums with jazz-pop pianist and vocalist Ray Charles. On one of those albums, *Soul Brothers,* Jackson returned for the only time in his recording career to his first instrument, the guitar. Jackson's 1961 duet album with guitarist Wes Montgomery was termed "a stunner" by Ron Wynn of the *All Music Guide to Jazz.*

Jackson's solo career flourished in the 1960s, and continued unabated for the rest of the twentieth century. He remained active as a musician until just before his death. Recording for Pablo and other labels in a great variety of styles, Jackson's albums maintained a remarkable consistency. He essayed vocals on the 1978 Original Jazz Classics album *Soul Believer,* which ventured into modern jazz-pop territory with its synthesizer accompaniments, and toured and recorded in the 1980s with the reunited Modern Jazz Quartet.

Even in the 1990s, half a century after his first recording dates, Jackson released several widely acclaimed albums, notably 1994's *The Prophet Speaks.* "The Prophet" had been a more serious nickname that had flourished alongside the familiar "Bags." Jackson's last album, a collaboration with pianist Oscar Peterson and bassist Ray Brown entitled *The Very Tall Band,* was released on the Telarc label in 1999. On October 9, 1999, Jackson died of liver cancer in New York.

Selected discography

Bluesology, Savoy, 1949.
The First Q, Savoy, 1952.
Opus de Jazz, Savoy, 1955.
Plenty Plenty Soul, Atlantic, 1957.
Soul Brothers, Atlantic, 1957 (with Ray Charles).
Bean Bags, Atlantic, 1958.
Bags and Trane, Atlantic, 1959 (with John Coltrane).
Bags Meets Wes, Original Jazz Classics, 1961 (with Wes Montgomery).
Live at the Village Gate, Original Jazz Classics, 1963.
Sunflower, CTI, 1973.
Soul Believer, Original Jazz Classics, 1978.
Night Mist, Pablo, 1980.
Mostly Duke, Pablo, 1982.
Reverence and Compassion, Qwest, 1993.
The Prophet Speaks, Qwest, 1994.
The Very Tall Band, Telarc, 1999.

Sources

Books

Contemporary Musicians, volume 15, Gale, 1996.
Erlewine, Michael, et al., eds., *The All Music Guide to Jazz,* Miller Freeman, 1998.
Kernfeld, Barry, ed. *The New Grove Dictionary of Jazz,* Macmillan, 1988.
Lyons, Len, and Don Perlo, *Jazz Portraits,* Morrow, 1989.

Periodicals

Down Beat, November 1999, p. 24.

—James M. Manheim

Ronny Jordan

1962—

Acid jazz guitarist

Down Beat magazine called Ronny Jordan "one of acid jazz's early instrumental heroes." Jordan was one of the first guitarists in the early 1990s to fuse open jazz improvisations with funk and hip hop rhythms. The experiment offended jazz purists, but the resulting "acid jazz," spread quickly from London to New York, San Francisco, and across the United States. Although the record industry was slow to catch on to the movement, and the purists rejected the new formula, Jordan's 1992 debut album *The Antidote,* became one of the most popular records to emerge from London's acid jazz scene. "I'm not a hard-nosed jazz purist," Jordan told *Guitar Player,* which may have been the understatement of his career.

Jordan was born in 1962 in London, England. His parents were of Jamaican descent. A self-taught guitarist, Jordan first picked up the instrument at the age of four, and was playing live shows at the age of 15. He was exposed to gospel groups like the Soul Stirrers and Andrae Crouch. Jordan's first public performances were with gospel acts in and around London. His father, a minister, disapproved of his son leading a musician's life. To appease him, Jordan went to college and earned a business degree. Before devoting himself to his music full-time, Jordan worked "straight" jobs for many years.

The outbreak of British funk during the 1980s inspired Jordan to start exploring different types of music beyond his gospel roots. At some point, he developed a fascination with jazz. His influences included Charlie Christian, Wes Montgomery, and Grant Green. Although Jordan loved jazz, he was also fond of 1970s funk groups like Sly & The Family Stone, Parliament/Funkadelic, and Tower of Power. "I was split down the middle," he told *Guitar Player.*

Jordan started experimenting after college and combined his two loves, jazz and funk. When hip hop began to take off, he started incorporating that into the mix as well. Jordan's experiments resulted in the song "After Hours," on which he played all of the instruments. This single was one of the first recordings of the music genre that would come to be known as "acid jazz."

The term "acid jazz" applies to a style of music created by disc jockeys in London. The music recreated sounds from the 1970s era, complete with the "wah-wah" guitar and Hammond organ that exemplified the work of artists such as Roy Ayers and Donald Byrd. However, Jordan believes that it is impossible to recapture that old sound. "So rather than calling my music acid jazz," he told *Guitar Player,* "I refer to it as 'music for the head and feet.'" Jazz purists hated the new sound. They believed that jazz should not be fused with funk, hip-hop, rap, and R&B. In an interview with *Guitar Player,* Jordan counted contemporary jazz musician Wynton Marsalis among his critics.

Initially, record companies showed no interest in producing acid jazz recordings. "After Hours" was rejected by several British record companies. After Jordan recorded a compelling reworking of legendary jazz artist Miles Davis's classic "So What," the attitudes of record company executives began to change. Jordan

At a Glance . . .

Born November 29, 1962 in London, England.

Career: Guitarist; credited as a pioneer of acid jazz; released the albums: *The Quiet Revolution,* 1993; *Bad Brothers,* 1995; *Light to Dark,* 1996; *A Brighter Day,* 1999.

Addresses: *Record label*—Blue Note Records, 304 Park Ave. South,Third Floor, New York, NY, 10010.

took Davis's cool sense of jazz improvisation and updated it with hip-hop rhythms. His version of "So What" became a hit on London's underground music scene. Jordan soon landed a record deal with Island Records, and released his debut album, *The Antidote,* in 1992. *The Antidote* was influential, and the acid jazz movement began to spread. Jordan also found success when he teamed with hip-hop artist Guru on 1993's *Jazzmatazz, Volume 1.* Jordan's guitar work was featured prominently on the record, and it became a best seller. *Jazzmatazz* brought acid jazz into the mainstream, and made it a viable genre. In 1995, Jordan appeared on *Jazzmatazz, Volume 2.*

By the time that Jordan released his follow-up to *The Antidote,* the popularity of acid jazz was beginning to wane. *Down Beat* magazine credited his 1994 release, *The Quiet Revolution,* for it's guest appearances by hip-hop artists Guru, Dana Bryant, and vocalist Fay Simpson. It also noted that, without the hip-hop rhythms, Jordan's music "goes limp." In 1995, Jordan released *Bad Brothers,* which contained remixes of his earlier work. Although critical response to the album was lukewarm, Jordan continued to perform before enthusiastic crowds throughout North America, Europe, Japan, Australia, and Southeast Asia.

In 1999, Jordan signed a new contract with the legendary jazz label Blue Note. His Blue Note debut, *A Brighter Day,* was released in March of 2000. The album explores many styles of music, including trip-hop, bossa-nova, and the sounds of Brazil and India, and pays homage to British acid jazz. "I really feel this record is giving me the first opportunity to show all that I can do," Jordan remarked in his Blue Note biography. On one track, Jordan teamed with one of his heroes, Roy Ayers, on a new version of Ayers's classic "Mystic Voyage." *A Brighter Day* was recorded in New York City, and featured many local musicians. "This album has a more organic feel to it than anything I've done before," Jordan noted in his Blue Note biography. "The energy of the New York musicians was very conducive to what I wanted to do in taking my music to the next level." Although Jordan understands the criticism he gets from jazz purists for mixing a new formula, he has a different historical outlook. "Remember, jazz started out as street music," he told *Guitar Player.* "Benny Goodman, Charlie Christian, and Django Reinhardt were the '30s equivalent of rave and house. Their urban feel was very close to what hip hop is today. They're both based in reality."

Selected discography

The Antidote, Island, 1992.
The Quiet Revolution, 4th & Broadway, 1993.
Bad Brothers, Island, 1995.
Light to Dark, Fourth & Broadway, 1996.
A Brighter Day, Blue Note, 2000.

Sources

Periodicals

Guitar Player, February 1994, p.23.
Down Beat, January 1994, p.49; January 1997, p. 58.

Other

Additional information for this profile was obtained from the " Ronny Jordan" Homepage, http://www.ronnyjordan.com (May 13, 2000); and the entry on "Ronny Jordan," from AMG All Music Guide, http://www.allmusic.com (May 13, 2000).

—Brenna Sanchez

Marjorie Stewart Joyner

1896–1994

Businesswoman, community leader, inventor

A true pillar of her Chicago South Side community, Marjorie Stewart Joyner affected the lives of many African Americans with her altruistic endeavors for most of her ninety-eight years. She worked with First Lady Eleanor Roosevelt to combat racial segregation and discrimination. She organized and for six decades directed the annual Bud Billiken parade in the city's African-American neighborhoods; it grew to become the nation's largest gathering of its type. She was a close associate of pioneering African American educator Mary McLeod Bethune and became a key supporter of Bethune-Cookman College. And perhaps most famously, she was an important figure in the history of African American beauty culture and the inventor of a permanent-wave machine.

Joyner was born Marjorie Stewart in the Blue Ridge Mountains near Monterey, Virginia, on October 24, 1896, the granddaughter of slaves. She grew up in poverty—only four of the thirteen Stewart children survived infancy—but her father was a schoolteacher who had worked with the famous African American educator Booker T. Washington and harbored higher ambitions. The family moved to Dayton, Ohio, in 1904, where Joyner's father landed a teaching job in a white school. But her parents divorced soon afterward, and Joyner bounced between various family members.

Studied Under Madame C. J. Walker

Her education was frequently interrupted, and when she moved to Chicago to be with her mother in 1912, it was further derailed by cleaning and waitressing jobs. Joyner attended Englewood High School on the South Side, but did not receive her high school diploma until 1935 (she did earn a music-school certificate in 1924). She reaffirmed her faith in the value of education when she went to college as a senior citizen and received a B.S. degree from Bethune-Cookman college at the age of 77. Joyner met her future husband, who later became a podiatrist, when he roller-skated past her home; the two married in 1916 and had two daughters.

Becoming the first African American graduate of Chicago's A.B. Molar Beauty School, Joyner opened a salon of her own in 1916. Her first customers were white, but the turning point of her career came when she enrolled in a hair-styling class with Madame C. J. Walker, the grandmother of the African American hair-care industry and reputedly America's first African

At a Glance . . .

Born October 24, 1896, near Monterey, VA; died December 27, 1994, in Chicago, IL; daughter of George Emmanuel Stewart, a schoolteacher, and Annie Daugherty Stewart; married Robert S. Joyner, 1916; children: Anne Joyner Fook, Barbara Joyner Powell. *Education:* Bethune-Cookman College, B. S., 1973; Chicago Musical College, certificate in dramatic art and expression, 1924; several cosmetology degrees. *Religion:* attended African Methodist Episcopal churches; co-founded non-denominational Cosmopolitan Community Church, early 1930s.

Career: Hair salon executive, activist, philanthropist, and community leader. Enrolled inclasses of famed hair-care entrepreneur Madame C. J. Walker, 1916; worked extensively with Walker as agent until Walker's death, 1919; national supervisor for more than 200 Walker beauty schools, late 1910s; later vice president of company; helped write Illinois cosmetology laws, 1924; granted patent for permanent wave machine, 1928; organized first Bud Billiken Parade, Chicago, 1929, and chaired parade committee for decades; organized National Council ofNegro Women, 1935; worked with First Lady Eleanor Roosevelt, late 1930s and early 1940s; organized educational trip to Paris for 195 black cosmetologists, 1954; worked extensively as fundraiser for Bethune-Cookman College later in career.

Awards: Honorary Doctor of Humanities degree, Bethune-Cookman College, 1961; named one of Five Outstanding Achievers, National Council of Negro Women, 1990; birthday named Dr. Marjorie Stewart Joyner Day in Chicago, 1990; subject of museum exhibitions atSmithsonian Institution in Washington, D.C. and at several other major museums.

American female millionaire. Joyner took the class at her mother- in-law's behest. According to her recollections quoted in *Notable Black American Women*, Joyner botched a hair styling job she undertook on her mother-in-law: "When I got through with her hair she looked like an accident going somewhere to happen. She said you can't do anything with my hair, but... I am going to give you money to go down to [Walker's] class; she is teaching how to do black hair."

Walker quickly recognized her student's intelligence and energy and signed her on as an instructor and agent. Joyner helped Walker spread her methods and products across the Midwest, and was instrumental in the Walker Company's rapid growth. By the time of Walker's death in 1919, Joyner was a national supervisor for more than 200 Madame C. J. Walker beauty schools. She helped write Illinois' first cosmetology laws in 1924, and four years later registered a patent on a permanent-wave machine, a device that automated parts of Walker's hair-straightening procedure. A noted hair stylist herself, Joyner did styling work for such African American celebrities as Billie Holliday, Ethel Waters, and opera star Marian Anderson.

Joyner remained with the Walker firm for more than fifty years, and always credited her hair-styling experience with developing her imagination and her problem-solving abilities. She developed a host of other products, including the "Satin Tress" preparation, the predecessor of the now-ubiquitous hair relaxer. But later in life she broadened the scope of her energies to include more community-oriented and philanthropic endeavors. Part of the reason was that despite her success, she had been touched by the segregation and institutionalized racial discrimination that permeated American life.

"They talk about Rosa Parks having to sit in the back of a bus in Montgomery, Alabama," Joyner was quoted as saying by the *Chicago Tribune*. "Well, how would you like to ride all night in a baggage car with a corpse?" she continued. On her way to a speaking engagement in Texas from Cairo, Illinois, Joyner was told to leave the whites-only cars of the train in which she was riding. Since no blacks-only seating was available, Joyner had to ride in the train's baggage car. Resting her feet on a long box to get comfortable, she was later horrified to realize that it was a casket.

After experiences like that, Joyner was inspired to devote her considerable organizational talents to laying down the roots of what eventually became the civil rights movement. She became an associate of First Lady Eleanor Roosevelt in the 1930s, and the two women made headlines by attending an integrated-audience concert by the Bethune-Cookman choir and facing down threats of Ku Klux Klan violence. During World War II, Roosevelt named Joyner to a women's leadership post on the Democratic National Committee. Joyner was also a founding member of the National Council of Negro Women in 1935. She was acquainted with democratic U.S. presidents from Franklin D. Roosevelt to Jimmy Carter.

Many Chicagoans know Joyner as the "Matriarch of the Bud Billiken Parade," an annual event begun by the *Chicago Defender*, the city's venerable African American-owned newspaper, as a benefit for its young delivery carriers. Bud Billiken is a figure in African

American folklore who works as a protector of children. Joyner organized the first parade in 1929, and under her decades-long leadership it grew into a central festival event in Chicago's African American community. Later Joyner became the director of the newspaper's Chicago Defender Charities, overseeing food and clothing drives and social-agency fundraising. Joyner's fame spread when she organized a widely reported trip to Paris by 195 young African American cosmetologists to learn new techniques; she had been frustrated at the slow pace at which U.S. beauty colleges admitted African American students.

Joyner was also notable as a fundraiser for Bethune-Cookman College, an institution in Daytona Beach, Florida, that was instrumental in opening up higher education opportunities for young African American women. Much of her time in later years was spent fundraising for the school; the United Beauty School Owners and Teachers, an organization Joyner herself had founded after being cold-shouldered by white trade associations, donated hundreds of thousands of dollars. Joyner gained another patrician admirer in multimillionaire New York governor Nelson Rockefeller, a major donor who helped make possible the college's expansion, and in the 1970s a residence hall was named after her.

Marjorie Stewart Joyner died of heart failure at her South Side home on December 27, 1994, at the age of ninety-eight. Until her death she went every day to her office at the *Defender,* and every Sunday to the Cosmopolitan Community Church, which she had helped to found. The *Chicago Tribune* noted that she had "touched the lives of millions of African Americans."

Sources

Books

MacDonald, Anne L., *Feminine Ingenuity and Invention in America,* Ballantine, 1992.

Smith, Jessie Carney, ed., *Notable Black American Women,* Book II, Gale, 1996.

Periodicals

Chicago Reader, September 11, 1992, p. 9.

Chicago Tribune, December 29, 1994, p. Chicagoland-11.

Jet, January 16, 1995, p. 54.

Mothering, Summer 1994, p. 98.

—James M. Manheim

Earl Lloyd

1928(?)—

Former professional basketball player

"People know who Jackie Robinson is. Why don't they know about Earl Lloyd?" Chicago sportscaster and former NBA player Johnny (Red) Kerr asked in an interview with *Sports Illustrated.* Lloyd himself, possessing of a modesty rare among basketball players of the present day, is quick to downplay the comparison, pointing out that he shared the spotlight in his debut year of 1950 with two other African American draftees. Nevertheless, Earl Lloyd has a place in history and in the record books as the first African-American player to take the court in an NBA basketball game, and his story offers more inspiration than he admits for those seeking to overcome barriers in their lives. Lloyd also went on to become the NBA's first non-playing African American coach later in his career.

Born circa 1928, Lloyd grew up in Alexandria, Virginia, living under the strict regime of Southern segregation in the era before civil rights. His selection in the 1950 NBA draft also marked for him a different and more personal milestone: he told the *Washington Times* that "[t]o that point I had never sat next to or even talked to a white person before." Lloyd attended all-black West Virginia State College. As a youth, he received some advice from his mother that he later recounted to *Sports Illustrated:* "Stupid people do stupid things," she told him. "Small people do small things. Don't let them get to you." It was advice he would need and heed later in his life.

A basketball standout at West Virginia State, Lloyd mulled an offer to take what he considered the only professional basketball opportunity open to him at the time: a slot with the razzle-dazzle, acrobatically inclined Harlem Globetrotters, whose on-court antics delighted basketball audiences of the day. But as Lloyd finished college in 1950, Jackie Robinson had broken baseball's color barrier three years before and had begun the long and arduous dismantling of the institutional racial segregation that pervaded American life. Lloyd's coach saw changes coming in other sports, and, perhaps mindful of the NBA scouts in the stands who were keeping an eye on his hot prospect, warned Lloyd to keep his options open.

Though Lloyd became the first African American player in the NBA, he was not the first one drafted. Boston Celtics coach Red Auerbach, who ironically was later responsible for building the great and largely-white dominated Celtics basketball dynasty of the 1980s, was the first basketball decision-maker to break

At a Glance . . .

Born ca. 1928; raised in Alexandria, VA; married, wife's name Charlita; children: Kevin, Kenneth. *Education:* earned education degree from West Virginia State College, 1950. *Military service:* U.S. Army, 1951-52.

Career: Professional basketball player and coach; one of three African Americans drafted by NBA teams, 1950; became NBA's first African American player to play on October 31, 1950, playing for Washington Capitols; signed with Syracuse Nationals, 1952; played on Nationals NBA champion team, 1955, as one of first two African Americans to win championship; signed with Detroit Pistons, 1958; became assistant coach with Pistons, 1960; became NBA's first African American non-playing coach with Pistons, 1971-73; workedas job-placement administrator, Detroit Public Schools, 1970s and 1980s; community liaison work with Bing Steel, Detroit, 1990s.

Addresses: *Office*—c/o Detroit Pistons, 2 Championship Dr., AuburnHills, MI 48326.

with tradition; the Celtics picked Duquesne forward Chuck Cooper in the second round of the 1950 NBA draft. Once the doors had been opened, two more African American players were picked. Nat (Sweetwater) Clifton, a Harlem Globetrotter forward was drafted by the New York Knickerbockers and became the first African American to sign an NBA contract.

Lloyd was selected by the Washington Capitols in the ninth round of the draft. He himself credited Auerbach for his own chance to enter the NBA. "I don't think you can put a price tag on what [Auerbach] has done for the black athlete," he told the *Washington Times.* "I believed then and I believe now that if Red Auerbach had not drafted Chuck Cooper, the Washington Capitols would not have drafted me," he continued. Reporting to the Capitols training camp, Lloyd faced a sharp period of adjustment.

"So first off, you're shocked," Lloyd told the *Detroit Free Press.* "When you get to camp, you're awestruck, because you're around these players you've heard about for years. And when you get treated like an inferior human being all of your life, you start to believe it... I said, 'What am I doing here?'" he recalled. But Lloyd had the mental discipline, and more important the skills, to ride out this period of self-doubt. "About the fifth day of training camp," he told the *Free Press,* "the light goes on and you say," 'Hey, these guys are no better than I am.' By the start of the regular season I was in the starting lineup."

On October 31, 1950, Lloyd became the NBA's first African American player to play when the Capitols took the court in Rochester, New York, against the Rochester Royals. Only 2,184 fans were in attendance, and this milestone in African-American history went unreported by the same national press that had closely scrutinized Jackie Robinson's debut three years earlier. One reason, Lloyd has pointed out, was that professional basketball was then in its infancy. Teams were located in out-of-the-way places, attendance was low, and national media coverage was sparse.

In Rochester, where the city's schools were already integrated and the fans used to seeing African American players, the game went off without incident. Things were not so pleasant at the Capitols' second game of the year, played at home against the Minneapolis Lakers. Lloyd's parents were in the crowd, and had to endure numerous racist remarks from disgruntled white fans. Things got even worse in Fort Wayne, Indiana, where Lloyd and a white teammate, walking off the court arm in arm after a Capitols' victory, were spit on by fans. "When you went to Fort Wayne to play," Lloyd told *Sports Illustrated,* "you had to do some emotional yoga to get ready because you knew what was coming." he continued.

Lloyd has repeatedly maintained that the challenges he faced were minor compared with those surmounted by Robinson. He pointed to the fact that while Robinson fought physically with his own teammates, he (Lloyd) was never even insulted with a racial slur on the court from a teammate or even from an opposing player. But Lloyd often faced difficulties in obtaining public accommodations when on the road with the Capitols. One night in Fort Wayne, the Van Orman Hotel refused to let him eat in its restaurant with the rest of the team. Capitols coach "Bones" McKinney tried to soften the blow by coming to eat in Lloyd's room, but Lloyd (quoted in the *Detroit Free Press)* told the coach, "No, you don't have to do this. There's no use both of us being miserable."

At times, Lloyd told *Sports Illustrated,* he "wanted to lash out at somebody." But he persisted, bringing a copy of *Down Beat* magazine on the road with him and seeking out jazz clubs, where all were made welcome. Other African American players joined the league and things got easier. Lloyd moved to the Syracuse Nationals in 1952, and when the Nationals won the NBA championships in 1955, Lloyd and teammate Jim Tucker became the first African Americans to win an NBA title. Nicknamed "The Big Cat" for his height and speed, Lloyd gained a reputation as a fine defensive player. He closed out his playing career with the Detroit Pistons from 1958 to 1960; over his pro career Lloyd averaged 8.4 points and 6.4 rebounds per game.

In the days before multimillion-dollar salaries and celebrity endorsements, professional athletes often had to begin new careers when their playing days were over. Lloyd, married and the father of two, stayed on in Detroit and became an assistant coach with the Pistons in 1960. In 1971 he notched a final first on his belt when he was named the team's coach: although Celtics star Bill Russell had broken coaching's color barrier when he served as the Celtics' player-coach in the late 1960s, Lloyd was the league's first non-playing African American coach.

Compiling a record of 22 wins and 55 losses, Lloyd was fired by the notoriously fickle Pistons in 1973 and dropped off the basketball radar screen. He moved into a job-placement career with Detroit Public Schools. The honors that began to flow his way began when his name appeared as the answer to a question on television's *Jeopardy* quiz show in 1988; the contestant at the time did not know Lloyd's name. In the 1990s Lloyd worked for the steel and auto-parts company of former Piston Dave Bing, who had played for Lloyd during his years at the helm of the Pistons. By the year 2000 he had retired to a home in Tennessee. "I can't count up to $5 million," he told the *Detroit Free Press,* "but it makes me feel good to know that I was part of contributing something to enable young black kids to make big money," he concluded.

Sources

Periodicals

Detroit Free Press, February 26, 1989, p. E9; January 14, 1992, p. D1; March 16, 2000, p. B2.

Insight on the News, March 29, 1999, p. 42.

Knight-Ridder/Tribune News Service, February 27, 2000.

Sports Illustrated, November 28, 1994, p. 8.

Washington Times, February 18, 1999, p. 1.

—James M. Manheim

Vicki Mabrey

1957(?)—

Television journalist

Vicki Mabrey may have been the "fresh face" on one of television's most talked-about news-magazine programs, but she earned her job as anchorwoman the hard way—by reporting standoffs and shootouts, floods, and internationally newsworthy events. The veteran journalist had the knack for being in the right place at the right time, leading to her coverage of some of the world's biggest news stories. When the spin-off of the legendary television news magazine "60 Minutes," entitled "60 Minutes II," debuted in 1999, Mabrey became the first African American woman to introduce herself as the show's trademark stopwatch began its 60-minute countdown.

The daughter of Barbara, a teacher, and Harold, a former civilian Army procurement officer, Mabrey is the oldest of three children. She also has two younger brothers, Lesley and Kevin. At the age of eight, Mabrey moved with her family from an inner-city neighborhood to Florissant, Missouri, then an all-white suburb of St. Louis. Instead of a welcoming committee, the Mabreys were greeted with a painted sign on their sidewalk that read, "White is right." Mabrey was also the first African American student to integrate the local elementary school. By the time she was a senior in high school, more African Americans had moved into the town, and the McCluer High School student body contained students of both races.

Mabrey graduated cum laude with a degree in political science from Howard University in 1977. Within four years, she had gotten married and moved to Baltimore. Mabrey found work as a real estate marketer, but quickly changed careers when she saw a college classmate working in local television news. Mabrey convinced the local CBS affiliate to give her a job, and went through the AFTRA reporter training program at WUSA-TV, the CBS affiliate in Washington, D.C. In 1983, the station hired her as a production assistant. "I think of the opportunities my grandparents didn't have," Mabrey told *Essence,* "and I have to grab every one." Within a year, she was working as an on-air general assignment reporter. She later became a Dallas-based correspondent for CBS News.

Mabrey's placement in Dallas marked the beginning of her success in journalism. In 1993, she received a tip that something was going to happen near Waco, Texas. Mabrey traveled to Waco, and covered the standoff between federal agents and Branch Davidian cult members. During a 55 day span, she provided

At a Glance . . .

Born c. 1957 in St. Louis, MO; married and divorced; *Education:* Howard University, B.A. in political science, cum laude, 1977.

Career: Real estate marketer, Baltimore, MD, 1981-83; production assistant,WBAL-TV, Baltimore, 1983-84; general assignment reporter, WBAL-TV, Baltimore, 1984-92; Dallas-based correspondent, CBS News, Dallas, 1992-95; correspondent, CBS News, London, England 1995-98; correspondent, "60 Minutes II," 1999-.

Awards: Emmy Award for coverage of the Atlanta Olympic bombing, 1996; Emmy Award for coverage of the crash of TWA Flight 800, 1996; two Emmy Awards for reporting for CBS News' coverage of the death of Princess Diana, 1997.

Addresses: *Office*—"60 Minutes II," 524 West 57th Street, New York, NY 10019.

often continuous on-air developments in the standoff. Mabrey was also sent to cover the severe flooding that devastated parts of the Midwest in 1993. The following year, she traveled to Haiti to provide coverage of the landing of American troops there after dictator Raul Cedras fled the country. The troops had entered Haiti to monitor the country's transition to a democratic government.

To London and Beyond

In 1995, a producer at CBS recommended Mabrey for a job at the network's London bureau. That year, CBS posted her in England as their London correspondent. In 1997, Mabrey covered the tragic car crash in Paris that killed Princess Diana. She won two Emmy awards for her coverage of the tragedy.

When CBS announced that it was producing a spin-off of its legendary news-magazine show "60 Minutes," applications for the new show's four resident correspondent spots quickly poured in. Mabrey e-mailed her request to "60 Minutes II" executive producer Jeff Fager. Although she thought that her chances of landing a spot on the show were slim, she was offered a position on "60 Minutes II." Mabrey was elated. "This is the job every broadcast journalist wants," she said in an interview with *Knight-Ridder/Tribune News Service*. However, she was saddened to learn that she would have to leave London and move to New York, where the show is taped. "I know I'll shed many tears when I leave my little house in London," Mabrey said in the same interview.

Every broadcast journalist may have wanted the "60 Minutes II" job, but Mabrey won it with her journalistic savvy and winning personality. Although she told *People* that Fager told her directly that she wasn't hired because she was African American, "I'm not naive enough to say race didn't play some part." Fager had his own reasons for hiring her. "She's warm, real, and you feel that as a viewer," he told *People*. Although Mabrey has a warm personality, she is not afraid to tackle difficult issues. On the debut edition of "60 Minutes II," Mabrey presented a report about children who died after receiving anesthesia at a dentist's office. A few weeks later, she offered a critical report about the controversial diet drug fen-phen. "She's not afraid to jump right into something," Fager commented in *People*.

Before "60 Minutes II" debuted, many network veterans resisted the idea of a spin-off of CBS' venerable news-magazine show "60 Minutes." Although the "60 Minutes II" team consisted of well respected journalists, some critics refused to accept the new show. Lawrie Mifflin, writing in the *New York Times*, defended "60 Minutes II" and remarked that "there is nothing second-string about the on-air team assembled for the latest CBS News magazine program." The show received favorable reviews, and eventually attracted a loyal following of viewers. Even though *People* criticized a few of the show's flaws—citing Mabrey for unnecessarily ambushing a dentist in the first show—the magazine called "60 Minutes II," overall, "a winner."

Compared to her fellow correspondents on "60 Minutes II"—Dan Rather, Bob Simon, and Charlie Rose—Mabrey was the show's "fresh face," as Fager told the *New York Times*. However, she credits her lack of recognition as an advantage. While most of the senior correspondents at CBS have worked their way up through the CBS ranks, as Mabrey did, "No one really knows me...I'm not coming in dragging a reputation I have to uphold," she told *Knight-Ridder/Tribune News Service*.

Sources

Periodicals

Essence, April 2000, p. 80.
Knight-Ridder/Tribune News Service, January 6, 1999.
New York Times, November 11, 1998.
People, March 1, 1999, p. 25; p.115.

Other

Additional information for this profile was obtained from CBS News Online at http://cbsnews.cbs.com (June 16, 2000).

—Brenna Sanchez

Edna Manley

1900–1987

Sculptor

"Her legacy extends beyond the expression of a personal artistic vision, to a vision of the realities and possibilities of a nation and a people," wrote Dena Merriam in *Sculpture Review* magazine. English-born sculptor Edna Manley became so entrenched in Jamaican culture that her work clearly grew to capture the spirit of the Caribbean island. She was wife to one Jamaican prime minister and mother to another. Often hailed as the "Mother of Jamaican art," Manley not only was Jamaica's foremost sculptor, but also was a pioneer for Jamaican art.

Manley's father, Harvey Swithenbank, was a Wesleyan clergyman, and married Ellie Shearer in 1895. Swithenbank met Shearer, who was Jamaican, while on a seven-year tour of duty on the island. Manley was born in 1900, in Bournemouth, England. Her father died when she was nine, and Manley's mother was left to raise nine children on her own. As the middle child, Manley was highly independent and spirited. Although her creative inclinations were clear early on, she was an impatient child and adolescent. She once attended several art schools in a two-year period, impatient with the limitations of training the schools offered.

When Manley was a teenager, she met her Jamaican cousin, Norman Washington Manley. A 21-year-old Rhodes Scholar and handsome champion athlete, he would be in England for two years to study at Oxford. Although Manley was charmed, she did not see Norman for four more years. Her next encounter with Norman occurred while he was on leave from military service in World War I, a weary soldier taking a break from battle. After the war, Norman returned to his studies at Oxford, and he and Manley developed a close friendship. Norman became her confidante, and the only person who could temper the young sculptor's restlessness. The couple's long discussions about art and regular trips to London museums and galleries helped Manley develop her views of art. They were married in 1921.

The Manleys sailed for Jamaica in 1922, just weeks before the birth of their first child, Douglas. Manley was anxious to start sculpting. "When I came to Jamaica I just was totally and absolutely inspired," she told David Boxer, a painter and director of the National Gallery of Jamaica, in an interview for *Americas* magazine. Manley's mother was Jamaican, and Manley had been raised with her mother's memories and stories of Jamaica.

The move to Jamaica had a profound impact on her work. She left the conventional animal studies of her London days behind, and her work took on a more "inspired formal elegance," according to Boxer. Manley's materials consisted mostly of native woods—she used yacca, mahogany, Guatemalan redwood, juniper cedar, and primavera. Some of the work dating from her first year on the island are *Beadseller,* and *Listener.* In describing *Beadseller,* Boxer said, "It was as if in one fell swoop, nearly a hundred years of sculptural development had been bridged: In this, her first work done in Jamaica, Edna seems to have given expression to her ideas about contemporary British sculpture with which she had saturated herself prior to leaving England."

At a Glance . . .

Born Edna Swithenbank, March 1,1900, in Bournemouth, England; died in 1987; married Norman Washington Manley, 1921 (died 1969); children: Douglas, Michael. *Education:* Regent Street Polytechnic, London, 1918-20; St. Martin's School of Art, London, 1920-22; Royal Academy, London, 1920-22.

Career: Sculptor; works exhibited regularly in England, 1927-80; first solo exhibition in Jamaica, 1937; exhibition, *Ten Jamaican Sculptors,* Commonwealth Institute, London, England, 1975; exhibition, *Edna Manley: The Seventies,* National Gallery of Jamaica,Jamaica, 1980; co-founder, teacher, Jamaica Art School, 1950.

Awards: Silver Musgrave Medal, Institute of Jamaica, Kingston, 1929; Gold Musgrave Medal, Institute of Jamaica, Kingston, 1943; honorary degree, University of the West Indies,1975; Order of Merit, National Awards, 1980; Fellow, Institute of Jamaica, Kingston, 1980.

Both pieces exhibited Manley's new, more expressive, and cubist style.

Between 1925 and 1929, Manley softened some of her geometric forms, replacing them with more massive, rounded ones. Her son, Michael, was born during this time. *Market Women,* a study of two voluptuous women sitting back to back, and *Demeter,* a carving of the mythical Earth Mother, are indicative of Manley's late-1920s influence. The 1930s saw another change in her sculptural style. She tamed her early-1920s cubist lines with rounder influences, and produced a new, definitive style that lasted into the 1940s.

Jamaica was facing many political changes during the late 1930s and early 1940s. Black Jamaicans were looking to do away with the old colonial system on the island. They were ready for a new social order, and voiced their displeasure with the colonial system through strikes, riots, food shortages, and protest marches. Manley's work of the time reflected this civil unrest. Works like *Prophet, Diggers, Pocomania,* and *Negro Aroused* "caught the inner spirit of our people and flung their rapidly rising resentment of the stagnant colonial order into vivid, appropriate sculptural forms," wrote poet M.G. Smith.

Accepted by Jamaicans

Although she'd been exhibiting her work in England since 1927, Manley didn't have her first solo show in Jamaica until 1937. The show ran for only five days, but almost a thousand people saw her work. The show marked a turning point in Jamaica's undeveloped art movement, and it prompted the first island-wide group show of Jamaican artists. Manley was also one of the founders of the new Jamaica School of Art. After premiering in Jamaica, her show opened in England, where it was received with much fanfare. It was the last time Manley's work would be shown in London for nearly 40 years.

While she was in London, Manley learned that the people of Jamaica had collected the money to buy *Negro Aroused.* Individuals pitched in whatever they could afford, and purchased the piece to start a national art collection. She was moved by this act, in part because it was such a difficult piece for her to create. "*Negro Aroused*,...was trying to create a national vision, and it nearly killed me, it was trying to put something into being that was bigger than myself and almost other than myself," Manley told *Sculpture Review.*

Nationalist feelings in Jamaica continued to rise. Norman Manley entered politics, and founded the Peoples' National Party in 1938. Although Manley was hesitant at first, she quickly accepted her husband's place—and her own—in Jamaican politics. She also designed *The Rising Sun* logo for the Peoples' National Party. The beginning of Jamaica's new government—and the fall of colonialism—was reflected in Manley's work, which at the time dealt with the cyclical, birth-and-death themes of the sun and moon. Her work was also heavily influenced by the nature that surrounded her at Nomdmi, the mountain retreat she had built with her husband.

The 1950s and 1960s were quiet times for Manley as an artist. Her husband became more involved with politics, and became chief minister of Jamaica in 1955. Manley's responsibilities as the wife of a politician left little time for art. In 1965, she created a statue of Paul Bogle to commemorate Jamaica's Morant Bay Rebellion. The statue was highly controversial because it was the first public statue of a black man in Jamaica. Manley also returned, in her personal carvings, to the animal sculptures she did as a young woman.

In 1969, Norman Manley died. He had helped Jamaica to achieve total independence from Britain and self government by 1962. Manley's carvings during this period were very personal—reflections on her husband's death, her pain, and sense of loss. She retreated to the mountains and created *Adios,* lovers in a last embrace, and *Woman,* an agonized woman alone. The end of this grieving period was marked by her creation of the triumphant *Mountain Women*. She had accepted the loss of her husband. "I felt that because my roots were here in Jamaica, I could survive," she told *Americas*. " It was my return to the world after that period of intense grief."

After creating several more profound carvings, including *Faun, Message,* and *Journey,* Manley gave her carving tools away to a young Jamaican sculptor and declared that she would never work with wood again. Instead, she worked with modeled terracotta or plaster casts. During the 1970s, the major themes of Manley's work were expressions of her "grandmother," or "old woman" image, of matriarchal society, and memories of her life with Norman.

But Manley did not leave politics completely after the death of her husband. Her son, Michael Norman, was elected as prime minister in the 1980s. Manley continued to sculpt until her death in 1987. Although a great deal of her work was intensely personal, she created a body of sculpture that embodies Jamaican culture and spirit. English novelist Sir Hugh Walpole, a collector of her work, spoke at the opening of her 1937 London show. "There is a very strange and curious spirit there and Mrs. Manley has got within that strange spirit," he remarked. "There is in Jamaica a beauty that finds its expression through her, that comes partly from the Jamaican material she uses, partly from her own individuality, and partly also, I think, from the sort of sense of beauty that the different people of Jamaica themselves possess." For Manley, expressing the beauty of Jamaica was second nature. "I carve as a Jamaican for Jamaica," she told *Americas,* "trying to understand our problems and living near to the heart of our people."

Sources

Books

Riggs, Thomas, ed., *St. James Guide to Black Artists,* St. James Press, 1997.

Periodicals

Americas, June-July 1980, p. 23
Sculpture Review, Winter 1996, p. 20.

—Brenna Sanchez

Greg Mathis

1960—

Television judge

As one of the several real-life judges who have moved into televised studio courtrooms as hosts of reality-based dispute-resolution shows, Greg Mathis enjoys solid ratings for his hour-long *Judge Mathis* television show. But the no-nonsense jurist had already tasted a certain degree of celebrity in his hometown, Detroit, as a former gang member who went to law school and was eventually elected as a judge; his life story became the basis for a local play. Mathis has always stressed that it was the wisdom and faith of a kind judge that helped change his life. Before he turned 40-years-old, Mathis's unusual life story had already attracted the attention of Hollywood producers. He negotiated a film and book deal with the Warner Entertainment Group, which created the *Judge Mathis* show.

Judge Mathis debuted in 1999 as one of several reality-based court television programs in syndication, and Mathis viewed the career move to television as part of a natural progression of his mission in life. "I had a commitment to changing lives," he told *Detroit News* television critic Tim Kiska about his time on the bench of Detroit's 36th District Court. "I think I was able to influence 15 to 20 people a week—a handful of lives. Now my inspirational justice might do the same thing for many more people in the living rooms of America."

Expelled from School

Mathis was born in 1960 in Detroit, one of four sons born to Alice Mathis. The family lived in one of the first federal housing projects in the United States, Herman Gardens, which by the time of his adolescence had earned a reputation as a tough, dangerous environment. Alice Mathis raised her sons there as a single mother, and worked two jobs—the midnight shift in a hospital as a nurse's aide, and as a cleaning woman during the day—in order to make ends meet. From an early age, Mathis had a problem with discipline, and was even expelled from elementary school. He attended three different high schools before dropping out in the tenth grade. "I fell victim to the peer pressures that went along with the environment," Mathis recalled in the *Detroit News.*

At the age of 15, Mathis became involved with an infamous Detroit gang, the Erroll Flynns. He quickly accumulated a juvenile criminal record for breaking and entering, purse-snatching, and shoplifting. When he was 17-years-old, he was arrested on a concealed-weapons charge and landed in the Wayne County Jail. His mother came to visit him there, and wept over the dismal turn his young life had already taken. "She told me she felt humiliated and hurt by my lifelong bad habits," Mathis told the *Detroit News.* He promised he would mend his ways and, fortunately for Mathis, his case came before a Wayne County Circuit Court judge named Charles Kaufman. The judge gave Mathis a choice between entering a maximum-security prison in Jackson, Michigan, or earning his General Equivalency Degree (GED). He chose the degree path, and soon began studying for the GED.

At a Glance . . .

Born April 5, 1960, in Detroit, MI; son of Alice Mathis; married to Linda (a school administrator); children: Camara, Gregory, Amir. *Education:* Eastern Michigan University, B.S., 1984; University of Detroit, J.D., 1988. *Politics:* Democrat.

Career: City Council, Detroit, MI, assistant to council member Clyde Cleveland,1984-88; Office of the Mayor of the City of Detroit, manager of neighborhood city hall, 1989-93; admitted to the bar of the State of Michigan, 1992; chief of staff, Detroit City Council member Brenda Scott, 1993; attorney in private practice, Detroit, 1993-95; 36th District Court of the State of Michigan, judge, 1995-98; host of *Judge Mathis,* a reality-based courtroom show, Warner Brothers Television, 1999-.

Awards: Man of the Year, Southern Christian Leadership Conference, 1995; specialtributes from the Michigan state legislature, from Detroit Mayor Dennis Archer, and from the Detroit City Council, all 1995.

Member: Reclaim Our Youth, chair, 1993-, Young Adults Asserting Themselves (YAAT), founder and chair, 1986-, National Rainbow Coalition.

Addresses: *Office*—c/o Warner Brothers Domestic Television, 4000 Warner Blvd., Burbank, CA 91522.

Pursued a Career in Law

Mathis's decision to turn his life around was strengthened by his mother's death from cancer not long after he made his promise to her. He earned his GED, and applied for admission to Eastern Michigan University. "I got there on the university's affirmative action program. My first couple of years at Eastern were tough," he recounted in the *Detroit News* interview with Kiska. Mathis earned a B.S. degree in 1984, and had become involved in local Detroit politics. He often took the bus from college in Ypsilanti, Michigan, about an hour outside of Detroit, to the downtown offices of Detroit City Council President Erma Henderson, where he worked as an unpaid intern. Mathis also worked for the mayoral campaigns of Coleman A. Young, the city's longtime mayor.

After graduating from Eastern Michigan, Mathis was hired as an assistant to another Detroit city council member, and began law school at the University of Detroit. He also co-founded an outreach program called Young Adults Asserting Themselves (YAAT) to help at-risk teens in the city find jobs. Mathis earned his law degree in 1988, and then passed the state bar exam. However, Michigan bar authorities were wary of his juvenile record, and prevented him from practicing law for four years. Mathis's life story intrigued some in the entertainment industry, and he was approached about selling his story for a made-for-television movie. In the meantime, Mathis ran a neighborhood city hall and served as the chief of staff for another Detroit city council member.

Inner City Miracle

Mathis eventually obtained his law license, and became an attorney in private practice in 1993. In 1994, he decided to run for a seat on the bench of the 36th District Court, Michigan's busiest court. Mathis won the election, becoming the youngest jurist ever elected to the bench of this court, which is located in downtown Detroit. "I'm living proof that people can change," he told *Detroit News* writer Kim Trent. "My being on the bench will show some of these hopeless black children that they can achieve, that they don't have to be in the streets."

Mathis spent three years as a judge, and always tried to provide the same guidance that Kaufman had given him. His inspirational story became the basis for a musical play, *Inner City Miracle,* which Mathis co-wrote with local playwright Ron Milner. The play, which featured several gospel-flavored numbers, chronicled Mathis's life from his Herman Gardens childhood to his success as an attorney. "The story here to me is the mother who did all she could to raise four boys in the projects and instill in us a foundation of education and spiritual values," Mathis told *Detroit Free Press* theater critic Lawrence DeVine. "But education and spiritual values, my mother taught me that; now we're using a show like this to help take that to the new young."

Mathis also related to DeVine that being a celebrity was a new experience for him, but he saw it as a continuation of his work with YAAT—which was the recipient of the show's ticket revenues—and other youth groups. "I wouldn't have wanted this except I thought it would inspire street youth to give up the street," he said in the *Free Press* interview. "To give them hope. To encourage young single mothers to have hope, and to encourage people to respect and help those single mothers."

In late 1998, Warner Brothers Domestic Television offered Mathis his own dispute-resolution show, which is filmed in Chicago and debuted on several stations across the United States early in 1999. Plaintiffs in Chicago's small-claims court are given the option of allowing Mathis to decide their case on television.

Judge Mathis is one of several reality-based court shows in syndication but, unlike the others, is one-hour in length. The show's format allows Mathis to review and adjudicate four different cases on each show. "I often try and provide those who come before me with successful living advice, in addition to a sentence," he told *Detroit Free Press* writer Darci McConnell. "When millions of viewers see that, hopefully they'll be able to take some of the advice and apply it to their own lives."

Back in his hometown of Detroit, Mathis has been mentioned as a potential candidate for the city's mayoral contest in 2001. Married to a school administrator in Detroit, he is also the father of three children. Just before the school year ended in 2000, Mathis toured several Detroit schools and spoke before the assembled students. "I know the challenges they face and it's really touching to inspire this group in particular," Mathis told a reporter from the *Detroit News,* Jeneil C. Johnson, who accompanied him on one visit. "If they keep the faith and believe in themselves, they can achieve their dreams and lead the world."

Selected writings

(With Ron Milner) *Inner City Miracle* (play), produced at the Masonic Temple, Detroit, 1997.

Sources

Broadcasting & Cable, January 11, 1999, pp. 42-43.
Detroit Free Press, November 10, 1997; December 28, 1998.
Detroit News, November 30, 1994, p. B3; November 12, 1997; February 3, 1998; January 6, 1999; September 11, 1999; June 9, 2000.

—Carol Brennan

Ralph Metcalfe

1910–1978

Olympic track star, Congressman

Ralph Metcalfe gained national attention as an African American pioneer not just in his first career as a sprinter known as "the world's fastest human," but also in his second, as a U.S. Congressman representing part of the city of Chicago. He was present at, and shaped the outcomes of, two of the most crucial conflicts of the twentieth century. His track-and-field career culminated in the 1936 Olympic Games in Berlin, Germany, where Metcalfe and fellow sprinter Jesse Owens dealt a crucial public-relations blow to Nazi dictator Adolf Hitler and his theories of white supremacy. Later, as a Chicago politician, Metcalfe broke with the city's Democratic machine to denounce the often racist tactics of the city's police department.

Born in Atlanta, Georgia, on May 30, 1910, Metcalfe was the third child of laborer Clarence Metcalfe and his wife Mamie. Like many other southern African Americans, the Metcalfes moved north in their search for a better quality of life in the Midwest's rapidly growing industrial cities. Clarence Metcalfe found work of the most difficult kind by taking a job at Chicago's notorious stockyards. Metcalfe's mother made dresses, and young Ralph was put to work part time to help the family make ends meet. The family's life was not easy, but it offered enough stability that Metcalfe was able to stay in Chicago's Tilden Technical High School and pursue the athletic skills that became obvious when he joined the school's track team at the age of 15.

A national high-school sprint champion in 1929, Metcalfe entered Marquette University. He quickly began to shatter National Collegiate Athletic Association (NCAA) records, becoming captain of the track team and winning the title of National Collegiate Champion for three years running between 1932 and 1934. Metcalfe made the 1932 U.S. Olympic team, winning the silver medal in the 100-meter dash after finishing in a famous record-time dead heat with Eddie Tolan, who was declared the winner after officials reviewed films of the race. Metcalfe also took the bronze in the 200-meter race. He excelled in intercollegiate competition over the next several years, winning NCAA championships in the 100- and 220-yard dashes in 1933 and 1934, and taking several Amateur Athletic Union (AAU) crowns.

Metcalfe gained more experience in international competition as part of a select U.S. track-and-field team. Despite his athletic stardom, he did not neglect his studies. In 1936, after winning election as senior class

At a Glance . . .

Born in Atlanta, GA, on May 30, 1910; died in Chicago, IL, on October 10, 1978. married Madalynne Fay Young on July 20, 1947; children: Ralph Jr. *Education:* Marquette University, B. Phil., 1936; University of Southern California, master's degree in physical education, 1939. *Military service:* U.S. Army, 1943-46.

Career: Champion sprinter and U.S. Congressional Representative. NCAA champion in 100- and 200-meter sprints, 1932, 1933, 1934; U.S. Olympic medalist in two events, LosAngeles Olympic Games, 1932; silver medal in 100-meter dash, gold medal in 400-meter relay, Berlin, Germany Olympic Games, 1936; track coach and instructor in several subjects, Xavier University, New Orleans, 1936-42; director, Chicago Department of Civil Rights, 1946-49;named to Illinois State Athletic Commission, 1949; elected alderman, Chicago City Council, 1955; U.S. congressman, 1970-78.

president, Metcalfe received his bachelor's degree. That fall Metcalfe competed for the United States once again in the Olympics, and found himself at a historic confluence of politics and sports. Nazi dictator Adolf Hitler had intended that the 1936 Olympic Games, which were held in Berlin, Germany, would be a showcase for his theories of white (or "Aryan") genetic superiority. The predominantly African American U.S. track squad arrived in Germany in an atmosphere charged with tension.

Little did Hitler know that Metcalfe and the legendary Jesse Owens would spoil those plans. Metcalfe, who maintained a lifelong friendship with Owens and spurred him to even greater athletic heights, took the silver medal in the 100-meter dash behind Owens. The two then joined forces on the U.S. 400-meter relay team, opening up a 15-meter margin over their nearest competition and setting a record that would last for 20 years, an eternity in track-and-field terms. The Olympic medal ceremony, at which Owens insisted that Metcalfe step onto the highest platform of the medal stage, crowned Metcalfe's track career.

From 1936 to 1942, Metcalfe coached track and taught physical education and political science at Xavier University, a historically black institution in New Orleans. Along the way, he worked toward a master's degree in physical education at the University of Southern California, earning that degree in 1939. Metcalfe's career as an educator was interrupted by the World War II military draft. He achieved the rank of first lieutenant in the Army, and received the Legion of Merit award for his work as a physical training officer with an Army transportation unit in Louisiana. Returning home to Chicago after the war, Metcalfe briefly sold insurance, but the wider world he had seen in the Army fired his ambition to work for equality between the races. He began to think about a career in politics, and landed two government jobs that helped to pave the way. From 1946 to 1949 he was the director of Chicago's newly created Department of Civil Rights, then a sub-agency of the Commission on Human Relations. In 1949, Metcalfe was named to the Illinois State Athletic Commission. That year, he began to work his way up the ladder of Chicago's famed Democratic Party machine, volunteering as an assistant precinct captain—a get-out-the-vote worker—in the city's Third Ward.

Four years of work in the political trenches were rewarded with an appointment as Third Ward committeeman in 1953. This was a position of considerable power in the Chicago political hierarchy because Democratic ward officials, not professional civil service employees, controlled the dispensing of city jobs. In 1955, Metcalfe was elected to the Chicago City Council. That year, a politically savvy young Irishman named Richard Daley was elected mayor. As a loyal cog in the Democratic machine, Metcalfe became a staunch Daley ally.

Metcalfe became one of the most powerful African American politicians in Chicago, rising to the chairmanship of the council's building and zoning committee. However, he was increasingly troubled by suggestions from black activists that he was acting as a puppet of the Democratic machine. This machine was dominated by white ethnic blocs and was seen as having done little to better the lot of Chicago's large African American population. When the South Side's longtime African American congressman, William Dawson, retired before the 1970 election cycle, Metcalfe won the Democratic primary to succeed him. With the support of the party machine, he also won handily in November. Metcalfe's election set the stage for a late-life conversion.

Chicago's police department was known for its ruthless treatment of African American residents, and Metcalfe irked Daley in 1972 by speaking out against police abuses. His break with Daley became permanent when he refused to support Daley's candidate for the post of Cook County state's attorney, Edward Hanrahan. Hanrahan had engineered a notorious 1969 police raid on Chicago's Black Panther party headquarters, which resulted in the death of activist Fred Hampton. Daley retaliated by supporting Metcalfe's primary opponents in subsequent primary elections, but Metcalfe's stature in the African American community was reaffirmed when he won reelection handily on three separate occasions.

According to *Notable Black American Men,* Metcalfe told a 1972 meeting of the activist group People United to Save Humanity (PUSH) that he had "turned black." Over his four terms in Congress, he emerged as a spokesman for liberal causes, championing job and housing bills, increased access to health care, and consumer protection. Metcalfe is also noted for his role in working out the treaty that eventually returned control of the Panama Canal to the country in which it is located. Metcalfe died of a probable heart attack at his home in Chicago on October 10, 1978. Many observers believe that his challenge to Mayor Daley paved the way for the election of Chicago's first African American mayor, Harold Washington, in 1982.

Sources

Books

Barone, Michael, Grant Ujifusa, and Douglas Matthews, *The Almanac of American Politics 1978,* Dutton, 1978.

Smith, Jessie Carney, ed., *Notable Black American Men,* Gale, 1999.

Who's Who Among Black Americans, Northbrook, IL: Who's Who, 1978.

Periodicals

Jet, October 10, 1994, p. 29.

New York Times, November 6, 1978.

Sports Illustrated, December 27, 1999.

—James M. Manheim

Chante Moore

1970(?)—

Vocalist

When singer Chante Moore released her first album, *Precious,* in 1992, it immediately hit the charts. Her follow-up albums, *A Love Supreme* (1994) and *This Moment Is Mine* (1999), have further established her reputation as a powerful singer and songwriter. Moore also gained fans when she performed on the soundtracks for the hit films *Waiting to Exhale* in 1995 and *How Stella Got Her Groove Back* in 1998. In 1995, Aldore D. Collier wrote in *Ebony* that "Chante Moore sensuously blends jazz, blues, and pop to woo and enrapture listeners with lush romantic ballads about ongoing, and in some cases, unrequited love. Her videos for hit songs such as 'It's Alright' and 'Love's Taken Over' are filled with passionate, dreamy images of sexy women professing undying and unyielding love."

Moore's third album, *This Moment Is Mine,* takes a slightly different approach. "The new record brought out a part of me that may have been missing from my first two albums," she told David Nathan of *Billboard.* "It shows that I'm not just a jazzy R&B singer, but that there are different and diverse ways for me to be produced." She also co-wrote 10 of the 12 songs on *This Moment Is Mine.* According to a reviewer for imusic.com, Moore "further hones the exceptional songwriting skills displayed on her first two albums, *Precious* and *A Love Supreme.* From the glistening first strains of 'If I Gave Love,' straight through to the towering affirmative closing of the title cut, it's evident *This Moment Is Mine* is the crown jewel of Chante Moore's illustrious career thus far."

Moore was born in San Francisco, California, the youngest daughter of Larry and Virginia Moore. Her father was a minister at the Church of God in Christ, and the family—which included an older brother, Kelvin, and an older sister, La Tendre—was deeply religious. The family was also musical: Moore's father played the piano, and her brother played the drums. As a child, Moore performed in the church choir, and loved to sing along to her parents' gospel records at home. "I sang all the time, all the time," she told Collier of *Ebony.* "My family used to make me be quiet. They would say, 'Shut up, Chante. Don't sing all the time.' I didn't care how I sounded. It was a release for me. I sang with all the gospel albums, primarily Andrae Crouch and Edwin Hawkins."

When Moore was 12-years-old, the family moved to San Diego. Four years later, she was asked to play Dorothy in a production of the musical *The Wiz,* an

At a Glance . . .

Born in San Francisco, CA; daughter of Larry Moore, a minister, and Virginia Moore; children: Sophia Milan Hardison.

Career: Recorded the solo albums *Precious,* 1992, *A Love Supreme,*1994, and *This Moment Is Mine,* 1999; contributed vocals to the film soundtracks for*Waiting to Exhale,* 1995 and *How Stella Got Her Groove Back,* 1998; acting roles in *The Fan,* 1996, and *Shake, Rattle, and Roll: An American Love Story,*1999.

Awards: Voted "Best Female Vocalist" and "Most Promising Newcomer" by *Blues & Soul* magazine, 1993.

Addresses: *Home*—Los Angeles, CA. *Office*—Silas/ MCARecords, 70 Universal City Plaza, 3rd Floor, Universal City, CA 91608.

adaptation of *The Wizard of Oz.* Despite the fact that she enjoyed singing, Moore had no idea that she had any musical talent at all until her performance in the show. "I think I sort of established some sort of measurement of my vocal ability. I didn't know I could touch people vocally," she told Collier of *Ebony.* "Some people said, 'You touched me and your voice is so beautiful, and I was crying at the end when you were singing.' And I'm like, 'Get out of here!'"

Moore had participated in beauty pageants and also tried modeling—but she realized that, at 5'4', she would have a limited future in that career. Flushed with success from her debut in *The Wiz,* she decided to pursue singing professionally. In San Diego, Moore performed in singing and dancing shows, while trying to meet people in the music industry. Her big break came in 1989, when singer El DeBarge saw her perform in the musical *Heat Wave* in Los Angeles. "It was a Motown production and some of their artists came by," Moore told Collier of *Ebony.* "El came backstage to say hello to us, and he and I became friends." DeBarge asked her to sing backup on the song "You Know What I Like," for his upcoming album *In the Storm.* Through her friendship with DeBarge, Moore became friends with his manager, who eventually agreed to manage her as well. "And I didn't even have my demo tape," she told *Ebony.* "I had a manager before I had a deal."

One month later, Moore landed a recording contract with MCA Records. Her debut album, *Precious,* featured seven songs that she had written. When it was released in 1992, it almost immediately went gold. Two songs from the album, "Love's Taken Over" and "It's Alright" became Top Five R&B hits. The first album was so successful that she was featured in a one-hour special, "Candlelight and You: Chante Moore Live" on the cable channel BET. Moore has been compared to vocalists such as Diana Ross, Roberta Flack, and Sade. According to B. Kimberly Taylor, writing in *Contemporary Musicians,* Moore "has seemingly incorporated elements of all three legendary singers: the dulcet tones of Ross, the thoughtful songwriting ability of Flack, and the smooth elegance of Sade." However, Moore told Sharon Dukes of *YSB* magazine, "I don't pattern myself after anyone in particular...I really sound like my mom!"

In 1993 Moore met Kadeem Hardison, a performer on the hit NBC sitcom "A Different World." Later, she and Hardison were asked to co-present an award at the NAACP Image Awards. "We had to go backstage after the awards presentation and talk to the press," Moore told Collier. "By the time we got to the press room, he grabbed my hand and he didn't let it go the whole night." Moore drew on her relationship with Hardison to write the songs for her next album, *A Love Supreme,* which was released in 1994. The album explores the theme of finding the right person, falling in love, and moving toward long-term commitment. Like *Precious, A Love Supreme* quickly went gold. The following year, Moore toured with legendary soul artist Barry White on his Icon World Tour.

Because of her background in gospel music, many people had expected Moore to pursue that genre first. However, she didn't want to be pigeonholed as a gospel artist. "I would love to record a gospel album," Moore told *Ebony,* "First I wanted to establish myself... .People think, 'Okay, you've got that talent. Don't let the devil use you, honey. Let the Lord use you.' But I do. In every interview I talk about the Lord."

Moore waited several years before releasing her third album, *This Moment Is Mine*—a risky move in the ever-changing music industry. "Mindful that people's musical tastes change...she [Moore] was a bit nervous, but very hopeful that fans would continue to embrace her after a layoff of several years," Collier wrote in *Ebony* in 1999. "And they have. Hers is one of the fastest-climbing albums on the charts." In an interview with David Nathan of *Billboard,* Moore explained her reason for delaying the release of *This Moment Is Mine,* "I wanted to wait for the right producers, and although it has been arduous, I'm glad I waited. As much as I've been gone, people have been welcoming me back with open arms, letting me know they've been waiting for this record."

For Moore, the lyrics in *This Moment Is Mine* reflect "personal experiences and those of people close to me," she told *Billboard.* "In between recording songs for the album, I've been transitioning from being a girl to being a mother." The album is dedicated to Moore's mother, Virginia, who died in 1995. Moore co-wrote 10 of the 12 songs on the album, including the hit single "Chante's Got a Man." The idea for the song, she related in *Ebony,* came from a conversation she had with producers Jimmy Jam and Terry Lewis while working on the album in Minneapolis. "Jimmy and Terry tease me a lot because I write a lot of happy songs and I'm always smiling. They were like, 'Come on, we need to write a sad song.' When they teased me, I said, 'Don't get mad at me because I got a man at home.' Jimmy was like, 'That's it! That's the name of the song.' That's how it came about." In fact, the song "Chante's Got a Man," which is about successful relationships between African American men and women, has inspired people to approach her on the street. "Most guys will come up to me and say, 'Thank you. We appreciate that a woman is not down on us. We appreciate you saying good things about us,'" Moore told Collier, "Women come up and they're like: 'So, how do I get a man?' or 'What do you think I should do?' It's funny. I just say, 'Well, love yourself. Be who you are.'"

In addition to her singing career, Moore has had a few small acting roles. She appeared in the film *The Fan* in 1996 and in a TV mini-series *Shake, Rattle, and Roll: An American Love Story* in 1999. While she would be interested in pursuing acting more seriously if the right role came along, Moore stated in *Ebony* that music will always be her top priority.

Moore credits her relationship with God for her success. "The Lord brought me to this," she told *Ebony.* "When people tell me, 'There's something special about you, I tell them it's the Lord, because I couldn't do this without him. He's [the one] who has blessed me."

Sources

Books

Contemporary Musicians, Gale Research, 1998.

Periodicals

Billboard, August 14, 1999; May 1, 1999.
Ebony, May 1995, Sept. 1999.
YSB, April 1995.

Other

Additional information for this profile was obtained from http://imusic.com

—Carrie Golus

Ernest "Dutch" Morial

1929–1989

Former mayor of New Orleans

In 1978, Ernest "Dutch" Morial was sworn in as the first African American mayor of New Orleans, Louisiana. A longtime civil rights activist in the city, Morial enjoyed an impressive career filled with many other firsts, including winning election to the state's House of Representatives as the first African American legislator in that body since the Reconstruction era. Morial died suddenly on Christmas Eve of 1989, but his son, Marc, continued his father's legacy of achievement when he was elected mayor of New Orleans in 1994. The elder Morial had once pointed out that the public sector was the ideal arena in which African Americans might, by default, gain a wealth of leadership skills. "Comparable white people will be presidents of private corporations, but the black has to be in the public sector to succeed," Morial told *U.S. News and World Report* writer Steve Huntley.

Morial was born in October of 1929, and was the youngest of six children. Walter, his father, was a cigar manufacturer, while his mother, Leonie, worked as a tailor. He grew up speaking French, as was common for many established African American New Orleans families during the era. The Morials were black Creoles, the descendants of free blacks who had found refuge in the liberal, European-minded port city of New Orleans. The family were practicing Roman Catholics, and Morial attended both public and parochial schools. At Xavier University—the customary training ground for middle-class African Americans in the city—he excelled academically, and earned his degree in 1951.

In 1954, Morial broke his first barrier in the pre-civil rights era of the Deep South when he became the first African American graduate of Louisiana State University School of Law. He then spent two years with the United States Army intelligence corps, and returned to his hometown to begin working as an attorney. During the late 1950s and early 1960s, he became deeply involved in the burgeoning civil rights movement, and won numerous discrimination cases involving the segregation of Louisiana public schools, New Orleans taxicabs, and the city's recreation department. "He was the last of a very important line of civil rights figures in New Orleans," a history professor in the city, Joseph Logsdon, told *New York Times* obituary writer Frances Frank Marcus. "He was part of a civil rights movement that went all the way back to Reconstruction."

Morial was also active in the New Orleans chapter of the National Association for the Advancement of Col-

At a Glance . . .

Born Ernest Nathan Morial, October 9, 1929, in New Orleans, LA; died of cardiopulmonary collapse, December 24, 1989, in New Orleans, LA; son of Walter (a cigar maker) and Leonie (a tailor) Morial; married Sybil Haydel; children: Marc, Jacques, Juli, Cheri, Monique. *Education:* Xavier University, B.A., 1951; Louisiana State University School of Law, J.D., 1954. *Politics:* Democrat. *Religion:* Roman Catholic. *Military service:* Spent two years with the U.S. Army intelligence corps, mid-1950s.

Career: Attorney in private practice, after 1955; appointed to post with the U.S.Attorney General in Louisiana, 1965; elected to Louisiana House of Representatives as a Democrat, 1967; appointed to Louisiana juvenile court, 1970; elected judge of Fourth CircuitCourt of Appeal, 1972; elected mayor of New Orleans, 1977, reelected, 1982; United States Conference of Mayors, president, 1982-86; Brook, Morial, and Cassibry (attorneys), partner, late1980s.

Member: Democratic National Committee; National Association for the Advancementof Colored People (president, New Orleans chapter, 1962-65).

ored People (NAACP), and served as the chapter president for three years. In 1965, he became the first African American to win appointment to the U.S. Attorney's office in Louisiana. Two years later, he ran as a Democrat and won a seat in the state House of Representatives, making him the first African American to serve in the legislature since the Reconstruction era just after the end of the American Civil War. As a member of the state House, Morial continued to strive for change, sponsoring a bill to eliminate the death penalty in Louisiana, and another that would have granted 18-year-olds the right to vote.

In 1969, Morial ran unsuccessfully for a seat on the New Orleans City Council, but the following year was appointed a judge on the bench of the state juvenile court—where, once again, he became the first African American to achieve that post. In 1972, Louisiana voters gave Morial another pioneering accomplishment with his election to the Fourth Circuit Court of Appeals. At the time, it made him the highest-ranking African American in Louisiana state government. "Dutch wouldn't bend his knee to anyone," Logsdon told the *New York Times*, "but he would cooperate with anyone on the basis of full equality."

Morial resigned from the Appeals Court bench when he decided to campaign for mayor of New Orleans in 1977. Racial barriers in the city, which were supposedly dismantled by federal civil-rights legislation in the 1960s, still existed in some quarters. Some white New Orleanians perceived Morial, with his impressive record of achievement, as being too overconfident for an African American man. Morial, who was running against an Italian American city council member, was forced to tread a thin line between white and African American voters because an overwhelmingly African American turnout might not yield victory. He also weathered some criticism for refusing to meet with white business and civic groups in the city. In November of 1977, Morial captured 51.5 percent of the vote and defeated Joseph V. DiRosa.

In his acceptance speech, the mayor-elect asserted that the victory "speaks eloquently for our city and indicates to the nation and to the South in particular that people in New Orleans recognize quality," according to a report written by Wayne King for the *New York Times*. Morial was sworn in the following spring as the first African American mayor of New Orleans. Although he had the largest constituency of any African American elected official in the South, he dismissed the significance of this achievement. Morial's primary goal was to turn New Orleans around and, as he was quoted as saying in the *New York Times*, alleviate the "urban ills which have created an underclass in American cities. It is not blackness, but executive ability that will solve the problems."

At the time of his election to the mayor's office, New Orleans was the third-poorest major American city. Morial was able to implement several measures and statutes to improve the city's economic health and quality of life. He cut 2,000 jobs out of the city's bloated bureaucracy, a strategy which he combined with general belt-tightening across all departments. Re-elected to a second term in 1982, Morial again captured nearly all of the African American vote and an impressive 14 percent of the white districts. By 1984, he had eliminated a $40-million deficit in the city's finances and balanced the budget. One of Morial's most impressive and lasting achievements during his eight years as mayor, however, was to secure federal funds to spur economic development in New Orleans. For instance, a $102 million appropriation led to the creation of a 7,500-acre industrial district which was predicted to lure over $1 billion in private investment to the city. In addition to the thousands of new jobs that were created, this development also sparked an unusual building boom in downtown New Orleans.

The New Orleans city charter specified that mayors could serve only two consecutive terms. Morial, who was riding a wave of voter approval, introduced a measure to amend the charter. However, his proposal was defeated by referendum in 1985. Morial returned to private practice, and continued his political activism from a more powerful platform—the Democratic National Committee. In 1988, he was invited to serve as senior advisor to the party's presidential candidate, Massachusetts governor Michael Dukakis.

Morial's many supporters in New Orleans tried to convince him to run for mayor in 1990, but he declined to enter the race. The city's problems had worsened since he left office, and "he realized the problems facing the next mayor would be enormous," noted the *New York Times.* During a week of unusually bitter cold weather in New Orleans, Morial left a friend's home and suffered an asthma attack from the cold air. This attack triggered a cardiopulmonary collapse, and he died on December 24, 1989. Morial was survived by his wife, Sybil, and five children. The Reverend Jesse Jackson followed the casket in the funeral procession, and thousands of New Orleanians who remembered their admirably uncompromising mayor lined the streets to mourn his death. Morial even managed to achieve another first after his death, when his son Marc was elected as mayor of New Orleans in 1994. It earned the two men a place in American mayoral history as the first African American father-son duo to lead a major city.

Sources

New Orleans Magazine, December 1993, p. 69.
New York Times, November 14, 1977; December 25, 1989, p. 64.
U.S. News and World Report, March 5, 1984, p. 68.

—Carol Brennan

Marion Motley

1920–1999

Former professional football player

In the late 1940s, African American athletes broke through the color barrier that prevented them from playing professional sports. The most famous example is Jackie Robinson, the first African American player in major league baseball. Less known is the story of Marion Motley, who joined the Cleveland Browns in 1946, becoming one of the first African Americans to play in the National Football League.

"What we did (in football) helped get Jackie into the major leagues," Motley was quoted as saying in a Knight-Ridder Newspapers wire story. "There was a quote from (Dodgers general manager) Branch Rickey, who said, 'If these men can play a contact sport like football, then Jackie Robinson can play baseball.' So we really opened the door in two sports." That achievement would be impressive enough, but Motley, a fullback and linebacker, accomplished far more in his eight years with the Browns. The team won five consecutive championships—four in the All-America Football Conference and one in the NFL—with Motley scoring five touchdowns. In the other three years, the team made it to the title game.

Motley led the NFL in rushing in 1950. One of the largest running backs of his era, he rushed for 4,720 yards in his career and averaged an astounding 5.7 yards per carry. Nevertheless, his top earnings as a professional football player were just $11,500 a year. Blanton Collier, assistant coach for the Browns and later head coach, told the *New York Times* that Motley was "the greatest all-around football player I ever saw. He had no equal as a blocker. He could run with anybody for 30 yards or so. And this man was a great, great linebacker." Paul Zimmerman, writing in *Sports Illustrated,* described Motley as "tireless, devastating, explosive. It's hard to see how you could play the game any better than he did." "I was fortunate to be able to be one of the few to excel at something I liked to do," Motley was quoted as saying in the *New York Times.* "I felt proud to be a black American. Just as Martin Luther King had a dream, let me tell you, without a dream, you can't accomplish anything."

Motley was born on June 5, 1920, in Lessburg, Georgia, and was the son of Shakeful and Blanche (Jones) Motley. When he was three-years-old, his family moved north to Canton, Ohio, where his father found work as a foundry molder. At Canton's McKinley High School, Motley played both basketball and football. During his three years as a star fullback, McKin-

At a Glance . . .

Born on June 5, 1920, Leesburg, GA; died on June 27, 1999, in Cleveland, OH; son of Shakeful and Blanche (Jones) Motley; married Eula Coleman, 1943; children: Raymond, Ronald, George. *Education:* studied at South Carolina State University, 1939-40; University of Nevada-Reno 1940-43. *Military service:* U.S. Navy.

Career: Steel worker, Republic Steel, 1943; played football for U.S. Navy Bluejackets,1945; fullback for the Cleveland Browns, 1946-54; linebacker for Pittsburgh Steelers, 1955;worked four years for the Cleveland Post Office; worked eight years as safety director for an Akron, OH construction company; worked ten years for State of Ohio Lottery; worked at the State of Ohio Department of Youth Services, Akron, OH.

Awards: All-AAFC fullback, 1946-48; selected to the All-Pro team, 1950; All-time AAFC leading rusher; inducted into the Professional Football Hall of Fame, 1968.

ley's football team lost only three times—all to archrival Massillon (Ohio) High School, which was coached by the legendary Paul Brown. Years later, Brown would coach Motley on two different teams: the U.S. Navy Bluejackets, and the Cleveland Browns.

After graduating from high school in 1939, Motley played football for a year at South Carolina State. In 1940, he transferred to the University of Nevada-Reno. During his three years playing for Nevada, the team achieved only a mediocre record, but Motley made some impressive long-distance touchdowns. In a game against San Francisco in 1942, he intercepted a pass and returned it 95 yards for a touchdown. That same year, *Illustrated Football Annual* included Motley on its "All-American Check List," and described him as "a 22-carat back."

After Motley injured his knee in 1943, he left college and returned to Canton, Ohio, where he worked for Republic Steel. "I burned scrap iron out of the steel with a torch, and it'd get awful hot up there on top of the steel where I worked," he was quoted as saying in *A Thinking Man's Guide to Pro Football*. "I honestly think all that heat mended my knee." The same year, Motley married Eula Coleman. The couple would raise three sons. He joined the U.S. Navy in 1944, and was assigned to the Great Lakes Naval Training Station.

In 1945, Motley played football for the U.S. Navy Bluejackets, which was coached by Paul Brown. In the season's final game, the Bluejackets routed Notre Dame by a score of 39-7, and Motley scored on a 44-yard run. "Notre Dame simply could not handle Motley that day," Brown was quoted as saying in the *Biographical Dictionary of American Sports*, "and even had trouble knocking him down as he ran several trap plays that became his specialty over the years."

In 1946, the All-America Football Conference was launched as a competitor to the NFL. One of the AAFC teams, the Cleveland Browns, recruited their first African American player, Bill Willis. At the time, there were only two African American players in the NFL, and none in the AAFC.

The Browns decided they needed to recruit another African American player to be Willis' roommate for away games, so they invited Motley to try out. "After a few practices, one of the white lineman, Mike Scarry, told Paul Brown, 'Either you get Motley for our side or I go over to his side,'" Motley later recalled in the *New York Times*. "After that, I didn't worry about being Bill Willis' roommate. I wanted to be the best fullback." Motley signed up with the Browns for $4,500 a year.

During his rookie season, the 26-year-old Motley averaged 8.2 yards per carry and scored five times. With Motley on the team, the Browns dominated the league, capturing All-America Football Conference titles every season between 1946 and 1949. Motley was the AAFC's all-time leading rusher, with 3,024 yards.

In 1950, the National Football League absorbed three AAFC teams—the Browns, the San Francisco 49ers and the Baltimore Colts—and the AAFC went out of business. Many football fans thought that the Browns would be outclassed in the NFL. However, Motley and the Browns—which included such all-time greats as quarterback Otto Graham, wide receivers Mac Speedie and Dante Lavelli, offensive tackle/kicker Lou Groza, and offensive guard Bill Willis—set out to prove them wrong. "None contributed more than the 6-foot-1-inch, 238-pound Motley, who was fast, explosive, and hard-working," Frank Litsky wrote in the *New York Times*.

In the Browns' first year in the NFL, Motley led the league in rushing, with 810 yards on 140 carries, and was selected to play in the first Pro Bowl. The Browns won the championship that year, defeating the Los Angeles Rams 30-28. They also reached the championship game each of the next three seasons.

While Motley possessed a sprinter's speed, he mostly ran plays inside the tackles. "He made most of his yardage on trap plays, on which a defensive lineman was allowed to penetrate the line of scrimmage, then was trapped, allowing Motley to run through the vacated area," Litsky wrote in the *New York Times*.

Motley averaged 5.7 yards per carry during his career. He also excelled on draw plays and screen passes, and was one of Cleveland's best defensive linebackers.

Motley was large enough to block defensive ends by himself, and quick enough to run away from—or run over—linebackers and cornerbacks. "He saved my life many a time," Hall of Famer and teammate Otto Graham told the (Cleveland) *Plain Dealer.* In the *Biographical Dictionary of American Sports,* Paul Brown praised Motley as "our greatest fullback ever because not only was he a great runner, but also no one ever blocked better—and no one ever cared more about his team."

Motley's commitment to the team also extended to its individual players. *In A Thinking Man's Guide to Pro Football,* Paul Zimmerman related a story that demonstrated Motley's kindness to teammate Joe Spencer. "One day after practice I was counting my pennies and trying to figure out the cheapest way to get home," Spencer said. "Marion didn't say a word—except 'Get in,' when he pulled up his car. So every day we used to drive to practice together and drive home, one of the greatest stars in the game and a guy just fighting to stay on the club. But that's the way he was. If you were his teammate, he would do anything for you."

As two of the first African American players in the NFL, Motley and Willis had to endure undisguised racism both on and off the field. "All the hate that Jackie Robinson faced in baseball, Motley and Willis faced first in football," Ray Didinger noted in a Knight-Ridder Newspapers wire story. "Like Robinson, they knew if they failed to produce, or if they fought back at those who cursed and spat on them, they would set back the cause of all black players." "It was rough for us on the field," Motley recalled in an interview with George Vecsey of the *New York Times.* "The officials called back touchdowns of mine. Players stepped on my hands so much that I still have scars on the backs of them." Football officials deliberately looked the other way as opponents stuck their fingers in his eyes, or punched him when he was lying on the ground.

Motley and Willis never complained to officials, or said anything to a player who had fouled them. Instead, their strategy was to go after that opponent—legally—in the next play. "We hit him hard enough that we didn't have to say anything," Motley told Ray Didinger of Knight-Ridder Newspapers. After his first year in the NFL, when Motley led the league in rushing, attitudes began to change. "One day, a guy stepped on my hand and the ref picked the ball up and walked off 15 yards," Motley recalled in an interview with Didinger. "The ref said, 'Personal foul. And if you do it again, you're out of the game.' I knew then I had respect."

During his last four seasons with the Browns, Motley's old knee injuries began to worsen. He was sidelined during the 1954 season, and was traded to the Pittsburgh Steelers the following year. Motley played five of the first six games, mostly as a blocking back for punts and field goals. "I felt my speed coming back when I ran the sprints," he was quoted as saying in *A Thinking Man's Guide to Pro Football.* "Then I hurt my knee again, and that was it. I told them I was through."

After retiring from football as an active player, Motley struggled to find a coaching job in the NFL. But while the league was ready to accept African American players, it did not provide a welcoming environment for the hiring of African American coaches. As Motley recalled in a 1982 interview with George Vecsey of the *New York Times,* he inquired about a coaching job with his old team, the Browns, only to have a team official ask, "Have you tried the steel mills?" Motley also expressed bitterness at his meager NFL salary, and the fact that the Browns continued to use plays he had originated, while refusing to let him coach. "They were ready to let me run with the ball," he told Vecsey. "But they weren't ready to pay me—or let me think." Motley worked briefly as a scout for the Washington Redskins, and coached a women's football team in 1967. However, his dream of coaching in the NFL would go unfulfilled.

In the years after his retirement from football, Motley held several different jobs. He worked for four years with the Cleveland Post Office. This was followed by eight years as safety director for a construction company in Akron, Ohio, and ten years with the State of Ohio Lottery. He ended his career at the State of Ohio Department of Youth Services in Akron.

Motley's accomplishments as a football player were not forgotten, however. In 1968, he became the second African American player to be voted into the Professional Football Hall of Fame. As his presenter, Motley chose Willis, his old teammate and roommate from the Browns. In the 1971 book *A Thinking Man's Guide to Pro Football,* Paul Zimmerman chose Motley as the greatest football player of all time. While Motley's statistics were impressive, "it's a kind of meaningless way of evaluating this remarkable player," Zimmerman wrote. "It would be like trying to describe a waterfall in terms of gallons per second, or a sunset in terms of light units."

On June 27, 1999, Motley died after a battle with prostate cancer. Fellow Hall of Famers Dante Lavelli, Lou Groza, Bill Willis, Leroy Kelly, Paul Warfield, Joe Perry, John Henry Johnson, Ollie Matson and Dick Lane were honorary pallbearers at his funeral. Shortly after Motley's death John Bankert, executive director of the Pro Football Hall of Fame told the (Cleveland) *Plain Dealer* that Motley was "a man of great courage and character. A champion in every respect, he represented pro football with dignity and pride. I am proud to have known him and called him 'friend.'"

Sources

Books

Biographical Dictionary of American Sports: Football, edited by David L. Porter, Greenwood Press, 1987.

A Thinking Man's Guide to Pro Football, by Paul Zimmerman, E. P. Dutton, 1971.

Periodicals

Detroit Free Press, June 28, 1999.

New York Times, Feb. 26, 1982; Sept. 25, 1997; June 28, 1999.

(Cleveland) *Plain Dealer,* June 30, 1999.

Sports Illustrated, July 5, 1999.

Other

Additional information for this profile was obtained from the *Knight-Ridder/Tribune News Service,* Oct. 19, 1995; and www.nfl.com

—Carrie Golus

Ozzie Newsome

1956—

Former professional football player, sports executive

Ozzie Newsome completed a remarkable journey from a small town in Alabama to the National Football League's ultimate shrine—the Hall of Fame. However, he was not content simply with his amazing success on the field. Newsome stayed in professional football as an executive with the Baltimore Ravens, and developed a reputation as a shrewd evaluator of talent. As vice president for player personnel for the Ravens, he is one of the most powerful African American executives in professional sports.

Newsome was born on March 16, 1956 in Muscle Shoals, Alabama, and was the third of five children. After winning the state football championship in high school, Newsome decided to attend the University of Alabama and play for legendary coach Paul "Bear" Bryant. In four years with the Crimson Tide, he played in 48 straight games. During Newsome's time at Alabama, the Crimson Tide won three Southeast Conference Championships and he was a consensus All-America. Not only did he finish his college career with 102 catches and 2,070 receiving yards, he revolutionized the game. Historically, the tight end served as a sixth offensive lineman whom the quarterback could dump the ball to if he was in trouble. However, Newsome's size, speed, and soft hands gave him the ability not only to block, but also outrun linebackers and go deep. The Cleveland Browns were so impressed with Newsome that they made him their first-round draft choice in 1978.

The Browns received a preview of Newsome's greatness the first time he touched the ball during an NFL game. Newsome took the ball on a reverse, bolted 33 yards, and scored a touchdown that helped to lift the Browns to a victory over the San Francisco 49ers. Once he reached the end zone, Newsome spiked the ball in celebration. He was immediately horrified by his spur-of-the-moment celebration as he told the Associated Press at his Hall of Fame press conference: "At Alabama, we were always taught to show our class. And when you got into the end zone, act like you'd been there before. I never did it [spike the ball after a touchdown] again, and Monday morning I called coach Bryant and apologized. He hadn't realized I had done it. He just appreciated that I was thoughtful enough to call him and let him know I had come out of character." After his rookie season in Cleveland, Newsome was named the Browns' Offensive Most Valuable Player, the first rookie in 25 years to accomplish that feat. He was named to the All-Pro team in 1979, an

At a Glance . . .

Born on March 16, 1956 in Muscle Shoals, AL; children: Michael. *Education:* Graduated from the University of Alabama.

Career: Played four years at the University of Alabama, 1974-77; selected in the first round of the NFL draft by the Cleveland Browns, 1978; was a fixture as the Brown's tightend and an offensive captain, 1978-90; vice president of player personnel for the Baltimore Ravens, 1996-.

Awards: First Team All-American, 1977; NFL All-Pro, 1979, 1984; selected to the Pro Bowl, 1982, 1985, 1986; received the Ed Block Courage Award, 1986; received the Whizzer White Award for community service, 1990; named to the College Football Hall of Fame, 1994; enshrined in the NFL's Hall of Fame, 1999.

Addresses: *Office*—c/o The Baltimore Ravens, 11001 Owings Mills Boulevard, Owings Mills, MD, 21117.

honor he would again receive after the 1984 season. In addition to these two all-league honors, Newsome was named to the Pro Bowl following the 1982, 1985, and 1986 seasons. During this period, the Browns played in three AFC championship games.

Newsome was not only talented, but extremely tough. In 1986, he won the Ed Block Courage award for playing in spite of injury and keeping his prolific receiving streak alive. He caught passes in 150 straight games, a streak that lasted almost a decade. After playing in parts of three decades, Newsome retired in 1990 after squeezing in one last honor—the NFL Players Association Whizzer White Award for community service. As offensive captain for the Browns, he racked up some startling achievements. Newsome played in 197 consecutive games, finishing his career as the most prolific tight end in NFL history. He made 662 receptions for 7,980 yards and 47 touchdowns. Perhaps the most amazing statistic is that in the last 557 times he touched the ball, Newsome did not fumble.

Following the end of his playing career, Newsome remained with the Browns first in a coaching role and then as part of the front office. Although his post-football career was going well in Cleveland, the team and its owner Art Modell were in a battle with the city over whether or not a new stadium should be built for the Browns. Modell threatened to move the team if he did not receive a new stadium. In 1996, he made good on his threat. The old Cleveland Browns moved to Baltimore and became the Baltimore Ravens. Newsome moved with the team to Baltimore. He told the Associated Press that the decision was a difficult one, "With me, it was an opportunity as a minority to get one of the highest-ranking jobs in professional sports." As vice president of player personnel, Newsome is responsible for the future of the Ravens franchise. In four drafts, he selected three Pro-Bowl caliber players—Jonathan Ogden, Ray Lewis, and Jermaine Lewis. While Newsome is proud of his role in Baltimore's success, he realizes that he must continue to produce and set an example of what an African American sports executive can accomplish. He told Thomas George of *The New York Times* about the pressure inherent in his job: "I've been evaluated all of my life, even though now my job is one of constant evaluation. There are blacks out there, former players and others, willing to climb their way up. A lot of people, owners included, are looking to see how I do. I am being compared closely with my peers."

The crowning achievement of Newsome's professional football career was his induction into the Hall of Fame in Canton, Ohio in August of 1999. Before the induction ceremony, Newsome nervously wondered how the Ohio-based crowd would react to a man who had been a Brown and then moved to Baltimore with Modell. He told Marla Ridenour of *Knight Ridder Newspapers* about his mind set going into the ceremony: "You expect the worst and you work from there. But it came down to something I learned from Coach Bryant. He said: 'In all circumstances, show your class.' As I thought about what can and cannot happen, I kept reminding myself, 'Just show your class.'" Newsome's fears proved to be groundless as the chant of "Ozzie, Ozzie, Ozzie," went up from the throngs of Browns' fans who attended the ceremony. In his long journey from Muscle Shoals, Alabama to the Hall of Fame, Newsome made the trip with grace and class.

Sources

The New York Times, August 7, 1999.

Other

Additional material for this profile was found on the worldwide web at http://cbs.sportsline.com/u/oneon one/ozzienewsome.html
http://nfl.com/news/990803hofbios.html
http://www.bergen.com/giants/hall08199908082.htm
http://cnnsi.com/football/nfl/news/1999/08/05/ newsome_hall_ap/

—Michael J. Watkins

Thandie Newton

1972—

Actress

Thandie Newton has established an impressive list of screen credits since making her film debut in 1992. Her work has run the gamut from "art house" pictures such as director Bernardo Bertolucci's *Besieged,* to Oprah Winfrey's highly touted production of *Beloved,* to the big budget action blockbuster *Mission: Impossible 2.* Although Newton has not yet broken through to stardom, it is just a matter of time before her name will go above the title. "With her physical gifts and intelligence, she could do whatever she wants," Edward Saxon, a co-producer of *Beloved,* said of Newton to Dan Jewel of *People.*

Thandie (pronounced Tan-dee) Newton was born in Zambia in 1972 to an English father, Nick, a lab technician and artist, and an Zimbabwean mother, Nyasha, a nurse. Newton's full first name is Thandiwe which means "beloved" in Zulu. When Newton was five years old her family, including her younger brother James, moved to England to escape political unrest in Africa. Newton was brought up in Penzance, a port city in southwest England, and experienced few racial problems during her childhood. "I am both Zimbabwean and English. I'm from nowhere. Because of my parents, however, I realized it was a strength, not a weakness. You're a bridge; you legitimize mixed raceness. Is it right? Natural? Beautiful? Yes. Race problems are just made up," Newton told *Time.*

In Hollywood, Newton has discovered that her background is sometimes an asset since it makes her difficult to classify. "I'm thrilled that I can get right past prejudgements. I walk into a room in L.A. and [the way people see me] might seem to be a racial thing. But as soon as I open my mouth, it isn't about being Black anymore. Suddenly it's about being English," Newton told Chuck Arnold of *People.* At other times she finds the movie industry is baffled by the idea of a dark skinned woman with a posh British accent. "I get stuff here in Hollywood. Really high-powered people who make really, really, really dodgy suggestions about what it is to be Black. Honestly, it would leave your mouth open. It's stupid, stupid, stupid!" Newton explained to *Time.*

Newton studied dancing at London's Arts Educational School as a teenager, but a back injury caused her to switch to the school's acting program. At 16, she auditioned for a part in the movie *Flirting,* a gentle story about Australian boarding school students in the 1960s. "I was dreadful," Newton said of her *Flirting*

At a Glance . . .

Born Thandiwe Newton in Zambia in 1972; daughter of Nick (a lab technician and artist) and Nyasha Newton (a nurse); married to Oliver Parker, a screenwriter. *Education:* Cambridge University, England, bachelor's degree in anthropology, 1994.

Career: Film actress; began acting career with *Flirting,* 1992. Other films include *Interview with the Vampire,* 1994; *Jefferson in Paris,* 1995; *The Young Americans,* 1995; *The Journey of August King,* 1996; *The Leading-Man,* 1997; *Gridlock'd,* 1997; *Loaded (a.k.a The Bloody Weekend),* 1997; *Beloved,* 1998; *Besieged,* 1999; *Mission: Impossible 2,* 2000; *ItWas an Accident,* 2000.

Addresses: *Home*—West London, England. *Agent*—Rick Nicita, Creative Artists Agency, 9830 Wilshire Blvd., Beverly Hills, CA 90212.

audition to Gregg Kilday of *Los Angeles Magazine.* "I thought acting meant that you had to orate and put on a disguise." Despite her low opinion of the audition, Newton got the part of a Ugandan exchange student who falls in love with a white boy, played by Noah Taylor. Jay Carr of the *Boston Globe* called *Flirting* "Solid, well-made coming of age stuff...the tenderly inscribed teens played by Taylor and Newton will live in your memory." *The Motion Picture Guide* added that "the exceptionally pretty Newton is graceful and charming" as the exchange student.

After the filming of *Flirting* was complete, the teenage Newton began affair with the movie's director, John Duigan, who was in his forties. It was a move that Newton now regrets. "Getting into the film business that young wasn't terrific. It is exploitative and there is a cut-off point. At the end of a shoot everyone disperses and you're left hanging. For me, coming from school and that sort of teacher-student dynamic, it was in the fabric of my being that I would say yes to a question," Newton told Ariel Swartley of the *New York Times.*

After finishing secondary school, Newton attended Cambridge University where she earned a degree in anthropology. While at Cambridge, Newton concentrated on academics and, as she told Kilday, looked upon acting as "something I did on holidays from school." Coincidentally, it was while Newton was studying the slave trade that she received two film offers which called for her to portray a slave. "I thought, 'How better to fuel my interest in this than to work in movies'?" Newton explained to Lisa Kennedy of *Interview.*

In *Jefferson in Paris,* which was released in 1995, Newton played Sally Hemings, the young slave owned by Thomas Jefferson. Directed by James Ivory and starring Nick Nolte as Jefferson, the controversial film portrayed Hemings as an alluring vixen who enjoys a warm relationship with her brooding master. In the 1996 film *The Journey of August King,* Newton played a runaway slave who is reluctantly assisted on her northward trek by a young white farmer, played by Jason Patric. The film was also directed by John Duigan. Although she has negative feelings about their romantic association, Newton has praise for Duigan's directorial talent. "John is a very good director, and he allowed me to see that film acting is subtle— sometimes you must do less than you would do in life," she told Kilday. Newton worked with Duigan a third time on the 1997 backstage drama *The Leading Man,* which co-starred Jon Bon Jovi.

Newton again portrayed a slave in *Beloved,* the 1998 screen version of the Toni Morrison novel. In this mystical film Newton played the title character, a ghost who haunts the memory of her grieving mother, played by Oprah Winfrey. The complicated role called for Newton to enact infant behavior, including smearing food over her face, vomiting, crying, and walking and talking as if she had just learned how. "You can do so much if you are uninhibited with your body. And your voice. To me, there's a melody behind every character's speech pattern," Newton explained to Swartley. *Beloved*'s director, Jonathan Demme, marveled at the croaking voice Newton developed for the character of Beloved. "The voice was a big part of the character, and she was literally brilliant," Demme told *Time.* Margo Jefferson of the *New York Times* called Newton's performance in *Beloved* "uncanny and amazingly bold...she is terrifying to watch." Michael O'Sullivan of the *Washington Post* wrote that Newton as Beloved "steals the show playing a part that is meant to be interpreted not just as tetched person or a ghost of the dead but as a metaphor for the vestiges of a horrific past." Newton does not consider the prevalence of slave roles as evidence of Hollywood's limited view of African Americans. "People say, 'Oh, you've played a slave girl three times,' but I say: 'Get over it. Just look at the films. They're all completely different," she told Swartley.

Newton's list of leading men includes the late Tupac Shakur. The two appeared together in the 1997 sardonic comedy *Gridlock'd,* which was directed by Vondie Curtis-Hall. Shakur played a musician who tries to overcome his drug addiction after a singer friend (Newton) overdoses. Newton said to *Time* about Shakur, "I was rude to him. 'What's that tatoo?' I'd ask him. We had a flirty-rude relationship."

In director Bernardo Bertolucci's 1999 drama *Besieged,* Newton played an African medical student living in Rome who is earning a living by working as a housekeeper for an eccentric English pianist, played by David Thewlis. Newton used her Zimbabwean mother as a model for the African character's style. "That's my mum. I would sit watching, especially in the mornings, when she would just get up out of bed and put on her cloth in such a swift movement," Newton said to Swartley.

Newton's first worked with Tom Cruise in 1994's *Interview with the Vampire,* a film in which Newton had a small role. Cruise was so impressed with Newton that her name was quickly mentioned for the role of his leading lady in *Mission Impossible 2.* The lead female role was especially important since Cruise and director John Woo wanted to give the film a stronger romantic story line than most other action films. Initially, Newton was not enthusiastic about being "the girl" in an action thriller. "When Tom and John Woo asked me to audition, they said it would have a love story. I said 'Yeah, yeah, yeah. The girl's going to be screaming while the men are showing off their muscles," Newton told *Time.* Once Newton was signed to the part of international jewel thief Nyah Hall, the script was rewritten with Newton's classy style in mind. "We actually designed the character around her. She exuded an elegance and intelligence that this character needed," Cruise explained to *Time.*

In preparation for the role of Nyah Hall, Newton wrote a lengthy biography or "backstory" for the character, but ended up throwing it away before filming started. "Who the character was meant nothing at all. Where she was from meant nothing. Everything's about the moment. The instincts of the characters, how they respond to the situation...it was quite mythical in a way," Newton told Swartley.

Upon its debut in theaters in May of 2000, *Mission: Impossible 2* was a box office smash. The film grossed $70 million during its first week in release. Most critics enjoyed the film's heart-stopping action sequences and praised Newton's beauty, but few considered the love story strong enough to be an effective display of Newton's acting talent.

Newton has been married since 1998 to Oliver Parker, a British screenwriter she met when working on a British television film. "I was completely and immediately besotted," Newton was quoted by Jewel as telling *OK Magazine* about her meeting with Parker. Newton turned down a role in a big budget screen version of the popular 1970s series *Charlie's Angels* in order to appear in *It Was an Accident,* a modest budget film written by Parker and set for release in late 2000. Newton and Parker, who live in West London, are expecting their first child at about the same time. Newton is looking forward to motherhood. She told Swartley, "I think when you are called to protect something, a child, instinctively you feel more powerful."

Sources

Books

Motion Picture Guide 1993 (films of 1992). New York: Baseline, 1993.

Periodicals

Boston Globe, November 20, 1992, p. 41.

Entertainment Weekly, June 26, 1998, p. 24.

Interview, November 1998, p. 52.

Los Angeles Magazine, March 1999, p. 106.

New York Times, October 19, 1998, p. E1; May 21, 2000, p. Arts and Leisure, p. 23-24.

People, February 24, 1997, p. 144; June 12, 2000, p. 69-70.

Time, May 29, 2000, p. 70.

Washington Post, March 22, 1996, p. B7; October 16, 1998, p. N48; June 11, 1999, p. C5.

—Mary Kalfatovic

Jeffrey Osborne

1948—

Rhythm and blues vocalist

The 1980s were a golden age of African American vocal artistry, sandwiched between the disco-dominated 1970s and the spoken-word hip-hop experimentation of the 1990s. From car radios and concert stages everywhere bloomed big, romantic voices, well schooled in both singing technique and pure romantic appeal. One of the best-selling recording artists among the crop of 1980s balladeers was Jeffrey Osborne, who notched five gold or platinum albums with sales of over 500,000 units each.

Osborne was born on March 9, 1948, in Providence, Rhode Island. More than those of most other artists, his was an upbringing steeped in musical traditions, and several of his siblings also went on to make music professionally. Osborne's father, Clarence "Legs" Osborne, was a big-band trumpeter who played with the Duke Ellington, Count Basie, and Lionel Hampton bands. He could have had an even more distinguished career had he not opted to spend more time with his family. Clarence Osborne died when Jeffrey was 13-years-old.

Moved to Los Angeles

After his father's death, Osborne switched from trumpet to drums, and two years later, he kept the family musical tradition alive by moving to Los Angeles in search of a musical career. He had the blessing of his mother, who was a descendant of the Native American Pequot tribe. She had always nurtured his musical side, encouraging him to perform renditions of Johnny Mathis songs at parties while he was still a youngster.

Before he ever sang professionally, Osborne was a drummer. Not long after arriving in Los Angeles, he landed a guest slot on drums for a live performance with the soon-to-be-famous soul group the O'Jays, and ended up performing with the band for two weeks. That brush with musical greatness kept Osborne going through several years of musical apprenticeship. Back home in Providence in 1969, he went to a performance by a group called Love Men Ltd. that was in sudden need of a drummer—their usual drummer was arrested for fighting with an audience member during

At a Glance . . .

Born March 9, 1948, in Providence, RI; father's name Clarence "Legs" Osborne; married to Sheri; children: Tiffany, Dawn, and Jeanine.

Career: Popular recording artist, songwriter, and producer. Joined group Love Men Ltd., 1969; group renamed LTD; became lead vocalist for LTD, early 1970s; with LTD, recorded "Love Ballad," 1976; with LTD, recorded "Every Time I Turn Around (Back in Love Again), "1977; made debut as solo artist with the album *Jeffrey Osborne,* 1982; scored five gold or platinum albums, 1980s and early 1990s; with Dionn eWarwick, recorded "Love Power," 1987; released CD *That's forSure,* 2000.

Addresses: *Publishing company*—Almo-Irving Publishing Company, 1358 N. LaBrea, Hollywood, CA 90028.

the show's intermission. Osborne filled in, was signed to a contract, and went back to Los Angeles with the band, where they altered their name to LTD. They explained to their female fans that the initials stood for Love, Togetherness, and Devotion.

Bookings for the band were lean at first, as LTD served as the backup group for a female impersonator. However, several members of LTD were southern soul veterans who had backed the 1960s soul duo Sam & Dave on horns and had an ear for potential vocal power. The rich tenor voice of their new drummer impressed them, and Osborne was encouraged to take vocal solos with LTD. Finally, Osborne became the group's lead vocalist. He stayed with LTD for 11 years, contributing vocals to six hit albums and to such individual song successes as "Love Ballad" (1976) and "(Every Time I Turn Around) Back in Love Again" (1977). Although the latter was a bigger hit originally, "Love Ballad" became a signature tune for Osborne, and he was still singing it in concerts a quarter of a century later.

LTD experienced some crossover success in addition to its stellar performance on African American pop charts. Toward the end of the 1970s, buoyed by session work for such artists as Smokey Robinson, Osborne began to consider a solo career. In contrast to the straight R&B inclinations of his bandmates, Osborne wanted to move in the direction of a more pop-oriented style. He chose as a producer the jazz-pop keyboard player George Duke, whose work was perfectly suited to, and indeed formed much of the musical basis for, the romantic "Quiet Storm" style of the early 1980s. Osborne could not have made a better choice, for Duke provided him with low-key but sophisticated backing that showcased his smoothly soaring vocals to maximum advantage.

Osborne's debut solo album, *Jeffrey Osborne,* was released on the A&M label in 1982, in the midst of strong competition from similarly-styled vocal powerhouses such as Luther Vandross and Teddy Pendergrass. It yielded three hit singles, of which one, the wedding-ready "On the Wings of Love," cracked the pop top 30 and also became an international hit. His next three album releases— *Stay with Me Tonight,* (1983) *Don't Stop,* (1984) and *Emotional,* (1986)—likewise offered radio-ready material and sold well. Osborne placed nine singles in the top three positions of *Billboard*'s R&B chart, with several crossing over to pop as well.

A multi-talented musician, Osborne wrote or co-wrote many of his hits. He also began to branch out into production, co-producing his 1988 album release *One Love—One Dream.* That disc yielded the biggest R&B hit of his career, "She's on the Left." His highest pop chart performances came with "You Should Be Mine (The Woo Woo Song)," from *Emotional,* and with a 1987 duet with Dionne Warwick, "Love Power." That song, composed by legendary pop tunesmith Burt Bacharach, offered Osborne a chance to demonstrate his interpretive skills, which stacked up well against those of veteran pop vocalist Warwick.

For a variety of reasons, Osborne's career faltered after the release of *One Love—One Dream.* Jumping into other endeavors such as producing albums for other artists, he took two years to release a follow-up, *Only Human.* For that album he moved to a new label, Arista, which backed Osborne with high-tech accompaniments less suited to his style. "In pushing Osborne into a livelier dance vein," noted *People* reviewer David Hiltbrand, "[Arista head Clive] Davis has handed this booming balladeer some bum steers." The ultimate cause of Osborne's decline may simply have been a change in musical tastes—African American music of the 1990s had a harder edge than the music of Osborne's prime years.

The title track of *Only Human* reached number three on the R&B charts, giving Osborne what may remain his last top ten hit. Osborne left Arista in 1994, and did not cut another album until the Modern label holiday release *Something Warm for Christmas* in 1997. In 1999 he signed with the Private label, which also was working to resuscitate the careers of one-time romantic icons Barry White, Peabo Bryson, and James Ingram. His first album for the label, *That's for Sure,* was released in 2000. Produced and largely composed by Osborne himself, the album included a live version of "Love Ballad" as well as new music.

Selected discography

Jeffrey Osborne, A&M, 1982.
Stay with Me Tonight, A&M, 1983.
Don't Stop, A&M, 1984.
Emotional, A&M, 1986.
One Love: One Dream, A&M, 1988.
Only Human, Arista, 1991.
Something Warm for Christmas, Modern, 1997.
That's for Sure, Private Music, 2000.

Sources

Books

Larkin, Colin, ed., *The Enyclopedia of Popular Music,* Muze UK, 1998.
Nite, Norm N., with Charles Crespo, *Rock On: The Illustrated Encyclopedia of Rock n' Roll,* Harper & Row, 1985.
Romanowski, Patricia, and Holly George-Warren, eds., *The New Rolling Stone Encyclopedia of Rock and Roll,* Fireside, 1995.
Tee, Ralph, *Soul Music: Who's Who,* Prima Publishing, 1992.

Periodicals

Billboard, January 15, 2000, p. 25.
People, September 19, 1988, p. 22; February 4, 1991, p. 19.

Other

Additional information for this profile was obtained from http://www.allmusic.com

—James M. Manheim

Charley Pride

1938(?)—

Country music vocalist

Many African Americans have crossed the color line in their respective fields of endeavor, winning respect and fame throughout American society for their persistence, for their belief in equality and justice, and for sheer guts. Perhaps none other, however, has had a career that so completely overcame negative expectations as that of Charley Pride, country music's first and only major African American star. Pride made his mark not only by breaking into a white-dominated world, but also by succeeding brilliantly. He was among the best-selling country vocalists of the 1960s and 1970s, and enjoyed an enduring career that stretched over parts of four decades.

Pride's own autobiography, *Pride,* is unclear as to his actual birthdate, but most sources agree that he was born on March 18, 1938. Named Charl Frank Pride by his father, he received the name Charley when a clerk mistyped his birth certificate. Pride grew up in the Mississippi Delta, in the small town of Sledge, as one of eleven children in a sharecropper's family. The children, he wrote in his autobiography, "slept three and four to a bed, lying alternately head to foot."

As a child, Pride endured not only the worst indignities that Southern segregation could dish out, but also unrelenting physical abuse from his father. Two breezes of influence from the outside seemed to carry suggestions of a different life. Pride shared one of these inspirational influences with many other African American young people of his time: a gifted athlete named Jackie Robinson. Pride was greatly impressed by Robinson, who became the first African American player to enter baseball's major leagues. The other inspiration was more unusual. Pride, along with his family, listened to the weekly Saturday-night broadcasts of country music's long-running *Grand Ole Opry* radio program, which was transmitted on station WSM out of Nashville.

While it was not uncommon for African Americans in the South to listen to country music from time to time—jazz and pop vocalist Ray Charles described similar listening sessions from his own childhood—Pride's interest went much deeper. Born with a talent for mimicry, he quickly mastered the nasal yet sonorous singing styles of top country vocalists of the day such as Hank Williams and Roy Acuff. Pride's siblings were

At a Glance . . .

Born Charl Pride on March 18, 1938, in Sledge, MS; son of Mack Pride, a sharecropper farmer; married, wife's name Rozene; children: Kraig, Dion, and Angela. *Military service:* U.S. Army, 1956-58.

Career: Country singer, guitarist, and former professional baseball player; played inNegro Leagues in Detroit, Memphis, and Birmingham, Alabama, 1955-56 and 1958-59; played baseball and worked as tin smelter in Montana, 1960-63; began singing in night clubs around1962; recorded debut album for RCA label, 1967; topped country and pop charts with hit single "Kiss an Angel Good Morning," 1970; moved to 16th Avenue label, 1987.

Awards: Several Grammy awards. Entertainer of the Year and Male Vocalist of the Year, Country Music Association, 1970; Top Male Artist of the Decade (1970s), *CashBox* magazine, 1980; inducted into Country Music Hall of Fame, 2000.

Addresses: *Booking agent*—Cecca Productions, P.O. Box 670507, DallasTX 75367

mystified by his desire to sing country music. A natural musician, Pride amused himself by constructing simple musical instruments out of such materials as combs and pieces of wire. At the age of 14, he bought his first guitar.

Despite his interest in music, Pride first turned to baseball as his ticket out of Sledge. "As far as I was concerned, my future was in baseball," he wrote in his autobiography. "Once I saw what Jackie Robinson did, that was my goal." Pride won a spot with the Memphis Red Sox and the Birmingham Black Barons in the old Negro Leagues, and excelled even when these teams faced off against major league squads in exhibition play. Following military service in the U.S. Army in 1956 and 1957, Pride made repeated attempts to break into the majors. However, he became frustrated because the number of African Americans who were allowed to play major league baseball was still small. Newly married, Pride settled for an offer from the owner of a small semi-professional team in Montana, the Missoula Timberjacks. The baseball job came with a price, working a dangerous, demanding shift in a smelting plant.

Pride sang the national anthem at baseball games and occasionally performed a country song or two between innings. He was greatly encouraged by the audience's positive response, and soon began to round out his income by singing in taverns. At a concert in the early 1960s, he filled a slot at a Helena, Montana concert hosted by country stars Red Foley and Red Sovine. Sovine was impressed with Pride's performance, and gave him the telephone number of his booking agent in Nashville. In the meantime, Pride still tried to earn a spot in the major leagues. In 1963 he tried out for the New York Mets, but was rejected. Given a bus ticket back to Montana by the team, Pride traveled by way of Nashville and acquired the services of a manager, Jack Johnson. Two years passed before Pride was signed to the RCA label in Nashville, and executives at the label moved gingerly to promote their new artist. His first single, the murder ballad "Snakes Crawl at Night," was released without any accompanying photo publicity. Pride's rich baritone voice was so steeped in the traditions of country music, that most audiences did not realize he was African American. Initially, RCA would not allow Pride to record love songs such as the sentimental classic "Green, Green Grass of Home". The song referred to a woman with "hair of gold and lips like cherries," and executives feared that white audiences would react negatively to hearing Pride sing of a love affair with a blonde-haired woman.

Pride's first several singles became hits and, by 1966, his career was in full bloom. During live performances, he won the audience over with his vocal stylings and genial sense of humor. Before a crucial Detroit concert, Pride and manager Johnson devised the trademark joke in which he mentioned his "permanent tan." During the late 1960s, when tensions were running high over riots in several American cities, Pride's remarkable rapport with audiences ensured that his concerts would be free of any racial violence. Pride joined a tour organized by rising "outlaw" singer-songwriter Willie Nelson, who gave Pride important support during the early stages of his career.

Pride soon became a fixture on the country music scene. With the release of a 1969 collection of his singles, *The Best of Charley Pride,* the singer hit the coveted Number One position on country music sales charts. In 1970, Pride released "Kiss an Angel Good Morning," which crossed over to pop audiences and reached the pop top 20. The song, in which Pride delivers the folksy advice "Kiss an angel good morning/And love her like the devil when you get back home", remains one of his most popular hits. In 1971, Pride swept the Country Music Association's Male Vocalist of the Year and Entertainer of the Year awards.

Pride's string of hit singles and albums was virtually unbroken throughout the 1970s. *Cash Box* magazine named Pride country music's top male vocalist of the decade. At several points in his career, he struggled with depression. However, he always bounced back and turned to medication only after being hospitalized in 1989. In the early 1980s, Pride released the Hank Williams tribute album *There's a Little Bit of Hank in Me.* Pride had always had an affinity for Williams's songs, and later recorded a rambunctious version of the Williams song "Kaw-Liga". The song tells the story of a wooden antique-store Indian who is unable to verbalize his love for a similar female figure. The female figure is eventually purchased by a customer and taken away.

During the late 1980s, Pride's popularity faded somewhat with the rise of newer, rock-oriented country styles. He became a leader of a group of older, established singers who were critical of country radio stations for ignoring the legends of the genre. Pride continued to hold on to his devoted base of fans, however. In 1992, he opened a theater in Branson, Missouri, a country music-oriented tourist town geared to older travelers. That year, he was inducted into the roster of the Grand Ole Opry in Nashville—a high honor among country music traditionalists. Twenty-five years earlier, Pride had become the first African American singer to appear on the Opry stage. In the year 2000, he became the first African American member of the Country Music Hall of Fame.

Selected discography

Country Charley Pride, RCA, 1966.
The Pride of Country Music, RCA, 1967.
Songs of Pride...Charley, That Is, RCA, 1968.
Charley Pride—In Person, RCA, 1968.
Christmas in My Home Town, RCA, 1970.
Charley Pride Sings Heart Songs, RCA, 1971.
Songs of Love by Charley Pride, RCA, 1973.
Charley, RCA, 1975.
Sunday Morning with Charley Pride, RCA, 1976.
She's Just an Old Love Turned Memory, RCA, 1977.
Burgers and Fries, RCA, 1978.
You're My Jamaica, RCA, 1979.
There's a Little Bit of Hank in Me, RCA, 1980.
Roll On Mississippi, RCA, 1981.
Night Games, RCA, 1983.
The Power of Love, RCA, 1984.
After All This Time, 16th Avenue, 1987.
I'm Gonna Love Her on the Radio, 16th Avenue, 1988.
The Essential Charley Pride, RCA, 1997.

Sources

Books

Contemporary Musicians, volume 4, Gale, 1991.
Larkin, Colin, ed., *The Encyclopedia of Popular Music,* Muze UK, 1998.
Pride, Charley, with Jim Henderson, *Pride: The Charley Pride Story,* Morrow, 1994.
Smith, Jessie Carney, ed., *Notable Black American Men,* Gale, 1999.
Stambler, Irwin, and Grelun Landon, *The Encyclopedia of Folk, Country & Western Music,* St. Martin's, 1983.

Periodicals

Country Music, July-August 1996, p. 64.
Jet, August 9, 1999.

—James M. Manheim

J. Saunders Redding

1906–1988

Professor, author, literary critic

Professor and author J. Saunders Redding was a pioneering critic in the field of African American literature. During his long academic career, he published ten books, ranging from literary criticism to fiction to memoir, as well as numerous essays. His best-known works include *To Make a Poet Black* (1939), a critical literary survey; *No Day of Triumph* (1942), an autobiographical book about the lives of African Americans in the South; and *Stranger and Alone* (1950), a novel.

Redding is believed to be the first African American faculty member to teach at an Ivy League university—Brown University in Providence, Rhode Island. He also taught at several colleges and universities in the South and the Northeast, where he helped to establish African American studies programs. "Both as an educator and as a writer, Redding has been an integral part of the two American worlds—the black and the white," Arthur P. Davis wrote in *From the Dark Tower: Afro-American Writers, 1900-1960.* Pancho Savery, writing in the *Dictionary of Literary Biography,* described Redding as "Afro-American literature's primary literary historian" as well as its "first great scholar-critic." According to Savery, "Redding is not solely a pioneer in the field; decades after his initial critical statements were made, his work is still the standard by which others are measured."

However, in the 1960s and 1970s, Redding came under fire by younger, more radical African American literary critics. He had approached the work of African American writers in the same way that he criticized literature from the Western tradition. Later critics advocated a "black aesthetic," a special set of criteria to evaluate African American writing. One such critic, Amiri Baraka, was quoted in the *Dictionary of Literary Biography* as saying that Redding's views were "basically supportive of the oppression of the Afro-American nation and white chauvinism in general."

Nonetheless, even critics who disagreed with Redding acknowledged his early contributions to the discipline. Darwin Turner called *To Make a Poet Black* "the best single volume of criticism by a black," while Joan R. Sherman was quoted as saying in the *Dictionary of Literary Biography* that Redding was "the dean of Afro-American literary critics." According to Davis, writing in *From the Dark Tower,* "Redding...helped to prepare the ground for the black Renaissance of the sixties."

At a Glance . . .

Born Jay Saunders Redding, Oct. 13, 1906, Wilmington, DE; died March 2, 1988 in Ithaca, NY; son of Lewis Alfred and Mary Ann (Holmes) Redding; married Esther Elizabeth James, a teacher; children: Conway Holmes, and Lewis Alfred II. *Education:* Brown University, Ph.B., 1928, M.A., 1932; additional graduate work at Columbia University.

Career: Instructor in English, Morehouse College, 1928-31; instructor in English, Louisville Municipal College, 1934-36; head of English department, Southern University,1936-38; professor, Hampton Institute, 1943-67; fellow in humanities, Duke University,1964-65; director of the division of research and publications, National Endowment for theHumanities, 1966-69; professor of American history and civilization, George Washington University, 1969-70; Ernest I. White Professor Emeritus of American Studies and Humane Letters, Cornell University, 1970-75.

Selected awards: Rockefeller Foundation Fellow, 1939-40; Guggenheim Fellow,1944-45, 1959-60; Mayflower Award for Distinguished Writing, 1944; honorary degrees from Brown University and Hobart College.

Member: American Society of African Culture (executive council), College English Association, Phi Beta Kappa, Sigma Pi Phi.

Redding was born in Wilmington, Delaware on October 13, 1906, the third of seven children. Both his mother, Mary Ann (Holmes) Redding, and his father, Lewis Alfred Redding, had graduated from Howard University. The Reddings lived in a middle-class, predominantly white neighborhood. His father supported the family by working at the postal service, as well as doing various odd jobs during vacations and after his regular work hours. In addition, he was secretary of the Wilmington branch of the National Association for the Advancement of Colored People, and founded the first YMCA for African Americans in Wilmington.

Redding recalled in *No Day of Triumph* that both of his parents struggled with inner conflicts about their race. His mother was "in rage and tears" when another African American family moved into the neighborhood. Meanwhile, his father was driven by an insatiable need to prove himself to his white neighbors and colleagues. "Surrounded by whites both at home and at work, he was driven by an intangible something, a merciless, argus-eyed spiritual enemy that stalked his every movement and lurked in every corner," Redding wrote in *No Day of Triumph*.

As a young child, Redding was educated at home. He first attended school in the third grade. Redding later attended Howard High School which, until 1951, was the only high school in Delaware that would admit African Americans. In high school, he participated in drama, journalism, and basketball, and excelled at speech and debate.

During this time, Redding's mother died. When he graduated from high school in 1923, at the age of 16, his father sent him to the predominantly African American Lincoln University in Pennsylvania. In the Redding family, all of the children were expected to pursue higher degrees. "College education was preordained," Redding wrote in his entry in *Contemporary Authors*. Unhappy at Lincoln, Redding transferred to Brown University at the end of his freshman year. Brown University was the alma mater of his older brother, Louis, who would later become Delaware's first African American lawyer, and a powerful opponent of segregation.

As a student at Brown, Redding decided to major in English, and began his first attempts at writing for publication. "It was at college that I began to give serious attention to writing, not as a career but because I liked it; though heaven knows why, since even then the effort used to tear me apart," he wrote in his entry in *Contemporary Authors*. He won several scholarships and prizes in public speaking, and was elected to the Phi Beta Kappa honor society.

After earning a degree from Brown in 1928, Redding joined the faculty of Morehouse College in Atlanta, Georgia, as an English instructor. The following year, he married Esther Elizabeth James, a teacher. However, he did not flourish at Morehouse. The administration considered him to be too radical, while he thought the college was much too conservative and pretentious. Redding was fired in 1931. He returned to Brown to pursue graduate work, supported by scholarships and his wife's earnings. In 1932, he received a master's degree in English and American literature. From 1932 to 1934, he did further graduate work at Columbia University in New York.

In 1934, Redding accepted a lecturer's position at Louisville Municipal College in Louisville, Kentucky. The following year, his first son was born. In 1936, the Redding family moved to Baton Rouge, Louisiana, where Redding served as chair of the English department at Southern University. During his time at Southern, he began working on his first book of literary criticism, which would become *To Make a Poet Black*.

In 1938 the family moved again, this time to Elizabeth City, North Carolina, where Redding became the chair of the English department at the State Teachers College. The following year, Redding published *To Make a Poet Black*, a survey of African American literature from the 1700s through the Harlem Renaissance. "*To Make a Poet Black* is really a pioneer work in the field of Negro literature...," Arthur P. Davis wrote in *From the Dark Tower* in 1974. "At the time it appeared, very few critics concerned themselves with Negro American literature." In the book, Redding recognized African American literature as worthy of serious study, while at the same time criticizing most of it for what he considered to be its artistic shortcomings.

In 1941, Redding received a prestigious Rockefeller Fellowship to produce a book about African Americans in the South. To research the book, he traveled through the southern states, interviewing African Americans of all classes. The result was the autobiographical work *No Day of Triumph,* which received a Mayflower Award. Wallace Stegner, reviewing the book in a 1942 issue of the *Atlantic,* described *No Day of Triumph* as "an angry and honest and compassionate book..., perhaps the sanest and most eloquent study of the Negro American that has appeared." "Most critics consider *No Day of Triumph* Redding's best volume," Arthur P. Davis wrote in *From the Dark Tower,* "A combination of autobiography and reportage, the work is a brilliant report on the condition of Southern Negroes in the year that it was planned and written."

In 1943 Redding accepted a position at Hampton Institute in Virginia, where he would be based for more than 20 years. In 1944 he won a Guggenheim Fellowship, and took a leave from Hampton to begin writing his first novel, *Stranger and Alone.* The following year, Redding's second son was born.

Redding continued to work on *Stranger and Alone* for two more years, after returning to his duties at Hampton. In 1949, on another leave from Hampton, he was a visiting full professor at his alma mater, Brown University. According to historian Henry Louis Gates, by teaching at Brown, Redding became the first African American faculty member of an Ivy League university. In 1950, *Stranger and Alone* was published. The novel told the story of Shelton Howden, the son of an African American mother and white father, who struggles to fit in to the white world. Although some critics faulted the book's organization, *Stranger and Alone* earned praise for its emotional power. The following year, Redding published *On Being Negro in America*, another autobiographical work. In the book, "Redding expresses the attitude of most black intellectuals of America—their attitude toward integration, toward Communism as a way out, toward the 'deep sickness' which they found in America...," Arthur P. Davis wrote in *From the Dark Tower.* "As a writer I feel that my first obligation is to truth," Redding remarked in *Contemporary Authors.* "Since life is tragically short, there is only so much truth one can experience and know about in the wholly personal and intimate way that is necessary to the writer....Even the little truth that one can know is generally unpleasant, and insofar as I have told the truth in them, my books have not been pleasant."

During the summer of 1952, Redding traveled to India at the request of the State Department. In India, he lectured about American life, and met with politicians, writers, intellectuals, and journalists. He later wrote about his experiences in the book *An American in India,* published in 1954.

In 1955, Redding accepted the position of Johnson Professor of Literature at Hampton Institute. Three years later, he published *The Lonesome Road*, which used the biographies of well-known African Americans to trace the transition from slavery to relative social equality. "He has a real talent for giving life and meaning to historic episodes," Arthur P. Davis wrote *in From the Dark Tower.* "Moreover, he has insight into historic characters; he looks at them with the eye of a dramatist, and he brings them alive, emphasizing their peculiarities as well as their outstanding qualities."

In 1959, Redding took another leave from Hampton, having won a second Guggenheim Fellowship. He took additional periods of leave from 1964 to 1965, when he was a fellow in humanities at Duke University in North Carolina, and from 1966 to 1967, when he served as director of the division of research and publications at the National Endowment for the Humanities.

In 1967, Redding published *The Negro,* an analysis of the role of African Americans in American society. That same year, he resigned his position at Hampton, and continued to work at the National Endowment for the Humanities. Two years later, Redding was appointed professor of American history and civilization at George Washington University in Washington D.C.

In 1970, Redding became Ernest I. White Professor Emeritus of American Studies and Humane Letters at Cornell University. In accepting this position, he became the first African American professor in Cornell University's College of Arts and Sciences. He also published the book *Cavalcade,* an anthology of African American literature, which he co-edited with A. P. Davis. Redding taught at Cornell for five years, and retired in 1975.

During the 1970s, Redding was a member of the Haverford Group, an informal circle of influential African Americans, who met to discuss ways of discouraging racial segregation. The group included Robert C. Weaver, the former Secretary of Housing and Urban Development; William Hastie, the first African American federal judge; psychologist Kenneth B. Clark; and historian John Hope Franklin. Redding and other members of the group also worked at the Joint Center for Political Studies in Washington, where they helped to develop strategies for coping with racism.

Redding died of heart failure on March 2, 1988 at his home in Ithaca, New York. He was 81 years old. "Urbane, moderate, scholarly, Saunders Redding, as both writer and person, exemplifies the best of that middle-class background from which he comes and of the classical education which he received," Arthur P. Davis wrote in *From the Dark Tower* in 1974. "For three decades his voice has been the voice of protest...but always the cultured voice of a well-educated and wise observer of the American racial scene."

Selected writings

To Make a Poet Black, 1939.
No Day of Triumph, 1942.
Stranger and Alone, 1950.
They Came in Chains: Americans from Africa, 1950, revised 1973.
On Being Negro in America, 1951.
An American in India: A Personal Report on the Indian Dilemma and the Nature of Her Conflicts, 1954.
The Lonesome Road: The Story of the Negro's Part in America, 1958.
The Negro, 1967.
Of Men and the Writing of Books, 1969.
Negro Writing and the Political Climate, 1970.

Sources

Books

Dictionary of Literary Biography, edited by Gregory S. Jay, Gale Research, 1988.
From the Dark Tower: Afro-American Writers, 1900-1960, by Arthur P. Davis, Howard University Press, 1974.

Periodicals

New York Times, March 5, 1988.

—Carrie Golus

Louis L. Redding

1901–1998

Attorney

During the civil rights era, Louis L. Redding was one of a group of lawyers who dismantled the structure of legal segregation in the South. As Delaware's first African American lawyer, Redding struggled to ensure that his African American clients received equal treatment in the eyes of the law. Beginning in the late 1940s, he successfully fought for the right of African American students to attend the high-quality schools reserved for whites.

Redding won several important cases in Delaware, including *Parker v. University of Delaware* (1950), which marked the first time that a state-funded university was desegregated by court order. Four years later, Redding was one of a team of lawyers who argued the *Brown v. Board of Education* case in front of the U.S. Supreme Court. The court's historic ruling in that case struck down the "separate but equal rule," and led to the desegregation of public schools throughout the nation.

In a memorial in *IN RE,* the newsletter of the Delaware State Bar Association, Irving Morris praised Redding's courage and leadership in the fight against institutionalized racism. "We, in our state, would have continued in our old ways, blind to the discrimination and the lack of freedom in our own community," Morris wrote. "Louis L. Redding courageously came forward to help us. He assumed the leadership of the effort to strike down the debilitating restrictions which doomed so many to lives of despair."

Louis Lorenzo Redding was born in 1901 in Alexandria, Virginia. He was the son of Mary Ann (Holmes) Redding and Lewis Alfred Redding, who were both graduates of Howard University. This achievement was all the more impressive given that Lewis Redding's mother had been a slave. When Redding was a small child, the family moved to Wilmington, Delaware, where they settled in a middle-class, mostly white neighborhood. Redding's father supported the family by working at the postal service, as well as doing various odd jobs during vacations and after his regular work hours.

Both of Redding's parents valued education highly, and encouraged their children to excel at school. Later, two of Redding's sisters would become school teachers, while his younger brother, Jay Saunders Redding, would become the first African American faculty member at an Ivy League university.

As a student in Wilmington, Redding attended segregated schools, including Howard High School, the only high school for African Americans in the state. Decades later, Redding would successfully sue for the right of African American students to attend schools where they lived, rather than taking long bus rides into the city to attend Howard.

After graduating from high school, Redding went on to study at an Ivy League institution, Brown University in Providence, Rhode Island. He excelled at Brown, and when he graduated with a bachelor's degree in 1923, he delivered the commencement address. In the early

At a Glance . . .

Born in 1901 in Alexandria, VA; died on September 29, 1998. son of Lewis Alfred Redding and Mary Ann (Holmes) Redding; married Ruth Albert Cook Redding (divorced); married Gwendolyn Carmen Kiah; children: Ann, Rupa, and Judith. *Education:* Brown University, AB, 1923; Harvard University Law School, JD, 1928.

Career: Vice principal, Fessenden Academy, Ocala, Florida, 1923-24; teacher, Morehouse College, 1924-25; attorney at law, State of Delaware, 1929-98; public defender, State of Delaware, 1965-84.

Member: American Bar Association, National Bar Association.

Awards: Honorary law degree from Brown University.

1920s, Redding had a brief career as an educator. From 1923 to 1924, he was vice principal of Fessenden Academy in Ocala, Florida. From 1924 to 1925, he taught at Morehouse College in Atlanta, Georgia. Redding then won a scholarship to Harvard Law School, where he began to pursue the career that would make him famous.

In Delaware, however, Redding's prestigious education mattered much less than the color of his skin. On vacation from law school, he once wandered into the court house in Wilmington and took a convenient seat. When the guard pointed out the section reserved for African Americans, Redding refused to move and was thrown out of the courthouse.

In 1928, Redding received his law degree from Harvard. At the urging of his father, he decided to return to Delaware to practice law. The following year, Redding became the first African American admitted to the bar in Delaware. "Black Delaware badly needed his services," Richard Kluger wrote in *Simple Justice: The History of Brown v. Board of Education and Black America's Struggle for Equality.* In Delaware, most of the best lawyers focused on corporate law, while the white lawyers who did accept African American clients often charged exorbitant fees. "He [Redding] fought, largely alone, for the civil rights and liberties of black Delawareans by throwing all of his superior training and bottomless energy into representing them." Redding would continue to be the only African American lawyer in Delaware for more than 25 years. "The path he traveled was a lonely one for few at the Bar welcomed him," Irving Morris wrote in *IN RE,* "But he made no complaint. There was no one to whom he could complain. He persevered."

By 1949, Redding had 20 years of legal experience behind him, and was ready to mount a challenge to the Jim Crow laws of his home state. That year, 30 students at the Delaware State College for Negroes applied to the all-white University of Delaware. After they were rejected—on the basis that an all-African American college had been provided for their education—they approached Redding about suing for admission.

Redding initially wrote to the university's board of trustees, who refused to alter their decision. The following year, Redding went to court to argue *Parker v. University of Delaware.* He was assisted by Jack Greenberg, the first white lawyer to be hired by the NAACP. Redding would work with Greenberg on several historic cases, including *Brown v. Board of Education.*

After listening to their arguments, the judge visited both the white and African American colleges. Finding the all-African American college to be "grossly inferior," he ordered the plaintiffs to be admitted to the all-white University of Delaware. It was the first time in the nation's history that a university was desegregated by court order.

Redding next turned his attention to Delaware's public schools. Under a segregated educational system, African American children often had to travel long distances to attend school, sometimes passing by superior white schools on their way. With Greenberg again at his side, Redding sought to bring down this system.

In 1951, Redding and Greenberg brought two cases to the court: *Belton v. Gebhart,* which concerned high school education, and *Bulah v. Gebhart,* which concerned elementary education. Redding lined up an impressive list of witnesses, including the acclaimed psychiatrist Frederic Wertham, who testified that segregated education severely damaged the mental health of African American children. The judge listened to the arguments, visited the schools in question, and in 1952 ordered that African American students be immediately admitted to white schools. For the first time, a segregated white public school in the United States had been ordered by a court of law to admit African American children.

However, while the state of Delaware had agreed to desegregate universities, it refused to accept integrated public schools, and therefore decided to appeal the ruling. Eventually, Redding's cases were combined with the *Brown v. Board of Education* case, which was from Kansas, and other similar cases from Virginia and South Carolina. In 1954, the U.S. Supreme Court agreed to hear the combined *Brown v. Board of Education* case.

The Delaware case was the last to be heard by the Court. Redding kept his arguments short, since many of the constitutional issues had already been cited by the other lawyers on the team. He simply argued that temporary solutions would not work, and the state should be permanently banned from segregating its students. In a historic decision, the Supreme Court struck down the "separate but equal" doctrine, desegregating public schools throughout the United States.

However, the struggle against racial segregation did not end with the *Brown v. Board of Education* decision. Returning to Delaware, Redding fought to force the state to abide by the Supreme Court's ruling. "Through the years of the struggle in Delaware, neither a single school board, nor any of the attorneys for the school boards, nor the state board, nor the successive attorney generals and their deputies, nor any governor, nor the general assembly came forward to stand by Louis L. Redding's side in opposition to the evil of racism in the public schools of Delaware," Irving Morris wrote in *IN RE*, "The harsh fact is millions of dollars we could have spent for the education of all children we instead spent to defend racial segregation in our public schools."

Redding would return to the Supreme Court once more, to argue the case of *Burton v. Wilmington Parking Authority*. The court again agreed with Redding, ruling that a building funded by public money could not discriminate against its customers because of their race. In 1965, Redding became a public defender for the state of Delaware, and fought for the rights of poor clients for nearly 20 years. He retired in 1984, after 55 years of practicing law. On September 29, 1998, Redding died at the age of 96.

Following his death, Normal Lockman wrote in the *News Journal* (New Castle, Delaware) that " Redding made the term "racial equality" mean something at a time when black Americans were routinely—and legally—denied full citizenship...One of the first things he did was refuse to practice in racially segregated courtrooms. From that point forward he waged legal war on segregation—de jure or de facto—and won." Irving Morris, writing in *IN RE*, added that "Some may say that all he did was to help those who desperately needed help and that is so, and, indeed, commendable in and of itself. But Louis Redding did far more. The fact is what he did was to help all of us, black and white, regardless of our station in life, confront our prejudices so that we may overcome the racism in our midst which bars us from becoming the free society we seek to achieve."

In 1999, six months after Redding's death, the University of Delaware established a professorship in his name. According to a university press release, the Louis L. Redding Chair for the Study of Law and Public Policy "will be filled by a scholar, teacher and community leader who will continue Mr. Redding's commitment to the use of the law to achieve social justice for all Americans." It was a fitting tribute to the man who had helped to desegregate the University of Delaware nearly 50 years earlier.

Sources

Books

Simple Justice: The History of Brown v. Board of Education and Black America's Struggle for Equality, by Richard Kluger, Alfred A. Knopf, 1976.

Periodicals

IN RE: (newsletter of the Delaware State Bar Association), November 1998, www.dsba.org

New York Times, Oct. 2, 1998.

News Journal (New Castle, Delaware), Feb. 3, 1999.

Other

Additional information for this profile was obtained from a University of Delaware press release dated Feb. 3, 1999, and accessible at www.udel.edu

—Carrie Golus

Oscar Robertson

1938—

Former basketball player, businessman

Considered to be one of the greatest basketball players of all time, Oscar Robertson has triumphed off the court as well. He oversees three successful businesses in Ohio and is often asked to provide commentary on issues ranging from civil rights to the current state of basketball. His 1999 book, *The Art of Basketball,* showcases the basic fundamentals that Robertson believes a good basketball player must possess. It was these fundamentals that allowed Robertson to achieve the unsurpassed feat of averaging a "tripledouble" during the entire 1961-62 season. The tripledouble is achieved by reaching double digits in points, rebounds and assists during a game. Many players have accomplished a tripledouble during a game, but nobody has maintained the average for a whole season except Robertson.

Born Oscar Palmer Robertson in Charlotte, Tennessee, the Robertson family moved to Indianapolis when Oscar was four, where his father worked for the city sanitation department. Near his home in the city's African American ghetto was a rundown basketball court known as the "dust bowl." It was here that the young Robertson shot tin cans and then old tennis balls through the hoops because the family couldn't afford a real basketball. At the age of 11, he received his first basketball, which was going to be thrown away by a family for whom his mother worked as a maid. The basketball and Robertson became inseparable.

Robertson's love for basketball grew when he entered Crispus Attucks High School, an all-African American school that had no gym. Coach Ray Crowe instilled the basics of the game into his team, and when Robertson combined those qualities with his years of incessant street practice, the Attucks Tigers had found a new leader. During his junior and senior years, Robertson led the team to a 45-game winning streak and two state championships. In 1956, Robertson was named Indiana's "Mr. Basketball." As the first African American school to win the Indiana state title, Robertson and his Attucks teammates received national attention and Robertson was heavily recruited by more than 30 colleges.

Robertson decided to attend the University of Cincinnati because it was fairly close to his family in Indianapolis and because of the tough schedule that the Bearcats played. He again emerged as a team leader, and took his team to new heights. The Bearcats reached the Final Four during his last two years, but

At a Glance . . .

Born Oscar Palmer Robertson on November 24, 1938 in Charlotte, TN; son of Henry Bailey Robertson and Mazell Bell Robertson; married Yvonne Crittenden, June 25, 1960. children: Shana, Tia, Mari. *Education:* University of Cincinnati, BBA, 1960.

Career: Co-captain, U.S. Olympic basketball team, 1960; professional basketball player for the Cincinnati Royals, 1960-70, Milwaukee Bucks 1970-74; president of the National Basketball Player's Association, 1964-74; president and CEO, Oscar Robertson Construction, 1975-; president and CEO Orchem, Inc., 1981-; president and CEO, Orpack-Stone Corp., 1990-; president, NBA Retired Players Association, 1993-99; author, *The Art ofBasketball,* 1999.

Awards: *Sporting News* College Player of the Year, 1958, 1959, 1960;*Sporting News* All-Star First Team, 1958, 1959, 1960; Gold medal, U.S. Olympicbasketball team, 1960; NBA Rookie of the Year, 1961; All-NBA First Team, 1961-69; NBAAll-Star Game MVP, 1961, 1964, 1969; NBA Most Valuable Player, 1964; Naismith Memorial Basketball Hall of Fame, 1979; NBA 35th Anniversary All-Star Team, 1980; Olympic Hall ofFame, 1984; Oscar Robertson statue on the campus of the University of Cincinnati, 1994;College Player of the Year Award renamed the Oscar Robertson Trophy, 1998; named one of the Greatest Athletes of the 20th Century, *Sport Illustrated,* 1999; named Indiana Living Legend, 1999; named one of the 50 Greatest Athletes of the Century, ESPN, 1999; OhioGovernor's Award, 1999.

Addresses: *Office*—Orchem, Inc., 4923 Mulhauser Rd., Fairfield, OH45014.

were defeated both times by the University of California. As an individual player, Robertson set 14 NCAA records and averaged close to 34 points per game. He won the national scoring title three times, and was named an All-American in each of his three varsity seasons. Additionally, Robertson was named College Player of the Year three years in a row—the first person to win that award three times—and in 1998 the award was named the Oscar Robertson Trophy. It was also during his years at Cincinnati where he earned the nickname, "the Big O."

While Robertson excelled on the court and in the classroom, he had no control over the racial tensions which existed in the Midwest and the South during the 1950s. As the first African American to play for Cincinnati, Robertson was subjected to the humiliation of racism on numerous occasions. Often, while on the road with his team, Robertson was not permitted to stay at the same hotel with his teammates and would stay by himself in a college dorm. Even in Cincinnati, where he was a star on the University of Cincinnati campus, there were many theaters and restaurants that refused to serve him. This rampant racism bothered Robertson so much that during his junior and senior years, he considered an offer to play for the Harlem Globetrotters. He stayed in school, however, and graduated with a bachelor's degree in business in 1960.

In the summer of 1960 Robertson co-captained the U.S. Olympic basketball team, a team that is considered by some to be the greatest amateur team ever put together for the Olympics. The United States finished the competition with an undefeated record, and won the gold medal. Upon returning from the Olympics, Robertson signed a three-year contract worth $100,000 to play professionally for the Cincinnati Royals (now the Sacramento Kings). As with his previous teams, Robertson was an immediate stand-out.

Robertson earned Rookie of the Year honors for the 1960-61 season and was named Most Valuable Player at the first of his 12 consecutive trips to the NBA All-Star game. The following year Robertson scored a feat which has yet to be matched when he averaged a tripledouble for the entire season (30.8 points, 12.5 rebounds and 11.4 assists). As Ken Shouler pointed out in his book *The Experts Pick Basketball's Best 50 Players in the Last 50 Years,* Robertson just missed averaging a tripledouble the other four of his first five years in the NBA. Robertson credited his high school coach Ray Crowe and his insistence on fundamentals for his success in professional basketball. "Even the so-called 'natural' has to work on things," he explained to Shouler. "I did have the fundamentals down when I entered pro ball. Once you get into pro ball, you don't have time to think, 'If a guy does this, I do that.' You do things instinctively."

In 1964, Robertson was named league MVP while winning MVP honors for the second time at the All-Star game and leading the Royals to their best season ever with a 55-25 record. Still, the Royals could never advance beyond the second round of the playoffs despite Robinson's efforts. "Oscar always made the big play, the right play," former Los Angeles Laker Elgin Baylor explained to Shouler. "When you played against Oscar you not only faced an opponent with a tremendous amount of talent and physical skills, but you were also up against a finely tuned pro basketball mind. Oscar was smarter than any pro player I have ever faced." Also in 1964, Robertson became president of the NBA player's union, a position he held until his retirement from playing in 1974.

Although Robertson and the Royals continued to post winning records during the late 1960s, they were not a championship caliber team. During the 1969-70 season, new Royals coach Bob Cousy wanted to trade Robertson to the Baltimore Bullets, a trade Robertson vetoed by staging a two-week hold out. In April of 1970, Robertson approved a trade that sent him to the Milwaukee Bucks, a fiery, young team that included Lew Alcindor—who later changed his name to Kareem Abdul-Jabbar. With Robertson on the roster, the Bucks advanced to the NBA Finals in 1971. The Bucks went on to sweep the Bullets in four games, and Robinson had won his first NBA championship. In 1974 the Bucks again charged to the NBA Finals, but lost to the Boston Celtics in seven games. Robertson retired from basketball shortly after the defeat.

Although his playing days were over, Robertson was still involved with professional basketball for the next two years as the result of a 1970 lawsuit against the NBA that he filed as president of the player's union. The anti-trust suit challenged the merger of the NBA and American Basketball Association (ABA), the college draft and the NBA's reserve clause that prohibited free agency. In 1976, the suit was settled. The NBA and ABA were allowed to merge, while the college draft remained intact. Drafted players were given the option of refusing to join the team that drafted them and reentering the draft one year later. Teams were no longer required to provide compensation when signing a free agent, which encouraged the signing of more free agents and led to higher salaries for players. The issue became known as "the Oscar Robertson Rule."

Following his retirement from basketball, Robertson returned to the Cincinnati area where he became a prominent businessman and participant in a number of charitable and community activities. He made headlines in 1997 when he donated a kidney to his daughter Tia, who had been suffering from lupus, a disease in which the body's immune system becomes overactive and attacks tissues and organs, particularly the kidneys. His daughter's illness prompted Robertson to become involved with the National Lupus Foundation and the National Kidney Foundation, for whom he acts as an advocate for organ donation.

As the 20th century drew to a close, Robertson began to appear on "Greatest Athletes of the Century" lists, including those presented by *Sports Illustrated* and ESPN. He maintained a vigorous pace in both his business and charitable activities. Robinson also authored *The Art of Basketball,* a book designed to teach the fundamentals of basketball to youngsters. Like his old high school coach Ray Crowe, Robertson stresses the fundamentals not only in basketball, but in daily life. As he wrote in *The Art of Basketball:* "Listen to people in authority—parents, teachers, coaches. They can offer you insights and information. Strive to become as good an athlete as you can, but remember, that education is equally important... .Take pride in being a well-educated athlete instead of the alternative. It makes for a more balanced and successful life."

Sources

Books

Bayne, Bijan C., *Sky Kings: Black Pioneers of Professional Basketball,* Grolier Publishing, 1988.

Robertson, Oscar, *The Art of Basketball,* Oscar Robertson Media Ventures, 1999.

Shouler, Kenneth A., *The Experts Pick Basketball's Best 50 Players in the Last 50 Years,* AllSport Books, 1996.

Periodicals

Cincinnati Post, April 5, 1999.

Indianapolis Star, March 20, 1955.

Jet, August 2, 1993, p.36.

New York Daily News, July 31, 1997.

New York Times, September 17, 1989, p. S-1; November 7, 1998, p. A-15.

People, May 26, 1997, p.52; December 29, 1997, p. 148.

Other

Additional information for this profile was obtained from www.ESPN.com; www.NBA.com/history/robert son_bio.html; and www.thebigO.com

—Brian Escamilla

Bobby Rush

1946—

Politician

A leader of the militant Black Panther Party in the 1960s who narrowly escaped with his life after a notorious police raid on the party's Chicago headquarters, Bobby Rush became part of the city's political establishment, winning election to the city council and then to the U.S. House of Representatives. In the process, he moderated some of his militant beliefs. The former gun-toting radical emerged as a leading spokesman for gun control after the murder of his son in 1999 and, as a Congressman, supported the positions of the Illinois business community on several key issues. Yet Rush saw no total metamorphosis in his evolution from community activist to mainstream politician. "I am consistent in working on behalf of [black] people," he told *Black Enterprise,* "and my move into politics was gradual."

Rush was born in Albany, Georgia, on November 23, 1946, but grew up in Chicago. Although the venerable African American community of the city's South Side would later become his political base, Rush grew up on the city's North Side. He was a member of the Boy Scouts, and got an early introduction to politics from his mother, who ironically was a precinct-level organizer for the Republican Party. When Rush won election to Congress in 1992, it was from one of the most Democratic-leaning districts in the entire United States.

Founded Panthers Chicago Chapter

After dropping out of high school, Rush joined the U.S. Army in 1963 and became involved in the great civil-rights struggles of the 1960s. He worked in civil-disobedience campaigns in the South, and founded the Chicago chapter of the Black Panthers in 1967. His son, Huey, was named after Panther leader Huey Newton. "We were reacting to police brutality, to the historical relationship between African-Americans and recalcitrant racist whites," Rush later told *People.* "We needed to arm ourselves." Indeed, Rush might have felt his suspicions justified when Chicago police raided a Panther meeting in 1969, killing two local party leaders. One of them was a young organizer, Fred Hampton, whom Rush himself had recruited. Rush could easily have been killed in the same hail of police bullets, but he survived.

Although he was imprisoned for six months in 1972 on a weapons charge, Rush also worked energetically on the non-violent projects that built support for the

At a Glance . . .

Born in Albany, Georgia, on November 23, 1946; raised in Chicago. Married, wife's name Carolyn. *Education:* Roosevelt University, Chicago, B.A. with honors, 1973; University of Illinois, M.A., 1994; McCormick Seminary, M.A., 1998. *Military Service:* U.S. Army, 1963–68. *Religion:* Baptist.

Career: United States Congressional Representative, First District of Illinois. JoinedStudent Non-Violent Coordinating Committee, 1966; worked on civil-disobedience campaigns in the southern United States; founded Chicago chapter, Black Panther Party, 1967; directed Panther-funded low-income medical clinic 1970–73; worked in insurance sales; elected Chicago city alderman from Second Ward, 1983; elected to U.S. House, 1992; ran unsuccessfully for mayor of Chicago, 1999.

Addresses: *Office*—U.S. House of Representatives, 131 Cannon House Office Building, Washington, DC 20515.

Panthers in African American communities. He coordinated a medical clinic that offered sickle-cell anemia testing on an unprecedented scale. Rush returned to school and graduated with honors from Chicago's Roosevelt University in 1973. A year later he left the Panthers, who were already in decline. "We started glorifying thuggery and drugs," he told *People.* That was distasteful to the deeply religious Rush, who in the 1990s resumed his education at McCormick Seminary and received a master's degree in theology.

Rush sold insurance for a time in the 1970s, and ran for a seat on Chicago's city council in 1974. The first of several black militants who later sought political office, he was defeated. In the early 1980s, however, Chicago's political life was transformed by the ascendancy of U.S. Representative Harold Washington, a brilliant orator and a charismatic figure who united the city's African American community. Washington was elected mayor of Chicago in 1983, ending decades of control by the city's white-ethnic political machine. That year, Rush was elected alderman from the Second Ward on Chicago's South Side.

A strong supporter of Washington, Rush showed himself to be as effective an organizer in the political arena as he had been on the streets with the Black Panthers. Throughout the 1980s and 1990s, he amassed an army of loyal precinct workers who could deliver large voter turnouts not only for his own campaigns, but also for those of other politicians he supported. As a result, Rush began to forge larger alliances not only within African American political circles but across racial lines. After Washington died suddenly while in office, the mayoralty reverted to Irish-American Richard Daley, son of the city's mayor from 1955 to 1978. Despite his previous ties to Washington, Rush worked effectively with Daley as well.

In 1992, Rush challenged incumbent Representative Charles Hayes for the Congressional seat in the Illinois First District, which included the heart of the South Side African American community plus a smattering of predominantly Irish-American wards to the southwest. Aided by a check-overdraft scandal that embroiled Hayes, Rush won the primary in March by a three-percentage-point margin, gaining white support thanks to the endorsement of Illinois House Speaker Michael Madigan. He waltzed to victory in November in this overwhelmingly Democratic area.

Rush took liberal positions in Congress, offering especially strong criticism of President Bill Clinton's welfare cuts in 1996. He was quoted in the *Almanac of American Politics* as saying that requiring public housing residents to perform community service amounted to "involuntary servitude." Because of his seat on the powerful Commerce committee, Rush also played host to numerous members of the Illinois business community. He became an astute negotiator: "When they come to sit down and discuss their interests with me," he told *Black Enterprise,* "I reach into my pocket and bring out my list [of pet projects]. Then we see where there are areas of mutual support and agreement."

"Only when African Americans own businesses, be they ma and pa shops or megasize companies," Rush continued in *Black Enterprise,* "will they be able to withstand the winds of [political] change that sweep periodically across America." Rush continued to focus on gaining more and more political influence. Observing Rush's South Side organization and the increasing number of races elsewhere in Chicago in which Rush became involved, *Chicago* magazine noted that "a politician who does all that ain't playin' beanbag."

After considering a mayoral run in 1995, Rush jumped into the 1999 race for mayor against Richard Daley. Rush charged that Daley was neglecting the city's neighborhoods in favor of its glittering downtown core. Rush tried to rally the same coalition of African Americans and white liberals that had elected Washington, but his campaign against Daley was hampered by a lack of funds and by Daley's own wide popularity. Daley's administration had been much more inclusive of minorities than had that of his famous father. In the election of February 1999, Daley won by a 72-to-28 percent margin, taking 45 percent of the African American vote and dealing Rush his first electoral defeat in many years.

Rush's 29-year-old son, Huey, was murdered by alleged robbers in front of his South Side home in October of 1999. Rush was devastated by his son's death. "I always thought it was going to be me who wouldn't get to 30," he told *People.* He stepped up his legislative efforts in favor of handgun control, telling *People* that "I'm committed to making sure that his life was not given in vain." Rush has sponsored or co-sponsored over 30 gun-control measures in Congress. After running for mayor and facing publicity over past unpaid taxes, he attracted opposition in the Democratic primary of April 2000, but triumphed over two opponents. "I'm going to get back to work," Rush told *Jet.* "We've got a lot we have to accomplish in these next few days, next few weeks, few months, few years."

Sources

Books

Barone, Michael, and Grant Ujifusa, *The Almanac of American Politics 2000,* National Journal, 1999.

Periodicals

Black Enterprise, November 1995, p. 28.
Crain's Chicago Business, November 30, 1998, p. 1.
Chicago, June 1994, p. 24.
Ebony, August 1996, p. 108.
Jet, April 10, 2000.
People, May 22, 2000, p. 115.

—James M. Manheim

Betty Shabazz

1936–1997

Registered nurse, health administrator, educator, activist

When Betty Shabazz married the dynamic civil rights leader Malcolm X, she could not anticipate the extent of her husband's fame or the course that their lives would take. Shabazz was catapulted into the American consciousness and the media spotlight following her husband's assassination in 1965 by three members of the Nation of Islam. Formerly an esteemed leader of the Nation, Malcolm broke with the black nationalist organization in 1963, after revising his separatist ideals and embracing a new philosophy of global unity. His young widow, pregnant with twin daughters at the time of his murder, was left to raise them—and their four sisters—by herself. In the ensuing years, Shabazz avoided publicity when she could, opting instead to provide a quiet, normal home life and full education for her children.

Betty was an adopted child who grew up in a fairly sheltered, middle-class household in Detroit, Michigan. She went to the local Methodist church with her parents on Sundays, parties on some Saturday nights with church friends, and movies on Fridays. While attending Northern High School, she joined the Del Sprites, a sorority affiliate. After high school graduation, she attended Tuskegee Institute in Alabama and encountered her first racial hostilities, which she didn't understand, and her parents refused to acknowledge. "They thought [the problems] were my fault," she later wrote in an autobiographical portrait printed in *Essence* magazine. After two years in Alabama, she moved to New York City to attend nursing school at Brooklyn State Hospital.

While at school in New York, a friend invited her to hear Malcolm X speak at an Islamic temple. When this friend said she'd arrange for them to be introduced after his speech, Betty's initial reaction was "big deal," she related in *Essence* in 1992. "But then," she continued, "I looked over and saw this man on the extreme right aisle sort of galloping to the podium. He was tall, he was thin, and the way he was galloping it looked as though he was going someplace much more important than the podium... .Well, he got to the podium—and I sat up straight. I was impressed with him." They were introduced later, and she became even more impressed. They talked about the racism she encountered in Alabama, and she began to understand its causes, pervasiveness, and effects. Soon, Betty was attending all of Malcolm's lectures. By the time she graduated from nursing school in 1958, she was a member of the Nation of Islam.

At a Glance . . .

Born May 28, 1936; died June 23, 1997, in Bronx, NY; adopted and raised by the Sanders family in Detroit, MI; married Malcolm X (formerly known as Malcolm Little; later took the name El-Hajj Malik El-Shabazz; a civil rights activist), 1958; children: Attallah, Qubilah, Ilyasah, Gamilah, Malaak, Malikah. *Education:* Attended Tuskegee Institute; Brooklyn State Hospital School of Nursing, R.N. and B.A, 1958; received master's degree in public health administration from Jersey City State College; University of Massachusetts at Amherst, Ph.D. in education administration, 1975.

Career: Medgar Evers College, City University of New York, Brooklyn, associate professor of health administration, beginning 1976; became director of Department of Communications and Public Relations.

Member: Delta Sigma Theta.

Awards: Betty Shabazz Cultural Center was established at Mount Holyoke College.

Betty Shabazz explained in *Essence,* "I never 'dated' Malcolm as we think of it because at the time single men and women in the Muslims did not 'fraternize' as they called it. Men and women always went out in groups." In addition, Malcolm was busy with a relentless schedule of speaking engagements for the Nation of Islam. Nevertheless, their connection grew strong. Soon after she finished nursing school, Malcolm, who was traveling the country at the time, called her from Detroit and proposed. Before the week was out, they were married.

The marriage did not last as long as either had hoped. On February 21, 1965, while speaking at the Audubon Ballroom in Harlem, he was gunned down. Shabazz had brought their four daughters to hear him speak that day. As the first of the 16 bullets that tore into Malcolm's body rang out, she threw her children down and covered them with her own body. After the shots, Shabazz tried to get to Malcolm, but someone held her back. When she finally did reach him, he was dead, and she wondered if she would survive herself.

For three weeks, Shabazz did not sleep. She kept seeing her husband's body fall. "I really don't know where I'd be today if I had not gone to Mecca to make Hajj [a spiritual pilgrimage] shortly after Malcolm was assassinated," she confided in *Essence.* "Two young doctors—one from Harvard and the other from Dartmouth—invited me to go to Mecca in my husband's stead. And that is what helped put me back on track. I remembered Malcolm saying, 'Don't look back and don't cry. Remember, Lot's wife turned into a pillar of salt.' I began to understand the meaning of that statement." She also had six daughters to raise. The twin daughters were born seven months after their father's death; Attallah, Malcolm and Betty's eldest daughter, was only six at the time of the assassination. After returning from Mecca, Shabazz did not allow herself to grieve further—at least not visibly; her children needed her strength. "The girls knew only that something terrible had happened," she told *Look* magazine a few years after Malcolm's death. "After the shock, as I became aware again, I tried to soothe them. I couldn't let them see hysteria on my part. Later, I learned that I had to adopt a personality of positiveness and high humor. For, if I laughed, they laughed.... I learned that I couldn't even express sadness around them. I didn't want them to worry." Shabazz threw herself into the care and education of her children. They studied French and Arabic, as well as ballet. Attallah even took classes in medicine offered to children by Columbia University.

The Shabazz children also studied black history. "Malcolm was a firm believer in the value and importance of our heritage. He believed that we have valuable and distinct cultural traditions which need to be institutionalized so that they can be passed on to our heirs." Shabazz further explained her educational perspective to *Ebony* in 1969: "I... want them to travel so they can know more about Africa, the West Indies and the Middle East. I want them to go to some of the places that their father visited. In this way I feel they will broaden their scope and become of maximum use to themselves, their families, and their people.

Although raising and educating her daughters took up most of her time, Shabazz still managed to further her education. Between 1970 and 1975, she completed a master's degree in public health administration and received a doctorate in education from the University of Massachusetts at Amherst. In 1976, she joined the faculty of Medgar Evers College in Brooklyn as associate professor of health administration. Shortly thereafter, she became director of the school's Department of Communications and Public Relations.

Although Shabazz made occasional appearances on behalf of civil rights, she remained a private person, preferring the intimacy of her family and close friends to any suggestion of public life. She was, however, "committed to the broadest possible distribution [of Malcolm's message]" as she told *Publishers Weekly* in 1991. She also wanted to protect his image from base commercialization. Shabazz served as a consultant on the Spike Lee film *Malcolm X,* which was released in 1992, and also hired a licensing firm to help maintain some control over the use of his name. She entered into several legal battles over copyright infringements of his writings, name, and the symbol X. As she told the *Washington Post,* the marketing of Malcolm's image had "gotten out of hand."

In 1994, nearly 30 years after the assassination of Malcolm X, Shabazz spoke out for the first time against the Nation of Islam and linked Nation leader Louis Farrakhan to his death. Farrakhan denied the allegations, claiming only that the turbulent, racially hostile atmosphere of the 1960s was responsible for Malcolm's death.

In January of 1995 Shabazz's daughter, Qubilah, was arrested for hiring a hit man to kill Farrakhan. The hit man turned out to be a government informer. Suprisingly, Farrakhan defended Qubilah and claimed that she had been duped by government agents who wanted to sow discord within the Nation of Islam and throughout the African American community. In May of that year, Shabazz and Farrakhan ended their bitter feud by shaking hands at a fundraiser at the Apollo Theater in Harlem. The fundraiser had been arranged by Farrakhan to help pay for Qubilah Shabazz's legal fees. In October of 1995, Shabazz spoke at the Million Man March in Washington, D.C. Farrakhan was the main organizer of the march.

Although Qubilah was not sent to prison for her part in the plot to assassinate Farrakhan, she was required to undergo psychological counseling and treatment for drug and alcohol abuse for a two-year period. During this time Qubilah's 12-year-old son, Malcolm, was sent to live with Shabazz at her home in Yonkers, New York. Angered that he was forced to live with his grandmother, Malcolm set fire to her home on June 1, 1997. Shabazz suffered third-degree burns over 80 percent of her body. For the next three weeks, she remained in extremely critical condition at Jacobi Medical Center in Bronx, New York, and underwent five operations to replace burned tissue. On June 23, 1997, Shabazz passed away. Her grandson was placed in a juvenile detention center for 18 months.

More than 2,000 mourners attended a memorial service for Shabazz at New York City's Riverside Church where several speakers, including Coretta Scott King, Myrlie Evers-Williams, poet Maya Angelou, actor-activist Ossie Davis, New York City mayor Rudolph Giuliani, and U.S. Representative Maxine Waters remembered Shabazz for her strength, warm personality, and love for her children. In a statement released after Shabazz's death, civil rights leader Jesse Jackson declared that "she never stopped giving and she never became cynical. She leaves today the legacy of one who epitomized hope and healing."

Sources

Ebony, June 1969, p. 172; February 1984, p. 127.
Essence, May 1979, p. 88; February 1985, p. 12.
Jet, October 5, 1992, p. 36; April 5, 1993, p. 46.
Look, March 4, 1969, p. 74.
Publishers Weekly, August 9, 1991, p. 13; October 18, 1991, p. 14.
Rolling Stone, November 30, 1989, p. 76.
Variety, November 23, 1992, p. 62.
Washington Post, November 18, 1992, p. C1.

Other

Additional information for this profile was taken from an Associated Press wire report dated April 3, 1994.

—Robin Armstrong and David G. Oblender

Horace Silver

1928—

Jazz pianist and composer

Pianist and composer Horace Silver, a pre-eminent founder of what became known as hard bop or soul jazz, emerged in the 1950s as noted instrumentalist and bandleader. Steeped in blues and a student of a church organist, Silver drew upon many sources for his musical vision, including Latin sounds that imbued his music with an intoxicating rhythmic quality. His inventive writing for small group settings featuring a saxophone-trumpet front line became a model for jazzmen of the post bop era. During a period when most jazz recording dates became "blowing sessions" in which the participants played unrehearsed standards and "head arrangements," Silver maintained, within his small groups, a sense of unique compositional form, and his tightly rehearsed groups became known for their impeccable sense of swing, while retaining a soulfully powerful sound. Many of Silver's compositions such as "The Preacher," "Juicy Lucy," "Nica's Dream," "Sister Sadie," and "Filthy McNasty" have become modern jazz classics and continue to find their way into the repertoires of jazz artists around the world.

Horace Ward Martin Tavares Silver was born on September 9, 1928 in Norwalk, Connecticut. Silver's father, John Tavares Silver, hailed from the Cape Verde Islands—a former Portuguese colony off the west coast of Africa—and worked at the Norwalk Tire Factory. A violinist and guitarist, he played music at family parties. Silver first studied the classical keyboard under the direction of a church organist. As a member of the Norwalk High School band, he played tenor saxophone under the influence of Lester Young. During his second year in high school, he took up the baritone saxophone, while pursuing his piano studies.

After graduating from high school, Silver continued playing piano, and primarily studied blues and boogie woogie players. His early training included memorizing Avery Parrish's classic blues solos on Erskine Hawkins's recording of "After Hours." Silver also studied the music of Charlie Parker and jazz pianists Art Tatum and Teddy Wilson. As he later recounted in *Talking Jazz,* "Teddy Wilson I copied a little of his stuff. I could copy stuff off the record. I couldn't catch all of it... .I bought a couple of Teddy Wilson piano folios and tried to practice out them... .Art Tatum piano folios were impossible for me to read. I couldn't get through them, there were so many thirty-second, sixty-forth notes, it looked like somebody took some ink and just threw it at the paper." Instead, Silver concentrated on studying

At a Glance . . .

Born Horace Ward Martin Tavares, September 9, 1928, in Norwalk, CT; son of John Tavares (factory worker) and Gertrude (a domestic worker).

Career: Discovered by Stan Getz in 1950 and performed and recorded with Getz until 1951; became a member of New York City's jazz scene and recorded as session musician for the Savoy label; made first solo recordings for the Blue Note label, 1952; led a group at Minton's Playhouse and recorded as a member of Art Blakey's Quintet, 1954; recorded solo release with Blakey and Jazz Messengers, 1954-55; subsequently recorded with the group under Blakey's leadership, 1954-56; pursued solo career, 1957; recorded a number of Blue Note albums, 1960s and 1970s; founded Silveto Productions and recorded music related to holistic healing, 1981; toured with small groups, 1980s; recorded for various labels, 1990s.

Awards: Won the New Star piano category of *Down Beat* magazine's International Critic's Poll, 1954.

Addresses: *Office*—Silveto Productions Inc., 18326 Clifftop Way, Malibu, California, 90265-5628.

the music of bebop piano genius Bud Powell. He soon discovered the works of one of Powell's mentors, Thelonious Monk, who, as Thomas Owens emphasized in *Bebop The Music and Its Players,* influenced "Silver's fast tremolos and dry pedal-free ballads, but also in the stiff-fingered percussive technique both men share—the oddest approach to the keyboard attack and fingering in jazz."

In 1950, while performing with Harold Holt in Hartford, Connecticut, Silver was discovered by saxophonist Stan Getz. Getz hired him for a group that toured extensively between 1950 and 1951. Within weeks of an August 1951 studio session, Silver left Getz's group in order to establish himself in New York City's flourishing jazz scene. By performing at Birdland, he was able to accompany many of the leading jazz talents of the day. In *Song of the Hawk,* Silver recalled playing Birdland with "Hawk [Coleman Hawkins] and bassist Curly Russell— once with Roy Eldridge and Art Blakey, once with Howard McGhee and Art Taylor. It was a privilege and an honor. Like most great artists, Hawk showed not only genius but consistency." During the early 1950s, he performed with saxophonist Lester Young and bebop bassist Oscar Pettiford.

Silver's first sides as a leader for the Blue Note label, a company he would have a steady working relationship for the next 40 years, were a series of trio dates from 1952 and 1953. These recordings featured Art Blakey and the varied bass accompaniment of Gene Ramey, Curly Russell, and Percy Heath. These early efforts captured a number of Silver's original compositions such as "Quicksilver," "Safari," and "Opus De Funk." Around the same time he debuted on the Blue Note label, Silver took part in numerous sessions for the Savoy label. On these recordings, he performed with saxophonists Lou Donaldson and Al Cohn. In 1954, Silver led a quartet at Minton's Playhouse with saxophonist Hank Mobley and bassist Doug Watkins. In February of 1954, he appeared as a member of the Art Blakey Quintet for the Blue Note album *At Night At Birdland Vol. I* and *Vol. II.* Under Blakey's leadership, Silver joined trumpeter Clifford Brown, Lou Donaldson, and bassist Curly Russell for a showcase of hard bop which included his three original compositions "Split Kick," "Quicksilver," and "Myreh." Nick Catalano, author of *Clifford Brown: The Life and Art of the Legendary Jazz Trumpeter,* emphasized that the *Birdland* album "has become a jazz classic for many reasons; the brilliant improvisations, the innovative Silver compositions, the quintessential hard bop musical statements, and the production standards by Rudy Van Gelder and Blue Note."

In 1954, Silver led a Blue Note recording band under the name The Jazz Messengers. The Jazz Messengers was a quintet that included his Minton's sidemen Mobely and Watkins along with Blakey and trumpeter Kenny Dorham. Although Blakey had led a big band called the Jazz Messengers in 1947, the formation of this smaller cooperative unit marked the official debut of a band that, under Blakey's subsequent leadership, would become a premiere showcase of young jazz talent. Cut in two sessions in December of 1954 and February of 1955, *Horace Silver and the Jazz Messengers* featured six original Silver compositions including "The Preacher," a groundbreaking number of what became known as hard bop or soul jazz. An immensely popular number among jazz musicians, "The Preacher" was described by Ira Gitler in the album's liner notes as "an earthy swinger", and derived its melody from "Show Me the Way to Go Home."

During 1954, Silver also took part in Prestige recording dates led by Miles Davis. As Davis explained in his memoir, *Miles,* "I liked the way Horace played piano....He put fire under my playing." In March of 1954, Davis recorded with Silver, Blakey, and bassist Percy Heath. "Silver's presence on Davis' Blue Note date and also on his next three recording sessions during this prolific spring," commented Jack Chambers in *Milestones,* "gave him exactly the kind of exposure he needed. His immediate blossoming as a major talent further enhanced Davis' reputation as a jazz mentor." Several Davis-led sessions held in March and April of 1954 yielded material that was included on the albums

Blue Haze and *Walkin.'* Silver returned to the studio with Davis in late June of 1954, and appeared on the album *Miles Davis and The Jazz Giants: Bag's Groove* with tenor saxophonist Sonny Rollins, Percy Heath, and drummer Kenny Clarke.

Silver won the New Star piano category of *Down Beat* magazine's International Critic's Poll in 1954. Over the next two years, he found himself in great demand as a Blue Note session pianist. In 1955 he recorded with saxophonist Milt Jackson, Gigi Gryce, and Kenny Clarke, and also appeared with an eight-piece band (including the conga playing of Carlos "Potato" Valdes) on Dorham's Blue Note album *Afro-Cuban.* Under the leadership of Art Blakey, Silver, Dorham, and Watkins appeared together at a club date in November of 1955. The session was released as the live recordings, *The Jazz Messengers at the Cafe Bohemia Vol. I* and *Vol. II.* Silver's next two recording sessions with Art Blakey took place in April and May of 1956, and were released as the Columbia album *Art Blakey, The Jazz Messengers.* The album featured Dorham's trumpet replacement, Donald Byrd, in addition to Mobely and Watkins. "It is my opinion," stated drummer Kenny Washington in the liner notes to *The Jazz Messengers,* "that by the time these 1956 Columbia sides were released the Messengers had found a sound of their own. Credit must also be given to Horace Silver for this direction." In September of 1956, Silver provided the piano accompaniment for bassist Paul Chambers's Blue Note release, *Whims of Chambers.* The recording also included Donald Byrd, John Coltrane, Kenny Burrell, and Philly Joe Jones.

In 1956, Silver left The Jazz Messengers to form his own group with Mobley and trumpeter Art Farmer. During the following year, he continued to record with artists like Sonny Rollins. Silver's late 1958 release *Further Explorations*— which featured Farmer, saxophonist Clifford Jordan, bassist Teddy Kotick and drummer Louis Hayes—represented, according to David Rosenthal in *Hard Bop,* "the most successful crystallization of his style as a pianist, composer, and bandleader... .At the time it was recorded, the quintet had been playing together for many months and had evolved into one of the best-integrated combos in jazz." Silver's 1959 Blue Note album, *Blowin' The Blues Away,* became a fiery showcase of original compositions featuring saxophonist Blue Mitchell, trumpeter Junior Cook, bassist Gene Taylor, and drummer Louis Hayes. From the album's break neck title track, "The Baghdad Blues" to the beautiful ballad "Peace" and the classic and often covered "Sister Sadie" the unit, whether in its quintet or trio setting, played some of the finest music of the hard bop era. "Apropos of all the talk about 'soul' and 'funk' lately," discussed Ira Gitler in the liner notes to *Blowin' The Blues Away,* "it is interesting to note that with Horace Silver, the one who has them in abundant amounts, they have always been natural qualities and never the result of self-conscious striving."

Though a premiere exponent of soul jazz, Silver's music did not limit itself to a blues and gospel influenced sound. As Thomas Owens asserted in *Bebop: The Music and Its Players,* "For every down-home 'funky' tune there is one or more that in no way fits the 'funky' stereotype." Silver's musical repertoire, noted Rosenthal in *Hard Bop,* contained "some of modern jazz's most poignant ballads... .In addition, he was something of an innovator in his compositions, venturing into time signatures (like the 6/8 he used in his major hits, 'Senor Blues') and bar lengths (like the 16-6-16 structure of 'Swingin' Samaba') that broke with jazz's traditional Tin Pan Alley-derived-two-bar A-A-B-A formula." In *The History of Jazz,* Ted Gioia also explained that many of Silver's compositions reflected a "refreshing diversity" of 6/8 rhythms and "jazz waltzes" and "Caribbean-Latin Hybrids." The latter style found its way into Silver's music following a trip to Rio de Janeiro when he heard the authentic playing of bossa nova. Inspired by Brazilian music, he decided to incorporate the bossa nova sound as well as the folk music of his father's Cape Verdean heritage into his jazz compositions. In 1963, Silver debuted his Caribbean and Latin-tinged material on Blue Note's *Song For My Father.* The album became one of the company's best-selling recordings and stayed on the charts for many weeks. It was also named by *Down Beat* magazine readers as one of the top five jazz albums of the year. Cut in three sessions, the album captured two different quintets, one with trumpeter Carmell Jones, Joe Henderson, Teddy Smith, and Roger Humphries—and the other with Mitchell, Cook, Gene Taylor, and Roy Brooks. In May of 1963, *Silver's Serenade* was released. The album contained five original Sliver compositions, along with the Mitchell-Cook front line and the rhythm section of Taylor and Brooks.

In 1964, Silver recruited saxophonist Joe Henderson and, the following year, added trumpeter Woody Shaw to his band. In *History of Jazz,* Gioia stated "Horace Silver's mid-1960s combo might have challenged Blakey's supremacy in the hard-bop idiom, if it had only lasted longer. Its front line of saxophonist Joe Henderson and trumpeter Woody Shaw featured two of the most promising younger jazz talents of the day." The horns of Shaw and Henderson, augmented by guest trombonist J.J. Johnson, provided the accompaniment for Silver's Blue Note album, *The Cape Verdean Blues.* Recorded in the fall of 1965, the album showcased five original numbers and continued Silver's foray into Latin-Caribbean influences. "Listening to these sides," commented Leonard Feather in the album's liner notes, "one can understand easily why Horace Silver's success pattern has taken him forward uninterruptedly for almost ten years. The Horace Silver Quintet albums are predictable only to the extent that one can foretell their general character. Horace Silver is one composer who is never content to rest on past achievements." A mix of soul jazz and Latin sounds, Silver's 1966 Blue Note release, *The Jody Grind,* exhibited his artistic consistency as composer and bandleader. Apart from the bluesy title track, the album contains the original compositions "Mary Lou" and "Mexican Hip Dance."

Because of its versatility and modern edge, Silver's music influenced musical trends outside mainstream jazz. John Storm Roberts, in his book *Latin Jazz: The First of the Fusions,* commented that during the 1970s "Silver's soul-Latin mix would give another shot in the arm to the movement toward a funk-Latin jazz fusion." During the 1980s, Silver's Latin-tinged music reached London discos, and influenced many of "the Young Lions" of the new acoustic jazz school. However, as Stuart Nicholson observed in *Jazz: The 1980s Resurgence,* "Silver...failed to capitalize on the bebop revival of the 1980s in the way several of his contemporaries did." In 1981, Silver formed Silveto Records. As he explained in *Talking Jazz,* the label was devoted to "self-help, holistic, metaphysical music" intended to integrate "a trilogy, consisting of spirit, mind and body." Among the best of his Silveto recordings was *Music to Ease Your Disease.* This album featured Silver's former saxophonist Junior Cook, trumpeter Clark Terry, bassist Billy Drummond, and drummer Billy Hart. Silver returned to his hard bop roots during the 1990s, and recorded the Columbia releases *It's Got to Be Funky* in 1993 and *Pencil Packin' Papa* in 1994. He also recorded *The Hardbop Grandpop!* in 1996 and *Jazz Has a Sense of Humor* in 1999 for the Impulse! label. His 1997 Silveto release, *A Prescription For the Blues,* featured the horns of Michael and Randy Brecker, bassist Ron Carter, and longtime sideman Louis Hayes. Silver's music was included on a Blue Note remix release in 1998, and appeared as part of the company's three CD compilation, *The Blue Note Years.*

A musician whose musical career spanned from hardbop to a modern sound drenched in a "funky" earthiness and Latin-Caribbean sound, Silver has created a formidable and influential style by distilling the kinetic energy of bebop into a music of emotional intensity and beauty. In his book *Talking Jazz,* Ben Sidran noted, "To this day jazz players 'quote' his [Silver's] writing and playing, and many of the young lions, those emerging in the popular press, try their best to imitate his compositional devices and to reinvent the Horace Silver sound."

Selected discography

Horace Silver and the Jazz Messengers, Blue Note, 1955.
Six Pieces of Silver, Blue Note, 1956.
Further Exlporations, Blue Note, 1958.
Blowin' the Blues Away, Blue Note, 1959.
Horace-Scope, Blue Note, 1960.
Tokyo Blues, Blue Note, 1962.
Silver's Serenade, Blue Note, 1963.
Song For My Father, Blue Note, 1964.
The Horace Sliver Quintet Plus J.J. Johnson, The Cape Verdean Blues, Blue Note, 1965.
The Jody Grind, Blue Note, 1966.
Serenade to a Soul Sister, Blue Note, 1968.
Spiritualizing the Senses, Silveto, 1983.
It's Got to Be Funky, Columbia, 1993.
Hardbop Grandpop, Impulse!, 1996.
Prescription For the Blues, Impulse!, 1997.
Jazz Has a Sense of Humor, Impulse!, 1999.
Horace Silver Retrospective, Blue Note, 1999.

with Miles Davis

Miles Davis, Blue Haze, Prestige, 1954.
Miles, United Artists, 1954.
Miles Davis Allstars, Prestige, 1954.
Miles Davis and The Jazz Giants, Bags' Groove, Prestige, 1954.

with others

Stan Getz: Birdland Sessions, 1952.
Al Cohn, Cohn's Tones, Savoy, 1953.
Art Farmer, Art Farmer Septet, 1953.
A Night at Birdland With the Art Blakey Quintet Vol. 1 and 2, Blue Note, 1954.
The Jazz Messengers at the Cafe Bohemia, Vol. 1 and 2, Blue Note, 1955.
Kenny Dorham, Afro-Cuban, Blues Note, 1955.
Kenny Clarke, Bohemia After Dark, Savoy, 1955.
Gigi Gryce, Nica's Tempo, Savoy, 1955.
Art Blakey and The Jazz Messengers, Columbia, 1956.
The Jazz Message of Hank Mobley, Savoy, 1956.
Paul Chambers, Whims of Chambers, Blue Note, 1956.
Sonny Rollins Vol. Two, Blue Note, 1957.

Sources

Books

Catalano, Nick, *Clifford Brown: The Life and Art of the Legendary Jazz Trumpeter,* Oxford University Press, 2000.
Chambers, Jack, with new introduction, *Milestones: The Music and Times of Miles Davis,* Da Capo, 1998.
Chilton, John, *The Song of the Hawk: The Life and Recordings of Coleman Hawkins,* Ann Arbor, University of Michigan Press, 1990.
Davis, Miles with Qunicy Troupe, *Miles, The Autobiography,* Touchstone Books, 1990.
Gioia, Ted. *The History of Jazz,* Oxford University Press, 1997.
Maggin, Donald L., *Stan Getz: A Life in Jazz,* Quill, 1996.
Owens, Thomas, *Bebop, The Music and Its Players,* Oxford University Press, 1993.

Roberts, John Storm, *Latin Jazz: The of the First Fusions 1880's to Today,* Schirmer Books, 1999.

Rosenthal, David H., *Hard Bop: Jazz and Black Music 1955-1965,* Oxford University Press, 1992.

Sidran, Ben, *Talking Jazz: An Oral History,* Da Capo, 1995.

Other

Additional information for this profile was obtained from the liner notes by Ira Gitler *Horace Silver and the Jazz Messengers* and *Blowin' the Blues Away;* Kenny Washington, *Art Blakey and the Jazz Messengers;* and a telephone conversation with Horace Silver, Malibu, California, June 21, 2000.

—John Cohassey

Barbara A. Sizemore

1927—

Educator

Barbara Sizemore is a woman for whom the restrictions placed on African American achievement actually led her to her life's calling. A classical languages major with a gift for Latin, Sizemore dreamed of becoming a translator with the United Nations. But in 1947, when she graduated from Northwestern University, teaching was one of the few professional avenues open to African American women, and it is within the realm of education that Sizemore has reached the highest level of professional achievement.

Barbara Laffoon Sizemore was born in December 17, 1927 in Chicago, Illinois. Her parents, Sylvester and Delilah Laffoon, had moved to Chicago from Terre Haute, Indiana in search of jobs and a better life. However, shortly after Barbara was born, the Great Depression destroyed any opportunities for economic advancement and forced her family to return home. It was in Terre Haute, 72 miles southwest of Indianapolis, that Sizemore spent her formative years.

For an African American living in Terre Haute in the 1930s, daily life mimicked that of northern Kentucky; that is to say, while Indiana had never been a slave state, Jim Crow laws were strictly enforced. Sizemore still vividly recalls the segregation of her childhood: her inability to try on clothes at a store or to eat at lunch counters, seats at the back of the bus, theater tickets only in the balcony. Her elementary and middle schools, from kindergarten through the eighth grade, were also segregated. Throughout these years, all of her teachers were highly-educated African Americans. Despite the obstacles presented by segregation, Sizemore received an excellent education.

It was not until the ninth grade that Sizemore attended an integrated school. She quickly deduced that the segregation of the community at large had deeply penetrated into the school structure. In an interview with *Contemporary Black Biography,* Sizemore recounted her initial placement in section 9B3, the highest section available to African American students. When her mother was dismayed at the ease with which Sizemore sailed through her coursework, she marched into the school and demanded that her daughter be placed in the most advanced ninth grade section. However, according to Sizemore, "white supremacy" prevented this move, and she was elevated only to section 9B2.

At a Glance . . .

Born Barbara Ann Laffoon December 17, 1927 in Chicago, IL; daughter of Sylvester and Delilah Laffoon; married and divorced; children: six. *Education:* Northwestern University, Evanston, IL, BA in classical languages, 1947, MA in elementary education, 1954; University of Chicago, Chicago, IL, Ph.D. in educational administration, 1979.

Career: Teacher, Chicago Public Schools, 1947-62; served as principal of Anton Dvorak Elementary School, Chicago, IL; principal, Forrestville High School, Chicago, IL; director, Woodlawn Experimental School District; associate secretary of the American Association of School Administrators, Arlington, VA 1972-73; superintendent of schools,Washington, D.C., 1973-75; educational consultant, 1975-77; associate professor, professor, interim chairperson, Department of Black Community, Research and Education, University of Pittsburgh, Pittsburgh, PA, 1977-92; professor emerita, University of Pittsburgh, 1992-; dean, School of Education, DePaul University, Chicago, IL, 1992-98; professor emerita, DePaul University, 1998-.

Selected awards: Charles D. Moody Service Award, National Alliance of Black SchoolEducators, 1999; Harold Delaney Educational Leadership Award, American Association of Higher Education, 1999; New Jersey Association of Parent Coordinators Award, 2000.

Selected memberships: Delta Sigma Theta; Urban League; NAACP; Phi Delta Kappa; board member, Consortium on Chicago School Research, 1992-.

Addresses: *Office*—School of Education, DePaul University—Levan Zoic, 2320 N. Kenmore Avenue, Chicago, IL 60614.

In 1935, Sizemore's father was killed in an accident. Her mother remarried in 1940, and the family moved to Evanston, Illinois in 1943. At the time, Sizemore was a senior in high school, ranked number one in her class, and was president of the national honor society. Concerned that her daughter would lose her number one ranking, Sizemore's mother paid the state of Illinois to allow her to graduate from Wiley High School in Terre Haute, the same school from which Sizemore's parents had graduated.

In return, Sizemore spent the final semester of her senior year at Evanston Township High School, "the most racist place I have ever been," she told *CBB.* "It was as if the teachers were trying to make me fit into the stereotype of the Black student that they had in their heads." For instance, she was assigned more difficult work than her white classmates. In a contest to judge students' performance of a sonnet, Sizemore tied for first place with a white student. In order to declare one winner, the teacher assigned each finalist a new project. While the white student was asked to prepare a Milton sonnet with a simple structural scheme, Sizemore was instructed to learn the first 22 lines of Chaucer's *The Canterbury Tales*—in Old English. When the Women's Club of Evanston was prepared to present the graduating senior with the highest marks in social studies with a $500.00 cash prize, Sizemore's social studies teacher did not give any A grades to her students so that Sizemore, the leading candidate, could not claim the prize.

Sizemore's mother would not allow such blatant racism to detract from her plan to ensure that her daughter would earn a college degree. Both of Sizemore's parents had graduated from Indiana State Teacher's College. During Sizemore's senior year, her mother worked as a domestic for a dentist who was president of the Northwestern University Alumni Association, and she asked him for assistance. Sizemore's mother told her employer about her daughter's ability to speak Latin. In an interview with *CBB,* Sizemore wittily commented that being able to speak Latin fluently was comparable to "being born in the 20th century with a gift for being the world's best chariot driver." While speaking Latin may have seemed anachronistic, it proved critical to her future. The dentist told Sizemore's mother that Northwestern University offered a classical language scholarship, and encouraged her daughter to apply for it. However, Sizemore was informed that the scholarship could not be presented to an African American. Unwilling to accept this outcome, the dentist researched the award more closely and ensured that Sizemore received the scholarship.

Sizemore attended Northwestern from 1944 until 1947. Her experience at the university was not a happy one. Appalled by the racism that was prevalent on the campus, Sizemore helped to form a group called Students for Educational Equality in 1946. The group was composed mostly of African Americans and Jews, who also faced racism on campus. One day, Sizemore recalled in an interview with *CBB,* the group picketed the university president's home. She looked to the west, and saw a person approaching her. "That looks like my mother," Sizemore recounted to *CBB.* Her mother was working at the Great Lakes Naval Training Station, and had traveled to the campus. Sizemore's mother grabbed her daughter and dragged her from the protest. She begged Sizemore to protest only after she had received her degree. Other mothers also appeared on the scene, and the protest was disbanded.

Despite her unhappiness, Sizemore remained at Northwestern. Upon graduating in 1947 with a bachelor of arts degree in classical languages, she immediately began to teach in the Chicago public schools. Initially, Sizemore taught English and reading to the mentally disadvantaged and Spanish in an elementary school. In 1954, she earned a master's degree in elementary education from Northwestern. Sizemore eventually left teaching in 1963 to become principal of the Anton Dvorak Elementary School. She became the first African American woman to be appointed principal of a Chicago school. In 1965, Sizemore became the principal of Forrestville High School. As Nancy Arnez explained in *The Besieged School Superintendent,* by this time Sizemore's "creative spirit had reached its stride as she initiated efforts to turn Forrestville from a gangland oasis into an innovative hiatus for the creative energies of her students, using the arts as a vehicle for learning the basic skills."

After four years at Forrestville, Sizemore embraced a new challenge in 1969 when she became director and district superintendent of the Woodlawn Experimental Schools Project. She also served as an instructor at Northwestern's Center for Inner City Studies, an innovate multi-disciplinary, multi-ethnic graduate school program located on Chicago's impoverished South Side. When the project went bankrupt in 1971, Sizemore became the coordinator for proposal development within the Department of Government Funded Programs for the Chicago public schools. In 1973, she left the Chicago public school system to become the associate secretary of the American Association of School Administrators in Arlington, Virginia. One year later, Sizemore was elected superintendent of schools for the District of Columbia public school system. The election marked the first time that an African American woman had been chosen to head a public school system in a major city, and Sizemore was thrust into the national spotlight. In *The Besieged School Superintendent,* Arnez remarked that Sizemore was elected superintendent of schools in Washington, D.C. because of her impressive accomplishments as a principal in Chicago and her philosophy of education. This philosophy was based on the principle of equal education for all students. As Arnez noted in her book, Sizemore argued that "All can learn equally in general only as they can learn differently...what we need is an educational system for people, all of whom are different instead of one for people who are assumed to be alike. All talent then becomes significant in an institution where there is justice for all."

Given this core value, Sizemore fervently believed that the organizational structure—the teaching and learning environment—had to be changed so that schools met the needs of all students as they mature. She also held that public schools do not fully utilize the talents of African American students. In Sizemore's opinion, the situation demanded a reconstruction of the teaching/learning environment along multi-modal (containing children of different ethnicity, age, and size within the group), multi-lingual, and multi-cultural lines. In interviews leading to her selection as superintendent, Sizemore also articulated additional systemic changes, including non-grading, team teaching, a K-12 integrated structure, curriculum changes, and an administrative team concept, which she hoped to implement.

During her tenure as superintendent of the Washington, D.C. public school system, Sizemore tackled several highly visible and politicized issues, including the abolishment of standardized testing and the decentralization of the school system. Standardized tests, she believed, reflected a bias toward Anglo-Saxon values and placed minority students at a disadvantage. As Arnez further explained in *The Besieged School Superintendent,* Sizemore emphatically held that these tests were not used "as tools for learning what special services or extra resources each child needs to meet his special 'growth rates, development patterns, learning styles, cultural heritage and sociolinguistic experiences.'"

Sizemore pushed ahead with her plans to restructure the District of Columbia school system. On July 1, 1974, she authorized the decentralization of the school system into six regions. The system, as Sizemore envisioned it, would provide multi-age, multi-level groupings within individual classrooms. She also sought to flatten the administrative hierarchy by involving parents, administrators, community leaders, teachers, and students in a collaborative decision-making body that would help to set and achieve educational goals.

After two controversial years as school superintendent, Sizemore was fired by the District of Columbia school on October 9, 1975. As Arnez remarked to Ann Bradley of *Education Week,* Sizemore was "before her time...she's a brilliant person. She tried to do some things in D.C. that people couldn't accept. The fact that she could stand up to authority is one of the things that frightened people. Her approach to Congress was not one of supplication and of begging. She was just putting forth, in a strong manner, the kinds of things she had in mind to help these nonachieving students achieve...[No one expected] that she would openly challenge the school board and demand that a majority Black school system serve the needs of Black children, and that curriculum be designed to fit that need."

Sizemore told *CBB* that she "didn't know the first thing about D.C." before her arrival. She also called Washington, D.C. "a colony." Governed by Congress or, as Sizemore remarked to *CBB,* its "racist white power structure," citizens have no power to enforce their own decisions. Even their elected congressional representatives have no power to vote. Her behavior as superintendent, Sizemore told *CBB,* did not reflect this reality until it was too late. "I pretended I had power to make decisions when I didn't have power to do anything. It took too long for reality to burst into my consciousness to allow me to make good decisions and, by the time that it did, I had made too many bad ones." The D.C. Board of Education, moreover, also pretended to wield power that it did not possess. When the Board discussed the decentralization of the public school system, Sizemore thought they were serious and believed that such a move would make a difference. In truth, however, the school board feared change and predominantly voiced support for the status quo. "What they really wanted," Sizemore told *CBB,* "was for me to fire the people they didn't like and hire those they did."

Needless to say, Sizemore's experience within the Washington D.C. public school system greatly affected her world view. Previously, she believed that democracy was esteemed as the highest value in the United States, and that American citizens truly sought equality of opportunity and access for everyone. Sizemore came to believe, however, that capitalism and the pursuit of wealth actually stood as this nation's most cherished values. As an economic system, capitalism does not allow for equality. Instead, some will benefit greatly from the system, while others are victimized by it. When this realization became clear, Sizemore found a context for the nation's focus and insistence on standardized testing, as well as her next mission. "Once I understood this," Sizemore told *CBB,* "my mission became clear: help African Americans to pass the tests."

From 1975 until 1992, Sizemore taught at the University of Pittsburgh. During her tenure, she conducted research on schools that effectively served low-income African American children. Sizemore returned to Chicago in 1992, and assumed a professorship at DePaul University. As Dean of the School of Education, she created her School Achievement Structure (SAS) program, which is designed to enable African American students to compete successfully on any standardized exam. As Sizemore remarked in an article for *Catalyst—Chicago,* "School improvement will not happen until the school employees make student achievement their highest priority and agree to cooperate and collaborate in changing their educational routines to attain it." SAS laid out ten routines dealing with assessment, student placement, curriculum pacing and acceleration, monitoring, measuring, discipline, instruction, evaluation, professional development, and decision making. Assimilating SAS into the curriculum would, according to Sizemore, help low-achieving schools in Chicago convert into high performers.

SAS, at its fundamental level, embodied a complete reversal of Sizemore's position while in Washington. No longer arguing for the abolishment of national standardized testing, she now put forth a curriculum in which standardized tests dictated the course of daily classwork. Within this structure, Sizemore's SAS program helped to determine progress and enable students to move quickly through specific, pre-determined tasks.

In 1995, the Illinois State Legislature gave control of the Chicago Public Schools to the mayor. Paul Vallas was chosen as CEO of the public school system. He immediately asked Sizemore to serve as his chief education officer because he was impressed with her vision, commitment, and dedication. As Vallas commented to Bradley in *Education Week,* "Barbara takes over schools that no one wants to take and makes them work. Period. They have nowhere to go but up. Everybody wants to take the elementary schools, and nobody wants the high schools. She's the only one with the guts." Sizemore declined Vallas' offer, but promised to help him close the achievement gap between minority and majority children.

Sizemore is also deeply committed to teaching children how to read. A talented reading teacher, she is harsh in her criticism of schools. As she insisted in an interview with *Education Week,* "There is too much laxness in our schools. The fear of the progressive people is that teachers will get caught up in the mechanics. Their own flaw is that they don't teach the kids how to read."

Sizemore continues to serve as a consultant to Vallas. Test scores in her targeted schools have started to rise, fueling renewed optimism in the SAS program. Schools in Indianapolis and Dallas/Fort Worth have also enlisted the help of this dynamic and strong-willed woman. With ever-increasing attention being focused on the poor condition of public schools in the United States, Sizemore may once again stand in the national spotlight.

Selected writings

The Politics of Decentralization: A Case Study of the Public Schools of the District of Columbia, 1979.

The Ruptured Diamond: The Politics of the Decentralization of the District of Columbia Public Schools, University Press of America, 1981.

Sources

Books

Arnez, Nancy, *The Besieged School Superintendent,* University of America Press, 1981.

Periodicals

Catalyst – Chicago, September 1998.

Education Week, March 13, 1996.

Other

Additional information for this profile was obtained from an interview with *Contemporary Black Biography* on June 21, 2000.

—Lisa S. Weitzman

Mary Carter Smith

1919—

Storyteller, educator

Before the 1970s, few Americans knew the meaning of the word "griot". Mary Carter Smith helped to change that. Perhaps no other individual has done more to bring traditional African stories, poems and songs to life across the United States. Her contribution to the continuation of African oral tradition in America has been significant. Since the beginning of Smith's career, interest in African history and heritage has blossomed. She is also the state of Maryland's official "griot," or African storyteller.

Mary Carter Smith was born Mary Rogers Ward on February 10, 1919 in Birmingham, Alabama. She and her mother, Eartha Nowden, a domestic worker, lived with Eartha's mother, Mary Deas Nowden. Smith never developed much of a relationship with her father, Rogers Ward. Eartha Nowden and Rogers Ward eventually divorced. When Mary was four years old, Eartha married Warren Coleman, and Mary was renamed Mary Rogers Coleman. One year later, Warren Coleman died of tuberculosis. Smith's mother married her third husband, Earl Knight, and the family moved to New York. Tragically, Knight shot Eartha Nowden to death less than a year after they married. Smith was left in the care of her grandmother.

Moved to Ohio

Meanwhile, Smith's uncles had moved north in search of better jobs. One of them, known as Brother, settled in Youngstown, Ohio, and invited Smith and her grandmother to live with him. While living in Youngstown, Smith became an avid reader and excellent student. When she wasn't reading, she was telling stories she had created or learned from her grandmother. Throughout most of the 1920s, Smith would visit her aunts during the summer months. In 1927 her uncles moved to New Jersey in search of better jobs, and Smith and her grandmother went to live in West Virginia with Smith's aunt, Sally Lou Nowden Coleman.

Two years later, Smith's life would again be touched by tragedy when her grandmother became seriously ill with cancer. In 1932, she succumbed to the disease. By this time Smith was living with another aunt, Willie Nowden McAdory—known inside the family as Aunt Booby—in the West Virginia town of Edwight. In 1934, the McAdorys were run out of Edwight by anti-union goons who were hostile to the labor organizing activities of Aunt Booby's coal miner husband Norman McAdory. They relocated to Idamay in upstate

At a Glance . . .

Born Mary Rogers Ward on February 10, 1919, in Birmingham, AL; daughter of Eartha Nowden (a domestic worker) and Rogers Ward; married Ulysses J. Carter, 1946 (divorced 1951); married Elias Raymond Smith, 1960 (widowed 1962); children: Ricardo Rogers Carter (deceased). *Education:* Coppin Teachers College, BS, 1942.

Career: Teacher and librarian, Baltimore Public Schools, 1942-73; professional storyteller, 1969-, full-time beginning 1973; producer and host, *Griot for the Young and Young at Heart* radio show, WEAA-FM, 1975- ; founded Citizen's Coalition of Baltimore, 1981.

Awards: Sojourner Truth Award, 1965; Distinguished Alumni Citation, Coppin State College, 1966; Community Service Award, National Council of Jewish Women, 1967; Distinguished Teacher Award, National Council of Negro Women, 1968; Distinguished WomanAward, Delta Theta Sigma Sorority, 1973; National Citation, Phi Delta Kappa, Inc., 1976; namedBaltimore's Official Griot, 1983; Keeper of the Flame Aware, Maryland Writers' Council, 1983; Twenty Women of Distinction, African-American Women's PoliticalCaucus, 1983; Beautiful Black Woman Award, Towson State University, 1985; installed in Baltimore Great Blacks in Wax Museum, 1989; named Maryland's Official Griot, 1991; named America's Mother Griot, National Association of Black Storytellers, 1994.

Addresses: *Office*—PO Box 11484, Baltimore, MD 21239.

West Virginia. One year later, Aunt Booby went blind, and the family moved to Baltimore so that she could receive treatment for her condition. Smith attended her last two years of high school at Baltimore's Frederick Douglass High. At Douglass, she continued to develop her emerging storytelling skills by participating in the school drama and speech clubs.

After graduating from high school in 1938, Smith enrolled at Coppin Teachers College in Baltimore. In 1942, she earned her elementary education degree from Coppin. She immediately went to work as an elementary school teacher and librarian in Baltimore's inner-city schools, a career that would last 31 years. In 1946, after a brief courtship, she married Ulysses J. Carter and took the name Mary Coleman Carter. Her only child, Ricardo Rogers Carter, was born two years later. Unlike many teachers of that period, Smith returned to work only a year after the birth of her son. Less than five years into her marriage to Ulysses Carter, the couple divorced. Smith was now a single parent.

Although the Baltimore public schools had a high percentage of African American students, the system did not offer classes on African culture or heritage. Smith sought to change this situation. She began to dress in dashikis and adorned herself in traditional ornamental bracelets and necklaces. She also became a serious collector of traditional African stories, poems, and songs. In addition to teaching her students about their African heritage, Smith became involved in their lives outside of the classroom by providing emotional support to troubled students.

Smith married again in 1960. Her second husband, Elias Raymond Smith, was an old acquaintance from West Virginia whom Smith had dated years earlier. Smith reestablished contact with him when she learned that his first wife had died, and they married a short time later. Less than two years later, Smith suffered yet another tragic loss when Elias Smith died of kidney failure. In 1966, she began publishing poetry that she had written. Her books of poetry include *Town Child* and *Laugh a Little, Cry a Lot.*

In 1969, two events changed Smith's life. She traveled to Ghana, the first of her many trips to Africa, and immersed herself in the native culture. Secondly, she also discovered that she could receive payment for telling stories and reciting poetry in public. Smith contacted an agent, and was quickly hired as an emergency replacement for a poet who had to cancel an appearance in Augusta, Georgia. Her performance was a hit, and marked the beginning of Smith's career as a professional storyteller.

In 1971, Smith took a leave of absence from teaching to pursue storytelling on a full-time basis. Her popularity as a storyteller increased, and she performed at schools, churches, festivals and other venues. By 1973, it became clear to Smith that she had to decide between careers in teaching or storytelling. After 31 years of teaching in the Baltimore public schools, she left to become a full-time storyteller of traditional African tales.

Soon after leaving the Baltimore school system, Smith became the hostess of a Maryland Public Television show entitled "Black Is." During the mid-1970s, interest in African culture increased following the publication of Alex Haley's novel, *Roots.* In 1977, an award-winning film based on the novel was aired on national television. Smith was introduced to Haley, who told her that she was a "griot," the traditional word for African storyteller. In fact, Haley began referring to Smith as "my American griot." In 1975, Smith launched a radio show on WEAA-FM in Baltimore. The name of the show, for which Smith served as creator, producer and host, was *Griot for the Young and Young of Heart.* The show continued to air throughout the 1990s.

Smith was again burdened by tragedy in 1978 when her only child, Ricardo, was stabbed to death in a Baltimore bar. Rather than letting herself be destroyed by grief, Smith incorporated the emotional impact of losing her son to violence into her art. She often included the story of her son's death in her presentations.

Smith's popularity and acclaim continued to grow during the 1980s. She became an activist, founding the Citizen's Coalition of Baltimore in 1981, and spearheading the movement to observe Martin Luther King, Jr.'s birthday. In 1983, Smith was named as "Baltimore's Official Griot." That same year, she co-founded the National Association of Black Storytellers with fellow storyteller Linda Goss. In 1989, Baltimore's Great Blacks in Wax Museum immortalized Smith in wax. Two years later, Smith became the state of Maryland's official griot. In 1994, she was named "America's Mother Griot" by the National Association of Black Storytellers.

In 1998, Smith was inducted into the Maryland Women's Hall of Fame. Her influence, however, has reached far beyond the borders of Maryland. During the summer of 1999, she traveled to Ghana for the first international conference on storytelling. Smith has crossed both geographical and generational barriers. Through her work with children, a new generation of griots has been created. Smith's efforts will ensure that future generations can enjoy the beauty of traditional African stories, songs, and poems.

Selected writings

Opinionated, Beacon Press, 1966.
Laugh a Little, Cry a Lot, Young Publications, 1967.
A Few Words, Aframa Agency, 1971.
Vibes, Nordika Publications, 1974.
(with Alice McGill and Elmira Washington) *The Griots' Cookbook: Rare and Well-Done,* C.H. Fairfax, 1985.

Sources

Books

Beckles, Frances N., *20 Black Women,* Gateway Press, 1978.
Hajdusiewicz, Babs Bell, *Mary Carter Smith, African-American Storyteller,* Enslow, 1995.

Periodicals

Baltimore Business Journal, December 27, 1991, p. 1.
Baltimore Sun, October 10, 1994, p. 1B; December 29, 1995, p. 1E; July 11, 1999, p. 2B.
Washington Post, April 20, 1989, p. M1.

—Robert R. Jacobson

Mildred D. Taylor

1943—

Writer

Mildred Delois Taylor is a critically acclaimed author of children's novels. Most of her works, which are based on her own family history, revolve around the close-knit Logan family, an African American family that rises above the indignities of racism through courage and love. In 1977, Taylor won the Newbery Medal, the most prestigious award in children's literature, for her historical novel *Roll of Thunder, Hear My Cry.* Since 1977, Taylor's fiction continued to portray the effects of racism counterbalanced with courage and love. In doing so, her fiction defied the "political correctness" of the 1990s.

Taylor was born at home on September 13, 1943 in Jackson, Mississippi, where she joined her older sister Wilma. Their paternal great-grandfather, the son of a white Alabama plantation owner and a slave woman, had become a successful farmer in Mississippi. His large extended family thrived despite the racism they encountered. Yet Taylor's parents, Wilbert and Deletha, wanted their daughters to grow up in a less racist society. Delois, as her family called Mildred, was only four months old when they, like thousands of other southern African American families, boarded a segregated train bound for the North. Upon arriving in Toledo, Ohio, the Taylors stayed with friends until they earned enough money to buy a large duplex on a busy commercial street. This house soon became home to aunts, uncles, and cousins, who eventually moved away from Mississippi in search of a better life.

Taylor enjoyed being surrounded by so many family members, who gave her attention when her parents were busy. Her neighborhood, with its café and movie theater, provided plenty of entertainment, and the Taylor family enjoyed several other forms of recreation, as well, such as storytelling. Taylor vividly stored in her memory the tales she heard at family gatherings. Many of these stories would later play an important role in her novels. In the author's note to *Roll of Thunder, Hear My Cry,* Taylor acknowledged her debt to this oral history and to her father in particular, "By the fireside in our northern home or in the South where I was born, I learned a history not then written in books but one passed from generation to generation on the steps of moonlit porches and beside dying fires in one-room houses, a history of great-grandparents and of slavery and of the days following slavery; of those who lived still not free, yet who would not let their spirits be enslaved. From my father the storyteller I learned to respect the past, to respect my own heritage and myself."

In addition to the oral stories, books played an important role in Taylor's life from an early age. An avid reader, she devoured book after book. "I can't remember when I received the very first book of my own," she recalled in a speech at the American Booksellers Convention, which was published in *Booklist.* "I remember how proud my parents were that I loved so much to read." Reading, at times, caused trouble for Taylor. "I got into trouble at night when I would sit in the closet when I was supposed to have long been asleep. I got into trouble during the daytime, too, when I would be sitting somewhere hidden, when I was suppose to have been doing my chores."

At a Glance . . .

Born Mildred Delois Taylor, September 13, 1943, in Jackson, MS; daughter of Wilbert Lee and Deletha Marie Taylor; married Errol Zeal-Daly, August, 1972 (divorced, 1975); children: P. Lauren. *Education:* University of Toledo, B.Ed., 1965; University of Colorado, M.A., 1969.

Career: Novelist; English and history teacher with the Peace Corps, Tuba City, AZ,1965, and Yirgalem, Ethiopia, 1965-67, recruiter, 1967-68, instructor, 1968; University ofColorado, Boulder, study skills coordinator, 1969-71; proofreader and editor, Los Angeles, CA,1971-73.

Awards: First prize (African-American category), Council on Interracial Books forChildren, 1973; Outstanding Book of the Year Citation, *New York Times,* 1975, andJane Addams Honor Citation, 1976, all for *Song of the Trees;* Notable Book Citation,American Library Association, 1976, National Book Award (finalist), Honor Book Citation,*Boston Globe Horn Book,* 1977, Jane Addams Honor Citation, 1977, Newbery Medal,1977, and Buxtehuder Bulle Award, 1985, for *Roll of Thunder, Hear My Cry;*Outstanding Book of the Year Citation, *New York Times,* 1981, Jane Addams HonorCitation, *New York Times,* 1982, American Book Award nomination, 1982, and CorettaScott King Award, 1982, for *Let the Circle Be Unbroken;* Coretta Scott King Award, andFiction Award, *Boston Globe-Horn Book,* 1988, for *The Friendship;* NotableBook Citation, *New York Times,* 1987, and Christopher Award, 1988, for *The GoldCadillac;* Coretta Scott King Award, 1990, for *The Road to Memphis;* ALAN Awardfor Significant Contribution to Young Adult Literature, National Council of Teachers of English,1997.

Addresses: *Residence*— Boulder, CO. *Office*— c/o DialBooks, 2 Park Ave., New York, NY 100176.

Nine years after arriving in Toledo, the Taylor family moved into a more residential neighborhood. Taylor was the only African American student in her grade school class. As a result, she worked even harder to excel academically because she did not want anyone to blame her failures on her race. Her father continually stressed to his daughter that she could do anything that she set out to do if she worked hard enough. At around the age of 10, Taylor decided that she wanted to be an author, and that she would visit other parts of the world. However, writing did not come easily for Taylor. For many years, she struggled to find her voice.

When Taylor enrolled as a freshman at Scott High School in 1957, the civil rights movement was becoming an important force for change in American society. Taylor was aware of the existence of racism, having seen its effects in the South during her family's vacation trips to visit relatives in Mississippi and hearing her family tell their stories. Racism reared its ugly head in her high school when the election of an African American student as the homecoming queen caused an uproar.

Although roughly half of the entire student population was made up of African American students, Taylor was the only African American in her college preparatory classes. She was a class officer, editor of the school newspaper, and the only African American student from her school to be elected to the National Honor Society. During these years, Taylor also focused on learning to write well. However, her models for literary quality were classics written by white male authors, and their style did not lend itself to the stories Taylor wanted to tell. With the encouragement of her father and one of her high school teachers, Taylor entered a citywide fiction contest. Although she did not win the contest, she discovered that she was most comfortable writing stories in the first-person narrative style.

After graduating from high school in 1961, Taylor enrolled at the University of Toledo. She pursued a teaching degree with a major in English and minor in history in order to placate her parents, who insisted that she earn a practical degree rather than one in creative writing. During her high school and college years, Taylor wrote and submitted many fictional pieces but received only rejection notices because she did not yet know how to polish her work. When she did get the attention of a publisher for her novel *Dark People, Dark World,* Taylor did not accept the editor's demand for revision and the novel remained unpublished.

Despite her father's opposition, Taylor planned to enter the Peace Corps after earning her degree. Eventually, Taylor's father gave his approval. The two years that Taylor spent in Ethiopia were a happy time for her because she was easily accepted into Ethiopian society, the countryside was much like that of the American South, and she had escaped the pervasive racism of the United States. Although she was tempted to remain in Africa, Taylor returned to the United States when her two-year tour ended. For a time, she recruited and trained other Peace Corps workers. Taylor then pursued a master of arts degree in journalism at the University of Colorado at Boulder, where she was active in the Black Student Alliance. After earning her degree, she worked for nine months improving the Black Studies program at the university.

In 1971 Taylor relocated to Los Angeles, California, where she lived off of her savings for a year while she wrote. When her savings ran low, she worked temporary jobs. The following year, Taylor married Errol Zea-Daly, whom she would divorce three years later. She also declined an offer to report the news for CBS, somehow knowing that her future lay in writing books, not news reports. Taylor realized that she could not thrive in isolation, so she worked at various jobs to give herself a social outlet. In the fall of 1973, Taylor discovered a writing contest sponsored by the Council on Interracial Books for Children. As the deadline for submitting entries quickly approached, she revised a story she had previously written in the third person, recasting it in the first person. Her story of an African American father who defends his land from illegal logging by a white man won the contest. The story also launched Taylor's writing career when it was published by Dial as *Song of the Trees.* With this tale, Taylor created the Logan family that would remain the basis of her body of work.

One year later Taylor finished the novel *Roll of Thunder, Hear My Cry,* in which she more fully developed the characters she had created in *Song of the Trees.* Taylor predicted to her father that *Roll of Thunder, Hear My Cry* would win the Newbery Medal, an award presented by the American Library Association for the most outstanding book for children written during the previous year. Taylor was correct, although her father did not live to see her receive the award. He died several months before the American Library Association's Newbery Medal selection committee announced that Taylor was the winner of the 1977 award. In her acceptance speech, Taylor acknowledged her debt to her parents for their unfailing support, and to her larger family for the inspiration of their courageous lives and stories. The following year, ABC television aired a three-part miniseries adapted from *Roll of Thunder, Hear My Cry.* By winning the Newbery Medal, Taylor's novel would remain in publication for decades and her later works would get immediate attention from editors. With this status, Taylor gained the financial means to devote herself entirely to writing.

During the 1980s and 1990s, Taylor published a steady stream of novels about the Logan family and members of the nearby community. The Logan series of novels includes the following titles: *The Land, The Well, Song of the Trees, The Friendship, Roll of Thunder, Hear My Cry, Let the Circle Be Unbroken, The Road to Memphis,* and *Logan.* The release of *Logan* marked the end of the Logan family saga.

Challenged Racism

Taylor modeled many of the characters in her novels after her own relatives, often making them composites of several family members. She blended fact with fiction in the same way that Alex Haley created "faction" in his novel *Roots.* After her father's death, Taylor relied more heavily on historical research because she had lost her greatest source of information about her family history. The importance of family ties and respect for the land are evident in most of Taylor's works, as are the damaging aspects of racism. However, Taylor consistently balances her painful representation of racism with hope. "In the writing of my books I have tried to present not only a history of my family, but the effects of racism, not only to the victims of racism but also to the racists themselves," Taylor explained in her acceptance speech for the 1997 ALAN Award. "I have recounted events that were painful to write and painful to be read, but I had hoped they brought more understanding."

Many critics have praised Taylor's books for their powerful realism and relevancy. They are not universally admired, however. In her ALAN speech, Taylor bemoaned the fact that some people have challenged her novels by maintaining that her portrayal of racism is too harsh for young readers. She even admitted that while writing *The Land,* she debated about using words that would have been used in the late nineteenth century because readers might object to them. "But just as I have had to be honest with myself in the telling of all my stories," Taylor remarked, "I realize I must be true to the feelings of the people about whom I write and true to the stories told. My stories might not be 'politically correct,' so there will be those who will be offended, but as we all know, racism is offensive."

Sources

Books

Crowe, Chris, *Presenting Mildred Taylor*, Twayne (New York), 1999.

Taylor, Mildred, essay in *Something About the Author Autobiography Series,* volume 5, Gale (Detroit), pp. 267-86.

Periodicals

ALAN Review, Spring, 1998.

Booklist, December 1, 1990, p. 740.

—Jeanne M. Lesinski

Debi Thomas

1967—

Olympic figure skater

In 1986, Debi Thomas became the first African American to win senior championship titles in both American and world figure skating competitions, an achievement all the more unusual given the sport's country-club image. Thomas, who was only 18-years-old at the time, had already spent half of her life in training, and was also a pursuing an education at Stanford University as well. Known for her fearless, confident jumps, she was a favorite for the gold medal in women's figure skating at the 1988 Winter Olympic Games in Calgary, Canada. However, she was bested by her East German rival Katarina Witt.

Born in March of 1967, Thomas spent her early life in Poughkeepsie, New York, during a time when her mother, Janice Thomas, was working for computer giant IBM as a program analyst. The family—which included Thomas's father, McKinley, and a half-brother—moved to San Jose, California, when both McKinley and Janice Thomas were offered jobs with one of the new-technology companies that helped create what would become Silicon Valley. The Thomases were one of the few African American families in their neighborhood, and Thomas's early life was further challenged in 1974 when her parents divorced.

Junior-High School Dropout

After attending an Ice Follies show as a toddler, Thomas told her mother that she wanted to skate for a living. She put on her first pair of ice skates at the age of five, and won her first competition four years later, the same year that she began taking formal lessons. The following year, she signed on with a Scottish coach, Alex McGowan, who still guided Thomas's career when she trained for the Olympics. However, the costs of skates, lessons, competition fees, travel, and costumes quickly added up. Thomas's mother sometimes found it difficult to raise her children and fund the $25,000-a-year sport as a single parent. At times, Thomas had to stop lessons for weeks at a stretch.

In the elitist world of teen figure skating, Thomas encountered discrimination both overt and subtle. On one occasion, the family returned home from a competition to find a cross burning on their lawn. Judges often gave better marks to Thomas's competitors who had not attempted the technically difficult jumps that Thomas landed so flawlessly. She persevered, however, and became known for her self-assured style as a skater. At the age of 12, Thomas advanced all the way

At a Glance . . .

Born March 25, 1967, in Poughkeepsie, NY; daughter of McKinley Thomas (a computer program manager) and Janice Thomas (a computer program analyst); married Brian Vanden Hogen, March 15, 1988 (divorced 1991); married Chris Bequette (an attorney), 1996; children: Luc. *Education:* Stanford University, bachelor's degree, 1991; Northwestern University, M.D., 1998.

Career: Amateur figure skater, 1980-92; professional figure skater, 1992-96.

Awards: National Sports Festival, 1985, winner; United States Ladies Figure Skating champion, 1986; World Figure Skating Championships, first-place female winner, 1986; bronze medalist in women's figure skating, Winter Olympic Games, 1988.

Addresses: *Home*—Little Rock, AR.

to the national novice finals, where she won a silver medal. Her mother than allowed her to finish the eighth grade by taking correspondence courses so that she could devote more time to her training. Unfortunately, Thomas fared poorly in the junior ladies' competition that year. "Right then I decided I wasn't going to put the rest of my life on the line in front of some judges who might not like my yellow dress," Thomas recalled in an interview with *Time*'s Tom Callahan. Both Thomas and her mother vowed never again to allow skating to come before education.

Thomas attended high school in San Mateo, California, not far from a rink where she and McGowan spent several hours a week training. For four years, her mother drove 150 miles a day between the rink and Thomas's high school, her own job, and the family home. Thomas napped or did her homework in the car; she also made her own dresses for competitions. Despite her heavy extracurricular schedule, Thomas earned excellent grades, and was accepted to Harvard, Princeton and Stanford universities. In the fall of 1985, she entered Stanford University in Palo Alto, California.

In February of 1986, Thomas won the senior women's title at the U.S. Figure Skating Championships by successfully completing five triple jumps, an impressive athletic performance. She became the first African American to win a non-novice title, and the media seized upon the story of the hardworking Stanford freshman who planned to become a doctor after she competed in the Winter Olympics. Thomas's success was all the more remarkable in light of the fact that very few skaters at this level attended college while training, due to the full-time demands of figure skating. Thomas was studying medical microbiology at the time, a challenging program for any student. Her coach complained that she had no time to run, work out with weights, or do any other off-ice training. "She isn't able to eat or sleep at proper hours," McGowan told *Sports Illustrated* writer E.M. Swift. "When Debi arrives at the rink for training, she's exhausted."

Won a World Championship

Thomas's celebrity status received an added boost when she took the world championship title from Katarina Witt, an East German skater who had won the gold medal at the 1984 Winter Olympic Games in Sarajevo, Yugoslavia. Much of the media attention focused on Thomas as a minority in a sport that was traditionally dominated by the wealthy. Although she had no predecessors to follow, Thomas told Callahan in *Time* that "I never felt I had to have a role model... I didn't think I had to see a black woman do this to believe it's possible."

During her sophomore year, Thomas found it a bit more difficult to keep up the difficult pace of college and competition. In early 1987, she lost both her national title to Jill Trenary and her world championship crown to Witt. Beginning in the summer of 1987, Thomas took a leave of absence from school and began training in Boulder, Colorado, in preparation for the 1988 Olympic Games. On a visit to New York, she worked on her choreography with ballet dancer Mikhail Baryshnikov. She also planned an appearance in Calgary, the site of the 1988 Winter Olympics, that would feature her interpretation of a selection from the Bizet opera *Carmen* in her artistic program.

When Thomas arrived in Calgary in early 1988, she was the subject of a great deal of media attention. No American woman had won a gold medal in figure skating since Dorothy Hamill in 1976, and Witt had also selected a number from *Carmen* as well. "Every time I open the papers, they're trying to make this thing between me and Katarina," *Time* journalist Jill Smolowe quoted her as saying. "It bugs me. We're just two people." During the Olympic competition, Witt stood very close to the ice in order to intimidate Thomas during her performance. The pressure affected Thomas, and she made a small error during the first minute of her performance. She was never able to recover completely. Witt won the gold medal again, while Canadian skater Elizabeth Manley took the silver. Thomas captured the bronze medal, and became the first African American to win a medal in the any Winter Olympic sport.

"Thomas deserved credit for maintaining considerable poise in the face of all the preshow hype, as did Witt," wrote Smolowe in *Time.* Thomas later admitted that she dreaded having to compete in the world championships only a few weeks after the Winter Olympics. The world championships marked the final time that Witt, Thomas, and several other top Olympic skaters would compete as amateurs. "The three weeks after the Olympics were probably the hardest of my life," Thomas told *Sports Illustrated*'s Swift. "I cried every day." She also remarked in *Sports Illustrated* that the support she received from others helped to ease her disappointment for failing to win the gold medal. "I felt I'd let down the whole U.S.," said Thomas. "But then I got so many letters of support. I realized it really didn't matter that much that I didn't win the gold."

In the world championships held in Budapest, Hungary, Thomas competed surprisingly well against Witt. She also celebrated her 21st birthday there, and revealed that she had married a few days earlier. Over the next four years, Thomas divided her time between her studies at Stanford and a professional career with Stars on Ice. She earned her bachelor's degree in 1991, and retired from skating the following year to enter the medical degree program at Northwestern University. Her marriage did not last. However, in early 1996, a handsome man recognized her in an airport, waved to her, and later sent her a letter. Thomas wrote back to him and, after only dating for a month, married Arkansas attorney Chris Bequette. Thomas completed medical school in 1997, and gave birth to a son, Luc, that same summer.

Sources

People, September 16, 1996, p. 197.

Sports Illustrated, February 17, 1986, p. 22.; March 17, 1986, p. 54; March 31, 1986, p. 28; January 8, 1988, p. 38.

Time, February 15, 1988, p. 44; March 7, 1988, p. 64; April 4, 1988, p. 34.

—Carol Brennan

Isiah Thomas

1961—

Former professional basketball player, entrepreneur

To many sports fans and writers, Isiah Thomas was the best small man ever to play professional basketball. The six-foot-one-inch Thomas served as a point guard for the Detroit Pistons from 1981 to 1994, earning a spot on the All-Star roster for 12 consecutive years and leading his team to back-to-back NBA championships in 1989 and 1990. Thomas, who joined the Pistons when he was just 19, was a ruthless competitor on the court but dedicated himself to civic causes and social issues in his spare time. The passing of the years eroded Thomas's playing ability and his reputation as a good-natured, accessible superstar, but his competitive drive and dedication to the game of basketball cannot be questioned.

Detroit Free Press columnist Charlie Vincent called Thomas "the spirit and the heart and the soul of a team that wormed its way into our hearts. He came with a smile that made us all think he was a choirboy but showed us, in time, that—on the floor—he could be an assassin." Vincent added that Thomas "showed a generation of Detroit fans how a winner behaves. He has given us memories of glory and of leadership and courage." Thomas retired from basketball on May 11, 1994, following months of speculation about his future and a rumored $55-million retirement package. "This has been a great life for me," Thomas told reporters. "I think I enjoyed myself more than any other player who ever came through the NBA." Thomas was expected to become a color commentator for televised basketball coverage and to devote more time to his extensive business dealings.

"I'm in love with basketball," Thomas once told *Sports Illustrated.* "It's my release. It's my outlet. If I get mad, I go shoot. It's my freedom. It's my security. It's my drug; it's my high." Thomas's love of the game has at times bordered on obsession. As a rookie Piston point guard in 1981, he set a goal of being part of an NBA championship team. At times, that goal seemed out of reach no matter how hard Thomas played as an individual. Time and maturity seasoned his game, however, and he finally led the Pistons to their first-ever championship in 1989. *Sport* magazine contributor Johnette Howard wrote: "Like many other superstars—at least the smart ones—Thomas learned long ago that piling up statistics is less intriguing than chasing or craving what he cannot guarantee. Like winning. By that measure, regardless of what anyone else says, he is an unqualified success."

At a Glance . . .

Born Isiah Lord Thomas III, April 30, 1961, in Chicago, IL; son of Isiah Lord II (a plant foreman) and Mary (a civil service employee) Thomas; married Lynn Kendall (a teacher), 1985; children: two. *Education:* Indiana University, B.A., 1987.

Career: Professional basketball player with Detroit Pistons, 1981-94. Member of U.S.Olympic basketball team, 1980; vice-president of National Basketball Association Players Association, 1986-89, president, 1989-94; vice president of basketball operations, Toronto Raptors, 1994-97; NBA analyst and sportscaster, NBC Sports, 1997-; chairman and chief executive officer, Continental Basketball Association, 1999-00; Indiana Pacers, coach, 2000-.

Selected awards: Named to NBA All-Star Team, 1982-92; named All-Star Game Most Valuable Player, 1984 and 1986; Elected to the Basketball Hall of Fame, 2000.

Addresses: *Office*—Continental Basketball Association, Two Arizona Center, 400 North 5th Street, Suite 1425, Phoenix, AZ 85004.

Isiah Lord Thomas III grew up in the heart of Chicago's West Side ghetto, the youngest of seven boys and two girls born to Mary and Isiah Thomas II. "He was well behaved, but spoiled," Mary Thomas told *Sports Illustrated.* "I can't say I didn't treat him special. He was the baby. He got special attention." Isiah II was a plant supervisor who pushed his children to read, barred them from watching anything but educational television, and lectured them to stick together and protect one another. When Isiah III was an infant, his father lost his job as a supervisor at International Harvester and could not find comparable work elsewhere. He was forced to work as a janitor at extremely reduced wages, and the stress of his disappointment caused friction in the family. "My father was frustrated by his intelligence," Thomas told *Gentleman's Quarterly.* "He was a black man coming up in the Twenties, Thirties and Forties. Being very intelligent and not being able to express that intelligence made him a very angry man. Sometimes he took that anger out on our family."

Eventually, Isiah II and Mary Thomas separated, and the childrearing duties fell primarily to Mary. She was a strict disciplinarian who required her children to be home by the time the street lights came on. Born a Baptist, she turned the family toward Catholicism and thus came under the wing of a local church, Our Lady of Sorrows, and its schools. Fearlessly protective of her family, there was little that Mary Thomas would not do to shield her children from the gangs that prowled their neighborhood's streets. Once she chased gang members from her front porch with a shotgun when they came to recruit her sons. Her courage and determination—especially where Isiah III was concerned—were the subject of a 1987 made-for-television movie.

Thomas spent most of his free time playing basketball at tiny Gladys Park, next to Chicago's Eisenhower Expressway. According to Ira Berkow in the *New York Times,* the young Thomas was a "prodigy in basketball the way Mozart was in music. At age three, Amadeus was composing on a harpsichord; at three, Isiah could dribble and shoot baskets." Thomas was tutored by his older brothers, some of whom were top-notch players in their own right. Thomas recalled those days fondly in *Sports Illustrated.* "Go anywhere on the West Side and say, 'Meet me at the court,' and they'd know what you were talking about," he said. "That's where I really learned to play. There were some basketball players there. You could always get a game there. Any time of day, any time of night. Me and my brothers used to go over there with snow shovels in the winter so we could play."

When Thomas was 12, the street gangs began moving in more ferociously, and some of his older brothers succumbed to the lure of drug abuse and crime. Mary Thomas moved the family five miles west to Menard Avenue, but trouble seemed to follow. "Those were probably the worst times as a kid," Thomas told *Sports Illustrated.* "We very rarely had heat. We had an oil furnace but no money to buy oil. In the winter, it was always cold, and you had to sleep all the time with your clothes on. Everything broke down in the house once we bought it... . I mean everything was a disaster." Sleeping in a closet and eating food donated by concerned church members, Thomas was tempted to follow the lead of his brothers and turn to drug dealing as a way out of poverty. His brothers and his mother convinced him otherwise. They told him that he might well lead the family into better circumstances with his basketball skills.

Most of the coaches in the Chicago area considered Thomas too small to have any significant impact on a basketball program, but Thomas's brothers persuaded coach Gene Pingatore of St. Joseph High School to give Isiah a sports scholarship. St. Joseph was located in a white suburb of Chicago. Thomas had to commute three hours each way to and from school, taking three buses and arriving home well after dark. He struggled to acquire discipline in the classroom and on the court and, by his junior year, he led St. Joseph to a second-place finish in the state high school championship tournament. As a senior, Thomas was one of the most coveted college prospects in the nation.

More than 100 colleges recruited Thomas. His family wanted him to stay home and attend DePaul, but he chose to go to Indiana University and play for temperamental coach Bob Knight. Thomas made All-Big Ten his freshman year and was named a consensus All-American as a sophomore. That year he led the Hoosiers to the NCAA championship game, where Indiana routed the North Carolina Tar Heels, 63-50. With 23 points in the championship match, Thomas was named NCAA tournament Most Valuable Player. Despite his All-Star performance as a freshman and sophomore, Thomas was not happy at Indiana. He and Knight clashed frequently. Finally, in 1981—on the advice of his friend Magic Johnson—Thomas decided to leave college and apply for the NBA draft.

Thomas was selected second in the opening round of the 1981 NBA draft by the Detroit Pistons, a hopelessly foundering organization that had won only 37 of 164 games the previous two seasons. At the tender age of 19, Thomas became burdened with the chore of rescuing the NBA's worst team. A *Detroit News* headline hailed him as "Isiah the Savior," and Pistons season ticket sales jumped 50 percent. Even the club brass talked about making the NBA Finals as they announced Thomas's four-year, $1.6 million contract. Undaunted by the expectations, Thomas turned in a successful rookie season, averaging 17 points per game and leading his team in assists and steals. He improved further in his second season, averaging nearly 23 points and 8 assists per game. Both years he represented the Pistons at the All-Star Game.

Through his first four years in Detroit, Thomas consistently outplayed his teammates. He was the first player in league history to be voted to the All-Star team in his first five seasons, and in 1984 and 1986 his performances in the All-Star game were so spectacular that he was named the contest's Most Valuable Player. By 1984 he had managed to guide the Pistons to their first winning record in seven seasons, and he was given a new ten-year, $12 million contract that was specifically designed to keep him in Detroit for his entire career. He responded to this vote of confidence in the 1984-85 season by compiling an NBA-record 1,123 assists, an average of 13.1 per game.

Not only did Thomas shine on the court, he also earned the affection of basketball fans everywhere—and especially in Detroit—for his well-publicized anti-crime work, his open dedication to his family, and his accessibility to the media. Howard noted of Thomas: "Half the beat reporters in the NBA had his home phone number, and it wasn't uncommon for him to sit for an hour after a practice, talking about some societal issue such as racism or his latest take on the game." Perhaps inevitably, however, pressures began to mount on the affable superstar as the Detroit Pistons became a legitimate playoff contender in 1986. A turning point in the evolution of Isiah Thomas occurred during the 1987 Eastern Conference finals against the Boston Celtics.

Under new head coach Chuck Daly, the Detroit Pistons improved enough to challenge for the 1987 NBA championship. That year, Thomas averaged almost 20 points per game in the playoffs as the Pistons advanced to an Eastern Conference showdown with the Celtics. The winner of the best-of-seven series would advance to the NBA playoffs—something the Pistons had never done. The series was hard-fought and seethed with emotion. By Game Five each team had won twice, and as Game Five drew to a close, the Pistons clung to a one-point lead and had possession of the ball. With one second left to play, Thomas in-bounded the ball. His pass was stolen by Larry Bird of the Celtics. Bird lobbed the ball to teammate Dennis Johnson, who scored the winning basket as the buzzer sounded. The dramatic loss stunned the Pistons, who went on to lose the series in seven games.

Just after Detroit's loss to the Celtics, another Piston, rookie Dennis Rodman, told reporters that Larry Bird was "overrated" because he was white. Asked to comment on his teammate's statement, Thomas responded that while Bird was a "very, very good basketball player," if he were black he would be "just another good guy." The backlash among media and fans was immediate. Even though Thomas apologized to Bird at a press conference—and clarified his remarks by explaining that he felt an inherent racial bias existed in basketball—his reputation was severely damaged. Howard wrote in 1992 that in the wake of that controversy, "neither [Thomas] nor his image has ever been the same." Howard added: "Looking back on it now, Thomas' greatest sin might've been that his thinking and candor put him ahead of his time."

Thomas's honeymoon with the media ended just as the Pistons achieved their greatest success. Beginning in 1987, the Pistons adopted surly tactics both on- and off-court that led to their being nicknamed the "Bad Boys." With Thomas as team captain, the "Bad Boys" turned in a strong 1987-88 season and capped the year with an Eastern Conference Finals victory over the Celtics and a bruising, seven-game championship run versus the Los Angeles Lakers. Playing with a jammed finger, a bruised eye, facial cuts, and a badly sprained ankle, Thomas threatened to steal the series for the Pistons, especially in Game Six, when he scored 43 points and 8 assists. Los Angeles won the championship in seven games, but the Pistons—and Thomas—had finally shed their losing image. The next two seasons would belong to Detroit.

With Isiah Thomas at the height of his ability, the Pistons won the NBA championship in 1989 and again in 1990. These championship teams were often embroiled in controversy, both for their aggressive style of play and for their combative attitudes off-court. *Rolling Stone* contributor Jeff Coplon wrote that the "Bad Boys" were perceived nationwide as "goons, thugs, terrorists... . When they took the court, a hockey game broke out. Normally placid opponents... blew up bumps into scuffles, scuffles into brawls. In the cultish NBA, if the Celtics were white America's team, and the Lakers were Club Hollywood, the Pistons belonged to Qaddafi... . Piston-bashing was suddenly a blood sport—especially among those most threatened by Detroit's rise." In 1988-89 Detroit compiled the best regular-season record in the NBA, winning 65 of 82 games. A six-game Eastern Conference Finals victory against Michael Jordan and the Chicago Bulls set the stage for another showdown with the Lakers. This time, the Pistons swept Los Angeles in four games and returned to Detroit with the championship.

Even greater triumph awaited Thomas the following year as Detroit's "Bad Boys" advanced again to the championship series, this time against the Portland Trail Blazers. In a series remembered for its physical play, the Pistons won in just five games to clinch back-to-back championship victories. *Sports Illustrated* correspondent Jack McCallum credited the strong Detroit showing to Thomas. The Piston captain, wrote McCallum, "kept the tempo at a controlled, even pace, which disrupted the fast-breaking...Trail Blazers. And when he wasn't doing that, he was creating something from nothing, with long-distance jump shots, body-twisting drives and steals in the open floor.... By the time the Pistons had beaten the Blazers... to clinch their second straight championship... there was only one great guard still playing basketball—Isiah Lord Thomas III."

Thomas was named Most Valuable Player of the 1990 championship series. Returning home to celebrate with his wife, he discovered that he was the target of media scrutiny for alleged gambling improprieties. Although no formal charges were brought against him, the negative publicity only alienated him further from the media and fans he had once courted so gallantly. As regular season play began in the 1990s, Thomas's statistics fell off somewhat, and he began spending more time alone with his family. He was sidelined in the 1991-92 season after receiving a blow to the head in a game against the Utah Jazz. Also, Thomas was probably the best-known NBA player who was not selected for the celebrated 1992 U.S. Olympic basketball team, allegedly because of pressure from reigning basketball superstar Michael Jordan, with whom Thomas had long feuded. That omission was particularly difficult for Thomas, because he had been a member of a 1980 Olympic basketball team that was forced to boycott the Olympics by President Carter.

Through these and other controversies, Thomas remained the Pistons' team captain. He also served a four-year stint as the president of the NBA Players Association. As he ended his eleventh season in the NBA, Thomas reflected on his career in *Sport* magazine: "You gotta understand," he said. "I'm 6-1. If I was 6-9, I could be 'nice.' If I was 6-9, or 6-6 and could jump out of the building, I could be nice. But being 6-1, having to try to be successful in a league where everyone else is 6-7, 6-8, 6-9, you've got to have a little fire in your gut, or you'll be like every other 6-1 guy is supposed to be in the league—average. I didn't want to be average... . You have to do what you have to do. And I had no problems doing that."

As a team, the Pistons' fortunes ebbed as those of the Chicago Bulls rose. The Pistons were defeated by the Bulls in the Eastern Conference Finals in 1991, crushing their hopes for a third straight NBA title and prompting calls for "rebuilding." In December of 1993, rumors suggested that Thomas was about to leave the Pistons for the New York Knicks. Instead, on January 7, 1994, the Pistons called a press conference to announce that Thomas had signed a long-term contract that would take him past retirement. "This is one of the happiest days of my career, and one of the happiest days of my life," Thomas told the *Detroit Free Press* when the agreement was announced. Soon after the contract was signed, more rumors circulated that Thomas would retire at the end of the season.

On April 19, 1994, Isiah Thomas played his last game as a Detroit Piston, although his retirement would not become official until May 11. Thomas left his final game in the third quarter with a torn Achilles tendon, after scoring 12 points and serving up 6 assists against the Orlando Magic. Reflecting on his years in the NBA, Thomas told Vincent, "I have no regrets. As a basketball player, you gave everything to your sport, gave everything to the organization and to the team you played for. You leave it all out on the floor. So it's not disappointing to me at all." Following his retirement party, Thomas ended rumors about his taking a front-office position with the Pistons franchise, telling reporters, "All the jobs were full."

Thomas met many of the goals he set for himself as a rookie in the NBA—and exceeded even his own sky-high expectations. The leader in every category in the history of the Pistons' franchise, Thomas also left the game as the fourth all-time NBA leader in assists and steals, and the 28th all-time leader in scoring. Thomas retired with 18,822 career points, 9,061 assists, and 1,861 steals in 979 games. Thomas told *Jet* magazine: "I'm living the dream I had since I was a little boy. How many kids, especially kids who grew up as poor as I did, ever live to see their dreams come true? I'm just lucky I've had the opportunity."

Following his retirement from the NBA, Thomas turned his attention to becoming a successful businessman and entrepreneur. Along with his business partners, he purchased American Speedy Printing Centers, Inc. With Thomas serving as principal shareholder and co-chairman of the board of directors, American

Speedy Printing Centers emerged from bankruptcy to become a highly profitable company. In 1994 he became a principal investor in OmniBanc Corp, the nation's first multistate African American owned bank holding company. The goal of OmniBanc was to revitalize economically disadvantaged inner cities communities. As Thomas remarked in *American Banker,* "Anytime you have the chance to revitalize the community that you came from...it's a very exciting challenge and a very exciting opportunity."

Moved to Toronto

On May 24, 1994, Thomas was introduced as the head of basketball operations for the expansion Toronto Raptors, the first NBA franchise located outside the United States. As part of his duties, he was charged with helping to shape the team, which debuted during the 1995-96 season. At a press conference in Toronto at the time of his announcement, Thomas remarked, "I think it's the dream of most professional athletes...to make this kind of cross-over once the playing days are over... .I'm so excited to get on with the job at hand."

In late 1997, Thomas abruptly resigned as general manager of the Toronto Raptors and left town. Rumors circulated that Thomas's relationship with Raptors majority owner Allan Slaight had soured after Thomas failed to purchase sole ownership of the team. Although Thomas owned a nine percent share of the Raptors, he wanted complete control of the organization. His sudden departure dealt a severe blow to the team's morale. As Raptors forward Walt Williams told *Maclean's,* "Isiah is a big part of why a lot of the guys are here."

Shortly after leaving the Raptors, Thomas signed a deal with NBC in December of 1997 to become an analyst for NBA games. With experience as both a player and NBA executive, NBC felt that Thomas would bring an interesting perspective to the job. Although Thomas was excited about the new opportunity, he had almost no experience as a broadcaster and realized that he had much to learn. As quoted by *Jet* magazine, Thomas remarked, "I understand that I come into this as a rookie, that I'm very young and very green. I don't come into this professing to be the top guy, but as a young guy with a lot of talent."

Became Owner of the CBA

Thomas had long professed a desire to purchase his own NBA franchise. That goal had gone unfulfilled. However, in 1999, Thomas purchased the nine-team Continental Basketball Association (CBA). Suddenly, he was the sole owner of nine franchises scattered across the United States. Thomas voiced his plans for the CBA in *Black Enterprise,* "My goal is to one day form an official affiliation with the NBA where each team will have its own CBA team and you can call up or send down players, similar to what they have in baseball." He also planned to expand the CBA and increase its visibility through increased promotion and marketing. "Our goal is to continue to grow the league through acquisitions and mergers. We've looked at some cities...and there's considerable interest in smaller cities wanting to have the second-best league in the world playing in their towns." Unfortunately, Thomas will never see the affiliation come to pass as owner. He sold the CBA, so he could become the next coach of the Indiana Pacers. Now, he has the chance to become a part of another championship-winning NBA team.

In May of 2000, Thomas was elected to the Basketball Hall of Fame in his first year of eligibility. This distinction placed him alongside other Detroit sports legends such as Al Kaline, Ty Cobb, and Gordie Howe. At a press conference held at the Palace of Auburn Hills, the same arena where Thomas led the Pistons to championship glory, his trademark competitiveness shone through. As reported in the *Detroit Free Press,* Thomas remarked, "I kid Magic and Jordan all the time that if I was taller, they never would've gotten the championship from me. If I had been 6-5 or 6-6, I would have killed all of those guys all of the time." The press conference also featured a five minute video highlighting some of Thomas's greatest moments on a basketball court. After watching the video, Thomas quipped in the *Detroit Free Press,* "I look at that video and I think to myself, 'Man, I was good.'"

Sources

American Banker, October 20, 1994, p. 6.
Black Enterprise, November, 1999, p. 28.
Boston Globe, November 1, 1981; April 26, 1985; June 7, 1987.
Chicago Tribune, February 8, 1987.
Detroit Free Press, April 25, 1987; April 28, 1987; January 4, 1994, p. D1; January 8, 1994, p. B3; April 20, 1994, pp. 1E, 6E; May 12, 1994, pp. 1A, 6A, 1C, 8C-10C; May 25, 2000, p. 1A.
Detroit News, October 11, 1981.
Dollars & Sense, May 1994, pp. 21-22.
Ebony, May 1990.
Gentleman's Quarterly, February 1988, pp. 190-193, 238-242.
Inside Sports, April 1984, p. 64; November 1987, p. 21; June 1994, pp. 38-39.
Jet, December 11, 1989, pp. 36-38; October 22, 1990, p. 48; October 14, 1991, p. 49; January 31, 1994, p. 48.
Los Angeles Daily News, June 19, 1988.
Los Angeles Herald Examiner, June 6, 1987.
Los Angeles Times, February 10, 1986; June 7, 1988; June 11, 1988; June 20, 1988.
Maclean's, December 1, 1997.
Newsday, June 2, 1987; May 30, 1988.
Newsweek, December 14, 1981, p. 130.

New York Times, April 27, 1981; June 2, 1987; January 8, 1994, p. 32; January 9, 1994, sec. 8, p. 5.

Oakland Press (Michigan), April 3, 1994; April 4, 1994, p. D1; April 18, 1994, p. B1; April 24, 1994, pp. D1-D2, D13-D14.

Philadelphia Daily News, June 15, 1988.

Philadelphia Inquirer, June 7, 1988.

Rolling Stone, May 4, 1989.

Sport, February 1986, p. 59; May 1988, p. 24; June 1992, pp. 66-70.

Sports Illustrated, January 19, 1987; May 18, 1987; June 25, 1990, pp. 32-36; January 21, 1991, p. 46; January 17, 1994, p. 71.

—Mark Kram and David G. Oblender

Bennie G. Thompson

1948—

Congressman from Mississippi

A longtime politician and grassroots political activist, Bennie G. Thompson has been a member of the United States Congress since 1993. Representing Mississippi's second congressional district, a mostly African American, rural, and economically distressed area, Thompson has made economic opportunity, and discrimination on account of race, gender, and class his chief issues. Unlike his predecessor in the second district seat, Mike Espy, Thompson has made few attempts to reach out to white voters or curry favor with conservative white businessmen and landowners. He believes that the struggle for African American civil rights is not over, and is a firm supporter of affirmative action programs. "For most of us who are over forty-five, we never had new textbooks in our community, we never had the opportunity to play in a public playground or swim in a public swimming pool, and so some of us take very seriously the notion of affirmative action because this was the only opportunity that many of us ever received," Thompson was quoted by *CQ's Politics in America 2000* as having told his Congressional colleagues.

Thompson was born in Bolton, Mississippi, a small town about fifteen miles west of Jackson, in 1948. His mother, Annie Laura, was a school teacher. His father, Will, who died when Thompson was a teenager, worked as an auto mechanic. Although the family's income was modest, the Thompsons were still better off than the average African American family in Bolton, most of whom were dependent upon the region's agricultural enterprises. Thompson attended segregated local public schools and had little contact with Bolton's white population. "You hear stories about blacks and whites being so close down south, but Bolton was always two separate communities. I *never* had a single white friend. Once, when I was about eleven, I went into town to get a part for my bicycle. The man at the store didn't have it, and he asked me if that was all. I said 'Yes,' and he said 'What you say, nigger? Didn't no one ever teach to you say yessuh to a white man?' That's how it was," Thompson told Joe Klein of *Esquire.*

After graduating from high school Thompson attended Tougaloo College, an all-African American liberal arts college in Mississippi. Thompson told *CQ's Politics in America 2000* that Tougaloo College "was there to open its arms to me [when] the number of colleges I could attend [was] significantly limited by the racial

At a Glance . . .

Born on January 28, 1948 in Bolton, MS; son of Will Thompson (an auto mechanic), and Annie Laura Thompson (a teacher); married to London Johnson Thompson (a teacher); children: one daughter. *Education:* Tougaloo College, Tougaloo, MS, B.A. in political science, 1968; Jackson State University, Jackson, MS, M.A., 1972; also completed extensive coursework towards a doctorate in public administration at the University of Southern Mississippi. *Religion:* Methodist.

Career: Worked briefly as a public school teacher in Madison, MS. Began political career as a member of the board of aldermen, Bolton, MS, 1969-73; mayor of Bolton, MS,1973-80, supervisor of Hinds County, MS, 1980-93. Congressman from Mississippi's second district, 1993-; serves on the House Committee on the Budget and the House Committeeon Agriculture.

Member: Board of trustees, Tougaloo College; board of directors, Southern Regional Council; board of directors, Housing Assistance Council.

Awards: Honorary doctor of laws degree from Claflin College; citations from the Housing Assistance Council and the National Black Nurses Foundation.

Addresses: *Home*— Bolton, MS. *Office*—1408 Longworth House Office Building, Washington, DC 20515.

segregation that was endemic in the South." At Tougaloo, Thompson joined the Student Nonviolent Coordinating Committee (SNCC), and spent much of his free time registering African American voters throughout the Mississippi Delta. He also worked on civil rights activist Fannie Lou Hamer's unsuccessful congressional campaign. It was Hamer's inspirational example that led Thompson to consider a career in politics. Also, his work in voter registration made him see that the lack of African American politicians was a major reason for African American apathy towards the electoral process. Thompson received a bachelor's degree in political science from Tougaloo in 1968.

In 1969, while employed as a teacher in nearby Madison, Mississippi, Thompson ran for the board of aldermen in his hometown of Bolton. He won a seat on the board (as did two other African Americans), but white local officials refused to accept the results of the election. Thompson and the other African American candidates filed a legal suit and a court order ultimately forced local officials to relent. "Within a few weeks after we won that," Thompson said of the court battle to Klein, "I was fired from my teaching job for being a negative influence...and the draft board—the all-white draft board—decided to send me off to Vietnam. I challenged both of those things in court, too." Thompson was never reinstated as a teacher but he did manage, through various appeals, to avoid military conscription.

Thompson is proud of the fact that he stayed in Mississippi after finishing college. Typically, educated southern African Americans went to the North or to California where racism was less oppressive and career opportunities were wider. "There are things I just can't find words for...This place is important to me," Thompson said of Bolton to Klein.

Became Mayor of Bolton

In 1973, Thompson was elected mayor of Bolton. An all-African American board of aldermen was elected along with him. Considering that local laws had effectively barred African Americans from voting in Mississippi until the 1960s, this was a breathtaking change in the political landscape. White incumbents challenged the election results in court, but Thompson and the other African Americans prevailed. As mayor of Bolton, Thompson had streets paved, housing renovated, and a new city hall constructed. He also had the town's real estate reevaluated by a property appraiser. The findings showed that white officials had been deliberately undervaluing their property for years in order to avoid higher taxes. Many whites looked up the reevaluation as an act of revenge, but Thompson saw it as way of sweeping out corruption.

Thompson was criticized for focusing too much of his attention on Bolton's poorest citizens, nearly all of whom were African American, while neglecting the concerns of the town's more affluent white population. He defended his actions by pointing out that the poor were in the greatest need. "If I have two roads, a paved road with potholes in a white neighborhood and an unpaved one in a Black neighborhood, my priority is the unpaved road. Equality doesn't mean spending the same amount of money on Blacks and whites. It means giving Blacks the same quality of service as whites," Thompson told Klein.

Moving up the ladder of local politics, Thompson was elected to the Hinds County Board of Supervisors in 1979. His "good government" attitude went with him to the county board and brought him into an unlikely alliance with fellow supervisor Frank Bryan, a white Republican. "Bennie Thompson believes in open, honest, fair, taxpayer-responsive government that is open to scrutiny. Of course, he and I disagree on a whole bunch of other stuff like social programs, but we agree on things like open meetings and making county government more efficient," Bryan told Klein.

In the 1980s, an African American majority congressional district was created in Mississippi. Running along the Mississippi River, the second district begins at Tunica County at the Arkansas border and goes south nearly to Natchez. Nine of Mississippi's ten poorest counties are included in the second district. When Mike Espy was elected to the second district seat in 1986, he became the first African American congressman from Mississippi since the Reconstruction era after the Civil War. A political moderate from a well-to-do family in the funeral parlor business, Espy formed alliances with white power brokers in the Mississippi Delta and received a significant share of white votes.

In early 1993, Espy vacated his seat in the House of Representatives to become secretary of agriculture in the Clinton administration. A special election was called to fill the second district seat. Thompson, who had considered running for Congress when the African American-majority second district was first created but declined in favor of continuing in local politics, decided it was time to move onto the national scene. Although Thompson was one of the most prominent and powerful politicians in the state, he was seen as too rough-edged in his manner to be effective in Washington, and too much of a "black radical" to get enough of the white vote that was deemed necessary for victory. The early Democratic favorite in the second district race was Henry Espy, Mike Espy's brother and the mayor of Clarksdale, who had the same smooth, middle-of-the-road style as his brother. The Democratic field also included Unita Blackwell, mayor of Mayersville, and James Meredith, a political activist who made history in the early 1960s when he became the first African American to attend the University of Mississippi. On the Republican side, the only candidate was Hayes Dent, an advisor to Mississippi Governor Kirk Fordice.

In an all-party primary election held in March of 1993, Dent, who had no rival for the Republican and conservative vote, came out on top with 34 percent of the total vote. Thompson was second with 28 percent, and Espy was third with 20 percent. Since election rules stated that only the top two primary candidates, regardless of party, could go on to the April runoff election, Espy and the other Democratic candidates threw their support to Thompson.

Thompson's victory in the final election was not assured since Republicans, although they are a minority in the second district, traditionally come to the polls in strong numbers. Also, it was unclear whether the non-partisan moderate voters who had supported Mike Espy in the past, and had voted for Henry Espy in the primary, would be comfortable with the more abrasive and politically left-wing Thompson. "It goes back to voter turnout and which one can pick up the loose change out there on the table," Chip Reynolds, a spokesman for the Mississippi Republican Party, told Kitty Cunningham of *Congressional Quarterly*.

While Dent's campaign targeted moderate crossover voters, Thompson focused his attention on getting out as much of the African American vote as possible. He organized volunteers to spread the word at African American churches and among church-related women's groups. A special push was made on Easter Sunday, which fell two days before the runoff election. "If we can touch all those bases on Sunday, then all we'll have to do is go vote on Tuesday," Thompson was quoted by Kenneth J. Cooper of the *New York Times* as telling his supporters. During their bitter campaign, Dent characterized Thompson as a big spending liberal who was not supportive of the region's agricultural business interests. Thompson countered that agriculture profits went primarily to white businessmen and did not necessarily raise the standard of living of the average citizen. "We want to help agriculture. But we want agriculture to help everybody in this area," Thompson explained to Cooper.

Thompson won the runoff election, garnering 55 percent of the vote to Dent's 45 percent. The vote ran along racial lines, with Thompson receiving very few white votes. "I hope to bridge that gap, but right now it's still very much divided," Thompson said of the racial polarization in a post-election statement that was quoted in *Congressional Quarterly*.

In 1994 and 1996, the Republican Party presented two African American candidates for the second district seat (Bill Jordan, an attorney, in 1994; Danny Covington, a former Congressional aide, in 1996), but the incumbent Thompson easily won reelection both times. In 1998, the GOP ran no candidate against Thompson and his only opposition was the Libertarian Party's William Chipman, whom he easily defeated.

As a member of Congress, Thompson has not modified the liberal views he advocated as a local politician. He has been strongly critical of budget cuts in federal poverty programs. "It makes no sense to force the poorest of Americans to go without food stamps, school lunches and baby formula in order to balance the budget and then turn around and give wealthy campaign contributors a huge tax cut," he told his fellow House Budget Committee members, as quoted by *CQ's Politics in America 2000*. As head of a Congressional Black Caucus task force on tobacco use, Thompson maintained that because tobacco companies had marketed their products to African American consumers, a share of the billions of dollars paid by the tobacco industry in lawsuits should be set aside for African American oriented programs, including anti-smoking campaigns. He also called for moderation in anti-tobacco legislation since the livelihoods of many African American farmers and merchants are dependent on tobacco sales. "We must position the minority community in this country so that it benefits proportionately from a tobacco bill," Thompson told Michael A. Fletcher of the *Washington Post.*

In 1998, Thompson lodged a protest against the Mississippi Department of Wildlife, Fisheries, and Parks because only eight percent of the department's employees were African American, while more than one-third of the population of Mississippi is African American. Thompson noted that most of the African Americans who were employed by the department were low level workers and aides. "It is difficult for me to believe that the agency could not find enough qualified Blacks in a state that is 36 percent Black. It is statistically impossible unless you maintain a pattern or practice of racial discrimination," Thompson told *Jet.*

In 1999, Thompson led the drive to honor the nine African American students who integrated Little Rock's Central High School in 1957 while facing opposition so fierce that troops had to be called in to ensure their safety. In a White House ceremony, the "Little Rock Nine" were awarded medals. According to *Jet*, Thompson called the ceremony a "rite of passage" that acknowledged the students' bravery.

Thompson's closest friends in Congress are fellow Black Caucus members Earl Hilliard of Alabama and James Clyburn of South Carolina. Known as the "Three Dudes," Thompson, Hilliard, and Clyburn discuss politics during their morning walks together. Thompson is married to the former London Johnson, a teacher, and is the father of one child. In his spare time, Thompson enjoys fishing in the waters back home in Mississippi.

Sources

Books

Barone, Michael, and Grant Ujifusa. *The Almanac of American Politics 2000.* Washington, DC: National Journal, 1999.

CQ's Politics in America 2000. Washington, DC: Congressional Quarterly, 1999.

Congressional Quarterly Almanac 1993. Washington, DC: Congressional Quarterly, 1994.

Periodicals

Congressional Quarterly, April 3, 1993, p. 859; April 17, 1993, pp. 970-971.

Esquire, December 1985, pp. 258-262.

Jet, June 28, 1996, p. 10; January 26, 1998, p. 47; December 20, 1999, p. 10.

The Nation, July 5, 1999, p. 16.

New York Times, April 14, 1993, p. A14.

Washington Post, April 11, 1993, p. A12; May 17, 1998, p. A8.

Other

Additional information for this profile was obtained from Bennie G. Thompson's office website at www.house.gov/thompson

—Mary Kalfatovic

John W. Thompson

1949—

Corporate executive

Reaching the age of 50 is often a major milestone in a person's life and career, and that was certainly true for corporate executive John W. Thompson. He had spent his entire career in business working for a single employer, industry giant, IBM. In the 28 years with them, he had risen steadily through the management ranks from his entry level position as a salesperson. With each new position, the number of employees and the size of the budget he managed increased, until by 1993, Thompson was one of the senior executives with the company. His name had even been mentioned in print sources as a potential candidate for the company's top position.

Yet, despite his bedrock solid standing at IBM, Thompson left IBM to take on a new position. On April 14, 1999, only 10 days before his 50th birthday, Symantec Corporation, a California software company, announced that Thompson had accepted an offer to become its new president and chief executive officer (CEO). Within two weeks, Thompson moved to California and began his reign at Symantec.

A Chance to Take Charge

Symantec is based in Cupertino, California, part of an area so crowded with software companies, microchip manufacturers, and Internet startups that it is known worldwide as Silicon Valley. In the fast-paced computer industry, Symantec, which began in 1983, had senior status as a company. However, despite its experience and its solid niche as a manufacturer of antivirus and utility software, the company was not thriving. It was facing intense competition, and, while the company was healthy financially, its performance was sluggish. New investors were not being attracted to the company. The company had been under the leadership of the same CEO since its founding, software pioneer Gordon Eubanks, but Eubanks was resigning to head a new software startup company.

At the same time that Symantec was looking for new energy, Thompson was laying down a strong track record in his position as general manager of IBM's Americas unit, a division with $37 billion in annual sales and 30,000 employees. In the two years he had been in this position, a major leadership position within the IBM corporate structure, Thompson had greatly increased the area's profitability, and both employee morale and customer satisfaction in his division had reached record levels. His name was mentioned some-

At a Glance . . .

Born at Fort Dix, New Jersey (where his father was stationed) April 24, 1949, son of John H. Thompson and Eunice Thompson; married Sandi Thompson; children: John E., Ayanna Thompson Prather. *Education:* Received his undergraduate degree in business from Florida A & M University, 1971; masters degree in management sciences from MIT's Sloan School of Management, 1982.

Career: Began working as a sales representative for IBM in Florida in 1971, became an IBM branch office manager in Atlanta, 1975-79; transferred to IBM in Boston as regional administrative assistant and later as regional marketing director, 1980-84; moved to IBM-headquarters in White Plains to become assistant to the chief executive officer and the chairman,1984; became director of IBM's Midwest operations, 1990; named head of marketing for IBM's U.S. operations, 1993; appointed general manager of IBM's personal-software products, 1994-98; named general manager of IBM Americas, 1997-99; president, chief executive officer, and chairman of the board for Symantec Corp, 1999-.

Member: Board of directors for NiSORCE (Northern Indiana Public Services Company), headed the fund-raiser for Teach for America in the Bay area, member of the board of directors for Fortune Brands, Inc; former chair of the Florida A & M Industry Cluster; served on the Illinois Governor's Human Resource Advisory Council.

Addresses: *Office*—Symantec, 20330 Stevens Creek Boulevard,Cupertino, CA 95014.

times as a possible eventual successor to IBM's chief, Louis Gerstner.

Despite his successes, Thompson wanted a chance to be the person at the helm. As he approached 50, he found himself scanning the horizon for a new position, one where he would be the one ultimately responsible for whether a company succeeded or failed—in his terms, a place to practice his craft. The ideal company for him to head, he determined, would be a software company, so that he could put his knowledge about building sales and marketing to good use. The company would be an established company, not a start-up. Thompson felt that his greatest successes had been in taking leadership of an ailing division at IBM and turning it into a healthy enterprise. He saw himself as "more of a remodeler than a manager of new construction."

When he was approached by Symantec's board members with an offer, it met his requirements precisely. By the time the discussions were over, Symantec had also agreed to make Thompson not only president and CEO but also the chair of the board of directors. He was without a doubt going to be the guy in charge.

One of Thompson's first moves at Symantec was to focus the company's objectives on one area, that of Internet security. Symantec, the manufacturer of such popular consumer software titles as Norton's Disk Doctor, was already involved in utility software for consumers, but it was involved in other areas as well. Thompson set a single unifying goal for the company, to become the leading company in the world in Internet security technology.

There are two areas of Internet security. One area, content security, involves protecting individuals and companies from attacks on information that is on their computers or moving through company networks. Anti-virus software, software that inoculates networks against attacks by computer viruses, and e-mail scanning software, programs that screen information being shared via e-mail, are examples of utilities of this type. A second area of Internet security is operational security, which involves setting up computer systems in ways that will protect them from potential harm.

Thompson took several steps his first year to ratchet up Symantec's emphasis on Internet security. He moved to sell off some company divisions that were not security-related and to acquire three smaller companies that were already focused on Internet security, he sank more resources into growing the sections of the company that produced Internet security solutions for corporate customers and that developed new content security products, and he increased the company's international business operations.

His timing was perfect. In 1999 and 2000, companies and individual computers users alike had been alerted to risks to their computers by dire warnings of Y2K computer system breakdowns as clocks rolled from 1999 to 2000 on New Year's Eve. Aggressive e-mail worms and viruses, like the Melissa and I Love You viruses wreaked havoc with company networks by automatically sending e-mails to everyone in a user's e-mail address book and clogging company networks. And in spring of 2000, hackers using a fairly simple program clogged major Internet sites Yahoo.com and Amazon.com for hours. Other devices besides computers and computer networks proved to be vulnerable as well. Mobile telephones in Spain and Microsoft's TV-based Internet browser were also disrupted by worms and viruses. All of these threats helped increase the appeal of a market strategy centered on Internet security solutions. Thompson's decision to increase the emphasis at Symantec on corporate security solutions was especially fruitful: by the end of his first year as CEO, the corporate segment of the company's revenues had increased from 30% to 46%. His moves made Symantec more attractive to investors, who saw the corporate market as more profitable than the consumer market. During Thompson's first year, the value of a share of Symantec's stock increased from $13 a share to around $70 a share and revenues rose between 22% and 40% each quarter.

By the end of his first year "practicing his craft," Thompson was leading Symantec confidently and assertively, using the abilities that he had developed and practiced through his education and in his long career at IBM. An army brat, Thompson was born in 1949 on the military base at Fort Dix, New Jersey where his father was stationed. After a few more military transfers, the family settled in the West Palm Beach area of Florida about the time that Thompson was ready to start school. Thompson went to Lincoln High school (later renamed Kennedy High). He was, according to his own account, a hellion in high school, but managed to learn how to play the clarinet well enough to be offered a scholarship to Lincoln University in Missouri. When he got there, he learned to his dismay that a stipulation of the scholarship was that he had to major in music, an idea that did not appeal to him. So, he transferred to Florida A & M University, influenced by an accounting professor who was also a family friend, and he became a business major, graduating in 1971. IBM was recruiting sales representatives on campus, and he accepted a job offer from them, figuring that his gift of gab along with his business degree would make sales a good choice.

At IBM in Florida, not only was he the only African American in the office, he also stood out because of his large moustache and even larger Afro, a marked departure from the conservative IBM style of dress. His attitude was that his competence was more relevant than his conformity. As he became more experienced, however, he realized that sometimes he could be beaten out of a sale by someone who was equally competent and who conformed as well. So he adopted a mainstream professional appearance and has never looked back.

His sales career with IBM lead to his first management position, managing an IBM sales office in Atlanta. By 1980, he had moved to Boston as administrative assistant to the regional manager, and three years later he was director of marketing for the region. IBM sent him to MIT's Sloan School of Management for an intensive 12 month MBA program designed especially for mid-career executives. By 1984, he had moved to IBM headquarters in White Plains where he worked in the chairman's office as an assistant, an experience he describes as akin to getting a second master's in business administration with a concentration on IBM.

From this point, each position he was given at IBM involved greater responsibility, a larger budget, and a bigger pool of employees to manage. His positions in the next decade and a half included director of IBM's Midwest operations, head of marketing for all IBM's U.S. business, general manager of IBM's personal software products, and director of and general manager of IBM Americas. In terms of shaping his leadership strategy, probably the most significant of these appointments was as director of Midwest operations, an assignment he was given in 1990 during a period when IBM was in a slump and undergoing a major corporate shakeup. At that time, IBM's Midwest sales force were all "jacks of all trades." He reorganized them into teams, with each team specializing in one specific area of customer need. Because they got to concentrate on one area, the teams became more proficient at their jobs and did a better job of serving customers. Customer satisfaction increased and so did the morale of the sales force.

The strategies that Thompson used at IBM are evident at Symantec: listen to the customers and align the company's mission with their needs, hire a talented work force, make sure that every employee knows the company's mission, and provide leadership in the area that is the company's focus. In his view, companies that both respond well to their customers and provide leadership are the ones that survive and thrive in a competitive marketplace. As Symantec continues to break new grounds in Internet security, both the computer industry and the business field will play close attention to John Thompson.

Sources

Periodicals

Black Enterprise, June, 1997, p.80.
San Francisco Examiner, May 2, 1999, B.1.
Wall Street Journal, August 19, 1999, B6.

Other

Additional information for this profile was obtained from Barron's Online, http://www.barrons.com; Bloomberg.com, http://www.bloomberg.com; CNET News, http://news.com; PR Newswire, http://www.prnewswire.com; Redherring.com, http://www.redherring.com; Symantec Press Center, http://www.symantec.com/PressCenter; The Wall Street Transcript, http://www.twst.com; and an interview with *Contemporary Black Biography*, June, 2000.

—Rory Donnelly

Morgan Tsvangirai

1952(?)—

Opposition leader

In the late 1990s, Morgan Tsvangirai emerged as a surprisingly formidable political challenger inside Zimbabwe, a nation of 11 million in south central Africa. Once a miner, Tsvangirai headed the country's largest trade union for a decade, but growing dissatisfaction in the country spurred the formation of a movement opposing Zimbabwe's aging, autocratic president, Robert Mugabe. Tsvangirai was one of the founders of the Movement for Democratic Change (MDC), and was formally elected its leader in the party's first conference in early 2000. In the spring of that year, a wave of politically-motivated violence swept through Zimbabwe, and Tsvangirai—not for the first time in his life—became the target of a plan to silence him through official intimidation. "He may yet follow in the proud African tradition of trade union leaders who become presidents," noted Anton La Guardia, Zimbabwe correspondent for the British *Telegraph* newspaper.

Tsvangirai was born in the early 1950s in what was then called Southern Rhodesia, and was the first of nine children in a poor rural family. At the time, Southern Rhodesia was a self-governing colony of the British empire. Over the course of the next decade, a black nationalist movement gathered strength inside Rhodesia, and began agitating for independence and black majority rule. Southern Rhodesia, however, was dominated politically and economically by English settlers with large agricultural land holdings, thanks to laws dating back to the early 1930s. As the independence movement grew, the white government became increasingly hostile to calls for the political enfranchisement of blacks. A white conservative prime minister, elected in 1964, led the country into a battle with the British crown, who supported the black nationalists. In 1965, Rhodesia's white government declared its independence from the British crown, which the Queen and Parliament viewed as an act of rebellion.

Rhodesia's declaration of independence brought scorn from the international community. In 1968 the United Nations Security Council voted, for the first time in its history, to impose economic sanctions on the country. In 1970, by the time Tsvangirai had left school while still an adolescent to work in the country's rich nickel mines in order to support his family, Rhodesia had become a republic. However, political power remained in the hands of the former colonial settlers. A stalemate ensued, and a protracted guerrilla war against the Rhodesian government endured over the next decade.

At a Glance . . .

Born c. 1952, in Southern Rhodesia (now Zimbabwe). *Politics:* Movement for Democratic Change.

Career: Miner in Zimbabwe's nickel mines since the late 1960s; became active in miners' union; elected secretary general of Zimbabwe Congress of Trade Unions(ZCTU), 1988; elected president of Movement for Democratic Change (MDC), January, 2000.

Addresses: *Office*—c/o Embassy of Zimbabwe, 1608 New Hampshire Ave. NW, Washington, DC 20009.

Finally, in 1979, a settlement was reached after negotiations with guerrilla leaders Joshua Nkomo and Robert Mugabe. Their two groups united to form the Zimbabwe African National Union "Patriotic Front" (ZANU-PF), and the country was re-named Zimbabwe.

Rhodesian blacks like Tsvangirai voted for the first time in February of 1980, and chose Mugabe as their president. The constitution, which had been ratified one year earlier, still allowed Zimbabwe's white minority certain rights, especially regarding property ownership of the country's most valuable acreage. Over the next decade, Mugabe consolidated political power, and forced out men like Nkomo who had become threats to his power. Violence and unrest occurred in the countryside during the 1980s, as widespread corruption, fuel shortages, inflation, and wage shrinkage kept most Zimbabweans mired in poverty.

Problems also arose among Zimbabwe's tribal factions, especially in the area of Matabeleland, home to the smaller of Zimbabwe's two main African ethnicities, the Ndebele. Related to the Zulu of South Africa, and in Zimbabwe only since the 1840s, the Ndebele make up about 16 percent of the population. A Ndebele opposition group fomented discord against the government, which was dominated by the Shona ethnic group. The Shona retaliated harshly, and earned condemnation from international human-rights organizations.

Tsvangirai spent ten years working in the nickel mines, and was an ardent ZANU-PF member in the early years of independence. He even served as a political commissar for the party at his workplace. However, Mugabe became increasingly despotic and many Zimbabweans grew resentful. Although elections were generally fair, the Mugabe government possessed total control over the newspapers and television stations. This left very few means by which opposition parties could get their message across. ZANU-PF politicians held nearly all of the seats in Zimbabwe's legislative body, the House of Assembly.

Life Endangered

By 1988, after having risen through the ranks of the organized labor movement, Tsvangirai was elected secretary-general of Zimbabwe's largest coalition of trade unions, the Zimbabwe Congress of Trade Unions (ZCTU). Rejecting the dominance of ZANU-PF, Tsvangirai and other union leaders focused their energies on making the well-structured union movement a voice for political power. With 700,000 members, the ZCTU became a formidable foe of the Mugabe government. In 1989, Tsvangirai was jailed for a few weeks by the government—whose human-rights abuses had continued to earn international scorn—after being accused of spying on behalf of South Africa.

A few years later, Tsvangirai began leading strikes against harsh government measures, such as punitive tax hikes and price increases. In December of 1997, he organized a successful anti-tax protest—the Mugabe administration had planned to increase revenues in order to fund pensions for veterans of Zimbabwe's guerrilla war for independence in the 1970s—and a few days later, was attacked in his ZCTU office by unknown thugs. He was severely beaten, and his assailants even attempted to throw him out of the tenth-story window.

These tactics did not deter Tsvangirai or the rest of the ZCTU leadership, however, and they continued to organize strikes throughout 1998. The movement gained strength, in part, because of the dire situation within Zimbabwe: unemployment hovered at 50 percent, and nearly 2,000 Zimbabweans died from AIDS each week. In late 1999, the Movement for Democratic Change was founded, and at its first national congress, Tsvangirai was chosen to head the opposition party on January 30, 2000. As a crowd of 4,000 people chanted "Chinja," or "change," Tsvangirai affirmed the MDC's intention to loosen the ZANU-PF's stranglehold on the country. "I hope they disappear into the dustbin of history, because their betrayal of this country has been a treasonable offence," Tsvangirai was quoted as saying, according to David Blair of the British *Telegraph* newspaper. The journalist also reported that a delegate to the congress declared to him, "Tsvangirai is the only one who can save us from this government."

In a nationwide referendum held in February of 2000, Mugabe suffered a clear defeat when voters rejected his proposed constitutional changes. The plan would have expanded his presidential powers, and allowed the seizure of land from white farmers without compensation. A powerful group of war veterans had clamored for increased land ownership, and found support for their cause with the Mugabe government. "Grappling with political and economic crises and falling popularity ahead of parliamentary elections next month, the government has been accused by critics of using land redistribution to win votes among poor blacks and thus fanning racial and political animosities," explained *New York Times* journalist Henri E. Cauvin.

The MDC opposed the land-seizure plan, and won support from the economically powerful white farmers. The majority of the country's commercial farms—about 4,500 in all—were white-owned, and occupied the most fertile land in country. This small minority, however, also played an important role in Zimbabwe's economy, since the tobacco and cotton exports from such farms bring in much-needed hard currency. Tsvangirai noted that the economic situation in Zimbabwe was so dismal that the land-for-veterans issue was irrelevant. "Poverty, unemployment, debt problems, and corruption have a terrible effect on the standard of living of 75 percent of the people," he told the *New York Times*'s Jane Perlez. "When you talk of land in that sea of poverty it's meaningless. What does land do if you haven't got a meal?"

The rejection of the February referendum gave Mugabe his first electoral defeat since 1980, and the MDC geared up to win support for their candidates in upcoming parliamentary elections that were originally scheduled for May of 2000. Increases in voter registration, however, made the Mugabe government wary, and thousands began flocking to MDC rallies. White farmers gave financial support to the MDC, an alliance that was called the first real reconciliation of blacks and whites in Zimbabwe since the independence era two decades earlier.

In April of 2000, squatters organized by the veterans' groups began occupying white-owned farms, and deadly skirmishes resulted. Nearly all of those killed were blacks who supported the MDC, however. The car of two MDC supporters was firebombed, killing two, and other members of the MDC died under mysterious circumstances, including Tsvangirai's own driver. After an independent newspaper in Harare, the capital city, described the deaths as politically motivated, its offices were firebombed. It was feared that the civil unrest would lead to a declaration of a state of emergency and then rule by decree, which would mean that the parliamentary elections could be indefinitely postponed.

Tsvangirai visited Washington D.C. to ask for help in mid-April of 2000, and made it clear that he and the MDC hoped for a peaceful end to the conflict, not outright warfare with Mugabe. "As much as I would like to take an aggressive stand, that's what he's looking for," Tsvangirai told the *New York Times*'s Perlez. "He's looking to be made a martyr." By early May, 13 Zimbabweans had died, and 1,100 white-owned farms had been occupied by force. Tsvangirai spoke that week at a large rally outside Harare, and urged MDC followers to keep a low profile, to feign support for the Mugabe government "as long as on voting day your X is for the MDC," Tsvangirai said, according to an Associated Press report that appeared in the *New York Times.*

Sources

New York Times, April 3, 2000; April 19, 2000; April 20, 2000; April 30, 2000; May 2, 2000.

Telegraph (U.K.), January 31, 2000; February 16, 2000; May 14, 2000.

Other

Additional information for this profile was provided by the United States Department of State web site at http://www.state.gov

—Carol Brennan

A. J. Verdelle

1960—

Novelist

A. J. Verdelle burst upon the literary scene in 1995 with *The Good Negress,* a coming-of-age story that became one of the most acclaimed novels of the 1990s. Until then, Verdelle had pursued a career as a statistics consultant that seemingly gave few hints of what was to come. In fact, Verdelle drew heavily upon her own life experiences in the book. Written mostly in southern African American dialect, *The Good Negress* brought to life the linguistic divide in the African American community between speakers of different forms of the English language, and contained powerful reflections on the conflicts that education might set in motion in the life of a brilliant, but uneducated young African American woman.

Verdelle was born in Washington, D.C., in 1960 to A. Y. Jones and Patricia Howell Jones. Verdelle was the middle name of her maternal grandmother. Her family had lived in Washington, D.C. for three generations, but as a child Verdelle often visited relatives in Detroit, the setting for *The Good Negress.* When a male cousin in Detroit was jailed, Verdelle told a *Chicago Tribune* interviewer, she "nearly had a nervous breakdown." When she asked her mother what they could do, her mother replied that "[t]his 'do anything,' that's for white people who have money. I'm paying for your school and I need you to calm down and study." Verdelle personally experienced racism early on in grade school. When her white schoolmates were assigned to wash blackboards, she was sent to clean toilets—an episode that found its way in revised form into *The Good Negress.*

Verdelle attended a private Catholic girls' high school in Washington, D.C., and her parents instilled in her a sense of the value of education and a belief in her own capabilities. "I was raised to be a superwoman," she told the *Tribune.* "My mother raised me to believe I could do everything." However, it was an education of a practical kind that her parents sought. As Verdelle told the *Tribune* interviewer, "I felt shut up. I felt shut up a lot. When I was nine I said I wanted to be a writer. My mother told me I had to grow up and figure out how to put food on the table. I did exactly what my mother said."

After finishing high school, Verdelle enrolled at the University of Chicago, perhaps the most purely bookish and intellectual of the nation's elite colleges and universities. Though she had been labeled rambunctious by her high school administration and had never really fit in—"That school was not ready for a smart African-American girl, especially not such a dark one," she told the *Tribune*—Verdelle had come to a sense of her own intellectual abilities. At the University of Chicago, however, she found herself struggling academically. Disoriented and lost, she refused to quit, although it took her until her senior year to earn her first A grade.

Verdelle graduated with a bachelor's degree in 1982 and went on for an master's degree at the University of Chicago. After earning her master's degree in 1986, she took her mother's practical admonitions to heart and embarked upon a career quite distant from her own creative aspirations. Verdelle had studied statistics

At a Glance . . .

Born 1960 in Washington, DC; daughter of A.Y. and Patricia (Howell) Jones; took middle name of maternal grandmother for last name. *Education:* University of Chicago, B.A., 1982; University of Chicago, M.A., 1986; Bard College, M.F.A., 1993.

Career: Novelist and essayist. Statistics consultant specializing in minority concerns,Brooklyn, NY, 1988-95; freelance writer, 1995-; novel *The Good Negress* published by Algonquin Books, 1995; Bunting fellow in creative writing, Radcliffe College, 1996; lecturer in-creative writing, Princeton University, late 1990s.

Awards: Finalist in first fiction category, *Los Angeles Times* book prizes, PEN/Faulkner finalist, cited among Books of the Year, New York Public Library, VursellAward, American Academy of Arts and Letters, all for *The Good Negress,* 1995; WhitingWriters Award, 1996.

Addresses: *Home*—New Orleans, LA, and New York, NY;*Agent*—Wendy Weil Agency, Inc., 232 Madison Ave., Suite 1300, New York, NY10016.

and, after a move to Brooklyn, New York, founded her own statistics consulting firm in 1988. She also joined the American Statistical Association and the American Women's Economic Development Corporation, and devoted herself to the task of making a living. The firm is devoted to research that explores the situations faced by women and minority groups.

It didn't take long for Verdelle to get back to writing, however. She enrolled in a graduate writing program at Bard College, where she would eventually earn a masters in fine arts degree in 1993. Verdelle set to work on what would become *The Good Negress,* rising early in the morning every day for 14 months to work on the book. The novel went down several blind alleys. At one point she tossed a two-thirds-completed draft into the trash, dissolved into tears, and began again. *The Good Negress* eventually went through six complete drafts, with Verdelle crediting her training as a statistician for the discipline needed to complete it. "Life is hard work," she observed in an interview with the *Santa Fe New Mexican.* Verdelle may have been her own severest critic, but there were hurdles to overcome before the novel could be published. A key feature of the book is its use of contrasts between different linguistic levels, and Verdelle found that publishers were put off by the book's use of dialect. One editor told her to rewrite the main character's stream of consciousness into standard English. Verdelle did so, but couldn't live with the results—they went counter to the book's core. "I was trying to write about how smart you could be in a language that is not considered standard English," she told the *Chicago Tribune.*

Verdelle succeeded brilliantly at conveying the intelligence of her novel's central character, Denise Palms. Palms, who is 12-years-old in 1963, is raised in the country in Virginia by her grandmother, but comes to live with her pregnant mother and her two older brothers in Detroit. Against the backdrop of her brothers' struggles against the circumscribed identities available to African American men in the 1960s, Palms comes into contact with a Detroit teacher, Gloria Pearson. Pearson recognizes her intelligence, tries to divert her away from manual work, and endeavors to teach her standard English. Verdelle used a complex narrative structure in the novel, jumping backward and forward in time and employing transitions between levels of language in order to show the development of Denise's unique identity.

The Good Negress was a technical tour de force, and won wide acclaim for its author. Most encouraging of all were the words of Pulitzer Prize–winning novelist Toni Morrison, who called the book "truly extraordinary". Morrison's comment, emblazoned on the cover of the book's paperback edition, attracted many readers to the book. Verdelle joined Morrison as a faculty member at Princeton University's prestigious writing department, and the novel won several awards, including the Vursell Award of the American Academy of Arts and Letters in 1995 and the Whiting Writers Award, a $30,000 grant given to developing writers of exceptional talent, the following year. *The Good Negress* was also a finalist for a PEN/Faulkner award.

Verdelle and her companion, the concert producer Alexa Birdsong, divide their time between New Orleans and New York City. In both cities, Verdelle immersed herself in libraries and historical archives, compiling material for a new novel. The new novel is a sprawling historical work about African American cowboys who made their way to the American West in the years before the Civil War. Provisionally titled *Meanwhile Back at the Ranch,* the novel is slated for publication in 2000 or 2001. "I was interested in understanding the propertied perspective of both the African-American and the horse, the breadth and expanse of the nation, and the march toward the end of the century," Verdelle told *In Review,* a website devoted to the current activities of Princeton faculty. "And the notion of African-American psychology underpins it all."

Selected writings

The Good Negress, Algonquin, 1995.

Sources

Books

Contemporary Authors, volume 152, Gale, 1997.

Periodicals

Chicago Tribune, April 24, 1995, p. Tempo-1.
Detroit Free Press, April 12, 1995, p. E3.
The Nation, January 27, 1997, p. 5.
Publishers Weekly, November 4, 1996, p. 10.
Santa Fe New Mexican, November 27, 1998.

Other

Additional information for this profile was obtained from http://www.princeton.edu/~paw (current activities of Princeton faculty)

—James M. Manheim

Benny Waters

1902–1998

Jazz musician, vocalist, and arranger

Benny Waters was an indomitable jazz master whose musical career began in early childhood and spanned every decade of the 20th century. Continuing to perform up to within two months of his death, he was considered to be the oldest regularly performing musician in the United States. Waters was also one of a dwindling number of jazz musicians whose recording careers dated back to the inception of jazz in the 1920s. His passing left only five other surviving artists of that era: Benny Carter, Rosey McHargue, Spiegel Willcox, Lionel Hampton, and Claude "Fiddler" Williams.

Waters was an accomplished saxophonist, clarinetist, vocalist, and arranger. He played and recorded with many of the jazz greats of the 1920s, 1930s, and 1940s. His interest in carousing often overshadowed attention to his career, and although it never kept him from playing music, it did limit the renown that might otherwise have been his. His popularity in the United States was further limited by a 40-year sojourn in Europe. Waters embarked on a European tour with a Dixieland band led by Jimmy Archey in 1952, but did not return to the United States until 1992. He was quite popular in Europe, especially France, where he settled.

Returning to the United States for medical care, Waters underwent cataract surgery in 1992 that left him blind. He was soon back at work, however, maintaining an amazing calendar of performances–averaging about 100 a year–and a new generation of Americans discovered Waters. Playing classic swing, usually on a tenor sax, he continually surprised his audiences. Critics, awed by his longevity, were even more astonished by the strength and vitality of his playing. "[Waters] is," wrote Don Heckman of the *Los Angeles Times* in 1997, "a walking compendium of jazz. But there is nothing archaic about his playing or his energy, which offer convincing testimony to the idea that creativity knows no age limits."

Benjamin Arthur Waters was born on January 23, 1902, in the small crossroads town of Brighton, Maryland. He was the youngest of seven children born to Edward and Frances Waters. The family greatly enjoyed music. Mary Schumacher noted in the *Washington Post* in 1998 that Frances Waters "couldn't carry a tune but was always belting out some hymn or other. Waters's father, on the other hand, would...sing perfect

At a Glance . . .

Born Benjamin Arthur Waters January 23, 1902, in Brighton, MD; died August 11, 1998, in Columbia, MD; son of Edward and Frances Waters; married and divorced twice. *Education:* New England Conservatory of Music, Boston, MA. *Religion:* Christian Science.

Career: Jazz musician, vocalist, arranger; played with Charlie Miller Band, c. 1920-23; played with Charlie Johnson Orchestra, 1926-33; played with house band, Apollo Theater, Harlem, c. 1934; played with Fletcher Henderson, Oran Page, 1930's; played with Jimmie-Lunceford, 1942; headed own band in Red Mill, New York City, 1942-43; headed own band in California, 1944-47; joined Jimmy Archey's Dixieland band, 1949-52; freelance musicianin Europe, 1952-92; co-founded and toured with the Statesmen of Jazz, 1994-97.

Awards: Chevalier, Ministry of Culture, France, 1996.

barbershop harmonies on Sunday mornings while everyone else was in church." Waters discovered his own musical talent very early in life. By his own account, he began to play the pipe organ at the age of three. He soon progressed to piano, and then to reed instruments, which he learned from reading a book. Waters was giving piano recitals at age seven, and had mastered E-flat clarinet one year later. He was featured in local performances, and was billed as a child prodigy. During these adolescent years, Waters often performed with a brother who played the trumpet. The two played in a country band and also performed at dances and house parties.

As Michael Bourne noted in *Down Beat* in 1997, "What's remarkable about Waters's musical life is that he was first playing jazz as jazz was being invented. He couldn't learn from books or magazines, records or radio, and the music being played was barely called 'jazz' back then." Waters told Bourne, "I actually didn't hear that much jazz. I was playing what was called jazz... I'd play religious songs for my mother, and in the gaps and little spaces of a song I'd make a little improvisation. And my mother would say, 'Stop that jazz, Benny!'"

As a teenager, Waters moved to Haverford, Pennsylvania to live with an aunt. However, he continued to perform with his brother. They played at dances and gave classical concerts at the Philadelphia Academy of Music. Waters mastered alto, soprano, baritone, and tenor saxophone, and was a regular member of the Charlie Miller dance band from 1918 to 1921. At the age of 18, Waters entered the New England Conservatory of Music in Boston, where he studied theory and arrangement for three years. He was an excellent student, and also established a strong reputation as a private tutor. In fact, Waters taught clarinet to Harry Carney, who would go on to play baritone saxophone in Duke Ellington's orchestra for half a century. In addition, Waters played with Johnny Hodges while attending the Conservatory.

During the 1920s, Waters formally embarked on a career as an inveterate sideman, working with some of the biggest names of the era. He recorded with Joe "King" Oliver, and, joining Charlie Johnson's Orchestra in Atlantic City in 1926, Waters worked with Jabbo Smith, Sidney DeParis, and Benny Carter. He remained with Johnson's orchestra until 1933, playing mostly at Small's Paradise club in Harlem. Johnson passed up a golden opportunity in 1927, when the band was offered a position as the house band at the Cotton Club, complete with a regular radio broadcast. Johnson turned the offer down because the wages were too low, and the position was accepted by Duke Ellington, who became famous because of the radio broadcast.

In 1934, Waters played in the Apollo Theater's house orchestra. The band accompanied a young Ella Fitzgerald in her Apollo debut, when she won an amateur talent contest. "She did real well," Waters remembered for *Down Beat* in 1997. "We would have given Ella the prize ourselves if the band had been judges." Also during the 1930s, Waters replaced saxophone legend Coleman Hawkins in the reed section of Fletcher Henderson's orchestra, and played with Oran "Hot Lips" Page as well.

Waters freelanced during the 1940s, playing notably with Jimmie Lunceford in 1942. He then headed his own bands, first in New York for two years, and then in California, between 1944 and 1947. Returning to New York, Waters played for a time with Roy Milton, and then joined trombonist Jimmy Archey's Dixieland band in 1949.

Waters traveled to Europe in 1942 while on tour with Archey's band, and decided to stay. He spent the next 40 years as an expatriate, living and working mainly in Paris. Waters had a 15-year stint at La Cigale, a café in the red-light district of Paris. He was a regular performer, and jammed with whomever came to sit in. The list of visiting musicians included Sonny Criss, Dexter Gordon, Thelonius Monk, and Bud Powell. Waters decided to go solo in 1969–at the age of 67–and worked throughout Europe. He played in festivals all over the world, and became a favorite in Britain and Germany. Waters began making annual trips back to the United States in 1979. He published a memoir in

1985, *The Key to a Jazzy Life.* Paula Span noted in the *Washington Post* that the book "records a career punctuated with drunken episodes, myriad girlfriends, the occasional brawl, two volatile marriages and divorces." Although he claimed not to have fathered any children, Waters admitted in his memoir that it was a subject open to debate.

In 1970, with his health suffering from his excessive taste for alcohol, Waters quit drinking. "I never did get so drunk that I couldn't play," he pointed out to Span. He added, "If a guy is down, tired and sleepy and he's got to do a show, it's possible a couple of drinks'll spry him up. But then you lose control."

In 1992, Waters was injured in an auto accident in Germany and also underwent surgery to remove cataracts. When he was unable to raise his insurance to cover the operation, he decided to move back to the United States, where Medicare would pay for it. Waters moved into an apartment in Hollis, Queens, a neighborhood that has been home to many jazz musicians over the years. Although the cataract surgery left him blind, Waters hit the road again as soon as his strength returned. He averaged 100 dates a year and attracted a new generation of fans. He continued to practice at least one hour every day, as he always had. In 1998, *Down Beat* quoted Waters as saying, "You are never too old to learn. The more you practice, the better you get." Audiences were always surprised that his music was so "modern." "They expect you to play real old-timey," Waters explained to the *Washington Post* in 1998. "When you don't, then they're knocked out."

Waters finally began to receive acclaim in the United States after four decades abroad. Reviews of his performances were extremely positive. *Music Central '96* described him as "a spirited soloist," and said, "Waters possesses a dazzling technique underscored by a fervent feeling for the blues. His enthusiasm, skill and intensity would be creditable in a jazzman of any age...." Jazz deejay Alex Leak stated in 1998, "Benny is still fresh after 96 years. He's an icon.... He's history."

In 1995 Waters helped found the venerated Statesmen of Jazz, a performing band of musicians older than 65. The roster included Waters, Claude Williams, Milt Hinton, Joe Wilder, and Buddy Tate, among others. As its oldest member, Waters was the band's patriarch. He toured throughout Europe, Japan, and the United States as a member of the Statesmen of Jazz.

Waters celebrated his 95th birthday with an evening of jazz at Birdland in Manhattan, with a band that featured Mike LeDonne, Howard Alden, Steve Blailock, Ed Locke, and Earl May. The evening's music was recorded and released as a CD entitled *Birdland Birthday: Live at 95.* In a 1998 review of the album, John McDonough wrote in *Down Beat,* "He [Waters] plays it straight down the middle with a sympathetic but contemporary rhythm section, and his strong, gritty-on-demand sound in all registers neither asks nor gives any quarter." McDonough continued, "His intonation and control are clear and hard as a rock as he twists notes with a raw lyricism. It's that sound more than his ideas that regularly carr[ies] his solos to a boil on track after track."

Waters gave his last performance in Manhattan in June of 1998. The following month, he moved back to Maryland. On August 11, 1998, Waters died of a heart attack in a hospital in Columbia, Maryland and was buried in Sandy Spring, Maryland. He had been a living jazz legend, a largely unrecognized but significant contributor to the genre. Waters treated his musicianship as one long learning curve. His legacy is not only as a great jazz architect, but as a man who continued to contribute vitally to the world of music long after others were content to age in obscurity. Waters played because of his enduring love for jazz.

Selected writings

The Key to a Jazzy Life, Toulouse, Arts Graphiques, 1985.

Selected discography

Preston Jackson and Benny Waters in Stockholm, Kenneth, 1974.
On the Sunny Side of the Street, JSP, 1981.
When You're Smiling, Hep, 1981.
From Paradise (Small's) to Shangri-La, Muse, 1987.
Memories of the Twenties, Stomp Off, 1990.
(with Statesmen of Jazz), *Statesmen of Jazz,* Arbor, 1995.
Birdland Birthday: Live at 95, Enja, 1997.
Benny Waters: Freddy Randall Jazz Band, Jazzology, 1998.
Live at the Pawnshop, Opus 3, 1999.

Sources

Books

Feather, Leonard. *The Encyclopedia of Jazz.* New York: Bonanza Books, 1969.
Who's Who Among African Americans, 12th Edition. Edited by Ashyia N. Henderson and Shirelle Phelps. Detroit, Gale, 1999.

Periodicals

Down Beat, May 1997, p.12; May 1998, p.63; July 1998, p.44; October, 1998, p.18.
Los Angeles Times, January 6, 1991, Calendar, p.57; December 19, 1997, Calendar, p.30.
Nashville Scene, September 28, 1998.
New York Times, August 13, 1998.
Time, August 24, 1998, p.35.
Washington Post, May 16, 1998, p.D1; May 21, 1998, p.M1; August 14, 1998, p.B8.

Other

Additional information for this profile was obtained from Hot Jazz Management Production at http://www.2.los.com/[]hotjazz/waters.hm; and http://elvispelvis.com/bennywaters.htm

—Ellen Dennis French

Melvin Watt

1945—

Congressman from North Carolina

North Carolina U.S. Representative Melvin Watt stood at the center of one of the most divisive American political controversies of the 1990s: the debate over whether redistricting should be used to create political-district boundary lines enclosing large African American majorities, thereby guaranteeing African American political representation. The man at the vortex of the storm was no political opportunist, but a superbly qualified attorney who has been noted for taking principled stands even when they were politically dangerous. Even after the boundary lines of his district were redrawn, Watt won re-election in his new white-majority district, defying the usual voting patterns based along racial lines.

Watt was born on August 26, 1945. He grew up on the outskirts of Charlotte in a tin-roofed shack without electricity or indoor plumbing. Education took him quickly out of these modest surroundings. Watt graduated from Charlotte's York Road High School in 1963 and then moved on to the University of North Carolina at Chapel Hill. Desegregation of the large southern state universities, a process marked by contention and sometimes violence, had been underway for only a few years, and Watt was one of only a few African American students enrolled. Nevertheless he compiled an excellent academic record, and graduated with a business administration degree in 1967.

Even more impressive was his conquest of the curriculum at Yale University Law School, one of the most competitive and tradition-bound institutions in the country. Watt finished the program in only three years, receiving his degree in 1970 and passing the bar exam in the District of Columbia that same year. In 1971 he moved back to North Carolina, passed the bar exam in that state, and began a career in civil rights law. Watt joined the firm of Chambers, Stein, Ferguson, and Becton and served there until his election to Congress in 1992. By joining numerous civic organizations in Charlotte and winning election to the presidency of the Mecklenburg County Bar Association, he built a valuable network of contacts. In 1989 Watt invested in a Charlotte restaurant and hotel complex, and became the owner of a nursing home.

Politics seemed a natural choice for Watt, and he served a term in the North Carolina state senate between 1984 and 1986. Family obligations temporarily halted his political career, and he vowed not to run for office again until his two sons, Brian and Jason,

At a Glance . . .

Born August 26, 1945, near Charlotte, NC; married, wife's name Eulada; children: two sons. *Education:* University of North Carolina at Chapel Hill, B.S. in business administration, 1967; Yale University, J.D., 1970. *Religion:* Presbyterian.

Career: Practiced civil rights law with the firm of Chambers, Stein, Ferguson, andBecton, 1971-92; elected to North Carolina Senate, 1984; temporarily left politics to concentration family, late 1980s; campaign manager, Harvey Gantt for Senate campaign, 1990; elected to House of Representatives from the Twelfth District of North Carolina, 1992; re-elected in 1994,1996, and 1998; member, House Banking and Financial Services Committee.

Addresses: *Office*—1230 Longworth House Office Building, Washington, DC 20515.

had finished high school. Watt's devotion to his family paid off, as both sons followed their father to Yale. He kept a hand in politics, though, managing the Charlotte city council and mayoral campaigns of a fellow rising star in African-American politics, Harvey Gantt.

Gantt made headlines when he became the mayor of Charlotte, North Carolina, and jumped into the 1990 race for the U.S. Senate seat held by longtime Republican Senator Jesse Helms, one of the most conservative politicians in America at the national level. Watt received a trial by fire in national politics when he signed on to manage Gantt's campaign. Helms, who is widely acknowledged to have run an ugly campaign that inflamed racial passions, won reelection. However, Watt gained status within North Carolina's Democratic party organization that he would use in his own bid for a Congressional seat two years later.

After the 1990 census, the North Carolina state legislature created a new Twelfth Congressional District with a 57 percent African American majority. African American politicians including Watt supported the change, and were joined by white Republicans who saw an opportunity to dilute Democratic voting strength in adjacent districts. The new district snaked along Interstate 85, encompassing predominantly African American neighborhoods in cities from Gastonia through Charlotte and Winston-Salem to Durham. The bizarre shape of the district attracted national attention. One candidate who joined Watt in the race for the seat complained, according to the *New York Times*, that he could "drive down I-85 with both car doors open and his every person in the district."

Watt defeated three other candidates in the 1992 Democratic primary, and cruised to victory in November. He and fellow first-time Representative Eva Clayton became the first African Americans to be sent to Congress from North Carolina since 1901, at the end of the Reconstruction era. Watt proclaimed that he was "saddened that it took 92 years" to break the color barrier once again, according to the *Almanac of American Politics.*

In Congress, Watt emerged as one of the nation's most staunchly liberal legislators, and became a strong ally of President Bill Clinton. On the issue of health care he went even further than Clinton, supporting a Canadian-style government plan. Watt also strongly resisted bills that would restrict civil liberties. He opposed a series of bills that strengthened the hand of law enforcement in dealing with juvenile offenders, and voted against a measure to fence off the U.S.–Mexican border. In 1996 Watt was the only member of Congress to vote against the "Megan's Law" a bill requiring convicted sex offenders to register with local law enforcement agencies upon their release from prison. He even crossed swords occasionally with North Carolina's powerful tobacco lobby. "On one issue after another," noted the *Almanac of American Politics,* "he [Watt] has risked unpopular stands to defend principle."

More notorious than any of Watt's activities in Congress was the protracted battle over the makeup of his district, which was still going on in the year 2000 as the new census was being taken. First, a federal lawsuit challenged the boundaries of the Twelfth District, under which Watt had run in 1992, as impermissible under statutes that required congressional districts to be compact and contiguous. The Supreme Court in 1996 declared those boundaries unconstitutional and, in 1997, the North Carolina legislature responded by shaving the ends off the district. This failed to satisfy a new panel of federal judges and, in 1998, the legislature devised yet another plan that reduced the proportion of African American voters in the district to 36 percent.

During Watt's reelection campaign, in which Republicans attacked Watt as an ultra-liberal and focused on his vote against Megan's Law (a position he eventually abandoned), he reaped the benefits of incumbency. He illustrated to voters the benefits he could bring to Charlotte's large banking industry through his position on the House Banking Committee. Watt won reelection to Congress in 1998 by a 56 to 42 percent margin. He took 69 percent of the vote in predominantly Republican Mecklenburg County, and made significant gains among white voters. Watt had done what few African American politicians and no Southern liberals had ever managed: he had won election in a white-majority district.

The redistricting battle continued to make headlines when a U.S. district court threw out the new boundaries. However, their decision was overturned by the U.S. Supreme Court, which ordered the reinstatement of the state legislature's 1997 plan. "Clearly, Mr. Watt's constituents are exasperated," observed the *New York Times,* which noted that Watt had the unenviable task of spreading the word of the decision among his constituents. Although Watt's political future seemed to depend in some measure on the 2000 elections and the future makeup of North Carolina's state government, he had already shown an ability to cross lines of party and race. The *Almanac of American Politics* noted that "he [Watt] has proven to be a tough contender."

Sources

Books

Barone, Michael, and Grant Ujifusa, *The Almanac of American Politics 2000,* National Journal, 1999.

Joint Committee on Printing, United States Congress, *1997-1998 Official Congressional Directory,* United States Government Printing Office, 1997.

Periodicals

Jet, January 11, 1999, p. 4; April 10, 2000, p. 8.

New York Times, April 29, 2000.

Time, November 2, 1992, p. 44.

Other

Additional information for this profile was obtained from http://www.house.gov/watt/bio_mel.htm

—James M. Manheim

Clarence Williams III

1939—

Actor

After a star turn on one of the most popular shows of the late 1960s, *The Mod Squad,* Clarence Williams III returned to the stage, and eventually landed roles in feature films. Over his long career, he has developed into an intense character actor. In films such as *Purple Rain, 52 Pick-up, Deep Cover* and *Against the Wall,* Williams has portrayed mysterious and often sinister characters.

After a long career on the Broadway stage, Williams landed one of the hippest parts on late-1960's television. He played undercover cop Linc Hayes on the television series *The Mod Squad,* which ran from 1968 to 1973. Williams starred with fellow unknown actors Peggy Lipton and Michael Cole. In its day, *The Mod Squad* was an innovative show, one that redefined fashion, hairstyles, and language.

Most actors try to make the leap from television into film, but Williams returned to the stage after *The Mod Squad* went off the air. He told *Entertainment Weekly* that he turned down film offers for many years because he was not impressed by the roles available to African American actors. Williams had no interest in playing one-dimensional characters in action-movies, or "blaxploitation" films, as they were called. "They gave a lot of people the chance to work," he told *Entertainment Weekly.* "I just didn't want to do them." Instead of becoming a blaxploitation action-movie star, Williams co-starred on Broadway in *Night and Day* with Maggie Smith in 1979.

Finally, in 1984, a legitimate role presented itself to Williams in Prince's biographic film *Purple Rain.* Williams played the musician's tortured father. Once a very talented musician himself, the character becomes alcoholic and abusive to his wife and son, called The Kid, who was played by Prince.

Two years later, in the 1986 adaptation of novelist Elmore Leonard's book *52 Pick-Up,* Williams starred opposite Roy Scheider and Ann-Margaret. Williams played a "spaced-out thug," according to the *Entertainment Weekly*'s review of the film on video. But, compared to Scheider and Ann-Margaret's "cold fish" characters, Williams and the other supporting actors were "hot potatoes." Another critic from *People* agreed with *Entertainment Weekly*, remarking that some supposedly intense scenes between the stars seem "tired and bored," while only the villains, played by Williams and John Glover, "have any energy."

At a Glance . . .

Born August 26,1945, near Charlotte, NC; married, wife's name Eulada; children: two sons. *Education:*University of North Carolina at Chapel Hill, B.S. in business administration, 1967, Yale University, J.D., 1970. *Religion* Presbyterian.

Career: Practiced civil rights law with the firm of Chambers, Stein, Ferguson, and Becton, 1971-92; elected to North Carolina Senate, 1984; temporarily left politics to concentration family, late 1980s; campaign manager, Harvey Gantt for Senate campaign, 1990; elected to House of representatives for the Twelfth District of North Carolina, 1992; re-elected in 1994, 1996, and 1998; member House Banking and Financial services Committee..

Addresses: *Office*—1230 Longworth House Office Building, Washington, DC 20515.

In 1994, Williams appeared in a cable television movie entitled *Against the Wall.* The film is based on a true story about a violent inmate revolt that occurred at New York's Attica prison in 1971. Thirty-two inmates and 11 guards who had been taken hostage died when law enforcement officials stormed the prison. Williams played one of the inmates who takes a young guard hostage. *People* called the violence in the film "unsparingly brutal," and noted that director John Frankenheimer "keeps the tension cranked up."

In 1995, Williams starred in the campy African American horror film, *Tales from the Hood.* He starred as the film's host, a ghoulish, dazed mortuary caretaker named Mr. Simms. *Entertainment Weekly,* which called the film a "black Twilight Zone," called Williams' hilarious character a "funkzombie Vincent Price."

In the 1997 made-for-TV movie *George Wallace,* Williams performed brilliantly. The two- part film was a biography of George Wallace, a conservative four-term governor of Alabama and former presidential candidate who was known for his segregationist beliefs. Based on the 1968 biography by Marshall Frady, the production received favorable reviews. *Time* magazine writer Joel Stein wrote that the mini-series, like its subject, "isn't afraid to give it to you straight, unpleasantness and all." Stein wrote that Williams did a "fine job," considering that he played what Stein called the film's "silliest" part. Williams played Archie, Wallace's African American servant who represents a combination of all of the African American people Wallace ever knew.

Williams started off the year 2000 with a role in the film *Reindeer Games.* The movie also featured two of Hollywood's hottest young stars, Ben Affleck and Charlize Theron. Williams played a small-time criminal who wants to make a big score. *Reindeer Games* also starred Gary Sinise and Dennis Farina. It marked the sixth time that Williams starred in a film directed by John Frankenheimer. Frankheimer also directed *52 Pick-up, George Wallace,* and *Against the Wall.* In *Reindeer Games,* which is set in northern Michigan during the Christmas holidays, Williams and Sinise force a young ex-convict to help them rob a casino. The film's plot contains many unexpected twists and turns, and relies heavily on the element of surprise.

Williams has a tremendous work ethic, and is highly regarded by filmmakers because he is a talented and reliable actor. "Everybody's waiting for a pot of gold to drop out of the sky and not work for a living," he told *Jet.* "I work a great deal. People come to me because they know they can get a good performance and a big bang for their buck."

Sources

Books

Kondek, Joshua, ed., *Contemporary Theatre, Film and Television,* Volume 26, Gale Group, 2000.

Mapp, Edward, ed., *Directory of Blacks in the Performing Arts,* Scarecrow Press, 1990.

Periodicals

Entertainment Weekly, April 1, 1994, p. 37; June 2, 1995; May 31, 1996.

Jet, February 28, 2000, p. 64.

People, November 24, 1986, p. 10; March 28, 1994, p. 15.

Time, August 25, 1997, p. 74.

Other

Additional information for this profile was obtained from "Clarence Williams III," *Internet Movie Database,* at http://www.imdb.com (May 13, 2000); and "The Mod Squad," *E! Online,* http://www .eonline.com (May 13, 2000).

—Brenna Sanchez

Edwin T. Witt

1920—

Physician

While not perceiving himself as either a hero or a victim, Edwin Witt stands a role model for the youth of today. Raised in Birmingham, Alabama during the Great Depression, Witt struggled to overcome rampant racism, poverty, and a highly dysfunctional family. He ultimately succeeded in achieving his dream of becoming a physician.

Edwin Witt was born on January 9, 1920, the first of three children born to Thomas Jesse and Virginia Alberta Ogletree Witt. Witt spent his childhood in South Woodlawn, Alabama, which was located six miles south of downtown Birmingham. Birmingham was a city notorious for its preservation of segregation and white supremacy. Racism and the restrictions which it inherently implied clearly defined Witt's youth. While his neighborhood was approximately 80 percent white, social contacts existed for business purposes only. Like many of his generation, Witt vividly recalled not being permitted to buy popcorn in the movie theater lobbies, having to sit in the balcony, and being prohibited from sitting at the drug store's soda fountain.

Woodlawn, Alabama's African American community was close-knit and relatively stable. Approximately 99 percent of Witt's neighbors were two-parent families who owned their homes and held good jobs. Moreover, as Witt described in his autobiography, *Witt's End,* "Every neighborhood adult had an automatic parental surrogate disciplinary license to chastise any child they knew for any kind of misbehavior without rebuke from the child's parents."

Following the end of World War I in 1918, Witt's father found employment at the Red Ore Mines in Huffman, Alabama. When the mines were closed in 1923, he purchased a horse and wagon and began to sell fruits and vegetables. With his route and customer base well-established, Witt's father then capitalized on the demand for liquor generated by Prohibition and began to sell whiskey from his cart. The money earned from this business helped to sustain the family throughout the Depression, and allowed them to survive without public assistance. Forever an entrepreneur, Witt's father later sold watermelons from a stand outside the family home, and established a barbecue next to it from which his wife sold spareribs and soft drinks.

Witt's life was affected most drastically when his father added a new dimension to his business: selling a

At a Glance . . .

Born Edwin T. Witt January 9, 1920; son of Thomas Jesse Witt and Virginia Alberta Ogletree Witt; married Cordelia Witt, June 1956. *Education:* Miles College, Birmingham, AL, B.A., 1943; Meharry Medical College, Nashville, TN, M.D., 1946; National Institute of Mental Health Fellowship, Pediatric Psychiatry, Los Angeles County General Hospital, 1964-65.

Career: Internship, Harlem Hospital, New York, NY, 1946-47; general practice,Birmingham, AL, 1947-53; pediatric residency, Meharry Medical College, 1953; pediatricresidency, Kern General Hospital, Bakersfield, CA, 1954; pediatric practice, Los Angeles, CA,1955-76; school physician, Los Angeles Unified School District, 1967-76; private pediatricpractice, Las Vegas, NV, 1976-80.

Selected memberships: Phi Beta Sigma Fraternity; president, Charles R. Drew MedicalSociety.

Addresses: *Home*—8714 SVL Box, Victorville, CA 92392.

mind-altering and highly addictive form of whiskey commonly known as "hooch." As Witt recalled, his father became addicted to hooch. Family life at the Witt household became increasingly chaotic as his father's consumption escalated. Witt and his mother were the chief victims, both emotionally and physically, of his father's latest enterprise. Moreover, as a result of his father's active bootlegging, the family was subjected to the indignity of numerous police searches and raids.

In order to escape his abusive father, Witt began to spend increasing amounts of time with his maternal grandmother, a woman whom he adored. When Witt was six years old, his grandmother contracted pneumonia, and Dr. P.S. Moten came daily to visit her. During these consultations, Witt found himself mesmerized by the stethoscope, and particularly by the ear pieces, which he was convinced were horns. From this point forward, the sciences forever piqued his curiosity, and Witt unfailingly kept his sights pointed in the direction of a medical career. Interestingly, while Witt's parents were both literate and his father read the daily *Birmingham News,* the Witt household did not contain any books. The annual *Almanac,* which was sent to every household, stood as the only magazine. Not surprisingly, then, his parents never encouraged his academic pursuits.

Although Witt's parents were incapable of nurturing his budding interest in the medical profession, he found other supporters within his community. As Witt recounted in his autobiography, from the "professional demeanor and the smell of alcohol saturated cotton balls used to cleanse the skin before an injection" of Dr. Broughton, to Dr. A. G. Martin, a general practitioner who encouraged Witt to study medicine, to Mrs. Susie Felton, a rural elementary school teacher, Witt found strong sources of inspiration and motivation.

Following completion of Patterson Elementary School in 1933, Witt attended Industrial High School, located five miles north of downtown Birmingham. Although Woodlawn High was located less than one mile from his home, he was forced to attend Industrial because it was the only high school for African Americans in the area during the 1920s and 1930s. Instead of enjoying a short, six-block walk to school, Witt spent three hours daily commuting on the streetcar.

Witt had always dreamed of attending Tuskegee Institute, founded by Booker T. Washington, in Tuskegee, Alabama. However, he had no means of earning the necessary tuition. Because he could not attend Tuskegee Institute, Witt decided not to pursue a college education. Because few jobs were available, he spent the next two years playing card games such as rise and fly whist with other unemployed neighbors and friends.

In 1939, two years after graduating from high school, a first-grade classmate offered Witt his 36-customer paper route with *The Birmingham Post,* one of the city's two evening newspapers. As Witt recounted in *Witt's End,* the "crowning point of my paper route" was a contest sponsored by the branch office manager to increase the number of subscribers. During the contest week, Witt serviced 102 people, with 66 new customers continuing their subscriptions at week's end. Concurrently, in the summer of 1939, he found employment at the Merita Bakery, initially unloading 100-pound sacks of flour from a railroad box car and then sweeping the floors of the oven room.

At the same time, Witt's father expanded his illegal activities by becoming a "station man" in various numbers games. Because he possessed an extensive record with the Birmingham police, Witt's father asked his son to visit the homes of players, write down their numbers, and transport all of the bets to a headquarters located downtown. Anxious to please his father, Witt agreed. Despite the fact that he was helping his father, he was still the recipient of both physical and verbal abuse. Witt was ultimately expelled from the family home for three months.

Through his paper route and work at the bakery, Witt was able to accumulate a small bankroll. Still shy of the amount necessary for an entire year of tuition at Tuskegee, he had saved enough money to cover the \$35.00 entrance fee and \$35.00 quarterly charge needed to enroll at Miles College, a four-year African American Methodist Episcopal school located south of Birmingham. At the urging of two friends, he enrolled in the pre-med program at Miles College in September of 1939. He almost left the college immediately after he was caught helping a fellow student cheat on an entrance math exam. As he later recounted in his autobiography, the only thing that really forced Witt to stay was a large sign pasted onto the wall of the college that read, "Fees paid to the college will not be refunded." "I had worked too hard for that thirty-five dollars to forfeit it." he recalled in *Witt's End.*

Witt remained in school and, on May 23, 1943, graduated cum laude with a bachelor of arts degree from Miles College. His only disappointment on that special day was that his mother was not present to share in his accomplishment. She had died early in his senior year. Witt then took another giant step towards realizing his life-long dream of becoming a doctor when he began classes at Meharry Medical College in Nashville, Tennessee on June 23, 1943. He was one of only 66 students chosen from an applicant pool of 660. Having received a deferment from the draft in 1941, Witt then benefitted from the Department of the Army's take-over of all 125 medical and dental schools in the country. In order to ensure adequate medical and dental personnel to cover wartime needs, the government agreed to assume all costs of medical education. As a result, Witt was able to complete his medical schooling at Meharry Medical College.

Witt was sent to Fort Benning, Georgia, and inducted into the Army Specialized Training Program as a private. He promptly began to study medicine and military science. Despite the conclusion of World War II in 1945, the Army agreed to finance the conclusion of his studies. Witt remained in uniform, performed regular Army duties, studied military science for two hours weekly, and participated in daily drills, reveille, and retreat. On June 6, 1946, he graduated from Meharry, tenth in a class of 60 students, and received an honorable Army discharge. He was placed in the inactive Army Reserves for five years, with the rank of First Lieutenant, Medical Corps, and was subject to active duty call-up at any time during that period.

From 1946 until 1947, Witt followed a general internship at Harlem Hospital in New York. He then applied for a residency as an ear, eye, nose, and throat doctor (which at the time were grouped as one specialty). When he did not receive the appointment, Witt returned to the Birmingham area and established a general practice in Fairfield, Alabama in July of 1947. Unsure about remaining in the Birmingham area, the Army once again intervened to decide Witt's fate. He was called up by the Army in July of 1949 and sent to Fort Bliss, Texas. The base had not had an African American medical officer for 100 years, and Witt did not see another African American for the first three months that he was stationed there. As he later recounted in an interview with *Contemporary Black Biography,* his only thought was, "The Lord has forsaken me!" As a first lieutenant, Witt was assigned to the general dispensary and predominantly treated headaches and backaches. After ten months there, he requested and received an overseas assignment to Europe. Witt was stationed as a captain in the urology department of William Beaumont General Hospital in Wurzburg, West Germany for the remaining 14 months of his assignment. The assignment allowed him to escape service in the Korean War.

When his Army tour of duty ended in 1951, Witt established an office for general practice in downtown Birmingham. Sadly, he discovered that the racism and segregation he had experienced there during his childhood was still in force. After two years in private practice, Witt returned to Meharry Medical College in 1953 for a one-year pediatric residency, followed by an additional year at Kern General Hospital in Bakersfield, California. Upon completion of his residency, Witt joined a colleague in establishing a private practice in the Los Angeles/Watts area. While serving as president of the Charles R. Drew Medical Society and continuing his private practice, he also became affiliated with the new Martin Luther King, Jr. Hospital in Willowbrook, California. He later served for 17 years as a pediatrician with the Los Angeles City School System. In 1964, Witt took a sabbatical to complete a one-year fellowship awarded by the National Institute of Mental Health at the Los Angeles County General Hospital's psychiatric service. In 1976, Witt and his wife, Cordelia, moved to Las Vegas, Nevada, where he opened a pediatric practice which he maintained until his retirement on December 31, 1980.

After six relaxing years in Las Vegas, Witt yearned to write his autobiography. The result of his eight to ten years of labor is *Witt's End.* He wrote the autobiography completely in long-hand, and his wife dutifully typed each page. In the book, Witt examined his own life in incredible detail, and vividly recalled the events and people who influenced his life. As he told *CBB,* he also wrote *Witt's End* for all children "who begin to find themselves down and out and don't think they have anywhere to go."

Witt's End also emphasizes the importance of getting an education as a means of escaping the racism that still exists in the United States. As Witt explained to *CBB,* the book "is dedicated to all boys, girls, adolescents, and parents of the world, rich and poor. Study and make ready by doing well in school and some day your chance will come. Get that high school diploma and college degree. Just hang them on the wall if you want to delay using them. They can always be activated and utilized whenever you are ready." In a warm, personable, unpretentious way, Witt holds up his own life as an embodiment of one who overcame the systemic prejudice of Alabama's social and educational institutions, and surmounted the challenges and disappointments of his childhood to succeed in realizing his dreams.

Sources

Books

Witt's End, E&C Publishers, 1996.

Periodicals

Los Angeles Sentinel, June 24, 1999, p. C-7.

Other

Additional information for this profile was obtained from an interview with *Contemporary Black Biography,* June 2000; and press releases prepared by Edwin Witt's literary agent.

—Lisa S. Weitzman

Cumulative Nationality Index

Volume numbers appear in Bold

American
Aaron, Hank **5**
Abdul-Jabbar, Kareem **8**
Abernathy, Ralph David **1**
Abu-Jamal, Mumia **15**
Adams Early, Charity **13**
Adams, Floyd, Jr. **12**
Adams, Oleta **18**
Adams, Sheila J. **25**
Adams, Yolanda **17**
Adkins, Rutherford H. **21**
Agyeman, Jaramogi Abebe **10**
Ailey, Alvin **8**
Al-Amin, Jamil Abdullah **6**
Albright, Gerald **23**
Alexander, Archie Alphonso **14**
Alexander, Clifford **26**
Alexander, Joyce London **18**
Alexander, Margaret Walker **22**
Alexander, Sadie Tanner Mossell **22**
Ali, Muhammad **2, 16**
Allen, Byron **3, 24**
Allen, Debbie **13**
Allen, Ethel D. **13**
Allen, Marcus **20**
Allen, Tina **22**
Amos, John **8**
Amos, Wally **9**
Anderson, Elmer **25**
Anderson, Jamal **22**
Anderson, Marian **2**
Andrews, Benny **22**
Andrews, Bert **13**
Andrews, Raymond **4**
Angelou, Maya **1, 15**
Ansa, Tina McElroy **14**
Anthony, Wendell **25**
Archer, Dennis **7**
Arkadie, Kevin **17**
Armstrong, Louis **2**
Armstrong, Robb **15**
Armstrong, Vanessa Bell **24**
Arrington, Richard **24**
Asante, Molefi Kete **3**
Ashe, Arthur **1, 18**
Ashford, Emmett **22**
Ashford, Nickolas **21**
Ashley-Ward, Amelia **23**
Austin, Patti **24**
Avant, Clarence **19**
Ayers, Roy **16**
Badu, Erykah **22**
Bailey, Radcliffe **19**
Bailey, Xenobia **11**
Baisden, Michael **25**
Baker, Anita **21**
Baker, Dusty **8**
Baker, Ella **5**
Baker, Gwendolyn Calvert **9**
Baker, Houston A., Jr. **6**
Baker, Josephine **3**
Baker, LaVern **26**
Baker, Thurbert **22**
Baldwin, James **1**
Bambara, Toni Cade **10**
Banks, Jeffrey **17**
Banks, Tyra **11**
Banks, William **11**
Baraka, Amiri **1**
Barboza, Anthony **10**
Barden, Don H. **9, 20**
Barkley, Charles **5**
Barney, Lem **26**
Barrett, Andrew C. **12**
Barry, Marion S. **7**
Barthe, Richmond **15**
Basie, Count **23**
Basquiat, Jean-Michel **5**
Bassett, Angela **6, 23**
Bates, Daisy **13**
Bates, Peg Leg **14**
Baugh, David **23**
Baylor, Don **6**
Beach, Michael **26**
Beals, Jennifer **12**
Beals, Melba Patillo **15**
Bearden, Romare **2**
Bechet, Sidney **18**
Beckford, Tyson **11**
Belafonte, Harry **4**
Bell, Derrick **6**
Bell, Robert Mack **22**
Bellamy, Bill **12**
Belle, Albert **10**
Belle, Regina **1**
Belton, Sharon Sayles **9, 16**
Ben-Israel, Ben Ami **11**
Benjamin, Regina **20**
Bennett, Lerone, Jr. **5**
Berry, Bertice **8**
Berry, Halle **4, 19**
Berry, Mary Frances **7**
Bethune, Mary McLeod **4**
Beverly, Frankie **25**
Bickerstaff, Bernie **21**
Biggers, John **20**
Bing, Dave **3**
Bishop Jr., Sanford D. **24**
Black, Keith Lanier **18**
Blackwell, Unita **17**
Blake, Asha **26**
Blanks, Billy **22**
Blige, Mary J. **20**
Bluford, Guy **2**
Bluitt, Juliann S. **14**
Bolden, Charles F., Jr. **7**
Bolin, Jane **22**
Bolton, Terrell D. **25**
Bond, Julian **2**
Bonds, Barry **6**
Bontemps, Arna **8**
Booker, Simeon **23**
Borders, James **9**
Bosley, Freeman, Jr. **7**
Boston, Kelvin E. **25**
Boston, Lloyd **24**
Bowe, Riddick **6**
Bowser, Yvette Lee **17**
Boyd, John W., Jr. **20**
Boyd, T. B. III **6**
Boykin, Keith **14**
Bradley, Ed **2**
Bradley, Thomas **2, 20**
Brandon, Barbara **3**
Brandon, Terrell **16**
Brandy **14**
Braugher, Andre **13**
Braun, Carol Moseley **4**
Braxton, Toni **15**
Brazile, Donna **25**
Brimmer, Andrew F. **2**
Briscoe, Connie **15**
Brock, Lou **18**
Brooke, Edward **8**
Brooks, Avery **9**
Brooks, Gwendolyn **1**
Brown, Charles **23**
Brown, Corrine **24**
Brown, Donald **19**
Brown, Elaine **8**
Brown, Erroll M. **23**
Brown, Foxy **25**
Brown, James **22**
Brown, Jesse **6**
Brown, Jim **11**
Brown, Joyce F. **25**

Brown, Lee Patrick **1, 24**
Brown, Les **5**
Brown, Marie Dutton **12**
Brown, Ron **5**
Brown, Sterling **10**
Brown, Tony **3**
Brown, Wesley **23**
Brown, Willie L., Jr. **7**
Brown, Zora Kramer **12**
Bruce, Isaac **26**
Brunson, Dorothy **1**
Bryant, John **26**
Bryant, Kobe **15**
Bryant, Wayne R. **6**
Buckley, Victoria (Vikki) **24**
Bullard, Eugene **12**
Bullins, Ed **25**
Bullock, Steve **22**
Bumbry, Grace **5**
Bunche, Ralph J. **5**
Burke, Selma **16**
Burnett, Charles **16**
Burrell, Thomas J. **21**
Burris, Chuck **21**
Burris, Roland W. **25**
Burroughs, Margaret Taylor **9**
Burton, LeVar **8**
Busby, Jheryl **3**
Butler, Jerry **26**
Butler, Leroy III **17**
Butler, Octavia **8**
Butler, Paul D. **17**
Butts, Calvin O., III **9**
Byrd, Donald **10**
Byrd, Michelle **19**
Byrd, Robert **11**
Cadoria, Sherian Grace **14**
Caesar, Shirley **19**
Cain, Herman **15**
Callender, Clive O. **3**
Calloway, Cab **14**
Camp, Kimberly **19**
Campanella, Roy **25**
Campbell, Bebe Moore **6, 24**
Campbell, Bill **9**
Campbell, E. Simms **13**
Campbell, Tisha **8**
Canada, Geoffrey **23**
Cannon, Katie **10**
Carew, Rod **20**
Carroll, Diahann **9**
Carson, Benjamin **1**
Carson, Julia **23**
Carson, Lisa Nicole **21**
Carter, Anson **24**
Carter, Betty **19**
Carter, Cris **21**
Carter, Mandy **11**
Carter, Regina **23**
Carter, Rubin **26**
Carter, Stephen L. **4**
Carter, Vince **26**
Carver, George Washington **4**
Cary, Lorene **3**
CasSelle, Malcolm **11**
Catlett, Elizabeth **2**
Cayton, Horace **26**
Chamberlain, Wilt **18**
Chambers, Julius **3**
Chapman, Jr., Nathan A. **21**
Chapman, Tracy **26**
Chappell, Emma **18**
Charles, Ray **16**
Chase-Riboud, Barbara **20**
Chavis, Benjamin **6**
Cheadle, Don **19**
Chenault, Kenneth I. **4**
Chideya, Farai **14**
Childress, Alice **15**
Chinn, May Edward **26**
Chisholm, Shirley **2**
Christian, Spencer **15**
Christian-Green, Donna M. **17**
Chuck D **9**
Clark, Celeste **15**
Clark, Joe **1**
Clark, Kenneth B. **5**
Clark, Patrick **14**
Clark, Septima **7**
Clark-Sheard, Karen **22**
Clarke, Hope **14**
Clarke, John Henrik **20**
Clash, Kevin **14**
Clay, William Lacy **8**
Clayton, Constance **1**
Clayton, Eva M. **20**
Clayton, Xernona **3**
Claytor, Helen **14**
Cleage, Pearl **17**
Cleaver, Eldridge **5**
Cleaver, Emanuel **4**
Clements, George **2**
Clendenon, Donn **26**
Cleveland, James **19**
Clifton, Lucille **14**
Clinton, George **9**
Clyburn, James **21**
Coachman, Alice **18**
Cobbs, Price M. **9**
Cochran, Johnnie L., Jr. **11**
Cohen, Anthony **15**
Colbert, Virgis William **17**
Cole, Johnnetta B. **5**
Cole, Nat King **17**
Cole, Natalie Maria **17**
Coleman, Bessie **9**
Coleman, Donald A. **24**
Coleman, Leonard S., Jr. **12**
Colemon, Johnnie **11**
Collins, Albert **12**
Collins, Barbara-Rose **7**
Collins, Cardiss **10**
Collins, Marva **3**
Coltrane, John **19**
Combs, Sean "Puffy" **17**
Comer, James P. **6**
Cone, James H. **3**
Connerly, Ward **14**
Conyers, John, Jr. **4**
Conyers, Nathan G. **24**
Cook, Samuel DuBois **14**
Cook, Suzan D. Johnson **22**
Cook, Toni **23**
Cooper, Anna Julia **20**
Cooper, Cynthia **17**
Cooper, Edward S. **6**
Cooper, J. California **12**
Cornelius, Don **4**
Cosby, Bill **7, 26**
Cosby, Camille **14**
Cose, Ellis **5**
Cottrell, Comer **11**
Cowans, Adger W. **20**
Crawford, Randy **19**
Crew, Rudolph F. **16**
Crockett, Jr., George **10**
Cross, Dolores E. **23**
Crothers, Scatman **19**
Crouch, Stanley **11**
Crowder, Henry **16**
Cullen, Countee **8**
Cummings, Elijah E. **24**
Cunningham, Evelyn **23**
Cunningham, Randall **23**
Currie, Betty **21**
Curry, George E. **23**
Curry, Mark **17**
Curtis, Christopher Paul **26**
Curtis-Hall, Vondie **17**
Dandridge, Dorothy **3**
Daniels-Carter, Valerie **23**
Darden, Christopher **13**
Dash, Julie **4**
Davidson, Jaye **5**
Davidson, Tommy **21**
Davis, Allison **12**
Davis, Angela **5**
Davis, Anthony **11**
Davis, Benjamin O., Sr. **4**
Davis, Benjamin O., Jr. **2**
Davis, Danny K. **24**
Davis, Ed **24**
Davis, Miles **4**
Davis, Ossie **5**
Davis, Piper **19**
Davis, Terrell **20**
Dawes, Dominique **11**
Dawkins, Wayne **20**
Days, Drew S., III **10**
de Passe, Suzanne **25**
Dee, Ruby **8**
Delaney, Beauford **19**
Delany, Bessie **12**
Delany, Sadie **12**
Delany, Samuel R., Jr. **9**
Dellums, Ronald **2**
Devers, Gail **7**
Devine, Loretta **24**
Dickens, Helen Octavia **14**
Dickerson, Ernest R. **6, 17**
Dickey, Eric Jerome **21**
Diggs, Charles C. **21**
Diggs, Taye **25**
Diggs-Taylor, Anna **20**
Dinkins, David **4**
Divine, Father **7**
Dixon, Julian C. **24**
Dixon, Margaret **14**
Dixon, Sharon Pratt **1**
Dixon, Willie **4**
Doby, Sr., Lawrence Eugene **16**
Dodson, Howard, Jr. **7**
Doley, Harold, Jr. **26**
Donegan, Dorothy **19**
Dorsey, Thomas **15**
Douglas, Aaron **7**
Dove, Rita **6**
Dove, Ulysses **5**
Downing, Will **19**
Dr. Dre **10**
Draper, Sharon M. **16**
Dre, Dr. **14**
Drew, Charles Richard **7**
Drexler, Clyde **4**
Driskell, David C. **7**
Driver, David E. **11**
DuBois, Shirley Graham **21**
DuBois, W. E. B. **3**
Ducksworth, Marilyn **12**
Duke, Bill **3**
Duke, George **21**
Dumars, Joe **16**
Dunbar, Paul Laurence **8**
Duncan, Michael Clarke **26**
Duncan, Tim **20**

Dungy, Tony **17**
Dunham, Katherine **4**
Dupri, Jermaine **13**
Dutton, Charles S. **4, 22**
Dyson, Michael Eric **11**
Early, Gerald **15**
Edelin, Ramona Hoage **19**
Edelman, Marian Wright **5**
Edley, Christopher **2**
Edmonds, Kenneth "Babyface" **10**
Edmonds, Terry **17**
Edmonds, Tracey **16**
Edward, Melvin **22**
Edwards, Harry **2**
Edwards, Teresa **14**
Elder, Larry **25**
Elder, Lee **6**
Elders, Joycelyn **6**
Ellerbe, Brian **22**
Ellington, Duke **5**
Ellington, E. David **11**
Elliott, Sean **26**
Ellison, Ralph **7**
Elmore, Ronn **21**
Epps, Omar **23**
Erving, Julius **18**
Esposito, Giancarlo **9**
Espy, Mike **6**
Eubanks, Kevin **15**
Europe, James Reese **10**
Evans, Darryl **22**
Evans, Faith **22**
Evans, Harry **25**
Evans, Mari **26**
Everett, Francine **23**
Evers, Medgar **3**
Evers, Myrlie **8**
Faison, George **16**
Farmer, Forest J. **1**
Farmer, James **2**
Farr, Mel, Sr. **24**
Farrakhan, Louis **2, 15**
Fats Domino **20**
Fattah, Chaka **11**
Fauntroy, Walter E. **11**
Fauset, Jessie **7**
Favors, Steve **23**
Feelings, Tom **11**
Ferguson, Roger W. **25**
Fielder, Cecil **2**
Fields, C. Virginia **25**
Fields, Cleo **13**
Fishburne, Larry **4, 22**
Fitzgerald, Ella **1, 18**
Flack, Roberta **19**
Foster, Henry W., Jr. **26**
Frazier, E. Franklin **10**
Frazier, Joe **19**
Freeman, Al, Jr. **11**
Freeman, Charles **19**
Freeman, Harold P. **23**
Freeman, Marianna **23**
Freeman, Morgan **2, 20**
French, Albert **18**
Friday, Jeff **24**
Fudge, Ann **11**
Fulani, Lenora **11**
Fuller, Charles **8**
Fuller, S. B. **13**
Fuller, Solomon Carter, Jr. **15**
Gaines, Ernest J. **7**
Gaither, Alonzo Smith (Jake) **14**
Gantt, Harvey **1**
Garnett, Kevin **14**
Garrison, Zina **2**
Gary, Willie E. **12**
Gaston, Arthur G. **4**
Gates, Henry Louis, Jr. **3**
Gates, Sylvester James, Jr. **15**
Gaye, Marvin **2**
Gayle, Helene D. **3**
Gentry, Alvin **23**
George, Nelson **12**
Gibson, Althea **8**
Gibson, Johnnie Mae **23**
Gibson, Josh **22**
Gibson, Kenneth Allen **6**
Gibson, William F. **6**
Giddings, Paula **11**
Gillespie, Dizzy **1**
Gilliam, Frank **23**
Gilliam, Sam **16**
Giovanni, Nikki **9**
Gist, Carole **1**
Givens, Robin **4, 25**
Glover, Danny **1, 24**
Glover, Nathaniel, Jr. **12**
Glover, Savion **14**
Goines, Donald **19**
Goldberg, Whoopi **4**
Golden, Marita **19**
Golden, Thelma **10**
Goldsberry, Ronald **18**
Gomes, Peter J. **15**
Gomez-Preston, Cheryl **9**
Goode, Mal **13**
Goode, W. Wilson **4**
Gooden, Dwight **20**
Gooding, Jr., Cuba **16**
Gordon, Dexter **25**
Gordon, Ed **10**
Gordone, Charles **15**
Gordy, Berry, Jr. **1**
Goss, Tom **23**
Gossett, Louis, Jr. **7**
Gourdine, Simon **11**
Graham, Lawrence Otis **12**
Graham, Stedman **13**
Gravely, Samuel L., Jr. **5**
Graves, Denyce **19**
Graves, Earl G. **1**
Gray, F. Gary **14**
Gray, William H. III **3**
Green, Al **13**
Green, Dennis **5**
Greene, Joe **10**
Greenfield, Eloise **9**
Gregory, Dick **1**
Gregory, Frederick D. **8**
Grier, Pam **9**
Grier, Roosevelt **13**
Griffey, Ken, Jr. **12**
Griffith, Mark Winston **8**
Griffith, Yolanda **25**
Grimké, Archibald H. **9**
Guillaume, Robert **3**
Guinier, Lani **7**
Gumbel, Bryant **14**
Gumbel, Greg **8**
Gunn, Moses **10**
Guy, Jasmine **2**
Guy, Rosa **5**
Guy-Sheftall, Beverly **13**
Guyton, Tyree **9**
Gwynn, Tony **18**
Hailey, JoJo **22**
Hailey, K-Ci **22**
Hale, Clara **16**
Hale, Lorraine **8**
Haley, Alex **4**
Haley, George Williford Boyce **21**
Hall, Elliott S. **24**
Hall, Lloyd A. **8**
Hamblin, Ken **10**
Hamer, Fannie Lou **6**
Hamilton, Virginia **10**
Hammer, M. C. **20**
Hammond, Fred **23**
Hampton, Fred **18**
Hampton, Henry **6**
Hampton, Lionel **17**
Hancock, Herbie **20**
Handy, W. C. **8**
Hannah, Marc **10**
Hansberry, Lorraine **6**
Hansberry, William Leo **11**
Hardaway, Anfernee (Penny) **13**
Hardison, Bethann **12**
Hardison, Kadeem **22**
Harkless, Necia Desiree **19**
Harmon, Clarence **26**
Harper, Frances Ellen Watkins **11**
Harrell, Andre **9**
Harrington, Oliver W. **9**
Harris, Alice **7**
Harris, Barbara **12**
Harris, E. Lynn **12**
Harris, Eddy L. **18**
Harris, Jay T. **19**
Harris, Leslie **6**
Harris, Marcelite Jordon **16**
Harris, Monica **18**
Harris, Patricia Roberts **2**
Harris, Robin **7**
Harsh, Vivian Gordon **14**
Harvard, Beverly **11**
Harvey, Steve **18**
Haskins, Clem **23**
Hastie, William H. **8**
Hastings, Alcee L. **16**
Hathaway, Donny **18**
Hawkins, Coleman **9**
Hawkins, Erskine **14**
Hawkins, La-Van **17**
Hawkins, Steven **14**
Hawkins, Tramaine **16**
Hayden, Palmer **13**
Hayden, Robert **12**
Hayes, Isaac **20**
Hayes, James C. **10**
Hayes, Roland **4**
Haynes, George Edmund **8**
Haynes, Marques **22**
Haywood, Margaret A. **24**
Heard, Gar **25**
Hedgeman, Anna Arnold **22**
Height, Dorothy I. **2, 23**
Hemphill, Essex **10**
Hemsley, Sherman **19**
Henderson, Cornelius Langston **26**
Henderson, Gordon **5**
Henderson, Wade J. **14**
Hendricks, Barbara **3**
Hendrix, Jimi **10**
Henry, Aaron **19**
Henson, Matthew **2**
Henson, Matthew **2**
Herenton, Willie W. **24**
Herman, Alexis M. **15**
Hernandez, Aileen Clarke **13**
Hickman, Fred **11**
Higginbotham, A. Leon, Jr. **13, 25**
Hightower, Dennis F. **13**
Hill, Anita **5**
Hill, Bonnie Guiton **20**

Hill, Calvin **19**
Hill, Grant **13**
Hill, Janet **19**
Hill, Jessie, Jr. **13**
Hill, Lauryn **20**
Hill, Oliver W. **24**
Hillard, Terry **25**
Hilliard, David **7**
Hilliard, Earl F. **24**
Himes, Chester **8**
Hinderas, Natalie **5**
Hine, Darlene Clark **24**
Hines, Gregory **1**
Hinton, William Augustus **8**
Holder, Eric H., Jr. **9**
Holdsclaw, Chamique **24**
Holiday, Billie **1**
Holland, Endesha Ida Mae **3**
Holland, Robert, Jr. **11**
Holmes, Larry **20**
Holyfield, Evander **6**
Hooks, Benjamin L. **2**
hooks, bell **5**
Hope, John **8**
Horne, Lena **5**
House, Son **8**
Houston, Charles Hamilton **4**
Houston, Cissy **20**
Houston, Whitney **7**
Howard, Desmond **16**
Howard, Juwan **15**
Howard, M. William, Jr. **26**
Howlin' Wolf **9**
Hrabowski, Freeman A. III **22**
Hudlin, Reginald **9**
Hudlin, Warrington **9**
Hudson, Cheryl **15**
Hudson, Wade **15**
Huggins, Larry **21**
Hughes, Albert **7**
Hughes, Allen **7**
Hughes, Langston **4**
Hughley, D.L. **23**
Humphrey, Bobbi **20**
Humphries, Frederick **20**
Hunt, Richard **6**
Hunter-Gault, Charlayne **6**
Hurston, Zora Neale **3**
Hutchinson, Earl Ofari **24**
Hutson, Jean Blackwell **16**
Hyman, Earle **25**
Hyman, Phyllis **19**
Ice Cube **8**
Ice-T **6**
Iceberg Slim **11**
Ingram, Rex **5**
Innis, Roy **5**
Irving, Larry, Jr. **12**
Isley, Ronald **25**
Iverson, Allen **24**
Jackson, Alexine Clement **22**
Jackson, Fred James **25**
Jackson, George **14**
Jackson, George **19**
Jackson, Isaiah **3**
Jackson, Janet **6**
Jackson, Jesse **1**
Jackson, Jesse, Jr. **14**
Jackson Lee, Sheila **20**
Jackson, Mahalia **5**
Jackson, Mannie **14**
Jackson, Maynard **2**
Jackson, Michael **19**
Jackson, Millie **25**
Jackson, Milt **26**
Jackson, Reggie **15**
Jackson, Samuel L. **8, 19**
Jackson, Sheneska **18**
Jackson, Shirley Ann **12**
Jacob, John E. **2**
Jakes, Thomas "T.D." **17**
James, Daniel Jr. **16**
James, Etta **13**
James, Juanita **13**
James, Rick **19**
James, Sharpe **23**
Jamison, Judith **7**
Jarreau, Al **21**
Jarvis, Charlene Drew **21**
Jefferson, William J. **25**
Jeffries, Leonard **8**
Jemison, Mae C. **1**
Jenifer, Franklyn G. **2**
Jenkins, Beverly **14**
Jenkins, Ella **15**
Jimmy Jam **13**
Joe, Yolanda **21**
John, Daymond **23**
Johnson, Beverly **2**
Johnson, Charles **1**
Johnson, Charles S. **12**
Johnson, Earvin "Magic" **3**
Johnson, Eddie Bernice **8**
Johnson, Jack **8**
Johnson, James Weldon **5**
Johnson, John H. **3**
Johnson Jr., Harvey **24**
Johnson, Michael **13**
Johnson, Norma L. Holloway **17**
Johnson, Robert **2**
Johnson, Robert L. **3**
Johnson, Robert T. **17**
Johnson, Virginia **9**
Johnson, William Henry **3**
Jones, Bill T. **1**
Jones, Bobby **20**
Jones, Carl **7**
Jones, Cobi N'Gai **18**
Jones, Elaine R. **7**
Jones, Elvin **14**
Jones, Ingrid Saunders **18**
Jones, James Earl **3**
Jones, Lois Mailou **13**
Jones, Marion **21**
Jones, Quincy **8**
Jones, Star **10**
Joplin, Scott **6**
Jordan, Barbara **4**
Jordan, June **7**
Jordan, Michael **6, 21**
Jordan, Montell **23**
Jordan, Vernon E. **3**
Josey, E. J. **10**
Joyner-Kersee, Jackie **5**
Joyner, Marjorie Stewart **26**
Joyner, Matilda Sissieretta **15**
Joyner, Tom **19**
Julian, Percy Lavon **6**
Just, Ernest Everett **3**
Justice, David **18**
Kani, Karl **10**
Karenga, Maulana **10**
Kearse, Amalya Lyle **12**
Keith, Damon J. **16**
Kelly, Patrick **3**
Kelly, R. **18**
Kendricks, Eddie **22**
Kennedy, Adrienne **11**
Kennedy, Florynce **12**
Keyes, Alan L. **11**
Khan, Chaka **12**
Khanga, Yelena **6**
Kilpatrick, Carolyn Cheeks **16**
Kimbro, Dennis **10**
Kimbro, Henry A. **25**
Kincaid, Jamaica **4**
King, B. B. **7**
King, Barbara **22**
King, Bernice **4**
King, Coretta Scott **3**
King, Dexter **10**
King, Don **14**
King, Gayle **19**
King, Martin Luther, Jr. **1**
King, Martin Luther, III **20**
King, Yolanda **6**
Kirby, George **14**
Kirk, Ron **11**
Kitt, Eartha **16**
Kitt, Sandra **23**
Knight, Gladys **16**
Knight, Suge **11**
Komunyakaa, Yusef **9**
Kotto, Yaphet **7**
Kountz, Samuel L. **10**
Kravitz, Lenny **10**
Kunjufu, Jawanza **3**
L.L. Cool J **16**
La Salle, Eriq **12**
LaBelle, Patti **13**
Lafontant, Jewel Stradford **3**
Lampkin, Daisy **19**
Lane, Charles **3**
Lane, Vincent **5**
Langhart, Janet **19**
Lankford, Ray **23**
Larkin, Barry **24**
Larsen, Nella **10**
Lassiter, Roy **24**
Latimer, Lewis H. **4**
Lawless, Theodore K. **8**
Lawrence, Jacob **4**
Lawrence, Jr., Robert H. **16**
Lawrence-Lightfoot, Sara **10**
Lawrence, Martin **6**
Lawson, Jennifer **1**
Leary, Kathryn D. **10**
Leavell, Dorothy R. **17**
Lee, Annie Francis **22**
Lee, Barbara **25**
Lee, Canada **8**
Lee, Joie **1**
Lee-Smith, Hughie **5, 22**
Lee, Spike **5, 19**
Leffall, LaSalle, Jr. **3**
Leland, Mickey **2**
Lemmons, Kasi **20**
Leon, Kenny **10**
Leonard, Sugar Ray **15**
Lester, Julius **9**
Levert, Gerald **22**
Lewellyn, J. Bruce **13**
Lewis, Byron E. **13**
Lewis, Carl **4**
Lewis, David Levering **9**
Lewis, Delano **7**
Lewis, Edmonia **10**
Lewis, Edward T. **21**
Lewis, John **2**
Lewis, Reginald F. **6**
Lewis, Samella **25**
Lewis, Shirley A. R. **14**
Lewis, Terry **13**
Lewis, Thomas **19**
Lincoln, Abbey **3**

Little, Benilde **21**
Little Richard **15**
Little, Robert L. **2**
Lloyd, Earl **26**
Locke, Alain **10**
Lofton, Kenny **12**
Logan, Onnie Lee **14**
Long, Nia **17**
Lorde, Audre **6**
Lott, Ronnie **9**
Louis, Errol T. **8**
Louis, Joe **5**
Love, Darlene **23**
Love, Nat **9**
Lover, Ed **10**
Lowery, Joseph **2**
Lucas, John **7**
Lymon, Frankie **22**
Lyons, Henry **12**
Lyttle, Hulda Margaret **14**
Mabley, Moms **15**
Mabrey, Vicki **26**
Madhubuti, Haki R. **7**
Madison, Joseph E. **17**
Major, Clarence **9**
Mallett, Jr., Conrad **16**
Malone, Annie **13**
Malone, Karl A. **18**
Manigault, Earl "The Goat" **15**
Manley, Audrey Forbes **16**
Marable, Manning **10**
Marrow, Queen Esther **24**
Marsalis, Wynton **16**
Marshall, Bella **22**
Marshall, Paule **7**
Marshall, Thurgood **1**
Martin, Louis E. **16**
Mase **24**
Massenburg, Kedar **23**
Massey, Walter E. **5**
Master P **21**
Mathis, Greg **26**
Mathis, Johnny **20**
Maxwell **20**
Mayfield, Curtis **2**
Maynard, Robert C. **7**
Maynor, Dorothy **19**
Mays, Benjamin E. **7**
Mays, Willie **3**
McBride, Bryant **18**
McCabe, Jewell Jackson **10**
McCall, Nathan **8**
McCarty, Oseola **16**
McClurkin, Donnie **25**
McCoy, Elijah **8**
McCray, Nikki **18**
McDaniel, Hattie **5**
McDonald, Audra **20**
McDonald, Erroll **1**
McDonald, Gabrielle Kirk **20**
McDougall, Gay J. **11**
McEwen, Mark **5**
McGee, Charles **10**
McGriff, Fred **24**
McGruder, Robert **22**
McKay, Claude **6**
McKay, Nellie Yvonne **17**
Mckee, Lonette **12**
McKinney, Cynthia Ann **11**
McKinnon, Isaiah **9**
McKissick, Floyd B. **3**
McKnight, Brian **18**
McMillan, Terry **4, 17**
McNair, Ronald **3**
McNair, Steve **22**
McNeil, Lori **1**
McPhail, Sharon **2**
McQueen, Butterfly **6**
Meek, Carrie **6**
Meeks, Gregory **25**
Meredith, James H. **11**
Metcalfe, Ralph **26**
Mfume, Kweisi **6**
Micheaux, Oscar **7**
Millender-McDonald, Juanita **21**
Miller, Bebe **3**
Miller, Cheryl **10**
Mills, Florence **22**
Mingus, Charles **15**
Mitchell, Arthur **2**
Mitchell, Brian Stokes **21**
Mitchell, Corinne **8**
Mitchell, Russ **21**
Monica **21**
Monk, Thelonious **1**
Moon, Warren **8**
Moore, Chante **26**
Moore, Melba **21**
Moore, Shemar **21**
Moorer, Michael **19**
Morgan, Garrett **1**
Morgan, Joe Leonard **9**
Morgan, Rose **11**
Morial, Ernest "Dutch" **26**
Morial, Marc **20**
Morrison, Toni **2, 15**
Morton, Joe **18**
Moses, Edwin **8**
Moses, Gilbert **12**
Moses, Robert Parris **11**
Mosley, Walter **5, 25**
Moss, Carlton **17**
Moss, Randy **23**
Moten, Etta **18**
Motley, Constance Baker **10**
Motley, Marion **26**
Mourning, Alonzo **17**
Moutoussamy-Ashe, Jeanne **7**
Mowry, Jess **7**
Muhammad, Elijah **4**
Muhammad, Khallid Abdul **10**
Murphy, Eddie **4, 20**
Murray, Cecil **12**
Murray, Eddie **12**
Murray, Lenda **10**
Muse, Clarence Edouard **21**
Myers, Walter Dean **8**
N'Namdi, George R. **17**
Nanula, Richard D. **20**
Napoleon, Benny N. **23**
Naylor, Gloria **10**
Ndegéocello, Me'Shell **15**
Nelson, Jill **6**
Neville, Aaron **21**
Newcombe, Don **24**
Newsome, Ozzie **26**
Newton, Huey **2**
Nicholas, Fayard **20**
Nicholas, Harold **20**
Nichols, Nichelle **11**
Norman, Jessye **5**
Norman, Maidie **20**
Norman, Pat **10**
Norton, Eleanor Holmes **7**
Notorious B.I.G. **20**
O'Leary, Hazel **6**
O'Neal, Shaquille **8**
O'Neil, Buck **19**
Oglesby, Zena **12**
Ogletree, Jr., Charles **12**
Osborne, Jeffrey **26**
Owens, Jesse **2**
Owens, Major **6**
Pace, Orlando **21**
Page, Alan **7**
Page, Clarence **4**
Paige, Satchel **7**
Painter, Nell Irvin **24**
Parker, Charlie **20**
Parker, Pat **19**
Parks, Bernard C. **17**
Parks, Gordon **1**
Parks, Rosa **1**
Parsons, James **14**
Parsons, Richard Dean **11**
Patrick, Deval **12**
Patterson, Floyd **19**
Patterson, Frederick Douglass **12**
Patterson, Louise **25**
Payne, Allen **13**
Payne, Donald M. **2**
Payton, Benjamin F. **23**
Payton, Walter **11, 25**
Peck, Carolyn **23**
Peete, Calvin **11**
Peete, Holly Robinson **20**
Pendergrass, Teddy **22**
Peoples, Dottie **22**
Perez, Anna **1**
Perkins, Edward **5**
Perkins, Tony **24**
Perrot, Kim **23**
Person, Waverly **9**
Petry, Ann **19**
Phifer, Mekhi **25**
Pickett, Bill **11**
Pinchback, P. B. S. **9**
Pinkett, Jada **10**
Pinkney, Jerry **15**
Pinkston, W. Randall **24**
Pippen, Scottie **15**
Pippin, Horace **9**
Pleasant, Mary Ellen **9**
Poitier, Sidney **11**
Porter, James A. **11**
Poussaint, Alvin F. **5**
Powell, Adam Clayton, Jr. **3**
Powell, Bud **24**
Powell, Colin **1**
Powell, Debra A. **23**
Powell, Maxine **8**
Powell, Mike **7**
Pratt, Geronimo **18**
Price, Frederick K.C. **21**
Price, Glenda **22**
Price, Hugh B. **9**
Price, Kelly **23**
Price, Leontyne **1**
Pride, Charley **26**
Primus, Pearl **6**
Prince **18**
Pritchard, Robert Starling **21**
Procope, Ernesta **23**
Prothrow-Stith, Deborah **10**
Pryor, Richard **3, 24**
Puckett, Kirby **4**
Quarles, Benjamin Arthur **18**
Quarles, Norma **25**
Quarterman, Lloyd Albert **4**
Queen Latifah **1, 16**
Raines, Franklin Delano **14**
Ralph, Sheryl Lee **18**
Ramsey, Charles H. **21**
Rand, A. Barry **6**
Randall, Dudley **8**

Randle, Theresa **16**
Randolph, A. Philip **3**
Rangel, Charles **3**
Rashad, Ahmad **18**
Rashad, Phylicia **21**
Raspberry, William **2**
Rawls, Lou **17**
Razaf, Andy **19**
Reagon, Bernice Johnson **7**
Reason, J. Paul **19**
Reddick, Lawrence Dunbar **20**
Redding, J. Saunders **26**
Redding, Louis L. **26**
Redding, Otis **16**
Redmond, Eugene **23**
Reed, Ishmael **8**
Reese, Della **6, 20**
Reeves, Rachel J. **23**
Reid, Irvin D. **20**
Rhames, Ving **14**
Rhodes, Ray **14**
Rhone, Sylvia **2**
Ribbs, Willy T. **2**
Ribeiro, Alfonso **17**
Rice, Condoleezza **3**
Rice, Jerry **5**
Rice, Linda Johnson **9**
Rice, Norm **8**
Richardson, Nolan **9**
Richie, Leroy C. **18**
Richmond, Mitch **19**
Riggs, Marlon **5**
Riley, Helen Caldwell Day **13**
Ringgold, Faith **4**
Rivers, Glenn "Doc" **25**
Roach, Max **21**
Roberts, Marcus **19**
Roberts, Robin **16**
Roberts, Roy S. **14**
Robertson, Oscar **26**
Robeson, Eslanda Goode **13**
Robeson, Paul **2**
Robinson, Bill "Bojangles" **11**
Robinson, David **24**
Robinson, Eddie G. **10**
Robinson, Frank **9**
Robinson, Jackie **6**
Robinson, Max **3**
Robinson, Patrick **19**
Robinson, Rachel **16**
Robinson, Randall **7**
Robinson, Sharon **22**
Robinson, Smokey **3**
Robinson, Spottswood W. III **22**
Robinson, Sugar Ray **18**
Roche, Joyce M. **17**
Rochon, Lela **16**
Rock, Chris **3, 22**
Rodgers, Johnathan **6**
Rodman, Dennis **12**
Rogers, John W., Jr. **5**
Roker, Al **12**
Rolle, Esther **13, 21**
Rollins, Jr., Howard E. **16**
Ross, Diana **8**
Rowan, Carl T. **1**
Rowell, Victoria **13**
Rudolph, Wilma **4**
Rupaul **17**
Rush, Bobby **26**
Rushen, Patrice **12**
Russell, Bill **8**
Russell, Herman Jerome **17**
Russell-McCloud, Patricia A. **17**
Rustin, Bayard **4**
Saar, Alison **16**
Saint James, Synthia **12**
Samara, Noah **15**
Sampson, Charles **13**
Sanchez, Sonia **17**
Sanders, Joseph R., Jr. **11**
Sapphire **14**
Savage, Augusta **12**
Sayles Belton, Sharon, **9, 16**
Scott, Robert C. **23**
Scott, Sr., Wendell Oliver **19**
Sengstacke, John **18**
Shabazz, Betty **7, 26**
Shakur, Tupac **14**
Sharpton, Al **21**
Sheffield, Gary **16**
Sherrod, Clayton **17**
Shipp, E. R. **15**
Silas, Paul **24**
Silver, Horace **26**
Simmons , Ruth J. **13**
Simone, Nina **15**
Simpson, O. J. **15**
Simpson, Valerie **21**
Sinbad, **1, 16**
Singletary, Mike **4**
Singleton, John **2**
Sinkford, Jeanne C. **13**
Sister Souljah **11**
Sizemore, Barbara A. **26**
Sklarek, Norma Merrick **25**
Slater, Rodney E. **15**
Sleet, Moneta, Jr. **5**
Smaltz, Audrey **12**
Smiley, Tavis **20**
Smith, Anna Deavere **6**
Smith, Barbara **11**
Smith, Bessie **3**
Smith, Clarence O. **21**
Smith, Emmitt **7**
Smith, Jane E. **24**
Smith, John L. **22**
Smith, Joshua **10**
Smith, Mary Carter **26**
Smith, Roger Guenveur **12**
Smith, Tubby **18**
Smith, Will **8, 18**
Smith, Willi **8**
Sneed, Paula A. **18**
Snipes, Wesley **3, 24**
Sowell, Thomas **2**
Spaulding, Charles Clinton **9**
Spikes, Dolores **18**
Sprewell, Latrell **23**
St. Jacques, Raymond **8**
St. John, Kristoff **25**
Stallings, George A., Jr. **6**
Stanford, John **20**
Stanton, Robert **20**
Staples, Brent **8**
Staupers, Mabel K. **7**
Steele, Claude Mason **13**
Steele, Shelby **13**
Stephens, Charlotte Andrews **14**
Steward, Emanuel **18**
Stewart, Alison **13**
Stewart, Kordell **21**
Stewart, Maria W. Miller **19**
Stewart, Paul Wilbur **12**
Stokes, Carl B. **10**
Stokes, Louis **3**
Stone, Chuck **9**
Stone, Toni **15**
Stout, Juanita Kidd **24**
Strawberry, Darryl **22**
Street, John F. **24**
Stringer, C. Vivian **13**
Sudarkasa, Niara **4**
Sullivan, Leon H. **3**
Sullivan, Louis **8**
Summer, Donna **25**
Sweat, Keith **19**
Swoopes, Sheryl **12**
Swygert, H. Patrick **22**
Sykes, Roosevelt **20**
Tamia **24**
Tanner, Henry Ossawa **1**
Tate, Eleanora E. **20**
Tate, Larenz **15**
Taulbert, Clifton Lemoure **19**
Taylor, Billy **23**
Taylor, Charles **20**
Taylor, Kristin Clark **8**
Taylor, Lawrence **25**
Taylor, Meshach **4**
Taylor, Mildred D. **26**
Taylor, Regina **9**
Taylor, Susan L. **10**
Taylor, Susie King **13**
Terrell, Dorothy A. **24**
Terrell, Mary Church **9**
Thigpen, Lynne **17**
Thomas, Alma **14**
Thomas, Clarence **2**
Thomas, Debi **26**
Thomas, Derrick **25**
Thomas, Frank **12**
Thomas, Franklin A. **5**
Thomas, Isiah **7, 26**
Thomas, Rufus **20**
Thomas, Vivien **9**
Thompson, Bennie G. **26**
Thompson, John W. **26**
Thompson, Tazewell **13**
Thompson, Tina **25**
Thurman, Howard **3**
Thurman, Wallace **16**
Till, Emmett **7**
Tillman, George, Jr. **20**
Tolliver, William **9**
Toomer, Jean **6**
Towns, Edolphus **19**
Townsend, Robert **4, 23**
Tribble, Israel, Jr. **8**
Trotter, Monroe **9**
Tubbs Jones, Stephanie **24**
Tubman, Harriet **9**
Tucker, C. DeLores **12**
Tucker, Chris **13, 23**
Tucker, Cynthia **15**
Tucker, Rosina **14**
Turnbull, Walter **13**
Turner, Henry McNeal **5**
Turner, Tina **6**
Tyree, Omar Rashad **21**
Tyson, Cicely **7**
Tyson, Neil de Grasse **15**
Uggams, Leslie **23**
Underwood, Blair **7**
Unseld, Wes **23**
Upshaw, Gene **18**
Usher **23**
Usry, James L. **23**
Utendahl, John **23**
Van Peebles, Mario **2**
Van Peebles, Melvin **7**
Vance, Courtney B. **15**
VanDerZee, James **6**
Vandross, Luther **13**
Vanzant, Iyanla **17**

Vaughan, Sarah **13**
Vaughn, Mo **16**
Verdelle, A. J. **26**
Vereen, Ben **4**
Vincent, Marjorie Judith **2**
Von Lipsey, Roderick K. **11**
Waddles, Charleszetta (Mother) **10**
Wagner, Annice **22**
Walker, A'lelia **14**
Walker, Albertina **10**
Walker, Alice **1**
Walker, Cedric "Ricky" **19**
Walker, Herschel **1**
Walker, Madame C. J. **7**
Walker, Maggie Lena **17**
Walker, T. J. **7**
Wallace, Michele Faith **13**
Wallace, Phyllis A. **9**
Wallace, Sippie **1**
Ward, Lloyd **21**
Warfield, Marsha **2**
Warner, Malcolm-Jamal **22**
Warwick, Dionne **18**
Washington, Booker T. **4**
Washington, Denzel **1, 16**
Washington, Dinah **22**
Washington, Fredi **10**
Washington, Grover, Jr. **17**
Washington, Harold **6**
Washington, Laura S. **18**
Washington, MaliVai **8**
Washington, Patrice Clarke **12**
Washington, Val **12**
Wasow, Omar **15**
Waters, Benny **26**
Waters, Ethel **7**
Waters, Maxine **3**
Watkins, Levi, Jr. **9**
Watkins, Perry **12**
Watkins, Shirley R. **17**
Watkins, Walter C. **24**
Watson, Bob **25**
Watson, Johnny "Guitar" **18**
Watt, Melvin **26**
Wattleton, Faye **9**
Watts, J. C., Jr. **14**
Watts, Rolonda **9**
Wayans, Damon **8**
Wayans, Keenen Ivory **18**
Weathers, Carl **10**
Weaver, Robert C. **8**
Webb, Veronica **10**
Webb, Wellington **3**
Webber, Chris **15**
Wells-Barnett, Ida B. **8**
Wells, James Lesesne **10**
Welsing, Frances Cress **5**
Wesley, Dorothy Porter **19**
Wesley, Valerie Wilson **18**
West, Cornel **5**
West, Dorothy **12**
West, Togo D., Jr. **16**
Westbrook, Peter **20**
Wharton, Clifton R., Jr. **7**
Wheat, Alan **14**
Whitaker, Forest **2**
Whitaker, Mark **21**
Whitaker, Pernell **10**
White, Barry **13**
White, Bill **1**
White, Jesse **22**
White, Lois Jean **20**
White, Michael R. **5**
White, Reggie **6**
White, Walter F. **4**
Whitfield, Fred **23**
Whitfield, Lynn **18**
Wideman, John Edgar **5**
Wilder, L. Douglas **3**
Wiley, Ralph **8**
Wilkens, Lenny **11**
Wilkins, Roger **2**
Wilkins, Roy **4**
Williams, Anthony **21**
Williams, Bert **18**
Williams, Billy Dee **8**
Williams, Clarence, III **26**
Williams, Daniel Hale **2**
Williams, Doug **22**
Williams, Evelyn **10**
Williams, George Washington **18**
Williams, Gregory **11**
Williams, Hosea Lorenzo **15**
Williams, Joe **5, 25**
Williams, Maggie **7**
Williams, Mary Lou **15**
Williams, Montel **4**
Williams, O. S. **13**
Williams, Patricia J. **11**
Williams, Paul R. **9**
Williams, Robert F. **11**
Williams, Samm-Art **21**
Williams, Serena **20**
Williams, Sherley Anne **25**
Williams, Vanessa L. **4, 17**
Williams, Venus **17**
Williams, Walter E. **4**
Williams, William T. **11**
Williams, Willie L. **4**
Williamson, Mykelti **22**
Wilson, August **7**
Wilson, Cassandra **16**
Wilson, Flip **21**
Wilson, Nancy **10**
Wilson, Phill **9**
Wilson, Sunnie **7**
Wilson, William Julius **20**
Winans, BeBe **14**
Winans, CeCe **14**
Winans, Marvin L. **17**
Winans, Vickie **24**
Winfield, Dave **5**
Winfield, Paul **2**
Winfrey, Oprah **2, 15**
Witt, Edwin T. **26**
Wolfe, George C. **6**
Wonder, Stevie **11**
Woodard, Alfre **9**
Woodruff, Hale **9**
Woods, Granville T. **5**
Woods, Tiger **14**
Woodson, Carter G. **2**
Woodson, Robert L. **10**
Worrill, Conrad **12**
Wright, Bruce McMarion **3**
Wright, Deborah C. **25**
Wright, Louis Tompkins **4**
Wright, Richard **5**
Wynn, Albert R. **25**
X, Malcolm **1**
Yoba, Malik **11**
Young, Andrew **3**
Young, Coleman **1, 20**
Young, Jean Childs **14**
Young, Whitney M., Jr. **4**
Youngblood, Johnny Ray **8**

Angolan
Bonga, Kuenda **13**
Savimbi, Jonas **2**

Bahamian
Ingraham, Hubert A. **19**

Batswana
Masire, Quett **5**

Belizian
Jones, Marion **21**

Beninois
Hounsou, Djimon **19**
Kerekou, Ahmed (Mathieu) **1**
Mogae, Festus Gontebanye **19**
Soglo, Nicéphore **15**

Bermudian
Gordon, Pamela **17**
Smith, Jennifer **21**

Brazilian
da Silva, Benedita **5**
Nascimento, Milton **2**
Pelé **7**
Pitta, Celso **17**

British
Abbott, Diane **9**
Bassey, Shirley **25**
Campbell, Naomi **1**
Christie, Linford **8**
Davidson, Jaye **5**
Henry, Lenny **9**
Jean-Baptiste, Marianne **17**
Jordan, Ronny **26**
Julien, Isaac **3**
Lindo, Delroy **18**
Newton, Thandie **26**
Pitt, David Thomas **10**
Seal **14**
Taylor, John (David Beckett) **16**

Burkinabé
Somé, Malidoma Patrice **10**

Burundian
Ndadaye, Melchior **7**
Ntaryamira, Cyprien **8**

Cameroonian
Kotto, Yaphet **7**
Milla, Roger **2**

Canadian
Bell, Ralph S. **5**
Carnegie, Herbert **25**
Fuhr, Grant **1**
Johnson, Ben **1**
McKegney, Tony **3**
O'Ree, Willie **5**
Reuben, Gloria **15**
Richards, Lloyd **2**

Cape Verdean
Evora, Cesaria **12**

Chadian
Habré, Hissène **6**

Costa Rican
McDonald, Erroll **1**

Cuban
León, Tania **13**
Quirot, Ana **13**

Dominican
Charles, Mary Eugenia **10**
Sosa, Sammy **21**

Dutch
Liberia-Peters, Maria Philomena **12**

Ethiopian
Haile Selassie **7**
Meles Zenawi **3**

French
Baker, Josephine **3**
Baldwin, James **1**
Bonaly, Surya **7**
Noah, Yannick **4**
Tanner, Henry Ossawa **1**

Gabonese
Bongo, Omar **1**

Gambian
Jammeh, Yahya **23**

Ghanaian
Annan, Kofi Atta **15**
DuBois, Shirley Graham **21**
Jawara, Sir Dawda Kairaba **11**
Nkrumah, Kwame **3**
Rawlings, Jerry **9**
Rawlings, Nana Konadu Agyeman **13**

Guinea-Bissauan
Vieira, Joao **14**

Guinean
Conté, Lansana **7**
Touré, Sekou **6**

Guyanese
Beaton, Norman **14**
Jagan, Cheddi **16**
van Sertima, Ivan **25**

Haitian
Aristide, Jean-Bertrand **6**
Auguste, Rose-Anne **13**
Charlemagne, Manno **11**
Christophe, Henri **9**
Danticat, Edwidge **15**
Jean, Wyclef **20**
Pascal-Trouillot, Ertha **3**
Pierre, Andre **17**
Siméus, Dumas M. **25**

Italian
Esposito, Giancarlo **9**

Ivorian
Bedie, Henri Konan **21**
Houphouët-Boigny, Félix **4**

Jamaican
Ashley, Maurice **15**
Belafonte, Harry **4**
Ewing, Patrick A. **17**
Fagan, Garth **18**
Garvey, Marcus **1**
Johnson, Ben **1**
Manley, Edna **26**
Marley, Bob **5**
McKay, Claude **6**
Morrison, Keith **13**
Patterson, Orlando **4**
Patterson, P. J. **6, 20**
Perry, Ruth **19**
Tosh, Peter **9**

Kenyan
Kenyatta, Jomo **5**
Mazrui, Ali A. **12**
Moi, Daniel **1**

Liberian
Fuller, Solomon Carter, Jr. **15**
Perry, Ruth **15**
Sawyer, Amos **2**
Taylor, Charles **20**

Malawian
Banda, Hastings Kamuzu **6**
Muluzi, Bakili **14**

Malian
Touré, Amadou Toumani **18**

Mozambican
Chissano, Joaquim **7**
Machel, Graca Simbine **16**
Machel, Samora Moises **8**
Mutola, Maria **12**

Namibian
Mbuende, Kaire **12**
Nujoma, Samuel **10**

Nigerian
Abacha, Sani **11**
Achebe, Chinua **6**
Arinze, Francis Cardinal **19**
Azikiwe, Nnamdi **13**
Babangida, Ibrahim **4**
Fela **1**
Obasanjo, Olusegun **5, 22**
Olajuwon, Hakeem **2**
Onwueme, Tess Osonye **23**
Rotimi, Ola **1**
Sade **15**
Soyinka, Wole **4**

Puerto Rican
Schomburg, Arthur Alfonso **9**

Russian
Khanga, Yelena **6**

Rwandan
Bizimungu, Pasteur **19**
Habyarimana, Juvenal **8**

Senegalese
Diop, Cheikh Anta **4**
Diouf, Abdou **3**
Mboup, Souleymane **10**
N'Dour, Youssou **1**
Sané, Pierre Gabriel **21**
Sembène, Ousmane **13**
Senghor, Léopold Sédar **12**

Sierra Leonean
Kabbah, Ahmad Tejan **23**

Somali
Ali Mahdi Mohamed **5**
Iman **4**

South African
Biko, Steven **4**
Buthelezi, Mangosuthu Gatsha **9**
Hani, Chris **6**
Luthuli, Albert **13**
Mabuza, Lindiwe **18**
Makeba, Miriam **2**
Mandela, Nelson **1, 14**
Mandela, Winnie **2**
Masekela, Barbara **18**
Masekela, Hugh **1**
Mathabane, Mark **5**
Mbeki, Thabo Mvuyelwa **14**
Nyanda, Siphiwe **21**
Nzo, Alfred **15**
Ramaphosa, Cyril **3**
Sisulu, Sheila Violet Makate **24**
Thugwane, Josia **21**
Tutu, Desmond **6**

Sudanese
Bol, Manute **1**
Wek, Alek **18**

Tanzanian
Mkapa, Benjamin **16**
Mongella, Gertrude **11**
Mwinyi, Ali Hassan **1**
Nyerere, Julius **5**
Rugambwa, Laurean **20**

Togolese
Eyadéma, Gnassingbé **7**
Soglo, Nicéphore **15**

Trinidadian
Carmichael, Stokely **5, 26**
Guy, Rosa **5**
Nakhid, David **25**
Primus, Pearl **6**

Ugandan
Museveni, Yoweri **4**
Mutebi, Ronald **25**

Upper Voltan
Sankara, Thomas **17**

West Indian
Innis, Roy **5**
Kincaid, Jamaica **4**
Staupers, Mabel K. **7**
Pitt, David Thomas **10**
Taylor, Susan L. **10**
Walcott, Derek **5**

Zairean
Kabila, Laurent **20**
Mobutu Sese Seko **1**
Mutombo, Dikembe **7**
Ongala, Remmy **9**

Zambian
Kaunda, Kenneth **2**

Cumulative Occupation Index

Volume numbers appear in Bold

Art and design

Allen, Tina **22**
Andrews, Benny **22**
Andrews, Bert **13**
Armstrong, Robb **15**
Bailey, Radcliffe **19**
Bailey, Xenobia **11**
Barboza, Anthony **10**
Barnes, Ernie **16**
Barthe, Richmond **15**
Basquiat, Jean-Michel **5**
Bearden, Romare **2**
Biggers, John **20**
Brandon, Barbara **3**
Brown, Donald **19**
Burke, Selma **16**
Burroughs, Margaret Taylor **9**
Camp, Kimberly **19**
Campbell, E. Simms **13**
Catlett, Elizabeth **2**
Chase-Riboud, Barbara **20**
Cowans, Adger W. **20**
Delaney, Beauford **19**
Douglas, Aaron **7**
Driskell, David C. **7**
Edwards, Melvin **22**
Ewing, Patrick A.**17**
Feelings, Tom **11**
Gantt, Harvey **1**
Gilliam, Sam **16**
Golden, Thelma **10**
Guyton, Tyree **9**
Harkless, Necia Desiree **19**
Harrington, Oliver W. **9**
Hayden, Palmer **13**
Hope, John **8**
Hudson, Cheryl **15**
Hudson, Wade **15**
Hunt, Richard **6**
Hutson, Jean Blackwell **16**
John, Daymond **23**
Johnson, William Henry **3**
Jones, Lois Mailou **13**
Kitt, Sandra **23**
Lawrence, Jacob **4**
Lee, Annie Francis **22**
Lee-Smith, Hughie **5, 22**
Lewis, Edmonia **10**
Lewis, Samella **25**
Manley, Edna **26**
McGee, Charles **10**
Mitchell, Corinne **8**
Morrison, Keith **13**
Moutoussamy-Ashe, Jeanne **7**
N'Namdi, George R. **17**
Pierre, Andre **17**
Pinkney, Jerry **15**
Pippin, Horace **9**
Porter, James A. **11**
Ringgold, Faith **4**
Saar, Alison **16**
Saint James, Synthia **12**
Sanders, Joseph R., Jr. **11**
Savage, Augusta **12**
Serrano, Andres **3**
Shabazz, Attallah **6**
Simpson, Lorna **4**
Sklarek, Norma Merrick **25**
Sleet, Moneta, Jr. **5**
Tanner, Henry Ossawa **1**
Thomas, Alma **14**
Tolliver, William **9**
VanDerZee, James **6**
Walker, A'lelia **14**
Walker, Kara **16**
Wells, James Lesesne **10**
Williams, Billy Dee **8**
Williams, O. S. **13**
Williams, Paul R. **9**
Williams, William T. **11**
Woodruff, Hale **9**

Business

Abdul-Jabbar, Kareem **8**
Ailey, Alvin **8**
Al-Amin, Jamil Abdullah **6**
Alexander, Archie Alphonso **14**
Allen, Byron **24**
Amos, Wally **9**
Avant, Clarence **19**
Baker, Dusty **8**
Baker, Ella **5**
Baker, Gwendolyn Calvert **9**
Banks, Jeffrey **17**
Banks, William **11**
Barden, Don H. **9, 20**
Barrett, Andrew C. **12**
Bennett, Lerone, Jr. **5**
Bing, Dave **3**
Borders, James **9**
Boston, Kelvin E. **25**
Boston, Lloyd **24**
Boyd, John W., Jr. **20**
Boyd, T. B., III **6**
Brimmer, Andrew F. **2**
Brown, Les **5**
Brown, Marie Dutton **12**
Brunson, Dorothy **1**
Bryant, John **26**
Burrell, Thomas J. **21**
Burroughs, Margaret Taylor **9**
Busby, Jheryl **3**
Cain, Herman **15**
CasSelle, Malcolm **11**
Chamberlain, Wilt **18**
Chapman, Jr., Nathan A. **21**
Chappell, Emma **18**
Chenault, Kenneth I. **4**
Clark, Celeste **15**
Clark, Patrick **14**
Clay, William Lacy **8**
Clayton, Xernona **3**
Cobbs, Price M. **9**
Colbert, Virgis William **17**
Coleman, Donald A. **24**
Connerly, Ward **14**
Conyers, Nathan G. **24**
Cornelius, Don **4**
Cosby, Bill **7, 26**
Cottrell, Comer **11**
Daniels-Carter, Valerie **23**
Davis, Ed **24**
de Passe, Suzanne **25**
Delany, Bessie **12**
Delany, Sadie **12**
Divine, Father **7**
Doley, Harold Jr. **26**
Dre, Dr. **14**
Driver, David E. **11**
Ducksworth, Marilyn **12**
Edelin, Ramona Hoage **19**
Edmonds, Tracey **16**
Elder, Lee **6**
Ellington, E. David **11**
Evans, Darryl **22**
Evers, Myrlie **8**
Farmer, Forest J. **1**
Farr, Mel Sr. **24**
Farrakhan, Louis **15**
Fauntroy, Walter E. **11**
Fletcher, Alphonse, Jr. **16**
Franklin, Hardy R. **9**
Friday, Jeff **24**
Fudge, Ann **11**
Fuller, S. B. **13**
Gaston, Arthur G. **4**

Gibson, Kenneth Allen **6**
Goldsberry, Ronald **18**
Gordon, Pamela **17**
Gordy, Berry, Jr. **1**
Goss, Tom **23**
Graham, Stedman **13**
Graves, Earl G. **1**
Griffith, Mark Winston **8**
Hale, Lorraine **8**
Hamer, Fannie Lou **6**
Hammer, M. C. **20**
Handy, W. C. **8**
Hannah, Marc **10**
Hardison, Bethann **12**
Harrell, Andre **9**
Harris, Alice **7**
Harris, E. Lynn **12**
Harris, Monica **18**
Harvey, Steve **18**
Hawkins, La-Van **17**
Henderson, Gordon **5**
Henry, Lenny **9**
Hightower, Dennis F. **13**
Hill, Bonnie Guiton **20**
Hill, Calvin **19**
Hill, Janet **19**
Hill, Jessie, Jr. **13**
Holland, Robert, Jr. **11**
Holmes, Larry **20**
Houston, Whitney **7**
Hudlin, Reginald **9**
Hudlin, Warrington **9**
Hudson, Cheryl **15**
Hudson, Wade **15**
Huggins, Larry **21**
Ice Cube **8**
Jackson, George **19**
Jackson, Mannie **14**
Jackson, Michael **19**
James, Juanita **13**
John, Daymond **23**
Johnson, Eddie Bernice **8**
Johnson, John H. **3**
Johnson, Robert L. **3**
Jones, Bobby **20**
Jones, Carl **7**
Jones, Ingrid Saunders **18**
Jones, Quincy **8**
Jordan, Michael **6, 21**
Jordan, Montell **23**
Joyner, Marjorie Stewart **26**
Julian, Percy Lavon **6**
Kelly, Patrick **3**
Kimbro, Dennis **10**
King, Dexter **10**
King, Don **14**
Knight, Suge **11**
Lane, Vincent **5**
Langhart, Janet **19**
Lawless, Theodore K. **8**
Lawson, Jennifer **1**
Leary, Kathryn D. **10**
Leavell, Dorothy R. **17**
Lee, Annie Francis **22**
Leonard, Sugar Ray **15**
Lewellyn, J. Bruce **13**
Lewis, Byron E. **13**
Lewis, Delano **7**
Lewis, Edward T. **21**
Lewis, Reginald F. **6**
Lott, Ronnie **9**
Louis, Errol T. **8**
Lucas, John **7**
Madhubuti, Haki R. **7**
Malone, Annie **13**
Marshall, Bella **22**
Massenburg, Kedar **23**
Master P **21**
Maynard, Robert C. **7**
McCabe, Jewell Jackson **10**
McCoy, Elijah **8**
McDonald, Erroll **1**
Micheaux, Oscar **7**
Morgan, Garrett **1**
Morgan, Joe Leonard **9**
Morgan, Rose **11**
Nanula, Richard D. **20**
Nichols, Nichelle **11**
Parks, Gordon **1**
Parsons, Richard Dean **11**
Payton, Walter **11, 25**
Peck, Carolyn **23**
Perez, Anna **1**
Pleasant, Mary Ellen **9**
Powell, Maxine **8**
Price, Frederick K.C. **21**
Price, Hugh B. **9**
Procope, Ernesta **23**
Queen Latifah **1, 16**
Ralph, Sheryl Lee **18**
Rand, A. Barry **6**
Reeves, Rachel J. **23**
Rhone, Sylvia **2**
Rice, Linda Johnson **9**
Rice, Norm **8**
Richie, Leroy C. **18**
Roberts, Roy S. **14**
Robertson, Oscar **26**
Robeson, Eslanda Goode **13**
Robinson, Jackie **6**
Robinson, Rachel **16**
Robinson, Randall **7**
Roche, Joyce M. **17**
Rodgers, Johnathan **6**
Rogers, John W., Jr. **5**
Ross, Diana **8**
Russell, Bill **8**
Russell, Herman Jerome **17**
Russell-McCloud, Patricia **17**
Saint James, Synthia **12**
Samara, Noah **15**
Sanders, Dori **8**
Sengstacke, John **18**
Siméus, Dumas M. **25**
Simmons, Russell **1**
Sinbad, **1, 16**
Smith, Barbara **11**
Smith, Clarence O. **21**
Smith, Jane E. **24**
Smith, Joshua **10**
Smith, Willi **8**
Sneed, Paula A. **18**
Spaulding, Charles Clinton **9**
Stewart, Paul Wilbur **12**
Sullivan, Leon H. **3**
Taylor, Kristin Clark **8**
Taylor, Susan L. **10**
Terrell, Dorothy A. **24**
Thomas, Franklin A. **5**
Thomas, Isiah **7, 26**
Thompson, John W. **26**
Tribble, Israel, Jr. **8**
Trotter, Monroe **9**
Utendahl, John **23**
Van Peebles, Melvin **7**
VanDerZee, James **6**
Walker, A'lelia **14**
Walker, Cedric "Ricky" **19**
Walker, Madame C. J. **7**
Walker, Maggie Lena **17**
Walker, T. J. **7**
Ward, Lloyd **2**
Washington, Val **12**
Wasow, Omar **15**
Watkins, Walter C. Jr, **24**
Wattleton, Faye **9**
Wek, Alek **18**
Wells-Barnett, Ida B. **8**
Wharton, Clifton R., Jr. **7**
White, Walter F. **4**
Wiley, Ralph **8**
Williams, O. S. **13**
Williams, Paul R. **9**
Williams, Walter E. **4**
Wilson, Phill **9**
Wilson, Sunnie **7**
Winfrey, Oprah **2, 15**
Woodson, Robert L. **10**
Wright, Deborah C. **25**
Yoba, Malik **11**

Dance

Ailey, Alvin **8**
Allen, Debbie **13**
Baker, Josephine **3**
Bates, Peg Leg **14**
Beals, Jennifer **12**
Byrd, Donald **10**
Clarke, Hope **14**
Davis, Sammy Jr. **18**
Dove, Ulysses **5**
Dunham, Katherine **4**
Fagan, Garth **18**
Glover, Savion **14**
Guy, Jasmine **2**
Hammer, M. C. **20**
Hines, Gregory **1**
Horne, Lena **5**
Jackson, Michael **19**
Jamison, Judith **7**
Johnson, Virginia **9**
Jones, Bill T. **1**
McQueen, Butterfly **6**
Miller, Bebe **3**
Mills, Florence **22**
Mitchell, Arthur **2**
Moten, Etta **18**
Muse, Clarence Edouard **21**
Nicholas, Fayard **20**
Nicholas, Harold **20**
Nichols, Nichelle **11**
Powell, Maxine **8**
Primus, Pearl **6**
Ribeiro, Alfonso, **17**
Robinson, Bill "Bojangles" **11**
Rolle, Esther **13, 21**
Vereen, Ben **4**
Walker, Cedric "Ricky" **19**
Washington, Fredi **10**
Williams, Vanessa L. **4, 17**

Education

Achebe, Chinua **6**
Adkins, Rutherford H. **21**
Alexander, Margaret Walker **22**
Archer, Dennis **7**
Aristide, Jean-Bertrand **6**
Asante, Molefi Kete **3**
Baker, Gwendolyn Calvert **9**
Baker, Houston A., Jr. **6**
Bambara, Toni Cade **10**
Baraka, Amiri **1**
Barboza, Anthony **10**
Bell, Derrick **6**
Berry, Bertice **8**

Berry, Mary Frances **7**
Bethune, Mary McLeod **4**
Biggers, John **20**
Black, Keith Lanier **18**
Bluitt, Juliann S. **14**
Bosley, Freeman, Jr. **7**
Boyd, T. B., III **6**
Brooks, Avery **9**
Brown, Joyce F. **25**
Brown, Sterling **10**
Brown, Wesley **23**
Burke, Selma **16**
Burroughs, Margaret Taylor **9**
Burton, LeVar **8**
Butler, Paul D. **17**
Callender, Clive O. **3**
Campbell, Bebe Moore **6, 24**
Cannon, Katie **10**
Carnegie, Herbert **25**
Carver, George Washington **4**
Cary, Lorene **3**
Catlett, Elizabeth **2**
Cayton, Horace **26**
Clark, Joe **1**
Clark, Kenneth B. **5**
Clark, Septima **7**
Clarke, John Henrik **20**
Clayton, Constance **1**
Clements, George **2**
Clifton, Lucille **14**
Cobbs, Price M. **9**
Cohen, Anthony **15**
Cole, Johnnetta B. **5**
Collins, Marva **3**
Comer, James P. **6**
Cone, James H. **3**
Cook, Samuel DuBois **14**
Cook, Toni **23**
Cooper, Anna Julia **20**
Cooper, Edward S. **6**
Cosby, Bill **7, 26**
Cottrell, Comer **11**
Crew, Rudolph F. **16**
Cross, Dolores E. **23**
Crouch, Stanley **11**
Cullen, Countee **8**
Davis, Allison **12**
Davis, Angela **5**
Days, Drew S., III **10**
Delany, Sadie **12**
Delany, Samuel R., Jr. **9**
Dickens, Helen Octavia **14**
Diop, Cheikh Anta **4**
Dixon, Margaret **14**
Dodson, Howard, Jr. **7**
Douglas, Aaron **7**
Dove, Rita **6**
Dove, Ulysses **5**
Draper, Sharon M. **16**
Driskell, David C. **7**
Dyson, Michael Eric **11**
Early, Gerald **15**
Edelin, Ramona Hoage **19**
Edelman, Marian Wright **5**
Edley, Christopher **2**
Edwards, Harry **2**
Elders, Joycelyn **6**
Ellison, Ralph **7**
Evans, Mari **26**
Fauset, Jessie **7**
Favors, Steve **23**
Foster, Henry W., Jr. **26**
Franklin, John Hope **5**
Franklin, Robert M. **13**
Frazier, E. Franklin **10**
Freeman, Al, Jr. **11**
Fuller, Solomon Carter, Jr. **15**
Gaines, Ernest J. **7**
Gates, Henry Louis, Jr. **3**
Gates, Sylvester James, Jr. **15**
Giddings, Paula **11**
Giovanni, Nikki **9**
Golden, Marita **19**
Gomes, Peter J. **15**
Greenfield, Eloise **9**
Guinier, Lani **7**
Guy-Sheftall, Beverly **13**
Hale, Lorraine **8**
Handy, W. C. **8**
Hansberry, William Leo **11**
Harkless, Necia Desiree **19**
Harris, Alice **7**
Harris, Jay T. **19**
Harris, Patricia Roberts **2**
Harsh, Vivian Gordon **14**
Hayden, Robert **12**
Haynes, George Edmund **8**
Herenton, Willie W. **24**
Hill, Anita **5**
Hill, Bonnie Guiton **20**
Hine, Darlene Clark **24**
Hinton, William Augustus **8**
Holland, Endesha Ida Mae **3**
hooks, bell **5**
Hope, John **8**
Houston, Charles Hamilton **4**
Hrabowski, Freeman A. III **22**
Humphries, Frederick **20**
Hunt, Richard **6**
Hutson, Jean Blackwell **16**
Jackson, Fred James **25**
Jarvis, Charlene Drew **21**
Jeffries, Leonard **8**
Jenifer, Franklyn G. **2**
Jenkins, Ella **15**
Johnson, Hazel **22**
Johnson, James Weldon **5**
Jones, Bobby **20**
Jones, Ingrid Saunders **18**
Jones, Lois Mailou **13**
Joplin, Scott **6**
Jordan, Barbara **4**
Jordan, June **7**
Josey, E. J. **10**
Just, Ernest Everett **3**
Karenga, Maulana **10**
Keith, Damon J. **16**
Kennedy, Florynce **12**
Kilpatrick, Carolyn Cheeks **16**
Kimbro, Dennis **10**
Komunyakaa, Yusef **9**
Kunjufu, Jawanza **3**
Lawrence, Jacob **4**
Lawrence-Lightfoot, Sara **10**
Lee, Annie Francis **22**
Leffall, LaSalle, Jr. **3**
Lester, Julius **9**
Lewis, David Levering **9**
Lewis, Samella **25**
Lewis, Shirley A. R. **14**
Lewis, Thomas **19**
Liberia-Peters, Maria Philomena **12**
Locke, Alain **10**
Lorde, Audre **6**
Lyttle, Hulda Margaret **14**
Madhubuti, Haki R. **7**
Major, Clarence **9**
Manley, Audrey Forbes **16**
Marable, Manning **10**
Marsalis, Wynton **16**
Marshall, Paule **7**
Masekela, Barbara **18**
Massey, Walter E. **5**
Maynard, Robert C. **7**
Maynor, Dorothy **19**
Mays, Benjamin E. **7**
McCarty, Oseola **16**
McKay, Nellie Yvonne **17**
McMillan, Terry **4, 17**
Meek, Carrie **6**
Meredith, James H. **11**
Millender-McDonald, Juanita **21**
Mitchell, Corinne **8**
Mongella, Gertrude **11**
Moore, Melba **21**
Morrison, Keith **13**
Morrison, Toni **15**
Moses, Robert Parris **11**
N'Namdi, George R. **17**
Norman, Maidie **20**
Norton, Eleanor Holmes **7**
Ogletree, Jr., Charles **12**
Onwueme, Tess Osonye **23**
Owens, Major **6**
Page, Alan **7**
Painter, Nell Irvin **24**
Patterson, Frederick Douglass **12**
Patterson, Orlando **4**
Payton, Benjamin F. **23**
Porter, James A. **11**
Poussaint, Alvin F. **5**
Price, Glenda **22**
Primus, Pearl **6**
Quarles, Benjamin Arthur **18**
Reagon, Bernice Johnson **7**
Reddick, Lawrence Dunbar **20**
Redding, J. Saunders **26**
Redmond, Eugene **23**
Reid, Irvin D. **20**
Ringgold, Faith **4**
Robinson, Sharon **22**
Robinson, Spottswood **22**
Russell-McCloud, Patricia **17**
Satcher, David **7**
Schomburg, Arthur Alfonso **9**
Shabazz, Betty **7, 26**
Shange, Ntozake **8**
Shipp, E. R. **15**
Simmons, Ruth J. **13**
Sinkford, Jeanne C. **13**
Sisulu, Sheila Violet Makate **24**
Sizemore, Barbara A. **26**
Smith, Anna Deavere **6**
Smith, John L. **22**
Smith, Mary Carter **26**
Smith, Tubby **18**
Soyinka, Wole **4**
Spikes, Dolores **18**
Stanford, John **20**
Steele, Claude Mason **13**
Steele, Shelby **13**
Stephens, Charlotte Andrews **14**
Stewart, Maria W. Miller **19**
Stone, Chuck **9**
Sudarkasa, Niara **4**
Sullivan, Louis **8**
Swygert, H. Patrick **22**
Taylor, Susie King **13**
Terrell, Mary Church **9**
Thomas, Alma **14**
Thurman, Howard **3**
Tribble, Israel, Jr. **8**
Tucker, Rosina **14**
Turnbull, Walter **13**
Tutu, Desmond **6**

Tyson, Neil de Grasse **15**
Usry, James L. **23**
van Sertima, Ivan **25**
Walcott, Derek **5**
Wallace, Michele Faith **13**
Wallace, Phyllis A. **9**
Washington, Booker T. **4**
Watkins, Shirley R. **17**
Wattleton, Faye **9**
Wells-Barnett, Ida B. **8**
Wells, James Lesesne **10**
Welsing, Frances Cress **5**
Wesley, Dorothy Porter **19**
West, Cornel **5**
Wharton, Clifton R., Jr. **7**
White, Lois Jean **20**
Wilkins, Roger **2**
Williams, Gregory **11**
Williams, Patricia J. **11**
Williams, Sherley Anne **25**
Williams, Walter E. **4**
Wilson, William Julius **22**
Woodruff, Hale **9**
Woodson, Carter G. **2**
Worrill, Conrad **12**
Young, Jean Childs **14**

Fashion
Bailey, Xenobia **11**
Banks, Jeffrey **17**
Banks, Tyra **11**
Barboza, Anthony **10**
Beals, Jennifer **12**
Beckford, Tyson **11**
Berry, Halle **4, 19**
Brown, Joyce F. **25**
Campbell, Naomi **1**
Davidson, Jaye **5**
Henderson, Gordon **5**
Iman **4**
John, Daymond **23**
Johnson, Beverly **2**
Jones, Carl **7**
Kani, Karl **10**
Kelly, Patrick **3**
Powell, Maxine **8**
Robinson, Patrick **19**
Rochon, Lela **16**
Rowell, Victoria **13**
Smaltz, Audrey **12**
Smith, Barbara **11**
Smith, Willi **8**
Walker, T. J. **7**
Webb, Veronica **10**
Wek, Alek **18**

Film
Amos, John **8**
Baker, Josephine **3**
Banks, Tyra **11**
Bassett, Angela **6, 23**
Beach, Michael **26**
Beals, Jennifer **12**
Belafonte, Harry **4**
Bellamy, Bill **12**
Berry, Halle **4, 19**
Braugher, Andre **13**
Brown, Jim **11**
Brown, Tony **3**
Burnett, Charles **16**
Byrd, Michelle **19**
Byrd, Robert **11**
Calloway, Cab **14**
Campbell, Naomi **1**
Campbell, Tisha **8**
Carroll, Diahann **9**
Carson, Lisa Nicole **21**
Cheadle, Don **19**
Clash, Kevin **14**
Cosby, Bill **7, 26**
Crothers, Scatman **19**
Curry, Mark **17**
Curtis-Hall, Vondie **17**
Dandridge, Dorothy **3**
Dash, Julie **4**
Davidson, Jaye **5**
Davidson, Tommy **21**
Davis, Ossie **5**
Davis, Sammy, Jr. **18**
de Passe, Suzanne **25**
Dee, Ruby **8**
Devine, Loretta **24**
Dickerson, Ernest **6, 17**
Diggs, Taye **25**
Dr. Dre **10**
Driskell, David C. **7**
Duke, Bill **3**
Duncan, Michael Clarke **26**
Dunham, Katherine **4**
Dutton, Charles S. **4, 22**
Epps, Omar **23**
Esposito, Giancarlo **9**
Evans, Darryl **22**
Everett, Francine **23**
Fishburne, Larry **4**
Fox, Vivica A. **15**
Foxx, Jamie **15**
Foxx, Redd **2**
Franklin, Carl **11**
Freeman, Al, Jr. **11**
Freeman, Morgan **2, 20**
Friday, Jeff **24**
Fuller, Charles **8**
George, Nelson **12**
Givens, Robin **4, 25**
Glover, Danny **1, 24**
Glover, Savion **14**
Goldberg, Whoopi **4**
Gooding, Cuba, Jr. **16**
Gordon, Dexter **25**
Gordy, Berry, Jr. **1**
Gossett, Louis, Jr. **7**
Gray, F. Gary **14**
Grier, Pam **9**
Guillaume, Robert **3**
Gunn, Moses **10**
Guy, Jasmine **2**
Hampton, Henry **6**
Hardison, Kadeem **22**
Harris, Leslie **6**
Harris, Robin **7**
Hayes, Isaac **20**
Hemsley, Sherman **19**
Henry, Lenny **9**
Hill, Lauryn **20**
Hines, Gregory **1**
Horne, Lena **5**
Hounsou, Djimon **19**
Houston, Whitney **7**
Hudlin, Reginald **9**
Hudlin, Warrington **9**
Hughes, Albert **7**
Hughes, Allen **7**
Ice Cube **8**
Iman **4**
Ingram, Rex **5**
Jackson, George **19**
Jackson, Janet **6**
Jackson, Samuel L. **8, 19**
Jean-Baptiste, Marianne **17**
Johnson, Beverly **2**
Jones, James Earl **3**
Jones, Quincy **8**
Julien, Isaac **3**
King, Regina **22**
Kirby, George **14**
Kitt, Eartha **16**
Kotto, Yaphet **7**
Kunjufu, Jawanza **3**
L. L. Cool J **16**
La Salle, Eriq **12**
LaBelle, Patti **13**
Lane, Charles **3**
Lawrence, Martin **6**
Lee, Joie **1**
Lee, Spike **5, 19**
Lemmons, Kasi **20**
Lewis, Samella **25**
Lincoln, Abbey **3**
Lindo, Delroy **18**
Long, Nia **17**
Love, Darlene **23**
Lover, Ed **10**
Mabley, Jackie "Moms" **15**
Master P **21**
McDaniel, Hattie **5**
McKee, Lonette **12**
McQueen, Butterfly **6**
Micheaux, Oscar **7**
Moore, Chante **26**
Moore, Melba **21**
Moore, Shemar **21**
Morton, Joe **18**
Moses, Gilbert **12**
Moss, Carlton **17**
Murphy, Eddie **4, 20**
Muse, Clarence Edouard **21**
Newton, Thandie **26**
Nicholas, Fayard **20**
Nicholas, Harold **20**
Nichols, Nichelle **11**
Norman, Maidie **20**
Parks, Gordon **1**
Payne, Allen **13**
Phifer, Mekhi **25**
Pinkett, Jada **10**
Poitier, Sidney **11**
Prince **18**
Pryor, Richard **3**
Queen Latifah **1, 16**
Ralph, Sheryl Lee **18**
Randle, Theresa **16**
Reese, Della **6, 20**
Reuben, Gloria **15**
Rhames, Ving **14**
Riggs, Marlon **5**
Rochon, Lela **16**
Rock, Chris **3, 22**
Rolle, Esther **13, 21**
Rollins, Howard E., Jr. **16**
Ross, Diana **8**
Rowell, Victoria **13**
Rupaul **17**
Schultz, Michael A. **6**
Seal **14**
Sembène, Ousmane **13**
Shakur, Tupac **14**
Simpson, O. J. **15**
Sinbad **1, 16**
Singleton, John **2**
Smith, Anna Deavere **6**
Smith, Roger Guenveur **12**
Smith, Will **8, 18**
Snipes, Wesley **3, 24**
St. Jacques, Raymond **8**

St. John, Kristoff **25**
Tate, Larenz **15**
Taylor, Meshach **4**
Taylor, Regina **9**
Thigpen, Lynne **17**
Thurman, Wallace **16**
Tillman, George, Jr. **20**
Townsend, Robert **4, 23**
Tucker, Chris **13, 23**
Turner, Tina **6**
Tyson, Cicely **7**
Uggams, Leslie **23**
Underwood, Blair **7**
Usher **23**
Van Peebles, Mario **2**
Van Peebles, Melvin **7**
Vance, Courtney B. **15**
Vereen, Ben **4**
Warfield, Marsha **2**
Warner, Malcolm-Jamal **22**
Warwick, Dionne **18**
Washington, Denzel **1, 16**
Washington, Fredi **10**
Waters, Ethel **7**
Wayans, Damon **8**
Wayans, Keenen Ivory **18**
Weathers, Carl **10**
Webb, Veronica **10**
Whitaker, Forest **2**
Whitfield, Lynn **18**
Williams, Billy Dee **8**
Williams, Clarence, III **26**
Williams, Samm-Art **21**
Williams, Vanessa L. **4, 17**
Williamson, Mykelti **22**
Winfield, Paul **2**
Winfrey, Oprah **2, 15**
Woodard, Alfre **9**
Yoba, Malik **11**

Government and politics—international

Abacha, Sani **11**
Abbott, Diane **9**
Achebe, Chinua **6**
Ali Mahdi Mohamed **5**
Annan, Kofi Atta **15**
Aristide, Jean-Bertrand **6**
Azikiwe, Nnamdi **13**
Babangida, Ibrahim **4**
Baker, Gwendolyn Calvert **9**
Banda, Hastings Kamuzu **6**
Bedie, Henri Konan **21**
Berry, Mary Frances **7**
Biko, Steven **4**
Bizimungu, Pasteur **19**
Bongo, Omar **1**
Bunche, Ralph J. **5**
Buthelezi, Mangosuthu Gatsha **9**
Charlemagne, Manno **11**
Charles, Mary Eugenia **10**
Chissano, Joaquim **7**
Christophe, Henri **9**
Conté, Lansana **7**
da Silva, Benedita **5**
Diop, Cheikh Anta **4**
Diouf, Abdou **3**
Eyadéma, Gnassingbé **7**
Fela **1**
Gordon, Pamela **17**
Habré, Hissène **6**
Habyarimana, Juvenal **8**
Haile Selassie **7**
Haley, George Williford Boyce **21**
Hani, Chris **6**
Houphouët-Boigny, Félix **4**
Ingraham, Hubert A. **19**
Jagan, Cheddi **16**
Jammeh, Yahya **23**
Jawara, Sir Dawda Kairaba **11**
Kabbah, Ahmad Tejan **23**
Kabila, Laurent **20**
Kabunda, Kenneth **2**
Kenyatta, Jomo **5**
Kerekou, Ahmed (Mathieu) **1**
Liberia-Peters, Maria Philomena **12**
Luthuli, Albert **13**
Mabuza, Lindiwe **18**
Machel, Samora Moises **8**
Mandela, Nelson **1, 14**
Mandela, Winnie **2**
Masekela, Barbara **18**
Masire, Quett **5**
Mbeki, Thabo Mvuyelwa **14**
Mbuende, Kaire **12**
Meles Zenawi **3**
Mkapa, Benjamin **16**
Mobutu Sese Seko **1**
Mogae, Festus Gontebanye **19**
Moi, Daniel **1**
Mongella, Gertrude **11**
Mugabe, Robert Gabriel **10**
Muluzi, Bakili **14**
Museveni, Yoweri **4**
Mutebi, Ronald **25**
Mwinyi, Ali Hassan **1**
Ndadaye, Melchior **7**
Nkomo, Joshua **4**
Nkrumah, Kwame **3**
Ntaryamira, Cyprien **8**
Nujoma, Samuel **10**
Nyanda, Siphiwe **21**
Nyerere, Julius **5**
Nzo, Alfred **15**
Obasanjo, Olusegun **5, 22**
Pascal-Trouillot, Ertha **3**
Patterson, P. J. **6, 20**
Perkins, Edward **5**
Perry, Ruth **15**
Pitt, David Thomas **10**
Pitta, Celso **17**
Ramaphosa, Cyril **3**
Rawlings, Jerry **9**
Rawlings, Nana Konadu Agyeman **13**
Rice, Condoleezza **3**
Robinson, Randall **7**
Sampson, Edith S. **4**
Sankara, Thomas **17**
Savimbi, Jonas **2**
Sawyer, Amos **2**
Senghor, Léopold Sédar **12**
Smith, Jennifer **21**
Soglo, Nicephore **15**
Soyinka, Wole **4**
Taylor, Charles **20**
Taylor, John (David Beckett) **16**
Touré, Sekou **6**
Toure, Amadou Toumani **18**
Tsvangirai, Morgan **26**
Tutu, Desmond **6**
Vieira, Joao **14**
Wharton, Clifton R., Jr. **7**

Government and politics—U.S.

Adams, Floyd, Jr. **12**
Alexander, Archie Alphonso **14**
Alexander, Clifford **26**
Ali, Muhammad **2, 16**
Allen, Ethel D. **13**
Archer, Dennis **7**
Arrington, Richard **24**
Avant, Clarence **19**
Baker, Thurbert **22**
Barden, Don H. **9, 20**
Barrett, Andrew C. **12**
Barry, Marion S. **7**
Belton, Sharon Sayles **9, 16**
Berry, Mary Frances **7**
Bethune, Mary McLeod **4**
Blackwell, Unita **17**
Bond, Julian **2**
Bosley, Freeman, Jr. **7**
Boykin, Keith **14**
Bradley, Thomas **2**
Braun, Carol Moseley **4**
Brazile, Donna **25**
Brimmer, Andrew F. **2**
Brooke, Edward **8**
Brown, Corrine **24**
Brown, Elaine **8**
Brown, Jesse **6**
Brown, Lee Patrick **24**
Brown, Les **5**
Brown, Ron **5**
Brown, Willie L., Jr. **7**
Bryant, Wayne R. **6**
Buckley, Victoria (Vicki) **24**
Bunche, Ralph J. **5**
Burris, Chuck **21**
Burris, Roland W. **25**
Butler, Jerry **26**
Caesar, Shirley **19**
Campbell, Bill **9**
Carson, Julia **23**
Chavis, Benjamin **6**
Chisholm, Shirley **2**
Christian-Green, Donna M. **17**
Clay, William Lacy **8**
Clayton, Eva M. **20**
Cleaver, Eldridge **5**
Cleaver, Emanuel **4**
Clyburn, James **21**
Collins, Barbara-Rose **7**
Collins, Cardiss **10**
Connerly, Ward **14**
Conyers, John, Jr. **4**
Cose, Ellis **5**
Crockett, George, Jr. **10**
Cummings, Elijah E. **24**
Cunningham, Evelyn **23**
Currie, Betty **21**
Davis, Angela **5**
Davis, Benjamin O., Sr. **4**
Davis, Benjamin O., Jr. **2**
Davis, Danny K. **24**
Days, Drew S., III **10**
Dellums, Ronald **2**
Diggs, Charles R. **21**
Dinkins, David **4**
Dixon, Julian C. **24**
Dixon, Sharon Pratt **1**
Du Bois, W. E. B. **3**
Edmonds, Terry **17**
Elders, Joycelyn **6**
Espy, Mike **6**
Farmer, James **2**
Farrakhan, Louis **2**
Fattah, Chaka **11**
Fauntroy, Walter E. **11**
Ferguson, Roger W. **25**
Fields, C. Virginia **25**
Fields, Cleo **13**
Flake, Floyd H. **18**
Flipper, Henry O. **3**
Fortune, T. Thomas **6**
Franks, Gary **2**

Fulani, Lenora **11**
Gantt, Harvey **1**
Garvey, Marcus **1**
Gibson, Johnnie Mae **23**
Gibson, Kenneth Allen **6**
Gibson, William F. **6**
Goode, W. Wilson **4**
Gravely, Samuel L., Jr. **5**
Gray, William H., III **3**
Grimké, Archibald H. **9**
Guinier, Lani **7**
Haley, George Williford Boyce **21**
Hamer, Fannie Lou **6**
Harmon, Clarence **26**
Harris, Alice **7**
Harris, Patricia Roberts **2**
Harvard, Beverly **11**
Hastie, William H. **8**
Hastings, Alcee L. **16**
Hayes, James C. **10**
Henry, Aaron **19**
Herenton, Willie W. **24**
Herman, Alexis M. **15**
Hernandez, Aileen Clarke **13**
Hill, Bonnie Guiton **20**
Hilliard, Earl F. **24**
Holder, Eric H., Jr. **9**
Irving, Larry, Jr. **12**
Jackson, George **14**
Jackson, Jesse **1**
Jackson, Jesse, Jr. **14**
Jackson Lee, Sheila **20**
Jackson, Maynard **2**
Jackson, Shirley Ann **12**
Jacob, John E. **2**
James, Sharpe **23**
Jarvis, Charlene Drew **21**
Jefferson, William J. **25**
Johnson, Eddie Bernice **8**
Johnson, Harvey Jr. **24**
Johnson, James Weldon **5**
Johnson, Norma L. Holloway **17**
Johnson, Robert T. **17**
Jones, Elaine R. **7**
Jordan, Barbara **4**
Kennard, William Earl **18**
Keyes, Alan L. **11**
Kilpatrick, Carolyn Cheeks **16**
King, Martin Luther, III **20**
Kirk, Ron **11**
Lafontant, Jewel Stradford **3**
Lee, Barbara **25**
Leland, Mickey **2**
Lewis, Delano **7**
Lewis, John **2**
Mallett, Conrad, Jr. **16**
Marshall, Bella **22**
Marshall, Thurgood **1**
Martin, Louis E. **16**
McKinney, Cynthia Ann **11**
McKissick, Floyd B. **3**
Meek, Carrie **6**
Meeks, Gregory **25**
Meredith, James H. **11**
Metcalfe, Ralph **26**
Mfume, Kweisi **6**
Millender-McDonald, Juanita **21**
Morial, Ernest "Dutch" **26**
Morial, Marc **20**
Moses, Robert Parris **11**
Norton, Eleanor Holmes **7**
O'Leary, Hazel **6**
Owens, Major **6**
Page, Alan **7**
Patrick, Deval **12**
Patterson, Louise **25**
Payne, Donald M. **2**
Perez, Anna **1**
Perkins, Edward **5**
Pinchback, P. B. S. **9**
Powell, Adam Clayton, Jr. **3**
Powell, Colin **1**
Powell, Debra A. **23**
Raines, Franklin Delano **14**
Randolph, A. Philip **3**
Rangel, Charles **3**
Rice, Condoleezza **3**
Rice, Norm **8**
Robinson, Randall **7**
Rush, Bobby **26**
Rustin, Bayard **4**
Sampson, Edith S. **4**
Satcher, David **7**
Sayles Belton, Sharon **9**
Schmoke, Kurt **1**
Scott, Robert C. **23**
Sears-Collins, Leah J. **5**
Shakur, Assata **6**
Sharpton, Al **21**
Simpson, Carole **6**
Sisulu, Sheila Violet Makate **24**
Slater, Rodney E. **15**
Stanton, Robert **20**
Staupers, Mabel K. **7**
Stokes, Carl B. **10**
Stokes, Louis **3**
Stone, Chuck **9**
Street, John F. **24**
Sullivan, Louis **8**
Thomas, Clarence **2**
Thompson, Bennie G. **26**
Towns, Edolphus **19**
Tribble, Israel, Jr. **8**
Tubbs Jones, Stephanie **24**
Tucker, C. DeLores **12**
Turner, Henry McNeal **5**
Usry, James L. **23**
Von Lipsey, Roderick K. **11**
Wallace, Phyllis A. **9**
Washington, Harold **6**
Washington, Val **12**
Waters, Maxine **3**
Watkins, Shirley R. **17**
Watt, Melvin **26**
Watts, J. C., Jr. **14**
Weaver, Robert C. **8**
Webb, Wellington **3**
Wharton, Clifton R., Jr. **7**
Wheat, Alan **14**
White, Jesse **22**
White, Michael R. **5**
Wilder, L. Douglas **3**
Wilkins, Roger **2**
Williams, Anthony **21**
Williams, George Washington **18**
Williams, Hosea Lorenzo **15**
Williams, Maggie **7**
Wilson, Sunnie **7**
Wynn, Albert **25**
Young, Andrew **3**

Law

Alexander, Clifford **26**
Alexander, Joyce London **18**
Alexander, Sadie Tanner Mossell **22**
Archer, Dennis **7**
Banks, William **11**
Barrett, Andrew C. **12**
Baugh, David **23**
Bell, Derrick **6**
Berry, Mary Frances **7**
Bishop Jr., Sanford D. **24**
Bolin, Jane **22**
Bolton, Terrell D. **25**
Bosley, Freeman, Jr. **7**
Boykin, Keith **14**
Bradley, Thomas **2**
Braun, Carol Moseley **4**
Brooke, Edward **8**
Brown, Lee Patrick **1, 24**
Brown, Ron **5**
Brown, Willie L., Jr. **7**
Bryant, Wayne R. **6**
Burris, Roland W. **25**
Butler, Paul D. **17**
Campbell, Bill **9**
Carter, Stephen L. **4**
Chambers, Julius **3**
Clendenon, Donn **26**
Cochran, Johnnie L., Jr. **11**
Conyers, John, Jr. **4**
Crockett, George, Jr. **10**
Darden, Christopher **13**
Days, Drew S., III **10**
Diggs-Taylor, Anna **20**
Dinkins, David **4**
Dixon, Sharon Pratt **1**
Edelman, Marian Wright **5**
Edley, Christopher **2**
Ellington, E. David **11**
Espy, Mike **6**
Fields, Cleo **13**
Freeman, Charles **19**
Gary, Willie E. **12**
Gibson, Johnnie Mae **23**
Glover, Nathaniel, Jr. **12**
Gomez-Preston, Cheryl **9**
Graham, Lawrence Otis **12**
Grimké, Archibald H. **9**
Guinier, Lani **7**
Haley, George Williford Boyce **21**
Hall, Elliott S. **24**
Harris, Patricia Roberts **2**
Harvard, Beverly **11**
Hastie, William H. **8**
Hastings, Alcee L. **16**
Hawkins, Steven **14**
Haywood, Margaret A. **24**
Higginbotham, A. Leon, Jr. **13, 25**
Hill, Anita **5**
Hillard, Terry **25**
Hills, Oliver W. **24**
Holder, Eric H., Jr. **9**
Hooks, Benjamin L. **2**
Houston, Charles Hamilton **4**
Hunter, Billy **22**
Jackson Lee, Sheila **20**
Jackson, Maynard **2**
Johnson, James Weldon **5**
Johnson, Norma L. Holloway **17**
Jones, Elaine R. **7**
Jones, Star **10**
Jordan, Vernon E. **3**
Kearse, Amalya Lyle **12**
Keith, Damon J. **16**
Kennard, William Earl **18**
Kennedy, Florynce **12**
King, Bernice **4**
Kirk, Ron **11**
Lafontant, Jewel Stradford **3**
Lewis, Delano **7**
Lewis, Reginald F. **6**
Mallett, Conrad, Jr. **16**
Mandela, Nelson **1, 14**
Marshall, Thurgood **1**

Mathis, Greg 26
McDonald, Gabrielle Kirk 20
McDougall, Gay J. 11
McKinnon, Isaiah 9
McKissick, Floyd B. 3
McPhail, Sharon 2
Meeks, Gregory 25
Morial, Ernest "Dutch" 26
Motley, Constance Baker 10
Napoleon, Benny N. 23
Norton, Eleanor Holmes 7
O'Leary, Hazel 6
Ogletree, Charles, Jr. 12
Page, Alan 7
Parks, Bernard C. 17
Parsons, James 14
Parsons, Richard Dean 11
Pascal-Trouillot, Ertha 3
Patrick, Deval 12
Ramsey, Charles H. 21
Redding, Louis L. 26
Richie, Leroy C. 18
Robinson, Randall 7
Russell-McCloud, Patricia 17
Sampson, Edith S. 4
Schmoke, Kurt 1
Sears-Collins, Leah J. 5
Stokes, Carl B. 10
Stokes, Louis 3
Stout, Juanita Kidd 24
Taylor, John (David Beckett) 16
Thomas, Clarence 2
Thomas, Franklin A. 5
Tubbs Jones, Stephaie 24
Vanzant, Iyanla 17
Wagner, Annice 22
Washington, Harold 6
Watt, Melvin 26
Wilder, L. Douglas 3
Wilkins, Roger 2
Williams, Evelyn 10
Williams, Gregory 11
Williams, Patricia J. 11
Williams, Willie L. 4
Wright, Bruce McMarion 3
Wynn, Albert 25

Military

Abacha, Sani 11
Adams Early, Charity 13
Alexander, Margaret Walker 22
Babangida, Ibrahim 4
Bolden, Charles F., Jr. 7
Brown, Erroll M. 23
Brown, Jesse 6
Bullard, Eugene 12
Cadoria, Sherian Grace 14
Chissano, Joaquim 7
Christophe, Henri 9
Conté, Lansana 7
Davis, Benjamin O., Jr. 2
Davis, Benjamin O., Sr. 4
Europe, James Reese 10
Eyadéma, Gnassingbé 7
Flipper, Henry O. 3
Gravely, Samuel L., Jr. 5
Gregory, Frederick D. 8
Habré, Hissène 6
Habyarimana, Juvenal 8
Harris, Marcelite Jordan 16
Jackson, Fred James 25
James, Daniel, Jr. 16
Johnson, Hazel 22
Kerekou, Ahmed (Mathieu) 1
Lawrence, Robert H., Jr. 16
Nyanda, Siphiwe 21
Obasanjo, Olusegun 5, 22
Phelps, Shirelle 22
Powell, Colin 1
Pratt, Geronimo 18
Rawlings, Jerry 9
Reason, J. Paul 19
Stanford, John 20
Staupers, Mabel K. 7
Stokes, Louis 3
Touré, Amadou Toumani 18
Vieira, Joao 14
Von Lipsey, Roderick K. 11
Watkins, Perry 12
West, Togo, D., Jr. 16

Music

Adams, Oleta 18
Adams, Yolanda 17
Albright, Gerald 23
Anderson, Marian 2
Armstrong, Louis 2
Armstrong, Vanessa Bell 24
Ashford, Nickolas 21
Austin, Patti 24
Avant, Clarence 19
Ayers, Roy 16
Badu, Erykah 22
Baker, Anita 21
Baker, Josephine 3
Baker, LaVern 26
Basie, Count 23
Bassey, Shirley 25
Bechet, Sidney 18
Belafonte, Harry 4
Belle, Regina 1
Beverly, Frankie 25
Blige, Mary J. 20
Bonga, Kuenda 13
Brandy 14
Braxton, Toni 15
Brooks, Avery 9
Brown, Charles 23
Brown, Foxy 25
Bumbry, Grace 5
Busby, Jheryl 3
Butler, Jerry 26
Caesar, Shirley 19
Calloway, Cab 1
Campbell, Tisha 8
Carroll, Diahann 9
Carter, Betty 19
Carter, Regina 23
Chapman, Tracy 26
Charlemagne, Manno 11
Charles, Ray 16
Cheatham, Doc 17
Chuck D 9
Clark-Sheard, Karen 22
Cleveland, James 19
Clinton, George 9
Cole, Nat King 17
Cole, Natalie Maria 17
Collins, Albert 12
Coltrane, John 19
Combs, Sean "Puffy" 17
Cooke, Sam 17
Count Basie 23
Crawford, Randy 19
Crothers, Scatman 19
Crouch, Stanley 11
Crowder, Henry 16
Davis, Anthony 11
Davis, Miles 4
Davis, Sammy, Jr. 18
de Passe, Suzanne 25
Dixon, Willie 4
Donegan, Dorothy 19
Dorsey, Thomas 15
Downing, Will 19
Dr. Dre 10
Dre, Dr. 14
Duke, George 21
Dupri, Jermaine 13
Edmonds, Kenneth "Babyface" 10
Edmonds, Tracey 16
Ellington, Duke 5
Eubanks, Kevin 15
Europe, James Reese 10
Evans, Faith 22
Evora, Cesaria 12
Fats Domino 20
Fela 1
Fitzgerald, Ella 8, 18
Flack, Roberta 19
Foxx, Jamie 15
Franklin, Aretha 11
Franklin, Kirk 15
Gaye, Marvin 2
Gibson, Althea 8
Gillespie, Dizzy 1
Gordon, Dexter 25
Gordy, Berry, Jr. 1
Graves, Denyce 19
Gray, F. Gary 14
Green, Al 13
Hailey, JoJo 22
Hailey, K-Ci 22
Hammer, M. C. 20
Hammond, Fred 23
Hampton, Lionel 17
Hancock, Herbie 20
Handy, W. C. 8
Harrell, Andre 9
Hathaway, Donny 18
Hawkins, Coleman 9
Hawkins, Erskine 14
Hawkins, Tramaine 16
Hayes, Isaac 20
Hayes, Roland 4
Hendricks, Barbara 3
Hendrix, Jimi 10
Hill, Lauryn 20
Hinderas, Natalie 5
Holiday, Billie 1
Horne, Lena 5
House, Son 8
Houston, Cissy 20
Houston, Whitney 7
Howlin' Wolf 9
Humphrey, Bobbi 20
Hyman, Phyllis 19
Ice Cube 8
Ice-T 6
Isley, Ronald 25
Jackson, Fred James 25
Jackson, George 19
Jackson, Isaiah 3
Jackson, Janet 6
Jackson, Mahalia 5
Jackson, Michael 19
Jackson, Millie 25
Jackson, Milt 26
James, Etta 13
James, Rick 17
Jarreau, Al 21
Jean-Baptiste, Marianne 17
Jean, Wyclef 20
Jenkins, Ella 15
Jimmy Jam 13

Johnson, Beverly **2**
Johnson, James Weldon **5**
Johnson, Robert **2**
Jones, Bobby **20**
Jones, Elvin **14**
Jones, Quincy **8**
Joplin, Scott **6**
Jordan, Montell **23**
Jordan, Ronny **26**
Joyner, Matilda Sissieretta **15**
Joyner, Tom **19**
Kelly, R. **18**
Kendricks, Eddie **22**
Khan, Chaka **12**
King, B. B. **7**
King, Coretta Scott **3**
Kitt, Eartha **16**
Knight, Gladys **16**
Knight, Suge **11**
Kravitz, Lenny **10**
L.L. Cool J **16**
LaBelle, Patti **13**
León, Tania **13**
Lester, Julius **9**
Levert, Gerald **22**
Lewis, Terry **13**
Lincoln, Abbey **3**
Little Richard **15**
Love, Darlene **23**
Lover, Ed **10**
Lymon, Frankie **22**
Madhubuti, Haki R. **7**
Makeba, Miriam **2**
Marley, Bob **5**
Marrow, Queen Esther **24**
Marsalis, Wynton **16**
Mase **24**
Masekela, Hugh **1**
Massenburg, Kedar **23**
Master P **21**
Mathis, Johnny **20**
Maxwell **20**
Mayfield, Curtis **2**
Maynor, Dorothy **19**
McClurkin, Donnie **25**
McDaniel, Hattie **5**
McKee, Lonette **12**
McKnight, Brian **18**
Mingus, Charles **15**
Monica **21**
Monk, Thelonious **1**
Moore, Chante **26**
Moore, Melba **21**
Moses, Gilbert **12**
Moten, Etta **18**
Murphy, Eddie **4, 20**
Muse, Clarence Edouard **21**
N'Dour, Youssou **1**
Nascimento, Milton **2**
Ndegéocello, Me'Shell **15**
Neville, Aaron **21**
Nicholas, Fayard **20**
Nicholas, Harold **20**
Norman, Jessye **5**
Notorious B.I.G. **20**
O'Neal, Shaquille **8**
Ongala, Remmy **9**
Osborne, Jeffrey **26**
Parker, Charlie **20**
Parks, Gordon **1**
Pendergrass, Teddy **22**
Peoples, Dottie **22**
Perry, Ruth **19**
Powell, Maxine **8**
Powell,Bud **24**
Price, Kelly **23**
Price, Leontyne **1**
Pride, Charley **26**
Prince **18**
Pritchard, Robert Starling **21**
Queen Latifah **1, 16**
Ralph, Sheryl Lee **18**
Razaf, Andy **19**
Reagon, Bernice Johnson **7**
Reese, Della **6, 20**
Rhone, Sylvia **2**
Roach, Max **21**
Roberts, Marcus **19**
Robeson, Paul **2**
Robinson, Smokey **3**
Ross, Diana **8**
Rupaul **17**
Rushen, Patrice **12**
Sade **15**
Sangare, Oumou **18**
Seal **14**
Shakur, Tupac **14**
Silver, Horace **26**
Simmons, Russell **1**
Simone, Nina **15**
Simpson, Valerie **21**
Sister Souljah **11**
Smith, Bessie **3**
Smith, Will **8, 18**
Summer, Donna **25**
Sweat, Keith **19**
Sykes, Roosevelt **20**
Tamia **24**
Taylor, Billy **23**
Thomas, Rufus **20**
Tosh, Peter **9**
Turnbull, Walter **13**
Turner, Tina **6**
Uggams, Leslie **23**
Usher **23**
Vandross, Luther **13**
Vaughan, Sarah **13**
Vereen, Ben **4**
Walker, Albertina **10**
Walker, Cedric "Ricky" **19**
Wallace, Sippie **1**
Warwick, Dionne **18**
Washington, Dinah **22**
Washington, Grover, Jr. **17**
Waters, Benny **26**
Waters, Ethel **7**
Watson, Johnny "Guitar" **18**
White, Barry **13**
Williams, Bert **18**
Williams, Joe **5, 25**
Williams, Mary Lou **15**
Williams, Vanessa L. **4, 17**
Wilson, Cassandra **16**
Wilson, Nancy **10**
Wilson, Sunnie **7**
Winans, BeBe **14**
Winans, CeCe **14**
Winans, Marvin L. **17**
Winans, Vickie **24**
Wonder, Stevie **11**
Yoba, Malik **11**

Religion

Abernathy, Ralph David **1**
Adams, Yolanda **17**
Agyeman, Jaramogi Abebe **10**
Al-Amin, Jamil Abdullah **6**
Anthony, Wendell **25**
Arinze, Francis Cardinal **19**
Aristide, Jean-Bertrand **6**
Armstrong, Vanessa Bell **24**
Banks, William **11**
Bell, Ralph S. **5**
Ben-Israel, Ben Ami **11**
Boyd, T. B., III **6**
Butts, Calvin O., III **9**
Caesar, Shirley **19**
Cannon, Katie **10**
Chavis, Benjamin **6**
Cleaver, Emanuel **4**
Clements, George **2**
Cleveland, James **19**
Colemon, Johnnie **11**
Cone, James H. **3**
Cook, Suzan D. Johnson **22**
Divine, Father **7**
Dyson, Michael Eric **11**
Elmore, Ronn **21**
Farrakhan, Louis **2, 15**
Fauntroy, Walter E. **11**
Flake, Floyd H. **18**
Foreman, George **15**
Franklin, Kirk **15**
Franklin, Robert M. **13**
Gomes, Peter J. **15**
Gray, William H., III **3**
Green, Al **13**
Grier, Roosevelt **13**
Haile Selassie **7**
Harris, Barbara **12**
Hawkins, Tramaine **16**
Hayes, James C. **10**
Hooks, Benjamin L. **2**
Howard, M. William, Jr. **26**
Jackson, Jesse **1**
Jakes, Thomas "T.D." **17**
Jones, Bobby **20**
King, Barbara **22**
King, Bernice **4**
King, Martin Luther, Jr. **1**
Lester, Julius **9**
Little Richard **15**
Lowery, Joseph **2**
Lyons, Henry **12**
Mays, Benjamin E. **7**
McClurkin, Donnie **25**
Muhammad, Elijah **4**
Muhammad, Khallid Abdul **10**
Murray, Cecil **12**
Pierre, Andre **17**
Powell, Adam Clayton, Jr. **3**
Price, Frederick K.C. **21**
Reese, Della **6, 20**
Riley, Helen Caldwell Day **13**
Rugambwa, Laurean **20**
Shabazz, Betty **7, 26**
Sharpton, Al **21**
Somé, Malidoma Patrice **10**
Stallings, George A., Jr. **6**
Sullivan, Leon H. **3**
Thurman, Howard **3**
Turner, Henry McNeal **5**
Tutu, Desmond **6**
Vanzant, Iyanla **17**
Waddles, Charleszetta (Mother) **10**
Waters, Ethel **7**
West, Cornel **5**
White, Reggie **6**
Williams, Hosea Lorenzo **15**
Winans, BeBe **14**
Winans, CeCe **14**
Winans, Marvin L. **17**
X, Malcolm **1**
Youngblood, Johnny Ray **8**

Science and technology

Adkins, Rutherford H. **21**
Alexander, Archie Alphonso **14**
Allen, Ethel D. **13**
Auguste, Rose-Anne **13**
Banda, Hastings Kamuzu **6**
Benjamin, Regina **20**
Black, Keith Lanier **18**
Bluford, Guy **2**
Bluitt, Juliann S. **14**
Bolden, Charles F., Jr. **7**
Bullard, Eugene **12**
Callender, Clive O. **3**
Carson, Benjamin **1**
Carver, George Washington **4**
CasSelle, Malcolm **11**
Chinn, May Edward **26**
Christian, Spencer **15**
Cobbs, Price M. **9**
Coleman, Bessie **9**
Comer, James P. **6**
Cooper, Edward S. **6**
Davis, Allison **12**
Delany, Bessie **12**
Dickens, Helen Octavia **14**
Diop, Cheikh Anta **4**
Drew, Charles Richard **7**
Dunham, Katherine **4**
Elders, Joycelyn **6**
Ellington, E. David **11**
Fisher, Rudolph **17**
Flipper, Henry O. **3**
Foster, Henry W., Jr. **26**
Freeman, Harold P. **23**
Fulani, Lenora **11**
Fuller, Solomon Carter, Jr. **15**
Gates, Sylvester James, Jr. **15**
Gayle, Helene D. **3**
Gibson, Kenneth Allen **6**
Gibson, William F. **6**
Gregory, Frederick D. **8**
Hall, Lloyd A. **8**
Hannah, Marc **10**
Henderson, Cornelius Langston **26**
Henson, Matthew **2**
Hinton, William Augustus **8**
Irving, Larry, Jr. **12**
Jackson, Shirley Ann **12**
Jawara, Sir Dawda Kairaba **11**
Jemison, Mae C. **1**
Jenifer, Franklyn G. **2**
Johnson, Eddie Bernice **8**
Julian, Percy Lavon **6**
Just, Ernest Everett **3**
Kountz, Samuel L. **10**
Latimer, Lewis H. **4**
Lawless, Theodore K. **8**
Lawrence, Robert H., Jr. **16**
Leffall, LaSalle, Jr. **3**
Lewis, Delano **7**
Logan, Onnie Lee **14**
Lyttle, Hulda Margaret **14**
Manley, Audrey Forbes **16**
Massey, Walter E. **5**
Mboup, Souleymane **10**
McCoy, Elijah **8**
McNair, Ronald **3**
Morgan, Garrett **1**
O'Leary, Hazel **6**
Person, Waverly **9**
Pitt, David Thomas **10**
Poussaint, Alvin F. **5**
Prothrow-Stith, Deborah **10**
Quarterman, Lloyd Albert **4**
Riley, Helen Caldwell Day **13**
Robeson, Eslanda Goode **13**
Robinson, Rachel **16**
Roker, Al **12**
Samara, Noah **15**
Satcher, David **7**
Shabazz, Betty **7, 26**
Sinkford, Jeanne C. **13**
Staples, Brent **8**
Staupers, Mabel K. **7**
Sullivan, Louis **8**
Terrell, Dorothy A. **24**
Thomas, Vivien **9**
Tyson, Neil de Grasse **15**
Washington, Patrice Clarke **12**
Watkins, Levi, Jr. **9**
Welsing, Frances Cress **5**
Williams, Daniel Hale **2**
Williams, O. S. **13**
Witt, Edwin T. **26**
Woods, Granville T. **5**
Wright, Louis Tompkins **4**

Social issues

Aaron, Hank **5**
Abbott, Diane **9**
Abdul-Jabbar, Kareem **8**
Abernathy, Ralph David **1**
Abu-Jamal, Mumia **15**
Achebe, Chinua **6**
Adams, Sheila J. **25**
Agyeman, Jaramogi Abebe **10**
Al-Amin, Jamil Abdullah **6**
Alexander, Clifford **26**
Alexander, Sadie Tanner Mossell **22**
Ali, Muhammad, **2, 16**
Allen, Ethel D. **13**
Andrews, Benny **22**
Angelou, Maya **1**
Annan, Kofi Atta **15**
Anthony, Wendell **25**
Archer, Dennis **7**
Aristide, Jean-Bertrand **6**
Asante, Molefi Kete **3**
Ashe, Arthur **1, 18**
Auguste, Rose-Anne **13**
Azikiwe, Nnamdi **13**
Baisden, Michael **25**
Baker, Ella **5**
Baker, Gwendolyn Calvert **9**
Baker, Houston A., Jr. **6**
Baker, Josephine **3**
Baker, Thurbert **22**
Baldwin, James **1**
Baraka, Amiri **1**
Bates, Daisy **13**
Beals, Melba Patillo **15**
Belafonte, Harry **4**
Bell, Derrick **6**
Bell, Ralph S. **5**
Bennett, Lerone, Jr. **5**
Berry, Bertice **8**
Berry, Mary Frances **7**
Bethune, Mary McLeod **4**
Biko, Steven **4**
Blackwell, Unita **17**
Bolin, Jane **22**
Bond, Julian **2**
Bonga, Kuenda **13**
Bosley, Freeman, Jr. **7**
Boyd, John W., Jr. **20**
Boyd, T. B., III **6**
Boykin, Keith **14**
Braun, Carol Moseley **4**
Brooke, Edward **8**
Brown, Elaine **8**
Brown, Jesse **6**
Brown, Jim **11**
Brown, Lee P. **1**
Brown, Les **5**
Brown, Tony **3**
Brown, Zora Kramer **12**
Bryant, Wayne R. **6**
Bullock, Steve **22**
Bunche, Ralph J. **5**
Burroughs, Margaret Taylor **9**
Butler, Paul D. **17**
Butts, Calvin O., III **9**
Campbell, Bebe Moore **6, 24**
Canada, Geoffrey **23**
Carmichael, Stokely **5, 26**
Carter, Mandy **11**
Carter, Rubin **26**
Carter, Stephen L. **4**
Cary, Lorene **3**
Cayton, Horace **26**
Chavis, Benjamin **6**
Chideya, Farai **14**
Childress, Alice **15**
Chissano, Joaquim **7**
Christophe, Henri **9**
Chuck D **9**
Clark, Joe **1**
Clark, Kenneth B. **5**
Clark, Septima **7**
Clay, William Lacy **8**
Claytor, Helen **14**
Cleaver, Eldridge **5**
Clements, George **2**
Cobbs, Price M. **9**
Cole, Johnnetta B. **5**
Collins, Barbara-Rose **7**
Comer, James P. **6**
Cone, James H. **3**
Connerly, Ward **14**
Conté, Lansana **7**
Conyers, John, Jr. **4**
Cook, Toni **23**
Cooper, Anna Julia **20**
Cooper, Edward S. **6**
Cosby, Bill **7, 26**
Cosby, Camille **14**
Cose, Ellis **5**
Crockett, George, Jr. **10**
Crouch, Stanley **11**
Cummings, Elijah E. **24**
Cunningham, Evelyn **23**
da Silva, Benedita **5**
Dash, Julie **4**
Davis, Angela **5**
Davis, Danny K. **24**
Davis, Ossie **5**
Dee, Ruby **8**
Dellums, Ronald **2**
Dickerson, Ernest **6**
Diop, Cheikh Anta **4**
Divine, Father **7**
Dixon, Margaret **14**
Dodson, Howard, Jr. **7**
Dove, Rita **6**
Drew, Charles Richard **7**
Du Bois, W. E. B. **3**
DuBois, Shirley Graham **21**
Dunham, Katherine **4**
Early, Gerald **15**
Edelin, Ramona Hoage **19**
Edelman, Marian Wright **5**
Edley, Christopher **2**
Edwards, Harry **2**
Elder, Larry **25**
Elder, Lee **6**

Elders, Joycelyn **6**
Ellison, Ralph **7**
Esposito, Giancarlo **9**
Espy, Mike **6**
Europe, James Reese **10**
Evers, Medgar **3**
Evers, Myrlie **8**
Farmer, James **2**
Farrakhan, Louis **15**
Fauntroy, Walter E. **11**
Fauset, Jessie **7**
Fela **1**
Fields, C. Virginia **25**
Foreman, George **15**
Forman, James **7**
Fortune, T. Thomas **6**
Franklin, Hardy R. **9**
Franklin, John Hope **5**
Franklin, Robert M. **13**
Frazier, E. Franklin **10**
Fulani, Lenora **11**
Fuller, Charles **8**
Gaines, Ernest J. **7**
Garvey, Marcus **1**
Gates, Henry Louis, Jr. **3**
Gayle, Helene D. **3**
Gibson, Kenneth Allen **6**
Gibson, William F. **6**
Gist, Carole **1**
Goldberg, Whoopi **4**
Golden, Marita **19**
Gomez-Preston, Cheryl **9**
Gossett, Louis, Jr. **7**
Graham, Lawrence Otis **12**
Gregory, Dick **1**
Grier, Roosevelt **13**
Griffith, Mark Winston **8**
Grimké, Archibald H. **9**
Guinier, Lani **7**
Guy, Rosa **5**
Guy-Sheftall, Beverly **13**
Hale, Lorraine **8**
Haley, Alex **4**
Hall, Elliott S. **24**
Hamblin, Ken **10**
Hamer, Fannie Lou **6**
Hampton, Fred **18**
Hampton, Henry **6**
Hani, Chris **6**
Hansberry, Lorraine **6**
Hansberry, William Leo **11**
Harper, Frances Ellen Watkins **11**
Harrington, Oliver W. **9**
Harris, Alice **7**
Harris, Leslie **6**
Harris, Marcelite Jordan **16**
Harris, Patricia Roberts **2**
Hastings, Alcee L. **16**
Hawkins, Steven **14**
Haynes, George Edmund **8**
Hedgeman, Anna Arnold **22**
Height, Dorothy I. **2, 23**
Henderson, Wade J. **14**
Henry, Aaron **19**
Henry, Lenny **9**
Hernandez, Aileen Clarke **13**
Hill, Anita **5**
Hill, Jessie, Jr. **13**
Hill, Lauryn **20**
Hill, Oliver W. **24**
Hilliard, David **7**
Holland, Endesha Ida Mae **3**
Hooks, Benjamin L. **2**
hooks, bell **5**
Horne, Lena **5**
Houston, Charles Hamilton **4**
Howard, M. William, Jr. **26**
Hughes, Albert **7**
Hughes, Allen **7**
Hughes, Langston **4**
Hunter-Gault, Charlayne **6**
Hutchinson, Earl Ofari **24**
Hutson, Jean Blackwell **16**
Ice-T **6**
Iceberg Slim **11**
Iman **4**
Ingram, Rex **5**
Innis, Roy **5**
Jackson, Fred James **25**
Jackson, George **14**
Jackson, Janet **6**
Jackson, Jesse **1**
Jackson, Mahalia **5**
Jacob, John E. **2**
Jagan, Cheddi **16**
James, Daniel, Jr. **16**
Jean, Wyclef **20**
Jeffries, Leonard **8**
Johnson, Charles S. **12**
Johnson, Earvin "Magic" **3**
Johnson, James Weldon **5**
Jones, Elaine R. **7**
Jordan, Barbara **4**
Jordan, June **7**
Jordan, Vernon E. **3**
Josey, E. J. **10**
Joyner, Marjorie Stewart **26**
Joyner, Tom **19**
Julian, Percy Lavon **6**
Kaunda, Kenneth **2**
Keith, Damon J. **16**
Kennedy, Florynce **12**
Khanga, Yelena **6**
King, B. B. **7**
King, Bernice **4**
King, Coretta Scott **3**
King, Dexter **10**
King, Martin Luther, III **20**
King, Martin Luther, Jr. **1**
King, Yolanda **6**
Kitt, Eartha **16**
Lampkin, Daisy **19**
Lane, Charles **3**
Lane, Vincent **5**
Lee, Canada **8**
Lee, Spike **5, 19**
Leland, Mickey **2**
Lester, Julius **9**
Lewis, Delano **7**
Lewis, John **2**
Lewis, Thomas **19**
Little, Robert L. **2**
Lorde, Audre **6**
Louis, Errol T. **8**
Lowery, Joseph **2**
Lucas, John **7**
Madhubuti, Haki R. **7**
Madison, Joseph E. **17**
Makeba, Miriam **2**
Mandela, Nelson **1, 14**
Mandela, Winnie **2**
Manley, Audrey Forbes **16**
Marable, Manning **10**
Marley, Bob **5**
Marshall, Paule **7**
Marshall, Thurgood **1**
Martin, Louis E. **16**
Masekela, Barbara **18**
Masekela, Hugh **1**
Mathabane, Mark **5**
Maynard, Robert C. **7**
Mays, Benjamin E. **7**
McCabe, Jewell Jackson **10**
McCarty, Oseola **16**
McDaniel, Hattie **5**
McDougall, Gay J. **11**
McKay, Claude **6**
McKissick, Floyd B. **3**
McQueen, Butterfly **6**
Meek, Carrie **6**
Meredith, James H. **11**
Mfume, Kweisi **6**
Micheaux, Oscar **7**
Millender-McDonald, Juanita **21**
Mkapa, Benjamin **16**
Mongella, Gertrude **11**
Morial, Ernest "Dutch" **26**
Morrison, Toni **2**
Moses, Robert Parris **11**
Mosley, Walter **5, 25**
Motley, Constance Baker **10**
Moutoussamy-Ashe, Jeanne **7**
Mowry, Jess **7**
Muhammad, Elijah **4**
Muhammad, Khallid Abdul **10**
Ndadaye, Melchior **7**
Nelson, Jill **6**
Newton, Huey **2**
Nkrumah, Kwame **3**
Norman, Pat **10**
Norton, Eleanor Holmes **7**
Nzo, Alfred **15**
O'Leary, Hazel **6**
Obasanjo, Olusegun **5**
Oglesby, Zena **12**
Owens, Major **6**
Page, Alan **7**
Page, Clarence **4**
Paige, Satchel **7**
Parker, Pat **19**
Parks, Rosa **1**
Patterson, Frederick Douglass **12**
Patterson, Louise **25**
Patterson, Orlando **4**
Patterson, P. J. **6, 20**
Perkins, Edward **5**
Pitt, David Thomas **10**
Pleasant, Mary Ellen **9**
Poussaint, Alvin F. **5**
Powell, Adam Clayton, Jr. **3**
Pratt, Geronimo **18**
Price, Hugh B. **9**
Primus, Pearl **6**
Pritchard, Robert Starling **21**
Prothrow-Stith, Deborah **10**
Quarles, Benjamin Arthur **18**
Ramaphosa, Cyril **3**
Ramsey, Charles H. **21**
Rand, A. Barry **6**
Randolph, A. Philip **3**
Rangel, Charles **3**
Rawlings, Nana Konadu Agyeman **13**
Reagon, Bernice Johnson **7**
Reed, Ishmael **8**
Rice, Norm **8**
Riggs, Marlon **5**
Riley, Helen Caldwell Day **13**
Ringgold, Faith **4**
Robeson, Eslanda Goode **13**
Robeson, Paul **2**
Robinson, Jackie **6**
Robinson, Rachel **16**
Robinson, Randall **7**
Robinson, Sharon **22**
Robinson, Spottswood **22**

Rowan, Carl T. **1**
Rustin, Bayard **4**
Sampson, Edith S. **4**
Sané, Pierre Gabriel **21**
Sapphire **14**
Satcher, David **7**
Savimbi, Jonas **2**
Sawyer, Amos **2**
Sayles Belton, Sharon **9, 16**
Schomburg, Arthur Alfonso **9**
Seale, Bobby **3**
Senghor, Léopold Sédar **12**
Shabazz, Attallah **6**
Shabazz, Betty **7, 26**
Shakur, Assata **6**
Sifford, Charlie **4**
Simone, Nina **15**
Simpson, Carole **6**
Sister Souljah **11**
Sisulu, Sheila Violet Makate **24**
Sleet, Moneta, Jr. **5**
Smith, Anna Deavere **6**
Soyinka, Wole **4**
Stallings, George A., Jr. **6**
Staupers, Mabel K. **7**
Steele, Claude Mason **13**
Steele, Shelby **13**
Stewart, Alison **13**
Stewart, Maria W. Miller **19**
Stone, Chuck **9**
Sullivan, Leon H. **3**
Tate, Eleanora E. **20**
Taulbert, Clifton Lemoure **19**
Taylor, Mildred D. **26**
Taylor, Susan L. **10**
Terrell, Mary Church **9**
Thomas, Franklin A. **5**
Thomas, Isiah **7, 26**
Thompson, Bennie G. **26**
Thurman, Howard **3**
Thurman, Wallace **16**
Till, Emmett **7**
Toomer, Jean **6**
Tosh, Peter **9**
Tribble, Israel, Jr. **8**
Trotter, Monroe **9**
Tsvangirai, Morgan **26**
Tubman, Harriet **9**
Tucker, C. DeLores **12**
Tucker, Cynthia **15**
Tucker, Rosina **14**
Tutu, Desmond **6**
Tyree, Omar Rashad **21**
Underwood, Blair **7**
Van Peebles, Melvin **7**
Vanzant, Iyanla **17**
Vincent, Marjorie Judith **2**
Waddles, Charleszetta (Mother) **10**
Walcott, Derek **5**
Walker, A'lelia **14**
Walker, Alice **1**
Walker, Cedric "Ricky" **19**
Walker, Madame C. J. **7**
Wallace, Michele Faith **13**
Wallace, Phyllis A. **9**
Washington, Booker T. **4**
Washington, Fredi **10**
Washington, Harold **6**
Waters, Maxine **3**
Wattleton, Faye **9**
Wells-Barnett, Ida B. **8**
Wells, James Lesesne **10**
Welsing, Frances Cress **5**
West, Cornel **5**
White, Michael R. **5**
White, Reggie **6**
White, Walter F. **4**
Wideman, John Edgar **5**
Wilkins, Roger **2**
Wilkins, Roy **4**
Williams, Evelyn **10**
Williams, George Washington **18**
Williams, Hosea Lorenzo **15**
Williams, Maggie **7**
Williams, Montel **4**
Williams, Patricia J. **11**
Williams, Robert F. **11**
Williams, Walter E. **4**
Williams, Willie L. **4**
Wilson, August **7**
Wilson, Phill **9**
Wilson, Sunnie **7**
Wilson, William Julius **22**
Winfield, Paul **2**
Winfrey, Oprah **2, 15**
Wolfe, George C. **6**
Woodson, Robert L. **10**
Worrill, Conrad **12**
Wright, Louis Tompkins **4**
Wright, Richard **5**
X, Malcolm **1**
Yoba, Malik **11**
Young, Andrew **3**
Young, Jean Childs **14**
Young, Whitney M., Jr. **4**
Youngblood, Johnny Ray **8**

Sports

Aaron, Hank **5**
Abdul-Jabbar, Kareem **8**
Ali, Muhammad **2, 16**
Allen, Marcus **20**
Amos, John **8**
Anderson, Elmer **25**
Anderson, Jamal **22**
Ashe, Arthur **1, 18**
Ashford, Emmett **22**
Ashley, Maurice **15**
Baker, Dusty **8**
Barkley, Charles **5**
Barnes, Ernie **16**
Barney, Lem **26**
Baylor, Don **6**
Belle, Albert **10**
Bickerstaff, Bernie **21**
Bing, Dave **3**
Blanks, Billy **22**
Bol, Manute **1**
Bonaly, Surya **7**
Bonds, Barry **6**
Bowe, Riddick **6**
Brandon, Terrell **16**
Brock, Lou **18**
Brown, James **22**
Brown, Jim **11**
Bruce, Isaac **26**
Bryant, Kobe **15**
Butler, Leroy, III **17**
Campanella, Roy **25**
Carew, Rod **20**
Carnegie, Herbert **25**
Carter, Anson **24**
Carter, Cris **21**
Carter, Rubin **26**
Carter, Vince **26**
Chamberlain, Wilt **18**
Christie, Linford **8**
Clendenon, Donn **26**
Coachman, Alice **18**
Coleman, Leonard S., Jr. **12**
Cooper, Cynthia **17**
Cottrell, Comer **11**
Cunningham, Randall **23**
Davis, Piper **19**
Davis, Terrell **20**
Dawes, Dominique **11**
Devers, Gail **7**
Doby, Lawrence Eugene, Sr. **16**
Drew, Charles Richard **7**
Drexler, Clyde **4**
Dumars, Joe **16**
Duncan, Tim **20**
Dungy, Tony **17**
Edwards, Harry **2**
Edwards, Teresa **14**
Elder, Lee **6**
Ellerbe, Brian **22**
Elliott, Sean **26**
Erving, Julius **18**
Ewing, Patrick A. **17**
Farr, Mel Sr. **24**
Fielder, Cecil **2**
Flood, Curt **10**
Foreman, George **1, 15**
Frazier, Joe **19**
Freeman, Marianna **23**
Fuhr, Grant **1**
Gaither, Alonzo Smith (Jake) **14**
Garnett, Kevin **14**
Garrison, Zina **2**
Gentry, Alvin **23**
Gibson, Althea **8**
Gibson, Josh **22**
Gilliam, Frank **23**
Gooden, Dwight **20**
Goss, Tom **23**
Gourdine, Simon **11**
Green, Dennis **5**
Greene, Joe **10**
Gregg, Eric **16**
Grier, Roosevelt **1**
Griffey, Ken, Jr. **12**
Griffith, Yolanda **25**
Gumbel, Bryant **14**
Gumbel, Greg **8**
Gwynn, Tony **18**
Hardaway, Anfernee (Penny) **13**
Haskins, Clem **23**
Heard, Gar **25**
Hickman, Fred **11**
Hill, Calvin **19**
Hill, Grant **13**
Holdsclaw, Chamique **24**
Holmes, Larry **20**
Holyfield, Evander **6**
Howard, Desmond **16**
Howard, Juwan **15**
Hunter, Billy **22**
Iverson, Allen **24**
Jackson, Mannie **14**
Jackson, Reggie **15**
Johnson, Ben **1**
Johnson, Earvin "Magic" **3**
Johnson, Jack **8**
Johnson, Michael **13**
Jones, Cobi N'Gai **18**
Jones, Marion **21**
Jones, Roy Jr. **22**
Jordan, Michael **6, 21**
Joyner-Kersee, Jackie **5**
Justice, David **18**
Kimbro, Henry A. **25**
King, Don **14**
Lankford, Ray **23**
Larkin, Barry **24**

Lassiter, Roy **24**
Lee, Canada **8**
Leonard, Sugar Ray **15**
Leslie, Lisa **16**
Lewis, Carl **4**
Lloyd, Earl **26**
Lofton, Kenny **12**
Lott, Ronnie **9**
Louis, Joe **5**
Love, Nat **9**
Lucas, John **7**
Malone, Karl A. **18**
Manigault, Earl "The Goat" **15**
Master P **21**
Mays, Willie **3**
McBride, Bryant **18**
McCray, Nikki **18**
McGriff, Fred **24**
McKegney, Tony **3**
McNair, Steve **22**
McNeil, Lori **1**
Metcalfe, Ralph **26**
Milla, Roger **2**
Miller, Cheryl **10**
Moon, Warren **8**
Moorer, Michael **19**
Morgan, Joe Leonard **9**
Moses, Edwin **8**
Moss, Randy **23**
Motley, Marion **26**
Mourning, Alonzo **17**
Murray, Eddie **12**
Murray, Lenda **10**
Mutola, Maria **12**
Mutombo, Dikembe **7**
Nakhid, David **25**
Newcombe, Don **24**
Newsome, Ozzie **26**
Noah, Yannick **4**
O'Neal, Shaquille **8**
O'Neil, Buck **19**
O'Ree, Willie **5**
Olajuwon, Hakeem **2**
Owens, Jesse **2**
Pace, Orlando **21**
Page, Alan **7**
Paige, Satchel **7**
Patterson, Floyd **19**
Payton, Walter **11, 25**
Peck, Carolyn **23**
Peete, Calvin **11**
Pelé **7**
Perrot, Kim **23**
Pickett, Bill **11**
Pippen, Scottie **15**
Powell, Mike **7**
Pride, Charley **26**
Puckett, Kirby **4**
Quirot, Ana **13**
Rashad, Ahmad **18**
Rhodes, Ray **14**
Ribbs, Willy T. **2**
Rice, Jerry **5**
Richardson, Nolan **9**
Richmond, Mitch **19**
Rivers, Glenn "Doc" **25**
Robertson, Oscar **26**
Robinson, David **24**
Robinson, Eddie G. **10**
Robinson, Frank **9**
Robinson, Jackie **6**
Robinson, Sugar Ray **18**
Rodman, Dennis **12**
Rudolph, Wilma **4**
Russell, Bill **8**
Sampson, Charles **13**
Sanders, Barry **1**
Sanders, Deion **4**
Scott, Wendell Oliver, Sr. **19**
Sheffield, Gary **16**
Shell, Art **1**
Sifford, Charlie **4**
Silas, Paul **24**
Simpson, O. J. **15**
Singletary, Mike **4**
Smith, Emmitt **7**
Smith, Tubby **18**
Sosa, Sammy **21**
Sprewell, Latrell **23**
Steward, Emanuel **18**
Stewart, Kordell **21**
Stone, Toni **15**
Strawberry, Darryl **22**
Stringer, C. Vivian **13**
Swoopes, Sheryl **12**
Taylor, Lawrence **25**
Thomas, Debi **26**
Thomas, Derrick **25**
Thomas, Frank **12**
Thomas, Isiah **7, 26**
Thompson, Tina **25**
Thugwane, Josia **21**
Unseld, Wes **23**
Upshaw, Gene **18**
Walker, Herschel **1**
Washington, MaliVai **8**
Watson, Bob **25**
Watts, J. C., Jr. **14**
Weathers, Carl **10**
Webber, Chris **15**
Westbrook, Peter **20**
Whitaker, Pernell **10**
White, Bill **1**
White, Jesse **22**
White, Reggie **6**
Whitfield, Fred **23**
Wilkens, Lenny **11**
Williams, Doug **22**
Williams, Serena **20**
Williams, Venus Ebone **17**
Wilson, Sunnie **7**
Winfield, Dave **5**
Woods, Tiger **14**

Television

Allen, Byron **3**
Allen, Debbie **13**
Allen, Marcus **20**
Amos, John **8**
Arkadie, Kevin **17**
Banks, William **11**
Barden, Don H. **9**
Bassett, Angela **6, 23**
Beach, Michael **26**
Beaton, Norman **14**
Belafonte, Harry **4**
Bellamy, Bill **12**
Berry, Bertice **8**
Berry, Halle **4, 19**
Blake, Asha **26**
Boston, Kelvin E. **25**
Bowser, Yvette Lee **17**
Bradley, Ed **2**
Brandy **14**
Braugher, Andre **13**
Brooks, Avery **9**
Brown, James **22**
Brown, Les **5**
Brown, Tony **3**
Burnett, Charles **16**
Burton, LeVar **8**
Byrd, Robert **11**
Campbell, Tisha **8**
Carroll, Diahann **9**
Carson, Lisa Nicole **21**
Cheadle, Don **19**
Chideya, Farai **14**
Christian, Spencer **15**
Clash, Kevin **14**
Clayton, Xernona **3**
Cole, Nat King **17**
Cole, Natalie Maria **17**
Cornelius, Don **4**
Cosby, Bill **7, 26**
Crothers, Scatman **19**
Curry, Mark **17**
Curtis-Hall, Vondie **17**
Davidson, Tommy **21**
Davis, Ossie **5**
de Passe, Suzanne **25**
Dee, Ruby **8**
Devine, Loretta **24**
Dickerson, Ernest **6**
Diggs, Taye **25**
Dr. Dre **10**
Duke, Bill **3**
Dutton, Charles S. **4, 22**
Elder, Larry **25**
Erving, Julius **18**
Esposito, Giancarlo **9**
Eubanks, Kevin **15**
Evans, Harry **25**
Fishburne, Larry **4**
Foxx, Jamie **15**
Foxx, Redd **2**
Freeman, Al, Jr. **11**
Freeman, Morgan **2**
Gaines, Ernest J. **7**
Givens, Robin **4, 25**
Glover, Danny **3, 24**
Glover, Savion **14**
Goldberg, Whoopi **4**
Goode, Mal **13**
Gooding, Cuba, Jr. **16**
Gordon, Ed **10**
Gossett, Louis, Jr. **7**
Grier, Pam **9**
Guillaume, Robert **3**
Gumbel, Bryant **14**
Gumbel, Greg **8**
Gunn, Moses **10**
Guy, Jasmine **2**
Haley, Alex **4**
Hampton, Henry **6**
Hardison, Kadeem **22**
Harrell, Andre **9**
Harris, Robin **7**
Harvey, Steve **18**
Hayes, Isaac **20**
Hemsley, Sherman **19**
Henry, Lenny **9**
Hickman, Fred **11**
Hill, Lauryn **20**
Hinderas, Natalie **5**
Horne, Lena **5**
Hounsou, Djimon **19**
Hughley, D.L. **23**
Hunter-Gault, Charlayne **6**
Hyman, Earle **25**
Iman **4**
Ingram, Rex **5**
Jackson, George **19**
Jackson, Janet **6**
Jackson, Jesse **1**
Joe, Yolanda **21**

Johnson, Beverly **2**
Johnson, Robert L. **3**
Jones, Bobby **20**
Jones, James Earl **3**
Jones, Quincy **8**
Jones, Star **10**
King, Gayle **19**
King, Regina **22**
Kirby, George **14**
Kitt, Eartha **16**
Knight, Gladys **16**
Kotto, Yaphet **7**
L.L. Cool J **16**
La Salle, Eriq **12**
LaBelle, Patti **13**
Langhart, Janet **19**
Lawrence, Martin **6**
Lawson, Jennifer **1**
Lemmons, Kasi **20**
Lewis, Byron E. **13**
Lindo, Delroy **18**
Long, Nia **17**
Lover, Ed **10**
Mabrey, Vicki **26**
Mathis, Greg **26**
McDaniel, Hattie **5**
McEwen, Mark **5**
McKee, Lonette **12**
McQueen, Butterfly **6**
Miller, Cheryl **10**
Mitchell, Brian Stokes **21**
Mitchell, Russ **21**
Moore, Chante **26**
Moore, Melba **21**
Moore, Shemar **21**
Morgan, Joe Leonard **9**
Morton, Joe **18**
Moses, Gilbert **12**
Moss, Carlton **17**
Murphy, Eddie **4, 20**
Muse, Clarence Edouard **21**
Nichols, Nichelle **11**
Norman, Maidie **20**
Payne, Allen **13**
Peete, Holly Robinson **20**
Perkins, Tony **24**
Phifer, Mekhi **25**
Pinkett, Jada **10**
Pinkston, W. Randall **24**
Price, Frederick K.C. **21**
Price, Hugh B. **9**
Quarles, Norma **25**
Queen Latifah **1, 16**
Ralph, Sheryl Lee **18**
Randle, Theresa **16**
Rashad, Ahmad **18**
Rashad, Phylicia **21**
Reese, Della **6, 20**
Reuben, Gloria **15**
Ribeiro, Alfonso **17**
Roberts, Robin **16**
Robinson, Max **3**
Rochon, Lela **16**
Rock, Chris **3, 22**
Rodgers, Johnathan **6**
Roker, Al **12**
Rolle, Esther **13, 21**
Rollins, Howard E., Jr. **16**
Ross, Diana **8**
Rowan, Carl T. **1**
Rowell, Victoria **13**
Rupaul **17**
Russell, Bill **8**
Schultz, Michael A. **6**
Shaw, Bernard **2**
Simpson, Carole **6**
Simpson, O. J. **15**
Sinbad **1, 16**
Smiley, Tavis **20**
Smith, Barbara **11**
Smith, Roger Guenveur **12**
Smith, Will **8, 18**
St. Jacques, Raymond **8**
St. John, Kristoff **25**
Stewart, Alison **13**
Stokes, Carl B. **10**
Stone, Chuck **9**
Tate, Larenz **15**
Taylor, Meshach **4**
Taylor, Regina **9**
Thigpen, Lynne **17**
Townsend, Robert **4, 23**
Tucker, Chris **13, 23**
Tyson, Cicely **7**
Uggams, Leslie **23**
Underwood, Blair **7**
Usher **23**
Van Peebles, Mario **2**
Van Peebles, Melvin **7**
Vereen, Ben **4**
Warfield, Marsha **2**
Warner, Malcolm-Jamal **22**
Warwick, Dionne **18**
Washington, Denzel **1, 16**
Wattleton, Faye **9**
Watts, Rolonda **9**
Wayans, Damon **8**
Wayans, Keenen Ivory **18**
Weathers, Carl **10**
Whitfield, Lynn **1, 18**
Wilkins, Roger **2**
Williams, Billy Dee **8**
Williams, Clarence, III **26**
Williams, Montel **4**
Williams, Samm-Art **21**
Williams, Vanessa **4, 17**
Williamson, Mykelti **22**
Wilson, Flip **21**
Winfield, Paul **2**
Winfrey, Oprah **2, 15**
Yoba, Malik **11**

Theater

Ailey, Alvin **8**
Allen, Debbie **13**
Amos, John **8**
Andrews, Bert **13**
Angelou, Maya **1**
Arkadie, Kevin **17**
Armstrong, Vanessa Bell **24**
Baraka, Amiri **1**
Bassett, Angela **6, 23**
Beach, Michael **26**
Beaton, Norman **14**
Belafonte, Harry **4**
Borders, James **9**
Brooks, Avery **9**
Calloway, Cab **14**
Campbell, Naomi **1**
Campbell, Tisha **8**
Carroll, Diahann **9**
Cheadle, Don **19**
Childress, Alice **15**
Clarke, Hope **14**
Cleage, Pearl **17**
Curtis-Hall, Vondie **17**
Davis, Ossie **5**
Davis, Sammy, Jr. **18**
Dee, Ruby **8**
Devine, Loretta **24**
Diggs, Taye **25**
Duke, Bill **3**
Dunham, Katherine **4**
Dutton, Charles S. **4, 22**
Esposito, Giancarlo **9**
Europe, James Reese **10**
Fishburne, Larry **4**
Freeman, Al, Jr. **11**
Freeman, Morgan **2, 20**
Fuller, Charles **8**
Glover, Danny **1, 24**
Glover, Savion **14**
Goldberg, Whoopi **4**
Gordone, Charles **15**
Gossett, Louis, Jr. **7**
Graves, Denyce **19**
Grier, Pam **9**
Guillaume, Robert **3**
Gunn, Moses **10**
Guy, Jasmine **2**
Hansberry, Lorraine **6**
Harris, Robin **7**
Hemsley, Sherman **19**
Holland, Endesha Ida Mae **3**
Horne, Lena **5**
Hyman, Earle **25**
Hyman, Phyllis **19**
Ingram, Rex **5**
Jackson, Millie **25**
Jackson, Samuel L. **8, 19**
Jamison, Judith **7**
Jean-Baptiste, Marianne **17**
Jones, James Earl **3**
Joyner, Matilda Sissieretta **15**
King, Yolanda **6**
Kitt, Eartha **16**
Kotto, Yaphet **7**
La Salle, Eriq **12**
Lee, Canada **8**
Lemmons, Kasi **20**
Leon, Kenny **10**
Lincoln, Abbey **3**
Lindo, Delroy **18**
Mabley, Jackie "Moms" **15**
Marrow, Queen Esther **24**
McDaniel, Hattie **5**
McDonald, Audra **20**
McKee, Lonette **12**
McQueen, Butterfly **6**
Mills, Florence **22**
Mitchell, Brian Stokes **21**
Moore, Melba **21**
Moses, Gilbert **12**
Moss, Carlton **17**
Moten, Etta **18**
Muse, Clarence Edouard **21**
Nicholas, Fayard **20**
Nicholas, Harold **20**
Norman, Maidie **20**
Payne, Allen **13**
Powell, Maxine **8**
Primus, Pearl **6**
Ralph, Sheryl Lee **18**
Randle, Theresa **16**
Rashad, Phylicia **21**
Reese, Della **6, 20**
Rhames, Ving **14**
Richards, Lloyd **2**
Robeson, Paul **2**
Rolle, Esther **13, 21**
Rollins, Howard E., Jr. **16**
Rotimi, Ola **1**
Schultz, Michael A. **6**
Shabazz, Attallah **6**
Shange, Ntozake **8**

Smith, Anna Deavere **6**
Smith, Roger Guenveur **12**
Snipes, Wesley **3, 24**
Soyinka, Wole **4**
St. Jacques, Raymond **8**
Taylor, Meshach **4**
Taylor, Regina **9**
Thigpen, Lynne **17**
Thompson, Tazewell **13**
Thurman, Wallace **16**
Townsend, Robert **4, 23**
Tyson, Cicely **7**
Uggams, Leslie **23**
Underwood, Blair **7**
Van Peebles, Melvin **7**
Vance, Courtney B. **15**
Vereen, Ben **4**
Walcott, Derek **5**
Washington, Denzel **1, 16**
Washington, Fredi **10**
Waters, Ethel **7**
Whitaker, Forest **2**
Whitfield, Lynn **18**
Williams, Bert **18**
Williams, Billy Dee **8**
Williams, Clarence, III **26**
Williams, Samm-Art **21**
Williams, Vanessa L. **4, 17**
Williamson, Mykelti **22**
Wilson, August **7**
Winfield, Paul **2**
Wolfe, George C. **6**
Woodard, Alfre **9**

Writing
Abu-Jamal, Mumia **15**
Achebe, Chinua **6**
Al-Amin, Jamil Abdullah **6**
Alexander, Margaret Walker **22**
Andrews, Raymond **4**
Angelou, Maya **1, 15**
Ansa, Tina McElroy **14**
Aristide, Jean-Bertrand **6**
Arkadie, Kevin **17**
Asante, Molefi Kete **3**
Ashe, Arthur **1, 18**
Ashley-Ward, Amelia **23**
Azikiwe, Nnamdi **13**
Baisden, Michael **25**
Baker, Houston A., Jr. **6**
Baldwin, James **1**
Bambara, Toni Cade **10**
Baraka, Amiri **1**
Beals, Melba Patillo **15**
Bell, Derrick **6**
Bennett, Lerone, Jr. **5**
Berry, Mary Frances **7**
Bluitt, Juliann S. **14**
Bontemps, Arna **8**
Booker, Simeon **23**
Borders, James **9**
Boston, Lloyd **24**
Bradley, Ed **2**
Brimmer, Andrew F. **2**
Briscoe, Connie **15**
Brooks, Gwendolyn **1**
Brown, Elaine **8**
Brown, Les **5**
Brown, Marie Dutton **12**
Brown, Sterling **10**
Brown, Tony **3**
Brown, Wesley **23**
Bullins, Ed **25**
Bunche, Ralph J. **5**
Burroughs, Margaret Taylor **9**
Butler, Octavia **8**
Campbell, Bebe Moore **6, 24**
Carmichael, Stokely **5, 26**
Carter, Stephen L. **4**
Cary, Lorene **3**
Cayton, Horace **26**
Chamberlain, Wilt **18**
Chase-Riboud, Barbara **20**
Chideya, Farai **14**
Childress, Alice **15**
Clark, Kenneth B. **5**
Clark, Septima **7**
Cleage, Pearl **17**
Cleaver, Eldridge **5**
Clifton, Lucille **14**
Cobbs, Price M. **9**
Cohen, Anthony **15**
Cole, Johnnetta B. **5**
Comer, James P. **6**
Cone, James H. **3**
Cook, Suzan D. Johnson **22**
Cooper, Anna Julia **20**
Cooper, J. California **12**
Cosby, Bill **7, 26**
Cosby, Camille **14**
Cose, Ellis **5**
Crouch, Stanley **11**
Cullen, Countee **8**
Cunningham, Evelyn **23**
Curry, George E. **23**
Curtis, Christopher Paul **26**
Curtis-Hall, Vondie **17**
Danticat, Edwidge **15**
Davis, Allison **12**
Davis, Angela **5**
Davis, Miles **4**
Davis, Ossie **5**
Dawkins, Wayne **20**
de Passe, Suzanne **25**
Delany, Samuel R., Jr. **9**
Dickey, Eric Jerome **21**
Diop, Cheikh Anta **4**
Dodson, Howard, Jr. **7**
Dove, Rita **6**
Draper, Sharon M. **16**
Driskell, David C. **7**
Driver, David E. **11**
Du Bois, W. E. B. **3**
DuBois, Shirley Graham **21**
Dunbar, Paul Laurence **8**
Dunham, Katherine **4**
Dyson, Michael Eric **11**
Early, Gerald **15**
Edmonds, Terry **17**
Ellison, Ralph **7**
Elmore, Ronn **21**
Evans, Mari **26**
Farrakhan, Louis **15**
Fauset, Jessie **7**
Feelings, Tom **11**
Fisher, Rudolph **17**
Forman, James **7**
Fortune, T. Thomas **6**
Franklin, John Hope **5**
Franklin, Robert M. **13**
Frazier, E. Franklin **10**
French, Albert **18**
Fuller, Charles **8**
Gaines, Ernest J. **7**
Gates, Henry Louis, Jr. **3**
George, Nelson **12**
Gibson, Althea **8**
Giddings, Paula **11**
Giovanni, Nikki **9**
Goines, Donald **19**
Golden, Marita **19**
Graham, Lawrence Otis **12**
Greenfield, Eloise **9**
Griffith, Mark Winston **8**
Grimké, Archibald H. **9**
Guinier, Lani **7**
Guy, Rosa **5**
Guy-Sheftall, Beverly **13**
Haley, Alex **4**
Hamblin, Ken **10**
Hamilton, Virginia **10**
Hansberry, Lorraine **6**
Harkless, Necia Desiree **19**
Harper, Frances Ellen Watkins **11**
Harrington, Oliver W. **9**
Harris, Eddy L. **18**
Harris, Jay **19**
Harris, Leslie **6**
Harris, Monica **18**
Hayden, Robert **12**
Hemphill, Essex **10**
Henry, Lenny **9**
Henson, Matthew **2**
Hilliard, David **7**
Holland, Endesha Ida Mae **3**
hooks, bell **5**
Hrabowski, Freeman A. III **22**
Hudson, Cheryl **15**
Hudson, Wade **15**
Hughes, Langston **4**
Hunter-Gault, Charlayne **6**
Hurston, Zora Neale **3**
Iceberg Slim **11**
Jackson, Fred James **25**
Jackson, George **14**
Jackson, Sheneska **18**
Jenkins, Beverly **14**
Joe, Yolanda **21**
Johnson, Charles **1**
Johnson, Charles S. **12**
Johnson, James Weldon **5**
Johnson, John H. **3**
Jordan, June **7**
Josey, E. J. **10**
Just, Ernest Everett **3**
Karenga, Maulana **10**
Kennedy, Adrienne **11**
Kennedy, Florynce **12**
Khanga, Yelena **6**
Kimbro, Dennis **10**
Kincaid, Jamaica **4**
King, Coretta Scott **3**
King, Yolanda **6**
Kitt, Sandra **23**
Komunyakaa, Yusef **9**
Kotto, Yaphet **7**
Kunjufu, Jawanza **3**
Larsen, Nella **10**
Lawrence-Lightfoot, Sara **10**
Lawrence, Martin **6**
Lemmons, Kasi **20**
Lester, Julius **9**
Lewis, David Levering **9**
Lewis, Samella **25**
Little, Benilde **21**
Locke, Alain **10**
Lorde, Audre **6**
Louis, Errol T. **8**
Madhubuti, Haki R. **7**
Major, Clarence **9**
Makeba, Miriam **2**
Marshall, Paule **7**
Mathabane, Mark **5**
Maynard, Robert C. **7**
Mays, Benjamin E. **7**

McCall, Nathan **8**
McGruder, Robert **22**
McKay, Claude **6**
McMillan, Terry **4, 17**
Meredith, James H. **11**
Micheaux, Oscar **7**
Mitchell, Russ **21**
Morrison, Toni **2, 15**
Mosley, Walter **5, 25**
Moss, Carlton **17**
Moutoussamy-Ashe, Jeanne **7**
Mowry, Jess **7**
Myers, Walter Dean **8**
Naylor, Gloria **10**
Nelson, Jill **6**
Newton, Huey **2**
Nkrumah, Kwame **3**
Onwueme, Tess Osonye **23**
Owens, Major **6**
Page, Clarence **4**
Painter, Nell Irvin **24**
Parker, Pat **19**
Patterson, Orlando **4**
Petry, Ann **19**
Poussaint, Alvin F. **5**
Powell, Adam Clayton, Jr. **3**
Pryor, Richard **3**
Quarles, Benjamin Arthur **18**
Randall, Dudley **8**
Raspberry, William **2**
Reagon, Bernice Johnson **7**
Reddick, Lawrence Dunbar **20**
Redding, J. Saunders **26**
Redmond, Eugene **23**
Reed, Ishmael **8**
Riggs, Marlon **5**
Ringgold, Faith **4**
Robeson, Eslanda Goode **13**
Rodman, Dennis **12**
Rotimi, Ola **1**
Rowan, Carl T. **1**
Saint James, Synthia **12**
Sanchez, Sonia **17**
Sanders, Dori **8**
Sapphire **14**
Schomburg, Arthur Alfonso **9**
Seale, Bobby **3**
Sembène, Ousmane **13**
Senghor, Léopold Sédar **12**
Sengstacke, John **18**
Shabazz, Attallah **6**
Shakur, Assata **6**
Shange, Ntozake **8**
Shaw, Bernard **2**
Shipp, E. R. **15**
Simone, Nina **15**
Simpson, Carole **6**
Singleton, John **2**
Sister Souljah **11**
Smiley, Tavis **20**
Smith, Anna Deavere **6**
Smith, Barbara **11**
Smith, Mary Carter **26**
Somé, Malidoma Patrice **10**
Sowell, Thomas **2**
Soyinka, Wole **4**
St. John, Kristoff **25**
Staples, Brent **8**
Stewart, Alison **13**
Stone, Chuck **9**
Tate, Eleanora E. **20**
Taulbert, Clifton Lemoure **19**
Taylor, Kristin Clark **8**
Taylor, Mildred D. **26**
Taylor, Susan L. **10**
Thurman, Howard **3**
Toomer, Jean **6**
Townsend, Robert **4**
Trotter, Monroe **9**
Tucker, Cynthia **15**
Turner, Henry McNeal **5**
Turner, Tina **6**
Tutu, Desmond **6**
Tyree, Omar Rashad **21**
Tyson, Neil de Grasse **15**
Van Peebles, Melvin **7**
van Sertima, Ivan **25**
Verdelle, A. J. **26**
Walcott, Derek **5**
Walker, Alice **1**
Wallace, Michele Faith **13**
Wallace, Phyllis A. **9**
Washington, Booker T. **4**
Washington, Laura S. **18**
Waters, Ethel **7**
Wattleton, Faye **9**
Wayans, Damon **8**
Webb, Veronica **10**
Wells-Barnett, Ida B. **8**
Wesley, Dorothy Porter **19**
Wesley, Valerie Wilson **18**
West, Cornel **5**
West, Dorothy **12**
Wharton, Clifton R., Jr. **7**
Whitaker, Mark **21**
White, Walter F. **4**
Wideman, John Edgar **5**
Wiley, Ralph **8**
Wilkins, Roger **2**
Wilkins, Roy **4**
Williams, George Washington **18**
Williams, Patricia J. **11**
Williams, Robert F. **11**
Williams, Samm-Art **21**
Williams, Sherley Anne **25**
Wilson, August **7**
Wilson, William Julius **22**
Winans, Marvin L. **17**
Wolfe, George C. **6**
Woodson, Carter G. **2**
Worrill, Conrad **12**
Wright, Bruce McMarion **3**
Wright, Richard **5**
Young, Whitney M., Jr., **4**

Cumulative Subject Index

Volume numbers appear in Bold

AA
See Alcoholics Anonymous

AAAS
See American Association for the Advancement of Science

AARP
Dixon, Margaret **14**

ABC
See American Broadcasting Company

Academy awards
Austin, Patti **24**
Freeman, Morgan **2, 20**
Goldberg, Whoopi **4**
Gooding, Cuba, Jr. **16**
Gossett, Louis, Jr. **7**
Jean-Baptiste, Marianne **17**
McDaniel, Hattie **5**
Poitier, Sidney **11**
Prince **18**
Washington, Denzel **1, 16**
Wonder, Stevie **11**

A cappella
Cooke, Sam **17**
Reagon, Bernice Johnson **7**

ACDL
See Association for Constitutional Democracy in Liberia

ACLU
See American Civil Liberties Union

Acquired Immune Deficiency Syndrome (AIDS)
Ashe, Arthur **1, 18**
Gayle, Helene D. **3**
Hale, Lorraine **8**
Johnson, Earvin "Magic" **3**
Mboup, Souleymane **10**
Moutoussamy-Ashe, Jeanne **7**
Norman, Pat **10**
Riggs, Marlon **5**
Satcher, David **7**
Wilson, Phill **9**

Acting
Ailey, Alvin **8**
Allen, Debbie **13**
Amos, John **8**
Angelou, Maya **1, 15**
Armstrong, Vanessa Bell **24**
Baker, Josephine **3**
Banks, Tyra **11**
Bassett, Angela **6, 23**
Beach, Michael **26**
Beals, Jennifer **12**
Beaton, Norman **14**
Berry, Halle **4, 19**
Blanks, Billy **22**
Blige, Mary J. **20**
Borders, James **9**
Braugher, Andre **13**
Brooks, Avery **9**
Brown, Jim **11**
Caesar, Shirley **19**
Calloway, Cab **14**
Campbell, Naomi **1**
Campbell, Tisha **8**
Carroll, Diahann **9**
Carson, Lisa Nicole **21**
Cheadle, Don **19**
Childress, Alice **15**
Clarke, Hope **14**
Cole, Nat King **17**
Cole, Natalie Maria **17**
Combs, Sean "Puffy" **17**
Cosby, Bill **7, 26**
Crothers, Scatman **19**
Curry, Mark **17**
Curtis-Hall, Vondie **17**
Dandridge, Dorothy **3**
Davidson, Jaye **5**
Davis, Ossie **5**
Davis, Sammy Jr. **18**
Dee, Ruby **8**
Devine, Loretta **24**
Diggs, Taye **25**
Duke, Bill **3**
Duncan, Michael Clarke **26**
Dutton, Charles S. **4, 22**
Epps, Omar **23**
Esposito, Giancarlo **9**
Everett, Francine **23**
Fishburne, Larry **4, 22**
Fox, Vivica A. **15**
Foxx, Jamie **15**
Foxx, Redd **2**
Freeman, Al, Jr. **11**
Freeman, Morgan **2, 20**
Givens, Robin **4, 25**
Glover, Danny **1, 24**
Goldberg, Whoopi **4**
Gooding, Cuba, Jr. **16**
Gordon, Dexter **25**
Gossett, Louis, Jr. **7**
Grier, Pam **9**
Guillaume, Robert **3**
Gunn, Moses **10**
Guy, Jasmine **2**
Hammer, M. C. **20**
Hammond, Fred **23**
Hardison, Kadeem **22**
Harris, Robin **7**
Harvey, Steve **18**
Hayes, Isaac **20**
Hemsley, Sherman **19**
Henry, Lenny **9**
Hill, Lauryn **20**
Hines, Gregory **1**
Horne, Lena **5**
Hounsou, Djimon **19**
Houston, Whitney **7**
Hughley, D.L. **23**
Hyman, Earle **25**
Ice Cube **8**
Iman **4**
Ingram, Rex **5**
Jackson, Janet **6**
Jackson, Michael **19**
Jackson, Millie **25**
Jackson, Samuel L. **8, 19**
Jean-Baptiste, Marianne **17**
Jones, James Earl **3**
King, Regina **22**
Kirby, George **14**
Kitt, Eartha **16**
Knight, Gladys **16**
Kotto, Yaphet **7**
L. L. Cool J **16**
La Salle, Eriq **12**
Lane, Charles **3**
Lassiter, Roy **24**
Lawrence, Martin **6**
Lee, Canada **8**
Lee, Joie **1**
Lee, Spike **5, 19**
Lemmons, Kasi **20**
Lincoln, Abbey **3**
Lindo, Delroy **18**

Love, Darlene 23
Mabley, Jackie "Moms" 15
Marrow, Queen Esther 24
Master P 21
McDaniel, Hattie 5
McDonald, Audra 20
Mckee, Lonette 12
McQueen, Butterfly 6
Mitchell, Brian Stokes 21
Moore, Chante 26
Moore, Melba 21
Moore, Shemar 21
Morton, Joe 18
Moten, Etta 18
Murphy, Eddie 4, 20
Muse, Clarence Edouard 21
Newton, Thandie 26
Nicholas, Fayard 20
Nicholas, Harold 20
Nichols, Nichelle 11
Norman, Maidie 20
Notorious B.I.G. 20
Payne, Allen 13
Peete, Holly Robinson 20
Phifer, Mekhi 25
Pinkett, Jada 10
Poitier, Sidney 11
Prince 18
Pryor, Richard 3, 24
Queen Latifah 1, 16
Randle, Theresa 16
Rashad, Phylicia 21
Reese, Della 6, 20
Reuben, Gloria 15
Rhames, Ving 14
Ribeiro, Alfonso 17
Richards, Lloyd 2
Robeson, Paul 2
Rock, Chris 3, 22
Rolle, Esther 13, 21
Ross, Diana 8
Rowell, Victoria 13
Shakur, Tupac 14
Sinbad 1, 16
Smith, Anna Deavere 6
Smith, Barbara 11
Smith, Roger Guenveur 12
Smith, Will 8, 18
Snipes, Wesley 3, 24
St. Jacques, Raymond 8
St. John, Kristoff 25
Tamia 24
Tate, Larenz 15
Taylor, Meshach 4
Taylor, Regina 9
Thompson, Tazewell 13
Townsend, Robert 4, 23
Tucker, Chris 23
Turner, Tina 6
Tyson, Cicely 7
Uggams, Leslie 23
Underwood, Blair 7
Usher 23
Van Peebles, Mario 2
Van Peebles, Melvin 7
Vance, Courtney B. 15
Vereen, Ben 4
Warfield, Marsha 2
Washington, Denzel 1, 16
Washington, Fredi 10
Waters, Ethel 7
Wayans, Damon 8
Wayans, Keenen Ivory 18
Weathers, Carl 10
Webb, Veronica 10
Whitaker, Forest 2
Whitfield, Lynn 18
Williams, Bert 18
Williams, Billy Dee 8
Williams, Clarence, III 26
Williams, Joe 5, 25
Williams, Samm-Art 21
Williams, Vanessa L. 4, 17
Williamson, Mykelti 22
Wilson, Flip 21
Winfield, Paul 2
Winfrey, Oprah 2, 15
Woodard, Alfre 9
Yoba, Malik 11

Active Ministers Engaged in Nurturance (AMEN)
King, Bernice 4

Actuarial science
Hill, Jessie, Jr. 13

ACT UP
See AIDS Coalition to Unleash Power

Acustar, Inc.
Farmer, Forest 1

ADC

Adoption and foster care
Baker, Josephine 3
Clements, George 2
Gossett, Louis, Jr. 7
Hale, Clara 16
Hale, Lorraine 8
Oglesby, Zena 12

Adventures in Movement (AIM)
Morgan, Joe Leonard 9

Advertising
Barboza, Anthony 10
Burrell, Thomas J. 21
Campbell, E. Simms 13
Coleman, Donald A. 24
Johnson, Beverly 2
Jordan, Montell 23
Lewis, Byron E. 13
Roche, Joyce M. 17

Advocates Scene
Seale, Bobby 3

AFCEA
See Armed Forces Communications and Electronics Associations

Affirmative action
Berry, Mary Frances 7
Carter, Stephen L. 4
Higginbotham, Jr., A. Leon 13, 25
Maynard, Robert C. 7
Norton, Eleanor Holmes 7
Rand, A. Barry 6
Thompson, Bennie G. 26
Waters, Maxine 3

AFL-CIO
See American Federation of Labor and Congress of Industrial Organizations

African/African-American Summit
Sullivan, Leon H. 3

African American Catholic Congregation
Stallings, George A., Jr. 6

African American folklore
Bailey, Xenobia 11
Brown, Sterling 10
Driskell, David C. 7
Ellison, Ralph 7
Gaines, Ernest J. 7
Hamilton, Virginia 10
Hughes, Langston 4
Hurston, Zora Neale 3
Lester, Julius 9
Morrison, Toni 2, 15
Primus, Pearl 6
Tillman, George, Jr. 20
Williams, Bert 18

African American folk music
Handy, W. C. 8
House, Son 8
Johnson, James Weldon 5
Lester, Julius 9

African American history
Angelou, Maya 1, 15
Ashe, Arthur 1, 18
Bennett, Lerone, Jr. 5
Berry, Mary Frances 7
Burroughs, Margaret Taylor 9
Camp, Kimberly 19
Chase-Riboud, Barbara 20
Cheadle, Don 19
Clarke, John Henrik 20
Cooper, Anna Julia 20
Dodson, Howard, Jr. 7
Douglas, Aaron 7
Du Bois, W. E. B. 3
DuBois, Shirley Graham 21
Dyson, Michael Eric 11
Feelings, Tom 11
Franklin, John Hope 5
Gaines, Ernest J. 7
Gates, Henry Louis, Jr. 3
Haley, Alex 4
Harkless, Necia Desiree 19
Hine, Darlene Clark 24
Hughes, Langston 4
Johnson, James Weldon 5
Lewis, David Levering 9
Madhubuti, Haki R. 7
Marable, Manning 10
Morrison, Toni 2
Painter, Nell Irvin 24
Pritchard, Robert Starling 21
Quarles, Benjamin Arthur 18
Reagon, Bernice Johnson 7
Ringgold, Faith 4
Schomburg, Arthur Alfonso 9
Wilson, August 7
Woodson, Carter G. 2

African American Images
Kunjufu, Jawanza 3

African American literature
Andrews, Raymond 4
Angelou, Maya 1, 15
Baisden, Michael 25
Baker, Houston A., Jr. 6
Baldwin, James 1

Bambara, Toni Cade **1**
Baraka, Amiri **1**
Bontemps, Arna **8**
Briscoe, Connie **15**
Brooks, Gwendolyn **1**
Brown, Wesley **23**
Burroughs, Margaret Taylor **9**
Campbell, Bebe Moore **6, 24**
Cary, Lorene **3**
Childress, Alice **15**
Cleage, Pearl **17**
Cullen, Countee **8**
Curtis, Christopher Paul **26**
Dickey, Eric Jerome **21**
Dove, Rita **6**
Du Bois, W. E. B. **3**
Dunbar, Paul Laurence **8**
Ellison, Ralph **7**
Evans, Mari **26**
Fauset, Jessie **7**
Feelings, Tom **11**
Fisher, Rudolph **17**
Fuller, Charles **8**
Gaines, Ernest J. **7**
Gates, Henry Louis, Jr. **3**
Giddings, Paula **11**
Giovanni, Nikki **9**
Goines, Donald **19**
Golden, Marita **19**
Guy, Rosa **5**
Haley, Alex **4**
Hansberry, Lorraine **6**
Harper, Frances Ellen Watkins **11**
Himes, Chester **8**
Holland, Endesha Ida Mae **3**
Hughes, Langston **4**
Hurston, Zora Neale **3**
Iceberg Slim **11**
Joe, Yolanda **21**
Johnson, Charles **1**
Johnson, James Weldon **5**
Jordan, June **7**
Kitt, Sandra **23**
Larsen, Nella **10**
Lester, Julius **9**
Little, Benilde **21**
Lorde, Audre **6**
Madhubuti, Haki R. **7**
Major, Clarence **9**
Marshall, Paule **7**
McKay, Claude **6**
McKay, Nellie Yvonne **17**
McMillan, Terry **4, 17**
Morrison, Toni **2, 15**
Mowry, Jess **7**
Naylor, Gloria **10**
Painter, Nell Irvin **24**
Petry, Ann **19**
Pinkney, Jerry **15**
Randall, Dudley **8**
Redding, J. Saunders **26**
Redmond, Eugene **23**
Reed, Ishmael **8**
Ringgold, Faith **4**
Sanchez, Sonia **17**
Schomburg, Arthur Alfonso **9**
Shange, Ntozake **8**
Smith, Mary Carter **26**
Taylor, Mildred D. **26**
Thurman, Wallace **16**
Toomer, Jean **6**
Tyree, Omar Rashad **21**
Van Peebles, Melvin **7**
Verdelle, A. J. **26**
Walker, Alice **1**
Wesley, Valerie Wilson **18**
Wideman, John Edgar **5**
Williams, Sherley Anne **25**
Wilson, August **7**
Wolfe, George C. **6**
Wright, Richard **5**

African dance
Ailey, Alvin **8**
Fagan, Garth **18**
Primus, Pearl **6**

African folk music
Makeba, Miriam **2**
Nascimento, Milton **2**

African history
Chase-Riboud, Barbara **20**
Clarke, John Henrik **20**
Diop, Cheikh Anta **4**
Dodson, Howard, Jr. **7**
DuBois, Shirley Graham **21**
Hansberry, William Leo **11**
Harkless, Necia Desiree **19**
Jawara, Sir Dawda Kairaba **11**
Madhubuti, Haki R. **7**
Marshall, Paule **7**
van Sertima, Ivan **25**

African Methodist Episcopal Church (AME)
Flake, Floyd H. **18**
Murray, Cecil **12**
Turner, Henry McNeal **5**
Youngblood, Johnny Ray **8**

African National Congress (ANC)
Baker, Ella **5**
Hani, Chris **6**
Kaunda, Kenneth **2**
Luthuli, Albert **13**
Mandela, Nelson **1, 14**
Mandela, Winnie **2**
Masekela, Barbara **18**
Mbeki, Thabo Mvuyelwa **14**
Nkomo, Joshua **4**
Nyanda, Siphiwe **21**
Nzo, Alfred **15**
Ramaphosa, Cyril **3**
Tutu, Desmond **6**

African Women on Tour conference
Taylor, Susan L. **10**

Afro-American League
Fortune, T. Thomas **6**

Afrocentricity
Asante, Molefi Kete **3**
Biggers, John **20**
Diop, Cheikh Anta **4**
Hansberry, Lorraine **6**
Hansberry, William Leo **11**
Sanchez, Sonia **17**
Turner, Henry McNeal **5**

Agency for International Development (AID)
Gayle, Helene D. **3**
Perkins, Edward **5**
Wilkins, Roger **2**

A. G. Gaston Boys and Girls Club
Gaston, Arthur G. **4**

A. G. Gaston Motel
Gaston, Arthur G. **4**

Agricultural Development Council (ADC)
Wharton, Clifton R., Jr. **7**

Agriculture
Boyd, John W., Jr. **20**
Carver, George Washington **4**
Espy, Mike **6**
Hall, Lloyd A. **8**
Masire, Quett **5**
Obasanjo, Olusegun **5**
Sanders, Dori **8**

AHA
See American Heart Association

AID
See Agency for International Development

AIDS
See Acquired Immune Deficiency Syndrome

AIDS Coalition to Unleash Power (ACT UP)
Norman, Pat **10**

AIDS Health Care Foundation
Wilson, Phill **9**

AIDS Prevention Team
Wilson, Phill **9**

AIDS research
Mboup, Souleymane **10**

AIM
See Adventures in Movement

ALA
See American Library Association

Alcoholics Anonymous (AA)
Hilliard, David **7**
Lucas, John **7**

All Afrikan People's Revolutionary Party
Carmichael, Stokely **5, 26**
Moses, Robert Parris **11**

Alliance Theatre
Leon, Kenny **10**

Alpha & Omega Ministry
White, Reggie **6**

Alvin Ailey American Dance Theater
Ailey, Alvin **8**
Clarke, Hope **14**
Dove, Ulysses **5**
Faison, George **16**
Jamison, Judith **7**
Primus, Pearl **6**

Alvin Ailey Repertory Ensemble
Ailey, Alvin **8**
Miller, Bebe **3**

AME
See African Methodist Episcopal Church

AMEN
See Active Ministers Engaged in Nurturance

American Association for the Advancement of Science
Massey, Walter E. **5**

American Ballet Theatre
Dove, Ulysses **5**

American Basketball Association (ABA)
Chamberlain, Wilt **18**
Erving, Julius **18**

American Book Award
Baraka, Amiri **1**
Bates, Daisy **13**
Clark, Septima **7**
Gates, Henry Louis, Jr. **3**
Lorde, Audre **6**
Marshall, Paule **7**
Sanchez, Sonia **17**
Walker, Alice **1**

American Broadcasting Company (ABC)
Christian, Spencer **15**
Goode, Mal **13**
Jackson, Michael **19**
Joyner, Tom **19**
Roberts, Robin **16**
Robinson, Max **3**
Simpson, Carole **6**
Winfrey, Oprah **2, 15**

American Cancer Society
Ashe, Arthur **1, 18**
Leffall, LaSalle, Jr. **3**

American Civil Liberties Union (ACLU)
Baugh, David **23**
Norton, Eleanor Holmes **7**

American Communist Party
Patterson, Louise **25**

American Community Housing Associates, Inc.
Lane, Vincent **5**

American Enterprise Institute
Woodson, Robert L. **10**

American Express Company
Chenault, Kenneth I. **4**

American Express Consumer Card Group, USA
Chenault, Kenneth I. **4**

American Federation of Labor and Congress of Industrial Organizations (AFL-CIO)
Randolph, A. Philip **3**

American Heart Association (AHA)
Cooper, Edward S. **6**

American Library Association (ALA)
Franklin, Hardy R. **9**
Josey, E. J. **10**

American Negro Academy
Grimké, Archibald H. **9**
Schomburg, Arthur Alfonso **9**

American Nurses' Association (ANA)
Kennedy, Adrienne **11**
Staupers, Mabel K. **7**

American Red Cross
Bullock, Steve **22**

American Red Cross blood banks
Drew, Charles Richard **7**

American Society of Magazine Editors
Curry, George E. **23**

ANA
See American Nurses' Association

ANC
See African National Congress

Anglican church hierarchy
Tutu, Desmond **6**

Anthropology
Asante, Molefi Kete **3**
Bunche, Ralph J. **5**
Cole, Johnnetta B. **5**
Davis, Allison **12**
Diop, Cheikh Anta **4**
Dunham, Katherine **4**
Hansberry, William Leo **11**
Morrison, Toni **2, 15**
Primus, Pearl **6**
Robeson, Eslanda Goode **13**

Antoinette Perry awards
See Tony awards

Apartheid
Ashe, Arthur **18**
Berry, Mary Frances **7**
Biko, Steven **4**
Howard, M. William, Jr. **26**
Luthuli, Albert **13**
Makeba, Miriam **2**
Mandela, Nelson **1, 14**
Mandela, Winnie **2**
Masekela, Hugh **1**
Mathabane, Mark **5**
Mbeki, Thabo Mvuyelwa **14**
Mbuende, Kaire **12**
McDougall, Gay J. **11**
Nyanda, Siphiwe **21**
Nzo, Alfred **15**
Ramaphosa, Cyril **3**
Robinson, Randall **7**
Sullivan, Leon H. **13**
Tutu, Desmond **6**

Apollo 13
Williams, O. S. **13**

Arab-Israeli conflict
Bunche, Ralph J. **5**

ARCH
See Argonne National Laboratory-University of Chicago Development Corporation

Architecture
Gantt, Harvey **1**
Sklarek, Norma Merrick **25**
Williams, Paul R. **9**

Argonne National Laboratory
Massey, Walter E. **5**
Quarterman, Lloyd Albert **4**

Argonne National Laboratory-University of Chicago Development Corporation (ARCH)
Massey, Walter E. **5**

Ariel Capital Management
Rogers, John W., Jr. **5**

Arkansas Department of Health
Elders, Joycelyn **6**

Armed Forces Communications and Electronics Associations (AFCEA)
Gravely, Samuel L., Jr. **5**

Arthritis treatment
Julian, Percy Lavon **6**

Artists for a Free South Africa
Woodard, Alfre **9**

ASALH
See Association for the Study of Afro-American Life and History

ASH
See Association for the Sexually Harassed

Association for Constitutional Democracy in Liberia
Sawyer, Amos **2**

Association for the Sexually Harassed (ASH)
Gomez-Preston, Cheryl **9**

Association for the Study of Afro-American Life and History (ASALH)
Dodson, Howard, Jr. **7**
Woodson, Carter G. **2**

Astronauts
Bluford, Guy **2**
Bolden, Charles F., Jr. **7**
Gregory, Frederick D. **8**
Jemison, Mae C. **1**
Lawrence, Robert H., Jr. **16**
McNair, Ronald **3**

Atco-EastWest
Rhone, Sylvia **2**

Athletic administration
Goss, Tom **23**

Atlanta Baptist College
See Morehouse College

Atlanta Board of Education
Mays, Benjamin E. **7**

Atlanta Braves baseball team
Aaron, Hank **5**
Baker, Dusty **8**
Justice, David **18**
McGriff, Fred **24**
Sanders, Deion **4**

Atlanta Chamber of Commerce
Hill, Jessie, Jr. **13**

Atlanta City Council
Campbell, Bill **9**
Williams, Hosea Lorenzo **15**

Atlanta city government
Campbell, Bill **9**
Jackson, Maynard **2**
Williams, Hosea Lorenzo **15**
Young, Andrew **3**

Atlanta Falcons football team
Anderson, Jamal **22**
Sanders, Deion **4**

Atlanta Hawks basketball team
Silas, Paul **24**
Wilkens, Lenny **11**

Atlanta Life Insurance Company
Hill, Jessie, Jr. **13**

Atlanta Negro Voters League
Hill, Jessie, Jr. **13**

Atlanta Police Department
Brown, Lee Patrick **1, 24**
Harvard, Beverly **11**

Atlantic City city government
Usry, James L. **23**

Atlantic Records
Franklin, Aretha **11**
Rhone, Sylvia **2**

Aviation
Bullard, Eugene **12**
Coleman, Bessie **9**

"Back to Africa" movement
Turner, Henry McNeal **5**

Bad Boy Entertainment
Combs, Sean "Puffy" **17**
Notorious B.I.G. **20**

Ballet
Ailey, Alvin **8**
Allen, Debbie **13**
Dove, Ulysses **5**
Faison, George **16**
Johnson, Virginia **9**
Mitchell, Arthur **2**
Nichols, Nichelle **11**
Parks, Gordon **1**

Baltimore city government
Schmoke, Kurt **1**

Baltimore Colts football team
Barnes, Ernie **16**

Baltimore Elite Giants baseball team
Campanella, Roy **25**
Kimbro, Henry A. **25**

Baltimore Orioles baseball team
Baylor, Don **6**
Jackson, Reggie **15**
Robinson, Frank **9**

Banking
Boyd, T. B., III **6**
Brimmer, Andrew F. **2**
Bryant, John **26**
Chapman, Jr., Nathan A. **21**
Chappell, Emma **18**
Ferguson, Roger W. **25**
Griffith, Mark Winston **8**
Lawless, Theodore K. **8**
Louis, Errol T. **8**
Morgan, Rose **11**
Parsons, Richard Dean **11**
Utendahl, John **23**
Walker, Maggie Lena **17**
Watkins, Walter C. **24**
Wright, Deborah C. **25**

Baptist World Alliance Assembly
Mays, Benjamin E. **7**

Baptist
Gomes, Peter J. **15**

Barnett-Ader Gallery
Thomas, Alma **14**

Baseball
Aaron, Hank **5**
Anderson, Elmer **25**
Ashford, Emmett **22**
Baker, Dusty **8**
Baylor, Don **6**
Belle, Albert **10**
Bonds, Barry **6**
Brock, Lou **18**
Campanella, Roy **25**
Carew, Rod **20**
Clendenon, Donn **26**
Coleman, Leonard S., Jr. **12**
Cottrell, Comer **11**
Davis, Piper **19**
Doby, Lawrence Eugene **16**
Edwards, Harry **2**
Fielder, Cecil **2**
Flood, Curt **10**
Gibson, Josh **22**
Gooden, Dwight **20**
Gregg, Eric **16**
Griffey, Ken, Jr. **12**
Hammer, M. C. **20**
Jackson, Reggie **15**
Justice, David **18**
Kimbro, Henry A. **25**
Lankford, Ray **23**
Larkin, Barry **24**
Lofton, Kenny **12**
Mays, Willie **3**
McGriff, Fred **24**
Morgan, Joe Leonard **9**
Murray, Eddie **12**
Newcombe, Don **24**
O'Neil, Buck **19**
Paige, Satchel **7**
Pride, Charley **26**
Puckett, Kirby **4**
Robinson, Frank **9**
Robinson, Jackie **6**
Robinson, Sharon **22**
Sanders, Deion **4**
Sheffield, Gary **16**
Sosa, Sammy **21**
Stone, Toni **15**
Strawberry, Darryl **22**
Thomas, Frank **12**
Vaughn, Mo **16**
Watson, Bob **25**
White, Bill **1**
Winfield, Dave **5**

Basketball
Abdul-Jabbar, Kareem **8**
Barkley, Charles **5**
Bing, Dave **3**
Bol, Manute **1**
Brandon, Terrell **16**
Bryant, Kobe **15**
Carter, Vince **26**
Chamberlain, Wilt **18**
Cooper, Cynthia **17**
Drexler, Clyde **4**
Dumars, Joe **16**
Duncan, Tim **20**
Edwards, Harry **2**
Edwards, Teresa **14**
Ellerbe, Brian **22**
Elliott, Sean **26**
Ewing, Patrick A. **17**
Freeman, Marianna **23**
Garnett, Kevin **14**
Gentry, Alvin **23**
Gossett, Louis, Jr. **7**
Griffith, Yolanda **25**
Hardaway, Anfernee (Penny) **13**
Haskins, Clem **23**
Haynes, Marques **22**
Heard, Gar **25**
Hill, Grant **13**
Holdsclaw, Chamique **24**
Howard, Juwan **15**
Hunter, Billy **22**
Iverson, Allen **24**
Johnson, Earvin "Magic" **3**
Jones, Roy Jr. **22**
Jordan, Michael **6, 21**
Justice, David **18**
Kelly, R. **18**
Leslie, Lisa **16**
Lloyd, Earl **26**
Lofton, Kenny **12**
Lucas, John **7**
Malone, Karl A. **18**
Manigault, Earl "The Goat" **15**
Master P **21**
Miller, Cheryl **10**
Mourning, Alonzo **17**
Mutombo, Dikembe **7**
O'Neal, Shaquille **8**
Olajuwon, Hakeem **2**
Peck, Carolyn **23**
Pippen, Scottie **15**
Richardson, Nolan **9**
Richmond, Mitch **19**
Rivers, Glenn "Doc" **25**
Robertson, Oscar **26**
Robinson, David **24**
Russell, Bill **8**
Silas, Paul **24**

Smith, Tubby **18**
Sprewell, Latrell **23**
Stringer, C. Vivian **13**
Swoopes, Sheryl **12**
Thomas, Isiah **7, 26**
Thompson, Tina **25**
Unseld, Wes **23**
Webber, Chris **15**
Wilkens, Lenny **11**

BCALA
See Black Caucus of the American Library Association

BDP
See Botswana Democratic Party

Bear, Stearns & Co.
Fletcher, Alphonso, Jr. **16**

Beatrice International
See TLC Beatrice International Holdings, Inc.

Bebop
Carter, Betty **19**
Coltrane, John **19**
Davis, Miles **4**
Fitzgerald, Ella **8, 18**
Gillespie, Dizzy **1**
Gordon, Dexter **25**
Hancock, Herbie **20**
Jackson, Milt **26**
Parker, Charlie **20**
Powell, Bud **24**
Roach, Max **21**
Vaughan, Sarah **13**

Bechuanaland Protectorate Legislative Council
Masire, Quett **5**

Bedford-Stuyvesant Restoration Corporation
Thomas, Franklin A. **5**

Ben & Jerry's Homemade Ice Cream, Inc.
Holland, Robert, Jr. **11**

BET
See Black Entertainment Television

Bethann Management, Inc.
Hardison, Bethann **12**

Bethune-Cookman College
Bethune, Mary McLeod **4**
Joyner, Marjorie Stewart **26**

BFF
See Black Filmmaker Foundation

BGLLF
See Black Gay and Lesbian Leadership Forum

Billy Graham Evangelistic Association
Bell, Ralph S. **5**
Waters, Ethel **7**

Bing Steel, Inc.
Bing, Dave **3**
Lloyd, Earl **26**

Biology
Just, Ernest Everett **3**

Birth control
Elders, Joycelyn **6**
Williams, Maggie **7**

Bishop College
Cottrell, Comer **11**

BLA
See Black Liberation Army

Black Aesthetic
Baker, Houston A., Jr. **6**

Black American West Museum
Stewart, Paul Wilbur **12**

Black and White Minstrel Show
Henry, Lenny **9**

Black Arts movement
Giovanni, Nikki **9**

Black Cabinet
Hastie, William H. **8**

Black Caucus of the American Library Association (BCALA)
Josey, E. J. **10**

Black Christian Nationalist movement
Agyeman, Jaramogi Abebe **10**

Black Coaches Association (BCA)
Freeman, Marianna **23**

Black Consciousness movement
Biko, Steven **4**
Muhammad, Elijah **4**
Ramaphosa, Cyril **3**
Tutu, Desmond **6**

Black culturalism
Karenga, Maulana **10**

Black Economic Union (BEU)
Brown, Jim **11**

Black Enterprise
Brimmer, Andrew F. **2**
Graves, Earl G. **1**
Wallace, Phyllis A. **9**

Black Entertainment Television (BET)
Gordon, Ed **10**
Johnson, Robert L. **3**
Jones, Bobby **20**
Smiley, Tavis **20**

Black Filmmaker Foundation (BFF)
Hudlin, Reginald **9**
Hudlin, Warrington **9**
Jackson, George **19**

Black Gay and Lesbian Leadership Forum (BGLLF)
Wilson, Phill **9**

Black Guerrilla Family (BGF)
Jackson, George **14**

Black History Month
Woodson, Carter G. **2**

Black Horizons on the Hill
Wilson, August **7**

Black Liberation Army (BLA)
Shakur, Assata **6**
Williams, Evelyn **10**

Black literary theory
Gates, Henry Louis, Jr. **3**

Black Manifesto
Forman, James **7**

Black Muslims
Abdul-Jabbar, Kareem **8**
Ali, Muhammad **2, 16**
Farrakhan, Louis **2**
Muhammad, Elijah **4**
X, Malcolm **1**

Black nationalism
Baker, Houston A., Jr. **6**
Baraka, Amiri **1**
Carmichael, Stokely **5, 26**
Farrakhan, Louis **2**
Forman, James **7**
Garvey, Marcus **1**
Innis, Roy **5**
Muhammad, Elijah **4**
Turner, Henry McNeal **5**
X, Malcolm **1**

Black Panther Party (BPP)
Abu-Jamal, Mumia **15**
Al-Amin, Jamil Abdullah **6**
Brown, Elaine **8**
Carmichael, Stokely **5**
Cleaver, Eldridge **5**
Davis, Angela **5**
Forman, James **7**
Hampton, Fred **18**
Hilliard, David **7**
Jackson, George **14**
Newton, Huey **2**
Pratt, Geronimo **18**
Rush, Bobby **26**
Seale, Bobby **3**
Shakur, Assata **6**

Black Power movement
Al-Amin, Jamil Abdullah **6**
Baker, Houston A., Jr. **6**
Brown, Elaine **8**
Carmichael, Stokely **5, 26**
Dodson, Howard, Jr. **7**
Giovanni, Nikki **9**
McKissick, Floyd B. **3**
Stone, Chuck **9**

Blackside, Inc.
Hampton, Henry **6**

Black theology
Cone, James H. **3**

"Blood for Britain"
Drew, Charles Richard **7**

Blessed Martin House
Riley, Helen Caldwell Day **13**

Blood plasma research/preservation
Drew, Charles Richard **7**

Blues
Brown, Charles **23**
Collins, Albert **12**
Dixon, Willie **4**
Dorsey, Thomas **15**
Evora, Cesaria **12**
Handy, W. C. **8**
Holiday, Billie **1**
House, Son **8**
Howlin' Wolf **9**
Jean-Baptiste, Marianne **17**
King, B. B. **7**
Muse, Clarence Edouard **21**
Parker, Charlie **20**
Reese, Della **6, 20**
Smith, Bessie **3**
Sykes, Roosevelt **20**
Wallace, Sippie **1**
Washington, Dinah **22**
Waters, Ethel **7**
Watson, Johnny "Guitar" **18**
Williams, Joe **5, 25**
Wilson, August **7**

Blues Heaven Foundation
Dixon, Willie **4**

Blues vernacular
Baker, Houston A., Jr. **6**

Bobsledding
Moses, Edwin **8**

Bodybuilding
Murray, Lenda **10**

Booker T. Washington Business College
Gaston, Arthur G. **4**

Booker T. Washington Insurance Company
Gaston, Arthur G. **4**

Boston Bruins hockey team
O'Ree, Willie **5**

Boston Celtics basketball team
Russell, Bill **8**
Silas, Paul **24**

Boston Red Sox baseball team
Baylor, Don **6**
Vaughn, Mo **16**

Botany
Carver, George Washington **4**

Botswana Democratic Party (BDP)
Masire, Quett **5**
Mogae, Festus Gontebanye **19**

Boxing
Ali, Muhammad **2, 16**
Bowe, Riddick **6**
Carter, Rubin **26**
Foreman, George **1, 15**
Frazier, Joe **19**
Holmes, Larry **20**
Holyfield, Evander **6**
Johnson, Jack **8**
Jones, Roy Jr. **22**
King, Don **14**
Lee, Canada **8**
Leonard, Sugar Ray **15**
Louis, Joe **5**
Moorer, Michael **19**
Patterson, Floyd **19**
Robinson, Sugar Ray **18**
Steward, Emanuel **18**
Whitaker, Pernell **10**

Boys Choir of Harlem
Turnbull, Walter **13**

BPP
See Black Panther Party

Brazilian Congress
da Silva, Benedita **5**

Breast Cancer Resource Committee
Brown, Zora Kramer **12**

British House of Commons
Abbott, Diane **9**
Pitt, David Thomas **10**

British House of Lords
Pitt, David Thomas **10**

British Parliament
See British House of Commons

Broadcasting
Allen, Byron **3, 24**
Ashley, Maurice **15**
Banks, William **11**
Barden, Don H. **9, 20**
Bradley, Ed **2**
Brown, Les **5**
Brown, Tony **3**
Brunson, Dorothy **1**
Clayton, Xernona **3**
Cornelius, Don **4**
Davis, Ossie **5**
Elder, Larry **25**
Evans, Harry **25**
Goode, Mal **13**
Gumbel, Bryant **14**
Gumbel, Greg **8**
Hamblin, Ken **10**
Hickman, Fred **11**
Hunter-Gault, Charlayne **6**
Johnson, Robert L. **3**
Jones, Bobby **20**
Jones, Star **10**
Joyner, Tom **19**
Langhart, Janet **19**
Lawson, Jennifer **1**
Lewis, Delano **7**
Mabrey, Vicki **26**
Madison, Joseph E. **17**
McEwen, Mark **5**
Miller, Cheryl **10**
Mitchell, Russ **21**
Morgan, Joe Leonard **9**
Pinkston, W. Randall **24**
Quarles, Norma **25**
Roberts, Robin **16**
Robinson, Max **3**
Rodgers, Johnathan **6**
Russell, Bill **8**
Shaw, Bernard **2**
Simpson, Carole **6**
Simpson, O. J. **15**
Smiley, Tavis **20**
Stewart, Alison **13**
Stokes, Carl B. **10**
Watts, Rolonda **9**
White, Bill **1**
Williams, Montel **4**
Winfrey, Oprah **2, 15**

Broadside Press
Randall, Dudley **8**

Brooklyn Academy of Music
Miller, Bebe **3**

Brooklyn Dodgers baseball team
Campanella, Roy **25**
Newcombe, Don **24**
Robinson, Jackie **6**

Brotherhood of Sleeping Car Porters
Randolph, A. Philip **3**
Tucker, Rosina **14**

Brown v. Board of Education of Topeka
Bell, Derrick **6**
Clark, Kenneth B. **5**
Franklin, John Hope **5**
Hill, Oliver W. **24**
Houston, Charles Hamilton **4**
Marshall, Thurgood **1**
Motley, Constance Baker **10**
Redding, Louis L. **26**
Robinson, Spottswood W., III **22**

Buffalo Bills football team
Simpson, O. J. **15**

Bull-riding
Sampson, Charles **13**

Busing (anti-busing legislation)
Bosley, Freeman, Jr. **7**

Cabinet
See U.S. Cabinet

Cable News Network (CNN)
Chideya, Farai **14**
Hickman, Fred **11**
Quarles, Norma **25**
Shaw, Bernard **2**

California Angels baseball team
Baylor, Don **6**
Carew, Rod **20**
Robinson, Frank **9**
Winfield, Dave **5**

California State Assembly
Brown, Willie L., Jr. **7**
Dixon, Julian C. **24**
Lee, Barbara **25**
Millender-McDonald, Juanita **21**
Waters, Maxine **3**

Calypso
Belafonte, Harry **4**
Jean, Wyclef **20**

Canadian Football League (CFL)
Gilliam, Frank **23**
Moon, Warren **8**

Weathers, Carl **10**

Cancer research
Chinn, May Edward **26**
Clark, Celeste **15**
Freeman, Harold P. **23**
Leffall, LaSalle, Jr. **3**

Capital punishment
Hawkins, Steven **14**

Cardiac research
Watkins, Levi, Jr. **9**

CARE
Gossett, Louis, Jr. **7**
Stone, Chuck **9**

Caribbean dance
Ailey, Alvin **8**
Dunham, Katherine **4**
Fagan, Garth **18**
Nichols, Nichelle **11**
Primus, Pearl **6**

Cartoonists
Armstrong, Robb **15**
Brandon, Barbara **3**
Campbell, E. Simms **13**
Harrington, Oliver W. **9**

Catholicism
See Roman Catholic Church

CBEA
See Council for a Black Economic Agenda

CBC
See Congressional Black Caucus

CBS
See Columbia Broadcasting System

CBS Television Stations Division
Rodgers, Johnathan **6**

CDC
See Centers for Disease Control and Prevention

CDF
See Children's Defense Fund

CEDBA
See Council for the Economic Development of Black Americans

Celebrities for a Drug-Free America
Vereen, Ben **4**

Censorship
Butts, Calvin O., III **9**
Ice-T **6**

Centers for Disease Control and Prevention (CDC)
Gayle, Helene D. **3**
Satcher, David **7**

CFL
See Canadian Football League

CHA
See Chicago Housing Authority

Challenger
McNair, Ronald **3**

Chama cha Mapinduzi (Tanzania; Revolutionary Party)
Mkapa, Benjamin **16**
Mongella, Gertrude **11**
Nyerere, Julius **5**

Chamber of Deputies (Brazil)
da Silva, Benedita **5**

Chanteuses
Baker, Josephine **3**
Dandridge, Dorothy **3**
Horne, Lena **5**
Kitt, Eartha **16**
Moore, Melba **21**
Moten, Etta **18**
Reese, Della **6, 20**

Che-Lumumba Club
Davis, Angela **5**

Chemistry
Hall, Lloyd A. **8**
Humphries, Frederick **20**
Julian, Percy Lavon **6**

Chemurgy
Carver, George Washington **4**

Chesapeake and Potomac Telephone Company
Lewis, Delano **7**

Chess
Ashley, Maurice **15**

Chicago Bears football team
Page, Alan **7**
Payton, Walter **11, 25**
Singletary, Mike **4**

Chicago Bulls basketball team
Jordan, Michael **6, 21**
Pippen, Scottie **15**
Rodman, Dennis **12**

Chicago city government
Metcalfe, Ralph **26**
Washington, Harold **6**

Chicago Cubs baseball team
Sosa, Sammy **21**

Chicago Defender Charities
Joyner, Marjorie Stewart **26**

Chicago Eight
Seale, Bobby **3**

Chicago Housing Authority (CHA)
Lane, Vincent **5**

Chicago Negro Chamber of Commerce
Fuller, S. B. **13**

Chicago Police Department
Hillard, Terry **25**

Chicago Reporter
Washington, Laura S. **18**

Chicago Tribune
Page, Clarence **4**

Chicago White Sox baseball team
Doby, Lawrence Eugene, Sr. **16**
Thomas, Frank **12**

Child abuse prevention
Waters, Maxine **3**

Child psychiatry
Comer, James P. **6**

Child psychology
Hale, Lorraine **8**

Children's Defense Fund (CDF)
Edelman, Marian Wright **5**
Williams, Maggie **7**

Child Welfare Administration
Little, Robert L. **2**

Choreography
Ailey, Alvin **8**
Allen, Debbie **13**
Brooks, Avery **9**
Byrd, Donald **10**
de Passe, Suzanne **25**
Dove, Ulysses **5**
Dunham, Katherine **4**
Fagan, Garth **18**
Faison, George **16**
Glover, Savion **14**
Jamison, Judith **7**
Johnson, Virginia **9**
Jones, Bill T. **1**
Miller, Bebe **3**
Mitchell, Arthur **2**
Nicholas, Fayard **20**
Nicholas, Harold **20**
Primus, Pearl **6**

Christian Science Monitor
Khanga, Yelena **6**

Chrysler Corporation
Colbert, Virgis William **17**
Farmer, Forest **1**
Richie, Leroy C. **18**

Church for the Fellowship of All Peoples
Thurman, Howard **3**

Church of God in Christ
Franklin, Robert M. **13**
Hayes, James C. **10**

Cincinnati Reds baseball team
Larkin, Barry **24**
Morgan, Joe Leonard **9**
Robinson, Frank **9**

Cinematography
Dickerson, Ernest **6, 17**

Citadel Press
Achebe, Chinua **6**

Citizens Federal Savings and Loan Association
Gaston, Arthur G. **4**

City government—U.S.
Archer, Dennis **7**
Barden, Don H. **9, 20**
Barry, Marion S. **7**
Bosley, Freeman, Jr. **7**
Bradley, Thomas **2, 20**
Brown, Lee P. **1, 24**
Burris, Chuck **21**
Caesar, Shirley **19**
Campbell, Bill **9**
Clayton, Constance **1**
Cleaver, Emanuel **4**
Dinkins, David **4**
Dixon, Sharon Pratt **1**
Evers, Myrlie **8**
Fauntroy, Walter E. **11**
Fields, C. Virginia **25**
Gibson, Kenneth Allen **6**
Goode, W. Wilson **4**
Harmon, Clarence **26**
Hayes, James C. **10**
Jackson, Maynard **2**
James, Sharpe **23**
Jarvis, Charlene Drew **21**
Johnson, Eddie Bernice **8**
Johnson Jr., Harvey **24**
Kirk, Ron **11**
Mallett, Conrad, Jr. **16**
McPhail, Sharon **2**
Metcalfe, Ralph **26**
Millender-McDonald, Juanita **21**
Morial, Ernest "Dutch" **26**
Morial, Marc **20**
Powell, Adam Clayton, Jr. **3**
Powell, Debra A. **23**
Rice, Norm **8**
Sayles Belton, Sharon **9, 16**
Schmoke, Kurt **1**
Stokes, Carl B. **10**
Street, John F. **24**
Usry, James L. **23**
Washington, Harold **6**
Webb, Wellington **3**
White, Michael R. **5**
Williams, Anthony **21**
Young, Andrew **3**
Young, Coleman **1, 20**

Civil rights
Abbott, Diane **9**
Abernathy, Ralph **1**
Agyeman, Jaramogi Abebe **10**
Al-Amin, Jamil Abdullah **6**
Alexander, Clifford **26**
Ali, Muhammad **2, 16**
Angelou, Maya **1**
Anthony, Wendell **25**
Aristide, Jean-Bertrand **6**
Baker, Ella **5**
Baker, Houston A., Jr. **6**
Baker, Josephine **3**
Bates, Daisy **13**
Baugh, David **23**
Beals, Melba Patillo **15**
Belafonte, Harry **4**
Bell, Derrick **6**
Bennett, Lerone, Jr. **5**
Berry, Mary Frances **7**
Biko, Steven **4**
Bishop Jr., Sanford D. **24**
Bond, Julian **2**
Booker, Simeon **23**
Boyd, John W., Jr. **20**
Brown, Elaine **8**
Brown, Tony **3**
Brown, Wesley **23**
Campbell, Bebe Moore **6, 24**
Carmichael, Stokely **5, 26**
Carter, Mandy **11**
Carter, Rubin **26**
Carter, Stephen L. **4**
Cayton, Horace **26**
Chambers, Julius **3**
Chavis, Benjamin **6**
Clark, Septima **7**
Clay, William Lacy **8**
Cleaver, Eldridge **5**
Clyburn, James **21**
Cobbs, Price M. **9**
Cooper, Anna Julia **20**
Cosby, Bill **7, 26**
Crockett, George, Jr. **10**
Cunningham, Evelyn **23**
Davis, Angela **5**
Days, Drew S., III **10**
Dee, Ruby **8**
Diggs, Charles C. **21**
Diggs-Taylor, Anna **20**
Divine, Father **7**
Dodson, Howard, Jr. **7**
Du Bois, W. E. B. **3**
Edelman, Marian Wright **5**
Ellison, Ralph **7**
Evers, Medgar **3**
Evers, Myrlie **8**
Farmer, James **2**
Fauntroy, Walter E. **11**
Forman, James **7**
Fortune, T. Thomas **6**
Franklin, John Hope **5**
Gaines, Ernest J. **7**
Gibson, William F. **6**
Gregory, Dick **1**
Grimké, Archibald H. **9**
Guinier, Lani **7**
Haley, Alex **4**
Haley, George Williford Boyce **21**
Hall, Elliott S. **24**
Hamer, Fannie Lou **6**
Hampton, Fred **18**
Hampton, Henry **6**
Hansberry, Lorraine **6**
Harper, Frances Ellen Watkins **11**
Harris, Patricia Roberts **2**
Hastie, William H. **8**
Hawkins, Steven **14**
Hedgeman, Anna Arnold **22**
Height, Dorothy I. **2, 23**
Henderson, Wade J. **14**
Henry, Aaron **19**
Higginbotham, Jr., A. Leon **13, 25**
Hill, Jessie, Jr. **13**
Hill, Oliver W. **24**
Hilliard, David **7**
Holland, Endesha Ida Mae **3**
Hooks, Benjamin L. **2**
hooks, bell **5**
Horne, Lena **5**
Houston, Charles Hamilton **4**
Howard, M. William, Jr. **26**
Hughes, Langston **4**
Innis, Roy **5**
Jackson, Alexine Clement **22**
Jackson, Jesse **1**
James, Daniel, Jr. **16**
Johnson, Eddie Bernice **8**
Johnson, James Weldon **5**
Johnson, Norma L. Holloway **17**
Jones, Elaine R. **7**
Jordan, Barbara **4**
Jordan, June **7**
Jordan, Vernon E. **3**
Julian, Percy Lavon **6**
Kennedy, Florynce **12**
Kenyatta, Jomo **5**
King, Bernice **4**
King, Coretta Scott **3**
King, Martin Luther, Jr. **1**
King, Martin Luther, III **20**
King, Yolanda **6**
Lampkin, Daisy **19**
Lee, Spike **5, 19**
Lester, Julius **9**
Lewis, John **2**
Lorde, Audre **6**
Lowery, Joseph **2**
Makeba, Miriam **2**
Mandela, Nelson **1, 14**
Mandela, Winnie **2**
Martin, Louis E. **16**
Mays, Benjamin E. **7**
Mbeki, Thabo Mvuyelwa **14**
McDonald, Gabrielle Kirk **20**
McDougall, Gay J. **11**
McKissick, Floyd B. **3**
Meek, Carrie **6**
Meredith, James H. **11**
Metcalfe, Ralph **26**
Morial, Ernest "Dutch" **26**
Morrison, Toni **2, 15**
Moses, Robert Parris **11**
Motley, Constance Baker **10**
Mowry, Jess **7**
Ndadaye, Melchior **7**
Nelson, Jill **6**
Newton, Huey **2**
Nkomo, Joshua **4**
Norman, Pat **10**
Norton, Eleanor Holmes **7**
Nzo, Alfred **15**
Parks, Rosa **1**
Patrick, Deval **12**
Patterson, Louise **25**
Patterson, Orlando **4**
Perkins, Edward **5**
Pinchback, P. B. S. **9**
Pleasant, Mary Ellen **9**
Poitier, Sidney **11**
Powell, Adam Clayton, Jr. **3**
Price, Hugh B. **9**
Ramaphosa, Cyril **3**
Randolph, A. Philip **3**
Reagon, Bernice Johnson **7**
Redding, Louis L. **26**
Riggs, Marlon **5**
Robeson, Paul **2**
Robinson, Jackie **6**
Robinson, Rachel **16**
Robinson, Randall **7**
Robinson, Sharon **22**
Robinson, Spottswood W. III **22**
Rowan, Carl T. **1**
Rush, Bobby **26**
Rustin, Bayard **4**
Sané, Pierre Gabriel **21**
Seale, Bobby **3**
Shabazz, Attallah **6**
Shabazz, Betty **7, 26**

Shakur, Assata **6**
Simone, Nina **15**
Sisulu, Sheila Violet Makate **24**
Sleet, Moneta, Jr. **5**
Staupers, Mabel K. **7**
Sullivan, Leon H. **3**
Thompson, Bennie G. **26**
Thurman, Howard **3**
Till, Emmett **7**
Trotter, Monroe **9**
Tsvangirai, Morgan **26**
Turner, Henry McNeal **5**
Tutu, Desmond **6**
Underwood, Blair **7**
Washington, Booker T. **4**
Washington, Fredi **10**
Watt, Melvin **26**
Weaver, Robert C. **8**
Wells-Barnett, Ida B. **8**
Wells, James Lesesne **10**
West, Cornel **5**
White, Walter F. **4**
Wideman, John Edgar **5**
Wilkins, Roy **4**
Williams, Evelyn **10**
Williams, Hosea Lorenzo **15**
Williams, Robert F. **11**
Williams, Walter E. **4**
Wilson, August **7**
Wilson, Sunnie **7**
Wilson, William Julius **22**
Woodson, Robert L. **10**
X, Malcolm **1**
Yoba, Malik **11**
Young, Andrew **3**
Young, Jean Childs **14**
Young, Whitney M., Jr. **4**

Classical singers
Anderson, Marian **2**
Bumbry, Grace **5**
Hayes, Roland **4**
Hendricks, Barbara **3**
Norman, Jessye **5**
Price, Leontyne **1**

Clergy
Anthony, Wendell **25**
Caesar, Shirley **19**
Cleveland, James **19**
Cook, Suzan D. Johnson **22**
Gomes, Peter J. **15**
Howard, M. William, Jr. **26**
Jakes, Thomas "T.D." **17**
King, Barbara **22**
McClurkin, Donnie **25**
Reese, Della **6, 20**
Winans, Marvin L. **17**

Cleveland Browns football team
Brown, Jim **11**
Hill, Calvin **19**
Motley, Marion **26**
Newsome, Ozzie **26**

Cleveland Cavaliers basketball team
Brandon, Terrell **16**
Wilkens, Lenny **11**

Cleveland city government
Stokes, Carl B. **10**
White, Michael R. **5**

Cleveland Indians baseball team
Belle, Albert **10**
Doby, Lawrence Eugene, Sr. **16**
Justice, David **18**
Lofton, Kenny **12**
Murray, Eddie **12**
Paige, Satchel **7**
Robinson, Frank **9**

Clothing design
Bailey, Xenobia **11**
Henderson, Gordon **5**
John, Daymond **23**
Jones, Carl **7**
Kani, Karl **10**
Kelly, Patrick **3**
Robinson, Patrick **19**
Smith, Willi **8**
Walker, T. J. **7**

CNN
See Cable News Network

Coaching
Ashley, Maurice **15**
Baylor, Don **6**
Bickerstaff, Bernie **21**
Campanella, Roy **25**
Carew, Rod **20**
Dungy, Tony **17**
Ellerbe, Brian **22**
Freeman, Marianna **23**
Gaither, Alonzo Smith (Jake) **14**
Gentry, Alvin **23**
Gibson, Althea **8**
Green, Dennis **5**
Greene, Joe **10**
Haskins, Clem **23**
Heard, Gar **25**
Miller, Cheryl **10**
O'Neil, Buck **19**
Rhodes, Ray **14**
Richardson, Nolan **9**
Rivers, Glenn "Doc" **25**
Robinson, Eddie G. **10**
Russell, Bill **8**
Shell, Art **1**
Silas, Paul **24**
Smith, Tubby **18**
Stringer, C. Vivian **13**
White, Jesse **22**
Williams, Doug **22**

Coca-Cola Foundation
Jones, Ingrid Saunders **18**

COHAR
See Committee on Appeal for Human Rights

Collage
Andrews, Benny **22**
Bearden, Romare **2**
Driskell, David C. **7**

Colorado Rockies baseball team
Baylor, Don **6**

Columbia Broadcasting System (CBS)
Bradley, Ed **2**
Mabrey, Vicki **26**
McEwen, Mark **5**
Mitchell, Russ **21**
Pinkston, W. Randall **24**
Rashad, Phylicia **21**
Rodgers, Johnathan **6**
Taylor, Meshach **4**

Comedy
Allen, Byron **3, 24**
Amos, John **8**
Beaton, Norman **14**
Bellamy, Bill **12**
Berry, Bertice **8**
Campbell, Tisha **8**
Cosby, Bill **7, 26**
Curry, Mark **17**
Davidson, Tommy **21**
Davis, Sammy Jr. **18**
Foxx, Jamie **15**
Foxx, Redd **2**
Goldberg, Whoopi **4**
Gregory, Dick **1**
Harris, Robin **7**
Harvey, Steve **18**
Henry, Lenny **9**
Hughley, D.L. **23**
Kirby, George **14**
Lawrence, Martin **6**
Mabley, Jackie "Moms" **15**
McEwen, Mark **5**
Moore, Melba **21**
Murphy, Eddie **4, 20**
Pryor, Richard **3, 24**
Rashad, Phylicia **21**
Reese, Della **6, 20**
Rock, Chris **3, 22**
Schultz, Michael A. **6**
Sinbad **1, 16**
Smith, Will **8, 18**
Taylor, Meshach **4**
Townsend, Robert **4, 23**
Tucker, Chris **13, 23**
Warfield, Marsha **2**
Wayans, Damon **8**
Wayans, Keenen Ivory **18**
Wilson, Flip **21**

Comer Method
Comer, James P. **6**

Comic Relief
Goldberg, Whoopi **4**

Commission for Racial Justice
Chavis, Benjamin **6**

Committee on Appeal for Human Rights (COHAR)
Bond, Julian **2**

Communist party
Davis, Angela **5**
Du Bois, W. E. B. **3**
Jagan, Cheddi **16**
Wright, Richard **5**

Computer graphics
Hannah, Marc **10**

Computer science
Hannah, Marc **10**

Conceptual art
Allen, Tina **22**
Bailey, Xenobia **11**
Simpson, Lorna **4**

Concerned Black Men
Holder, Eric H., Jr. **9**

Conductors
Jackson, Isaiah **3**
Calloway, Cab **14**
León, Tania **13**

Congressional Black Caucus (CBC)
Christian-Green, Donna M. **17**
Clay, William Lacy **8**
Clyburn, James **21**
Collins, Cardiss **10**
Conyers, John, Jr. **4**
Dellums, Ronald **2**
Diggs, Charles C. **21**
Fauntroy, Walter E. **11**
Gray, William H. III **3**
Hastings, Alcee L. **16**
Johnson, Eddie Bernice **8**
Mfume, Kweisi **6**
Owens, Major **6**
Rangel, Charles **3**
Scott, Robert C. **23**
Stokes, Louis **3**
Thompson, Bennie G. **26**
Towns, Edolphus **19**

Congressional Black Caucus Higher Education Braintrust
Owens, Major **6**

Congress of Racial Equality (CORE)
Dee, Ruby **8**
Farmer, James **2**
Innis, Roy **5**
Jackson, Jesse **1**
McKissick, Floyd B. **3**
Rustin, Bayard **4**

Connerly & Associates, Inc.
Connerly, Ward **14**

Continental Basketball Association (CBA)
Thomas, Isiah **7, 26**

Convention People's Party (Ghana; CPP)
Nkrumah, Kwame **3**

Cook County Circuit Court
Sampson, Edith S. **4**

Cooking
Clark, Patrick **14**
Evans, Darryl **22**

CORE
See Congress of Racial Equality

Corporation for Public Broadcasting (CPB)
Brown, Tony **3**

Cosmetology
Cottrell, Comer **11**
Fuller, S. B. **13**
Morgan, Rose **11**
Powell, Maxine **8**
Roche, Joyce M. **17**
Walker, A'lelia **14**
Walker, Madame C. J. **7**

Council for a Black Economic Agenda (CBEA)
Woodson, Robert L. **10**

Council for Social Action of the Congregational Christian Churches
Julian, Percy Lavon **6**

Council for the Economic Development of Black Americans (CEDBA)
Brown, Tony **3**

Council on Legal Education Opportunities (CLEO)
Henderson, Wade J. **14**
Henry, Aaron **19**

Count Basie Orchestra
Williams, Joe **5, 25**

Country music
Pride, Charley **26**

Cow hand
Love, Nat **9**
Pickett, Bill **11**

CPB
See Corporation for Public Broadcasting

CPP
See Convention People's Party

Cress Theory of Color-Confrontation and Racism
Welsing, Frances Cress **5**

Crisis
Du Bois, W. E. B. **3**
Fauset, Jessie **7**
Wilkins, Roy **4**

Cross Colours
Jones, Carl **7**
Kani, Karl **10**
Walker, T. J. **7**

Crucial Films
Henry, Lenny **9**

Crusader
Williams, Robert F. **11**

CTRN
See Transitional Committee for National Recovery (Guinea)

Cubism
Bearden, Romare **2**

Culinary arts
Clark, Patrick **14**

Cultural pluralism
Locke, Alain **10**

Cumulative voting
Guinier, Lani **7**

Curator/exhibition designer
Camp, Kimberly **19**
Golden, Thelma **10**
Hutson, Jean Blackwell **16**
Sanders, Joseph R., Jr. **11**
Stewart, Paul Wilbur **12**

Cytogenetics
Satcher, David **7**

Dallas city government
Johnson, Eddie Bernice **8**
Kirk, Ron **11**

Dallas Cowboys football team
Hill, Calvin **19**
Smith, Emmitt **7**

Dallas Police Department
Bolton, Terrell D. **25**

Dance Theatre of Harlem
Johnson, Virginia **9**
Mitchell, Arthur **2**
Nicholas, Fayard **20**
Nicholas, Harold **20**
Tyson, Cicely **7**

DAV
See Disabled American Veterans

David M. Winfield Foundation
Winfield, Dave **5**

Daytona Institute
See Bethune-Cookman College

Dayton Philharmonic Orchestra
Jackson, Isaiah **3**

D.C. Black Repertory Theater
Reagon, Bernice Johnson **7**

Death Row Records
Dre, Dr. **14**
Hammer, M. C. **20**
Knight, Suge **11**
Shakur, Tupac **14**

De Beers Botswana
See Debswana

Debswana
Masire, Quett **5**

Defense Communications Agency
Gravely, Samuel L., Jr. **5**

Def Jam Records
Brown, Foxy **25**
Jordan, Montell **23**
L.L. Cool J **16**
Simmons, Russell **1**

Democratic National Committee (DNC)
Brown, Ron **5**
Brown, Willie L., Jr. **7**
Dixon, Sharon Pratt **1**
Fattah, Chaka **11**
Hamer, Fannie Lou **6**
Jordan, Barbara **4**
Joyner, Marjorie Stewart **26**
Mallett, Conrad, Jr. **16**
Martin, Louis E. **16**
Waters, Maxine **3**
Williams, Maggie **7**

Democratic National Convention
Allen, Ethel D. **13**
Brown, Ron **5**
Brown, Willie L., Jr. **7**
Dixon, Sharon Pratt **1**
Hamer, Fannie Lou **6**
Herman, Alexis M. **15**
Jordan, Barbara **4**
Millender-McDonald, Juanita **21**
Waters, Maxine **3**
Williams, Maggie **7**

Democratic Socialists of America (DSA)
West, Cornel **5**
Marable, Manning **10**

Dentistry
Bluitt, Juliann S. **14**
Delany, Bessie **12**
Sinkford, Jeanne C. **13**

Denver Broncos football team
Barnes, Ernie **16**
Davis, Terrell **20**

Denver city government
Webb, Wellington **3**

Denver Nuggets basketball team
Bickerstaff, Bernie **21**
Mutombo, Dikembe **7**

DePaul University
Sizemore, Barbara A. **26**

Depression/The Great Depression
Hampton, Henry **6**

Desert Shield
See Operation Desert Shield

Desert Storm
See Operation Desert Storm

Detective fiction
Himes, Chester **8**
Mosley, Walter **5, 25**
Wesley, Valerie Wilson **18**

Detroit City Council
Collins, Barbara-Rose **7**

Detroit city government
Archer, Dennis **7**
Crockett, George, Jr. **10**
Marshall, Bella **22**
Young, Coleman **1, 20**

Detroit entertainment
Wilson, Sunnie **7**

Detroit Golden Gloves
Wilson, Sunnie **7**

Detroit Lions football team
Barney, Lem **26**
Farr, Mel **24**
Sanders, Barry **1**

Detroit Pistons basketball team
Bing, Dave **3**
Dumars, Joe **16**
Gentry, Alvin **23**
Hill, Grant **13**
Lloyd, Earl **26**
Thomas, Isiah **7, 26**

Detroit Police Department
Gomez-Preston, Cheryl **9**
McKinnon, Isaiah **9**
Napoleon, Benny N. **23**

Detroit Tigers baseball team
Fielder, Cecil **2**

Diamond mining
Masire, Quett **5**

Dillard University
Cook, Samuel DuBois **14**

Dime Savings Bank
Parsons, Richard Dean **11**

Diplomatic Corps
See U.S. Diplomatic Corps

Directing
Thompson, Tazewell **13**
Warner, Malcolm-Jamal **22**

Disabled American Veterans (DAV)
Brown, Jesse **6**

Disco
Summer, Donna **25**

DNC
See Democratic National Committee

Documentary film
Byrd, Robert **11**
Dash, Julie **4**
Davis, Ossie **5**
Hampton, Henry **6**
Henry, Lenny **9**
Hudlin, Reginald **9**
Hudlin, Warrington **9**
Julien, Isaac **3**
Lee, Spike **5, 19**
Riggs, Marlon **5**

Donald Byrd/The Group
Byrd, Donald **10**

Drug abuse prevention
Brown, Les **5**
Clements, George **2**
Hale, Lorraine **8**
Harris, Alice **7**
Lucas, John **7**
Rangel, Charles **3**

Drug synthesis
Julian, Percy Lavon **6**

DSA
See Democratic Socialists of America

Dunham Dance Company
Dunham, Katherine **4**

DuSable Museum of African American History
Burroughs, Margaret Taylor **9**

Earthquake Early Alerting Service
Person, Waverly **9**

East St. Louis city government
Powell, Debra A. **23**

Ebenezer Baptist Church
King, Bernice **4**

Ebonics
Cook, Toni **23**

Ebony
Bennett, Lerone, Jr. **5**
Johnson, John H. **3**
Rice, Linda Johnson **9**
Sleet, Moneta, Jr. **5**

Ebony Museum of African American History
See DuSable Museum of African American History

Economic Community of West African States (ECOWAS)
Sawyer, Amos **2**

Economic Regulatory Administration
O'Leary, Hazel **6**

Economics
Boyd, T. B. III **6**
Brimmer, Andrew F. **2**
Brown, Tony **3**
Divine, Father **7**
Dodson, Howard, Jr. **7**
Gibson, William F. **6**
Hamer, Fannie Lou **6**
Hampton, Henry **6**
Machel, Graca Simbine **16**
Masire, Quett **5**
Raines, Franklin Delano **14**
Robinson, Randall **7**
Sowell, Thomas **2**
Sullivan, Leon H. **3**
Van Peebles, Melvin **7**
Wallace, Phyllis A. **9**
Wharton, Clifton R., Jr. **7**
White, Michael R. **5**
Williams, Walter E. **4**

ECOWAS
See Economic Community of West African States

Edelman Public Relations
Barrett, Andrew C. **12**

Editing
Curry, George E. **23**

Edmonds Entertainment
Edmonds, Kenneth "Babyface" **10**
Edmonds, Tracey **16**
Tillman, George, Jr. **20**

Edmonton Oilers hockey team
Fuhr, Grant **1**

Educational Testing Service
Stone, Chuck **9**

EEC
See European Economic Community

EEOC
See Equal Employment Opportunity Commission

Egyptology
Diop, Cheikh Anta **4**

Elder Foundation
Elder, Lee **6**

Emerge
Curry, George E. **23**

Emmy awards
Allen, Debbie **13**
Amos, John **8**
Ashe, Arthur **1, 18**
Belafonte, Harry **4**
Bradley, Ed **2**
Brown, James **22**
Brown, Les **5**
Clayton, Xernona **3**
Cosby, Bill **7, 26**
Curtis-Hall, Vondie **17**
Dee, Ruby **8**
Foxx, Redd **2**
Freeman, Al, Jr. **11**
Goldberg, Whoopi **4**
Gossett, Louis, Jr. **7**
Guillaume, Robert **3**
Gumbel, Greg **8**
Hunter-Gault, Charlayne **6**
Jones, James Earl **3**
La Salle, Eriq **12**
Mabrey, Vicki **26**
McQueen, Butterfly **6**
Moore, Shemar **21**
Parks, Gordon **1**
Pinkston, W. Randall **24**
Quarles, Norma **25**
Robinson, Max **3**
Rock, Chris **3, 22**
Rolle, Esther **13, 21**
St. John, Kristoff **25**
Stokes, Carl B. **10**
Taylor, Billy **23**
Thigpen, Lynne **17**
Tyson, Cicely **7**
Uggams, Leslie **23**
Wayans, Damon **8**
Whitfield, Lynn **18**
Williams, Montel **4**
Williams, Sherley Anne **25**
Winfrey, Oprah **2, 15**
Woodard, Alfre **9**

Endocrinology
Elders, Joycelyn **6**

Energy studies
Cose, Ellis **5**
O'Leary, Hazel **6**

Engineering
Alexander, Archie Alphonso **14**
Gibson, Kenneth Allen **6**
Hannah, Marc **10**
Henderson, Cornelius Langston **26**
McCoy, Elijah **8**
Williams, O. S. **13**

Environmental issues
Chavis, Benjamin **6**
Hill, Bonnie Guiton **20**

Epidemiology
Gayle, Helene D. **3**

Episcopal Diocese of Massachusetts
Harris, Barbara **12**

EPRDF
See Ethiopian People's Revolutionary Democratic Front

Equal Employment Opportunity Commission (EEOC)
Alexander, Clifford **26**
Hill, Anita **5**
Lewis, Delano **7**
Norton, Eleanor Holmes **7**
Thomas, Clarence **2**
Wallace, Phyllis A. **9**

ESPN
Roberts, Robin **16**

Essence
Lewis, Edward T. **21**
Parks, Gordon **1**
Smith, Clarence O. **21**
Taylor, Susan L. **10**
Wesley, Valerie Wilson **18**

Essence Communications
Lewis, Edward T. **21**
Smith, Clarence O. **21**
Taylor, Susan L. **10**

Essence, the Television Program
Taylor, Susan L. **10**

Ethiopian People's Revolutionary Democratic Front (EPRDF)
Meles Zenawi **3**

Eugene O'Neill Theater
Richards, Lloyd **2**

European Economic Community (EEC)
Diouf, Abdou **3**

Executive Leadership Council
Jackson, Mannie **14**

Exiled heads of state
Aristide, Jean-Bertrand **6**

Exploration
Henson, Matthew **2**

Eyes on the Prize series
Hampton, Henry **6**

Fairbanks city government
Hayes, James C. **10**

FAIRR
See Foundation for the Advancement of Inmate Rehabilitation and Recreation

Fair Share Agreements
Gibson, William F. **6**

Famine relief
See World hunger

Famous Amos Cookie Corporation
Amos, Wally **9**

FAN
See Forces Armées du Nord (Chad)

Fashion
Smaltz, Audrey **12**
Sade **15**

Fashion Institute of Technology (FIT)
Brown, Joyce F. **25**

FCC
See Federal Communications Commission

Federal Bureau of Investigation (FBI)
Gibson, Johnnie Mae **23**
Harvard, Beverly **11**

Federal Communications Commission (FCC)
Barrett, Andrew C. **12**
Hooks, Benjamin L. **2**
Kennard, William Earl **18**
Russell-McCloud, Patricia A. **17**

Federal Energy Administration
O'Leary, Hazel **6**

Federal Reserve Bank
Brimmer, Andrew F. **2**
Ferguson, Roger W. **25**

Fellowship of Reconciliation (FOR)
Farmer, James **2**
Rustin, Bayard **4**

Fencing
Westbrook, Peter **20**

Fiction
Alexander, Margaret Walker **22**
Ansa, Tina McElroy **14**
Baisden, Michael **25**
Briscoe, Connie **15**
Campbell, Bebe Moore **6, 24**
Chase-Riboud, Barbara **20**
Cleage, Pearl **17**
Curtis, Christopher Paul **26**
Danticat, Edwidge **15**
Harris, E. Lynn **12**
Jackson, Sheneska **18**
Jenkins, Beverly **14**
McMillan, Terry **4, 17**
Mosley, Walter **5, 25**
Tate, Eleanora E. **20**
Taylor, Mildred D. **26**
Verdelle, A. J. **26**
Williams, Sherley Anne **25**

Figure skating
Bonaly, Surya **7**
Thomas, Debi **26**

Film direction
Allen, Debbie **13**
Burnett, Charles **16**
Byrd, Robert **11**

Curtis-Hall, Vondie **17**
Dash, Julie **4**
Davis, Ossie **5**
Dickerson, Ernest **6, 17**
Duke, Bill **3**
Franklin, Carl **11**
Freeman, Al, Jr. **11**
Gray, F. Gary **14**
Harris, Leslie **6**
Hudlin, Reginald **9**
Hudlin, Warrington **9**
Hughes, Albert **7**
Hughes, Allen **7**
Jackson, George **19**
Julien, Isaac **3**
Lane, Charles **3**
Lee, Spike **5, 19**
Lemmons, Kasi **20**
Lewis, Samella **25**
Micheaux, Oscar **7**
Morton, Joe **18**
Moses, Gilbert **12**
Moss, Carlton **17**
Poitier, Sidney **11**
Riggs, Marlon **5**
Schultz, Michael A. **6**
Sembène, Ousmane **13**
Singleton, John **2**
Smith, Roger Guenveur **12**
St. Jacques, Raymond **8**
Tillman, George, Jr. **20**
Townsend, Robert **4, 23**
Underwood, Blair **7**
Van Peebles, Mario **2**
Van Peebles, Melvin **7**
Wayans, Damon **8**
Wayans, Keenen Ivory **18**

Film scores
Hancock, Herbie **20**
Jean-Baptiste, Marianne **17**
Jones, Quincy **8**
Prince **18**

Finance
Banks, Jeffrey **17**
Boston, Kelvin E. **25**
Bryant, John **26**
Chapman, Jr., Nathan A. **21**
Doley, Harold, Jr. **26**
Ferguson, Roger W. **25**
Fletcher, Alphonse, Jr. **16**
Griffith, Mark Winston **8**
Lawless, Theodore K. **8**
Louis, Errol T. **8**
Marshall, Bella **22**
Rogers, John W., Jr. **5**

Fisk University
Johnson, Charles S. **12**
Smith, John L. **22**

Florida A & M University
Gaither, Alonzo Smith (Jake) **14**
Humphries, Frederick **20**

Florida Marlins baseball team
Sheffield, Gary **16**

Florida state government
Brown, Corrine **24**
Meek, Carrie **6**
Tribble, Isreal, Jr. **8**

Flouride chemistry
Quarterman, Lloyd Albert **4**

Folk music
Chapman, Tracy **26**
Charlemagne, Manno **11**
Jenkins, Ella **15**
Wilson, Cassandra **16**

Football
Allen, Marcus **20**
Amos, John **8**
Anderson, Jamal **22**
Barney, Lem **26**
Brown, James **22**
Brown, Jim **11**
Bruce, Isaac **26**
Butler, LeRoy III **17**
Carter, Cris **21**
Cunningham, Randall **23**
Davis, Terrell **20**
Dungy, Tony **17**
Edwards, Harry **2**
Farr, Mel Sr. **24**
Gaither, Alonzo Smith (Jake) **14**
Gilliam, Frank **23**
Green, Dennis **5**
Greene, Joe **10**
Grier, Roosevelt **13**
Hill, Calvin **19**
Lott, Ronnie **9**
McNair, Steve **22**
Moon, Warren **8**
Moss, Randy **23**
Motley, Marion **26**
Newsome, Ozzie **26**
Pace, Orlando **21**
Page, Alan **7**
Payton, Walter **11, 25**
Rashad, Ahmad **18**
Rice, Jerry **5**
Robinson, Eddie G. **10**
Sanders, Barry **1**
Sanders, Deion **4**
Shell, Art **1**
Simpson, O. J. **15**
Singletary, Mike **4**
Smith, Emmitt **7**
Stewart, Kordell **21**
Taylor, Lawrence **25**
Thomas, Derrick **25**
Upshaw, Gene **18**
Walker, Herschel **1**
Watts, J. C., Jr. **14**
Weathers, Carl **10**
White, Reggie **6**
Williams, Doug **22**

FOR
See Fellowship of Reconciliation

Forces Armées du Nord (Chad; FAN)
Habré, Hissène **6**

Ford Foundation
Thomas, Franklin A. **5**
Franklin, Robert M. **13**

Ford Motor Company
Goldsberry, Ronald **18**

Foreign policy
Bunche, Ralph J. **5**
Rice, Condoleezza **3**
Robinson, Randall **7**

Forest Club
Wilson, Sunnie **7**

40 Acres and a Mule Filmworks
Dickerson, Ernest **6, 17**
Lee, Spike **5, 19**

Foster care
Hale, Clara **16**
Hale, Lorraine **8**

Foundation for the Advancement of Inmate Rehabilitation and Recreation (FAIRR)
King, B. B. **7**

Freedom Farm Cooperative
Hamer, Fannie Lou **6**

Free Southern Theater (FST)
Borders, James **9**

FRELIMO
See Front for the Liberation of Mozambique

French West Africa
Diouf, Abdou **3**

FRODEBU
See Front for Democracy in Burundi

FROLINAT
See Front de la Libération Nationale du Tchad (Chad)

FRONASA
See Front for National Salvation (Uganda)

Front de la Libération Nationale du Tchad (Chad; FROLINAT)
Habré, Hissène **6**

Front for Democracy in Burundi (FRODEBU)
Ndadaye, Melchior **7**
Ntaryamira, Cyprien **8**

Front for National Salvation (Uganda; FRONASA)
Museveni, Yoweri **4**

Front for the Liberation of Mozambique (FRELIMO)
Chissano, Joaquim **7**
Machel, Graca Simbine **16**
Machel, Samora Moises **8**

FST
See Free Southern Theater

Funk music
Ayers, Roy **16**
Clinton, George **9**
Watson, Johnny "Guitar" **18**

Fusion
Davis, Miles **4**
Jones, Quincy **8**

Gary, Williams, Parenti, Finney, Lewis & McManus
Gary, Willie E. **12**

Gary Enterprises
Gary, Willie E. **12**

Gassaway, Crosson, Turner & Parsons
Parsons, James **14**

Gay Men of Color Consortium
Wilson, Phill **9**

Genealogy
Dash, Julie **4**
Haley, Alex **4**

General Motors Corporation
Roberts, Roy S. **14**

Geometric symbolism
Douglas, Aaron **7**

Geophysics
Person, Waverly **9**

George Foster Peabody Broadcasting Award
Bradley, Ed **2**
Hunter-Gault, Charlayne **6**
Shaw, Bernard **2**

Georgia state government
Baker, Thurbert **22**
Bishop Jr., Sanford D. **24**
Bond, Julian **2**
Williams, Hosea Lorenzo **15**

Georgia State Supreme Court
Sears-Collins, Leah J. **5**

Glaucoma treatment
Julian, Percy Lavon **6**

Glidden Company
Julian, Percy Lavon **6**

Golden Globe awards
Allen, Debbie **13**
Bassett, Angela **23**
Carroll, Diahann **9**
Freeman, Morgan **2, 20**
Taylor, Regina **9**

Golden State Warriors basketball team
Edwards, Harry **2**
Lucas, John **7**
Sprewell, Latrell **23**

Golf
Elder, Lee **6**
Gibson, Althea **8**
Jackson, Fred James **25**
Peete, Calvin **11**
Richmond, Mitch **19**
Sifford, Charlie **4**
Webber, Chris **15**
Woods, Tiger **14**

Goodwill Games
Swoopes, Sheryl **12**

Gospel music
Adams, Oleta **18**
Adams, Yolanda **17**
Armstrong, Vanessa Bell **24**
Caesar, Shirley **19**
Clark-Sheard, Karen **22**
Cleveland, James **19**
Cooke, Sam **17**
Dorsey, Thomas **15**
Franklin, Aretha **11**
Franklin, Kirk **15**
Green, Al **13**
Hammond, Fred **23**
Hawkins, Tramaine **16**
Houston, Cissy **20**
Jackson, Mahalia **5**
Jakes, Thomas "T.D." **17**
Jones, Bobby **20**
Lassiter, Roy **24**
Little Richard **15**
Marrow, Queen Esther **24**
Mayfield, Curtis **2**
McClurkin, Donnie **25**
Monica **21**
Peoples, Dottie **22**
Reagon, Bernice Johnson **7**
Reese, Della **6, 20**
Walker, Albertina **10**
Washington, Dinah **22**
Winans, BeBe **14**
Winans, CeCe **14**
Winans, Marvin L. **17**
Winans, Vickie **24**

Grambling State University
Favors, Steve **23**

Grammy awards
Adams, Oleta **18**
Badu, Erykah **22**
Belafonte, Harry **4**
Blige, Mary J. **20**
Brandy **14**
Caesar, Shirley **19**
Chapman, Tracy **26**
Cleveland, James **19**
Cole, Natalie Maria **17**
Cosby, Bill **7, 26**
Davis, Miles **4**
Edmonds, Kenneth "Babyface" **10**
Ellington, Duke **5**
Fitzgerald, Ella **8**
Franklin, Aretha **11**
Gaye, Marvin **2**
Goldberg, Whoopi **4**
Hammer, M. C. **20**
Hathaway, Donny **18**
Hawkins, Tramaine **16**
Hill, Lauryn **20**
Houston, Cissy **20**
Houston, Whitney **7**
Isley, Ronald **25**
Jackson, Michael **19**
James, Etta **13**
Jean, Wyclef **20**
Jimmy Jam **13**
Jones, Bobby **20**
Jones, Quincy **8**
Kelly, R. **18**
Lewis, Terry **13**
Makeba, Miriam **2**
Murphy, Eddie **4, 20**
Norman, Jessye **5**
Price, Leontyne **1**
Pride, Charley **26**
Prince **18**
Queen Latifah **1, 16**
Reagon, Bernice Johnson **7**
Redding, Otis **16**
Robinson, Smokey **3**
Sade **15**
Smith, Will **8, 18**
Summer, Donna **25**
Turner, Tina **6**
Warwick, Dionne **18**
White, Barry **13**
Williams, Joe **5, 25**
Wilson, Nancy **10**
Winans, Marvin L. **17**
Wonder, Stevie **11**

Green Bay Packers football team
Butler, Leroy III **17**
Howard, Desmond **16**
White, Reggie **6**

Groupe de Recherche Choréographique del'Opéra de Paris
Dove, Ulysses **5**

Guardian
Trotter, Monroe **9**

Guitar
Hendrix, Jimi **10**
House, Son **8**
Howlin' Wolf **9**
Jean, Wyclef **20**
Johnson, Robert **2**
Jordan, Ronny **26**
King, B. B. **7**
Kravitz, Lenny **10**
Marley, Bob **5**
Mayfield, Curtis **2**
Ndegéocello, Me'Shell **15**
Ongala, Remmy **9**
Watson, Johnny "Guitar" **18**
Wilson, Cassandra **16**

Gulf War
Powell, Colin **1**
Shaw, Bernard **2**
Von Lipsey, Roderick K. **11**

Gurdjieff Institute
Toomer, Jean **6**

Gymnastics
Dawes, Dominique **11**
White, Jesse **22**

Hair care
Cottrell, Comer **11**
Fuller, S. B. **13**
Joyner, Marjorie Stewart **26**
Malone, Annie **13**
Roche, Joyce M. **17**
Walker, Madame C. J. **7**

Haitian refugees
Ashe, Arthur **1, 18**
Dunham, Katherine **4**
Jean, Wyclef **20**
Robinson, Randall **7**

Hale House
Hale, Clara **16**
Hale, Lorraine **8**

Harlem Globetrotters
Chamberlain, Wilt **18**
Haynes, Marques **22**
Jackson, Mannie **14**

Harlem Renaissance
Alexander, Margaret Walker **22**
Cullen, Countee **8**
Delaney, Beauford **19**
Ellington, Duke **5**
Fauset, Jessie **7**
Fisher, Rudolph **17**
Frazier, E. Franklin **10**
Hughes, Langston **4**
Hurston, Zora Neale **3**
Johnson, James Weldon **5**
Johnson, William Henry **3**
Larsen, Nella **10**
Locke, Alain **10**
McKay, Claude **6**
Mills, Florence **22**
Petry, Ann **19**
Thurman, Wallace **16**
Toomer, Jean **6**
VanDerZee, James **6**
West, Dorothy **12**

Harlem Writers Guild
Guy, Rosa **5**
Wesley, Valerie Wilson **18**

Harlem Youth Opportunities Unlimited (HARYOU)
Clark, Kenneth B. **5**

Harmonica
Howlin' Wolf **9**

Harriet Tubman Home for Aged and Indignet Colored People
Tubman, Harriet **9**

Harvard Law School
Bell, Derrick **6**
Ogletree, Charles, Jr. **12**

HARYOU
See Harlem Youth Opportunities Unlimited

Head Start
Edelman, Marian Wright **5**

Health care reform
Brown, Jesse **6**
Cooper, Edward S. **6**
Davis, Angela **5**
Gibson, Kenneth A. **6**
Norman, Pat **10**
Satcher, David **7**
Williams, Daniel Hale **2**

Heart disease
Cooper, Edward S. **6**

Heidelberg Project
Guyton, Tyree **9**

HEW
See U.S. Department of Health, Education, and Welfare

HHS
See U.S. Department of Health and Human Services

Historians
Berry, Mary Frances **7**
Chase-Riboud, Barbara **20**
Cooper, Anna Julia **20**
Diop, Cheikh Anta **4**
Dodson, Howard, Jr. **7**
Du Bois, W. E. B. **3**
Franklin, John Hope **5**
Gates, Henry Louis, Jr. **3**
Giddings, Paula **11**
Hansberry, William Leo **11**
Harkless, Necia Desiree **19**
Hine, Darlene Clark **24**
Marable, Manning **10**
Painter, Nell Irvin **24**
Patterson, Orlando **4**
Quarles, Benjamin Arthur **18**
Reagon, Bernice Johnson **7**
Reddick, Lawrence Dunbar **20**
Schomburg, Arthur Alfonso **9**
van Sertima, Ivan **25**
Williams, George Washington **18**
Woodson, Carter G. **2**

Hockey
Brown, James **22**
Carnegie, Herbert **25**
Fuhr, Grant **1**
McBride, Bryant **18**
McKegney, Tony **3**
O'Ree, Willie **5**

Homosexuality
Carter, Mandy **11**
Delany, Samuel R., Jr. **9**
Gomes, Peter J. **15**
Harris, E. Lynn **12**
Hemphill, Essex **10**
Julien, Isaac **3**
Lorde, Audre **6**
Norman, Pat **10**
Parker, Pat **19**
Riggs, Marlon **5**
Rupaul **17**
Wilson, Phill **9**

Honeywell Corporation
Jackson, Mannie **14**

House of Representatives
See U.S. House of Representatives

Houston Astros baseball team
Morgan, Joe Leonard **9**
Watson, Bob **25**

Houston Comets basketball team
Perrot, Kim **23**
Thompson, Tina **25**

Houston Oilers football team
McNair, Steve **22**
Moon, Warren **8**

Houston Rockets basketball team
Lucas, John **7**
Olajuwon, Hakeem **2**

Howard University
Jenifer, Franklyn G. **2**
Locke, Alain **10**
Mays, Benjamin E. **7**
Payton, Benjamin F. **23**
Porter, James A. **11**
Reid, Irvin D. **20**
Robinson, Spottswood W. III **22**
Swygert, H. Patrick **22**
Wells, James Lesesne **10**
Wesley, Dorothy Porter **19**

HRCF
See Human Rights Campaign Fund

Hubbard Hospital
Lyttle, Hulda Margaret **14**

HUD
See U.S. Department of Housing and Urban Development

Hugo awards
Butler, Octavia **8**
Delany, Samuel R., Jr. **9**

Hull-Ottawa Canadiens hockey team
O'Ree, Willie **5**

Human Rights Campaign Fund (HRCF)
Carter, Mandy **11**

Hurdles
Devers, Gail **7**

IBF
See International Boxing Federation

IBM
Thompson, John W. **26**

Ice skating
See Figure skating

Igbo people/traditions
Achebe, Chinua **6**

IHRLG
See International Human Rights Law Group

Illinois state government
Braun, Carol Moseley **4**
Burris, Roland W. **25**
Washington, Harold **6**
White, Jesse **22**

Illustrations
Biggers, John **20**
Campbell, E. Simms **13**
Hudson, Cheryl **15**
Kitt, Sandra **23**
Pinkney, Jerry **15**
Saint James, Synthia **12**

Imani Temple
Stallings, George A., Jr. **6**

IMF
See International Monetary Fund

Indiana state government
Carson, Julia **23**

Indianapolis 500
Ribbs, Willy T. **2**

Information technology
Smith, Joshua **10**

In Friendship
Baker, Ella **5**

Inkatha
Buthelezi, Mangosuthu Gatsha **9**

Institute for Black Parenting
Oglesby, Zena **12**

Institute for Journalism Education
Harris, Jay T. **19**
Maynard, Robert C. **7**

Institute for Research in African American Studies
Marable, Manning **10**

Institute of Positive Education
Madhubuti, Haki R. **7**

Institute of Social and Religious Research
Mays, Benjamin E. **7**

Institute of the Black World
Dodson, Howard, Jr. **7**

Insurance
Hill, Jessie, Jr. **13**
Procope, Ernesta **23**
Spaulding, Charles Clinton **9**

International Boxing Federation (IBF)
Ali, Muhammad **2, 16**
Moorer, Michael **19**
Whitaker, Pernell **10**

International Free and Accepted Masons and Eastern Star
Banks, William **11**

International Human Rights Law Group (IHRLG)
McDougall, Gay J. **11**

International Ladies' Auxiliary
Tucker, Rosina **14**

International Monetary Fund (IMF)
Babangida, Ibrahim **4**
Chissano, Joaquim **7**
Conté, Lansana **7**
Diouf, Abdou **3**
Patterson, P. J. **6, 20**

International Workers Organization (IWO)
Patterson, Louise **25**

Internet security
Thompson, John W. **26**

Inventions
Julian, Percy Lavon **6**
Latimer, Lewis H. **4**
McCoy, Elijah **8**
Morgan, Garrett **1**
Woods, Granville T. **5**

Investment management
Bryant, John **26**
Procope, Ernesta **23**
Rogers, John W., Jr. **5**
Utendahl, John **23**

Jackie Robinson Foundation
Robinson, Rachel **16**

Jamison Project
Jamison, Judith **7**

Jazz
Albright, Gerald **23**
Armstrong, Louis **2**
Austin, Patti **24**
Ayers, Roy **16**
Basie, Count **23**
Bechet, Sidney **18**
Belle, Regina **1**
Brooks, Avery **9**
Calloway, Cab **14**
Carter, Betty **19**
Carter, Regina **23**
Charles, Ray **16**
Cheatham, Doc **17**
Cole, Nat King **17**
Coltrane, John **19**
Count Basie **23**
Crawford, Randy **19**
Crothers, Scatman **19**
Crouch, Stanley **11**
Crowder, Henry **16**
Davis, Anthony **11**
Davis, Miles **4**
Donegan, Dorothy **19**
Downing, Will **19**
Duke, George **21**
Ellington, Duke **5**
Ellison, Ralph **7**
Eubanks, Kevin **15**
Fitzgerald, Ella **8, 18**
Gillespie, Dizzy **1**
Gordon, Dexter **25**
Hampton, Lionel **17**
Hancock, Herbie **20**
Hawkins, Coleman **9**
Holiday, Billie **1**
Hyman, Phyllis **19**
Jackson, Milt **26**
James, Etta **13**
Jarreau, Al **21**
Jones, Elvin **14**
Jones, Quincy **8**
Jordan, Ronny **26**
Lincoln, Abbey **3**
Madhubuti, Haki R. **7**
Marsalis, Wynton **16**
Mills, Florence **22**
Mingus, Charles **15**
Monk, Thelonious **1**
Moore, Melba **21**
Muse, Clarence Edouard **21**
Nascimento, Milton **2**
Parker, Charlie **20**
Powell, Bud **24**
Reese, Della **6, 20**
Roach, Max **21**
Roberts, Marcus **19**
Ross, Diana **8**
Silver, Horace **26**
Smith, Bessie **3**
Taylor, Billy **23**
Vaughan, Sarah **13**
Washington, Dinah **22**
Washington, Grover, Jr. **17**
Waters, Benny **26**
Watson, Johnny "Guitar" **18**
Williams, Joe **5, 25**
Williams, Mary Lou **15**
Wilson, Cassandra **16**
Wilson, Nancy **10**

Jet
Bennett, Lerone, Jr. **5**
Johnson, John H. **3**
Sleet, Moneta, Jr. **5**

John Lucas Enterprises
Lucas, John **7**

Johnson Publishing Company, Inc.
Bennett, Lerone, Jr. **5**
Booker, Simeon **23**
Johnson, John H. **3**
Rice, Linda Johnson **9**
Sleet, Moneta, Jr. **5**

Joint Chiefs of Staff
See U.S. Joint Chiefs of Staff

Journalism
Abu-Jamal, Mumia **15**
Ansa, Tina McElroy **14**
Ashley-Ward, Amelia **23**
Azikiwe, Nnamdi **13**
Barden, Don H. **9, 20**
Bennett, Lerone, Jr. **5**
Blake, Asha **26**
Booker, Simeon **23**
Borders, James **9**
Bradley, Ed **2**
Brown, Tony **3**
Campbell, Bebe Moore **6, 24**
Cayton, Horace **26**
Chideya, Farai **14**
Cose, Ellis **5**
Crouch, Stanley **11**
Cullen, Countee **8**
Cunningham, Evelyn **23**
Dawkins, Wayne **20**
Dunbar, Paul Laurence **8**
Edmonds, Terry **17**
Forman, James **7**
Fortune, T. Thomas **6**
Giddings, Paula **11**
Goode, Mal **13**
Gordon, Ed **10**
Grimké, Archibald H. **9**
Gumbel, Bryant **14**
Gumbel, Greg **8**
Hansberry, Lorraine **6**
Harrington, Oliver W. **9**
Harris, Jay **19**
Hickman, Fred **11**
Hunter-Gault, Charlayne **6**
Johnson, James Weldon **5**
Khanga, Yelena **6**
Lampkin, Daisy **19**
Leavell, Dorothy R. **17**

Lewis, Edward T. **21**
Mabrey, Vicki **26**
Martin, Louis E. **16**
Maynard, Robert C. **7**
McCall, Nathan **8**
McGruder, Robert **22**
McKay, Claude **6**
Mitchell, Russ **21**
Mkapa, Benjamin **16**
Nelson, Jill **6**
Page, Clarence **4**
Parks, Gordon **1**
Perez, Anna **1**
Perkins, Tony **24**
Pinkston, W. Randall **24**
Price, Hugh B. **9**
Quarles, Norma **25**
Raspberry, William **2**
Reed, Ishmael **8**
Reeves, Rachel J. **23**
Roberts, Robin **16**
Robinson, Max **3**
Rodgers, Johnathan **6**
Rowan, Carl T. **1**
Shaw, Bernard **2**
Shipp, E. R. **15**
Simpson, Carole **6**
Smith, Clarence O. **21**
Sowell, Thomas **2**
Staples, Brent **8**
Stewart, Alison **13**
Stokes, Carl B. **10**
Stone, Chuck **9**
Tate, Eleanora E. **20**
Taylor, Kristin Clark **8**
Taylor, Susan L. **10**
Thurman, Wallace **16**
Trotter, Monroe **9**
Tucker, Cynthia **15**
Wallace, Michele Faith **13**
Watts, Rolonda **9**
Webb, Veronica **10**
Wells-Barnett, Ida B. **8**
Wesley, Valerie Wilson **18**
Whitaker, Mark **21**
Wiley, Ralph **8**
Wilkins, Roger **2**
Williams, Patricia J. **11**

Journal of Negro History
Woodson, Carter G. **2**

Just Us Books
Hudson, Cheryl **15**
Hudson, Wade **15**

Kansas City Athletics baseball team
Paige, Satchel **7**

Kansas City Chiefs football team
Allen, Marcus **20**
Dungy, Tony **17**
Thomas, Derrick **25**

Kansas City government
Cleaver, Emanuel **4**

KANU
See Kenya African National Union

Karl Kani Infinity
Kani, Karl **10**

KAU
See Kenya African Union

KCA
See Kikuyu Central Association

Kenya African National Union (KANU)
Kenyatta, Jomo **5**

Kenya African Union (KAU)
Kenyatta, Jomo **5**

Kikuyu Central Association (KCA)
Kenyatta, Jomo **5**

King Center
See Martin Luther King Jr. Center for Nonviolent Social Change

Kraft General Foods
Fudge, Ann **11**
Sneed, Paula A. **18**

Kwanzaa
Karenga, Maulana **10**

Kwazulu Territorial Authority
Buthelezi, Mangosuthu Gatsha **9**

Ladies Professional Golfers' Association (LPGA)
Gibson, Althea **8**

LAPD
See Los Angeles Police Department

Latin American folk music
Nascimento, Milton **2**

Law enforcement
Alexander, Joyce London **18**
Bolton, Terrell D. **25**
Bradley, Thomas **2, 20**
Brown, Lee P. **1, 24**
Freeman, Charles **19**
Gibson, Johnnie Mae **23**
Glover, Nathaniel, Jr. **12**
Gomez-Preston, Cheryl **9**
Harvard, Beverly **11**
Hillard, Terry **25**
Johnson, Norma L. Holloway **17**
Johnson, Robert T. **17**
Keith, Damon J. **16**
McKinnon, Isaiah **9**
Napoleon, Benny N. **23**
Parks, Bernard C. **17**
Ramsey, Charles H. **21**
Schmoke, Kurt **1**
Thomas, Franklin A. **5**
Williams, Willie L. **4**

Lawyers' Committee for Civil Rights Under Law
McDougall, Gay J. **11**

LDF
See NAACP Legal Defense Fund

Leadership Conference on Civil Rights (LCCR)
Henderson, Wade J. **14**

League of Nations
Haile Selassie **7**

Leary Group Inc.
Leary, Kathryn D. **10**

"Leave No Child Behind"
Edelman, Marian Wright **5**

Lee Elder Scholarship Fund
Elder, Lee **6**

Legal Defense Fund
See NAACP Legal Defense Fund

Les Brown Unlimited, Inc.
Brown, Les **5**

Lexicography
Major, Clarence **9**

Liberation theology
West, Cornel **5**

Library science
Bontemps, Arna **8**
Franklin, Hardy R. **9**
Harsh, Vivian Gordon **14**
Hutson, Jean Blackwell **16**
Josey, E. J. **10**
Kitt, Sandra **23**
Larsen, Nella **10**
Owens, Major **6**
Schomburg, Arthur Alfonso **9**
Wesley, Dorothy Porter **19**

Lincoln University
Randall, Dudley **8**
Sudarkasa, Niara **4**

LISC
See Local Initiative Support Corporation

Literacy Volunteers of America
Amos, Wally **9**

Literary criticism
Baker, Houston A., Jr. **6**
Brown, Sterling **10**
Redding, J. Saunders **26**
Reed, Ishmael **8**
Wesley, Valerie Wilson **18**
West, Cornel **5**

"Little Paris" group
Thomas, Alma **14**

"Little Rock Nine"
Bates, Daisy **13**

Lobbying
Brooke, Edward **8**
Brown, Elaine **8**
Brown, Jesse **6**
Brown, Ron **5**
Edelman, Marian Wright **5**
Lee, Canada **8**
Mallett, Conrad, Jr. **16**
Robinson, Randall **7**

Local Initiative Support Corporation (LISC)
Thomas, Franklin A. **5**

Long jump
Lewis, Carl **4**
Powell, Mike **7**

Los Angeles city government
Bradley, Thomas **2, 20**
Evers, Myrlie **8**

Los Angeles Dodgers baseball team
Baker, Dusty **8**
Newcombe, Don **24**
Robinson, Frank **9**
Strawberry, Darryl **22**

Los Angeles Galaxy soccer team
Jones, Cobi N'Gai **18**

Los Angeles Lakers basketball team
Abdul-Jabbar, Kareem **8**
Bryant, Kobe **15**
Chamberlain, Wilt **18**
Johnson, Earvin "Magic" **3**

Los Angeles Police Department (LAPD)
Parks, Bernard C. **17**
Williams, Willie L. **4**

Los Angeles Raiders football team
Allen, Marcus **20**
Lott, Ronnie **9**
Shell, Art **1**

Los Angeles Sparks basketball team
Leslie, Lisa **16**

Lost-Found Nation of Islam
Ali, Muhammad **2, 16**
Farrakhan, Louis **2, 15**
Muhammad, Elijah **4**
Muhammad, Khallid Abdul **10**
X, Malcolm **1**

Louisiana state government
Fields, Cleo **13**
Morial, Ernest "Dutch" **26**
Pinchback, P. B. S. **9**

Louisiana State Senate
Fields, Cleo **13**
Jefferson, William J. **25**
Pinchback, P. B. S. **9**

LPGA
See Ladies Professional Golfers' Association

Lynching (anti-lynching legislation)
Johnson, James Weldon **5**
Till, Emmett **7**

Lyricist
Dunbar, Paul Laurence **8**
Fitzgerald, Ella **8**
Jean, Wyclef **20**
Johnson, James Weldon **5**

MacNeil/Lehrer NewsHour
Hunter-Gault, Charlayne **6**

Madame C. J. Walker Manufacturing Company
Joyner, Marjorie Stewart **26**
Walker, A'lelia **14**
Walker, Madame C. J. **7**

Major League Baseball Properties
Doby, Lawrence Eugene, Sr. **16**

Malawi Congress Party (MCP)
Banda, Hastings Kamuzu **6**

Manhattan Project
Quarterman, Lloyd Albert **4**

MARC Corp.
See Metropolitan Applied Research Center

March on Washington/Freedom March
Baker, Josephine **3**
Belafonte, Harry **4**
Bunche, Ralph J. **5**
Davis, Ossie **5**
Fauntroy, Walter E. **11**
Forman, James **7**
Franklin, John Hope **5**
Hedgeman, Anna Arnold **22**
Horne, Lena **5**
Jackson, Mahalia **5**
King, Coretta Scott **3**
King, Martin Luther, Jr. **1**
Lewis, John **2**
Meredith, James H. **11**
Randolph, A. Philip **3**
Rustin, Bayard **4**
Sleet, Moneta, Jr. **5**
Wilkins, Roy **4**
Young, Whitney M., Jr. **4**

Marie Brown Associates
Brown, Marie Dutton **12**

Martin Luther King Jr. Center for Nonviolent Social Change
Dodson, Howard, Jr. **7**
King, Bernice **4**
King, Coretta Scott **3**
King, Dexter **10**
King, Martin Luther, Jr. **1**
King, Yolanda **6**

Marxism
Baraka, Amiri **1**
Jagan, Cheddi **16**
Machel, Samora Moises **8**
Nkrumah, Kwame **3**
Sankara, Thomas **17**

Massachusetts state government
Brooke, Edward **8**

Masters Tournament
Elder, Lee **6**

Mathematics
Gates, Sylvester James, Jr. **15**

MAXIMA Corporation
Smith, Joshua **10**

Maxwell House Coffee Company
Fudge, Ann **11**

McCall Pattern Company
Lewis, Reginald F. **6**

MCP
See Malawi Congress Party

Medicine
Banda, Hastings Kamuzu **6**
Benjamin, Regina **20**
Black, Keith Lanier **18**
Callender, Clive O. **3**
Carson, Benjamin **1**
Chinn, May Edward **26**
Christian-Green, Donna M.**17**
Comer, James P. **6**
Cooper, Edward S. **6**
Dickens, Helen Octavia **14**
Drew, Charles Richard **7**
Elders, Joycelyn **6**
Fisher, Rudolph **17**
Foster, Henry W., Jr. **26**
Freeman, Harold P. **23**
Fuller, Solomon Carter, Jr. **15**
Gayle, Helene D. **3**
Gibson, William F. **6**
Hinton, William Augustus **8**
Jemison, Mae C. **1**
Kountz, Samuel L. **10**
Lawless, Theodore K. **8**
Leffall, LaSalle, Jr. **3**
Logan, Onnie Lee **14**
Pitt, David Thomas **10**
Poussaint, Alvin F. **5**
Satcher, David **7**
Sullivan, Louis **8**
Thomas, Vivien **9**
Watkins, Levi, Jr. **9**
Welsing, Frances Cress **5**
Williams, Daniel Hale **2**
Witt, Edwin T. **26**
Wright, Louis Tompkins **4**

Meharry Medical College
Foster, Henry W., Jr. **26**
Lyttle, Hulda Margaret **14**

Melanin theory of racism
See also Cress Theory of Color Confrontation and Racism

Men's movement
Somé, Malidoma Patrice **10**

Merce Cunningham Dance Company
Dove, Ulysses **5**

MESBICs
See Minority Enterprise Small Business Investment Corporations

Metropolitan Applied Research Center (MARC Corp.)
Clark, Kenneth B. **5**

MFDP
See Mississippi Freedom Democratic Party

Miami Dolphins football team
Greene, Joe **10**

Michael Jordan Foundation
Jordan, Michael **6, 21**

Michigan House of Representatives
Collins, Barbara-Rose **7**
Kilpatrick, Carolyn Cheeks **16**

Michigan State Supreme Court
Archer, Dennis **7**
Mallett, Conrad, Jr. **16**

Michigan State University
Wharton, Clifton R., Jr. **7**

Midwifery
Logan, Onnie Lee **14**
Robinson, Sharon **22**

Military police
Cadoria, Sherian Grace **14**

Miller Brewing Company
Colbert, Virgis William **17**

Millinery
Bailey, Xenobia **11**

Million Man March
Farrakhan, Louis **15**
Hawkins, La-Van **17**
Worrill, Conrad **12**

Milwaukee Braves baseball team
Aaron, Hank **5**

Milwaukee Brewers baseball team
Aaron, Hank **5**
Baylor, Don **6**
Sheffield, Gary **16**

Milwaukee Bucks basketball team
Abdul-Jabbar, Kareem **8**
Lucas, John **7**
Robertson, Oscar **26**

Minneapolis City Council
Sayles Belton, Sharon **9, 16**

Minneapolis city government
Sayles Belton, Sharon **9, 16**

Minnesota State Supreme Court
Page, Alan **7**

Minnesota Timberwolves basketball team
Garnett, Kevin **14**

Minnesota Twins baseball team
Baylor, Don **6**
Carew, Rod **20**
Puckett, Kirby **4**
Winfield, Dave **5**

Minnesota Vikings football team
Carter, Cris **21**
Cunningham, Randall **23**
Dungy, Tony **17**
Gilliam, Frank **23**
Green, Dennis **5**
Moon, Warren **8**
Moss, Randy **23**
Page, Alan **7**
Rashad, Ahmad **18**
Walker, Herschel **1**

Minority Business Resource Center
Hill, Jessie, Jr. **13**

Minority Enterprise Small Business Investment Corporations (MESBICs)
Lewis, Reginald F. **6**

Minstrel shows
McDaniel, Hattie **5**

Miss America
Vincent, Marjorie Judith **2**
Williams, Vanessa L. **4, 17**

Mississippi Freedom Democratic Party (MFDP)
Baker, Ella **5**
Blackwell, Unita **17**
Hamer, Fannie Lou **6**
Henry, Aaron **19**
Norton, Eleanor Holmes **7**

Mississippi state government
Hamer, Fannie Lou **6**

Miss USA
Gist, Carole **1**

MLA
See Modern Language Association of America

Model Inner City Community Organization (MICCO)
Fauntroy, Walter E. **11**

Modeling
Banks, Tyra **11**
Beckford, Tyson **11**
Berry, Halle **4, 19**
Campbell, Naomi **1**
Hardison, Bethann **12**
Hounsou, Djimon **19**
Houston, Whitney **7**
Iman **4**
Johnson, Beverly **2**
Langhart, Janet **19**
Leslie, Lisa **16**
Powell, Maxine **8**
Rochon, Lela **16**
Smith, Barbara **11**
Tamia **24**
Tyson, Cicely **7**
Webb, Veronica **10**
Wek, Alek **18**

Modern dance
Ailey, Alvin **8**
Allen, Debbie **13**
Byrd, Donald **10**
Dove, Ulysses **5**
Fagan, Garth **18**
Faison, George **16**
Jamison, Judith **7**
Kitt, Eartha **16**
Miller, Bebe **3**
Primus, Pearl **6**
Vereen, Ben **4**

Modern Language Association of America (MLA)
Baker, Houston A., Jr. **6**

Montgomery bus boycott
Abernathy, Ralph David **1**
Baker, Ella **5**
Jackson, Mahalia **5**
King, Martin Luther, Jr. **1**
Parks, Rosa **1**
Rustin, Bayard **4**

Montreal Expos
Doby, Lawrence Eugene, Sr. **16**

Morehouse College
Hope, John **8**
Mays, Benjamin E. **7**

Morna
Evora, Cesaria **12**

Morris Brown College
Cross, Dolores E. **23**

Moscow World News
Khanga, Yelena **6**
Sullivan, Louis **8**

Mother Waddles Perpetual Mission, Inc.
Waddles, Charleszetta (Mother) **10**

Motivational speaking
Brown, Les **5**
Kimbro, Dennis **10**
Russell-McCloud, Patricia **17**

Motown Records
Bizimungu, Pasteur **19**
Busby, Jheryl **3**
de Passe, Suzanne **25**
Gaye, Marvin **2**
Gordy, Berry, Jr. **1**
Jackson, George **19**
Jackson, Michael **19**
Kendricks, Eddie **22**
Massenburg, Kedar **23**
Powell, Maxine **8**
Robinson, Smokey **3**
Ross, Diana **8**
Wonder, Stevie **11**

Mouvement Revolutionnaire National pour la Developpement (Rwanda; MRND)
Habyarimana, Juvenal **8**

MOVE
Goode, W. Wilson **4**
Wideman, John Edgar **5**

Movement for Democratic Change (MDC)
Tsvangirai, Morgan **26**

MRND
See Mouvement Revolutionnaire National pour la Developpement

MTV Jams
Bellamy, Bill **12**

Multimedia art
Bailey, Xenobia **11**
Simpson, Lorna **4**

Muppets, The
Clash, Kevin **14**

Murals
Biggers, John **20**
Douglas, Aaron **7**
Lee-Smith, Hughie **5**
Walker, Kara **16**

Music Television (MTV)
Bellamy, Bill **12**
Chideya, Farai **14**

Musical composition
Ashford, Nickolas **21**
Blige, Mary J **20**
Bonga, Kuenda **13**
Braxton, Toni **15**
Caesar, Shirley **19**
Chapman, Tracy **26**
Charlemagne, Manno **11**
Charles, Ray **16**
Cleveland, James **19**
Cole, Natalie Maria **17**
Combs, Sean "Puffy" **17**
Davis, Anthony **11**
Davis, Miles **4**
Davis, Sammy Jr. **18**
Ellington, Duke **5**
Europe, James Reese **10**
Evans, Faith **22**
Fats Domino **20**
George, Nelson **12**
Gillespie, Dizzy **1**
Gordy, Berry, Jr. **1**
Green, Al **13**
Hailey, JoJo **22**
Hailey, K-Ci **22**
Hammer, M. C. **20**
Handy, W. C. **8**
Hathaway, Donny **18**
Hayes, Isaac **20**
Hill, Lauryn **20**
Humphrey, Bobbi **20**
Isley, Ronald **25**
Jackson, Fred James **25**
Jackson, Michael **19**
James, Rick **17**
Jean-Baptiste, Marianne **17**
Jean, Wyclef **20**
Jones, Quincy **8**
Joplin, Scott **6**
Jordan, Montell **23**
Jordan, Ronny **26**
Kelly, R. **18**
King, B. B. **7**
León, Tania **13**
Lincoln, Abbey **3**
Marsalis, Wynton **16**
Master P **21**
Maxwell **20**
McClurkin, Donnie **25**
Mitchell, Brian Stokes **21**
Monica **21**
Moore, Chante **26**
Muse, Clarence Edouard **21**
Ndegéocello, Me'Shell **15**
Osborne, Jeffrey **26**
Prince **18**
Pritchard, Robert Starling **21**
Reagon, Bernice Johnson **7**
Redding, Otis **16**
Roach, Max **21**
Rushen, Patrice **12**
Sangare, Oumou **18**
Silver, Horace **26**
Simone, Nina **15**
Simpson, Valerie **21**
Sweat, Keith **19**
Usher **23**
Van Peebles, Melvin **7**
Warwick, Dionne **18**
Washington, Grover, Jr. **17**

Music publishing
Combs, Sean "Puffy" **17**
Cooke, Sam **17**
Edmonds, Tracey **16**
Gordy, Berry, Jr. **1**
Handy, W. C. **8**
Humphrey, Bobbi **20**
Ice Cube **8**
Jackson, George **19**
Jackson, Michael **19**
James, Rick **17**
Knight, Suge **11**
Master P **21**
Mayfield, Curtis **2**
Prince **18**
Redding, Otis **16**
Ross, Diana **8**

Muslim Mosque, Inc.
X, Malcolm **1**

Mysteries
Himes, Chester **8**
Mosley, Walter **5, 25**
Wesley, Valerie Wilson **18**

NAACP
See National Association for the Advancement of Colored People

NAACP Legal Defense Fund (LDF)
Bell, Derrick **6**
Chambers, Julius **3**
Edelman, Marian Wright **5**
Guinier, Lani **7**
Jones, Elaine R. **7**
Julian, Percy Lavon **6**
Marshall, Thurgood **1**
Motley, Constance Baker **10**

NABJ
See National Association of Black Journalists

NAC
See Nyasaland African Congress

NACGN
See National Association of Colored Graduate Nurses

NACW
See National Association of Colored Women

NAG
See Nonviolent Action Group

NASA
See National Aeronautics and Space Administration

Nation
Wilkins, Roger **2**

Nation of Islam
See Lost-Found Nation of Islam

National Action Network
Sharpton, Al **21**

National Aeronautics and Space Administration (NASA)
Bluford, Guy **2**
Bolden, Charles F., Jr. **7**
Gregory, Frederick D. **8**
Jemison, Mae C. **1**
McNair, Ronald **3**
Nichols, Nichelle **11**

National Afro-American Council
Fortune, T. Thomas **6**

National Alliance Party (NAP)
Fulani, Lenora **11**

National Association for the Advancement of Colored People (NAACP)
Anthony, Wendell **25**
Baker, Ella **5**
Bates, Daisy **13**
Bell, Derrick **6**
Bond, Julian **2**
Bontemps, Arna **8**
Brooks, Gwendolyn **1**
Bunche, Ralph J. **5**
Chambers, Julius **3**
Chavis, Benjamin **6**
Clark, Kenneth B. **5**
Clark, Septima **7**
Days, Drew S., III **10**
Dee, Ruby **8**
DuBois, Shirley Graham **21**
Du Bois, W. E. B. **3**
Edelman, Marian Wright **5**
Evers, Medgar **3**
Evers, Myrlie **8**
Farmer, James **2**
Fuller, S. B. **13**
Gibson, William F. **6**
Grimké, Archibald H. **9**
Hampton, Fred **18**
Harrington, Oliver W. **9**
Henderson, Wade **14**
Hooks, Benjamin L. **2**
Horne, Lena **5**
Houston, Charles Hamilton **4**
Johnson, James Weldon **5**
Jordan, Vernon E. **3**
Lampkin, Daisy **19**
Madison, Joseph E. **17**
Marshall, Thurgood **1**
McKissick, Floyd B. **3**
McPhail, Sharon **2**
Meredith, James H. **11**
Moses, Robert Parris **11**
Motley, Constance Baker **10**
Owens, Major **6**
Rustin, Bayard **4**
Terrell, Mary Church **9**
Tucker, C. DeLores **12**
White, Walter F. **4**
Wilkins, Roger **2**
Wilkins, Roy **4**
Williams, Hosea Lorenzo **15**
Williams, Robert F. **11**
Wright, Louis Tompkins **4**

National Association of Black Journalists (NABJ)
Curry, George E. **23**
Dawkins, Wayne **20**
Harris, Jay T. **19**
Shipp, E. R. **15**
Stone, Chuck **9**
Washington, Laura S. **18**

National Association of Colored Graduate Nurses (NACGN)
Staupers, Mabel K. **7**

National Association of Colored Women (NACW)
Bethune, Mary McLeod **4**
Harper, Frances Ellen Watkins **11**
Lampkin, Daisy **19**
Terrell, Mary Church **9**

National Baptist Convention USA
Lyons, Henry **12**

National Baptist Publishing Board
Boyd, T. B., III **6**

National Baptist Sunday Church School and Baptist Training Union Congress
Boyd, T. B., III **6**

National Bar Association
Alexander, Joyce London **18**
Alexander, Sadie Tanner Mossell **22**
Archer, Dennis **7**
McPhail, Sharon **2**

National Basketball Association (NBA)
Abdul-Jabbar, Kareem **8**
Barkley, Charles **5**
Bing, Dave **3**
Bol, Manute **1**
Brandon, Terrell **16**
Bryant, Kobe **15**
Carter, Vince **26**
Chamberlain, Wilt **18**
Drexler, Clyde **4**
Duncan, Tim **20**
Elliott, Sean **26**
Erving, Julius **18**
Ewing, Patrick A. **17**
Garnett, Kevin **14**
Gourdine, Simon **11**
Hardaway, Anfernee (Penny) **13**
Heard, Gar **25**
Hill, Grant **13**
Howard, Juwan **15**
Hunter, Billy **22**
Johnson, Earvin "Magic" **3**
Jordan, Michael **6, 21**
Lucas, John **7**
Mourning, Alonzo **17**
Mutombo, Dikembe **7**
O'Neal, Shaquille **8**
Olajuwon, Hakeem **2**
Pippen, Scottie **15**
Rivers, Glenn "Doc" **25**
Robertson, Oscar **26**
Robinson, David **24**
Rodman, Dennis **12**
Russell, Bill **8**
Silas, Paul **24**
Sprewell, Latrell **23**
Thomas, Isiah **7, 26**
Webber, Chris **15**
Wilkens, Lenny **11**

National Basketball Players Association
Erving, Julius **18**
Ewing, Patrick A. **17**
Gourdine, Simon **11**
Hunter, Billy **22**

National Black Arts Festival (NBAF)
Borders, James **9**
Brooks, Avery **9**

National Black Farmers Association (NBFA)
Boyd, John W., Jr. **20**

National Black Gay and Lesbian Conference
Wilson, Phill **9**

National Black Gay and Lesbian Leadership Forum (NBGLLF)
Boykin, Keith **14**
Carter, Mandy **11**

National Book Award
Ellison, Ralph **7**
Haley, Alex **4**
Johnson, Charles **1**
Patterson, Orlando **4**

National Broadcasting Company (NBC)
Allen, Byron **3, 24**
Cosby, Bill **7, 26**
Gumbel, Bryant **14**
Hinderas, Natalie **5**
Jones, Star **10**
Rashad, Phylicia **21**
Reuben, Gloria **15**
Roker, Al **12**
Simpson, Carole **6**
Stokes, Carl B. **10**
Williams, Montel **4**
Wilson, Flip **21**

National Center for Neighborhood Enterprise (NCNE)
Woodson, Robert L. **10**

National Coalition of 100 Black Women
McCabe, Jewell Jackson **10**

National Coalition to Abolish the Dealth Penalty (NCADP)
Hawkins, Steven **14**

National Commission for Democracy (Ghana; NCD)
Rawlings, Jerry **9**

National Conference on Black Lawyers (NCBL)
McDougall, Gay J. **11**

National Council of Churches
Howard, M. William, Jr. **26**

National Council of Negro Women (NCNW)
Bethune, Mary McLeod **4**
Blackwell, Unita **17**
Cole, Johnnetta B. **5**
Hamer, Fannie Lou **6**
Height, Dorothy I. **2, 23**
Horne, Lena **5**
Lampkin, Daisy **19**
Sampson, Edith S. **4**
Smith, Jane E. **24**
Staupers, Mabel K. **7**

National Council of Nigeria and the Cameroons (NCNC)
Azikiwe, Nnamdi **13**

National Defence Council (Ghana; NDC)
Rawlings, Jerry **9**

National Democratic Party (Rhodesia)
Mugabe, Robert Gabriel **10**

National Earthquake Information Center (NEIC)
Person, Waverly **9**

National Endowment for the Arts (NEA)
Hemphill, Essex **10**
Serrano, Andres **3**
Williams, William T. **11**

National Equal Rights League (NERL)
Trotter, Monroe **9**

National Football League (NFL)
Allen, Marcus **20**
Barney, Lem **26**
Brown, Jim **11**
Bruce, Isaac **26**
Butler, Leroy III **17**
Cunningham, Randall **23**
Davis, Terrell **20**
Farr, Mel Sr. **24**
Gilliam, Frank **23**
Green, Dennis **5**
Greene, Joe **10**
Hill, Calvin **19**
Howard, Desmond **16**
Lott, Ronnie **9**
Moon, Warren **8**
Moss, Randy **23**
Motley, Marion **26**
Newsome, Ozzie **26**
Pace, Orlando **21**
Page, Alan **7**
Payton, Walter **11, 25**
Rhodes, Ray **14**
Rice, Jerry **5**
Sanders, Barry **1**
Sanders, Deion **4**
Shell, Art **1**
Simpson, O.J. **15**
Singletary, Mike **4**
Smith, Emmitt **7**
Stewart, Kordell **21**
Taylor, Lawrence **25**
Thomas, Derrick **25**
Upshaw, Gene **18**
Walker, Herschel **1**
White, Reggie **6**
Williams, Doug **22**

National Hockey League (NHL)
McBride, Bryant **18**
Fuhr, Grant **1**
McKegney, Tony **3**
O'Ree, Willie **5**

National Information Infrastructure (NII)
Lewis, Delano **7**

National Institute of Education
Baker, Gwendolyn Calvert **9**

National League
Coleman, Leonard S., Jr. **12**

National Minority Business Council
Leary, Kathryn D. **10**

National Museum of American History
Reagon, Bernice Johnson **7**

National Negro Congress
Bunche, Ralph J. **5**

National Negro Suffrage League
Trotter, Monroe **9**

National Organization for Women (NOW)
Kennedy, Florynce **12**
Hernandez, Aileen Clarke **13**

National Political Congress of Black Women
Chisholm, Shirley **2**
Tucker, C. DeLores **12**
Waters, Maxine **3**

National Public Radio (NPR)
Early, Gerald **15**
Lewis, Delano **7**
Abu-Jamal, Mumia **15**

National Resistance Army (Uganda; NRA)
Museveni, Yoweri **4**

National Resistance Movement
Museveni, Yoweri **4**

National Revolutionary Movement for Development
See Mouvement Revolutionnaire National pour la Developpment

National Rifle Association (NRA)
Williams, Robert F. **11**

National Science Foundation (NSF)
Massey, Walter E. **5**

National Security Council
Powell, Colin **1**
Rice, Condoleezza **3**

National Union for the Total Independence of Angola (UNITA)
Savimbi, Jonas **2**

National Union of Mineworkers (South Africa; NUM)
Ramaphosa, Cyril **3**

National Urban Coalition (NUC)
Edelin, Ramona Hoage **19**

National Urban League
Brown, Ron **5**
Haynes, George Edmund **8**
Jacob, John E. **2**
Jordan, Vernon E. **3**
Price, Hugh B. **9**
Young, Whitney M., Jr. **4**

National Women's Political Caucus
Hamer, Fannie Lou **6**

National Youth Administration (NYA)
Bethune, Mary McLeod **4**
Primus, Pearl **6**

Nature Boy Enterprises
Yoba, Malik **11**

NBA
See National Basketball Association

NBAF
See National Black Arts Festival

NBC
See National Broadcasting Company

NBGLLF
See National Black Gay and Lesbian Leadership Forum

NCBL
See National Conference on Black Lawyers

NCD
See National Commission for Democracy

NCNE
See National Center for Neighborhood Enterprise

NCNW
See National Council of Negro Women

NDC
See National Defence Council

NEA
See National Endowment for the Arts

Nebula awards
Butler, Octavia **8**
Delany, Jr., Samuel R. **9**

Negro American Labor Council
Randolph, A. Philip **3**

Negro American Political League
Trotter, Monroe **9**

Negro Digest
Johnson, John H. **3**

Negro Ensemble Company
Schultz, Michael A. **6**
Taylor, Susan L. **10**

Negro History Bulletin
Woodson, Carter G. **2**

Negro Leagues
Campanella, Roy **25**
Davis, Piper **19**
Gibson, Josh **22**
Kimbro, Henry A. **25**
O'Neil, Buck **19**
Paige, Satchel **7**
Pride, Charley **26**
Stone, Toni **15**

Negro Theater Ensemble
Rolle, Esther **13, 21**

Negro World
Fortune, T. Thomas **6**

NEIC
See National Earthquake Information Center

Neo-hoodoo
Reed, Ishmael **8**

Nequai Cosmetics
Taylor, Susan L. **10**

NERL
See National Equal Rights League

Netherlands Antilles
Liberia-Peters, Maria Philomena **12**

NetNoir Inc.
CasSelle, Malcolm **11**
Ellington, E. David **11**

Neurosurgery
Black, Keith Lanier **18**
Carson, Benjamin **1**

New Concept Development Center
Madhubuti, Haki R. **7**

New Dance Group
Primus, Pearl **6**

New Jersey Family Development Act
Bryant, Wayne R. **6**

New Jersey General Assembly
Bryant, Wayne R. **6**

New Jersey Nets
Doby, Lawrence Eugene, Sr. **16**

New Negro movement
See Harlem Renaissance

New York Age
Fortune, T. Thomas **6**

New York City government
Crew, Rudolph F. **16**
Dinkins, David **4**
Fields, C. Virginia **25**

New York Daily News
Cose, Ellis **5**

New York Drama Critics Circle Award
Hansberry, Lorraine **6**

New York Freeman
Fortune, T. Thomas **6**

New York Giants baseball team
Mays, Willie **3**

New York Giants football team
Taylor, Lawrence **25**

New York Globe
Fortune, T. Thomas **6**

New York Institute for Social Therapy and
Fulani, Lenora **11**

New York Jets football team
Lott, Ronnie **9**

New York Knicks basketball team
Ewing, Patrick A. **17**
Sprewell, Latrell **23**

New York Mets baseball team
Clendenon, Donn **26**

New York Nets basketball team
Erving, Julius **18**

New York Public Library
Dodson, Howard, Jr. **7**
Schomburg, Arthur Alfonso **9**

New York Shakespeare Festival
Gunn, Moses **10**
Wolfe, George C. **6**

New York State Senate
Motley, Constance Baker **10**
Owens, Major **6**

New York State Supreme Court
Wright, Bruce McMarion **3**

New York Stock Exchange
Doley, Harold, Jr. **26**

New York Sun
Fortune, T. Thomas **6**

New York Times
Hunter-Gault, Charlayne **6**
Price, Hugh B. **9**
Wilkins, Roger **2**

New York Yankees baseball team
Baylor, Don **6**
Jackson, Reggie **15**
Strawberry, Darryl **22**
Watson, Bob **25**
Winfield, Dave **5**

Newark city government
Gibson, Kenneth Allen **6**
James, Sharpe **23**

Newark Eagles
Doby, Lawrence Eugene, Sr. **16**

Newark Housing Authority
Gibson, Kenneth Allen **6**

NFL
See National Football League

Nguzo Saba
Karenga, Maulana **10**

NHL
See National Hockey League

Niagara movement
Du Bois, W. E. B. **3**
Hope, John **8**
Trotter, Monroe **9**

Nigerian Armed Forces
Abacha, Sani **11**
Babangida, Ibrahim **4**
Obasanjo, Olusegun **5, 22**

Nigerian literature
Achebe, Chinua **6**
Onwueme, Tess Osonye **23**
Rotimi, Ola **1**
Soyinka, Wole **4**

NII
See National Information Infrastructure

1960 Masks
Soyinka, Wole **4**

Nobel Peace Prize
Bunche, Ralph J. **5**
King, Martin Luther, Jr. **1**
Luthuli, Albert **13**
Tutu, Desmond **6**

Nobel Prize for literature
Soyinka, Wole **4**
Morrison, Toni **2, 15**
Walcott, Derek **5**

Nonviolent Action Group (NAG)
Al-Amin, Jamil Abdullah **6**

North Carolina Mutual Life Insurance
Spaulding, Charles Clinton **9**

North Pole
Henson, Matthew **2**

NOW
See National Organization for Women

NPR
See National Public Radio

NRA
See National Resistance Army (Uganda)

NRA
See National Rifle Association

NSF
See National Science Foundation

Nuclear energy
O'Leary, Hazel **6**
Quarterman, Lloyd Albert **4**

Nuclear Regulatory Commission
Jackson, Shirley Ann **12**

Nucleus
King, Yolanda **6**
Shabazz, Attallah **6**

NUM
See National Union of Mineworkers (South Africa)

Nursing
Auguste, Rose-Anne **13**
Johnson, Eddie Bernice **8**
Johnson, Hazel **22**
Larsen, Nella **10**
Lyttle, Hulda Margaret **14**
Riley, Helen Caldwell Day **13**
Robinson, Rachel **16**
Robinson, Sharon **22**
Shabazz, Betty **7, 26**
Staupers, Mabel K. **7**
Taylor, Susie King **13**

Nutrition
Clark, Celeste **15**
Gregory, Dick **1**
Watkins, Shirley R. **17**

NYA
See National Youth Administration

Nyasaland African Congress (NAC)
Banda, Hastings Kamuzu **6**

Oakland Athletics baseball team
Baker, Dusty **8**
Baylor, Don **6**
Jackson, Reggie **15**
Morgan, Joe Leonard **9**

Oakland Raiders football team
Howard, Desmond **16**
Upshaw, Gene **18**

Oakland Tribune
Maynard, Robert C. **7**

OAU
See Organization of African Unity

OECS
See Organization of Eastern Caribbean States

Office of Civil Rights
See U.S. Department of Education

Office of Management and Budget
Raines, Franklin Delano **14**

Office of Public Liaison
Herman, Alexis M. **15**

Ohio House of Representatives
Stokes, Carl B. **10**

Ohio state government
Brown, Les **5**
Stokes, Carl B. **10**
Williams, George Washington **18**

Ohio State Senate
White, Michael R. **5**

OIC
See Opportunities Industrialization Centers of America, Inc.

Olympics
Ali, Muhammad **2, 16**
Bonaly, Surya **7**
Bowe, Riddick **6**
Carter, Vince **26**
Christie, Linford **8**
Coachman, Alice **18**
Dawes, Dominique **11**
Devers, Gail **7**
Edwards, Harry **2**
Edwards, Teresa **14**
Ewing, Patrick A. **17**
Garrison, Zina **2**
Griffith, Yolanda **25**
Hardaway, Anfernee (Penny) **13**
Hill, Grant **13**
Holyfield, Evander **6**
Johnson, Ben **1**
Johnson, Michael **13**
Joyner-Kersee, Jackie **5**
Leslie, Lisa **16**
Lewis, Carl **4**
Malone, Karl A. **18**
Metcalfe, Ralph **26**
Miller, Cheryl **10**
Moses, Edwin **8**
Mutola, Maria **12**
Owens, Jesse **2**
Pippen, Scottie **15**
Powell, Mike **7**
Quirot, Ana **13**
Robertson, Oscar **26**
Rudolph, Wilma **4**
Russell, Bill **8**
Swoopes, Sheryl **12**
Thomas, Debi **26**
Thugwane, Josia **21**
Westbrook, Peter **20**
Whitaker, Pernell **10**
Wilkens, Lenny **11**

Oncology
Leffall, LaSalle, Jr. **3**

One Church, One Child
Clements, George **2**

OPC
See Ovambo People's Congress

Opera
Anderson, Marian **2**
Brooks, Avery **9**
Bumbry, Grace **5**
Davis, Anthony **11**
Graves, Denyce **19**
Hendricks, Barbara **3**
Joplin, Scott **6**
Joyner, Matilda Sissieretta **15**
Maynor, Dorothy **19**
McDonald, Audra **20**
Norman, Jessye **5**
Price, Leontyne **1**

Operation Desert Shield
Powell, Colin **1**

Operation Desert Storm
Powell, Colin **1**

Operation HOPE
Bryant, John **26**

OPO
See Ovamboland People's Organization

Opportunities Industrialization Centers of America, Inc. (OIC)
Sullivan, Leon H. **3**

Organization of African States
Museveni, Yoweri **4**

Organization of African Unity (OAU)
Diouf, Abdou **3**
Haile Selassie **7**
Kaunda, Kenneth **2**
Kenyatta, Jomo **5**
Nkrumah, Kwame **3**
Nujoma, Samuel **10**
Nyerere, Julius **5**
Touré, Sekou **6**

Organization of Afro-American Unity
X, Malcolm **1**

Organization of Eastern Caribbean States (OECS)
Charles, Mary Eugenia **10**

Orisun Repertory
Soyinka, Wole **4**

Orlando Magic basketball team
Erving, Julius **18**
O'Neal, Shaquille **8**
Rivers, Glenn "Doc" **25**

Orlando Miracle basketball team
Peck, Carolyn **23**

Osteopathy
Allen, Ethel D. **13**

Ovambo People's Congress (South Africa; OPC)
Nujoma, Samuel **10**

Ovamboland People's Organization (South Africa; OPO)
Nujoma, Samuel **10**

Page Education Foundation
Page, Alan **7**

Paine College
Lewis, Shirley A. R. **14**

Painting
Andrews, Benny **22**
Bailey, Radcliffe **19**
Barthe, Richmond **15**
Basquiat, Jean-Michel **5**
Bearden, Romare **2**
Biggers, John **20**
Campbell, E. Simms **13**
Cowans, Adger W. **20**
Delaney, Beauford **19**
Douglas, Aaron **7**
Driskell, David C. **7**
Ewing, Patrick A. **17**
Flood, Curt **10**
Gilliam, Sam **16**
Guyton, Tyree **9**
Harkless, Necia Desiree **19**
Hayden, Palmer **13**
Johnson, William Henry **3**
Jones, Lois Mailou **13**
Lawrence, Jacob **4**
Lee, Annie Francis **22**
Lee-Smith, Hughie **5, 22**
Lewis, Samella **25**
Major, Clarence **9**
McGee, Charles **10**
Mitchell, Corinne **8**
Pierre, Andre **17**
Pippin, Horace **9**
Porter, James A. **11**
Ringgold, Faith **4**
Tanner, Henry Ossawa **1**
Thomas, Alma **14**
Tolliver, William **9**
Wells, James Lesesne **10**
Williams, Billy Dee **8**
Williams, William T. **11**
Woodruff, Hale **9**

Pan-Africanism
Carmichael, Stokely **5, 26**
Clarke, John Henrik **20**
Du Bois, W. E. B. **3**
Garvey, Marcus **1**
Haile Selassie **7**
Kenyatta, Jomo **5**
Madhubuti, Haki R. **7**
Marshall, Paule **7**
Nkrumah, Kwame **3**
Nyerere, Julius **5**
Touré, Sekou **6**
Turner, Henry McNeal **5**

Pan African Orthodox Christian Church
Agyeman, Jaramogi Abebe **10**

Parents of Watts (POW)
Harris, Alice **7**

Parti Démocratique de Guinée (Guinea
Touré, Sekou **6**

Parti Démocratique de la Côte d'Ivoire (Democratic Party of the Ivory Coast; PDCI)
Houphouët-Boigny, Félix **4**

Parti Démocratique de la Côte d'Ivoire (Democratic Party of the
Bedie, Henri Konan **21**

Partido Africano da Independencia da Guine e Cabo Verde (PAIGC)
Vieira, Joao **14**

Party for Unity and Progress (Guinea; PUP)
Conté, Lansana **7**

PATC
See Performing Arts Training Center

Pathology
Fuller, Solomon Carter, Jr. **15**

Patriot Party
Fulani, Lenora **11**

Patriotic Alliance for Reconstruction and Construction (PARC)
Jammeh, Yahya **23**

PBS
See Public Broadcasting Service

PDCI
See Parti Démocratique de la Côte d'Ivoire (Democratic Party of the Ivory Coast)

PDG
See Parti Démocratique de Guinée (Guinea Democratic Party)

Peace and Freedom Party
Cleaver, Eldridge **5**

Peace Corps
See U.S. Peace Corps

Peace Mission
Divine, Father **7**

Pediatrics
Carson, Benjamin **1**
Elders, Joycelyn **6**
Witt, Edwin T. **26**

Peg Leg Bates Country Club
Bates, Peg Leg **14**

Pennsylvania state government
Allen, Ethel D. **13**

People Organized and Working for Economic Rebirth (POWER)
Farrakhan, Louis **2**

People United to Serve Humanity (PUSH)
Jackson, Jesse **1**
Jackson, Jesse, Jr. **14**

People's Association Human Rights
Williams, Robert F. **11**

People's Liberation Army of Namibia (PLAN)
Nujoma, Samuel **10**

People's National Party (Jamaica; PNP)
Patterson, P. J. **6, 20**

People's Progressive Party (PPP)
Jagan, Cheddi **16**
Jawara, Sir Dawda Kairaba **11**

Performing Arts Training Center (PATC)
Dunham, Katherine **4**

PGA
See Professional Golfers' Association

Phelps Stokes Fund
Patterson, Frederick Douglass **12**

Philadelphia City Council
Allen, Ethel D. **13**

Philadelphia city government
Goode, W. Wilson **4**
Street, John F. **24**

Philadelphia Eagles football team
Cunningham, Randall **23**
Rhodes, Ray **14**
White, Reggie **6**

Philadelphia Phillies baseball team
Morgan, Joe Leonard **9**

Philadelphia public schools
Clayton, Constance **1**

Philadelphia 76ers basketball team
Barkley, Charles **5**
Bol, Manute **1**
Chamberlain, Wilt **18**
Erving, Julius **18**
Iverson, Allen **24**
Lucas, John **7**

Philadelphia Warriors
Chamberlain, Wilt **18**

Philanthropy
Cosby, Bill **7, 26**
Cosby, Camille **14**
Golden, Marita **19**
Malone, Annie **13**
McCarty, Oseola **16**
Pleasant, Mary Ellen **9**
Reeves, Rachel J. **23**
Thomas, Franklin A. **5**
Waddles, Charleszetta (Mother) **10**
Walker, Madame C. J. **7**
White, Reggie **6**
Wonder, Stevie **11**

Philosophy
Baker, Houston A., Jr. **6**
Davis, Angela **5**
Toomer, Jean **6**
West, Cornel **5**

Phoenix Suns basketball team
Barkley, Charles **5**
Heard, Gar **25**

Photography
Andrews, Bert **13**
Barboza, Anthony **10**
Cowans, Adger W. **20**
Lester, Julius **9**
Moutoussamy-Ashe, Jeanne **7**
Parks, Gordon **1**
Robeson, Eslanda Goode **13**
Serrano, Andres **3**
Simpson, Lorna **4**
Sleet, Moneta, Jr. **5**
Tanner, Henry Ossawa **1**
VanDerZee, James **6**

Photojournalism
Ashley-Ward, Amelia **23**
Moutoussamy-Ashe, Jeanne **7**
Parks, Gordon **1**
Sleet, Moneta, Jr. **5**

Physical therapy
Elders, Joycelyn **6**

Physics
Adkins, Rutherford H. **21**
Gates, Sylvester James, Jr. **15**
Jackson, Shirley Ann **12**
Massey, Walter E. **5**
Tyson, Neil de Grasse **15**

Piano
Basie, Count **23**
Cole, Nat King **17**
Donegan, Dorothy **19**
Duke, George **21**
Ellington, Duke **5**
Fats Domino **20**
Hancock, Herbie **20**
Hayes, Isaac **20**
Hinderas, Natalie **5**
Joplin, Scott **6**
Monk, Thelonious **1**
Powell, Bud **24**
Pritchard, Robert Starling **21**
Roberts, Marcus **19**
Silver, Horace **26**
Sykes, Roosevelt **20**
Taylor, Billy **23**
Vaughan, Sarah **13**
Williams, Mary Lou **15**

Pittsburgh Pirates baseball team
Bonds, Barry **6**
Clendenon, Donn **26**

Pittsburgh Steelers football team
Dungy, Tony **17**
Greene, Joe **10**
Stewart, Kordell **21**

PLAN
See People's Liberation Army of Namibia

Planned Parenthood Federation of America Inc.
Wattleton, Faye **9**

Playwright
Arkadie, Kevin **17**
Baldwin, James **1**
Bullins, Ed **25**
Cheadle, Don **19**
Childress, Alice **15**
Cleage, Pearl **17**
Evans, Mari **26**
Gordone, Charles **15**
Hansberry, Lorraine **6**
Hughes, Langston **4**
Jean-Baptiste, Marianne **17**
Kennedy, Adrienne **11**
Moss, Carlton **17**
Onwueme, Tess Osonye **23**
Sanchez, Sonia **17**
Thurman, Wallace **17**
Walcott, Derek **5**
Williams, Samm-Art **21**
Wilson, August **7**

PNP
See People's National Party (Jamaica)

Poet laureate (U.S.)
Dove, Rita **6**

Poetry
Alexander, Margaret Walker **22**
Angelou, Maya **1, 15**
Bontemps, Arna **8**
Cleage, Pearl **17**
Clifton, Lucille **14**
Dove, Rita **6**
Evans, Mari **26**
Harkless, Necia Desiree **19**
Harper, Frances Ellen Watkins **11**
Hayden, Robert **12**
Hughes, Langston **7**
Jackson, Fred James **25**
Lorde, Audre **6**
Parker, Pat **19**
Randall, Dudley **8**
Redmond, Eugene **23**
Sanchez, Sonia **17**
Sapphire **14**
Senghor, Léopold Sédar **12**
Smith, Mary Carter **26**
van Sertima, Ivan **25**
Williams, Sherley Anne **25**

Politics
Alexander, Archie Alphonso **14**
Baker, Thurbert **22**
Belton, Sharon Sayles **9, 16**
Bishop Jr., Sanford D. **24**
Blackwell, Unita **17**
Brazile, Donna **25**
Brown, Corrine **24**
Buckley, Victoria (Vikki) **24**
Burris, Chuck **21**
Burris, Roland W. **25**
Butler, Jerry **26**
Chideya, Farai **14**
Christian-Green, Donna M. **17**
Clayton, Eva M. **20**
Connerly, Ward **14**
Cummings, Elijah E. **24**
Currie, Betty **21**
Dixon, Julian C. **24**
Edmonds, Terry **17**
Fields, C. Virginia **25**
Gordon, Pamela **17**
Henry, Aaron **19**
Herenton, Willie W. **24**
Hilliard, Earl F. **24**
Ingraham, Hubert A. **19**
Jackson Lee, Sheila **20**
James, Sharpe **23**
Jammeh, Yahya **23**
Jarvis, Charlene Drew **21**
Jefferson, William J. **25**
Johnson Jr., Harvey **24**
Kabbah, Ahmad Tejan **23**
Lee, Barbara **25**
Meeks, Gregory **25**
Metcalfe, Ralph **26**
Millender-McDonald, Juanita **21**
Morial, Ernest "Dutch" **26**
Morial, Marc **20**
Obasanjo, Olusegun **22**
Perry, Ruth **15**
Powell, Debra A. **23**
Rush, Bobby **26**
Scott, Robert C. **23**
Sisulu, Sheila Violet Makate **24**
Smith, Jennifer **21**
Thompson, Bennie G. **26**
Touré, Amadou Toumani **18**
Tsvangirai, Morgan **26**
Watt, Melvin **26**
Watts, J. C., Jr. **14**
Wheat, Alan **14**
White, Jesse **22**
Williams, Anthony **21**
Williams, George Washington **18**
Wynn, Albert R. **25**

Pop music
Ashford, Nickolas **21**
Bassey, Shirley **25**
Blige, Mary J. **20**
Cole, Nat King **17**
Combs, Sean "Puffy" **17**
Duke, George **21**
Edmonds, Kenneth "Babyface" **10**
Franklin, Aretha **11**
Franklin, Kirk **15**
Hailey, JoJo **22**
Hailey, K-Ci **22**
Hammer, M. C. **20**
Hayes, Isaac **20**
Hill, Lauryn **20**
Houston, Cissy **20**
Houston, Whitney **7**
Humphrey, Bobbi **20**
Isley, Ronald **25**
Jackson, Janet **6**
Jackson, Michael **19**
James, Rick **17**
Jarreau, Al **21**
Jean, Wyclef **20**
Jones, Quincy **8**
Jordan, Montell **23**
Kelly, R. **18**
Kendricks, Eddie **22**
Khan, Chaka **12**
Love, Darlene **23**
Massenburg, Kedar **23**
Mathis, Johnny **20**
Monica **21**
Moore, Chante **26**
Neville, Aaron **21**
Osborne, Jeffrey **26**
Prince **18**
Robinson, Smokey **3**
Rupaul **17**
Sade **15**
Seal **14**
Senghor, Léopold Sédar **12**
Simpson, Valerie **21**
Summer, Donna **25**
Sweat, Keith **19**
Turner, Tina **6**
Usher **23**
Washington, Dinah **22**
Washington, Grover, Jr. **17**
Washington, Val **12**
White, Barry **13**
Williams, Vanessa L. **4, 17**
Wilson, Nancy **10**
Wonder, Stevie **11**

Portland Trail Blazers basketball team
Drexler, Clyde **4**
Wilkens, Lenny **11**

POW
See Parents of Watts

POWER
See People Organized and Working for Economic Rebirth

PPP
See People's Progressive Party (Gambia)

Presbyterianism
Cannon, Katie **10**

Pride Economic Enterprises
Barry, Marion S. **7**

Printmaking
Wells, James Lesesne **10**

Prison ministry
Bell, Ralph S. **5**

Pro-Line Corp.
Cottrell, Comer **11**

Professional Golfers' Association (PGA)
Elder, Lee **6**
Sifford, Charlie **4**

Progressive Labour Party
Smith, Jennifer **21**

Proposition 209
Connerly, Ward **14**

Psychiatry
Cobbs, Price M. **9**
Comer, James P. **6**
Fuller, Solomon Carter, Jr. **15**
Poussaint, Alvin F. **5**
Welsing, Frances Cress **5**

Psychology
Brown, Joyce F. **25**
Fulani, Lenora **11**
Staples, Brent **8**
Steele, Claude Mason **13**

Public Broadcasting Service (PBS)
Brown, Les **5**
Davis, Ossie **5**
Duke, Bill **3**
Hampton, Henry **6**
Hunter-Gault, Charlayne **6**
Lawson, Jennifer **1**
Riggs, Marlon **5**
Wilkins, Roger **2**

Public housing
Hamer, Fannie Lou **6**
Lane, Vincent **5**

Public relations
Barden, Don H. **9, 20**
Edmonds, Terry **17**
Graham, Stedman **13**
Hedgeman, Anna Arnold **22**
McCabe, Jewell Jackson **10**
Perez, Anna **1**
Pritchard, Robert Starling **21**
Rowan, Carl T. **1**
Taylor, Kristin Clark **8**
Williams, Maggie **7**

Public television
Brown, Tony **3**

Publishing
Achebe, Chinua **6**
Ashley-Ward, Amelia **23**

Baisden, Michael **25**
Barden, Don H. **9, 20**
Bates, Daisy **13**
Boston, Lloyd **24**
Boyd, T. B. III **6**
Brown, Marie Dutton **12**
Dawkins, Wayne **20**
Driver, David E. **11**
Ducksworth, Marilyn **12**
Giddings, Paula **11**
Graves, Earl G. **1**
Harris, Jay **19**
Harris, Monica **18**
Hill, Bonnie Guiton **20**
Hudson, Cheryl **15**
Hudson, Wade **15**
James, Juanita **13**
Johnson, John H. **3**
Jones, Quincy **8**
Kunjufu, Jawanza **3**
Lawson, Jennifer **1**
Leavell, Dorothy R. **17**
Lewis, Edward T. **21**
Lorde, Audre **6**
Madhubuti, Haki R. **7**
Maynard, Robert C. **7**
McDonald, Erroll **1**
Morgan, Garrett **1**
Myers, Walter Dean **8**
Parks, Gordon **1**
Perez, Anna **1**
Randall, Dudley **8**
Sengstacke, John **18**
Smith, Clarence O. **21**
Tyree, Omar Rashad **21**
Vanzant, Iyanla **17**
Walker, Alice **1**
Washington, Laura S. **18**
Wells-Barnett, Ida B. **8**
Williams, Patricia J. **11**

Pulitzer prize
Brooks, Gwendolyn **1**
Dove, Rita **6**
Fuller, Charles **8**
Gordone, Charles **15**
Haley, Alex **4**
Komunyakaa, Yusef **9**
Lewis, David Levering **9**
Morrison, Toni **2, 15**
Page, Clarence **4**
Shipp, E. R. **15**
Sleet, Moneta, Jr. **5**
Walker, Alice **1**
Wilkins, Roger **2**
Wilson, August **7**

PUP
See Party for Unity and Progress (Guinea)

Puppeteer
Clash, Kevin **14**

PUSH
See People United to Serve Humanity

Quiltmaking
Ringgold, Faith **4**

Race car driving
Ribbs, Willy T. **2**
Scott, Sr., Wendell Oliver **19**

Race relations
Abbott, Diane **9**
Achebe, Chinua **6**
Alexander, Clifford **26**
Anthony, Wendell **25**
Asante, Molefi Kete **3**
Baker, Ella **5**
Baker, Houston A., Jr. **6**
Baldwin, James **1**
Beals, Melba Patillo **15**
Bell, Derrick **6**
Bennett, Lerone, Jr. **5**
Bethune, Mary McLeod **4**
Booker, Simeon **23**
Bosley, Freeman, Jr. **7**
Boyd, T. B. III **6**
Brown, Elaine **8**
Bunche, Ralph J. **5**
Butler, Paul D. **17**
Butts, Calvin O., III **9**
Carter, Stephen L. **4**
Cary, Lorene **3**
Cayton, Horace **26**
Chavis, Benjamin **6**
Clark, Kenneth B. **5**
Clark, Septima **7**
Cobbs, Price M. **9**
Cochran, Johnnie L., Jr. **11**
Cole, Johnnetta B. **5**
Comer, James P. **6**
Cone, James H. **3**
Conyers, John, Jr. **4**
Cook, Suzan D. Johnson **22**
Cook, Toni **23**
Cosby, Bill **7, 26**
Cunningham, Evelyn **23**
Darden, Christopher **13**
Davis, Angela **5**
Davis, Benjamin O., Sr. **4**
Davis, Benjamin O., Jr. **2**
Dee, Ruby **8**
Dellums, Ronald **2**
Divine, Father **7**
DuBois, Shirley Graham **21**
Dunbar, Paul Laurence **8**
Dyson, Michael Eric **11**
Edelman, Marian Wright **5**
Elder, Lee **6**
Ellison, Ralph **7**
Esposito, Giancarlo **9**
Farmer, James **2**
Farrakhan, Louis **2**
Fauset, Jessie **7**
Franklin, John Hope **5**
Fuller, Charles **8**
Gaines, Ernest J. **7**
Gibson, William F. **6**
Goode, W. Wilson **4**
Graham, Lawrence Otis **12**
Gregory, Dick **1**
Grimké, Archibald H. **9**
Guinier, Lani **7**
Guy, Rosa **5**
Haley, Alex **4**
Hall, Elliott S. **24**
Hampton, Henry **6**
Hansberry, Lorraine **6**
Harris, Alice **7**
Hastie, William H. **8**
Haynes, George Edmund **8**
Hedgeman, Anna Arnold **22**
Henry, Aaron **19**
Henry, Lenny **9**
Hill, Oliver W. **24**
Hooks, Benjamin L. **2**
hooks, bell **5**
Hope, John **8**
Howard, M. William, Jr. **26**
Ingram, Rex **5**
Innis, Roy **5**
Jeffries, Leonard **8**
Johnson, James Weldon **5**
Jones, Elaine R. **7**
Jordan, Vernon E. **3**
Khanga, Yelena **6**
King, Bernice **4**
King, Coretta Scott **3**
King, Martin Luther, Jr. **1**
King, Yolanda **6**
Lane, Charles **3**
Lee-Smith, Hughie **5, 22**
Lee, Spike **5, 19**
Lorde, Audre **6**
Mandela, Nelson **1, 14**
Martin, Louis E. **16**
Mathabane, Mark **5**
Maynard, Robert C. **7**
Mays, Benjamin E. **7**
McDougall, Gay J. **11**
McKay, Claude **6**
Meredith, James H. **11**
Micheaux, Oscar **7**
Mosley, Walter **5, 25**
Muhammad, Khallid Abdul **10**
Norton, Eleanor Holmes **7**
Page, Clarence **4**
Perkins, Edward **5**
Pitt, David Thomas **10**
Poussaint, Alvin F. **5**
Price, Frederick K.C. **21**
Price, Hugh B. **9**
Robeson, Paul **2**
Robinson, Spottswood W. III **22**
Sampson, Edith S. **4**
Shabazz, Attallah **6**
Sifford, Charlie **4**
Simpson, Carole **6**
Sister Souljah **11**
Sisulu, Sheila Violet Makate **24**
Smith, Anna Deavere **6**
Sowell, Thomas **2**
Spaulding, Charles Clinton **9**
Staples, Brent **8**
Steele, Claude Mason **13**
Taulbert, Clifton Lemoure **19**
Till, Emmett **7**
Tutu, Desmond **6**
Tyree, Omar Rashad **21**
Walcott, Derek **5**
Walker, Maggie **17**
Washington, Booker T. **4**
Washington, Harold **6**
Wells-Barnett, Ida B. **8**
Welsing, Frances Cress **5**
West, Cornel **5**
Wideman, John Edgar **5**
Wiley, Ralph **8**
Wilkins, Roger **2**
Wilkins, Roy **4**
Williams, Gregory **11**
Williams, Hosea Lorenzo **15**
Williams, Patricia J. **11**
Williams, Walter E. **4**
Wilson, Sunnie **7**
Wright, Richard **5**
Young, Whitney M., Jr. **4**

Radio
Abu-Jamal, Mumia **15**
Banks, William **11**

Booker, Simeon **23**
Dee, Ruby **8**
Dr. Dre **10**
Elder, Larry **25**
Fuller, Charles **8**
Goode, Mal **13**
Gumbel, Greg **8**
Hamblin, Ken **10**
Joe, Yolanda **21**
Joyner, Tom **19**
Keyes, Alan L. **11**
Lewis, Delano **7**
Lover, Ed **10**
Madison, Joseph E. **17**
Moss, Carlton **17**
Samara, Noah **15**
Smiley, Tavis **20**
Taylor, Billy **23**

Ragtime
Europe, James Reese **10**
Joplin, Scott **6**

Rainbow Coalition
Chappell, Emma **18**
Jackson, Jesse **1**
Jackson, Jesse, Jr. **14**

Rap music
Baker, Houston A., Jr. **6**
Brown, Foxy **25**
Butts, Calvin O., III **9**
Chuck D. **9**
Combs, Sean "Puffy" **17**
Dr. Dre **10**
Dre, Dr. **14**
Dupri, Jermaine **13**
Dyson, Michael Eric **11**
Gray, F. Gary **14**
Hammer, M. C. **20**
Harrell, Andre **9**
Hill, Lauryn **20**
Ice Cube **8**
Ice-T **6**
Jean, Wyclef **20**
Jones, Quincy **8**
Knight, Suge **11**
Lover, Ed **10**
Mase **24**
Master P **21**
Notorious B.I.G. **20**
O'Neal, Shaquille **8**
Queen Latifah **1, 16**
Shakur, Tupac **14**
Simmons, Russell **1**
Sister Souljah **11**
Smith, Will **8, 18**
Tucker, C. DeLores **12**

Rassemblement Démocratique Africain (African Democratic Rally; RDA)
Houphouët-Boigny, Félix **4**
Touré, Sekou **6**

Rastafarianism
Haile Selassie **7**
Marley, Bob **5**
Tosh, Peter **9**

RDA
See Rassemblement Démocratique Africain (African Democratic Rally)

Real estate development
Barden, Don H. **9, 20**
Brooke, Edward **8**
Lane, Vincent **5**
Marshall, Bella **22**
Russell, Herman Jerome **17**

Recording executives
Avant, Clarence **19**
Busby, Jheryl **3**
Combs, Sean "Puffy" **17**
de Passe, Suzanne **25**
Dupri, Jermaine **13**
Gordy, Berry, Jr. **1**
Harrell, Andre **9**
Jackson, George **19**
Jimmy Jam **13**
Jones, Quincy **8**
Knight, Suge **11**
Lewis, Terry **13**
Massenburg, Kedar **23**
Master P **21**
Mayfield, Curtis **2**
Queen Latifah **1, 16**
Rhone, Sylvia **2**
Robinson, Smokey **3**
Simmons, Russell **1**

Record producer
Albright, Gerald **23**
Ayers, Roy **16**
Blige, Mary J. **20**
Combs, Sean "Puffy" **17**
de Passe, Suzanne **25**
Dre, Dr. **14**
Duke, George **21**
Dupri, Jermaine **13**
Edmonds, Kenneth "Babyface" **10**
Hailey, JoJo **22**
Hailey, K-Ci **22**
Hammond, Fred **23**
Hill, Lauryn **20**
Ice Cube **8**
Jackson, George **19**
Jackson, Michael **19**
Jean, Wyclef **20**
Jimmy Jam **13**
Jones, Quincy **8**
Kelly, R. **18**
Lewis, Terry **13**
Master P **21**
Osborne, Jeffrey **26**
Prince **18**
Queen Latifah **1, 16**
Sweat, Keith **19**
Vandross, Luther **13**
White, Barry **13**

Reggae
Marley, Bob **5**
Perry, Ruth **19**
Tosh, Peter **9**

Republican National Convention
Allen, Ethel D. **13**

Republic of New Africa (RNA)
Williams, Robert F. **11**

Restaurants
Cain, Herman **15**
Daniels-Carter, Valerie **23**
Hawkins, La-Van **17**
Smith, Barbara **11**

Revolutionary Party of Tanzania
See Chama cha Mapinduzi

Rheedlen Centers for Children and Families
Canada, Geoffrey **23**

Rhythm and blues/soul music
Adams, Oleta **18**
Ashford, Nickolas **21**
Austin, Patti **24**
Ayers, Roy **16**
Badu, Erykah **22**
Baker, Anita **21**
Baker, LaVern **26**
Belle, Regina **1**
Beverly, Frankie **25**
Blige, Mary J. **20**
Brandy **14**
Braxton, Toni **15**
Brown, Charles **23**
Busby, Jheryl **3**
Butler, Jerry **26**
Campbell, Tisha **8**
Charles, Ray **16**
Clinton, George **9**
Combs, Sean "Puffy" **17**
Cooke, Sam **17**
Downing, Will **19**
Dre, Dr. **14**
Dupri, Jermaine **13**
Edmonds, Kenneth "Babyface" **10**
Evans, Faith **22**
Fats Domino **20**
Foxx, Jamie **15**
Franklin, Aretha **11**
Gaye, Marvin **2**
Green, Al **13**
Hailey, JoJo **22**
Hailey, K-Ci**22**
Hammer, M. C. **20**
Hathaway, Donny **18**
Hayes, Isaac **20**
Hill, Lauryn **20**
Houston, Cissy **20**
Houston, Whitney **7**
Hyman, Phyllis **19**
Isley, Ronald **25**
Jackson, Janet **6**
Jackson, Michael **19**
Jackson, Millie **25**
James, Etta **13**
James, Rick **17**
Jarreau, Al **21**
Jean, Wyclef **20**
Johnson, Robert **2**
Jones, Quincy **8**
Jordan, Montell **23**
Kelly, R. **18**
Kendricks, Eddie **22**
Knight, Gladys **16**
Levert, Gerald **22**
Little Richard **15**
Massenburg, Kedar **23**
Master P **21**
Maxwell **20**
Mayfield, Curtis **2**
McKnight, Brian **18**
Monica **21**
Moore, Chante **26**
Moore, Melba **21**
Ndegéocello, Me'Shell **15**
Neville, Aaron **21**
Notorious B.I.G. **20**
Pendergrass, Teddy **22**

Price, Kelly **23**
Prince **18**
Redding, Otis **16**
Robinson, Smokey **3**
Ross, Diana **8**
Sade **15**
Simpson, Valerie **21**
Sweat, Keith **19**
Tamia **24**
Thomas, Rufus **20**
Turner, Tina **6**
Usher **23**
Vandross, Luther **13**
White, Barry **13**
Williams, Vanessa L. **4, 17**
Wilson, Cassandra **16**
Wilson, Nancy **10**
Wonder, Stevie **11**

RNA
See Republic of New Africa

Rock and Roll Hall of Fame
Brown, Charles **23**
Franklin, Aretha **11**
Isley, Ronald **25**
James, Etta **13**
Wonder, Stevie **11**

Rockefeller Foundation
Price, Hugh B. **9**

Rock music
Clinton, George **9**
Fats Domino **20**
Hendrix, Jimi **10**
Ice-T **6**
Kravitz, Lenny **10**
Little Richard **15**
Lymon, Frankie **22**
Prince **18**
Turner, Tina **6**

Rockets
Williams, O. S. **13**

Rodeo
Pickett, Bill **11**
Sampson, Charles **13**
Whitfield, Fred **23**

Roman Catholic Church
Arinze, Francis Cardinal **19**
Aristide, Jean-Bertrand **6**
Clements, George **2**
Guy, Rosa **5**
Rugambwa, Laurean **20**
Stallings, George A., Jr. **6**

Royal Ballet
Jackson, Isaiah **3**

Royalty
Christophe, Henri **9**
Mutebi, Ronald **25**

RPT
See Togolese People's Rally

Rush Artists Management Co.
Simmons, Russell **1**

Russell-McCloud and Associates
Russell-McCloud, Patricia A. **17**

St. Louis Rams football team
Bruce, Isaac **26**
Pace, Orlando **21**

SAA
See Syndicat Agricole Africain

SACC
See South African Council of Churches

Sacramento Kings basketball team
Russell, Bill **8**

Sacramento Monarchs basketball team
Griffith, Yolanda **25**

SADCC
See Southern African Development Coordination Conference

Southeastern University
Jarvis, Charlene Drew **21**

St. Louis Browns baseball team
Paige, Satchel **7**

St. Louis Cardinals baseball team
Baylor, Don **6**
Brock, Lou **18**
Flood, Curt **10**
Lankford, Ray **23**

St. Louis city government
Bosley, Freeman, Jr. **7**
Harmon, Clarence **26**

St. Louis Hawks basketball team
See Atlanta Hawks basketball team

San Antonio Spurs basketball team
Duncan, Tim **20**
Elliott, Sean **26**
Lucas, John **7**
Robinson, David **24**

San Diego Chargers football team
Barnes, Ernie **16**

San Diego Conquistadors
Chamberlain, Wilt **18**

San Diego Gulls hockey team
O'Ree, Willie **5**

San Diego Hawks hockey team
O'Ree, Willie **5**

San Diego Padres baseball team
Gwynn, Tony **18**
McGriff, Fred **24**
Sheffield, Gary **16**
Winfield, Dave **5**

San Francisco 49ers football team
Edwards, Harry **2**
Green, Dennis **5**
Lott, Ronnie **9**
Rice, Jerry **5**
Simpson, O. J. **15**

San Francisco Giants baseball team
Baker, Dusty **8**
Bonds, Barry **6**
Mays, Willie **3**
Morgan, Joe Leonard **9**
Robinson, Frank **9**
Strawberry, Darryl **22**

Sankofa Film and Video
Julien, Isaac **3**

Saturday Night Live
Murphy, Eddie **4, 20**
Rock, Chris **3, 22**

Saxophone
Albright, Gerald **23**
Bechet, Sidney **18**
Coltrane, John **19**
Gordon, Dexter **25**
Hawkins, Coleman **9**
Parker, Charlie **20**
Washington, Grover, Jr. **17**
Waters, Benny **26**

Schomburg Center for Research in Black Culture
Andrews, Bert **13**
Dodson, Howard, Jr. **7**
Hutson, Jean Blackwell **16**
Reddick, Lawrence Dunbar **20**
Schomburg, Arthur Alfonso **9**

School desegregation
Fortune, T. Thomas **6**
Hamer, Fannie Lou **6**

Science fiction
Bell, Derrick **6**
Butler, Octavia **8**
Delany, Samuel R., Jr. **9**

SCLC
See Southern Christian Leadership Conference

Sculpture
Allen, Tina **22**
Bailey, Radcliffe **19**
Barthe, Richmond **15**
Biggers, John **20**
Brown, Donald **19**
Burke, Selma **16**
Catlett, Elizabeth **2**
Chase-Riboud, Barbara **20**
Edwards, Melvin **22**
Guyton, Tyree **9**
Hunt, Richard **6**
Lewis, Edmonia **10**
Lewis, Samella **25**
Manley, Edna **26**
McGee, Charles **10**
Ringgold, Faith **4**
Saar, Alison **16**
Savage, Augusta **12**
Shabazz, Attallah **6**

Seattle city government
Rice, Norm **8**

Seattle Mariners baseball team
Griffey, Ken, Jr. **12**

Seattle Supersonics basketball team
Bickerstaff, Bernie **21**
Lucas, John **7**
Russell, Bill **8**
Silas, Paul **24**
Wilkens, Lenny **11**

Second Republic (Nigeria)
Obasanjo, Olusegun **5**

Seismology
Person, Waverly **9**

Senate Confirmation Hearings
Ogletree, Charles, Jr. **12**

Sesame Street
Clash, Kevin **14**
Glover, Savion **14**

Sexual harassment
Gomez-Preston, Cheryl **9**
Hill, Anita **5**
Thomas, Clarence **2**

Shrine of the Black Madonna
Agyeman, Jaramogi Abebe **10**

Sickle cell anemia
Satcher, David **7**

Sierra Leone People's Party (SLPP)
Kabbah, Ahmad Tejan **23**

Silicon Graphics Incorporated
Hannah, Marc **10**

Siméus Foods International
Siméus, Dumas M. **25**

Slavery
Asante, Molefi Kete **3**
Bennett, Lerone, Jr. **5**
Chase-Riboud, Barbara **20**
Cooper, Anna Julia **20**
Douglas, Aaron **7**
Du Bois, W. E. B. **3**
Dunbar, Paul Laurence **8**
Gaines, Ernest J. **7**
Haley, Alex **4**
Harper, Frances Ellen Watkins **11**
Johnson, Charles **1**
Morrison, Toni **2, 15**
Muhammad, Elijah **4**
Patterson, Orlando **4**
Pleasant, Mary Ellen **9**
Stephens, Charlotte Andrews **14**
Stewart, Maria W. Miller **19**
Taylor, Susie King **13**
Tubman, Harriet **9**
X, Malcolm **1**

SNCC
See Student Nonviolent Coordinating Committee

Soccer
Jones, Cobi N'Gai **18**
Milla, Roger **2**
Nakhid, David **25**
Pelé **7**

Social disorganization theory
Frazier, E. Franklin **10**

Social science
Berry, Mary Frances **7**
Bunche, Ralph J. **5**
Cayton, Horace **26**
Clark, Kenneth B. **5**
Cobbs, Price M. **9**
Frazier, E. Franklin **10**
Harris, Eddy L. **18**
Haynes, George Edmund **8**
Lawrence-Lightfoot, Sara **10**
Marable, Manning **10**
Steele, Claude Mason **13**
Woodson, Robert L. **10**

Social work
Auguste, Rose-Anne **13**
Berry, Bertice **8**
Canada, Geoffrey **23**
Dunham, Katherine **4**
Fields, C. Virginia **25**
Hale, Clara **16**
Hale, Lorraine **8**
Harris, Alice **7**
Haynes, George Edmund **8**
King, Barbara **22**
Lewis, Thomas **19**
Little, Robert L. **2**
Robinson, Rachel **16**
Waddles, Charleszetta (Mother) **10**
Young, Whitney M., Jr. **4**

Socialist Party of Senegal
Diouf, Abdou **3**

Soledad Brothers
Jackson, George **14**

Soul City, NC
McKissick, Floyd B. **3**

Soul Train
Cornelius, Don **4**

South African Communist Party
Hani, Chris **6**

South African Council of Churches (SACC)
Tutu, Desmond **6**

South African Defence Force (SADF)
Nujoma, Samuel **10**

South African literature
Mathabane, Mark **5**

South African Students' Organization
Biko, Steven **4**

Southern African Development Community (SADC)
Mbuende, Kaire **12**

Southern African Development Coordination Conference (SADCC)
Masire, Quett **5**
Numjoma, Samuel **10**

Southern African Project
McDougall, Gay J. **11**

Southern Christian Leadership Conference (SCLC)
Abernathy, Ralph **1**
Angelou, Maya **1, 15**
Baker, Ella **5**
Chavis, Benjamin **6**
Dee, Ruby **8**
Fauntroy, Walter E. **11**
Hooks, Benjamin L. **2**
Jackson, Jesse **1**
King, Martin Luther, Jr. **1**
King, Martin Luther, III **20**
Lowery, Joseph **2**
Moses, Robert Parris **11**
Rustin, Bayard **4**
Williams, Hosea Lorenzo **15**
Young, Andrew **3**

South West African People's Organization (SWAPO)
Nujoma, Samuel **10**

Space Shuttle
Bluford, Guy **2**
Bolden, Charles F., Jr. **7**
Gregory, Frederick D. **8**
Jemison, Mae C. **1**
McNair, Ronald **3**

Spectroscopy
Quarterman, Lloyd Albert **4**

Spelman College
Cole, Johnnetta B. **5**
Price, Glenda **22**

Spingarn medal
Aaron, Hank **5**
Ailey, Alvin **8**
Anderson, Marian **2**
Angelou, Maya **15**
Bethune, Mary McLeod **4**
Bradley, Thomas **2, 20**
Brooke, Edward **8**
Bunche, Ralph J. **5**
Carver, George Washington **4**
Clark, Kenneth B. **5**
Cosby, Bill **7, 26**
Davis, Sammy Jr. **18**
Drew, Charles Richard **7**
Du Bois, W. E. B. **3**
Ellington, Duke **5**
Evers, Medgar **3**
Grimké, Archibald H. **9**
Haley, Alex **4**
Hastie, William H. **8**
Hayes, Roland **4**
Higginbotham, Jr., A. Leon **13, 25**
Hinton, William Augustus **8**
Hooks, Benjamin L. **2**
Horne, Lena **5**
Houston, Charles Hamilton **4**
Hughes, Langston **4**
Jackson, Jesse **1**
Johnson, James Weldon **5**
Johnson, John H. **3**
Jordan, Barbara **4**
Julian, Percy Lavon **6**
Just, Ernest Everett **3**
King, Martin Luther, Jr. **1**
Lawless, Theodore K. **8**
Lawrence, Jacob **4**
Marshall, Thurgood **1**
Mays, Benjamin E. **7**

Parks, Gordon **1**
Parks, Rosa **1**
Powell, Colin **1**
Price, Leontyne **1**
Randolph, A. Philip **3**
Robeson, Paul **2**
Robinson, Jackie **6**
Staupers, Mabel K. **7**
Sullivan, Leon H. **3**
Weaver, Robert C. **8**
White, Walter F. **4**
Wilder, L. Douglas **3**
Wilkins, Roy **4**
Williams, Paul R. **9**
Woodson, Carter **2**
Wright, Louis Tompkins **4**
Wright, Richard **5**
Young, Andrew **3**
Young, Coleman **1, 20**

Spirituals
Anderson, Marian **2**
Hayes, Roland **4**
Jackson, Mahalia **5**
Joyner, Matilda Sissieretta **15**
Norman, Jessye **5**
Reese, Della **6, 20**
Robeson, Paul **2**

Sports psychology
Edwards, Harry **2**

State University of New York System
Wharton, Clifton R., Jr. **7**

Stonewall 25
Norman, Pat **10**

Structural Readjustment Program
Babangida, Ibrahim **4**

Student Nonviolent Coordinating Committee (SNCC)
Al-Amin, Jamil Abdullah **6**
Baker, Ella **5**
Barry, Marion S. **7**
Blackwell, Unita **17**
Bond, Julian **2**
Carmichael, Stokely **5, 26**
Clark, Septima **7**
Crouch, Stanley **11**
Davis, Angela **5**
Forman, James **7**
Hamer, Fannie Lou **6**
Holland, Endesha Ida Mae **3**
Lester, Julius **9**
Lewis, John **2**
Moses, Robert Parris **11**
Norton, Eleanor Holmes **7**
Poussaint, Alvin F. **5**
Reagon, Bernice Johnson **7**

Sundance Film Festival
Harris, Leslie **6**

Supreme Court
See U.S. Supreme Court

Supreme Court of Haiti
Pascal-Trouillot, Ertha **3**

Surrealism
Ellison, Ralph **7**
Lee-Smith, Hughie **5, 22**

SWAPO
See South West African People's Organization

Sweet Honey in the Rock
Reagon, Bernice Johnson **7**

Syndicat Agricole Africain (SAA)
Houphouët-Boigny, Félix **4**

Synthetic chemistry
Julian, Percy Lavon **6**

Tampa Bay Buccaneers football team
Dungy, Tony **17**
Williams, Doug **22**

Tanga Consultative Congress (Tanzania)
Nujoma, Samuel **10**

Tanganyikan African National Union (TANU)
Nyerere, Julius **5**

TANU
See Tanganyikan African National Union

Tanzanian African National Union (TANU)
See Tanganyikan African National Union

Tap dancing
Bates, Peg Leg **14**
Glover, Savion **14**
Hines, Gregory **1**

TBS
See Turner Broadcasting System

Teachers Insurance and Annuity Association and the College Retirement Equities Fund (TIAA-CREF)
Wharton, Clifton R., Jr. **7**

Teaching
Alexander, Margaret Walker **22**
Clarke, John Henrik **20**
Early, Gerald **15**
Gates, Sylvester James, Jr. **15**
Humphries, Frederick **20**
Jackson, Fred James **25**
Norman, Maidie **20**
Redmond, Eugene **23**
Smith, John L. **22**

TEF
See Theological Education Fund

Television
Arkadie, Kevin **17**
Beach, Michael **26**
Blake, Asha **26**
Bowser, Yvette Lee **17**
Burnett, Charles **16**
Carson, Lisa Nicole **21**
Cheadle, Don **19**
Cosby, Bill **7, 26**
Curtis-Hall, Vondie **17**
de Passe, Suzanne **25**
Diggs, Taye **25**
Elder, Larry **25**
Eubanks, Kevin **15**
Evans, Harry **25**
Givens, Robin **4, 25**
Hardison, Kadeem **22**
Hemsley, Sherman **19**
Hill, Lauryn **20**
Hughley, D.L. **23**
Hyman, Earle **25**
Jackson, George **19**
Joe, Yolanda **21**
Jones, Bobby **20**
Mathis, Greg **26**
Mitchell, Brian Stokes **21**
Mitchell, Russ **21**
Moss, Carlton **16**
Phifer, Mekhi **25**
Price, Frederick K. C. **21**
Quarles, Norma **25**
Rock, Chris **3, 22**
Rollins, Howard E. Jr., **17**
Smiley, Tavis **20**
Snipes, Wesley **3, 24**
Thigpen, Lynne **17**
Usher **23**
Williams, Clarence, III **26**
Williamson, Mykelti **22**

Tennessee Titans football team
McNair, Steve **22**

Tennis
Ashe, Arthur **1, 18**
Garrison, Zina **2**
Gibson, Althea **8**
Lucas, John **7**
McNeil, Lori **1**
Noah, Yannick **4**
Washington, MaliVai **8**
Williams, Samm-Art **21**
Williams, Serena **20**
Williams, Venus **17**

Texas House of Representatives
Johnson, Eddie Bernice **8**
Wilson, Flip **21**

Texas Rangers baseball team
Cottrell, Comer **11**

Texas State Senate
Johnson, Eddie Bernice **8**
Jordan, Barbara **4**

Theological Education Fund (TEF)
Gordon, Pamela **17**
Tutu, Desmond **6**

Theology
Franklin, Robert M. **13**

Third World Press
Madhubuti, Haki R. **7**

Threads 4 Life
Jones, Carl **7**
Kani, Karl **10**
Walker, T. J. **7**

TIAA-CREF
See Teachers Insurance and Annuity Association and the College Retirement Equities Fund

Time-Warner Inc.
Parsons, Richard Dean **11**

TLC Beatrice International Holdings, Inc.
Lewis, Reginald F. **6**

TLC Group L.P.
Lewis, Reginald F. **6**

Today
Gumbel, Bryant **14**

Togolese Army
Eyadéma, Gnassingbé **7**

Togolese People's Rally (RPT)
Eyadéma, Gnassingbé **7**

Tonight Show, The
Eubanks, Kevin **15**

Tony awards
Allen, Debbie **13**
Belafonte, Harry **4**
Carroll, Diahann **9**
Clarke, Hope **14**
Faison, George **16**
Fishburne, Larry **4, 22**
Horne, Lena **5**
Hyman, Phyllis **19**
Jones, James Earl **3**
McDonald, Audra **20**
Moore, Melba **21**
Richards, Lloyd **2**
Thigpen, Lynne **17**
Uggams, Leslie **23**
Vereen, Ben **4**
Wilson, August **7**
Wolfe, George C. **6**

Toronto Blue Jays baseball team
McGriff, Fred **24**
Winfield, Dave **5**

Toronto Raptors basketball team
Carter, Vince **26**
Thomas, Isiah **7, 26**

Track and field
Christie, Linford **8**
Devers, Gail **7**
Johnson, Michael **13**
Jones, Marion **21**
Joyner-Kersee, Jackie **5**
Lewis, Carl **4**
Metcalfe, Ralph **26**
Moses, Edwin **8**
Mutola, Maria **12**
Owens, Jesse **2**
Powell, Mike **7**
Quirot, Ana **13**
Rudolph, Wilma **4**
Thugwane, Josia **21**

TransAfrica, Inc.
Robinson, Randall **7**

Transition
Soyinka, Wole **4**

Transitional Committee for National Recovery (Guinea; CTRN)
Conté, Lansana **7**

Transplant surgery
Callender, Clive O. **3**
Kountz, Samuel L. **10**

"Trial of the Century"
Cochran, Johnnie L., Jr. **11**
Darden, Christopher **13**
Simpson, O.J. **15**

Trinidad Theatre Workshop
Walcott, Derek **5**

Trumpet
Armstrong, Louis **2**
Davis, Miles **4**
Ellison, Ralph **7**
Gillespie, Dizzy **1**

Turner Broadcasting System (TBS)
Clayton, Xernona **3**

Tuskegee Airmen
James, Daniel, Jr. **16**
Patterson, Frederick Douglass **12**

Tuskegee Experiment Station
Carver, George Washington **4**

Tuskegee University
Payton, Benjamin F. **23**

U.S. Department of Agriculture
Watkins, Shirley R. **17**
Williams, Hosea Lorenzo **15**

U.S. Diplomatic Corp
Haley, George Williford Boyce **21**

U.S. District Court judge
Diggs-Taylor, Anna **20**
Keith, Damon J. **16**
Parsons, James **14**

UCC
See United Church of Christ

UFBL
See Universal Foundation for Better Living

UGA
See United Golf Association

Umkhonto we Sizwe
Hani, Chris **6**
Mandela, Nelson **1, 14**

UN
See United Nations

UNCF
See United Negro College Fund

Uncle Nonamé Cookie Company
Amos, Wally **9**

Underground Railroad
Cohen, Anthony **15**

Unemployment and Poverty Action Committee
Forman, James **7**

UNESCO
See United Nations Educational, Scientific, and Cultural Organization

UNIA
See United Negro Improvement Association

UNICEF
See United Nations Children's Fund

Unions
Clay, William Lacy **8**
Crockett, George, Jr. **10**
Europe, James Reese **10**
Farmer, James **2**
Hilliard, David **7**
Ramaphosa, Cyril **3**
Randolph, A. Philip **3**
Touré, Sekou **6**

UNIP
See United National Independence Party

UNITA
See National Union for the Total Independence of Angola

United Bermuda Party
Gordon, Pamela **17**

United Church of Christ (UCC)
Chavis, Benjamin **6**

United Democratic Front (UDF)
Muluzi, Bakili **14**

United Golf Association (UGA)
Elder, Lee **6**
Sifford, Charlie **4**

United Methodist Church
Lewis, Shirley A. R. **14**

United National Independence Party (UNIP)
Kaunda, Kenneth **2**

United Nations (UN)
Annan, Kofi Atta **15**
Bunche, Ralph J. **5**
Diouf, Abdou **3**
Lafontant, Jewel Stradford **3**
McDonald, Gabrielle Kirk **20**
Mongella, Gertrude **11**
Perkins, Edward **5**
Sampson, Edith S. **4**
Young, Andrew **3**

United Nations Children's Fund (UNICEF)
Baker, Gwendolyn Calvert **9**
Belafonte, Harry **4**
Machel, Graca Simbine **16**

United Nations Educational, Scientific, and Cultural Organization (UNESCO)
Diop, Cheikh Anta **4**
Frazier, E. Franklin **10**
Machel, Graca Simbine **16**

United Negro College Fund (UNCF)
Boyd, T. B. III **6**
Edley, Christopher **2**
Gray, William H. III **3**
Jordan, Vernon E. **3**
Mays, Benjamin E. **7**
Patterson, Frederick Douglass **12**

United Negro Improvement Association (UNIA)
Garvey, Marcus **1**

United Parcel Service
Washington, Patrice Clarke **12**

United Somali Congress (USC)
Ali Mahdi Mohamed **5**

United States Football (USFL)
White, Reggie **6**
Williams, Doug **22**

United Workers Union of South Africa (UWUSA)
Buthelezi, Mangosuthu Gatsha **9**

Universal Foundation for Better Living (UFBL)
Colemon, Johnnie **11**
Reese, Della **6, 20**

University of California administration
Massey, Walter E. **5**

University of Colorado administration
Berry, Mary Frances **7**

University of Michigan administration
Goss, Tom **23**

UniverSoul Circus
Walker, Cedric "Ricky" **19**

Urban League (regional)
Adams, Sheila J. **25**
Clayton, Xernona **3**
Jacob, John E. **2**
Mays, Benjamin E. **7**
Young, Whitney M., Jr. **4**

Urban renewal
Archer, Dennis **7**
Barry, Marion S. **7**
Bosley, Freeman, Jr. **7**
Collins, Barbara-Rose **7**
Harris, Alice **7**
Lane, Vincent **5**
Waters, Maxine **3**

US
Karenga, Maulana **10**

U.S. Air Force
Davis, Benjamin O., Jr. **2**
Gregory, Frederick D. **8**
Harris, Marcelite Jordan **16**
James, Daniel, Jr. **16**

U.S. Armed Forces Nurse Corps
Staupers, Mabel K. **7**

U.S. Army
Cadoria, Sherian Grace **14**
Davis, Benjamin O., Sr. **4**
Flipper, Henry O. **3**
Jackson, Fred James **25**
Johnson, Hazel **22**
Powell, Colin **1**
Stanford, John **20**
Watkins, Perry **12**
West, Togo D., Jr. **16**

U.S. Attorney's Office
Lafontant, Jewel Stradford **3**

U.S. Basketball League (USBL)
Lucas, John **7**

USBL
See U.S. Basketball League

USC
See United Somali Congress

U.S. Cabinet
Brown, Ron **5**
Elders, Joycelyn **6**
Espy, Mike **6**
Harris, Patricia Roberts **2**
Herman, Alexis M. **15**
O'Leary, Hazel **6**
Slater, Rodney E. **15**
Sullivan, Louis **8**
Weaver, Robert C. **8**

U.S. Circuit Court of Appeals
Hastie, William H. **8**
Keith, Damon J. **16**

U.S. Coast Guard
Brown, Erroll M. **23**

U.S. Commission on Civil Rights
Berry, Mary Frances **7**

U.S. Court of Appeals
Higginbotham, A. Leon, Jr. **13, 25**
Kearse, Amalya Lyle **12**

USDA
See U.S. Department of Agriculture

U.S. Department of Agriculture (USDA)
Espy, Mike **6**

U.S. Department of Commerce
Brown, Ron **5**
Irving, Larry, Jr. **12**
Person, Waverly **9**
Wilkins, Roger **2**

U.S. Department of Defense
Tribble, Israel, Jr. **8**

U.S. Department of Education
Hill, Anita **5**
Hill, Bonnie Guiton **20**
Thomas, Clarence **2**
Tribble, Israel, Jr. **8**

U.S. Department of Energy
O'Leary, Hazel **6**

U.S. Department of Health and Human Services (HHS)
See also U.S. Department of Health, Education, and Welfare

U.S. Department of Health, Education, and Welfare (HEW)
Bell, Derrick **6**
Berry, Mary Frances **7**
Harris, Patricia Roberts **2**
Johnson, Eddie Bernice **8**
Sullivan, Louis **8**

U.S. Department of Housing and Urban Development (HUD)
Harris, Patricia Roberts **2**
Weaver, Robert C. **8**

U.S. Department of Justice
Bell, Derrick **6**
Campbell, Bill **9**
Days, Drew S., III **10**
Guinier, Lani **7**
Holder, Eric H., Jr. **9**
Lafontant, Jewel Stradford **3**
Lewis, Delano **7**
Patrick, Deval **12**
Wilkins, Roger **2**

U.S. Department of Labor
Crockett, George, Jr. **10**
Herman, Alexis M. **15**

U.S. Department of Social Services
Little, Robert L. **2**

U.S. Department of State
Bethune, Mary McLeod **4**
Bunche, Ralph J. **5**
Keyes, Alan L. **11**
Lafontant, Jewel Stradford **3**
Perkins, Edward **5**
Rice, Condoleezza **3**
Wharton, Clifton R., Jr. **7**

U.S. Department of the Interior
Person, Waverly **9**

U.S. Department of Veterans Affairs
Brown, Jesse **6**

U.S. Diplomatic Corps
Grimké, Archibald H. **9**
Harris, Patricia Roberts **2**
Stokes, Carl B. **10**

USFL
See United States Football League

U.S. Geological Survey
Person, Waverly **9**

U.S. House of Representatives
Bishop Jr., Sanford D. **24**
Brown, Corrine **24**
Carson, Julia **23**
Chisholm, Shirley **2**
Clay, William Lacy **8**
Clayton, Eva M. **20**
Clyburn, James **21**
Collins, Barbara-Rose **7**
Collins, Cardiss **10**
Conyers, John, Jr. **4**

Crockett, George, Jr. **10**
Cummings, Elijah E. **24**
Dellums, Ronald **2**
Diggs, Charles C. **21**
Dixon, Julian C. **24**
Espy, Mike **6**
Fauntroy, Walter E. **11**
Fields, Cleo **13**
Flake, Floyd H. **18**
Ford, Harold E., Jr., **16**
Franks, Gary **2**
Gray, William H. III **3**
Hastings, Alcee L. **16**
Hilliard, Earl F. **24**
Jackson, Jesse, Jr. **14**
Jackson Lee, Sheila **20**
Jefferson, William J. **25**
Jordan, Barbara **4**
Kilpatrick, Carolyn Cheeks **16**
Lee, Barbara **25**
Leland, Mickey **2**
Lewis, John **2**
Meek, Carrie **6**
Meeks, Gregory **25**
Metcalfe, Ralph **26**
Mfume, Kweisi **6**
Millender-McDonald, Juanita **21**
Norton, Eleanor Holmes **7**
Owens, Major **6**
Payne, Donald M. **2**
Pinchback, P. B. S. **9**
Powell, Adam Clayton, Jr. **3**
Rangel, Charles **3**
Rush, Bobby **26**
Scott, Robert C. **23**
Stokes, Louis **3**
Towns, Edolphus **19**
Tubbs Jones, Stephanie **24**
Washington, Harold **6**
Waters, Maxine **3**
Watt, Melvin **26**
Wheat, Alan **14**
Wynn, Albert R. **25**
Young, Andrew **3**

U.S. Joint Chiefs of Staff
Powell, Colin **1**

U.S. Marines
Bolden, Charles F., Jr. **7**
Brown, Jesse **6**
Von Lipsey, Roderick K. **11**

U.S. Navy
Doby, Lawrence Eugene, Sr. **16**
Gravely, Samuel L., Jr. **5**
Reason, J. Paul **19**

U.S. Peace Corps
Days, Drew S., III **10**
Lewis, Delano **7**

U.S. Senate
Braun, Carol Moseley **4**
Brooke, Edward **8**
Dodson, Howard, Jr. **7**
Johnson, Eddie Bernice **8**
Pinchback, P. B. S. **9**

U.S. Supreme Court
Marshall, Thurgood **1**
Thomas, Clarence **2**

U.S. Surgeon General
Elders, Joycelyn **6**

U.S. Virgin Islands government
Hastie, William H. **8**

UWUSA
See United Workers Union of South Africa

Vaudeville
Bates, Peg Leg **14**
Davis, Sammy Jr. **18**
Johnson, Jack **8**
McDaniel, Hattie **5**
Mills, Florence **22**
Robinson, Bill "Bojangles" **11**
Waters, Ethel **7**

Veterinary science
Jawara, Sir Dawda Kairaba **11**
Patterson, Frederick Douglass **12**
Thomas, Vivien **9**

Vibe
Jones, Quincy **8**

Village Voice
Crouch, Stanley **11**

Virginia state government
Wilder, L. Douglas **3**

Virgina Squires basketball team
Erving, Julius **18**

Voodoo
Dunham, Katherine **4**
Guy, Rosa **5**
Hurston, Zora Neale **3**
Pierre, Andre **17**

Voting rights
Clark, Septima **7**
Forman, James **7**
Guinier, Lani **7**
Hamer, Fannie Lou **6**
Harper, Frances Ellen Watkins **11**
Hill, Jessie, Jr. **13**
Johnson, Eddie Bernice **8**
Lampkin, Daisy **19**
Mandela, Nelson **1, 14**
Moses, Robert Parris **11**
Terrell, Mary Church **9**
Trotter, Monroe **9**
Tubman, Harriet **9**
Wells-Barnett, Ida B. **8**
Williams, Hosea Lorenzo **15**
Woodard, Alfre **9**

Vulcan Realty and Investment Company
Gaston, Arthur G. **4**

Washington DC City Council
Jarvis, Charlene Drew **21**

WAAC
See Women's Auxiliary Army Corp

WAC
See Women's Army Corp

Walter Payton Inc.
Payton, Walter **11, 25**

War Resister's League (WRL)
Carter, Mandy **11**

Washington Capitols basketball team
Lloyd, Earl **26**

Washington Color Field group
Thomas, Alma **14**

Washington, DC City Council
Fauntroy, Walter E. **11**

Washington, DC city government
Barry, Marion S. **7**
Dixon, Sharon Pratt **1**
Fauntroy, Walter E. **11**
Jarvis, Charlene Drew **21**
Norton, Eleanor Holmes **7**
Williams, Anthony **21**

Washington Mystics basketball team
McCray, Nikki **18**

Washington Wizards basketball team
Bickerstaff, Bernie **21**
Heard, Gar **25**
Howard, Juwan **15**
Lucas, John **7**
Unseld, Wes **23**
Webber, Chris **15**

Washington Post
Maynard, Robert C. **7**
McCall, Nathan **8**
Nelson, Jill **6**
Raspberry, William **2**
Wilkins, Roger **2**

WBA
See World Boxing Association

WBC
See World Boxing Council

WCC
See World Council of Churches

Weather
Christian, Spencer **15**
McEwen, Mark **5**

Welfare reform
Bryant, Wayne R. **6**
Carson, Julia **23**
Williams, Walter E. **4**

West Indian folklore
Walcott, Derek **5**

West Indian folk songs
Belafonte, Harry **4**

West Indian literature
Guy, Rosa **5**
Kincaid, Jamaica **4**
Marshall, Paule **7**
McKay, Claude **6**
Walcott, Derek **5**

West Point
Davis, Benjamin O., Jr. **2**
Flipper, Henry O. **3**

West Side Preparatory School
Collins, Marva **3**

White House Conference on Civil Rights
Randolph, A. Philip **3**

Whitney Museum of American Art
Golden, Thelma **10**

WHO
See Women Helping Offenders

"Why Are You on This Planet?"
Yoba, Malik **11**

William Morris Talent Agency
Amos, Wally **9**

WillieWear Ltd.
Smith, Willi **8**

Wilmington 10
Chavis, Benjamin **6**

WOMAD
See World of Music, Arts, and Dance

Women Helping Offenders (WHO)
Holland, Endesha Ida Mae **3**

Women's Auxiliary Army Corps
See Women's Army Corp

Women's Army Corps (WAC)
Adams Early, Charity **13**
Cadoria, Sherian Grace **14**

Women's issues
Allen, Ethel D. **13**
Angelou, Maya **1, 15**
Baker, Ella **5**
Berry, Mary Frances **7**
Brown, Elaine **8**
Campbell, Bebe Moore **6, 24**
Cannon, Katie **10**
Charles, Mary Eugenia **10**
Chinn, May Edward **26**
Christian-Green, Donna M. **17**
Clark, Septima **7**
Cole, Johnnetta B. **5**
Cooper, Anna Julia **20**
Cunningham, Evelyn **23**
Dash, Julie **4**
Davis, Angela **5**
Edelman, Marian Wright **5**
Elders, Joycelyn **6**
Fauset, Jessie **7**
Giddings, Paula **11**
Goldberg, Whoopi **4**
Grimké, Archibald H. **9**
Guy-Sheftall, Beverly **13**
Hale, Clara **16**
Hale, Lorraine **8**
Hamer, Fannie Lou **6**
Harper, Frances Ellen Watkins **11**
Harris, Alice **7**
Harris, Leslie **6**
Harris, Patricia Roberts **2**
Height, Dorothy I. **2, 23**
Hernandez, Aileen Clarke **13**
Hill, Anita **5**
Hine, Darlene Clark **24**
Holland, Endesha Ida Mae **3**
hooks, bell **5**
Jackson, Alexine Clement **22**
Joe, Yolanda **21**
Jordan, Barbara **4**
Jordan, June **7**
Lampkin, Daisy **19**
Larsen, Nella **10**
Lorde, Audre **6**
Marshall, Paule **7**
McCabe, Jewell Jackson **10**
McMillan, Terry **4, 17**
Meek, Carrie **6**
Millender-McDonald, Juanita **21**
Mongella, Gertrude **11**
Morrison, Toni **2, 15**
Naylor, Gloria **10**
Nelson, Jill **6**
Nichols, Nichelle **11**
Norman, Pat **10**
Norton, Eleanor Holmes **7**
Painter, Nell Irvin **24**
Parker, Pat **19**
Rawlings, Nana Konadu Agyeman **13**
Ringgold, Faith **4**
Shange, Ntozake **8**
Simpson, Carole **6**
Smith, Jane E. **24**
Terrell, Mary Church **9**
Tubman, Harriet **9**
Vanzant, Iyanla **17**
Walker, Alice **1**
Walker, Maggie Lena **17**
Wallace, Michele Faith **13**
Waters, Maxine **3**
Wattleton, Faye **9**
Winfrey, Oprah **2, 15**

Women's National Basketball Association (WNBA)
Cooper, Cynthia **17**
Edwards, Teresa **14**
Griffith, Yolanda **25**
Holdsclaw, Chamique **24**
Leslie, Lisa **16**
McCray, Nikki **18**
Peck, Carolyn **23**
Perrot, Kim **23**
Swoopes, Sheryl **12**
Thompson, Tina **25**

Women's Strike for Peace
King, Coretta Scott **3**

Worker's Party (Brazil)
da Silva, Benedita **5**

Workplace equity
Hill, Anita **5**
Clark, Septima **7**
Nelson, Jill **6**
Simpson, Carole **6**

Works Progress Administration (WPA)
Alexander, Margaret Walker **22**
Baker, Ella **5**
Douglas, Aaron **7**
Dunham, Katherine **4**
Lawrence, Jacob **4**
Lee-Smith, Hughie **5, 22**
Wright, Richard **5**

World African Hebrew Israelite Community
Ben-Israel, Ben Ami **11**

World beat
Belafonte, Harry **4**
Fela **1**
N'Dour, Youssou **1**
Ongala, Remmy **9**

World Bank
Soglo, Nicéphore **15**

World Boxing Association (WBA)
Whitaker, Pernell **10**

World Boxing Council (WBF)
Whitaker, Pernell **10**

World Council of Churches (WCC)
Mays, Benjamin E. **7**
Tutu, Desmond **6**

World Cup
Milla, Roger **2**
Pelé **7**

World hunger
Belafonte, Harry **4**
Iman **4**
Jones, Quincy **8**
Leland, Mickey **2**
Masire, Quett **5**
Obasanjo, Olusegun **5**

World of Music, Arts, and Dance (WOMAD)
Ongala, Remmy **9**

WPA
See Works Progress Administration

WRL
See War Resister's League

Xerox Corp.
Rand, A. Barry **6**

Yab Yum Entertainment
Edmonds, Tracey **16**

Yale Child Study Center
Comer, James P. **6**

Yale Repertory Theater
Dutton, Charles S. **4, 22**
Richards, Lloyd **2**
Wilson, August **7**

Yale School of Drama
Dutton, Charles S. **4, 22**
Richards, Lloyd **2**

YMCA
See Young Men's Christian Associations

Yoruban folklore
Soyinka, Wole **4**
Vanzant, Iyanla **17**

Young Men's Christian Association (YMCA)
Butts, Calvin O., III **9**
Goode, Mal **13**
Hope, John **8**
Mays, Benjamin E. **7**

Young Negroes' Cooperative League
Baker, Ella **5**

Young Women's Christian Association (YWCA)
Baker, Ella **5**
Baker, Gwendolyn Calvert **9**
Clark, Septima **7**
Hedgeman, Anna Arnold **22**
Height, Dorothy I. **2, 23**
Jackson, Alexine Clement **22**
Jenkins, Ella **15**
Sampson, Edith S. **4**

Youth Pride Inc.
Barry, Marion S. **7**

Youth Services Administration
Little, Robert L. **2**

YWCA
See Young Women's Christian Association

ZANLA
See Zimbabwe African National Liberation Army

ZAPU
See Zimbabwe African People's Union

Zimbabwe African National Liberation Army (ZANLA)
Mugabe, Robert Gabriel **10**

Zimbabwe African People's Union (ZAPU)
Mugabe, Robert Gabriel **10**
Nkomo, Joshua **4**

Zimbabwe Congress of Trade Unions (ZCTU)
Tsvangirai, Morgan **26**

ZTA
See Zululand Territorial Authority

Zululand Territorial Authority (ZTA)
Buthelezi, Mangosuthu Gatsha **9**

Cumulative Name Index

Volume numbers appear in Bold

Johnson, Jack 1878-1946 **8**
"Deadwood Dick"
See Love, Nat
"The Goat"
See Manigault, Earl "The Goat"
Aaron, Hank 1934— **5**
Aaron, Henry Louis
See Aaron, Hank
Abacha, Sani 1943— **11**
Abbott, Diane (Julie) 1953— **9**
Abdul-Jabbar, Kareem 1947— **8**
Abdulmajid, Iman Mohame See Iman
Abernathy, Ralph David 1926-1990 **1**
Abu-Jamal, Mumia 1954— **15**
Achebe, (Albert) Chinua(lumogu) 1930— **6**
Adams Early, Charity (Edna) 1918— **13**
Adams, Floyd, Jr. 1945— **12**
Adams, Oleta 19(?)(?)— **18**
Adams, Sheila J. 1943— **25**
Adams, Yolanda 1961— **17**
Adkins, Rutherford H. 1924-1998 **21**
Adu, Helen Folasade
See Sade
Agyeman, Jaramogi Abebe 1911— **10**
Agyeman Rawlings, Nana Konadu 1948— **13**
Aiken, Loretta Mary
See Mabley, Jackie "Moms" **15**
Ailey, Alvin 1931-1989 **8**
Al-Amin, Jamil Abdullah 1943— **6**
Albright, Gerald 1947— **23**
Alcindor, Ferdinand Lewis
See Abdul-Jabbar, Kareem
Alexander, Archie Alphonso 1888-1958 **14**
Alexander, Joyce London 1949— **18**
Alexander, Clifford 1933— **26**
Alexander, Margaret Walker 1915-1998 **22**
Alexander, Sadie Tanner Mossell 1898-1989 **22**
Ali Mahdi Mohamed 1940— **5**
Ali, Muhammad 1942— **2, 16**
Allen, Byron 1961— **3, 24**
Allen, Debbie 1950— **13**
Allen, Ethel D. 1929-1981 **13**
Allen, Marcus 1960— **20**
Allen, Richard 1760-1831 **14**
Allen, Tina 1955— **22**
Amos, John 1941— **8**
Amos, Wally 1937— **9**
Anderson, Elmer 1941— **25**
Anderson, Jamal 1972 **22**
Anderson, Marian 1902 **2**
Andrews, Benny 1930— **22**
Andrews, Bert 1929-1993 **13**
Andrews, Raymond 1934-1991 **4**
Angelou, Maya 1928— **1, 15**
Anna Marie
See Lincoln, Abbey
Annan, Kofi Atta 1938— **15**
Ansa, Tina McElroy 1949— **14**
Anthony, Wendell 1950— **25**
Archer, Dennis (Wayne) 1942— **7**
Arinze, Francis Cardinal 1932— **19**
Aristide, Jean-Bertrand 1953— **6**
Arkadie, Kevin 1957— **17**
Armstrong, (Daniel) Louis 1900-1971 **2**
Armstrong, Robb 1962— **15**
Armstrong, Vanessa Bell 1953— **24**
Arnold, Monica
See Monica
Arrington, Richard 1934— **24**
Asante, Molefi Kete 1942— **3**
Ashe, Arthur Robert, Jr. 1943-1993 **1, 18**
Ashford, Emmett 1914-1980 **22**
Ashford, Nickolas 1942— **21**
Ashley, Maurice 1966— **15**
Ashley-Ward, Amelia 1957— **23**
Atkins, David
See Sinbad
Auguste, (Marie Carmele) Rose-Anne 1963— **13**
Austin, Patti 1948— **24**
Avant, Clarence 19(?)(?)— **19**
Ayers, Roy 1940— **16**
Azikiwe, Nnamdi 1904-1996 **13**
Babangida, Ibrahim (Badamasi) 1941— **4**
Babyface
See Edmonds, Kenneth "Babyface"
Badu, Erykah 1971(?)(?)— **22**
Bailey, Pearl Mae 1918-1990 **14**
Bailey, Radcliffe 1968— **19**
Bailey, Xenobia 1955(?)— **11**
Baisden, Michael 1963— **25**
Baker, Anita 1957(?)— **21**
Baker, Constance
See Motley, Constance Baker
Baker, Dusty 1949— **8**
Baker, Ella 1903-1986 **5**
Baker, George
See Divine, Father
Baker, Gwendolyn Calvert 1931— **9**
Baker, Houston A(lfred), Jr. 1943— **6**
Baker, Johnnie B., Jr.
See Baker, Dusty
Baker, Josephine 1906-1975 **3**
Baker, LaVern 1929-1997 **26**
Baker, Thurbert 1952— **22**
Baldwin, James 1924-1987 **1**
Bambara, Toni Cade 1939— **10**
Banda, (Ngwazi) Hastings Kamuzu 1898(?)— **6**
Banks, Jeffrey 1953— **17**
Banks, Tyra 1973— **11**
Banks, William (Venoid) 1903-1985 **11**
Baraka, Amiri 1934— **1**
Barboza, Anthony 1944— **10**
Barden, Don H. 1943— **9, 20**
Barkley, Charles (Wade) 1963— **5**
Barnes, Ernie 1938— **16**
Barney, Lem 1945— **26**
Barrett, Andrew C. 1942(?)— **12**
Barrow, Joseph Louis
See Louis, Joe
Barry, Marion S(hepilov, Jr.) 1936— **7**
Barthe, Richmond 1901-1989 **15**
Basie, Count 1904-1984 **23**
Basie, William James
See Basie, Count
Basie, William James
See Count Basie
Basquiat, Jean-Michel 1960-1988 **5**
Bassett, Angela 1959(?)— **6, 23**
Bassey, Shirley 1937— **25**
Bates, Clayton
See Bates, Peg Leg
Bates, Daisy (Lee Gatson) 1914(?)— **13**
Bates, Peg Leg 1907— **14**
Baugh, David 1947— **23**
Baylor, Don(ald Edward) 1949— **6**
Beach, Michael 1963— **26**
Beals, Jennifer 1963— **12**
Beals, Melba Patillo 1941— **15**
Bearden, Romare (Howard) 1912-1988 **2**
Beasley, Myrlie
See Evers, Myrlie
Beaton, Norman Lugard 1934-1994 **14**
Bechet, Sidney 1897-1959 **18**
Beck, Robert
See Iceberg Slim
Beckford, Tyson 1970— **11**
Bedie, Henri Konan 1934— **21**
Belafonte, Harold George, Jr.
See Belafonte, Harry

Belafonte, Harry 1927— **4**
Bell, Derrick (Albert, Jr.) 1930— **6**
Bell, Ralph S. 1934— **5**
Bell, Robert Mack 1943— **22**
Bellamy, Bill 1967— **12**
Belle, Albert (Jojuan) 1966— **10**
Belle, Regina 1963— **1**
Belton, Sharon Sayles 1951— **9, 16**
Ben-Israel, Ben Ami 1940(?)— **11**
Benjamin, Regina 1956— **20**
Bennett, Lerone, Jr. 1928— **5**
Berry, Bertice 1960— **8**
Berry, Halle 1967(?)— **4, 19**
Berry, Mary Frances 1938— **7**
Betha, Mason Durrell 1977(?)— **24**
Bethune, Mary (Jane) McLeod 1875-1955 **4**
Beverly, Frankie 1946— **25**
Bickerstaff, Bernard Tyrone 1944— **21**
Biggers, John 1924 **20**
Biko, Stephen
See Biko, Steven (Bantu)
Biko, Steven (Bantu) 1946-1977 **4**
Bing, Dave 1943— **3**
Bishop, Eric
See Foxx, Jamie
Bishop Jr., Sanford D. 1947— **24**
Bizimungu, Pasteur 1951— **19**
Black, Keith Lanier 1955— **18**
Blackwell, Unita 1933 **17**
Blair, Maxine
See Powell, Maxine
Blanks, Billy 1955(?)— **22**
Blake, Asha 1961(?)— **26**
Blige, Mary Jane 1971 **20**
Bluford, Guion Stewart, Jr.
See Bluford, Guy
Bluford, Guy 1942— **2**
Bluitt, Juliann Stephanie 1938— **14**
Bol, Manute 1963— **1**
Bolden, Charles F(rank), Jr. 1946— **7**
Bolin, Jane 1908— **22**
Bolton, Terrell D. 1959(?)— **25**
Bonaly, Surya 1973— **7**
Bond, (Horace) Julian 1940— **2**
Bonds, Barry (Lamar) 1964— **6**
Bonga, Kuenda 1942— **13**
Bongo, (El Hadj) Omar 1935— **1**
Bongo, Albert-Bernard
See Bongo, (El Hadj) Omar
Bontemps, Arna(ud Wendell) 1902-1973 **8**
Booker, Simeon 1918— **23**
Borders, James (Buchanan, IV) 1949— **9**
Bosley, Freeman (Robertson), Jr. 1954— **7**
Boston, Kelvin E. 1955(?)— **25**
Boston, Lloyd 1970(?)— **24**
Bowe, Riddick (Lamont) 1967— **6**
Bowser, Yvette Lee 1965(?)— **17**
Boyd, John W., Jr. 1965— **20**
Boyd, T(heophilus) B(artholomew), III 1947— **6**
Boykin, Keith 1965— **14**
Bradley, Ed(ward R.) 1941— **2**
Bradley, Thomas 1917— **2, 20**
Brandon, Barbara 1960(?)— **3**
Brandon, Thomas Terrell 1970— **16**
Brandy 1979— **14**
Braugher, Andre 1962(?)— **13**
Braun, Carol (Elizabeth) Moseley 1947— **4**
Braxton, Toni 1968(?)— **15**
Brazile, Donna 1959— **25**
Breedlove, Sarah
See Walker, Madame C. J.
Brimmer, Andrew F(elton) 1926— **2**
Briscoe, Connie 1952— **15**
Brock, Louis Clark 1939— **18**
Brooke, Edward (William, III) 1919— **8**
Brooks, Avery 1949— **9**
Brooks, Gwendolyn 1917— **1**
Brown, Andre
See Dr. Dre
Brown Bomber, The
See Louis, Joe
Brown, Charles 1922-1999 **23**
Brown, Corrine 1946— **24**
Brown, Donald 1963— **19**
Brown, Elaine 1943— **8**
Brown, Erroll M. 1950(?)— **23**
Brown, Foxy 1979— **25**
Brown, H. Rap
See Al-Amin, Jamil Abdullah
Brown, Hubert Gerold
See Al-Amin, Jamil Abdullah
Brown, James Willie, Jr.
See Komunyakaa, Yusef
Brown, James 1951— **22**
Brown, James 1933— **15**
Brown, James Nathaniel
See Brown, Jim
Brown, Jesse 1944— **6**
Brown, Jim 1936— **11**
Brown, Joyce F. 1946— **25**
Brown, Lee P(atrick) 1937— **1, 24**
Brown, Les(lie Calvin) 1945— **5**
Brown, Ron(ald Harmon) 1941— **5**
Brown, Sterling (Allen) 1901— **10**
Brown, Tony 1933— **3**
Brown, Wesley 1945— **23**
Brown, William Anthony
See Brown, Tony
Brown, Willie L., Jr. 1934— **7**
Brown, Zora Kramer 1949— **12**
Bruce, Isaac 1972— **26**
Brunson, Dorothy 1938— **1**
Bryant, John 1966— **26**
Bryant, Kobe 1978— **15**
Bryant, Wayne R(ichard) 1947— **6**
Buckley, Victoria (Vikki) 1947-1999 **24**
Bullard, Eugene Jacques 1894-1961 **12**
Bullins, Ed 1935— **25**
Bullock, Anna Mae
See Turner, Tina
Bullock, Steve 1936— **22**
Bumbry, Grace (Ann) 1937— **5**
Bunche, Ralph J(ohnson) 1904-1971 **5**
Burke, Selma Hortense 1900-1995 **16**
Burley, Mary Lou
See Williams, Mary Lou
Burnett, Charles 1944— **16**
Burnett, Chester Arthur
See Howlin' Wolf
Burnett, Dorothy 1905-1995 **19**
Burrell, Stanley Kirk
See Hammer, M. C.
Burrell, Thomas J. 1939— **21**
Burris, Chuck 1951— **21**
Burris, Roland W. 1937— **25**
Burroughs, Margaret Taylor 1917— **9**
Burton, LeVar(dis Robert Martyn) 1957— **8**
Busby, Jheryl 1949(?)— **3**
Buthelezi, Mangosuthu Gatsha 1928— **9**
Butler, Jerry 1939— **26**
Butler, Leroy, III 1968— **17**
Butler, Octavia (Estellle) 1947— **8**
Butler, Paul D. 1961— **17**
Butts, Calvin O(tis), III 1950— **9**
Byrd, Donald 1949— **10**
Byrd, Michelle 1965— **19**
Byrd, Robert (Oliver Daniel, III) 1952— **11**
Byron, JoAnne Deborah
See Shakur, Assata
Cade, Toni
See Bambara, Toni Cade
Cadoria, Sherian Grace 1940— **14**
Caesar, Shirley 1938— **19**
Cain, Herman 1945— **15**
Callender, Clive O(rville) 1936— **3**
Calloway, Cabell, III 1907-1994 **14**
Camp, Kimberly 1956— **19**
Campanella, Roy 1921-1993 **25**
Campbell, Bebe Moore 1950— **6, 24**
Campbell, Bill 1954— **9**
Campbell, Charleszetta Lena
See Waddles, Charleszetta (Mother)
Campbell, E(lmer) Simms 1906-1971 **13**
Campbell, Naomi 1970— **1**
Campbell, Tisha 1969— **8**
Canada, Geoffrey 1954— **23**
Canegata, Leonard Lionel Cornelius
See Lee, Canada
Cannon, Katie 1950— **10**
Carew, Rod 1945 **20**
Carmichael, Stokely 1941-1998 **5, 26**
Carnegie, Herbert 1919— **25**
Carroll, Diahann 1935— **9**
Carson, Benjamin 1951— **1**
Carson, Josephine
See Baker, Josephine
Carson, Julia 1938— **23**
Carson, Lisa Nicole 1969— **21**
Carter, Anson 1974— **24**
Carter, Ben
See Ben-Israel, Ben Ami
Carter, Betty 1930— **19**
Carter, Cris 1965— **21**
Carter, Mandy 1946— **11**
Carter, Regina 1966(?)— **23**
Carter, Rubin 1937— **26**
Carter, Stephen L(isle) 1954— **4**
Carter, Vince 1977— **26**
Carver, George Washington 1861(?)-1943 **4**
Cary, Lorene 1956— **3**
CasSelle, Malcolm 1970— **11**
Catlett, Elizabeth 1919— **2**
Cayton, Horace 1903-1970 **26**
Chamberlain, Wilton Norman 1936— **18**
Chambers, Julius (LeVonne) 1936— **3**
Chapman, Jr., Nathan A. 1957— **21**
Chapman, Tracy 1964— **26**
Chappell, Emma C. 1941— **18**
Charlemagne, Emmanuel
See Charlemagne, Manno
Charlemagne, Manno 1948— **11**
Charles, Mary Eugenia 1919— **10**
Charles, Ray 1930— **16**
Chase-Riboud, Barbara 1939— **20**
Chavis, Benjamin (Franklin, Jr.) 1948— **6**
Cheadle, Don 1964— **19**
Cheatham, Doc 1905-1997 **17**
Chenault, Kenneth I. 1952— **4**
Chesimard, JoAnne (Deborah)
See Shakur, Assata
Chideya, Farai 1969— **14**
Childress, Alice 1920-1994 **15**
Chinn, May Edward 1896-1980 **26**
Chisholm, Shirley (Anita St. Hill) 1924— **2**
Chissano, Joaquim (Alberto) 1939— **7**
Christian-Green, Donna M. 1945— **17**
Christian, Spencer 1947— **15**
Christie, Linford 1960— **8**

Christophe, Henri 1767-1820 **9**
Chuck D 1960— **9**
Clark, Celeste (Clesteen) Abraham 1953— **15**
Clark, Joe 1939— **1**
Clark, Kenneth B(ancroft) 1914— **5**
Clark, Kristin
See Taylor, Kristin Clark
Clark, Patrick 1955— **14**
Clark, Septima (Poinsette) 1898-1987 **7**
Clark-Sheard, Karen 19(?)(?)— **22**
Clarke, Hope 1943(?)— **14**
Clarke, John Henrik 1915-1998 **20**
Clarke, Patrice Francise
See Washington, Patrice Clarke
Clash, Kevin 1961(?)— **14**
Clay, Cassius Marcellus, Jr.
See Ali, Muhammad
Clay, William Lacy 1931— **8**
Clayton, Constance 1937— **1**
Clayton, Eva M. 1934— **20**
Clayton, Xernona 1930— **3**
Claytor, Helen 1907— **14**
Cleage, Albert Buford
See Agyeman, Jaramogi Abebe
Cleage, Pearl Michelle 1934— **17**
Cleaver, (Leroy) Eldridge 1935— **5**
Cleaver, Emanuel (II) 1944— **4**
Clements, George (Harold) 1932— **2**
Clendenon, Donn 1935— **26**
Cleveland, James 1932(?)-1991 **19**
Clifton, Lucille 1936— **14**
Clinton, George (Edward) 1941— **9**
Clyburn, James 1940— **21**
Coachman, Alice 1923— **18**
Cobbs, Price M(ashaw) 1928— **9**
Cochran, Johnnie (L., Jr.) 1937— **11**
Cohen, Anthony 1963— **15**
Colbert, Virgis William 1939— **17**
Cole, Johnnetta B(etsch) 1936— **5**
Cole, Nat King 1919-1965 **17**
Cole, Natalie Maria 1950— **17**
Coleman, Bessie 1892-1926 **9**
Coleman, Donald A. 1952— **24**
Coleman, Leonard S., Jr. 1949— **12**
Colemon, Johnnie 1921(?)— **11**
Collins, Albert 1932-1993 **12**
Collins, Barbara-Rose 1939— **7**
Collins, Cardiss 1931— **10**
Collins, Marva 1936— **3**
Coltrane, John William 1926-1967 **19**
Combs, Sean J. 1969— **17**
Comer, James P(ierpont) 1934— **6**
Cone, James H. 1938— **3**
Connerly, Ward 1939— **14**
Conté, Lansana 1944(?)— **7**
Conyers, John, Jr. 1929— **4**
Conyers, Nathan G. 1932— **24**
Cook, Sam 1931-1964 **17**
Cook, Samuel DuBois 1928— **14**
Cook, Suzan D. Johnson 1957— **22**
Cook, Toni 1944— **23**
Cook, Wesley
See Abu-Jamal, Mumia
Cooks, Patricia 1944-1989 **19**
Cooper, Anna Julia 1858-1964 **20**
Cooper, Cynthia 1963— **17**
Cooper, Edward S(awyer) 1926— **6**
Cooper, J. California 19??— **12**
Cornelius, Don 1936— **4**
Cosby, Bill 1937— **7, 26**
Cosby, Camille Olivia Hanks 1944— **14**
Cosby, William Henry, Jr.
See Cosby, Bill
Cose, Ellis 1951— **5**
Cottrell, Comer 1931— **11**
Count Basie 1904-1984 **23**
Cowans, Adger W. 1936— **20**
Crawford, Randy 1952— **19**
Crawford, Veronica
See Crawford, Randy
Crew, Rudolph F. 1950(?)— **16**
Crockett, George (William), Jr. 1909— **10**
Cross, Dolores E. 1938— **23**
Crothers, Benjamin Sherman
See Crothers, Scatman
Crothers, Scatman 1910-1986 **19**
Crouch, Stanley 1945— **11**
Crowder, Henry 1895-1954(?) **16**
Cullen, Countee 1903-1946 **8**
Cummings, Elijah E. 1951— **24**
Cunningham, Evelyn 1916— **23**
Cunningham, Randall 1963— **23**
Currie, Betty 1939(?)— **21**
Curry, George E. 1947— **23**
Curry, Mark 1964— **17**
Curtis, Christopher Paul 1954(?)— **26**
Curtis-Hall, Vondie 1956— **17**
da Silva, Benedita 1942— **5**
Dandridge, Dorothy 1922-1965 **3**
Daniels-Carter, Valerie 19(?)(?)— **23**
Danticat, Edwidge 1969— **15**
Darden, Christopher 1957— **13**
Dash, Julie 1952— **4**
Davenport, Arthur
See Fattah, Chaka
Davidson, Jaye 1967(?)— **5**
Davidson, Tommy— **21**
Davis, Allison 1902-1983 **12**
Davis, Angela (Yvonne) 1944— **5**
Davis, Anthony 1951— **11**
Davis, Benjamin O(liver), Jr. 1912— **2**
Davis, Benjamin O(liver), Sr. 1877-1970 **4**
Davis, Danny K. 1941— **24**
Davis, Ed 1911-1999 **24**
Davis, Lorenzo "Piper" 1917-1997 **19**
Davis, Miles (Dewey, III) 1926-1991 **4**
Davis, Ossie 1917— **5**
Davis, Sammy, Jr. 1925-1990 **18**
Davis, Terrell 1972— **20**
Dawes, Dominique (Margaux) 1976— **11**
Dawkins, Wayne 1955 **20**
Days, Drew S(aunders, III) 1941— **10**
de Carvalho, Barcelo
See Bonga, Kuenda
de Passe, Suzanne 1948(?)— **25**
Dee, Ruby 1924— **8**
Delaney, Beauford 1901-1979 **19**
Delany, Annie Elizabeth 1891-1995 **12**
Delany, Samuel R(ay), Jr. 1942— **9**
Delany, Sarah (Sadie) 1889— **12**
Dellums, Ronald (Vernie) 1935— **2**
Devers, (Yolanda) Gail 1966— **7**
Devine, Loretta 1953— **24**
Devine, Major J.
See Divine, Father
Dickens, Helen Octavia 1909— **14**
Dickerson, Ernest 1952(?)— **6, 17**
Dickey, Eric Jerome 19(?)(?)— **21**
Diggs, Charles C. 1922-1998 **21**
Diggs, Taye 1972— **25**
Diggs-Taylor, Anna 1932— **20**
Dinkins, David (Norman) 1927— **4**
Diop, Cheikh Anta 1923-1986 **4**
Diouf, Abdou 1935— **3**
Divine, Father 1877(?)-1965 **7**
Dixon, Julian C. 1934— **24**
Dixon, Margaret 192(?)— **14**
Dixon, Sharon Pratt 1944— **1**
Dixon, Willie (James) 1915-1992 **4**
do Nascimento, Edson Arantes
See Pelé
Doby, Lawrence Eugene, Sr. 1924(?)— **16**
Dodson, Howard, Jr. 1939— **7**
Doley, Harold, Jr. 1947— **26**
Domini, Rey
See Lorde, Audre (Geraldine)
Donegan, Dorothy 1922-1998 **19**
Dorsey, Thomas Andrew 1899-1993 **15**
Douglas, Aaron 1899-1979 **7**
Dove, Rita (Frances) 1952— **6**
Dove, Ulysses 1947— **5**
Downing, Will 19(?)(?)— **19**
Dr. Dre **10**
Dr. J
See Erving, Julius Winfield, II
Draper, Sharon M. 1952— **16**
Dre, Dr. 1965?— **14**
Drew, Charles Richard 1904-1950 **7**
Drexler, Clyde 1962— **4**
Driskell, David C(lyde) 1931— **7**
Driver, David E. 1955— **11**
Du Bois, W(illiam) E(dward) B(urghardt) 1868-1963 **3**
DuBois, Shirley Graham 1907-1977 **21**
Ducksworth, Marilyn 1957— **12**
Duke, Bill 1943— **3**
Duke, George 1946— **21**
Dumars, Joe 1963— **16**
Dunbar, Paul Laurence 1872-1906 **8**
Duncan, Michael Clarke 1957— **26**
Duncan, Tim 1976— **20**
Dungy, Tony 1955— **17**
Dunham, Katherine (Mary) 1910(?)— **4**
Dupri, Jermaine 1972— **13**
Dutton, Charles S. 1951— **4, 22**
Dutton, Marie Elizabeth 1940— **12**
Dyson, Michael Eric 1958— **11**
Early, Deloreese Patricia
See Reese, Della
Early, Gerald (Lyn) 1952— **15**
Edelin, Ramona Hoage 1945— **19**
Edelman, Marian Wright 1939— **5**
Edley, Christopher (Fairfield, Sr.) 1928— **2**
Edmonds, Kenneth "Babyface" 1958(?)— **10**
Edmonds, Terry 1950(?)— **17**
Edmonds, Tracey 1967(?)— **16**
Edwards, Eli
See McKay, Claude
Edwards, Harry 1942— **2**
Edwards, Melvin 1937— **22**
Edwards, Teresa 1964— **14**
El-Hajj Malik El-Shabazz
See X, Malcolm
El-Shabazz, El-Hajj Malik
See X, Malcolm
Elder, (Robert) Lee 1934— **6**
Elder, Larry 1952— **25**
Elders, Joycelyn (Minnie) 1933— **6**
Ellerbe, Brian 1963— **22**
Ellington, Duke 1899-1974 **5**
Ellington, E. David 1960— **11**
Ellington, Edward Kennedy
See Ellington, Duke
Elliott, Sean 1968— **26**
Ellison, Ralph (Waldo) 1914-1994 **7**
Elmore, Ronn 1957— **21**
Epps, Omar 1973— **23**
Erving, Julius Winfield, II 1950— **18**
Esposito, Giancarlo (Giusseppi Alessandro) 1958— **9**
Espy, Alphonso Michael
See Espy, Mike
Espy, Mike 1953— **6**

Eubanks, Kevin 1957— **15**
Europe, (William) James Reese 1880-1919 **10**
Evans, Darryl 1961— **22**
Evans, Faith 1973(?)(?) **22**
Evans, Harry 1956(?)— **25**
Evans, Mari 1923— **26**
Everett, Francine 1917-1999 **23**
Everett, Ronald McKinley
See Karenga, Maulana
Evers, Medgar (Riley) 1925-1963 **3**
Evers, Myrlie 1933— **8**
Evora, Cesaria 1941— **12**
Ewing, Patrick Aloysius 1962— **17**
Eyadéma, (Étienne) Gnassingbé 1937— **7**
Fagan, Garth 1940—— **18**
Faison, George William 1946— **16**
Farmer, Forest J(ackson) 1941— **1**
Farmer, James 1920— **2**
Farr, Mel 1944— **24**
Farrakhan, Louis 1933— **2, 15**
Fats Domino 1928— **20**
Fattah, Chaka 1956— **11**
Fauntroy, Walter E(dward) 1933— **11**
Fauset, Jessie (Redmon) 1882-1961 **7**
Favors, Steve 1948— **23**
Feelings, T(h)om(a)s 1933— **11**
Fela 1938— **1**
Ferguson, Roger W. 1951— **25**
Fielder, Cecil (Grant) 1963— **2**
Fields, C. Virginia 1946— **25**
Fields, Cleo 1962— **13**
Fishburne, Larry 1962— **4, 22**
Fishburne, Laurence, III
See Fishburne, Larry
Fisher, Rudolph John Chauncey 1897-1934 **17**
Fitzgerald, Ella 1918-1996 **8, 18**
Flack, Roberta 1940— **19**
Flake, Floyd H. 1945— **18**
Fletcher, Alphonse, Jr. 1965— **16**
Flipper, Henry O(ssian) 1856-1940 **3**
Flood, Curt(is) 1963— **10**
Folks, Byron
See Allen, Byron
Forbes, Audrey Manley 1934— **16**
Ford, Harold Eugene, Jr. 1970— **16**
Foreman, George 1948— **1, 15**
Forman, James 1928— **7**
Fortune, T(imothy) Thomas 1856-1928 **6**
Foster, Henry W., Jr. 1933— **26**
Fox, Vivica A. 1964— **15**
Foxx, Jamie 1967— **15**
Foxx, Redd 1922-1991 **2**
Franklin, Aretha 1942— **11**
Franklin, Carl 1949— **11**
Franklin, Hardy R. 1929— **9**
Franklin, John Hope 1915— **5**
Franklin, Kirk 1970— **15**
Franklin, Robert M(ichael) 1954— **13**
Franks, Gary 1954(?)— **2**
Frazier, Edward Franklin 1894-1962 **10**
Frazier, Joe 1944— **19**
Freeman, Al(bert Cornelius), Jr. 1934— **11**
Freeman, Charles Eldridge 1933— **19**
Freeman, Harold P. 1933— **23**
Freeman, Marianna 1957— **23**
Freeman, Morgan 1937— **2, 20**
French, Albert 1943— **18**
Fresh Prince, The
See Smith, Will
Friday, Jeff 1964(?)— **24**
Fudge, Ann (Marie) 1951(?)— **11**
Fuhr, Grant 1962— **1**
Fulani, Lenora (Branch) 1950— **11**
Fuller, Charles (Henry) 1939— **8**
Fuller, S. B. 1895-1988 **13**
Fuller, Solomon Carter, Jr. 1872-1953 **15**
Gaines, Ernest J(ames) 1933— **7**
Gaither, Jake 1903-1994 **14**
Gantt, Harvey (Bernard) 1943— **1**
Garnett, Kevin 1976— **14**
Garrison, Zina 1963— **2**
Garvey, Marcus 1887-1940 **1**
Gary, Willie Edward 1947— **12**
Gaston, Arthur G(eorge) 1892— **4**
Gates, Henry Louis, Jr. 1950— **3**
Gates, Sylvester James, Jr. 1950— **15**
Gay, Marvin Pentz, Jr.
See Gaye, Marvin
Gaye, Marvin 1939-1984 **2**
Gayle, Helene D(oris) 1955— **3**
Gentry, Alvin 1954— **23**
George, Nelson 1957— **12**
Gibson, Althea 1927— **8**
Gibson, Johnnie Mae 1949— **23**
Gibson, Josh 1911-1947 **22**
Gibson, Kenneth Allen 1932— **6**
Gibson, William F(rank) 1933— **6**
Giddings, Paula (Jane) 1947— **11**
Gillespie, Dizzy 1917-1993 **1**
Gillespie, John Birks
See Gillespie, Dizzy
Gilliam, Frank 1934(?)— **23**
Gilliam, Sam 1933— **16**
Giovanni, Nikki 1943— **9**
Giovanni, Yolande Cornelia, Jr.
See Giovanni, Nikki
Gist, Carole 1970(?)— **1**
Givens, Robin 1965— **4, 25**
Glover, Danny 1948— **1, 24**
Glover, Nathaniel, Jr. 1943— **12**
Glover, Savion 1974— **14**
Goines, Donald 1937(?)-1974 **19**
Goldberg, Whoopi 1955— **4**
Golden, Marita 1950— **19**
Golden, Thelma 1965— **10**
Goldsberry, Ronald 1942— **18**
Gomes, Peter J(ohn) 1942— **15**
Gomez-Preston, Cheryl 1954— **9**
Goode, Mal(vin Russell) 1908-1995 **13**
Goode, W(oodrow) Wilson 1938— **4**
Gooden, Dwight 1964— **20**
Gooding, Cuba, Jr. 1968— **16**
Gordon, Dexter 1923-1990 **25**
Gordon, Ed(ward Lansing, III) 1960— **10**
Gordon, Pamela 1955— **17**
Gordone, Charles 1925-1995 **15**
Gordy, Berry, Jr. 1929— **1**
Goreed, Joseph
See Williams, Joe
Goss, Tom 1946— **23**
Gossett, Louis, Jr. 1936— **7**
Gourdine, Simon (Peter) 1940— **11**
Graham, Lawrence Otis 1962— **12**
Graham, Stedman 1951(?)— **13**
Gravely, Samuel L(ee), Jr. 1922— **5**
Graves, Denyce Antoinette 1964— **19**
Graves, Earl G(ilbert) 1935— **1**
Gray, F. Gary 1969— **14**
Gray, Frizzell
See Mfume, Kweisi
Gray, William H., III 1941— **3**
Green, Albert 1946— **13**
Green, Dennis 1949— **5**
Greene, Joe 1946— **10**
Greenfield, Eloise 1929— **9**
Gregg, Eric 1951— **16**
Gregory, Dick 1932— **1**
Gregory, Frederick D(rew) 1941— **8**
Grier, Pam(ala Suzette) 1949— **9**
Grier, Roosevelt (Rosey) 1932— **13**
Griffey, George Kenneth, Jr. 1969— **12**
Griffith, Mark Winston 1963— **8**
Griffith, Yolanda 1970— **25**
Grimké, Archibald H(enry) 1849-1930 **9**
Guarionex
See Schomburg, Arthur Alfonso
Guillaume, Robert 1927— **3**
Guinier, (Carol) Lani 1950— **7**
Gumbel, Bryant Charles 1948— **14**
Gumbel, Greg 1946— **8**
Gunn, Moses 1929-1993 **10**
Guy, Jasmine 1964(?)— **2**
Guy, Rosa 1925(?)— **5**
Guy-Sheftall, Beverly 1946— **13**
Guyton, Tyree 1955— **9**
Gwynn, Anthony Keith 1960— **18**
Habré, Hissène 1942— **6**
Habyarimana, Juvenal 1937-1994 **8**
Haile Selassie 1892-1975 **7**
Hailey, JoJo 1971— **22**
Hailey, K-Ci 1969— **22**
Hale, Clara 1902-1992 **16**
Hale, Lorraine 1926(?)— **8**
Haley, Alex (Palmer) 1921-1992 **4**
Haley, George Williford Boyce 1925— **21**
Hall, Elliott S. 1938(?)— **24**
Hall, Lloyd A(ugustus) 1894-1971 **8**
Hamblin, Ken 1940— **10**
Hamer, Fannie Lou (Townsend) 1917-1977 **6**
Hamilton, Virginia 1936— **10**
Hammer
See Hammer, M. C.
Hammer, M. C. 1963— **20**
Hammond, Fred 1960— **23**
Hampton, Fred 1948-1969 **18**
Hampton, Henry (Eugene, Jr.) 1940— **6**
Hampton, Lionel 1908(?)— **17**
Hancock, Herbie Jeffrey 1940— **20**
Handy, W(illiam) C(hristopher) 1873-1937 **8**
Hani, Chris 1942-1993 **6**
Hani, Martin Thembisile
See Hani, Chris
Hannah, Marc (Regis) 1956— **10**
Hansberry, Lorraine (Vivian) 1930-1965 **6**
Hansberry, William Leo 1894-1965 **11**
Hardaway, Anfernee (Deon)
See Hardaway, Anfernee (Penny)
Hardaway, Anfernee (Penny) 1971— **13**
Hardaway, Penny
See Hardaway, Anfernee (Penny)
Hardison, Bethann 19??— **12**
Hardison, Kadeem 1966— **22**
Harkless, Necia Desiree 1920— **19**
Harmon, Clarence 1940(?)— **26**
Harper, Frances E(llen) W(atkins) 1825-1911 **11**
Harrell, Andre (O'Neal) 1962(?)— **9**
Harrington, Oliver W(endell) 1912— **9**
Harris, "Sweet" Alice
See Harris, Alice
Harris, Alice 1934— **7**
Harris, Barbara 1930— **12**
Harris, E. Lynn 1957— **12**
Harris, Eddy L. 1956— **18**
Harris, James, III
See Jimmy Jam
Harris, Jay **19**
Harris, Leslie 1961— **6**
Harris, Marcelite Jordon 1943— **16**
Harris, Monica 1968— **18**
Harris, Patricia Roberts 1924-1985 **2**

Harris, Robin 1953-1990 **7**
Harsh, Vivian Gordon 1890-1960 **14**
Harvard, Beverly (Joyce Bailey) 1950— **11**
Harvey, Steve 1957— **18**
Haskins, Clem 1943— **23**
Hastie, William H(enry) 1904-1976 **8**
Hastings, Alcee Lamar 1936— **16**
Hathaway, Donny 1945-1979 **18**
Hawkins, Adrienne Lita
See Kennedy, Adrienne
Hawkins, Coleman 1904-1969 **9**
Hawkins, Erskine Ramsey 1914-1993 **14**
Hawkins, Jamesetta
See James, Etta
Hawkins, La-Van 1960(?)— **17**
Hawkins, Steven Wayne 1962— **14**
Hawkins, Tramaine Aunzola 1951— **16**
Hayden, Palmer 1890-1973 **13**
Hayden, Robert Earl 1913-1980 **12**
Hayes, Isaac 1942— **20**
Hayes, James C. 1946— **10**
Hayes, Roland 1887-1977 **4**
Haynes, George Edmund 1880-1960 **8**
Haynes, Marques 1926— **22**
Haywood, Margaret A. 1912— **24**
Heard, Gar 1948— **25**
Hedgeman, Anna Arnold 1899-1990 **22**
Hedgeman, Peyton Cole
See Hayden, Palmer
Height, Dorothy I(rene) 1912— **2, 23**
Hemphill, Essex 1957— **10**
Hemsley, Sherman 1938— **19**
Henderson, Cornelius Langston 1888(?)-1976 **26**
Henderson, Gordon 1957— **5**
Henderson, Natalie Leota
See Hinderas, Natalie
Henderson, Wade 1944(?)— **14**
Hendricks, Barbara 1948— **3**
Hendrix, James Marshall
See Hendrix, Jimi
Hendrix, Jimi 1942-1970 **10**
Hendrix, Johnny Allen
See Hendrix, Jimi
Henry, Aaron Edd 1922-1997 **19**
Henry, Lenny 1958— **9**
Henson, Matthew (Alexander) 1866-1955 **2**
Herenton, Willie W. 1940— **24**
Herman, Alexis Margaret 1947— **15**
Hernandez, Aileen Clarke 1926— **13**
Hickman, Fred(erick Douglass) 1951— **11**
Higginbotham, A(loyisus) Leon, Jr. 1928-1998 **13, 25**
Hightower, Dennis F(owler) 1941— **13**
Hill, Anita (Faye) 1956— **5**
Hill, Beatrice
See Moore, Melba
Hill, Bonnie Guiton 1941— **20**
Hill, Calvin 1947— **19**
Hill, Grant (Henry) 1972— **13**
Hill, Janet 1947— **19**
Hill, Jesse, Jr. 1927— **13**
Hill, Lauryn 1975(?)— **20**
Hill, Oliver W. 1907— **24**
Hill, Tamia
See Tamia
Hillard, Terry 1954— **25**
Hilliard, David 1942— **7**
Hilliard, Earl F. 1942— **24**
Himes, Chester 1909-1984 **8**
Hinderas, Natalie 1927-1987 **5**
Hine, Darlene Clark 1947— **24**
Hines, Gregory (Oliver) 1946— **1**
Hinton, William Augustus 1883-1959 **8**
Holder, Eric H., Jr. 1951(?)— **9**
Holdsclaw, Chamique 1977— **24**
Holiday, Billie 1915-1959 **1**
Holland, Endesha Ida Mae 1944— **3**
Holland, Robert, Jr. 1940— **11**
Holmes, Larry 1949— **20**
Holte, Patricia Louise
See LaBelle, Patti
Holyfield, Evander 1962— **6**
hooks, bell 1952— **5**
Hooks, Benjamin L(awson) 1925— **2**
Hope, John 1868-1936 **8**
Horne, Lena (Mary Calhoun) 1917— **5**
Hounsou, Djimon 1964— **19**
Houphouët-Boigny, Félix 1905— **4**
Houphouët, Dia
See Houphouët-Boigny, Félix
House, Eddie James, Jr.
See House, Son
House, Eugene
See House, Son
House, Son 1902-1988 **8**
Houston, Charles Hamilton 1895-1950 **4**
Houston, Cissy 19(?)(?)— **20**
Houston, Whitney 1963— **7**
Howard, Corinne
See Mitchell, Corinne
Howard, Desmond Kevin 1970— **16**
Howard, Juwan Antonio 1973— **15**
Howard, M. William, Jr. 1946— **26**
Howlin' Wolf 1910-1976 **9**
Hrabowski, Freeman A., III 1950— **22**
Hudlin, Reginald 1962(?)— **9**
Hudlin, Warrington, Jr. 1953(?)— **9**
Hudson, Cheryl 19(?)(?)— **15**
Hudson, Wade 1946— **15**
Huggins, Larry 1950— **21**
Hughes, (James Mercer) Langston 1902-1967 **4**
Hughes, Albert 1972— **7**
Hughes, Allen 1972— **7**
Hughley, Darryl Lynn 1964— **23**
Humphrey, Bobbi 1950— **20**
Humphries, Frederick 1935— **20**
Hunt, Richard (Howard) 1935— **6**
Hunter, Billy 1943— **22**
Hunter, Charlayne
See Hunter-Gault, Charlayne
Hunter-Gault, Charlayne 1942— **6**
Hunter, George William
See Hunter, Billy
Hurston, Zora Neale 1891-1960 **3**
Hutchinson, Earl Ofari 1945— **24**
Hutson, Jean Blackwell 1914— **16**
Hyman, Earle 1926— **25**
Hyman, Phyllis 1949(?)-1995 **19**
Ice Cube 1969(?)— **8**
Ice-T 1958(?)— **6**
Iceberg Slim 1918-1992 **11**
Iman 1955— **4**
Ingraham, Hubert A. 1947— **19**
Ingram, Rex 1895-1969 **5**
Innis, Roy (Emile Alfredo) 1934— **5**
Irving, Clarence (Larry) 1955— **12**
Isley, Ronald 1941— **25**
Iverson, Allen 1975— **24**
Jackson, Alexine Clement 1936— **22**
Jackson, Fred James 1950— **25**
Jackson, George Lester 1941-1971 **14**
Jackson, George 1960(?)— **19**
Jackson, Isaiah (Allen) 1945— **3**
Jackson, Janet 1966— **6**
Jackson, Jesse Louis, Jr. 1965— **14**
Jackson, Jesse 1941— **1**
Jackson Lee, Sheila 1950— **20**
Jackson, Mahalia 1911-1972 **5**
Jackson, Mannie 1939— **14**
Jackson, Maynard (Holbrook, Jr.) 1938— **2**
Jackson, Michael Joseph 1958— **19**
Jackson, Millie 1944— **25**
Jackson, Milt 1923-1999 **26**
Jackson, O'Shea
See Ice Cube
Jackson, Reginald Martinez 1946— **15**
Jackson, Samuel L. 1948— **8, 19**
Jackson, Sheneska 1970(?)— **18**
Jackson, Shirley Ann 1946— **12**
Jacob, John E(dward) 1934— **2**
Jagan, Cheddi 1918-1997 **16**
Jakes, Thomas "T.D." 1957— **17**
Jam, Jimmy
See Jimmy Jam
James, Daniel "Chappie", Jr. 1920-1978 **16**
James, Etta 1938— **13**
James, Juanita (Therese) 1952— **13**
James, Sharpe 1936— **23**
Jamison, Judith 1943— **7**
Jammeh, Yahya 1965— **23**
Jarreau, Al 1940— **21**
Jarvis, Charlene Drew 1941— **21**
Jawara, Sir Dawda Kairaba 1924— **11**
Jean-Baptiste, Marianne 1967(?)— **17**
Jean, Wyclef 1970— **20**
Jefferson, William J. 1947— **25**
Jeffries, Leonard 1937— **8**
Jemison, Mae C. 1957— **1**
Jenifer, Franklyn G(reen) 1939— **2**
Jenkins, Beverly 1951— **14**
Jenkins, Ella (Louise) 1924— **15**
Jimmy Jam 1959— **13**
Joe, Yolanda 19(?)(?)— **21**
John, Daymond 1969(?)— **23**
Johnson, "Magic"
See Johnson, Earvin "Magic"
Johnson, Ben 1961— **1**
Johnson, Beverly 1952— **2**
Johnson-Brown, Hazel W.
See, Johnson, Hazel
Johnson, Carol Diann
See Carroll, Diahann
Johnson, Caryn E.
See Goldberg, Whoopi
Johnson, Charles 1948— **1**
Johnson, Charles Spurgeon 1893-1956 **12**
Johnson, Charles Arthur
See St. Jacques, Raymond
Johnson, Earvin "Magic" 1959— **3**
Johnson, Eddie Bernice 1935— **8**
Johnson, Hazel 1927— **22**
Johnson, James William
See Johnson, James Weldon
Johnson, James Weldon 1871-1938 **5**
Johnson, John H(arold) 1918— **3**
Johnson, John Arthur
See Johnson, Jack
Johnson Jr., Harvey 1947(?)— **24**
Johnson, Marguerite
See Angelou, Maya
Johnson, Michael (Duane) 1967— **13**
Johnson, Norma L. Holloway 1932— **17**
Johnson, Robert L. 1946(?)— **3**
Johnson, Robert 1911-1938 **2**
Johnson, Robert T. 1948— **17**
Johnson, Virginia (Alma Fairfax) 1950— **9**
Johnson, William Henry 1901-1970 **3**
Jones, Bill T. 1952— **1**
Jones, Bobby 1939(?)— **20**
Jones, Carl 1955(?)— **7**

Jones, Cobi N'Gai 1970— **18**
Jones, Elaine R. 1944— **7**
Jones, Elvin 1927— **14**
Jones, Ingrid Saunders 1945— **18**
Jones, James Earl 1931— **3**
Jones, Le Roi
See Baraka, Amiri
Jones, Lillie Mae
See Carter, Betty
Jones, Lois Mailou 1905— **13**
Jones, Marion 1975— **21**
Jones, Quincy (Delight) 1933— **8**
Jones, Roy Jr. 1969— **22**
Jones, Ruth Lee
See Washington, Dinah
Jones, Sissieretta
See Joyner, Matilda Sissieretta
Jones, Star(let Marie) 1962(?)— **10**
Joplin, Scott 1868-1917 **6**
Jordan, Barbara (Charline) 1936— **4**
Jordan, June 1936— **7**
Jordan, Michael (Jeffrey) 1963— **6, 21**
Jordan, Montell 1968(?)— **23**
Jordan, Ronny 1962— **26**
Jordan, Vernon E(ulion, Jr.) 1935— **3**
Josey, E. J. 1924— **10**
Joyner, Jacqueline
See Joyner-Kersee, Jackie
Joyner-Kersee, Jackie 1962— **5**
Joyner, Marjorie Stewart 1896-1994 **26**
Joyner, Matilda Sissieretta 1869(?)-1933 **15**
Joyner, Tom 1949(?)— **19**
Julian, Percy Lavon 1899-1975 **6**
Julien, Isaac 1960— **3**
Just, Ernest Everett 1883-1941 **3**
Justice, David Christopher 1966— **18**
Kabbah, Ahmad Tejan 1932— **23**
Kabila, Laurent 1939 **20**
Kamau, Johnstone
See Kenyatta, Jomo
Kani, Karl 1968(?)— **10**
Karenga, Maulana 1941— **10**
Kaunda, Kenneth (David) 1924— **2**
Kearse, Amalya Lyle 1937— **12**
Keith, Damon Jerome 1922— **16**
Kelly, Patrick 1954(?)-1990 **3**
Kelly, R(obert) 1969(?)— **18**
Kelly, Sharon Pratt
See Dixon, Sharon Pratt
Kendricks, Eddie 1939-1992 **22**
Kennard, William Earl 1957— **18**
Kennedy, Adrienne 1931— **11**
Kennedy, Florynce Rae 1916— **12**
Kennedy, Lelia McWilliams Robinson 1885-1931 **14**
Kenyatta, Jomo 1891(?)-1978 **5**
Kerekou, Ahmed (Mathieu) 1933— **1**
Keyes, Alan L(ee) 1950— **11**
Khan, Chaka 1953— **12**
Khanga, Yelena 1962— **6**
Kilpatrick, Carolyn Cheeks 1945— **16**
Kimbro, Dennis (Paul) 1950— **10**
Kimbro, Henry A. 1912-1999 **25**
Kincaid, Jamaica 1949— **4**
King, B. B. 1925— **7**
King, Barbara 19(?)(?)— **22**
King, Bernice (Albertine) 1963— **4**
King, Coretta Scott 1929— **3**
King, Dexter (Scott) 1961— **10**
King, Don 1931— **14**
King, Gayle 1956— **19**
King, Martin Luther, III 1957— **20**
King, Martin Luther, Jr. 1929-1968 **1**
King, Regina 1971 **22**
King, Riley B.
See King, B. B.
King, Yolanda (Denise) 1955— **6**
Kirby, George 1924-1995 **14**
Kirk, Ron 1954— **11**
Kitt, Eartha Mae 1928(?) **16**
Kitt, Sandra 1947— **23**
Knight, Gladys Maria 1944— **16**
Knight, Marion, Jr.
See Knight, Suge
Knight, Suge 1966— **11**
Komunyakaa, Yusef 1941— **9**
Kotto, Yaphet (Fredrick) 1944— **7**
Kountz, Samuel L(ee) 1930-1981 **10**
Kravitz, Lenny 1964— **10**
Kravitz, Leonard
See Kravitz, Lenny
Kunjufu, Jawanza 1953— **3**
Kuti, Fela Anikulapo
See Fela
L. L. Cool J 1968— **16**
La Salle, Eriq 1962— **12**
LaBelle, Patti 1944— **13**
Lafontant, Jewel Stradford 1922— **3**
Lampkin, Daisy 1883(?)-1965 **19**
Lane, Charles 1953— **3**
Lane, Vincent 1942— **5**
Langhart, Janet 1941— **19**
Lankford, Raymond Lewis 1967— **23**
Larkin, Barry 1964— **24**
Larsen, Nella 1891-1964 **10**
Lassiter, Roy 1969— **24**
Latimer, Lewis H(oward) 1848-1928 **4**
Lawless, Theodore K(enneth) 1892-1971 **8**
Lawrence, Jacob (Armstead) 1917— **4**
Lawrence-Lightfoot, Sara 1944— **10**
Lawrence, Martin 1965— **6**
Lawrence, Robert Henry, Jr. 1935-1967 **16**
Lawson, Jennifer (Karen) 1946— **1**
León, Tania 1943— **13**
Leary, Kathryn D. 1952— **10**
Leavell, Dorothy R. 1944— **17**
Lee, Annie Francis 1935— **22**
Lee, Barbara 1946— **25**
Lee, Canada 1907-1952 **8**
Lee, Don L(uther)
See Madhubuti, Haki R.
Lee, Gabby
See Lincoln, Abbey
Lee, Joie 1962(?)— **1**
Lee, Shelton Jackson
See Lee, Spike
Lee-Smith, Hughie 1915— **5, 22**
Lee, Spike 1957— **5, 19**
Leffall, LaSalle (Doheny), Jr. 1930— **3**
Leland, George Thomas
See Leland, Mickey
Leland, Mickey 1944-1989 **2**
Lemmons, Kasi 1961— **20**
Leon, Kenny 1957(?)— **10**
Leonard, Sugar Ray 1956— **15**
Leslie, Lisa Deshaun 1972— **16**
Lester, Julius 1939— **9**
Levert, Gerald 1966— **22**
Lewellyn, J(ames) Bruce 1927— **13**
Lewis, (Frederick) Carl(ton) 1961— **4**
Lewis, (Mary) Edmonia 1845(?)-1911(?) **10**
Lewis, Byron E(ugene) 1931— **13**
Lewis, David Levering 1936— **9**
Lewis, Delano (Eugene) 1938— **7**
Lewis, Edward T. 1940— **21**
Lewis, John (Robert) 1940— **2**
Lewis, Reginald F. 1942-1993 **6**
Lewis, Samella 1924— **25**
Lewis, Shirley Ann Redd 1937— **14**
Lewis, Terry 1956— **13**
Lewis, Thomas 1939— **19**
Lincoln, Abbey 1930— **3**
Lindo, Delroy 1952— **18**
Little, Benilde 1958— **21**
Little, Malcolm
See X, Malcolm
Little Richard 1932— **15**
Little, Robert L(angdon) 1938— **2**
Lloyd, Earl 1928(?)— **26**
Locke, Alain (LeRoy) 1886-1954 **10**
Lofton, Kenneth 1967— **12**
Lofton, Ramona 1950— **14**
Logan, Onnie Lee 1910(?)-1995 **14**
Long, Nia 1970— **17**
Lord Pitt of Hampstead
See Pitt, David Thomas
Lorde, Audre (Geraldine) 1934-1992 **6**
Lott, Ronnie 1959— **9**
Louis, Errol T. 1962— **8**
Louis, Joe 1914-1981 **5**
Love, Darlene 1941— **23**
Love, Nat 1854-1921 **9**
Lover, Ed **10**
Lowery, Joseph E. 1924— **2**
Lucas, John 1953— **7**
Luthuli, Albert (John Mvumbi) 1898(?)-1967 **13**
Lyle, Marcenia
See Stone, Toni
Lymon, Frankie 1942-1968 **22**
Lyons, Henry 1942(?)— **12**
Lyttle, Hulda Margaret 1889-1983 **14**
Mabley, Jackie "Moms" 1897(?)-1975 **15**
Mabrey, Vicki 1957(?)— **26**
Mabuza, Lindiwe 1938— **18**
Machel, Graca Simbine 1945— **16**
Machel, Samora Moises 1933-1986 **8**
Madhubuti, Haki R. 1942— **7**
Madikizela, Nkosikazi Nobandle Nomzamo Winifred
See Mandela, Winnie
Madison, Joseph E. 1949— **17**
Mainor, Dorothy Leigh 1910(?)-1996 **19**
Major, Clarence 1936— **9**
Makeba, (Zensi) Miriam 1932— **2**
Malcolm X
See X, Malcolm
Mallett, Conrad, Jr. 1953— **16**
Malone, Annie (Minerva Turnbo Pope) 1869-1957 **13**
Malone, Karl A. 1963— **18**
Mandela, Nelson (Rolihlahla) 1918— **1, 14**
Mandela, Winnie 1934— **2**
Manigault, Earl "The Goat" 1943— **15**
Manley, Audrey Forbes 1934— **16**
Manley, Edna 1900-1987 **26**
Marable, Manning 1950— **10**
Marchand, Inga
See Foxy Brown
Marley, Bob 1945-1981 **5**
Marley, Robert Nesta
See Marley, Bob
Marrow, Queen Esther 1943(?)— **24**
Marrow, Tracey
See Ice-T
Marsalis, Wynton 1961— **16**
Marshall, Bella 1950— **22**
Marshall, Gloria
See Sudarkasa, Niara
Marshall, Paule 1929— **7**
Marshall, Thurgood 1908— **1**

Marshall, Valenza Pauline Burke
See Marshall, Paule
Martin, Louis Emanuel 1912-1997 **16**
Mase 1977(?)— **24**
Masekela, Barbara 1941— **18**
Masekela, Hugh (Ramopolo) 1939— **1**
Masire, Quett (Ketumile Joni) 1925— **5**
Massenburg, Kedar 1964(?)— **23**
Massey, Walter E(ugene) 1938— **5**
Master P 1970— **21**
Mathabane, Johannes
See Mathabane, Mark
Mathabane, Mark 1960— **5**
Mathis, Greg 1960— **26**
Mathis, Johnny 1935— **20**
Mauldin, Jermaine Dupri
See Dupri, Jermaine
Maxwell 1973— **20**
Mayfield, Curtis (Lee) 1942— **2**
Maynard, Robert C(lyve) 1937-1993 **7**
Maynor, Dorothy 1910-1996 **19**
Mays, Benjamin E(lijah) 1894-1984 **7**
Mays, William Howard, Jr.
See Mays, Willie
Mays, Willie 1931— **3**
Mazrui, Ali Al'Amin 1933— **12**
Mbeki, Thabo Mvuyelwa 1942— **14**
Mboup, Souleymane 1951— **10**
Mbuende, Kaire Munionganda 1953— **12**
McBride, Bryant Scott 1965— **18**
McCabe, Jewell Jackson 1945— **10**
McCall, Nathan 1955— **8**
McCarty, Osseola 1908— **16**
McClurkin, Donnie 1961— **25**
McCoy, Elijah 1844-1929 **8**
McCray, Nikki 1972— **18**
McDaniel, Hattie 1895-1952 **5**
McDonald, Audra 1970— **20**
McDonald, Erroll 1954(?)— **1**
McDonald, Gabrielle Kirk 1942— **20**
McDougall, Gay J. 1947— **11**
McEwen, Mark 1954— **5**
McGee, Charles 1924— **10**
McGriff, Fred 1963— **24**
McGruder, Robert 1942— **22**
McIntosh, Winston Hubert
See Tosh, Peter
McKay, Claude 1889-1948 **6**
McKay, Festus Claudius
See McKay, Claude
McKay, Nellie Yvonne 194(?)— **17**
McKee, Lonette 1952— **12**
McKegney, Tony 1958— **3**
McKinney, Cynthia Ann 1955— **11**
McKinnon, Ike
See McKinnon, Isaiah
McKinnon, Isaiah 1943— **9**
McKissick, Floyd B(ixler) 1922-1981 **3**
McKnight, Brian 1969— **18**
McMillan, Terry 1951— **4, 17**
McNair, Ronald (Ervin) 1950-1986 **3**
McNair, Steve 1973— **22**
McNeil, Lori 1964(?)— **1**
McPhail, Sharon 1948— **2**
McQueen, Butterfly 1911— **6**
McQueen, Thelma
See McQueen, Butterfly
Meek, Carrie (Pittman) 1926— **6**
Meeks, Gregory 1953— **25**
Meles Zenawi 1955(?)— **3**
Meredith, James H(oward) 1933— **11**
Messenger, The
See Divine, Father
Metcalfe, Ralph 1910-1978 **26**
Meyer, June
See Jordan, June
Mfume, Kweisi 1948— **6**
Micheaux, Oscar (Devereaux) 1884-1951 **7**
Milla, Roger 1952— **2**
Millender-McDonald, Juanita 1938— **21**
Miller, Bebe 1950— **3**
Miller, Cheryl 1964— **10**
Miller, Maria 1803-1879 **19**
Miller, Percy
See Master P
Mills, Florence 1896-1927 **22**
Mingus, Charles Jr. 1922-1979 **15**
Mitchell, Arthur 1934— **2**
Mitchell, Brian Stokes 1957— **21**
Mitchell, Corinne 1914-1993 **8**
Mitchell, Russ 1960— **21**
Mkapa, Benjamin William 1938— **16**
Mobutu, Joseph-Desire
See Mobutu Sese Seko (Nkuku wa za Banga)
Mobutu Sese Seko (Nkuku wa za Banga) 1930— **1**
Mogae, Festus Gontebanye 1939— **19**
Mohamed, Ali Mahdi
See Ali Mahdi Mohamed
Moi, Daniel (Arap) 1924— **1**
Mongella, Gertrude 1945— **11**
Monica 1980— **21**
Monk, Thelonious (Sphere, Jr.) 1917-1982 **1**
Moon, (Harold) Warren 1956— **8**
Moore, Bobby
See Rashad, Ahmad
Moore, Chante 1970(?)— **26**
Moore, Melba 1945— **21**
Moore, Shemar 1970— **21**
Moorer, Michael 1967— **19**
Morgan, Garrett (Augustus) 1877-1963 **1**
Morgan, Joe Leonard 1943— **9**
Morgan, Rose (Meta) 1912(?)— **11**
Morial, Ernest "Dutch" 1929-1989 **26**
Morial, Marc 1958— **20**
Morris, Stevland Judkins
See Wonder, Stevie
Morrison, Keith 1942— **13**
Morrison, Toni 1931— **2, 15**
Morton, Joe 1947— **18**
Moseka, Aminata
See Lincoln, Abbey
Moseley-Braun, Carol
See Braun, Carol (Elizabeth) Moseley
Moses, Edwin 1955— **8**
Moses, Gilbert, III 1942-1995 **12**
Moses, Robert Parris 1935— **11**
Mosley, Walter 1952— **5, 25**
Moss, Carlton 1909-1997 **17**
Moss, Randy 1977— **23**
Moten, Emma Barnett 1901— **18**
Motley, Constance Baker 1921— **10**
Motley, Marion 1920-1999 **26**
Mourning, Alonzo 1970— **17**
Moutoussamy-Ashe, Jeanne 1951— **7**
Mowry, Jess 1960— **7**
Mugabe, Robert Gabriel 1928— **10**
Muhammad, Elijah 1897-1975 **4**
Muhammad, Khallid Abdul 1951(?)— **10**
Muluzi, Elson Bakili 1943— **14**
Murphy, Eddie 1961— **4, 20**
Murphy, Edward Regan
See Murphy, Eddie
Murray, Cecil (Chip) 1929— **12**
Murray, Eddie 1956— **12**
Murray, Lenda 1962— **10**
Muse, Clarence Edouard 1889-1979 **21**
Museveni, Yoweri (Kaguta) 1944(?)— **4**
Mutebi, Ronald 1956— **25**
Mutola, Maria de Lurdes 1972— **12**
Mutombo, Dikembe 1966— **7**
Mwinyi, Ali Hassan 1925— **1**
Myers, Walter Milton
See Myers, Walter Dean
Myers, Walter Dean 1937— **8**
N'Dour, Youssou 1959— **1**
N'Namdi, George R. 1946— **17**
Nakhid, David 1964— **25**
Nanula, Richard D. 1960— **20**
Napoleon, Benny N. 1956(?)— **23**
Nascimento, Milton 1942— **2**
Naylor, Gloria 1950— **10**
Ndadaye, Melchior 1953-1993 **7**
Ndegeocello, Me'Shell 1968— **15**
Ndungane, Winston Njongonkulu 1941— **16**
Nelson, Jill 1952— **6**
Nelson, Prince Rogers
See Prince
Nettles, Marva Deloise
See Collins, Marva
Neville, Aaron 1941— **21**
Newcombe, Don 1926— **24**
Newsome, Ozzie 1956— **26**
Newton, Huey (Percy) 1942-1989 **2**
Newton, Thandie 1972— **26**
Ngengi, Kamau wa
See Kenyatta, Jomo
Nicholas, Fayard 1914— **20**
Nicholas, Harold 1921— **20**
Nichols, Grace
See Nichols, Nichelle
Nichols, Nichelle 1933(?)— **11**
Njongonkulu, Winston Ndungane 1941— **16**
Nkomo, Joshua (Mqabuko Nyongolo) 1917— **4**
Nkrumah, Kwame 1909-1972 **3**
Noah, Yannick (Simon Camille) 1960— **4**
Norman, Jessye 1945— **5**
Norman, Maidie 1912-1998 **20**
Norman, Pat 1939— **10**
Norton, Eleanor Holmes 1937— **7**
Norwood, Brandy
See, Brandy
Notorious B.I.G. 1972-1997 **20**
Nottage, Cynthia DeLores
See Tucker, C. DeLores
Ntaryamira, Cyprien 1955-1994 **8**
Nujoma, Samuel 1929— **10**
Nyanda, Siphiwe 1950— **21**
Nyerere, Julius (Kambarage) 1922— **5**
Nzo, Alfred (Baphethuxolo) 1925— **15**
O'Leary, Hazel (Rollins) 1937— **6**
O'Neal, Shaquille (Rashaun) 1972— **8**
O'Neil, Buck 1911— **19**
O'Neil, John Jordan
See O'Neil, Buck
O'Ree, William Eldon
See O'Ree, Willie
O'Ree, Willie 1935— **5**
Obasanjo, Olusegun 1937— **5, 22**
Oglesby, Zena 1947— **12**
Ogletree, Charles, Jr. 1933— **12**
Olajuwon, Akeem
See Olajuwon, Hakeem (Abdul Ajibola)
Olajuwon, Hakeem (Abdul Ajibola) 1963— **2**
Ongala, Ramadhani Mtoro
See Ongala, Remmy
Ongala, Remmy 1947— **9**

Onwueme, Tess Osonye 1955— **23**
Osborne, Jeffrey 1948— **26**
Ousmane, Sembène
See Sembène, Ousmane
Owens, Dana
See Queen Latifah
Owens, J. C.
See Owens, Jesse
Owens, James Cleveland
See Owens, Jesse
Owens, Jesse 1913-1980 **2**
Owens, Major (Robert) 1936— **6**
Pace, Orlando 1975— **21**
Page, Alan (Cedric) 1945— **7**
Page, Clarence 1947— **4**
Paige, Leroy Robert
See Paige, Satchel
Paige, Satchel 1906-1982 **7**
Painter, Nell Irvin 1942— **24**
Parker, Charlie 1920-1955 **20**
Parks, Bernard C. 1943— **17**
Parks, Gordon (Roger Alexander Buchanan) 1912— **1**
Parks, Rosa 1913— **1**
Parsons, James Benton 1911-1993 **14**
Parsons, Richard Dean 1948— **11**
Pascal-Trouillot, Ertha 1943— **3**
Patillo, Melba Joy 1941— **15**
Patrick, Deval Laurdine 1956— **12**
Patterson, Floyd 1935— **19**
Patterson, Frederick Douglass 1901-1988 **12**
Patterson, Louise 1901-1999 **25**
Patterson, Orlando 1940— **4**
Patterson, P(ercival) J(ames) 1936(?)— **6, 20**
Payne, Allen 1962(?)— **13**
Payne, Donald M(ilford) 1934— **2**
Payton, Benjamin F. 1932— **23**
Payton, Walter (Jerry) 1954—1999 **11, 25**
Peck, Carolyn 1966(?)— **23**
Peete, Calvin 1943— **11**
Peete, Holly Robinson 1965— **20**
Pelé 1940— **7**
Pendergrass, Teddy 1950 **22**
Penniman, Richard Wayne
See, Little Richard
Peoples, Dottie 19(?)(?) **22**
Perez, Anna 1951— **1**
Perkins, Anthony 1959?— **24**
Perkins, Edward (Joseph) 1928— **5**
Perrot, Kim 1967-1999 **23**
Perry, Rainford Hugh
See Perry, Lee "Scratch"
Perry, Ruth Sando 1939— **15**
Perry, Ruth 1936— **19**
Person, Waverly (J.) 1927— **9**
Peters, Maria Philomena 1941— **12**
Petry, Ann 1909-1997 **19**
Phifer, Mekhi 1975— **25**
Pickett, Bill 1870-1932 **11**
Pierre, Andre 1915— **17**
Pinchback, P(inckney) B(enton) S(tewart) 1837-1921 **9**
Pinkett, Jada 1971— **10**
Pinkney, Jerry 1939— **15**
Pinkston, W. Randall 1950— **24**
Pippen, Scottie 1965— **15**
Pippin, Horace 1888-1946 **9**
Pitt, David Thomas 1913-1994 **10**
Pitta, (do Nascimento), Celso (Roberto) 19(?)(?)— **17**
Pleasant, Mary Ellen 1814-1904 **9**
Poitier, Sidney 1927— **11**
Poole, Elijah
See Muhammad, Elijah
Porter, Countee Leroy
See, Cullin, Countee
Porter, James A(mos) 1905-1970 **11**
Poussaint, Alvin F(rancis) 1934— **5**
Powell, Adam Clayton, Jr. 1908-1972 **3**
Powell, Bud 1924-1966 **24**
Powell, Colin (Luther) 1937— **1**
Powell, Debra A. 1964— **23**
Powell, Maxine 1924— **8**
Powell, Michael Anthony
See Powell, Mike
Powell, Mike 1963— **7**
Pratt Dixon, Sharon
See Dixon, Sharon Pratt
Pratt, Geronimo 1947— **18**
Price, Frederick K.C. 1932— **21**
Price, Glenda 1939— **22**
Price, Hugh B. 1941— **9**
Price, Kelly 1973(?)— **23**
Price, Leontyne 1927— **1**
Pride, Charley 1938(?)— **26**
Primus, Pearl 1919— **6**
Prince 1958— **18**
Pritchard, Robert Starling 1927— **21**
Procope, Ernesta 19(?)(?)— **23**
Prothrow, Deborah Boutin
See Prothrow-Stith, Deborah
Prothrow-Stith, Deborah 1954— **10**
Pryor, Richard (Franklin Lennox Thomas) 1940— **3, 24**
Puckett, Kirby 1961— **4**
Quarles, Benjamin Arthur 1904-1996 **18**
Quarles, Norma 1936— **25**
Quarterman, Lloyd Albert 1918-1982 **4**
Queen Latifah 1970(?)— **1, 16**
Quirot, Ana (Fidelia) 1963— **13**
Raines, Franklin Delano 1949— **14**
Ralph, Sheryl Lee 1956— **18**
Ramaphosa, (Matamela) Cyril 1952— **3**
Ramsey, Charles H. 1948— **21**
Rand, A(ddison) Barry 1944— **6**
Randall, Dudley (Felker) 1914— **8**
Randle, Theresa 1967— **16**
Randolph, A(sa) Philip 1889-1979 **3**
Rangel, Charles (Bernard) 1930— **3**
Ras Tafari
See Haile Selassie
Rashad, Ahmad 1949— **18**
Rashad, Phylicia 1948— **21**
Raspberry, William 1935— **2**
Rawlings, Jerry (John) 1947— **9**
Rawls, Lou 1936— **17**
Raymond IV, Usher 1978(?)— **23**
Razaf, Andy 1895-1973 **19**
Razafkeriefo, Andreamentania Paul
See Razaf, Andy
Reagon, Bernice Johnson 1942— **7**
Reason, Joseph Paul 1943— **19**
Reddick, Lawrence Dunbar 1910-1995 **20**
Redding, J. Saunders 1906-1988 **26**
Redding, Louis L. 1901-1998 **26**
Redding, Otis, Jr. 1941— **16**
Redmond, Eugene 1937— **23**
Reed, Ishmael 1938— **8**
Reese, Della 1931— **6, 20**
Reeves, Rachel J. 1950(?)— **23**
Reid, Irvin D. 1941— **20**
Reuben, Gloria 19(?)(?)— **15**
Rhames, Ving 1961— **14**
Rhodes, Ray 1950— **14**
Rhone, Sylvia 1952— **2**
Ribbs, William Theodore, Jr.
See Ribbs, Willy T.
Ribbs, Willy T. 1956— **2**
Ribeiro, Alfonso 1971— **17**
Rice, Condoleezza 1954— **3**
Rice, Jerry 1962— **5**
Rice, Linda Johnson 1958— **9**
Rice, Norm(an Blann) 1943— **8**
Richards, Lloyd 1923(?)— **2**
Richardson, Elaine Potter
See Kincaid, Jamaica
Richardson, Nolan 1941— **9**
Richardson, Pat
See Norman, Pat
Richie, Leroy C. 1941— **18**
Richmond, Mitchell James 1965— **19**
Ridenhour, Carlton
See Chuck D.
Riggs, Marlon 1957— **5**
Riley, Helen Caldwell Day 1926— **13**
Ringgold, Faith 1930— **4**
Rivers, Glenn "Doc" 1961— **25**
Roach, Max 1924— **21**
Roberts, James
See Lover, Ed
Roberts, Marcus 1963— **19**
Roberts, Marthaniel
See Roberts, Marcus
Roberts, Robin 1960— **16**
Roberts, Roy S. 1939(?)— **14**
Robertson, Oscar 1938— **26**
Robeson, Eslanda Goode 1896-1965 **13**
Robeson, Paul (Leroy Bustill) 1898-1976 **2**
Robinson, Bill "Bojangles" 1878-1949 **11**
Robinson, David 1965— **24**
Robinson, Eddie G. 1919— **10**
Robinson, Frank 1935— **9**
Robinson, Jack Roosevelt
See Robinson, Jackie
Robinson, Jackie 1919-1972 **6**
Robinson, Luther
See Robinson, Bill "Bojangles"
Robinson, Max 1939-1988 **3**
Robinson, Rachel 1922— **16**
Robinson, Randall 1942(?)— **7**
Robinson, Sharon 1950— **22**
Robinson, Smokey 1940— **3**
Robinson, Spottswood W., III 1916-1998 **22**
Robinson, Sugar Ray 1921— **18**
Robinson, William, Jr.
See Robinson, Smokey
Roche, Joyce M. 1947— **17**
Rochon, Lela 1965(?)— **16**
Rock, Chris 1967(?)— **3, 22**
Rodgers, Johnathan (Arlin) 1946— **6**
Rodman, Dennis Keith 1961— **12**
Rogers, John W., Jr. 1958— **5**
Roker, Albert Lincoln, Jr. 1954(?)— **12**
Rolle, Esther 1920-1998 **13, 21**
Rollins, Howard Ellsworth 1950-1996 **16**
Ross, Araminta
See Tubman, Harriet
Ross, Diana 1944— **8**
Rotimi, (Emmanuel Gladstone) Ola(wale) 1938— **1**
Rowan, Carl T(homas) 1925— **1**
Rowell, Victoria 1962(?)— **13**
Rudolph, Wilma (Glodean) 1940— **4**
Rugambwa, Laurean 1912-1997 **20**
Rupaul 1960 **17**
Rush, Bobby 1946— **26**
Rushen, Patrice 1954— **12**
Russell, Bill 1934— **8**
Russell, Herman Jerome 1931(?)— **17**
Russell-McCloud, Patricia 1946— **17**

Russell, William Felton
See Russell, Bill
Rustin, Bayard 1910-1987 **4**
Saar, Alison 1956— **16**
Sade 1959— **15**
Saint James, Synthia 1949— **12**
Samara, Noah 1956— **15**
SAMO
See Basquiat, Jean-Michel
Sampson, Charles 1957— **13**
Sampson, Edith S(purlock) 1901-1979 **4**
Samuel, Sealhenry Olumide 1963— **14**
Sané, Pierre Gabriel 1948-1998 **21**
Sanchez, Sonia 1934— **17**
Sanders, Barry 1968— **1**
Sanders, Deion (Luwynn) 1967— **4**
Sanders, Dori(nda) 1935— **8**
Sanders, Joseph R(ichard, Jr.) 1954— **11**
Sanford, John Elroy
See Foxx, Redd
Sangare, Oumou 1968— **18**
Sankara, Thomas 1949-1987 **17**
Satcher, David 1941— **7**
Satchmo
See Armstrong, (Daniel) Louis
Savage, Augusta Christine 1892(?)-1962 **12**
Savimbi, Jonas (Malheiro) 1934— **2**
Sawyer, Amos 1945— **2**
Sayles Belton, Sharon 1952(?)— **9, 16**
Schmoke, Kurt (Lidell) 1949— **1**
Schomburg, Arthur Alfonso 1874-1938 **9**
Schomburg, Arturo Alfonso
See Schomburg, Arthur Alfonso
Schultz, Michael A. 1938— **6**
Scott, Coretta
See King, Coretta Scott
Scott, Robert C. 1947— **23**
Scott, Wendell Oliver, Sr. 1921-1990 **19**
Scruggs, Mary Elfrieda
See Williams, Mary Lou
Seal **14**
Seale, Bobby 1936— **3**
Seale, Robert George
See Seale, Bobby
Sears-Collins, Leah J(eanette) 1955— **5**
See Williams, Billy Dee
Selassie, Haile
See Haile Selassie
Sembène, Ousmane 1923— **13**
Senghor, Léopold Sédar 1906— **12**
Sengstacke, John Herman Henry 1912-1997 **18**
Serrano, Andres 1951(?)— **3**
Shabazz, Attallah 1958— **6**
Shabazz, Betty 1936-1997 **7, 26**
Shakur, Assata 1947— **6**
Shakur, Tupac Amaru 1971-1996 **14**
Shange, Ntozake 1948— **8**
Sharpton, Al 1954— **21**
Shaw, Bernard 1940— **2**
Sheffey, Asa Bundy
See Hayden, Robert Earl
Sheffield, Gary Antonian 1968— **16**
Shell, Art(hur, Jr.) 1946— **1**
Sherrod, Clayton 1944— **17**
Shipp, E. R. 1955— **15**
Sifford, Charlie (Luther) 1922— **4**
Silas, Paul 1943— **24**
Silver, Horace 1928— **26**
Siméus, Dumas M. 1940— **25**
Simmons, Russell 1957(?)— **1**
Simmons, Ruth J. 1945— **13**
Simone, Nina 1933— **15**
Simpson, Carole 1940— **6**
Simpson, Lorna 1960— **4**
Simpson, O. J. 1947— **15**
Simpson, Valerie 1946— **21**
Sinbad 1957(?)— **1, 16**
Singletary, Michael
See Singletary, Mike
Singletary, Mike 1958— **4**
Singleton, John 1968— **2**
Sinkford, Jeanne C. 1933— **13**
Sister Souljah 1964— **11**
Sisulu, Sheila Violet Makate 1948(?)— **24**
Sizemore, Barbara A. 1927— **26**
Sklarek, Norma Merrick 1928— **25**
Slater, Rodney Earl 1955— **15**
Sleet, Moneta (J.), Jr. 1926— **5**
Smaltz, Audrey 1937(?)— **12**
Smiley, Tavis 1964— **20**
Smith, Anna Deavere 1950— **6**
Smith, Arthur Lee, Jr.
See Asante, Molefi Kete
Smith, Barbara 1949(?)— **11**
Smith, Bessie 1894-1937 **3**
Smith, Clarence O. 1933— **21**
Smith, Emmitt (III) 1969— **7**
Smith, Jane E. 1946— **24**
Smith, Jennifer 1947— **21**
Smith, John L. 1938— **22**
Smith, Joshua (Isaac) 1941— **10**
Smith, Mary Carter 1919— **26**
Smith, Orlando
See Smith, Tubby
Smith, Roger Guenveur 1960— **12**
Smith, Tubby 1951— **18**
Smith, Walker, Jr.
See Robinson, Sugar Ray
Smith, Will 1968— **8, 18**
Smith, Willi (Donnell) 1948-1987 **8**
Sneed, Paula A. 1947— **18**
Snipes, Wesley 1962— **3, 24**
Soglo, Nicéphore 1935— **15**
Somé, Malidoma Patrice 1956— **10**
Sosa, Sammy 1968— **21**
Sowell, Thomas 1930— **2**
Soyinka, (Akinwande Olu)Wole 1934— **4**
Spaulding, Charles Clinton 1874-1952 **9**
Spikes, Dolores Margaret Richard 1936— **18**
Sprewell, Latrell 1970— **23**
St. Jacques, Raymond 1930-1990 **8**
St. John, Kristoff 1966— **25**
Stallings, George A(ugustus), Jr. 1948— **6**
Stanford, John 1938— **20**
Stanton, Robert 1940— **20**
Staples, Brent 1951— **8**
Staupers, Mabel K(eaton) 1890-1989 **7**
Steele, Claude Mason 1946— **13**
Steele, Shelby 1946— **13**
Stephens, Charlotte Andrews 1854-1951 **14**
Stevens, Yvette
See Khan, Chaka
Steward, Emanuel 1944— **18**
Stewart, Alison 1966(?)— **13**
Stewart, Kordell 1972— **21**
Stewart, Paul Wilbur 1925— **12**
Stokes, Carl B(urton) 1927— **10**
Stokes, Louis 1925— **3**
Stone, Charles Sumner, Jr.
See Stone, Chuck
Stone, Chuck 1924— **9**
Stone, Toni 1921-1996 **15**
Stout, Juanita Kidd 1919-1998 **24**
Strawberry, Darryl 1962— **22**
Street, John F. 1943(?)— **24**
Stringer, C. Vivian 1948— **13**
Sudarkasa, Niara 1938— **4**
Sullivan, Leon H(oward) 1922— **3**
Sullivan, Louis (Wade) 1933— **8**
Summer, Donna 1948— **25**
Sweat, Keith 1961(?)— **19**
Swoopes, Sheryl Denise 1971— **12**
Swygert, H. Patrick 1943— **22**
Sykes, Roosevelt 1906-1984 **20**
Tafari Makonnen
See Haile Selassie
Tamia 1975— **24**
Tanner, Henry Ossawa 1859-1937 **1**
Tate, Eleanora E. 1948— **20**
Tate, Larenz 1975— **15**
Taulbert, Clifton Lemoure 1945— **19**
Taylor, Billy 1921— **23**
Taylor, Charles 1948— **20**
Taylor, John (David Beckett) 1952— **16**
Taylor, Kristin Clark 1959— **8**
Taylor, Lawrence 1959— **25**
Taylor, Meshach 1947(?)— **4**
Taylor, Mildred D. 1943— **26**
Taylor, Regina 1959— **9**
Taylor, Susan L. 1946— **10**
Taylor, Susie King 1848-1912 **13**
Terrell, Dorothy A. 1945— **24**
Terrell, Mary (Elizabeth) Church 1863-1954 **9**
The Artist
See Prince
Thigpen, Lynne 19(?)(?)— **17**
Thomas, Alma Woodsey 1891-1978 **14**
Thomas, Clarence 1948— **2**
Thomas, Debi 1967— **26**
Thomas, Derrick 1967-2000 **25**
Thomas, Frank Edward, Jr. 1968— **12**
Thomas, Franklin A(ugustine) 1934— **5**
Thomas, Isiah (Lord III) 1961— **7, 26**
Thomas, Rufus 1917— **20**
Thomas, Vivien (T.) 1910-1985 **9**
Thompson, Bennie G. 1948— **26**
Thompson, John W. 1949— **26**
Thompson, Tazewell (Alfred, Jr.) 1954— **13**
Thompson, Tina 1975— **25**
Thugwane, Josia 1971— **21**
Thurman, Howard 1900-1981 **3**
Thurman, Wallace Henry 1902-1934 **16**
Till, Emmett (Louis) 1941-1955 **7**
Tillman, George, Jr. 1968— **20**
Tolliver, William (Mack) 1951— **9**
Toomer, Jean 1894-1967 **6**
Toomer, Nathan Pinchback
See Toomer, Jean
Tosh, Peter 1944-1987 **9**
Touré, Amadou Toumani 1948?— **18**
Touré, Sekou 1922-1984 **6**
Towns, Edolphus 1934— **19**
Townsend, Robert 1957— **23**
Townsend, Robert 1957— **4**
Tribble, Isreal, Jr. 1940— **8**
Trotter, (William) Monroe 1872-1934 **9**
Trouillot, Ertha Pascal
See Pascal-Trouillot, Ertha
Tsvangirai, Morgan 1952(?)— **26**
Tubbs Jones, Stephanie 1949— **24**
Tubman, Harriet 1820(?)-1913 **9**
Tucker, C. DeLores 1927— **12**
Tucker, Chris 1973(?)— **13, 23**
Tucker, Cynthia (Anne) 1955— **15**
Tucker, Rosina Budd Harvey Corrothers 1881-1987 **14**
Ture, Kwame
See Carmichael, Stokely
Turnbull, Walter 1944— **13**

Turner, Henry McNeal 1834-1915 **5**
Turner, Tina 1939— **6**
Tutu, Desmond (Mpilo) 1931— **6**
Tyree, Omar Rashad 1969— **21**
Tyson, Cicely 1933— **7**
Tyson, Neil de Grasse 1958— **15**
Uggams, Leslie 1943— **23**
Underwood, Blair 1964— **7**
Unseld, Wes 1946— **23**
Upshaw, Eugene, Jr. 1945— **18**
Usry, James L. 1922— **23**
Utendahl, John 1956— **23**
van Sertima, Ivan 1935— **25**
Van Peebles, Mario (Cain) 1957(?)— **2**
Van Peebles, Melvin 1932— **7**
Vance, Courtney B. 1960— **15**
VanDerZee, James (Augustus Joseph) 1886-1983 **6**
Vandross, Luther 1951— **13**
Vann, Harold Moore
See Muhammad, Khallid Abdul
Vanzant, Iyanla 1953— **17**
Vaughan, Sarah (Lois) 1924-1990 **13**
Vaughn, Mo 1967— **16**
Verdelle, A. J. 1960— **26**
Vereen, Ben(jamin Augustus) 1946— **4**
Vieira, Joao 1939— **14**
Vincent, Marjorie Judith 1965(?)— **2**
Von Lipsey, Roderick 1959— **11**
wa Ngengi, Kamau
See Kenyatta, Jomo
Waddles, Charleszetta (Mother) 1912— **10**
Waddles, Mother
See Waddles, Charleszetta (Mother)
Wagner, Annice 1937— **22**
Walcott, Derek (Alton) 1930— **5**
Walcott, Louis Eugene 1933— **2, 15**
See Farrakhan, Louis
Walker, Albertina 1929— **10**
Walker, Alice (Malsenior) 1944— **1**
Walker, Cedric "Ricky" 1953— **19**
Walker, Herschel (Junior) 1962— **1**
Walker, Kara 1969— **16**
Walker, Madame C. J. 1867-1919 **7**
Walker, Maggie Lena 1867(?)-1934 **17**
Walker, Nellie Marian
See Larsen, Nella
Walker, T. J. 1961(?)— **7**
Walker, Thomas "T. J."
See Walker, T. J.
Wallace, Michele Faith 1952— **13**
Wallace, Phyllis A(nn) 1920(?)-1993 **9**
Wallace, Ruby Ann
See Dee, Ruby
Wallace, Sippie 1898-1986 **1**
Wamutombo, Dikembe Mutombo Mpolondo Mukamba Jean Jacque
See Mutombo, Dikembe
Ward, Lloyd 1949— **21**
Warfield, Marsha 1955— **2**
Warner, Malcolm-Jamal 1970— **22**
Warwick, Dionne 1940— **18**
Washington, Booker T(aliaferro) 1856-1915 **4**
Washington, Denzel 1954— **1, 16**
Washington, Dinah 1924-1963 **22**
Washington, Fred(er)i(cka Carolyn) 1903-1994 **10**
Washington, Grover, Jr. 1943— **17**
Washington, Harold 1922-1987 **6**
Washington, Laura S. 1956(?)— **18**
Washington, MaliVai 1969— **8**
Washington, Patrice Clarke 1961— **12**
Washington, Valores James 1903-1995 **12**
Wasow, Omar 1970— **15**
Waters, Benny 1902-1998 **26**
Waters, Ethel 1895-1977 **7**
Waters, Maxine 1938— **3**
Watkins, Frances Ellen
See Harper, Frances Ellen Watkins
Watkins, Gloria Jean
See hooks, bell
Watkins, Levi, Jr. 1945— **9**
Watkins, Perry James Henry 1948-1996 **12**
Watkins, Shirley R. 1938— **17**
Watkins, Walter C. 1946 **24**
Watson, Bob 1946— **25**
Watson, Johnny "Guitar" 1935-1996 **18**
Watt, Melvin 1945— **26**
Wattleton, (Alyce) Faye 1943— **9**
Watts, Julius Caesar, Jr. 1957— **14**
Watts, Rolonda 1959— **9**
Wayans, Damon 1961— **8**
Wayans, Keenen Ivory 1958— **18**
Waymon, Eunice Kathleen
See Simone, Nina
Weathers, Carl 1948— **10**
Weaver, Robert C(lifton) 1907— **8**
Webb, Veronica 1965— **10**
Webb, Wellington, Jr. 1941— **3**
Webber, Chris 1973— **15**
Wek, Alek 1977— **18**
Wells-Barnett, Ida B(ell) 1862-1931 **8**
Wells, James Lesesne 1902-1993 **10**
Welsing, Frances (Luella) Cress 1935— **5**
Wesley, Valerie Wilson 194(?)— **18**
West, Cornel (Ronald) 1953— **5**
West, Dorothy 1907— **12**
West, Togo Dennis, Jr. 1942— **16**
Westbrook, Peter 1952— **20**
Wharton, Clifton R(eginald), Jr. 1926— **7**
Wheat, Alan Dupree 1951— **14**
Whitaker, "Sweet Pea"
See Whitaker, Pernell
Whitaker, Forest 1961— **2**
Whitaker, Mark 1957(?)— **21**
Whitaker, Pernell 1964— **10**
White, Barry 1944— **13**
White, Bill 1933(?)— **1**
White, Jesse 1934— **22**
White, Lois Jean 1938— **20**
White, Michael R(eed) 1951— **5**
White, Reggie 1961— **6**
White, Reginald Howard
See White, Reggie
White, Walter F(rancis) 1893-1955 **4**
White, William DeKova
See White, Bill
Whitfield, Fred 1967— **23**
Whitfield, Lynn 1954— **18**
Wideman, John Edgar 1941— **5**
Wilder, L(awrence) Douglas 1931— **3**
Wiley, Ralph 1952— **8**
Wilkens, Lenny 1937— **11**
Wilkens, Leonard Randolph
See Wilkens, Lenny
Wilkins, Roger (Wood) 1932— **2**
Wilkins, Roy 1901-1981 **4**
Williams, Anthony 1951— **21**
Williams, Bert 1874-1922 **18**
Williams, Billy Dee 1937— **8**
Williams, Carl
See Kani, Karl
Williams, Clarence, III 1939— **26**
Williams, Daniel Hale (III) 1856-1931 **2**
Williams, Doug 1955— **22**
Williams, Evelyn 1922(?)— **10**
Williams, George Washington 1849-1891 **18**
Williams, Gregory (Howard) 1943— **11**
Williams, Hosea Lorenzo 1926— **15**
Williams, Joe 1918-1999 **5, 25**
Williams, Maggie 1954— **7**
Williams, Margaret Ann
See Williams, Maggie
Williams, Mary Lou 1910-1981 **15**
Williams, Montel (B.) 1956(?)— **4**
Williams, O(swald) S. 1921— **13**
Williams, Patricia J. 1951— **11**
Williams, Paul R(evere) 1894-1980 **9**
Williams, Paulette Linda
See Shange, Ntozake
Williams, Robert Peter
See Guillaume, Robert
Williams, Robert F(ranklin) 1925— **11**
Williams, Samuel Arthur 1946— **21**
Williams, Serena 1981 **20**
Williams, Sherley Anne 1944-1999 **25**
Williams, Vanessa L. 1963— **4, 17**
Williams, Venus Ebone Starr 1980— **17**
Williams, Walter E(dward) 1936— **4**
Williams, William T(homas) 1942— **11**
Williams, William December
Williams, Willie L(awrence) 1943— **4**
Williamson, Lisa
See Sister Souljah
Williamson, Mykelti 1957— **22**
Willis, Cheryl
See Hudson, Cheryl
Wilson, August 1945— **7**
Wilson, Cassandra 1955— **16**
Wilson, Flip 1933-1998 **21**
Wilson, Nancy 1937— **10**
Wilson, Phill 1956-- **9**
Wilson, Sunnie 1908— **7**
Wilson, William Julius 1935— **22**
Wilson, William Nathaniel
See Wilson, Sunnie
Winans, Benjamin 1962— **14**
Winans, Marvin L. 1958— **17**
Winans, Priscilla 1964— **14**
Winans, Vickie 1953(?)— **24**
Winfield, Dave 1951— **5**
Winfield, David Mark
See Winfield, Dave
Winfield, Paul (Edward) 1941— **2**
Winfrey, Oprah (Gail) 1954— **2, 15**
Witt, Edwin T. 1920— **26**
Wofford, Chloe Anthony
See Morrison, Toni
Wolfe, George C. 1954— **6**
Wonder, Stevie 1950— **11**
Woodard, Alfre 1953— **9**
Woodruff, Hale (Aspacio) 1900-1980 **9**
Woods, Eldrick
See Woods, Tiger
Woods, Granville T. 1856-1910 **5**
Woods, Tiger 1975— **14**
Woodson, Carter G(odwin) 1875-1950 **2**
Woodson, Robert L. 1937— **10**
Wooldridge, Anna Marie
See Lincoln, Abbey
Worrill, Conrad 1941— **12**
Wright, Bruce McMarion 1918— **3**
Wright, Deborah C. 1958— **25**
Wright, Louis Tompkins 1891-1952 **4**
Wright, Richard 1908-1960 **5**
Wynn, Albert R. 1951— **25**
X, Malcolm 1925-1965 **1**
Yoba, (Abdul-)Malik (Kashie) 1967— **11**
Young, Andre Ramelle
See Dre, Dr.